DICKENS STUDIES ANNUAL
Essays on Victorian Fiction

DICKENS STUDIES ANNUAL
Essays on Victorian Fiction

EDITORS

Michael Timko
Fred Kaplan
Edward Guiliano

DICKENS
STUDIES
ANNUAL

Essays on Victorian Fiction

VOLUME
16

Edited by
Michael Timko, Fred Kaplan,
and Edward Guiliano

AMS PRESS
NEW YORK

DICKENS STUDIES ANNUAL

ISSN 0084-9812

International Standard Book Number
Series: 0-404-18520-7
Vol. 16: 0-404-18536-3

Dickens Studies Annual: Essays on Victorian Fiction welcomes essay and monograph-length contributions on Dickens as well as on other Victorian novelists and on the history or aesthetics of Victorian fiction. All manuscripts should be double-spaced, including footnotes, which should be grouped at the end of the submission, and should be prepared according to the format used in this journal. An editorial decision can usually be reached more quickly if two copies are submitted. The preferred editions for citations from Dickens' works are the Clarendon and the Norton Critical when available, otherwise the Oxford Illustrated Dickens or the Penguin.

Please send submission to the Editors, *Dickens Studies Annual,* Room 1522, Graduate School and University Center, City University of New York, 33 West 42nd Street, New York, N.Y. 10036: please send subscription inquiries to AMS Press, Inc., 56 East 13th Street, New York, N.Y. 10003.

Manufactured in the United States of America

Contents

List of Illustrations

Preface

This sixteenth volume of *Dickens Studies Annual* is the ninth to appear under its second generation of editors and in its modified editorial format. The *Annual* continues to contain a selection of essays ranging over many of Dickens' works and involving a variety of scholarly and critical approaches. A glance at this volume's table of contents confirms that the *Annual* remains an outlet for both established and emerging scholars, and that the subtitle, *Essays on Victorian Fiction* continues to be justified. Works by Thomas Carlyle, Wilkie Collins, George Eliot, and Mark Twain are treated in articles in Volume 16. The three essays dealing with Dickens and Twain grew out of papers delivered at the annual Dickens conference held each summer at the University of California at Santa Cruz.

One of the continuing gratifications of editing *DSA* has been the contact we make with and the support and cooperation we receive from colleagues around the world. All of our submissions receive multiple readings, and it is always a source of wonder and admiration when our one-page reader-report form comes back with several single-spaced pages of comments appended to it. Generous and gracious outside readers make our job as editors easier and enable us to provide those who submit articles with substantive reports and often, when merited, clear direction for revision. We deeply appreciate those who read essays for *DSA*.

We also appreciate those who have helped in other ways: the administrators at our respective colleges, the directors of the California Dickens Project, the staff of AMS Press—notably Gabriel Hornstein, President, William B. Long, Editor, and Robert Harris, Assistant Editor—as well as our own Editorial Assistants, Claire Pamplin and Debra Ann Suarez.

—The Editors

Notes on Contributors

HOWARD G. BAETZHOLD, Rebecca Clifton Reade Professor of English at Butler University is author of *Mark Twain and John Bull: The British Connection* (1970) and of numerous articles on Mark Twain and other literary figures. He is currently engaged in editing several volumes of *Middle Tales and Sketches (1871–1895)* and *Late Tales and Sketches (1896–1910)* for the Iowa-California Edition of the Works of Mark Twain.

CAROL BOCK is an assistant professor of English literature at the University of Minnesota, Duluth. Her publications include articles on Dickens, Dickinson, Charlotte Brontë, and D. G. Rossetti. She is currently at work on a book which studies the implied audiences in Charlotte Brontë's fiction.

WILLIAM M. BURGAN teaches in the English Department at Indiana University and is an associate editor of *Victorian Studies*. He has published a number of articles on Dickens, including one on manuscript revision in *Drood* which appeared in *DSA* 6, and is currently at work on a book on Dickens and the art of fictional setting.

DAVID M. CRAIG, an Associate Professor of Humanities at Clarkson University, has had articles appear in *The Centennial Review, The Henry James Review, Research Studies,* and elsewhere. He is presently finishing a book entitled *Tilting at Mortality: Joseph Heller's Fiction*.

JOHN DIZIKES is a Fellow of Cowell College, University of California at Santa Cruz, where he teaches American Studies and History. He is the author of two books, *Britain, Roosevelt and the New Deal* (1979) and *Sportsmen and*

Gamesmen (1981), and is currently writing a social history of opera in America.

EDWIN M. EIGNER, a frequent contributor to *DSA*, is the author of *Robert Louis Stevenson and Romantic Tradition* (Princeton, 1966), *The Metaphysical Novel in England and America* (California, 1978), and the co-editor of *Victorian Criticism of Fiction* (Cambridge, 1985). His most recent book, *The Dickens Pantomime*, which developed from articles first appearing in *DSA*, will be published by the University of California Press in 1988.

RICHARD FABRIZIO teaches English at Pace University, New York. His recent publications include articles on Moravia, the Oedipus theme, and the incest theme. He is currently working on a study of ancient and medieval art dealing with Oedipus.

JAMES R. KINCAID, Aerol Arnold Professor of English at the University of Southern California, is the author of books on Dickens, Tennyson, and Trollope—of several editions—and of many essays on literary theory, and Victorian literature and culture. He is currently at work on a book on Victorian pedophilia.

GEORGE LEVINE is Kenneth Burke Professor of English Literature and Director of the Center for the Critical Analysis of Contemporary Culture at Rutgers University. He is the author of *The Realistic Imagination* and of a forthcoming annotated bibliography of George Eliot for Harvester Press. The first volume in a series on Science and Literature which he is editing will appear from the University of Wisconsin Press this year.

RICHARD LETTIS is Professor of English at Long Island University, C. W. Post Campus. "Dickens and Drama" and an earlier article published in *DSA*, "Dickens and Art," are parts of a book entitled *The Dickens Aesthetic*, soon to be published by AMS Press.

JULIAN MASON is Professor (and former Chairman) in the English Department of the University of North Carolina at Charlotte. He is the author of over fifty articles, mostly in the fields of American literature and culture, and is the editor of *The Poems of Phillis Wheatley* (1966).

JEROME MECKIER, who teaches courses about both the Victorians and Moderns at the University of Kentucky, served as a sub-editor for the first seven volumes of *DSA*. In addition to *Aldous Huxley: Satire and Structure*, he has published widely on Waugh, Conrad, Lawrence, T.S. Eliot, Trollope, Collins, George Eliot, and others. His study *Hidden Rivalries in Victorian Fiction: Dickens, Realism, and Revaluation* will soon be published by the University Press of Kentucky.

MICHAEL TIMKO, Professor of English at Queens College and at the Graduate Center of The City University of New York and editor of *DSA*, has published widely on Victorian literature. His next book, a study of Tennyson and Carlyle (Macmillan), will appear this year.

ROBERT TRACY, Professor of English at the University of California, Berkeley, teaches courses in nineteenth- and twentieth-century literature, specializing in the literatures of Britain and Ireland. His *Trollope's Later Novels* (1978) is a standard work, and his *Stone* (1981), translations of early poems by the Russian poet Osip Mandelstam, has been well received. He is a recent Guggenheim Fellow and an active participant in the University of California Dickens Project.

Dickens, Carlyle, and the Chaos of Being

Michael Timko

That Carlyle had a great deal of influence on Dickens is well known, but I should like in this article to illustrate that Carlyle's influence on his young friend was far greater than we think. That will be the primary concern of the first part of my essay, which has to do chiefly with *Oliver Twist* as history. That Dickens was a writer of the nineteenth century, more specifically one closely identified with the Victorian period, is also well known, but again I should like both to insist and to illustrate that this identification is much closer than we think. To demonstrate this will be the chief concern of the second part of the essay.

Carlyle not only wrote history; he agonized over it. He always knew that one never could record that which really happened or those events that really took place. Also, as his comments on various historians and his own historical writings demonstrate, Carlyle worried about the purpose of writing history. What in fact was the historian trying to do as he wrote? Two key documents that provide some insight into Carlyle's ideas on history are his essays "On History" and "On History Again," both in *Fraser's,* the first in 1830, the second in 1833. *Oliver Twist,* we remember, was begun in 1837, although Kathleen Tillotson suggests that it might have been thought of as early as 1833. At any rate, Dickens no doubt knew of and read Carlyle's *Fraser* pieces, and the Carlylian approaches to and thoughts about Clio, "the eldest daughter of Memory, and chief of the Muses," are scattered throughout *Oliver,* which, after all, is a parish boy's progress, the history of his life and times. Indeed, Dickens himself wrote in his Preface to the third edition (1841), "I wished to shew, in little Oliver, the principle of Good surviving through every adverse circumstance, and triumphing at last." Dickens then goes on

1

to demonstrate in his remarks at least one Carlylian tenet in regard to the writing of history. "When I considered," says Dickens, "among what companions I could try him best, having regard to that kind of men into whose hands he would most naturally fall; I bethought myself of those who figure in these volumes. . . . It appeared to me that to draw a knot of such associates in crime as really do exist; to paint them in all their deformity, in all their wretchedness, in all the squalid poverty of their lives; to shew them as they really are, for ever skulking uneasily through the dirtiest paths of life, with the great, black, ghastly gallows closing up their prospects, turn them where they may; it appeared to me that to do this, would be to attempt a something which was greatly needed, and which would be a service to society. And therefore I did it as I best could" (Clarendon, lxii).

Behind these remarks, I believe, lies the shadow of Thomas Carlyle, who, according to Michael Goldberg, "remained a hero to Dickens throughout his life." Indeed, the bond between the two was so strong, Goldberg reminds us, that Dickens did not part company with him over the *Latter-Day Pamplets.* Dickens' "discipleship" was unshakeable: he would, he wrote Forster, "go at all times farther to see Carlyle than any man alive." Thomas Carlyle was "the man who had most influenced him" (Goldberg, 2).

Of particular interest at this point are Carlyle's ideas about history, most specifically about the relationship between history and the other arts, especially fiction. How does one present what really happened, the Truth? Dickens clearly is concerned with this question in *Oliver Twist;* he wants to show people as they really are and to discuss serious topics and ideas. Certainly he did not want his novels to be regarded as mere entertainments. *Pickwick* would suffice as a first work, but, as various critics have remarked, Dickens wanted his second novel to be a serious work, and Carlyle's ideas seemed pertinent and appropriate.

Without making Dickens entirely dependent on his older friend, what are those influences and ideas in this novel about the progress of a parish boy that can be said to be Carlylian? There are some rather obvious ones. Carlyle's greatest concerns deal with the concept of history itself, its essential purposes, and the way that one "writes" it—that is, the form of the genre itself. As he absorbed these various Carlylian ideas, Dickens began to understand that as a dedicated writer of novels he had to demonstrate that the writer of fiction could, indeed, be as much of a force for good as an historian. In fact, Dickens seems to be attempting to demonstrate that the writer of fiction, because of his special nature, could be even more influential, since he could depict even better than the historian the "Chaos of Being" that, according to Carlyle, was life itself.

It is not easy to pin down Carlyle on what he means by history. One can provide some representative quotations in order to convey his thoughts on the subject: 1. "History, as it lies at the root of all science, is also the first distinct product of man's spiritual nature; his earliest expression of what can be called Thought. It is a looking before and after; as, indeed, the coming Time already waits, unseen, yet definitely shaped, predetermined and inevitable, in the Time come; and only by the combination of both is the meaning of either completed" (80). 2. "In a certain sense all men are historians. . . . Our very speech is curiously historical" (80). 3. "Examine History, for it is 'Philosophy teaching by Experience' " (81). 4. "History is the essence of innumerable Biographies" (82).

As Carlyle himself would say, there are volumes in those thoughts, but I should like to emphasize two specific ideas they reveal about Carlyle and history. After a brief flirtation with the idea of becoming a writer of fiction and a period of writing essays and reviews, Carlyle soon opted for the writing of history. Peter Dale has put down the years of 1830–1832 as the years in which Carlyle was beginning to "discover his vocation as a historian after almost a decade of writing literary reviews" (48). Dale writes of Carlyle's "growing sense of the unreality, the uselessness of mere imaginative, 'fictive' writing"; and of his wondering about "more practical means of bringing about essential social and moral change" (49). Carlyle's turning to history, it seems, reflected his conviction that it was in that field and not in the "writing of criticism of 'fictive' literature that truth was to be found, the sort of truth that would at once explain the catastrophe of the modern age and deliver mankind from it" (50). These last statements admirably summarize Carlyle's view of the purposes of writing history: to examine the times in which he lived and to show the means of reforming it in terms that might be called "deliverance." One of the major thematic thrusts of *Oliver Twist* reflects these ideas. For Dickens in that novel, as for Carlyle in all his historical writings, history is philosophy teaching by experience.

The chief differences between these two like-minded writers are to be found in the form in which they present the truth. Is the historian, in fact, the better "seer" and "reformer" than the writer of fiction or of criticism? Carlyle thinks so, and he minces no words. If the task of all three is to see and reform, then the success of each depends on how clearly in the end the Truth is revealed. Obviously, then, the presentation is all-important. To Carlyle the problem involves two major elements: the clarity of the vision and the faithfulness of the representation of that vision in order to accomplish the necessary reform or deliverance.

For Carlyle early in his career the dilemma between Truth and Art became overwhelming. If history was philosophy teaching by experience and if it was the essence of innumerable biographies, it was inevitable that the writing of history must necessarily involve people and what people do, human actions and thoughts. The next step, for Carlyle, was logical: the one who came closest to depicting the Chaos of Being we call life deserved to be called the true Artist, and for Carlyle this was, in fact, the writer of history. In what would seem the most significant passage of his essays on history he wrote:

> The most gifted man can observe, still more can record, only the *series* of his own impressions; his observation, therefore, . . . must be *successive,* while the things done were often *simultaneous;* the things done were not a series, but a group. . . . Every single event is the offspring not of one, but of all other events, prior or contemporaneous, and will in its turn combine with all others to give birth to new: it is an ever-living, ever-working Chaos of Being. . . . And this Chaos, boundless as the habitation and duration of man, unfathomable as the soul and destiny of man, is what the historian will depict, and scientifically gauge, we may say, by threading it with single lines of a few ells in length!

The passage is, so far, an analysis of the historian's task, an impossible one. Carlyle, however, takes care to spell out the impossibility:

> For as all Action is, by its nature, to be figured as extended in breadth and in depth, as well as in length; that is to say, is based on Passion and Mystery, if we investigate its origin; and spreads abroad on all hands, modifying and modified; as well as advances towards completion,—so all Narrative is, by its nature, of only one dimension; only travels forward towards one, or towards successive points: Narrative is *linear,* Action is *solid.* . . . Truly, if History is Philosophy teaching by Experience, the writer fitted to compose History is hitherto an unknown man. The Experience itself would require All-knowledge to record it,—were the All-wisdom needful for such Philosophy as would interpret it, to be had for the asking.   (84–85)

While this passage indicates that for Carlyle the ideal Historian has not yet arrived, it does demonstrate what for him is the advantage of the historian over the writer of fiction, who, by the very title, is one who writes narrative. The writer of narrative is limited to putting down linear acts; action, which is solid, needs a writer who can see the whole. For Carlyle, that person is the ideal Historian, who had not yet appeared on the scene. Actually, he had, but had not yet been rightfully acknowledged; that was Carlyle himself, who was to spend the rest of his life attempting to convince everyone of that fact.

Dickens, however, grasped the opportunity to demonstrate that the writer of fiction was, in fact, the ideal Historian, the writer who, through the depiction of solid action, could serve as both seer and reformer, the artist who could portray better than anyone else the "Chaos of Being." By his ability to observe and depict the simultaneity of events and to show the passion and mystery that lay behind these various actions, the novelist could interpret them and, thus, present the Truth. The fiction writer is the Carlylian Artist, the "composer" of history in the Carlylian sense, the one who has an eye for the Whole, sees the organic connection of all events and actions. The history of an individual, a number of individuals, a family or families could, in this sense, be looked upon as a prophetic manuscript.

To see *Oliver Twist* as Dickens' response to Carlyle's call, even to view it in the most tentative terms, is to acknowledge more than ever both the hold that Carlyle had on Dickens and Dickens' own integrity as person and artist. Carlyle's "call" is both persuasive and moving. Indeed, in citing the novel as an attempt, through Oliver, to show the principle of Good triumphing and in defending his choice of wretched characters in all the "squalid poverty of their lives," in portraying them "as they really are," Dickens was "heroically" responding to Carlyle's call for the need to write not only of "courts and camps" but also of ordinary people and everyday events as well. In Carlyle's own words: "The rudest peasant has his complete set of Annual Registers legibly printed in his brain; and without the smallest training in Mnemonics, the proper pauses, subdivisions and subordinations of the little to the great, all introduced there" (96). Oliver Twist, in short, was as significant a character as Oliver Cromwell. Campbell stresses the same point: "While the whole shape of history may be hidden, vignettes of the lives and characters of individuals are always available, and this biographical interest colours all Carlyle's historical writings" (vii).

Dickens' artistic independence, however, clearly overshadows what may seem to be an apparent overattentiveness to Carlyle's message; he wants to call attention to the true nature of fiction, to its ability to reform society. With his usual confidence, he wanted to show Carlyle that only in the novel could the Idea of the Whole be discerned. Fiction was, indeed, to replace History as the means by which one could teach philosophy by experience. Actually, as has been suggested, Carlyle attempted in his historical writing to break the bonds of the model he inherited, the Enlightenment model of history as text, one that saw events as occurring within a "narrative continuum" of an "overarching story." In insisting that the historian be poet as well as scientist, Carlyle was emphasizing the need for the artist to be able to combine both the real and the "poetic" or mysterious, to demonstrate the limits of narrative. He himself, however, simply juxtaposed the two, expanding the range of "texts" on which historians could draw. However, expansion of texts did not result in combining poetry and science; it simply gave more scientific materials from which to draw (*VS*, 305).

What gives Carlyle's historical writing the appearance of poetry was his metaphorical approach, his view of the Chaos of Being. However, this view was simply Carlyle's own textualization of the Enlightenment view of history as narrative; he did not, as Hayden White reminds us, view history as an apparent Chaos which, in the Herderian view, was ultimately working its way towards total integration. Instead, Carlyle remained scientific rather than poetic, insisting on Fact and emphasizing biography. He wanted, in short, real people, real events. What one can view as his poetic attempts are simply the times in which he is revealed, in Traill's words, as a "splendid impressionist," as one who simply interjects at certain moments his own characteristic values, his notions of right and wrong. At these moments, as White insists, the stress is on "the novel and emergent, rather than on the achieved and inherited, aspects of cultural life. It made of history an arena in which new things can be seen to appear, rather than one in which old elements simply rearrange themselves endlessly in a finite set of possible combinations. But," and this point is significant, "it provided no rule by which the individual elements appearing in the field can be brought together in such ways as to encourage any confidence that *the whole process* has a comprehensible meaning" (149).

In *Oliver Twist* Dickens does encourage that confidence; he succeeds in combining both the scientific and poetic. Indeed, Dickens succeeds where Carlyle fails, the failure that White perceptively notes: "But Carlyle excluded any possibility of advancing beyond the (Metaphorical) insight that every life is both 'like every other' and at the same time 'utterly unique'." Carlyle, in other words, limited to facts, was unable to provide what he calls "poetic interest," which he defines as the "struggle of human Freewill against material Necessity, which every man's Life, by the mere circumstance that the man continues alive, will more or less victoriously exhibit,—is that which above all else . . . calls the Sympathy of mortal hearts into action; and whether as acted, or as represented and written of, not only is Poetry, but is the sole Poetry possible" (147). Dickens, in *Oliver Twist* and subsequent novels, provides Carlylian poetic interest, that which indeed calls the sympathy of mortal hearts into action. He surpassed Carlyle because he was able to demonstrate that to textualize history one must indeed encode person and topos, and, at the same time, reveal all-inclusively the struggle of human Freewill against material Necessity. His artistry lay in his ability to reveal "poetically" the Passion and Mystery that make up the Carlylian Chaos of Being.

One of the indications of Dickens' artistry in *Oliver* is his grounding the story in myth, thus encoding through emotional as well as logical means the "historical" importance of the story of Oliver. Dickens makes it not only his (Oliver's) story, the story of an orphan, but a story carrying various associations, including the mythic, moral, and fantastic, in short, the passion and mystery of life itself. While one can derive many associations simply in terms of Oliver's being an orphan, and all those fantastic stories written in that genre, the fact is that Dickens is writing on other levels. Jonathan Arac is especially helpful in his speculations about synecdoche, and, following his lead, one can begin to see the importance of humans and houses and hearts in Oliver's story/history. Not only is Dickens intent, as is Carlyle, on setting England's house in order, but the dwellings in his novels become important ethical and metaphorical icons. Home indeed is where the heart is, but very often a person has no choice in deciding just where his or her heart will reside. Various structures need to be changed, but very often the means to change them are difficult to obtain. I want to focus on this aspect of the novel, especially in homologic and isotopic terms, but first let me illustrate the richness of Dickens' allusive artistry on this synecdochic level.

Most of us, I think, are familiar with the heinous crime in Shakespeare's *Macbeth,* a crime that is homicidal but, while it may seem paradoxical, even more seriously is anti-synecdochic—that is, it is a crime committed against the noble ideal of the sanctity of one's home, especially when one has guests. At Lady Macbeth's urging (I refuse to go more deeply into that aspect of the deed), Macbeth murders his two guests. As he goes to do the deed, he hears the bell ring and exclaims, "Hear it not, Duncan; for it is a knell/That summons thee to heaven or to hell" (II, i, 63-64). After the murder, he looks at his hands: "This is a sorry sight" (II, ii, 21). It is at this point that the knocking at the gate occurs, the subject of that wonderful essay by Thomas DeQuincey. "Whence is that knocking?" asks the now doomed Macbeth; he continues: "How is't with me, when every noise apalls me? / What hands are here? Ha! they pluck out mine eyes. / Will all great Neptune's ocean wash this blood/Clean from my hand? No, this my hand will rather/The multitudinous seas incarnadine, / Making the green one red" (II, ii, 57–63).

I need not dwell on the similarity of this scene with the one in *Oliver Twist* as Bill Sikes brutally murders Nancy. I am not so much thinking of the blood and the effect of the deed on Bill himself; but, instead, of the way that Dickens emphasizes the anti-synecdochic aspect and the effect of the bright sun on the scene the next day, the equivalent of the knocking at the gate in Shakespeare's play. For the former, the anti-synecdochic, we recall the moving scene shortly before the murder as Rose tries to persuade Nancy to accept a "quiet asylum" somewhere, and Nancy refuses. "I must go home," says Nancy. " 'Home!' repeated the young lady, with great stress upon the word." " 'Home, lady,' rejoined the girl. 'To such a home as I have raised for myself with the work of my whole life' " (P, 415). Home and life are, indeed, the same in the novel, as they are in the time of Macbeth; to violate the sanctity of one is to violate the sanctity of the other.

In the same way the enormity of the crime is shown by Dickens with the emphasis on the brilliance of the morning sun on the bloody scene. Perhaps my point will become clear if I compare the opening lines of the chapter in Dickens with DeQuincey's words. Here is the latter: "Hence it is that when the deed is done—when the work of darkness is perfect, then the world of darkness passes away like a pageantry in the clouds: the knocking at the gate is heard; and it makes known audibly that the reaction has commenced: the human has made its reflux upon the fiendish: the pulses of life are beginning to beat again: and the re-establishment of the goings-on of the world in which we live, first makes us profoundly sensible of the awful parenthesis that had suspended them" (454). Here is Dickens:

> Of all bad deeds that, under cover of the darkness, had been committed within wide London's bounds since night hung over it, that was the worst. Of all the horrors that rose with an ill scent upon the morning air, that was the foulest and most cruel.
>
> The sun—the bright sun, that brings back, not light alone, but new life, and hope, and freshness to man—burst upon the crowded city in clear and radiant glory. . . . It lighted upon the room where the murdered woman lay. It did. He tried to shut it out, but it would stream in. If the sight had been a ghastly one in the dull morning, what was it, now, in all that brilliant light!   (423)

It is the sanctity of the synecdochic that Dickens is stressing, and he succeeds in demonstrating that concept in homologic terms; Oliver's story is his/story, his biography, and it is one that can be traced in his various attempts to find synecdochic peace, a home that represents his triumph over material Necessity. In Carlylian terms, Oliver's journey "home" calls forth from the reader the "Sympathy of mortal hearts into action"; Dickens' presentation of that journey is, again in Carlylian terms, "the sole Poetry possible." That "poetry," as I have suggested, has for its structural basis the isotopic and the homologic, for the synecdochic variations are expressed in these terms and are the key to Oliver's eventual triumph.

The variations are most vividly represented, in the novel, in two scenes that seem to some to represent Dickens at his most unpoetic level—that is to say, at his most melodramatic or, perish the term, Victorian. On the lowest end of the scale we see Oliver, after he has turned "wicious," dragged fighting and screaming and kicking into the dust-cellar of the Sowerberry establishment and then later left alone "in the silence and stillness of the gloomy workshop of the undertaker." Here we find Dickens, echoing Carlyle's definition of "Poetic interest," assuming the role of commentator and telling the reader exactly why Oliver's struggle should call the "Sympathy of mortal hearts into action": "He had listened to their taunts with a look of contempt; he had borne the lash without a cry: for he felt that pride swelling in his heart which would have kept down a shriek to the last, though they had roasted him alive. But now, when there were none to see or hear him, he fell upon his knees on the floor; and, hiding his face in his hands, wept such tears as, God send for the credit of our nature, few so young may ever have cause to pour out before him" (95).

At the other end of the homologic scale we see Monks and Fagin looking into Oliver's favorite room, the "little room in which he was accustomed to sit." Dickens' description strongly conveys the isotopic significance and the synecdochic emphasis one is to give to it:

> The little room in which he was accustomed to sit, when busy at his books, was on the ground-floor, at the back of the house. It was quite a cottage-room, with a lattice-window: around which were clusters of jessamine and honeysuckle, that crept over the casement, and filled the place with their delicious perfume. It looked into a garden, whence a wicket-gate opened into a small paddock; all beyond, was fine meadowland and wood. There was no other dwelling near, in that direction; and the prospect it commanded was very extensive.   (308)

If one is alert to the fine homologic variations, it comes as no surprise to find Dickens immediately bringing in at this point one of Oliver's other "homes," one that inspires in Oliver feelings and ideas associated with other places and events. "Suddenly, the scene changed; the air became close and confined; and he thought, with a glow of terror, that he was in the Jew's house again" (309). As with Nancy so with Oliver; where the home is there is one's life.

As I have suggested earlier, Oliver's story is the story of his synecdochic journey, and Dickens is careful to make certain that the reader make the integral connection between heart and home. The novel is not a picaresque novel, although one might find some resemblances between Oliver and Joseph

Andrews; and a swift survey of Oliver's history, particularly his search for a home, reveals a clear pattern. We (with Oliver) begin the journey at the place of his birth, the workhouse, one building among many other public buildings in a certain town. There is no time to elaborate on his treatment here, but I think the comments at the end of Chapter 1 and the beginning of Chapter 2 signify Dickens' own view of Oliver's first home: "What an excellent example of the power of dress, young Oliver Twist was! Wrapped in the blanket which had hitherto formed his only covering, he might have been the child of a nobleman or a beggar; it would have been hard for the haughtiest stranger to have fixed his station in society." Dickens obviously is under the influence of Thomas Carlyle's clothes philosophy. "But now that he was enveloped in the old calico robes, which had grown yellow in the same service, he was badged and ticketed, and fell into his place at once—a parish child—the orphan of a workhouse—the humble half-starved drudge—to be cuffed and buffeted through the world,—despised by all, and pitied by none" (47).

Oliver's next home, after eight or ten months as "victim of a systematic course of treachery and deception" in the workhouse, is with Mrs. Mann (a rather interesting name), to whom Oliver is "dispatched" by the authorities. Again, we need only a few details to get Dickens' sense of the synecdochic significance: "Everybody knows the story of another experimental philosopher, who had a great theory about a horse being able to live without eating. . . . He had got his own horse down to a straw a day, and would unquestionably have rendered him a very spirited . . . animal on nothing at all, if he had not died, four-and-twenty hours before he was to have had his first comfortable bait of air." Mrs. Mann would have no quarrel with that system: "at the very moment when a child had contrived to exist upon the smallest possible portion of the weakest possible food, it did perversely happen in eight and a half cases out of ten, either that it sickened from want and cold, or fell into the fire from neglect, or got half smothered by accident; in any one of which cases, the miserable little being was usually summoned into another world, and there gathered to the fathers it had never known in this" (48–49).

Oliver's early synecdochic experiences, in short, reflect Dickens' own concerns, so well expressed by Dickens himself in his preface to the third edition, in the novel itself, and summarized ably by Peter Fairclough in Appendix A of the Penguin edition. Oliver's early experience demonstrates the need for England to put its house in order, and it does so much more forcefully than historical fact. The rest of Oliver's story is one of synecdochic variation on this theme. Oliver, at nine, goes back to the workhouse. He then spends some time at the Sowerberry establishment, among the coffins and other paraphernalia associated with their trade; runs off to London and is taken "home" by Jack Dawkins; spends some time at home with Mr. Brownlow; and is taken once again to the Fagin establishment. From there he goes "on assignment" to the Maylie home, where he at last finds peace and rest.

From Oliver's travels and various domiciles we can note one or two important homologic differences and thus gain some notion of Dickens' attempt to gain our sympathy for both Oliver and other characters who reflect the author's concern for the heart and home of England itself. I think, for instance, that Dickens wants us to note carefully the contrast between Oliver's first and second stays at Fagin's home. Indeed, I think there is so much a difference, in both the regular and Derridian sense, that they can serve as a paradigm for the novel itself; certainly for the theme of the novel. On the first visit, after the perilous journey from the "underworld" of the Sowerberrys, Oliver is greeted with warmth and good fellowship; one sees many resemblances here to other scenes in many other novels. Fagin grins and makes a "low obeisance" to Oliver, shakes him by the hand, and hopes "he should have the honour of his intimate acquaintance." Oliver is given something to eat, a place near the fire, and a place to sleep. There is nothing during Oliver's first stay at Fagin's to suggest that he is not happy, certainly happier and better cared for than at any of his other earlier "homes."

Of course one reason for all this is Oliver's own "greenness," but the fact remains that he is better fed and better taken care of than in the workhouse or the Sowerberrys' place. His coming to know the true synecdochic nature of Fagin's "home" is delayed, in the Derridian sense, until his second stay, which comes after his sojourn in the Brownlow home, where he is shown for the first time in his life what kindness is truly like. For the first time he is home. However, he must also be shown the real "home" of Fagin, and thus he is taken back to Fagin's home, and his final homecoming is delayed until he goes to the Maylies.

The homologic difference between the two Fagin sojourns is immediately signalled by Dickens at the very beginning of Chapter 16: "The narrow streets and courts, at length, terminated in a large open space; scattered about which, were pens for beasts, and other indications of a cattle-market" (158). When Oliver meets Fagin the second time, Fagin again makes "a great number of low bows to the bewildered boy"; but this time, Dickens tells us, it is with "mock humility." For the first time in the novel, Fagin begins to beat Oliver and is prevented by Nancy from doing him harm. His second stay is, indeed, not much different from his previous sojourns in earlier homes, and at last Oliver comes to know the difference between home and home. Of course he will not come to know what home is really like until his stay at the Maylies; however, he does come to understand that Fagin's home is not home. It is, in fact, not much different from the workhouse or the Sowerberrys'. As Fagin describes the "unpleasant operation" of being hanged, Oliver's blood runs cold. For the first time, at liberty to wander about the house, he sees what a dirty, dismal, unappealing place it is. Oliver, sick at heart, "would crouch in the corner of the passage by the street-door, to be as near living people as he could; and would remain there, listening and counting the hours, until the Jew or the boys returned" (178–179).

What, then, is the synecdochic significance of all this? What is the difference between home and home? The difference, for Dickens, signifies the means by which England can put its own house in order, for where the home is there is the heart. Life and home are one, and the homologic differences of Oliver's homes reflect on a larger scale the sociological and spiritual differences Dickens and Carlyle saw in England itself. For Oliver, home carries the same meaning that it does for Nancy, and therein lies the true synecdochic *differance* for Dickens. Dickens in *Oliver Twist* demonstrates that the concept of home carries with it those qualities that reflect the poetic interest insisted on by Carlyle: the struggle of human Freewill against material Necessity, which every man's Life, by the mere circumstance that the man continues alive, will more or less victoriously exhibit.

We can end as we began—that is, we can look at two specific scenes in which are revealed those qualities that define home for Oliver, Nancy, and Dickens himself. This is not, of course, a new problem in Dickens studies; more than a few critics have puzzled over just what Dickens would posit against the deprivation of spirit he constantly saw and wrote about in England. In his Preface he talks of the "principle of Good surviving through every adverse circumstance, and triumphing at last"; in *Hard Times* he keeps saying that people must be amused. What is it that prompts Nancy to reject the help offered her and insist on going "home." What is home to Nancy? It is "such a home as I have raised for myself with the work of my whole life." We only know that home for her means being with Bill Sikes, to whom, as she tells him just before he brutally murders her, she has been true to the very end (422–423).

What is home to Oliver? In this instance Dickens has to resort to the most direct means he knows to get in contact with the reader, for if life often imitates art, then art must at times be larger than life in order to make an artistic point. How is one, for instance, to portray the passion and mystery that lie at the heart of this Chaos of Being? Dickens resorts, as I have said, to melodramatic gesture, to what Peter Brooks in his work on melodrama calls the "melodramatic sign." I need not go into detail about Brooks's thesis, but one of his main points is that by mid nineteenth century, with many of the conventional literary signs having exhausted their usefulness, the melodramatic sign became a useful signifier. My chief point here is that Dickens certainly came to rely heavily on it, especially as a "gesture toward a concealed world of meaning," a world that Brooks calls a "moral occult" of vague, Manichean forces of good and evil, the powers of which are sensed in a conventional repertory of oaths and epithets, formulaic characters, typed poses, and signifying gestures. Dickens masterfully uses this melodramatic gesture. In the scene I have just been discussing, Nancy, just before her death, raises herself to her knees, draws from her bosom Rose Maylie's white handkerchief, and holds it up to heaven (423). In one of the first scenes in the Maylie home Oliver is sick in bed and Rose comes in. She seats herself in a chair by the bedside, gathers Oliver's hair from his face, and, as "she stooped over him, her tears fell upon his forehead." After this "melodramatic sign," Oliver stirs, smiles in his sleep, "as though these marks of pity and compassion had awakened some pleasant dream of a love and affection he had never known" (268). With this melodramatic gesture we are prepared for Oliver's arrival home:

> So three months glided away; three months which, in the life of the most blessed and favoured of mortals, might have been unmingled happiness, and which, in Oliver's, were true felicity. With the purest and most amiable generosity on one side; and the truest, warmest, soul-felt gratitude on the other; it is no wonder that, by the end of that short time, Oliver Twist had become completely domesticated with the old lady and her niece, and that the fervent attachment of his young and sensitive heart, was repaid by their pride in, and attachment to, himself.   (292)

Is Dickens a better historian than Carlyle? Perhaps the question ought to be rephrased: Does Dickens approach Carlyle's ideal historian? That personage, we remember, was one who was both seer and reformer, who could observe and depict the simultaneity of events, solid action, to show the passion and the mystery that lay behind that action, who, finally, because of his eye for the Whole, could see the organic connection of events and actions. He was truly one who could take the story of an individual, his biography or history, and make that story serve as prophetic manuscript. He, in short, could get beyond fact and present the mystery of experience, the Chaos of

Being. Carlyle, we remember, could not get beyond the insight that every life is both "like every other" and at the same time "utterly unique." He rejected, in White's words, "any effort to find the meaning of human life outside humanity itself" (147). Dickens did not reject that effort, and in the story of Oliver he succeeds in demonstrating one possible way out of the Carlylian dilemma. For Dickens, the meaning of life is not bound by humanity itself; it is found through the recognition that there is, indeed, something beyond Fact itself.

As an historian, Carlyle was limited, finally coming to depend on some far-off apocalyptic event to "save" mankind. He was limited in that he could not recognize, in spite of his many affirmations, the spiritual nature of human beings. As a result he came to depend on strong leaders and might. Dickens, unlike Carlyle, both recognized and proclaimed the triumph of the spirit. He, in contrast to Carlyle, advanced beyond the metaphorical insight that every life is both like every other and at the same time utterly unique.

One of the most significant scenes, in this respect, is that in which Nancy tells her story to Rose and "the gentleman." When he describes the red mark that Monks has, Nancy says: "You know him!" The gentleman replies: "I think I do. . . . We shall see. Many people are singularly like each other. It may not be the same" (414). Of course it is true that many people are like each other, but surely Dickens is being Carlylian and more here: Monks is and is not like others; he is both unique and alike. A scene more revealing of Dickens' success as Carlylian historian is that seemingly insignificant one in which Mr. Bumble comes to rescue the Sowerberrys from Oliver, who has been locked in the coal-cellar. When Oliver tells all that he is not afraid of Mr. Bumble, Mrs. Sowerberry says that he must be mad. Mr. Bumble replies that it is not madness, it's meat. He goes on:

> "Meat, ma'am, meat," replied Bumble, with stern emphasis. "You've over-fed him, ma'am. You've raised a artificial soul and spirit in him, ma'am, unbecoming a person of his condition: as the board, Mrs. Sowerberry, who are practical philosophers, will tell you. What have paupers to do with soul or spirit? It's quite enough that we let 'em have live bodies." (93)

It is the genius of Dickens that often one finds profundity in seemingly comic, insignificant statements. The blending of the significant with the small, the comic with the tragic, the high with the low—all this attests to Dickens' artistry. It also reveals his ability to see the spiritual in the material, the spirit in the body. As Carlyle's ideal historian Dickens depicted what Carlyle called "solid action" as dramatically and as impressively as any artist. As such, he displayed more than any other artist in his time that gift of seeing the Whole. As such, he succeeded as much as any other artist in the Victorian period, often called the Carlylian era, in calling the sympathy of mortal hearts into action and vividly and truthfully making fiction take on the role of history in the Carlylian sense; he succeeded not simply in depicting the Chaos of Being but in giving it a comprehensible meaning.

WORKS CITED

Brooks, Peter. *The Melodramatic Imagination*. New Haven Conn.: Yale University Press, 1976.

Carlyle, Thomas. *Selected Essays*. Intro. Ian Campbell. London: J. M. Dent, 1915, 1972.

Dale, Peter. *The Victorian Critic and the Idea of History*. Cambridge, Mass.: Harvard University Press, 1977.

Dickens, Charles. *Oliver Twist*. Ed. Kathleen Tillotson. Oxford: Clarendon Press, 1966.

―――. *Oliver Twist*. Ed. Peter Fairclough. Intro. Angus Wilson. Harmondsworth: Penguin Books, 1966.

Goldberg, Michael. *Carlyle and Dickens*. Athens: Georgia University Press, 1972.

Prose of the Romantic Period. Ed. Carl Woodring. Boston: Houghton Mifflin, 1961.

Thesing, William B., and Denis Thomas. *"Victorian Studies* Alumni Conference, Indiana University, Bloomington." *Victorian Studies* 28 (Winter 1985): 305–308.

White, Hayden. *Metahistory*. Baltimore, Md.: Johns Hopkins University Press, 1973.

The Interplay of City and Self
in *Oliver Twist,*
David Copperfield,
and *Great Expectations*

David M. Craig

the city
the man, an identity, it can't be
otherwise—an
interpenetration both ways . . .
W. C. Williams, *Paterson*

In imagining the London experiences of his autobiographical heroes, Oliver, David, and Pip, Charles Dickens records his changing conception of the relationship between city and self. For Dickens, the terms of urban experience evolve as he becomes increasingly aware of the way in which reality is created by consciousness and consciousness is itself shaped by external reality. In *Oliver Twist,* the city and the self have discrete identities, as Dickens systematically detaches Oliver from his urban surroundings, the subjective world from the objective. In *David Copperfield,* the city has a subjective identity, as backdrop to David's desire to become the "hero of [his] own life" (1). Cast by David's memory or transfigured by his imagination, the city stands in relation to the hopes and fears of the self. Only in *Great Expectations* does Dickens fuse the identities of the city and self. Through the act of perception, views of the city are always conditioned and framed by the concerns of the self. Conversely, the city encloses consciousness itself so that acts of consciousness are always shaped by their urban context. In *Great Expectations,* then, city and self represent inseparable phenomena—much as observer and event do in the new physics.

Dickens makes explicit the connection between the identity of the city and the perceptions of its inhabitants in a notebook entry late in his career. He conceives the possibility of "representing London—or Paris, or any great place—in the new light of being actually unknown to all the people in the story, and only taking the colour of their fears and fancies and opinions. So getting a new aspect, and being unlike itself. An *odd* unlikeness to itself" (*Letters,* III: 788). This city exists in the minds of those who know or experience it. Such an urban novel would mirror the way in which urban residents know the city: the city they see as outside themselves is the mental representation of the experience of the city that is inside themselves. This transformation of the city into an *"odd* unlikeness to itself" identifies the true nature of the Dickensian city. As J. Hillis Miller says of the Dickens city: "[it] is, first of all, the co-presence of an unimaginable number of people in an entirely humanized world" (*World,* 293). If Dickens never actually wrote the novel of London or Paris that he postulates, he does record the London of the "fears," "fancies," and "opinions" of his autobiographical heroes. These "Londons"—as the Smithfield scenes of *Oliver Twist* and *Great Expectations* indicate—are worlds as different as their heroes Oliver and Pip.

By examining the urban experiences of Dickens' heroes as a relationship rather than as an event, I am departing from the thematic approaches of Alexander Welsh and F. S. Schwarzbach.[1] While Welsh and Schwarzbach provide the groundwork for this study by documenting the way in which the city operated as a catalytic agent for Dickens' imagination and the way in which his imagination responded differently to the country and the city, their readings render Dickens' London as a fixed reality. Focusing on Dickens' efforts to cope with the destructive London of his experience, Welsh and Schwarzbach reduce urban scenes as varied as the Smithfield scenes in *Oliver Twist* and *Great Expectations* to aspects of a single vision. Raymond Williams provides a more fruitful insight when he argues that the form of Dickens' novels unfolds "a way of seeing," because this formulation makes the city inseparable from Dickens' novelistic imagination (159). For Williams, this mode of seeing is ultimately social, a recognition of "relationships and connections . . . that are obscured, complicated, mystified, by the sheer rush and noise and miscellaneity of the new complex social order" (155). Unlike Williams, whose interest is in the vision, I want to focus on the process of seeing itself. As represented by *Oliver Twist, David Copperfield,* and *Great Expectations,* this process of seeing is more complicated than Williams's schema would indicate because it bonds the seer and the seen so that each shapes and is shaped by the other.

Oliver Twist, David Copperfield, and *Great Expectations* illuminate Dickens' increasingly self-conscious recognition of the interpenetration of city and self, for, as Berry Westburg argues, these novels "are systematically related" (xvi). They present striking similarities in their presentations of London and of urban experience.[2] On one level, there are suggestive geographical parallels, as for instance Dickens' use of Smithfield in *Oliver Twist* and *Great Expectations* as setting for the crucial scenes introducing the hero to the city. More importantly, Dickens reworks the same urban motifs in each successive novel. For example, Oliver's physical imprisonment in Fagin's lair becomes David's entrapment in his blacking house memories, which, in turn, becomes Pip's psychological entanglement in his own guilty consciousness. But the most important aspect for this study is the change in Dickens' style in representing moments of urban vision.[3] As a record of the dialogue between imagination and the city, Dickens' style embodies his recognition of a changing epistemological relationship between himself and the world. In this sense, style is an event, an experience; style is, to adapt Wallace Stevens, the "cry of its occasion / Part of the res itself and not about it" ("An Ordinary Evening in New Haven," xii: 473).

The shift in Dickens' style from the largely metonymic patterning of *Oliver Twist* to the metaphoric method of *Great Expectations* provides occasion and signal to the change in the way that his imagination conceives urban reality.[4] The metonymic style of *Oliver Twist* is dualistic, always distinguishing the subject from the object; the narrator's reportorial stance from that which he reports, Oliver's emotional responsiveness from the London world inside and out of Fagin's lair.[5] Dickens usually invests his rhetorical energy in the city as object of perception. Readers will recall the prominent role that extended passages of townscape description play in the scenes set at Jacob's island, at Smithfield, and in Fagin's den. By contrast, in *David Copperfield* a pattern of stylistic overlay juxtaposes two modes of consciousness often in the same passages, that of the youthful David with that of the narrator David.[6] Rhetorically, the subject, David, is always in the foreground and the object in the background, much as in the relationship between the actor and the backdrop on a stage. London scenes, so prominent in *Oliver Twist,* almost disappear. Even the famous account of the blacking factory occupies a scant four paragraphs, themselves foreshortened from Dickens' autobiographical formulation. This turn in Dickens' metonymic method places the city—as it exists in David's memories or as it is rendered by his imagination—in relation to the concerns of the self. The metaphoric mode of *Great Expectations* unites the city and the self by placing in the foreground the process of consciousness itself, both of Pip the youth and Pip the narrator. Ernst Cassirer's account of the making of metaphor provides a useful description of the kind of consciousness which the text reproduces: perceptual "excitement caused by some object in the outer world furnishes both the occasion and the means of its denomination" (89). This metaphoric process conjoins city and self, the object and subject of sensation, and in doing so concentrates meaning in the relationship between them. In *Great Expectations,* urban identity necessarily partakes of the reciprocal principles of city and self.

II

Detaching the observer from that which is observed, the metonymic style of *Oliver Twist* depicts city and self as separate realities. The Smithfield scene, in which Oliver and Sikes pass through the market on the way to rob the Maylies, provides a paradigmatic instance of the city as distinct from its observers, the narrator and Oliver. The narrator observes the churning market with the detachment of a reporter and chronicles its myriad details with the fidelity of a camera. Its energy challenges his ability to perceive and order. Hence his rhetorical structures embody his efforts to know—to classify, to sequence, and to order the tumultuous market:

> It was market-morning. The ground was covered, nearly ankle-deep, with filth and mire; a thick steam, perpetually rising from the reeking bodies of the cattle, and mingling with the fog, which seemed to rest upon the chimney-tops, hung heavily above. All the pens in the centre of the large area, and as many temporary pens as could be crowded into the vacant space, were filled with sheep; tied up to posts by the gutter side were long lines of beasts and oxen, three or four deep. Countrymen, butchers, drovers, hawkers, boys, thieves, idlers, and vagabonds of very low grade, were mingled together in a mass; the whistling of drovers, the barking of dogs, the bellowing and plunging of oxen, the bleating of sheep, the grunting and squeaking of pigs, the cries of hawkers, the shouts, oaths, and quarreling on all sides; the ringing of bells and roar of voices, that issued from every public-house; the crowding, pushing, driving, beating, whooping and yelling; the hideous and discordant din that resounded from every corner of the market; and the unwashed, unshaved, squalid, and dirty figures constantly running to and fro, and bursting in and out of the throng; rendered it a stunning and bewildering scene, which quite confounded the senses.   (153)

The passage presents an objective city, in contrast to the subjective city of the memorandum book, and works by enumerating and categorizing details: kinds of animals, varieties of people, and types of noise. The narrator's analysis gives the market the shape of the interpretive mind. Yet while each element in the classification schema is rendered individually, the totality becomes chaotic and confusing.[7] For example, the people, each classified so distinctly, become "mingled together in a mass" and the sounds combine to form the "hideous and discordant din." This anarchic world overcomes the order principles of the interpretive mind. Categorical distinctions disintegrate: "whistling drovers," "barking dogs," "bleating sheep," "cries of the hawkers" exist on the same level. The common element of this environment is noise, with human language just another variant. The collapse of the many details into a cacophonous whole negates the effort at classification, signifying a world which cannot be logically ordered and which dissolves upon analysis into shapelessness.

Like a solar flare, "crowding, pushing, driving," Smithfield reaches outward, its force threatening the narrative calm which attempts to contain, to form, and to analyze. Even in this early Dickens townscape, the object of perception is acting upon the subject. As the predominance of gerunds in the passage indicates, energy is the essential characteristic of the world. The gerunds provide a temporal representation of chaos—a continuous present that defies temporal order and sequence. The gerundial construction—a rhetorical synthesis of action and being—also illuminates the relationship between the narrative mind and the world. By literally rendering action as being, the gerunds provide moments of static perception, models of change. This rhetorical reordering of Smithfield's energy permits both the narrator and the reader to contemplate without becoming involved; it is the rhetoric of distance. Simultaneously, verbal nouns point to the limitations of language to represent and contain the anarchic market. They proclaim their own failure to represent motion as motion. The "stunning and bewildering scene . . . quite [confounding to the] senses" resists efforts at knowing, its energy and fluidity finally eluding the framing language of analysis and classification. Dickens' style undercuts the narrative control, pointing to an actuality that is beyond rational ordering.

Counterpoised to the narrator's rhetorical exploration is Oliver's movement through Smithfield, his urban journey. Dickens renders Oliver's journey with two comments which frame the extended passage of description: "from which latter place arose a tumult of discordant sounds that filled Oliver Twist with amazement" (153) and "Mr. Sikes, dragging Oliver after him, elbowed his way through the thickest of the crowd, and bestowed very little attention on the numerous sights and sounds, which so astonished the boy" (153). The syntax of each sentence emphasizes Oliver's passivity—that he is acted upon rather than acting and that the scene imposes itself upon his mind. Rhetorically, Smithfield, not Oliver, is the subject of this scene. The words "amazement" and "astonishment" point out Oliver's primarily emotional response to the marketplace—a reaction only half formulated by consciousness. His generalized reaction contrasts with the particularity of the narrator's analysis. In the journey, this Dickensian innocent is untainted by the world and knowledge. Unlike the narrator, who can bring the interpretive mind to bear on what he sees, Oliver cannot comprehend Smithfield; unlike the narrator, he can see with no possibility for knowing.

One terminus of the narrator's and Oliver's urban journeys is Fagin's lair, Dickens' imaginative center of London and the novel. If the metonymic style detaches the narrator and Oliver from the city, it emphasizes the interdependence between Fagin, the urban man, and his environment. In introducing Fagin, the narrator depicts him as inseparable from his context:

> The walls and ceiling of the room were perfectly black with age and dirt. There was a deal table before the fire: upon which were a candle, stuck in a ginger-beer bottle, two or three pewter pots, a loaf and butter, and a plate. In a frying-pan, which was on the fire, and which was secured to the mantleshelf by a string, some sausages were cooking; and standing over them, with a toasting-fork in his hand, was a very old shrivelled Jew, whose villainous-looking and repulsive face was obscured by a quantity of matted red hair. He was dressed in a greasy flannel gown, with his throat bare; and seemed to be dividing his attention between the frying-pan and a clothes-horse, over which a great number of silk handkerchiefs were hanging. Several rough beds made of old sacks were huddled side by side on the floor. Seated round the table were four or five boys, none older than the Dodger, smoking long clay pipes, and drinking spirits with the air of middle-aged men. These all crowded about their associate as he whispered a few words to the Jew; and then turned round and grinned at Oliver. So did the Jew himself, toasting-fork in hand. (56–57)

The narrative method is synecdochic (according to Jakobson, one of the characteristics of the metonymic style), with the table and its contents evoking the character of the room. The passage proceeds in a ''this-is-the-house-that-Jack-built'' fashion with a series of spatial connections all leading to the preparer of the domestic banquet, Fagin. The periodic sentence which introduces Fagin momentarily arrests the movement of the passage, suspending the reader's attention until the ''very old shrivelled Jew'' materializes. Introduced as an appendage to the frying pan, which is in turn connected to the wall, Fagin comes into existence inseparable from his surroundings. And yet clearly, he is the center of the scene, its source of energy and power. When Fagin focuses on Oliver in the final sentence of the paragraph, this center radiates outward, an ever-expanding ripple. Even the passive voice construction does not diminish Fagin's energy. When Fagin's attention turns to Oliver, Oliver is enclosed.

At once prison and refuge, Fagin's lair affords Oliver another perspective on the city, this time from the inside out.

> There was a back-garret window with rusty bars outside, which had no shutter; and out of this, Oliver often gazed with a melancholy face for hours together; but nothing was to be descried from it but a confused and crowded mass of house-tops, blackened chimneys, and gable-ends. Sometimes, indeed, a grizzly head might be seen, peering over the parapet-wall of a distant house: but it was quickly withdrawn again; and as the window of Oliver's observatory was nailed down, and dimmed with the rain and smoke of years, it was as much as he could do to make out the forms of the different objects beyond, without making any attempt to be seen or heard,—which he had as much chance of being, as if he had lived inside the ball of St. Paul's Cathedral.   (128–129)

This passage sets Oliver's confusion in relief.[8] Although he "gazes" upon the urban spectacle, he cannot apprehend what he sees. "The confused mass of house-tops, blackened chimneys, and gable-ends" are represented photographically—not filtered through Oliver's consciousness. The generalized details convey the confusion of the urban world: particulars proliferate, movement is always random, amid abundance there is only aloneness. Dickens' prose detaches Oliver from the very scene of which he is the observer. "Oliver's observatory" isolates him "as if he had lived inside the ball of St. Paul's Cathedral." This is one of the few metaphoric elements in the novel's townscape, and even it has a literal—not a metaphoric—referent. The simile calls attention to Dickens' willingness to expose the innocent to the city, but not to let it touch him; to let him gaze upon the city, but not to let him penetrate its mysteries.

There is an important exception to Dickens' systematic detachment of city and self, that in the story of Nancy and Sikes. In rendering deserted, fogenshrouded Smithfield, Dickens shifts his attention to the minds of his human observers. In doing so, he demonstrates the identification with the criminal that Edmund Wilson so brilliantly examined in "The Two Scrooges." At this point in his career Dickens cannot yet directly expose his hero to the night city, the alienating city, but can explore it in his guise as outlaw. Carefully detaching Oliver from Smithfield with the narrative hyperbole, "it [Smithfield] might have been Grosvenor Square, for anything Oliver knew to the contrary" (109), Dickens probes the city of Sikes's and Nancy's fears.

It was Smithfield that they were crossing. . . .

They [Sikes, Nancy, and Oliver] had hurried on a few paces, when a deep church-bell struck the hour. With its first stroke, his two conductors stopped, and turned their heads in the direction whence the sound proceeded.

"Eight o'clock, Bill," said Nancy, when the bell ceased.

"What's the good of telling me that; I can hear it, can't I!" replied Sikes.

"I wonder whether *they* can hear it," said Nancy.

"Of course they can," replied Sikes. "It was Bartlemy time when I was shopped; and there warn't a penny trumpet in the fair, as I couldn't hear the squeaking on. Arter I was locked up for the night, the row and din outside made the thundering old jail so silent, that I could almost have beat my brains out against the iron plates of the door."

"Poor fellows!" said Nancy. . . . "Oh, Bill, such fine young chaps as them!"   (109–110)

Sikes and Nancy understand Smithfield in a way that Oliver does not. Their impressions take shape in their remembrances of their Newgate colleagues, for to the consciousness of the criminal even the empty marketplace underscores his status as fugitive.[9] Yet as the reaction to the tolling bells indicates, Sikes and Nancy do not have the same experience of Smithfield. For Nancy the bells are the catalyst for her empathetic reminiscences, while for Sikes the silence between the tolling bells partakes of the ominous quiet of Newgate that made him want to beat his "brains out against the iron plates of the door." Nancy's sense of place is shaped by her loyalties to others, hence her pledge to remain faithful to Sikes if he is imprisoned: "I'd walk round and round the place [Newgate] till I dropped, if the snow was on the ground and I hadn't a shawl to cover me" (110). By contrast, for Sikes, the chiming clock frames the silent market—much as the "row and din [of the St. Bartholomew Fair] made the thundering old jail so silent."

Sikes's and Nancy's different reactions dramatize the subjective city that will later capture Dickens' attention in the memorandum book; their reactions also show why Schwarzbach is wrong when he argues that before *Edwin Drood* the Dickens city "is invested with tonal qualities independent of the novels' characters" (217). Nancy's plea to Sikes, "wait a minute," underscores the difference in their interpretations. By her plea, Nancy is telling Sikes of her loyalty to him and asking him to understand her "Smithfield." But of course Sikes cannot, for his "Smithfield" shares the silence of Newgate and prefigures the shape of death. His rejection of Nancy's sympathy on the grounds that only a "file and twenty yards of good stout rope" would help him reveals the workings of an alienated mind—a mind haunted by death and cut off from the sympathy it most needs (110). As their failure to communicate indicates, Sikes's and Nancy's interpretations of their Newgate memories place them in entirely different "Smithfields."

In the multiple Smithfields of Nancy, Sikes, the narrator, and Oliver, Dickens announces a central concern: exploring the relationship between the city's unaccommodating actuality and his protagonists' personal points of view. At root, his concern is epistemological, one of how best to know the city. In the novel's core story, Dickens contrasts the narrator's objective, taxonomic knowing and Oliver's subjective responsiveness—the latter which registers urban realities in the manner of a seismograph recording a far-off earthquake. By contrast, Dickens in the guise of outlaw can probe the alternative idea that city and self exist as relationship—that, as Sikes's and Nancy's Newgate memories demonstrate, the process of consciousness is necessarily shaped by its external context. Similarly, Sikes's and Nancy's Smithfield, while having an actual existence, cannot be entirely separated from their memories and perceptions. This city shaped by its viewers' needs and fears points to the London of David Copperfield's experience.

III

If the Oliver Twist story emphasizes the disjunction between the city's chaotic multiplicity and the hero's innocent consciousness, then *David Copperfield* brings the two into conjunction. The novel reproduces both the interpretative consciousness of the *Oliver Twist* narrator and the emotional innocence of Oliver's, but the two stories are joined with David's view of his youthful experience encased by the mature David's memories. When the two Davids view the city, there is an inward turn. The novel renders the central urban scenes—for instance, David's first passage through London, his time at Murdstone and Grinby's, and the search for Miss Emily—as interior events, experiences whose location is inside the self. In contrast to the simple metonymy of *Oliver Twist,* a pattern of overlay predominates in *David Copperfield*. This style juxtaposes past memories and present perspectives, thereby framing the external city with its subjective recording.

To the eyes of the youthful David, the city is the place of inclusion and confusion much as it was to Oliver. As he observes upon his first entrance into London, "we went on through a great noise and roar that confused my weary head beyond description" (74). Surrounded by this external tumult, David alternately casts the story of his triumph and falls asleep, overwhelmed by the welter of urban sensations. Appropriately, his first view of London records not the sights and sounds, but the city of his imagination where the heroes of literature were "constantly enacting and re-enacting their adventures" (71). In this formulation, David's story documents the growth of imagination, his *Prelude,* and the dangers that the city poses to imagination. The coach-house story of his first London visit unfolds both parts of this tale. With no one to meet him, David casts a tale of abandonment and identifies himself as "more solitary than Robinson Crusoe, who had nobody to look at him and see that he was solitary" (72). This identification signifies the problem the city poses for David—his absolute sense of isolation and the pain of a consciousness which cannot communicate its feelings to others.

David's account of his coach-house experiences fills out the story of his desertion: "I couldn't hope to remain there when I began to starve" (73). Sitting amid the bundles, boxes, and debris, David becomes to his own imagination one more bit of baggage waiting to be picked up. In this nightmare formulation David, unlike Oliver, has become part of the urban environment. The arrival of Mr. Mell—who picks up David "as if I were weighed, bought, delivered and paid for"—completes his story (73). This resolution unfolds one possible ending for his tale, being reduced from subject to object of his own narrative.[10] If imagination provides a way of expressing the fears of the emotional orphan uncared for by the world, it also intensifies his aloneness, making him want to extinguish consciousness. Positing a connection between the coach-house baggage and himself, David has liberated his imagination to explore the relationship between his experience and the world around him, between city and self. But this imaginative liberation also brings confinement as the surroundings impose themselves on his imagination so that he begins to see himself as a part of this setting, as coach-house refuse.

In rendering David's urban journey away from the London coach house toward Mr. Creakles's school, Dickens' narrative overlay blends past and present perspectives and dramatizes David's urban confinement. In contrast to David's transforming consciousness upon entering London, his mind now is passive. The ride produces only fragments of memory: "we went . . . over a bridge which, no doubt, was London Bridge (indeed I think he [Mr. Mell] told me so, but I was half asleep)" (72). During the journey, the reader never sees London more directly than this. Rather the narrative reproduces the overwhelming fatigue that David felt during the coach ride. This fatigue—a kind of twilight of consciousness—is not rendered as time past, but as sensation re-experienced. In the account of this sensation, the two Davids, youth and narrator, occupy the same narrative space, the stylistic overlay bringing the two into conjunction.

The account of the rest stop at Mrs. Fibbitson's almshouse in south London illustrates this conjunction of the two Davids and their two perspectives.

> My impression is, after many years of consideration, that there never can have been anybody in the world who played worse. He [Mr. Mell] made the most dismal sounds I have ever heard produced . . . but the influence of the strain upon me was, first, to make me think of all my sorrows until I could hardly keep my tears back; then to take away my appetite; and lastly, to make me so sleepy that I couldn't keep my eyes open. They begin to close again, and I begin to nod, as the recollection rises fresh upon me. Once more the little room, with its open corner cupboard, and its square-backed chairs, and its angular little staircase leading to the room above, and its three peacock's feathers displayed over the mantelpiece . . . fades from before me, and I nod, and sleep. The flute becomes inaudible, the wheels of the coach are heard instead, and I am on my journey. The coach jolts, I wake with a start, and the flute has come back again, and the Master of Salem House is sitting with his legs crossed, playing it dolefully, while the old woman of the house looks on delighted. She fades in her turn, and he fades, and all fades, and there is no flute, no Master, no Salem House, no David Copperfield, no anything but heavy sleep.(75–76)

For David the narrator, the memory of Mr. Mell's flute is the catalyst for re-experiencing the entire episode—the melancholy strains bringing back memories of Mrs. Fibbitson's parlor still ornamented by the peacock feathers, recalling the pain of desertion that David fights to suppress, and once again invoking the sleep that will momentarily relieve the pain. In the recollection—as in the troubled sleep of the youthful David—past, present, and future are co-presences. And in the recollection, David the narrator and David the youth have a composite identity. They respond similarly to the pain of the experience—the youth to the pain of abandonment by his mother, the man to the pain of the youth. Both want a sleep that will extinguish sensation. Neither awake, listening to Mell's flute, nor asleep can the Davids find rest or solace; neither can the narrative. A resting place comes only with the extinction of consciousness: "all fades, and there is no flute, no Master, no Salem House, *no David Copperfield,* no anything but heavy sleep" (my emphasis). Here sleep does not bring rest or comfort, only momentary ces-sation of the treasured modes of David's mental life, memory and imagination. With David so "dead asleep," the narrative momentarily has the quiescence of death. Yet even this momentary narrative silence takes its shape from "the great noise and uproar" that surrounds it, from the London outside Mrs. Fibbitson's (74).

The temptation to extinguish his troubled consciousness and David's fear of becoming one more bit of London debris give shape to his experiences in London. Again and again, he wonders what people think of him and records such comments as that of the one-eyed man in gaiters: "they had better put a brass collar round my neck, and tie me up in the stable" (72). Such comments are included because David wants to be recognized, and he believes that if people will only see him they will realize his preeminence. Thus in the blacking factory chapter David describes his efforts to buy a tavern keeper's best ale and the wife's kiss as fully as he does his time at Murdstone and Grinby's. For David (as for Dickens) the episode, especially the kiss, is important because it validates his sense of distinction. Many of the Micawber episodes in which David becomes friend and confidant also serve this function. As David begins to be seen by others, he becomes the subject of his life and emerges from the urban backdrop.

If the youthful David seeks liberation, the mature narrator finds only enclosure. The blacking factory, Murdstone and Grinby's, typifies these urban enclosures, for this youthful trauma has its imaginative formulation in the mature David's experience.[11] Dickens' revisions from his original, autobiographical account of the experience call attention to his changing intentions. In the autobiographical version, the passage presents a memory long avoided; in *Copperfield,* the memory frames even the present moment.

> The blacking warehouse was the last house on the left-hand side of the way, at old Hungerford Stairs. It was a crazy, tumble-down old house, abutting of course on the river, and literally overrun with rats. Its wainscotted rooms and its rotten floors and staircase, and the grey rats' swarming and scuffling coming up the stairs at all times, and the dirt and decay of the place, rise up visibly before me, as if I were there again. The counting-house was on the first floor, looking over the coal-barges and the river. There was a recess in it, in which I was to sit and work. (Forster I: 25)

> Murdstone and Grinby's warehouse was at the water-side. It was down in Blackfriars. Modern improvements have altered the place; but it was the last house at the bottom of a narrow street, curving down hill to the river, with some stairs at the end, where people took boat. It was a crazy old house with a wharf of its own, abutting on the water when the tide was in, and on the mud when the tide was out, and literally overrun with rats. Its panelled rooms, discoloured with the dirt and smoke of a hundred years, I dare say; its decaying floors and staircase; the squeaking and scuffling of the old grey rats down in the cellars; and the dirt and rottenness of the place; are things, not of many years ago, in my mind, but of the present instant. They are all before me, just as they were in the evil hour when I went among them for the first time, with my trembling hand in Mr. Quinion's. (154)

The passage from the autobiography is of the past, a past which impinges on the present only in that its images "rise up visibly before [one]." Yet even when pressing against the present, this past is held at a rhetorical distance.

The "as if" formulation of the simile "as if I were there again" signals that the details of Murdstone and Grinby's only can intrude on the present as the result of a deliberate act of mind. They remain at the distance of memory. By contrast, in the *Copperfield* passage the past encloses the present: "decaying floors and staircase . . . the squeaking and scuffling of the old grey rats [are] . . . of the present instant" still confining David. Unlike Oliver, whose enclosures were the physical and geographical reality of Fagin's den, David is enclosed by memories, memories which neither temporal nor geographical change affect. The *Copperfield* passage negates its initial assertion that "modern improvements have altered the place." In David's memory nothing has changed, and the physical details are as present as consciousness itself. It is not the blacking factory in which David "was to sit," rather the factory in which David's hand is still "trembling." As the image of David's trembling hand tells us, the scene does not locate the beginning of pain, but denominates David's continuing authorship of the self.

Unaltered by the accidents of historical change, the blacking factory is part of David's permanent psychic space. The narrative reproduces the mature David's, as well as the mature Dickens', active participations in the sensations of the child. Again Dickens' revisions from the autobiography are suggestive:

> The deep remembrance of the sense I had of being utterly *neglected and hopeless;* of the shame I felt in my position . . . cannot be written. My whole nature was so penetrated with the grief and humiliation of such considerations, that even now, famous and caressed and happy, I often forget in my dreams that I have a dear wife and children; even that I am a man; and wander desolately back to that time in my life.   (my emphasis, Forster I: 26–27)

> The deep remembrance of the sense I had, of being utterly without hope *now*—of the shame I felt in my position . . . cannot be written.   (my emphasis, 155)

The insertion of the word "now" and the deletions from the autobiographical account not only change the temporal character of the passage; they also call attention to David's narrative presence. The changes, particularly the omissions, dramatize what Dickens felt compelled to specify in the autobiography—the pain of insignificance and the fear of losing the self. The inserted "now" emphasizes the immediacy of the wounding, making the pain, fear, and guilt of the present moment. Dickens uses the *Copperfield* formulation of the passage to dramatize David's using a remembered "real" event to identify the self—not to show David wandering "back to that time in my life." Dickens' David narrates the tale in order to accommodate himself to the pain of the experience. By casting the city as backdrop to his own story and by dramatizing the hazards of urban enclosures, this David emerges as subject of his own narrative—something that the passive Oliver never became.

David's hard-won subjectivity demonstrates the successful interaction between his urban experience and his writing. Through the course of his narrative, David literally finds his way in the city, in this "Modern Babylon" as Micawber calls it. The welter of sensations occasioned by the city are organized and systematized. The blacking factory episode continues with David learning under Micawber's guidance "the names of streets and the shapes of corner houses . . . that [he] might find [his] way back easily [to the blacking factory]" (157). As his memoir *David Copperfield* demonstrates, these lessons in urban navigation are not lost on David, who returns at will to Murdstone and Grinby's. But Dickens' David not only traverses the city by mapping its geography, he also makes his way by "fit[ting] my old books to my altered life, and ma[king] stories for myself, out of the streets, and out of men and women" (168). For David, these urban fictions give London a familiar shape by imposing on its landscape a textual map that he already knows. If this David can no longer believe in London as the place where "all [his] favourite heroes . . . [were] constantly enacting and re-enacting"(71) their adventures, he can transform its "sordid things" and his "strange experiences" there into his own "imaginative world" (169).

In this imaginative re-formation of the city, David encounters not only the city, but also the self. David continues his memories of his London experiences during this time by turning, as he so often does in his narrative, to himself: "I set down this remembrance here, because it is an instance . . . [of] how some main points in the character I shall unconsciously develop, I suppose, in writing my life, were gradually forming all this while" (168). This passage juxtaposes his transcription of his life story with the development of his character in the past. Its rhetorical formulation makes David the author of his character. But David's authorship, his "development of [his] character," is an act of the present, an act of writing. Not that this authorship is detached from the past or from what he was before he began to compose his autobiography, but rather the mature rememberer David is as responsible for developing his character as the youthful David was. In this passage, then, as in much of Wordsworth's *Prelude,* memory and imagination are co-extensive realms, and they mix and mingle until neither David nor Dickens can distinguish between them. As David says at chapter's end in turning from the events of blacking factory days, "When my thoughts go back now, to that slow agony of my youth, I wonder how much of the histories I invented for such people hangs like a mist of fancy over well-remembered facts!" (169).

The mature David like his youthful counterpart can only accommodate himself to his pain by encasing urban experience in memory and imagination—just as he himself remains encased in blacking factory days. As Pip will discover, however, to transform the city either by memory or imagination will have its own dangers.

IV

By presenting townscape in *Great Expectations* as inseparable from the act of conceiving it, Dickens depicts the reciprocity of city and self. Unlike *David Copperfield,* which keeps David in the narrative foreground, *Great Expectations* places the process of consciousness itself in the foreground. Even more than David, Pip uses urban experience as both present occasion and vehicle for asserting the identity of the self. Townscape becomes the backdrop against which the drama of the self is played. His brief comment upon entering London for the first time is typical of his method of rendering the city: "I think I might have had some faint doubts, whether it [London] was not rather ugly, crooked, narrow, and dirty" (153). But the city also shapes the responses that it occasions. As occasion for and object of sensation, the city plays a crucial role in the way Pip defines his experience. If the London of *Great Expectations* takes the form of Pip's "fears and fancies and opinions," it also provides the mold which forms them.

The scene in Jaggers's office, which serves a function similar to that of the scene in Fagin's lair in *Oliver Twist* and the coach-house scene in *David Copperfield,* introduces the interplay between Pip and his urban surroundings.

> Mr. Jaggers's room was lighted by a skylight only, and was a most dismal place; the skylight, eccentrically patched like a broken head, and the distorted adjoining houses looking as if they had twisted themselves to peep down at me through it. There were not so many papers about, as I should have expected to see; and there were some odd objects about, that I should not have expected to see—such as an old rusty pistol, a sword in a scabbard, several strange-looking boxes and packages, and two dreadful casts on a shelf, of faces peculiarly swollen and twitchy about the nose. (154)

Rendering the office in synecdochic details, Pip has the particularity of vision that Oliver and David lack. His description reproduces the play of consciousness with the world: the likening of the skylight to a patched head or the adjoining houses to peeping Toms. Pip's transforming imagination (like the romantic imagination of the young David) replaces the reportorial objectivity of the *Oliver Twist* narrator. The verbs of the scene in Jaggers's office place Pip's mental actions and reactions in the foreground: "I should not have expected to see," "I fancied" (twice), "I . . . became frustrated," "I called to mind," "I wondered" (154–155). In the scene Pip has a novelistic imagination busy constructing its own plot. "Mr. Jaggers's own high back chair was of deadly black horse hair, with rows of brass nails round it like a coffin, and I fancied I could see how he leaned back in it, and bit his forefinger at his clients." When Pip sits in the client's chair, he becomes an actor in the imagined story.

Having animated the room, Pip finds himself the victim of his imaginative exercise, when his surroundings begin to enclose him. Pip is haunted by the life he has given to the fixtures of Jaggers's office. For instance, Pip notes that the two grotesque plaster statues above Jaggers's chair have "faces peculiarly swollen and twitchy about the nose." As he gazes on them further, he supplies them with a history, deciding that they are Jaggers's relatives, and finds himself wondering "why he stuck them [these plaster 'relatives'] on that dusty perch for the blacks and flies to settle on, instead of giving them a place at home" (155). Finally Pip flees the room because he cannot "bear the two casts on the shelf above Mr. Jaggers's chair" (155). This understated formulation mutes the emotion underlying the scene—Pip's feelings of being smothered and constricted by the room. The city provides the molds—the "casts"—with which Pip's claustrophobic imagination encloses him.

Pip's flight from Jaggers's office through Smithfield and Newgate, which provides his first extended urban views, exemplifies this interpenetration of city and self. In contrast to the narrative richness of the *Oliver Twist* vision of Smithfield, Pip's initial apprehension of the marketplace is rendered in a single sentence, a generalization that reduces the multiplicity of Smithfield to a single image—filth. "So, I came into Smithfield; and the shameful place, being all asmear with filth and fat and blood and foam, seemed to stick to me" (155). Unlike Oliver, Pip is experiencing Smithfield and is, to his own consciousness, contaminated by its filthy debris. Pip's feelings of uncleanliness call attention to the workings of the imaginative consciousness which fuses city and self. In the Smithfield sentence we observe the making of metaphor: "that concentration and heightening of simple sensory experience which finds release in the representation of subjective impulses and excitations in definite objective forms and figures" (Cassirer, 88). This projection of inner experience upon the world is precisely what Pip enacts when he tries to cleanse himself of Smithfield's "fat" and "foam" by turning toward St. Paul's. To the metaphoric imagination, the city becomes the external representation of the sensations of the self—the clinging "fat and foam," an iconic representation of Pip's emotional life, of the one constant in his experience, guilt. Smithfield has become a part of his self-consciousness. In the Smithfield passage, we can observe the interplay between city and self occurring on three simultaneous levels: his physical movement, his corresponding experiential movement, and the play of imagination which renders experience as metaphor.

On the first level, Pip's retreat from Smithfield transforms the townscape—Smithfield, Jaggers's office in Little Britain, Newgate, and St. Paul's—into a syntagmatic system in which the identity of each location is shaped by its proximity to its neighbors. Pip's movement towards St. Paul's through Newgate and back to Jaggers's office illustrates the workings of this system:

> So, I rubbed it [Smithfield's filth] off with all possible speed by turning into a street where I saw the great black dome of Saint Paul's bulging at me from behind a grim stone building which a bystander said was Newgate Prison. Following the wall of the jail, I found the roadway covered with straw to deaden the noise of passing vehicles; and from this, and from the quantity of people standing about smelling strongly of spirits and beer, I inferred that the trials were on.
> While I looked about me here, an exceedingly dirty and partially drunk minister of justice asked me if I would like to step in and hear a trial or so. . . . As I declined the proposal on the plea of an appointment, he was so good as to take me into a yard and show me . . . where people were publicly whipped, and then he showed me the Debtors' Door, out of which culprits came to be hanged. . . . Under these circumstances I thought myself well rid of him for a shilling.
> I dropped into the office to ask if Mr. Jaggers had come in yet. . . .
> (155–156)

As framed by Pip's perspective, the horror of Newgate is heightened by the blackness of St. Paul's looming behind it. And in this context, the church dome seems to take its blackness from the market refuse of Smithfield and the judicial corruption of Newgate. The succession of sites—the syntax of this geography—dramatizes Pip's flawed assumptions. By exposing him to increasingly appalling forms of corruption, this sequence unmasks Pip's illusory notions of progress. Ironically, while Pip's summary generalization of his walk, his "sickening idea of London," is entirely merited, he cannot see any connection between the city that he has just encountered and the London of his imagination—the setting which will seal and approve his aspirations toward gentility (156).

On the second level, Pip's experiential journey through Smithfield and

Newgate parallels his physical movement, as he continually confronts the feelings of contamination and enclosure that he hopes to dispel. The claustrophobic "dirt and dust" of Jaggers's office are replaced by the clinging blood and foam of Smithfield, which are in turn replaced by the judicial contamination of Newgate. Succumbing to the "partially drunk minister of justice['s]" invitation to see the gallows, Pip not only finds the most repulsive form of corruption and most constricting feelings of enclosure, but also perceives a pattern that recurs regularly and seems to shape his life. As Pip will observe on a subsequent visit to Newgate with Wemmick:

> I consumed the whole time in thinking how strange it was that I should be encompassed by all this taint of prison and crime; that, in my childhood out on our lonely marshes on a winter evening, I should have first encountered it; that it should have reappeared on two occasions, starting out like a stain that was faded but not gone; that it should . . . pervade my fortune and advancement. (249)

The suggestive irony of the verb "encompassed" dramatizes the interchange between Newgate and Pip's expectations as well as signifies his constricted and constricting view of experience. Like Miss Havisham, who enshrouds herself in the darkness of Satis House, the Pip who pursues his expectations darkens his consciousness, giving it the shape of nightmare. As the Newgate image makes clear, Pip's constricted imagination denies its very aspirations; in his imaginative enclosures, Pip gives himself no exit.

On the third level, Pip's language in the Smithfield and Newgate passages is metaphoric, yoking his subjective experience and the world as if they were equivalent realms. The metaphors are self-reflexive, calling attention to Pip's language rhythms and to the movement of his mind. His choice of verbs describes not only his movement through the city but also the movement of his consciousness: "would take a turn," "came into Smithfield," "rubbed it off by turning into," "dropped into the office," "strolled out again," "turned into Bartholomew Close" (155–156). Pip's physical and linguistic turns are always circular, revealing the rhythms of his life. Continually seeking release, he finds only the enclosure of the city and of his own mind. His circling consciousness continually eddies back to the two poles of his experience, Newgate and Estella. Also Pip's metaphoric imagination presents the creation of its experience, in the process of representing the experience itself. For example, when Pip perceives the physical corruption of Smithfield or the social corruption of Newgate, he simultaneously casts the form of his experience, the necessity for cleansing that he continually seeks but never finds.

Similarly, Pip's use of the verb "encompassed" during his second Newgate visit dramatizes both his guilty consciousness and his imaginative casting of his prison-house origins (the latter soon to be validated in Magwitch's revelations). As the Smithfield and Newgate narratives reveal, the self and the city are equivalent realms, Pip's guilty consciousness and the urban corruption.

Because city and self are equivalent realms, exploration of one allows exploration of the other. As rendered by Pip's mature imagination, the Jaggers's office-Smithfield-Newgate excursion represents this dual exploration. The journey has been from the city to the self and back again, from a perception of urban filth and corruption to the realization this perception is spawned by Pip's own guilt-constricted consciousness. To Pip's metaphoric consciousness, as well as to the mature Dickens, city and self are reciprocal principles: townscape partakes of the identity of the perceiver and in turn shapes the perceiver's consciousness.[12]

As medium for the dialogue between city and self, Charles Dickens' style in *Oliver Twist, David Copperfield,* and *Great Expectations* embodies his changing conception of the "identity of things." His successive redescriptions of the city constitute a series of epistemological events and a record of urban consciousness. In reseeing London, Dickens becomes increasingly unwilling to separate townscape from the consciousness that observes it. Not that the objective city disappears, for as the example of Smithfield suggests, its tumultuous reality troubles Pip as much as it did Oliver, the *Oliver Twist* narrator, and, of course, Dickens himself. But more important than the objective city is the contingent relationship between city and self. In Smithfield and the other urban locales of *Great Expectations,* Dickens approximates the only city that Pip can ever know, that of his fear, guilt, and desire. Pip metamorphoses this city into a "skylight, eccentrically patched like a broken head" or into clinging "fat and foam." Such metaphors not only refigure the city's existence, but also denominate the experience of the self. Pip's metamorphic language proclaims his consciousness and the subjectivity that David's narrative strives to achieve. Dickens' style reproduces Pip's metaphoric imagination, thereby conjoining the city and the self as dual creators of Pip's—and human—experience. Anticipating the Modernist view of such writers as William Carlos Williams, Charles Dickens forges the urban identity of city and self, "an interpenetration both ways."

NOTES

1. Grounding his argument on Dickens' journalistic and incidental pieces as well as on his fiction, Welsh persuasively argues that Dickens counterpoises the hearth and home to the modern city, which Dickens, inheriting the Christian tradition of his time, sees as a city of death. According to Welsh, Dickens' mythic rendering of domesticity "impose[s] its own religious construction of reality" (vi). Locating Dickens' understanding of urban experience at Warren's Blacking Factory, Schwarzbach traces Dickens' treatment of the city chronologically from the early novels, in which characters must flee the city in order to live, to the later novels, in which they learn to accommodate themselves to the urban world. He argues that in response to the trauma of his blacking factory experience Dickens creates a personal urban myth which sees the country past as a paradisal whole and the city present as an "objective correlative of Hell" (16). Only in *Our Mutual Friend* and *The Mystery of Edwin Drood* does Schwarzbach see Dickens' presentation of the city itself changing.
2. Readers interested in Dickens' use of actual London settings should see Chancellor, Dexter, and Fletcher.
3. See Stoehr (1–65) and Garis (1–30), who explore the relationship between Dickens' style and novelistic stance.
4. See Jakobson and Halle. In using the terms metonymic and metaphoric, I am drawing upon Jakobson's distinction between two modes of language and two modes of mind. According to Jakobson, the principle underlying metonymy is contiguity—in language especially syntactic contiguity and in mind contextual association and combination. In the metonymic mode, an author explores contiguous relationships: for instance, between characters and their context, plot and the atmosphere it evokes, space and time. The metonymic mode provides a kind of portraiture which represents a subject in relation to its context or which renders it by isolating its characteristic details. By contrast the principle underlying metaphor is substitution—in language especially semantic substitution and in mind symbolic transformation. In the metaphoric mode an author focuses on the sign or symbol, rather than on the referent. For this reason, Jakobson associates the metaphoric style with poetry or romance. In the metaphoric mode, an author operates symbolically, working by association or identification. In practice, as Jakobson indicates, both modes are continually operative, but at the level of "style, preference is given to one of the processes" (76).
5. There are a number of other studies which use Jakobson's terminology to investigate Dickens, most notably by Arac, Garrett, Miller ("The Fiction of Realism"), and Romano. Among these studies, Arac's pursues a tack most similar to my own, for he explores the relationship between stylistic effects and Dickens' search for a comprehensive social vision: "if narrative prose seemed innovative and disruptive, an agency of mobility and transformation, it also worked toward a totalizing understanding. Through the interplay of 'metaphor and metonymy,' local stylistic effects combined to build up the coherence of a book's world. . . . The search for continuity involved trying to see society as a whole extended to the search for figurative techniques to integrate a book" (8).
6. Professor Avrom Fleishman suggested the term "overlay" to describe Dickens' stylistic strategy of juxtaposing past and present moments within the same passage, even within the same sentence. This paper had its genesis in Professor Fleishman's "Literary Townscape" NEH seminar, and the ideas from his seminar are interwoven throughout my study.

7. The particularity of this description—its careful location in time and space—indicates that Stephen Marcus overstates his case when he argues: "*Oliver Twist*, however, issues from what we might call a generic imagination. . . . Even in describing so palpable a thing as the slums of London, Dickens repeatedly insists upon the labyrinthine, maze-like confusion of the streets, courts, and buildings" (63–64). This argument applies more to London as Oliver sees it, than to London as the omniscient narrator records it.

8. Readers of J. Hillis Miller's study of Dickens will recognize my debt to his analysis of this passage. Miller, however, sees Oliver as being much more active than I do in his perceptions of the world: "He [Oliver] spends long hours studying this disordered world, as if he had some faint chance of forcing it to yield up its secret which might be *his* secret too, the secret of his identity and the meaning of his life" (*World*, 54–55). Miller's analysis of Dickens' urban scenes has provided a stimulus for many of my own.

9. J. Hillis Miller's description of the metonymic logic of *Sketches by Boz* could also be applied to the underworld characters of *Oliver Twist*: "it is easy to see how, in the case of the *Sketches*, the predominance of metonymy reinforces that deterministic vision of man's life which is often said to be an essential aspect of realistic fiction. One narrative pattern recurring in the *Sketches* is an apparently inescapable progression of the city dwellers step by step toward starvation, sickness, degradation, crime, depravity, suicide, or execution. A character caught in this progression is 'impelled by sheer necessity, down the precipice that [has] led him to a lingering death' " ("The Fiction of Realism," 101).

10. As the novel's first sentence indicates, David's fear of losing his narrative preeminence and thus his self informs his story: "Whether I shall turn out to be the hero of my own life, or whether that station will be held by anybody else, these pages must show" (1). Written from the perspective of the present, this sentence tells us that David's subjectivity must be continually established.

11. In modifying interpretations of the blacking factory episode—particularly those of Forster, Wilson, and Marcus—Albert D. Hutter argues that the episode gains its importance from Dickens' adult perspective: "I have suggested . . . that he continued to use his adult memory of Warren's to preserve a sense of his own boyishness, his own identity as a child. . . . We tend to forget that Warren's was not, as most biographers would have us believe, the beginning; it is the subject of autobiographical reconstruction" (13–14). Like Hutter, I see the adult perspective as the crucially important one.

12. *Great Expectations* does not conclude Dickens' examination of urban experience, for he can only allow Pip to realize his identity in the city, not to make his living or life there. These will be the issues of *Our Mutual Friend*, his most ambitious urban novel. In a work in progress, Avrom Fleishman is exploring *Our Mutual Friend* as Dickens' utopian effort, showing how humane life is possible in the city.

WORKS CITED

Arac, Jonathan. *Commissioned Spirits*. New Brunswick, N.J.: Rutgers University Press, 1979.

Cassirer, Ernst. *Language and Myth*. 1946. New York: Dover, 1953.

Chancellor, E. Beresford. *The London of Charles Dickens*. London: Grant Richards, 1924.

Dexter, Walter. *The London of Charles Dickens*. New York: Dutton, 1924.

Dickens, Charles. *Oliver Twist*. 1838. London: Oxford University Press, 1949.

———. *David Copperfield*. 1850. London: Oxford University Press, 1948.

———. *Great Expectations*. 1861. London: Oxford University Press, 1953.

———. *The Letters of Charles Dickens*. Ed. Walter Drexler. Vol. III. Bloomsbury: Nonesuch Press, 1938. 3 vols.

Fletcher, Geoffrey. *The London Dickens Knew*. London: Hutchinson, 1970.

Forster, John. *The Life of Charles Dickens*. Vol. I. New York: Scribner's, 1927. 2 vols.

Garis, Robert. *The Dickens Theatre*. Oxford: Clarendon, 1965.

Garrett, Peter K. *The Victorian Multiplot Novel*. New Haven, Conn.: Yale University Press, 1980.

Hutter, Albert D. "Reconstructive Autobiography: The Experience at Warren's Blacking." *Dickens Studies Annual*, 6. Carbondale and Edwardsville: Southern Illinois University Press, 1977.

Jakobson, Roman, and Morris Halle. *Fundamentals of Language*. The Hague: Mouton, 1956.

Marcus, Steven. *Dickens from Pickwick to Dombey*. 1965. New York: Simon and Schuster, 1968.

Miller, J. Hillis. *Charles Dickens: The World of His Novels*. Cambridge, Mass.: Harvard University Press, 1958.

———. "The Fiction of Realism: *Sketches by Boz, Oliver Twist,* and Cruikshank's Illustrations." *Dickens Centennial Essays*. Eds. Ada Nesbet and Blake Nevius. Los Angeles: University of California Press, 1971.

Romano, John. *Dickens and Reality*. New York: Columbia University Press, 1978.

Schwarzbach, F. S. *Dickens and the City*. London: Athlone, 1979.

Stevens, Wallace. *The Collected Poems of Wallace Stevens*. New York: Knopf, 1971.

Stoehr, Taylor. *Dickens: The Dreamer's Stance*. Ithaca, N.Y.: Cornell University Press, 1965.

Welsh, Alexander, *The City of Dickens*. Oxford: Clarendon, 1971.

Westburg, Barry. *The Confessional Fiction of Dickens*. DeKalb: Northern Illinois University Press, 1977.

Williams, Raymond. *The Country and the City*. 1970. New York: Oxford University Press, 1973.

Wilson, Edmund. "The Two Scrooges." *The Wound and the Bow*. Cambridge, Mass.: Harvard University Press, 1941.

Death and the Gentleman:
David Copperfield
as Elegiac Romance

Edwin M. Eigner

Mortality and gentility, two concepts central to an understanding of *David Copperfield,* have become the subjects of important, recent studies of the nineteenth century. Philip Mason's *The English Gentleman: The Rise and Fall of an Ideal* (1982) and Robin Gilmour's *The Idea of the Gentleman in the Victorian Novel* (1981) both pay considerable attention to the works of Dickens, and Garrett Stewart's *Death Sentences: Styles of Dying in Victorian Fiction* (1984) uses *David Copperfield* as one of its primary texts. The themes appear to have little in common with one another and to require, indeed, quite different sorts of critical approaches, but still another recent book, *Elegiac Romance* (1983) by Kenneth A. Bruffee, although it deals with neither Dickens nor his times, provides nevertheless a way of discussing the pervasive Victorian aspiration toward gentility and the obsessive nineteenth-century preoccupation with the fear of death as they relate to one another in *David Copperfield,* the central novel in Dickens' career.

Most simply described, an elegiac romance is a first-person retrospective narration recounting the death of a romantic figure who has captured the imagination of the less heroic narrator. A few examples are *Moby-Dick, Heart of Darkness, The Great Gatsby,* Thomas Mann's *Doctor Faustus,* Ford Madox Ford's *The Good Soldier,* Salinger's "Seymour: An Introduction," R. P. Warren's *All the King's Men* and Saul Bellow's *Humboldt's Gift,* but Bruffee's impressive list of eighteen well-known novels and twice as many shorter pieces offers convincing proof that we have to do here with an important fictional construct, full of significance to some of our best writers. By virtue of the *apparent* heros, these works descend, according to Bruffee, from medieval exemplary romances. However, the down-to-earth writing styles and the self-effacement typical of the narrators, who, although they always turn out at last to be the true heroes, characteristically begin with the sincerely avowed purpose only of coming to terms with their grief by discovering its meaning, connect these important novels and stories with the nondidactic, unpretentious elegiac mode.

As the examples indicate, this apparently self-contradictory form belongs mainly to our own century. Moreover, *David Copperfield* is far too long and complex a novel to be summed up in terms of such a discreet and so relatively simple a genre. There is a great deal more in Dickens' novel than can be explained by it, or indeed by any single critical approach. It remains, nevertheless, that when we focus on the narrator's relationship with James Steerforth, *David Copperfield* displays most of the characteristics of an elegiac romance and can be profitably read as such.

Indeed, the novel's opening sentence—"Whether I shall turn out to be the hero of my own life, or whether that station will be held by anyone else, these pages must show"—is a sentiment that might almost have been spoken by Marlow or Nick Carraway or John Dowell or Gene Forrester of *A Separate Peace* or any of the other elegiac romance narrators who struggle to recapture, through their writing, the sense of identity and personal worth they lost through their ambiguous relationship with the hero. It is late in the novel, for instance, before Jack Burden of *All the King's Men* is ready to concede that "This has been the story of Willie Stark, but it is my story, too. For I have a story" (435); and Salinger's Buddy Glass castigates himself in the last paragraph for his "perpetual lust to share top billing with" his dead brother.

The role of David Copperfield in the novel that bears his name is similarly confusing. As Lawrence Frank writes, "Steerforth threatens to usurp our interest" (67), and, more significant, he threatens also to usurp the interest of the narrator. At times David appears to be writing an autobiography, and the complexities of the character self-revealed, either consciously or unconsciously, have proved fascinating to such acute critics as Barry Westburg and Sylvère Monod. At other times, he seems to operate merely as a window, an insignificant observer, reporting the far more interesting doings of the Heeps, the Strongs, the Peggottys, Micawbers, and Steerforths, and to be so uninteresting in his own right as to have led such a great Dickens enthusiast as George Bernard Shaw to conclude that David "might be left out of his biography altogether but for his usefulness as a stage confidant, a Horatio or Charles his friend: what they call on the stage a feeder" (31).

In *Charles Dickens: The World of His Novels,* J. Hillis Miller puts these two David Copperfields together in a way that will be useful to our discussion. Miller writes that "David has, during his childhood of neglect and misuse, been acutely aware of himself as a gap in being. . . . The center of David's life . . . is the search for some relationship to another person which will support his life, fill up the emptiness within him, and give him a substantial identity" (156–157). This is the quest of all the twentieth-century elegiac romance narrators, who, again like David, discover at the death of the other person that by attempting to complete themselves in this questionable fashion they appear to have lost themselves entirely. They then proceed, like David, to recount the story of the tragic loss, to elegize the heroic dead man, to puzzle over the meaning of the gut experience they have survived, and in the process, hopefully to free themselves of the fallen hero's quest, perhaps indeed of all heroic questing, and, in the end, to find their own true identities, to become, indeed, the heroes of their own lives, or to reject, once and for all, the romantic notion of heroism (Bruffee, 49–50).

David Copperfield had sought in his friendship with the arch-gentleman, James Steerforth, just such an identity-giving relationship as Miller describes, the intellectual companionship he somewhat peevishly complains of having missed in his marriage to Dora and which Dickens himself felt he had never been able to find. Friendships and would-be friendships abound in the novel. Murdstone begins his acquaintance with David by saying, "Come! Let us be the best friends in the world!" (16), and while David is wisely on his guard from this quarter, he usually welcomes the friendships that are constantly offered him throughout the novel. He "soon became the best of friends" with Mr. Dick (185), and he responds so positively when Mr. Wickfield refers to him as "our little friend" (189) that he soon finds himself "feeling friendly towards everybody" (192), including even the sinister Uriah Heep, who much later in the novel insists on the friendship then established:

> "This is indeed an unexpected pleasure! [says Heep]. To have, as I may say, all friends round Saint Paul's, at once, is a treat unlooked for! Mr. Copperfield, I hope I see you well, and—if I may umbly express myself so—friendly towards them as is ever your friends, whether or not." (637)

David's substitute father, Mr. Micawber, refers to Uriah as "your friend Heep" (224) or "our friend Heep" (482). Poor Micawber, embattled though he is, perceives friends everywhere, even in the razor he sometimes thinks of using to cut his own throat (224). He regards David as "the friend of . . . [my] youth, the companion of earlier days!" (348); and Mrs. Micawber tells David "You have never been a lodger. You have always been a friend" (149). David thinks himself "blest . . . in having . . . such a friend as Peggotty" (273), and, of course, his relationship with Agnes Wickfield sails under the flag of a "pure friendship" (737) until the very conclusion of the novel.

But it is, of course, Steerforth whom we and the narrator think of as "the friend" in the novel *David Copperfield*. Young David fastens onto this friendship as firmly and immediately as he does because, in the first place, Steerforth appears in his life at the moment when he is in most need of confirming his very nearly lost human identity. David's stepfather has beaten him like a dog, and David has responded, doglike, by biting his tormentor's hand. Now he walks around with a dog's sign tied to his back—"*Take care of him. He bites*" (67). In this state he is carried before Steerforth, "as before a magistrate," who enquires into the facts of the case and concludes "that it was 'a jolly shame;' for which," as David states, "I became bound to him ever afterwards" (72). Later on in the novel, when an older but still socially insecure David has been assigned a bed in "a little loft over a stable," Steerforth gives him a suitable, human identity once again. "Where," he demands of the innkeeper, "have you put my friend, Mr. Copperfield" (245). And David is immediately translated into a more genteel room "with an immense four-post bedstead in it, which was quite a little landed estate" (246).

Just what Steerforth sees in David besides an admiring plaything is perhaps somewhat more difficult to explain. Like most of the elegiac romance heroes Kenneth Bruffee describes, Steerforth does not reciprocate the affection entirely. At their reunion in London, for instance, David is overcome. " 'I never, never, never was so glad! My dear Steerforth, I am so overjoyed to see you!' " Steerforth is more restrained:" 'And I am rejoyced to see you, too!' he said, shaking my hands heartily. 'Why, Copperfield, old boy, don't be overpowered!' And yet he was glad too, I thought, to see how the delight I had in meeting him affected me" (245–246). After their final parting, David concedes that Steerforth's "remembrances of me . . . were light enough, perhaps, and easily dismissed" (388).

Like most romance heroes, Steerforth is too self-absorbed for satisfactory friendship, but, as his mother assures David, "he feels an unusual friendship for you" (253), and he is uncharacteristically solicitous of David's good opinion. " 'If anything should ever separate us'," he says at their parting, " 'you must think of me at my best. Come, let us make that bargain' " (373). George Bernard Shaw's belittling identification of David as a Horatio turns out to be inspired criticism. There is a great deal of Hamlet in James Steerforth, or at least he fancies so. Steerforth is broodingly suspicious of action, and he is cynically unable to direct his abundant energy to any goal except winning because he fails to see the value of any other goal. " 'As to fitfullness','' he says, " 'I have never learnt the art of binding myself to any of the wheels on which the Ixions of these days are turning round and round' '' (274). He even feels troubled by " 'a reproachful ghost' '' (273), and he misses the presence of " 'a judicious father' '' (274). The Hamlet-like James Steerforth wears David Copperfield in his heart of hearts because he thinks David, whom he nicknames Daisy, is free of the romantic passions which govern *him*, and because, like Hamlet and such elegiac romance heroes as Lord Jim, Jay Gatsby, Willie Stark of R. P. Warren's *All the King's Men,* and the mad editor of Nabokov's *Pale Fire,* he needs desperately to be understood aright and to have his story told. " 'I don't want to excuse myself;' '' Lord Jim says, " 'but I would like to explain—I would like somebody to under-stand—somebody—one person at least' '' (69). And on his deathbed, Willie Stark of *All the King's Men* tells his flunky and future biographer, " 'It might have been all different, Jack. . . . You got to believe that,' he said hoarsely. . . . 'You got to,' he said again. 'You got to believe that' '' (400).

David Copperfield becomes a novelist, a storyteller, because that was the identity James Steerforth, who had an equal need of justification, gave him when they were children back at Salem House School. Previously, in the lonely days at the Rookery, David sat upon his bed in solitude and read, as he says, "as if for life" (48). Now in his new friend's bedroom, to which David "belong[s]" (80) and where he feels "cherished as a kind of plaything" (81), Steerforth proposes that they "make some regular Arabian Nights of it" (79). David, as official storyteller to Steerforth, likens himself to "the Sultana Scheherazade" (80), who, of course, *told* stories for her life.[1]

Later on, when David becomes what he calls "a little laboring hind" (132) and feels in danger once again of losing both his class and his human identity, he makes use of this resource Steerforth had taught him when he tells "some astonishing fictions" (143) to the Orfling who works for the Micawbers. And, at the end of the novel, he will tunnel out from his grief for Steerforth by writing a story. It is significant that when David mentions working on his "first piece of fiction" he finds himself coming by accident "past Mrs. Steerforth's house" (567). And, while it is perhaps too much to say that the one surviving work of our fictional novelist may be a life of James Steerforth, curiously titled *David Copperfield,* it *is* true that when Dickens shortened his complex novel into an evening-long public reading, he omitted almost everything in the novel which did not relate to Steerforth, and he ended the reading with Steerforth's death.[2]

Kenneth Bruffee, whose book on elegiac romance is subtitled *Cultural Change and Loss of the Hero in Modern Fiction*, sees his genre as the most recent phase of a long tradition. In the medieval quest romance, he writes, our attention is directed "exclusively to the task and character of the aristocratic seeker, the knight . . . [whose] story is always courageous and serious . . . seldom ironic." In the second phase, invented by Cervantes, "the whole story becomes ironic," because the knight must now share the stage with Sancho Panza, and "the reader is never allowed to feel quite sure whose values Cervantes means us to share: the knight's or the squire's. . . . For the first time in the quest romance tradition, the conventions and values of feudal life, courtly love, and [the] heroic knightly quest receive serious criticism in the light of everyday experience" (32). In the modern or elegiac romance phase, as Bruffee sees it, the irony disappears once again as the squire, after a tremendous struggle, rids himself of his obsession with his hero, and in so doing, utterly rejects the corrupt values of the society that the hero represents, including the concept of heroism itself.

It follows from this line of thinking that an individual elegiac romance will become significant when the values of the romantic hero that obsess the narrator and that he finally comes to reject are of deep cultural importance. Thus Jay Gatsby and Lord Jim can be said to embody the false dreams of the societies they represent. It is not enough, therefore, simply to explain the psychological reasons for David Copperfield's decision to lose himself, so to speak, in James Steerforth. We must ask ourselves what social values Steerforth represents, and how he may be regarded not only as David's personal hero, but as a significant hero of the Victorian age, perhaps as *the* significant hero. When we have done this, we may also be able to see why he is so important to David, and why David must ultimately outgrow him.

Ellen Moers writes in her study of *The Dandy* that with Steerforth "Dickens for the first time draws a character whose 'aristocratic' temperament, manners, and attitudes play a major part in the novel. Steerforth the wicked seducer [of Little Em'ly]," she writes, "is merely a repetition of immature melodrama [such as Dickens had frequently made use of in earlier novels], but Steerforth the schoolboy hero of David Copperfield is Dickens's first attempt to deal with a problem that would bedevil him in maturity" as he dealt with such ambiguous, gentlemanly characters as James Harthouse, Henry Gowan, and Eugene Wrayburn (229–230). It is not quite accurate to say that there had been no admirable or admired gentleman in Dickens before Steerforth, but it is true, nevertheless, that in *David Copperfield,* for the first time in Dickens, the idea of gentility, represented by such a problematical figure, becomes the obsessive goal of the principal point-of-view character.

David's background may account for his social ambitions. Early in the novel Little Em'ly distinguishes between herself and David by noting, "your father was a gentleman and your mother is a lady" (30). David does not contradict her, but the reader knows that his mother was a governess, not a lady, before her marriage and that, as David's Aunt Betsey has pointed out, she and her husband "were not equally matched" (7). Perhaps David, like Dickens himself, was sensitive on this score of a servant ancestry, for, in contrast to such earlier heroes as Nicholas Nickleby and Oliver Twist, he behaves like a boy, and later on like a man, who is shamefully uncertain of his own position in society. His difficulty with servants, who almost always refuse contemptuously to accept his authority, is one of the great comic strands of the novel. When David's stepfather, who has told him that he is "not to associate with servants" (103), condemns him to become a laborer, David is devastated mainly at the loss of his social position:

> No words can express the secret agony of my soul as I sunk into this companionship; compared these henceforth every-day associates with those of my happier childhood—not to say with Steerforth and Traddles and the rest of those boys; and felt my hopes for growing up to be a learned and distinguished man, crushed in my bosom. (133)

Later when he is rescued and again finds genteel companions at Dr. Strong's school, "My mind ran upon what they would think, if they knew of my familiar acquaintance with the King's Bench Prison" (195). And still later he becomes morbidly afraid that his enemy Uriah Heep will discover these secrets from Micawber, and publicly taunt him with them, as indeed Heep does, when he calls Micawber, "the very scum of the world—as you yourself were, Copperfield, you know it, before anyone had charity on you" (640).

David's extraordinary sensitivity on the score of Heep has been noted by several critics, and usually interpreted, mistakenly, I believe, as an unconscious revelation of class consciousness on Dickens' own part. Thus, A. H. Gomme writes:

> [Heep's] writhings are real enough, but it is impossible at times to avoid a feeling of special pleading against him, of Dickens with a knife in Uriah. . . . It is made a point against him that not only does he pretend to a humiliation he does not own, but that he has a coarse accent and drops his aitches. . . . That . . . snobbery in Dickens as well as in David . . . becomes vicious in the scene in which David is obsessed by Heep's physical repulsiveness. (176)

In *Great Expectations,* where Pip feels a similar repulsion to the lower-class Orlick and where Orlick responds with the same emnity, readers have no trouble distinguishing between the class attitudes of the character and those of the author. The confusion exists in *David Copperfield* partly because it is an elegiac romance, while *Great Expectations* is not, and because what Barry A. Marks has called the writing time of a story, the months or years during which we are to suppose the narrator is putting his experience on paper so that he can "seek and express an understanding of it,"[3] is consequently more important. Pip-the-narrator at least believes that he has already achieved his wisdom, his maturity, his sense of his own identity long before he begins writing his autobiography. Thus he is able compassionately to condemn his own childish snobbery and to make us understand that neither he nor Dickens shares it. David Copperfield-the-narrator is in the *process* of learning about himself as he writes his own (or is it James Steerforth's?) life story, and since he does not yet understand his own class consciousness, his obsession with gentility, the blindness appears also to be that of Dickens, the creator of David-the-narrator as well as David-the-character, neither of whom is yet free of the hero-worship of Steerforth and a thralldom to the false values of gentility he represents.

David-the-narrator's excessive hatred of Uriah Heep is also understandable in terms of the behavior of David-the-character, which, if given an unfavorable construction—the sort of critical construction a Heep internalized in David's own psyche might put upon it—is not very easily distinguishable from the actions of Heep himself. In *Dickens and the Invisible World,* Harry Stone has written that Uriah personifies "David's most aggressive and covetous thoughts" (222). Certainly the two characters, both poor boys, are similarly determined to rise in the world. Keith Carabine believes that "Heep embodies and deflects those elements of David which . . . [he needs to] deny—namely his ambition and his sexuality" (161). And it must be admitted that as far as ambitious sexuality is concerned, neither David nor Heep is especially scrupulous in the business of secretly courting the daughter of his wealthy employer. Carabine sees Heep as "a rival and a double" of David's (161–162), and Harry Stone calls our attention to the Uriah-David rivalry over Bathsheba in the Bible, where, of course, King David, and not his subordinate Uriah, is the clear sexual aggressor. In light of this confusion and this combination of roles for Heep, we should note that David sees Uriah, as indeed Pip sees Orlick, in disgustingly phallic terms. The thought of his Agnes "outraged" by this "red-headed animal" makes David positively "giddy," so that Uriah "seemed to swell and grow before my eyes" (326).

Nevertheless, the aggressiveness and the aggressive sexuality of David or Heep are nothing when compared to these same qualities in Steerforth, a character David strives to exculpate as strongly as he works to incriminate Uriah. Steerforth, after all, succeeds in *his* seductions, and while he obviously disdains the tawdry business of rising in the world, he is clearly as determined as Heep is to win at any price:

> "Ride on! [he says] Rough-shod if need be, smooth-shod if that will do, but ride on! Ride over all obstacles, and win the race."
> "And win what race?" said I.
> "The race that one has started in," said he. "Ride on!" (364)

Dickens, who had already risen high enough by the time he was writing *David Copperfield* to enroll his eldest son at Eton, but who found himself still possessed by an excess of competitive energy, may have been as much or more disturbed by Steerforth's gratuitous aggression, when he saw it reflected in his own character, than he was by Uriah's self-help ambition.

Another servant who aspires to marry a woman David loves and against whom there is almost as much special pleading as there is against Heep is Steerforth's man, Littimer. Why, after all, should David hold Littimer more guilty and in so much greater contempt than he does Steerforth in the business of Little Em'ly's seduction? And what is so outrageous, after all, in Littimer's desire to marry Em'ly when Steerforth has cast her off? Is he not, as he represents himself, "a very respectable person, who was fully prepared to overlook the past, and who was at least as good [socially] as anybody the young woman could have aspired to in a regular way" (511)? As George Orwell says in defense of Heep, "Even villains have sexual lives" (41). It appears that, just as David prefers to revile Heep instead of himself for the sexual fantasies both of them cherish regarding Agnes, he also prefers, in the matter of Em'ly's seduction, to hate the servant Littimer rather than the gentleman Steerforth.

And David is not the only one who indulges this preference. Littimer (I almost said poor Littimer) is everybody's scapegoat. Miss Mowcher, who also, after all, assisted in the seduction, prays, "May the Father of all Evil confound him [Steerforth] . . . and *ten times more* confound that wicked servant" (395). Rosa Dartle, whom Steerforth had previously seduced, holds Littimer in such deep contempt after the Little Em'ly business that she will not permit him to address her (395). Steerforth insults him (572), and even Little Em'ly, meek though she is, tries to murder him (571). Daniel Peggotty, who can keep his powerful emotions under control when speaking of Steerforth, the man who has abused his hospitality and ruined his niece, boils over with rage whenever he thinks of "that theer spotted snake . . . may God confound him!" who tried, from his own point of view, at least, to make an honest woman of her (619).

What all these characters have in common with one another and with David is an absolute fascination with James Steerforth and the gentility he represents. Miss Mowcher is an indefatigable name-dropper, and Rosa is a sycophantic dependent. Daniel Peggotty may seem a much more self-respecting character, but he is so charmed by Steerforth from the moment of their first meeting at David's school that we can feel pretty sure he was more of an ally than Littimer in the business of his niece's seduction, albeit, of course, an unwitting one. Not only did he talk Steerforth up on every occasion—

> "There's a friend!" said Mr. Peggotty, stretching out his pipe. "There's a friend, if you talk about friends! Why, Lord love my heart alive, if it ain't a treat to look at him!"   (122)

—but it was he who first started Em'ly dreaming of becoming a lady when she was a small girl, wearing "a necklace of blue beads," which must have been a present from him.[4]

David's attraction to gentility is at least as strong as his need for friendship, and genteel people draw him out as easily as servants repel him. He finds his schoolmaster's daughter "in point of gentility not to be surpassed" (79), and Micawber impresses him "very much" at their first meeting with his "certain indescribable air of doing something genteel" (134). Both David and his biological mother come close on a number of occasions to acknowledging Peggotty—"that good and faithful servant, whom of all the people on earth I love the best" (113)—as his true mother (11, 13–14, 17, 53), and at one point Peggotty asserts her claim to act as David's motherly protector—"who has such a good right?" she asks—and she assures David "that the coach-fare to Yarmouth was always to be had for the asking" (212). But to accept Peggotty as his mother would mean an end to his dreams of gentility. Even Steerforth tells David that it is with Peggotty that he "naturally belong[s]" (265). And yet in his moments of deepest depression as "a little laboring hind" in London, he "never in any letter (though many passed between us) reveals the truth" to Peggotty (139), and when his situation becomes intolerable, David chooses to take his chances with Aunt Betsey, whom he has never seen and about whom he has heard nothing in the least bit encouraging, rather than come home to Peggotty, although he has to write a lie to Peggotty to get his Aunt's address and to borrow enough money to get to Dover in genteel fashion (151). As one critic writes, "David's walk to Dover is as irrepressible an assertion of individuality and the will to succeed as Heep's faith in his father's words, 'be 'umble, Uriah . . . and you'll get on' " (Carabine, 160). He also has a lot in common with Pip of *Great Expectations*. "I never could have derived anything like the pleasure from spending the money Mr. Dick had given me," David writes, "than I felt in sending a gold half-guinea to Peggotty, per post . . . to discharge the sum I had borrowed of her" (211). For David, as later for Pip, cutting the old, shameful though legitimate ties, is as important as weaving the new, highly questionable connections to the world of gentility.

With the help of his chosen mother, David, again like Pip, seems to have his fairy-tale wish of great expectations fulfilled. He gets a new name, becomes an heir, and is educated at a school for gentlemen. And when, like the hero of a fairy tale, he sets out into the great world to choose a genteel profession for himself, the first significant person he encounters, of course, is his old idol, the archetypal gentleman, whom he once chose over the skeleton-drawing Tommy Traddles and whom he soon acknowledges, in preference to Agnes Wickfield, as the guiding star of his existence (308). The profession David chooses, both at the suggestion of his lady Aunt, who wishes "to provide genteely" for him (299), and on the recommendation of his gentleman friend, could not be better suited to the goal he has set for himself. "A proctor is a gentlemanly sort of fellow," Steerforth tells David in a cancelled passage (293), and in a passage which was allowed to stand, Steerforth says, "On the whole, I would recommend you to take to Doctor's Commons kindly, David. They plume themselves on their gentility there" (293). So, in effect, it is Steerforth's advice that makes David a gentleman, just (and just as ambiguously) as it later makes Little Em'ly a lady.

Returning to the Em'ly plot and Daniel Peggotty's part in his niece's seduction, we can see just how Dickens connects his two themes of death and gentility, for it was Em'ly's concern to prevent her uncle's death that was the first cause of her dangerous ambition to become a lady. As she told the young David,

> "We should all be gentle folk together, then. Me, and uncle, and Ham, and Mrs. Gummidge. We wouldn't mind then, when there come stormy weather. Not for our own sakes, I mean. We would for the poor fishermen's, to be sure, and we'd help 'em with money when they come to any hurt. . . . I wake when it blows, and tremble to think of Uncle Dan and Ham, and believe I hear 'em crying out for help. That's why I should like so much to be a lady." (30–31)

This passage, one of the most poignant and meaningful in the novel, shows that for Dickens gentility was not only a question of social ambition or snobbish pride, but a life and death matter. In *Oliver Twist,* if you are not a gentleman, like Oliver, you are literally starved to death in the workhouse or hanged as a criminal. In *Bleak House* you are helplessly "moved on," carrying the plague that kills you. In *Great Expectations* the social alternatives are presented with a stunning simplicity: you can either be a hound (a gentleman) or a varment; if you do not run with the hunters, you must inevitably and unsuccessfully run from them. In *David Copperfield,* according to Little Em'ly's experience, if you are not a lady, all the men around you will be "Drowndead." On the night of her elopement with Steerforth, David, who is attending the death of Barkis, has "leisure to think . . . of pretty little Emily's dread of death" (379).

Steerforth and the gentility he both stands for and appears to offer, for he is ready "to swear she was born to be a lady" (284), seems to provide an escape from death and the grief death causes. I believe that Steerforth stands for something similar in David's mind also, and that this is why David is initially fascinated by Steerforth and so unwilling to condemn him even after he has been found unworthy. Steerforth the gentleman is thus the false cultural hero of Victorian England, the romantic knight whom the narrator of one of the century's most significant elegiac romances must reject for himself and his age, so that he and his readers can find their true identities in the face of their otherwise overwhelming and paralyzing fear of death.

Saul Bellow's *Humboldt's Gift,* perhaps more than any of the other works on Kenneth Bruffee's list, demonstrates that elegiac romance, like pastoral elegy, provides an opportunity for a serious inquiry into the general question of death. The subject had always fascinated Dickens, but nowhere more powerfully than in *David Copperfield,* where the narrator is, after all, a "posthumous child" (2), and where his story includes the deaths of his mother, his infant brother, the previous tenant of his London rooms, his aunt's estranged husband, his beloved nurse's husband and her nephew, his own first child, who is stillborn, his first wife, her father and even her dog, and, finally, his own best friend and alternate identity. Moreover, David's childhood sweetheart is an orphan, motivated, as we have seen, with the dread of death; his first wife's mother is dead; and so is the mother of his second wife, who has been brought up in a mausoleum, haunted by a father, overcome with what he calls "disease[d]" and sordid "grief" (493–494). As Garrett Stewart has noted, *David Copperfield* is the only work "before *Malone Dies* that has invented a new word for death [drowndead, and] . . . the novel has, beyond this, far more than a word to add to the idea of death as a test of wording'' (73).

If we are at first surprised at this quantity of deaths, it is perhaps because so few of them are actually rendered in the novel, so few of them directly witnessed by the narrator. I take this suppression to be in itself significant, for *David Copperfield* is a novel of suppressions, especially suppressions of death. Thus, Stewart suggests that Doctor Strong has been unable to get past the letter D in his unfinished dictionary because he cannot confront the word death. David apparently, or Dickens, cannot stand the sight of it, and so the writer who had sent Victorian England into profound mourning in his previous novel with the death of Paul Dombey and was to electrify them in his next book with the death of Jo the crossing-sweeper, shows David present at the dying moments only of the dog, Jip, and of the comic figure, Barkis. Moreover, both experiences are immediately overshadowed by so-called "Greater Loss[es]" (380), which David does not directly witness, the death of Dora and the elopement of Em'ly, who asks her family to "try to think as if I died when I was little and was buried somewhere" (386). When David remembers the last time he saw his mother alive, he writes, "I wish I had died. I wish I had died then with that feeling [of being loved?] in my heart!" (94). And soon his wish is symbolically fulfilled, although he has typically missed even his own death scene: When he describes his mother and his brother in their coffin, he thinks "The little creature in her arms was myself" (115).

David denies on the very first page of the novel that he was "privileged to see ghosts and spirits," but all the characters he subsequently introduces are referred to as "shadows" on the last page. Earlier he called them "phantoms" (541). The novel abounds with references to the ghosts in *Julius Caesar, Macbeth,* and especially *Hamlet.* Indeed, no other work of Dickens is so specter-ridden. The recollection of his unhappy youth, he writes, came upon David "without . . . invocation . . . like a ghost, and haunted happier times" (129), and after Steerforth's death David entered, what he calls "a long and gloomy night . . . haunted by the ghosts of many hopes, of many dear remembrances, many errors, many unavailing sorrows and regrets" (608).

As the presence as well as the denial of all this death in the novel would indicate, David Copperfield's reaction to death is both profound and ambiguous. "If ever a child were stricken with sincere grief," it was David at the news of his mother's death, yet he felt "distinguished" by it in the eyes of his schoolmates "and walked slowly" (107). When Mr. Spenlow dies David has "a lurking jealousy . . . of Death . . . [which might push him from his] ground in Dora's thoughts'' (475). But, on the whole, he has a nightmare dread which dates back to his association with the best parlor and Peggotty's account of his father's funeral there. The story of "how Lazarus was raised up from the dead" so frightened him as a child that his mother and Peggotty were obliged to take him out of bed and show him the quiet churchyard out the bedroom window, "with the dead all lying in their graves at rest, below the solemn moon" (12). It is, of course, his own death David fears. When he returns from his first trip to Yarmouth and thinks that his mother is dead, he feels as though he "were going to tumble down" (36), and this is precisely his sensation later on when he hears of Mr. Spenlow's death—"I thought it was the office reeling, and not I" (474). Spenlow, whose posthumous son-in-law David will soon become, is another character paralyzed at the thought of death. He has been psychologically unable to make out a will. But the subject of death is as fascinating to David and the others as it is horrifying. The death-dreading Em'ly goes to work for an undertaker, and David ends his search for a genteel profession by binding himself apprentice to a probate attorney.

Barry Westburg argues that David's stepfather, Mr. Murdstone, is the personification of Thanatos himself. Westburg writes:

> When David is told, "You have got a Pa!" he says, [that] "Something . . . connected with the grave in the churchyard, and the raising of the dead, seemed to strike me like an unwholesome wind." [Later,] when two of his associates greet Murdstone they say, "We thought you were dead!" He is dark of dress, skin, and whiskers and professes a mortifying religiosity. . . . Murdstone is the resurrection of death itself, of life's primal antithesis.   (46)

And as we have seen, it is Murdstone who initiates the friendship theme in the novel. " 'Come! Let us be the best friends in the world!' said the gentleman, laughing. 'Shake hands!' " (16).

David offers Murdstone only his left hand, but to Steerforth, the second gentleman of the novel, he gives both hand and soul wholeheartedly, and with Steerforth he does become "the best friends in the world." It is a strange substitution, as profoundly ironic as Little Em'ly turning to this same gentleman-sailor as a protection against being "drowndead." The warnings come quickly in both cases. On the first evening, Steerforth entertains Em'ly with "a story of a dismal shipwreck" (269), and David, who is introduced to Steerforth "under a shed in the playground" (72), spends *his* first night sitting with Steerforth in the bedroom, thinking of ghosts. We have previously seen that Steerforth gives David a life-saving, artist's identity at school, but we should note that if David is Scheherazade in the relationship, Steerforth is the Sultan, who may choose to spare, but whose more usual course is to execute his brides after the wedding night.

Michael Slater has suggested that the invention of Steerforth, "handsome and captivating, entrancing company, yet ultimately shallow, selfish and cruelly frivolous . . . enables Dickens to create David's Maria [Beadnell] figure, Dora Spenlow, untouched by the unhappy memories of the way in which his real-life original had tormented and ultimately failed him" (62–63). Dora, who dominates the second half of the novel almost as powerfully as Steerforth had the first, and whose plot was the only one besides Steerforth's that Dickens kept for his public reading of *David Copperfield,* is, with her attractive vivacity and gentility, yet another ironically fragile safety-net against death. David's association of Dora with life and gentility becomes comically clear in his shocked horror when his landlady likens his love for the doomed "Little Blossom" to the passion of a dead lodger, David's predecessor, for a working-class girl. "I must beg you," David says, expressing far more than snobbery, "not to connect the young lady in my case with a barmaid, or anything else of that sort, if you please" (341).

But it is more frequently to Steerforth directly that David, like Em'ly, looks for salvation. David refers to Steerforth as his "protector" (307). Steerforth, David says, "was a person of great power in my eyes" (76), power which I submit David believes will save him from the dominance of Murdstone and the spell of death, as, indeed, at their reunion at the London inn it rescues David from his "small bedchamber," which David describes as "shut up like a family vault" (243). Em'ly seems actually to expect something like a rebirth through Steerforth, hoping for the day when "he *brings me back* a lady" (386, my emphasis). That this appearance is delusive goes perhaps without much saying—Steerforth is himself "drowndead"—but *In Memoriam,* and a host of important literary works glorifying the gentleman give evidence that it was the culture's delusion as well as David's and Em'ly's. Robin Gilmour believes that Pip's great expectations represent "some of the deepest hopes, fears, and fantasies of Dickens's class and generation" (118), and Arnold Kettle writes that the "day-dream nature . . . of Steerforth, the Byronic super-man, aristocratic self-confidence and all, is revealed in the novel as no arbitrary personal 'weakness' in David's character, but as an important and complex social psychological problem of nineteenth-century England" (72–73). He seems, according to Lawrence Frank, "to have stepped out of David's dreams as the dazzling figure David wishes and fears to become" (92). "Steerforth was a myth," according to Garrett Stewart, "generated out of the . . . suspension of moral consciousness into which David was betrayed by his adolescent identification with his idol as the incarnated dream of invincible vitality and charm'' (78); i.e., of life and gentility.

After Steerforth rescued David from the vault-like room above the stable at the Golden Cross Inn, David, who had just seen a performance of *Julius Caesar*,'' fell asleep in a blissful condition, and dreamed of ancient Rome, Steerforth, and friendship, until the early morning coaches, rumbling out of the archway underneath, made me dream of thunder and the gods'' (247). Steerforth is, of course, the principal god in question, but David's and Em'ly's hope that he will confer some of his immortality on them does not reckon with the fact that he regards them and all servants and the children of servants as belonging to a different species from himself. Their "feelings," he assures one of his schoolmates, "are not like yours" (86), and when a member of his own class asks him if the Peggottys and people of that sort are "really animals and clods, and beings of a different order," he allows "with indifference," that "there's a pretty wide separation between them and us" (251). When Steerforth dismisses Ham Peggotty as "a chuckle-headed fellow," David, who has been vaguely worried about Steerforth since the latter's gratuitous humiliation of their unoffending schoolmaster, Mr. Mell, finds it possible, or perhaps necessary, to convince himself that his friend and protector is only hiding his sympathies for the poor by making a joke (271). Obviously Em'ly is capable of the same kind of self-delusion, until Steerforth unmistakably shows how he regards her by trying to arrange a marriage for her with his own servant.

Both David and Em'ly have passed through a sort of fairy-tale experience, which can be called the motif of the bad wish granted and which Dickens employed to structure a number of his novels, most obviously *The Haunted Man, Little Dorrit*, and *Great Expectations*. In such works the beneficent fairy, who is sometimes only implied, makes the wish come true so that the hero can learn its falseness and try to save himself by unwishing it. David and Em'ly both wished for gentility through Steerforth, and they both seemed about to have the desire fulfilled, but only so that, like Pip and the others, they might discover in time that the ambition was unworthy.

Em'ly began the necessary redemptive business of reversing the destructive wish when, after recovering from the fever which followed her flight from Steerforth and Littimer, she told the Italian children not to address her as " 'pretty lady' [*bella donna*] as the general way in that country is, and . . . taught 'em to call her 'Fisherman's daughter' instead'' (622). Then she became a servant at an inn in France. And finally, after her arrival in

England, she walked from Dover to London, literally reversing David's earlier painful and heroic march to gentility.

David's way back is more difficult because he has invested still more of himself even than Em'ly has in Steerforth and what he represents. She has been Steerforth's mistress and has lost her good name; but David, like the narrator of the twentieth-century elegiac romances, has allowed himself to become Steerforth's double, and it is not too much to say that he has lost his soul. After the seduction of Little Em'ly, which occurs at the precise center of the novel, David declares his cherished friend dead. He claims that Steerforth "fascinated me no longer" and that "the ties that bound me to him were broken" (388). Steerforth disappears physically from the next seven numbers of the novel, but his name recurs regularly in each monthly install-ment. And like Tennyson to the dead Hallam's door, David keeps returning during these pages—"in an attraction I could not resist" (445)—to the garden under Steerforth's window. After the drowning, which takes place in the next to last number, David mourns for Steerforth as a potential hero "who might have won the love and admiration of thousands, as he had won mine long ago" (696).

Robin Gilmour writes that "there is no real awakening of David's undis-ciplined heart in relation to Steerforth" because "Dickens's imagination is not really engaged [in *David Copperfield*] as it will be later in *Great Expec-tations* in exploring the processes of moral and emotional self-discovery" ("Memory," 39). I have been arguing a greater similarity between the two novels in question. According to my reading, David and Pip are alike not only in regard to their social ambition and the fear of death which sparks it in both instances, but, to an even larger extent, in the burden of guilt they share. Pip is made to feel guilty about being an orphan, about being a boy, about being a laborer, and he makes himself guilty by wishing himself into becoming a snobbish, persecuting gentleman. In the last third of *Great Ex-pectations,* Pip suffers various kinds of symbolic death, which have been seen as ritual attempts to expiate that guilt, to unwish the bad wish that had caused it. But in respect to guilt, David, I think, surpasses even Pip. As the projections on Littimer and Heep indicate, he feels guilty about his social background, about his ambition to rise above it, and about his sexual nature, which Dickens frequently saw as both motivation and means for social advancement. He even feels guilty about distrusting the perfidious Steerforth. More legitimately, perhaps, David appears to blame himself for his part in the seduction of Little Em'ly and for unconsciously wishing his unsatisfactory wife to death.[5] And the writing of *David Copperfield* can be seen as *David's* ritual attempt—the elegiac ritual, this time—to clear himself of this enormous load of guilt.

Elegy would seem to be a promising means of expiation in this case because the sins were all connected with the fascination for the dead Steerforth. It was David who introduced little Em'ly to her seducer and, according to John O. Jordan, gave her to Steerforth in an unconscious attempt to gain his idol's approval and thus rise in social class (69–70). Even the unsatisfactory wife recommended herself in the first place as a tangible representation of the Doctor's Commons gentility Steerforth had advised David to pursue. If David can come to terms with Steerforth through the act of writing *David Copperfield*, then he will perhaps have found the absolution he requires and will perhaps have unwished *his* evil wish.

And the ending of *David Copperfield*, which finds the hero comfortably married and the father of a growing family, might suggest that David's elegy has been more effective than the ritual expiations of Pip, who in the original version of *Great Expectations* remains a wanderer and a childless bachelor. Lawrence Frank believes that David has succeeded where Pip later fails, because at the end of *David Copperfield*—''at the successful end—one has come into possession of one's own story. At the end David's story stands in chronological and thematic coherence'' (92), whereas Pip recoils ''from his own imaginative achievement,'' glorifying Joe as he had previously falsified Miss Havisham (181). But I am not convinced that either hero really succeeds in overcoming his obsession with death, and Pip is, at least, a great deal clearer about the social significance of his guilt than David ever consciously becomes.

Nor, finally, am I certain that David Copperfield ever frees himself from his fascination for Steerforth, even after he has described the latter's death and supposedly ended the elegy. At the conclusion of the novel David has become a gentleman who keeps a respectful servant, and he has reached this station by exercising the identity of the storyteller which Steerforth has conferred on him as a schoolboy. *Steerforth's Gift*, Saul Bellow might have named the novel. There would be nothing wrong with this ending if the story that came before it had been in all respects an elegiac romance. But it seems to me that *if* David has attained the more significant ''station'' he wondered about in the first sentence of the novel, if he has, in fact, become the hero of his own life, he has done so not by acknowledging his alternate identity and then letting it go, like the narrator in Conrad's ''The Secret Sharer,'' not, as Frank maintains, by recognizing ''the failings of Steerforth without rejecting what is redeeming in him,'' thus acknowledging ''the ambiguity of his own moral condition in which good and bad intermingle'' (72). Rather, he asserts his identity at the conclusion by rigorously suppressing even the name of his rival.

David Copperfield, like most of Dickens' novels, was originally published in eighteen equal, monthly parts and a bonus nineteenth installment of one and a half times the normal length. Steerforth's death is recounted in the eighteenth number. The final ''double-number,'' seven chapters long, one-thirteenth of the entire novel, contains the most gratifyingly protracted set of curtain-calls in all of Dickens. Everyone is brought back for a final round of applause. Mr. Peggotty comes all the way from Australia so that we can learn not only about Em'ly, Martha, Mrs. Gummidge and the Micawbers, but even about Mr. Mell, whom we had long forgotten, and Mr. Creakle's son, who never appeared in the novel except to be briefly mentioned. Dickens even reminded himself in the Number Plan not to forget Aunt Betsey's donkeys. Most of the dead are recalled, including James Steerforth, whom David ''mourns for'' (696), but whom in this single case, he consistently avoids naming.

There are plenty of opportunities in the last seven chapters for David to write the name of Steerforth—he recollects the meeting at the Golden Cross Inn (702), he has an interview with Littimer, who mentions his master only through a reference to ''the sins of my former companions'' (730), and finally, in the last chapter, he encounters James's mother, whose name he also suppresses and who, in retaliation perhaps, has ''forgotten this *gentleman's* [David's] name'' (749, my emphasis). It has required considerable ingenuity on David's part to avoid writing the name of the character who has dominated so much of what has gone before. Perhaps Steerforth, the only major character in the novel without a counterpart in Dickens' biography and thus the only pure product of his imagination, is too powerful a force to be laid to rest, but an elegy which fails to commemorate does not legitimately permit a final shift of attention to an elegist, who free now for ''fresh woods and pastures new,'' can become a true hero of his own life.

I mentioned earlier that death scenes are scarce in *David Copperfield*—another important suppression—and that the only death scene of a human being at which David is himself present is that of Barkis. The last words of the dying man, ''Barkis is willin,'' are a reference to the private joke he shares with David, but, coming at this precise moment, they also express a willingness to face death, which the miserly Barkis had been previously reluctant to do.[6] The most obvious and significant suppression in the novel occurs in an earlier speech of Barkis's:

"It was as true," said Mr. Barkis, "as turnips is. It was as true," said Mr. Barkis, nodding his nightcap, which was his only means of emphasis, "as taxes is. And nothing's truer than them."

David has long since completed Barkis's suppressed thought, when he said "it is as certain as death" that greed and cunning will overreach itself (650), but he used this lesson not to redeem himself, but to cast into the teeth of his old scapegoat, Uriah Heep.

Garrett Stewart believes that David has "put his dead back together again" and has thus succeeded, where such suppressing characters as Mr. Dick and Doctor Strong failed, in completing "an articulate memorial or record" (80). I question whether he has even conceded that his dead are in fact dead. David-the-narrator tells us that he has been dreading "from the beginning of the narrative" (673) to recount the death of Steerforth, and when the doctor tells him of the approaching death of Dora, David-the-character "cannot master the thought of it" (656). This reluctance and inability is caused, perhaps, by the young David's failure, as Lawrence Frank would have it, to confront his mother's death. "Part of David," Frank writes, "has never left that room [at the Rookery], has remained within it, gazing longingly in dread and yearning at the graves in the churchyard" (66). If so, then it is unlikely that he ever does learn to make this confrontation, for his remembered image of Steerforth dead, like the image Peggotty leaves him of his dead mother, is of a child sleeping.

At least one critic shares my sense of disquiet at the ending of *David Copperfield*. Judith Wilt writes:

> the final pages seem to picture a "tranquility" achieved with "a better knowledge of myself" and Agnes. Yet the tranquility is a strange one. . . . David, in his last paragraph, imagines in the mirror of the future the hard-won "realities" melting from him "like shadows which I now dismiss." Further, this Prospero pictures Agnes, not joining him in a final Reality, but rather "pointing upward" where the restless heart rests at last. Perhaps.   (305)

The ambiguity suggests that the fear of death remains potent enough with David Copperfield, and perhaps also with Dickens, to prevent proper dismissal of the concept of gentility and of the gentleman who, as both the author and the narrator of this most penetrating study of death and gentility must surely know by now, cannot afford them the least protection.

NOTES

1. Sylvia Manning notes that "David's ability to tell stories is a saving social asset: his 'good memory' and his 'simple, earnest manner of narrating' win him a special position of storyteller to Steerforth." She goes on to say that "Just as the Sultana Scheherazade, whose image presides over the episode, told stories for her very life, her young successor David told them to save his sheltered niche—to save his boy's life—in the isolated world of Salem House" (331–332).
2. Samuel Clemens, who attended one of these performances, wrote that Dickens' reading of the storm scene "in which Steerforth lost his life was so vivid and so full of energetic action that the house was carried off its feet, so to speak" (175).
3. Marks, whose article anticipates Bruffee's by several years, does not distinguish between kinds of retrospective narrators, or between authors who attempt to discover meaning through this technique or discipline and those who use it merely as a device for "engaging the reader in order that he might be led to believe what he might otherwise have merely understood" (375). This last distinction seems crucial to me, and I could wish Bruffee himself had confronted it more directly. Romance asserts. Elegy seeks rather to discover.
4. In Hugh Walpole's fine scenario for the 1930s film version, we actually see Mr. Peggotty, played by Lionel Barrymore, give the necklace to Em'ly and tell her it comes from France.
5. Perhaps the most persuasive of the critics who have argued this point is Carl Bandelin, "David Copperfield: A Third Interesting Penitent," but Christopher E. Mulvey and Harry Stone also make strong cases for David's guilt.
6. George Anastaplo, writing on *A Christmas Carol*, argues that avarice should be regarded as "a determined attempt to fence oneself off from death" (127).

WORKS CITED

Anastaplo, George. *The Artist as Thinker: From Shakespeare to Joyce*. Chicago: Swallow Press, 1984.

Bandelin, Carl. "David Copperfield: A Third Interesting Penitent." *SEL* 16 (1976), 601–611.

Bruffee, Kenneth. *Elegiac Romance: Cultural Change and the Loss of the Hero in Modern Fiction*. Ithaca, N.Y.: Cornell University Press, 1983.

Carabine, Keith. "Reading *David Copperfield*." In *Reading the Victorian Novel: Detail Into Form*. London: Vision Press, 1980.

Clemens, Samuel. *The Autobiography of Mark Twain*. Ed. Charles Neider. New York: Harper, 1959.

Conrad, Joseph. *Lord Jim*. New York: Holt, Rinehart and Winston, 1965.

Dickens, Charles. *David Copperfield*. Ed. Nina Burgis. London: Oxford University Press, 1981.

Frank, Lawrence. *Charles Dickens and the Romantic Self*. Lincoln and London: University of Nebraska Press, 1984.

Gilmour, Robin. *The Idea of the Gentleman in the Victorian Novel*. London: Allen and Unwin, 1981.

———. "Memory in *David Copperfield.*" *Dickensian* 71 (1975), 38–42.

Gomme, A. H. *Dickens*. London: Evans, 1977.

Jordan, John O. "The Social Subtext of *David Copperfield.*" *Dickens Studies Annual* 14 (1985), 61–92.

Kettle, Arnold. "Thoughts on *David Copperfield.*" In *Review of English Studies* N.S. 2 (1961), 65–74.

Manning, Sylvia. "*David Copperfield* and Scheherazade: The Necessity of Narrative." *Studies in the Novel* 14 (1982), 327–336.

Marks, Barry A. "Retrospective Narrative in Nineteenth-Century American Literature." *College English* 30 (1970), 366–375.

Mason, Philip. *The English Gentleman: The Rise of an Ideal*. New York: William Morrow, 1982.

Miller, J. Hillis. *Charles Dickens: The World of His Novels*. Cambridge, Mass.: Harvard University Press, 1958.

Moers, Ellen. *The Dandy: Brummell to Beerbohm*. New York: Viking, 1959.

Monod, Sylvère. *Dickens the Novelist*. Norman: University of Oklahoma Press, 1968.

Mulvey, Christopher E. "*David Copperfield*: The Folk-Story Structure." *Dickens Studies Annual* 5 (1976), 74–94.

Orwell, George. "Charles Dickens." In *Dickens, Dali and Others*. New York and London: Harcourt Brace Jovanovich, 1973.

Salinger, J. D. *Raise High the Roofbeam Carpenter and Seymour: An Introduction*. New York: Bantam Books, 1981.

Shaw, George Bernard. "Epistle Dedicatory" to *Man and Superman*. Harmondsworth: Penguin, 1983.

Slater, Michael. *Dickens and Women*. London: J. M. Dent and Sons, 1983.

Stewart, Garrett. *Death Sentences: Styles of Dying in Victorian Fiction*. Cambridge, Mass.: Harvard University Press, 1984.

Stone, Harry. *Dickens and the Invisible World: Fairy Tales, Fantasy, and Novel-Making*. Bloomington: Indiana University Press, 1979.

Warren, Robert Penn. *All the King's Men*. New York: Bantam Books, 1981.

Westburg, Barry. *The Confessional Fictions of Charles Dickens*. DeKalb: Northern Illinois University Press, 1977.

Wilt, Judith. "Confusion and Consciousness in Dickens's Esther," *Nineteenth-Century Fiction* 32 (1977), 285–309.

Wonderful No-Meaning: Language and the Psychopathology of the Family in Dickens' *Hard Times*

Richard Fabrizio

I. THE ARGUMENT: "People live now in a way that I don't comprehend." Roger Carbury in Trollope, *The Way We Live Now* (1875).

Usually thought of as a satiric portrait of industrialization, weak in drama and feeble in characterization,[1] *Hard Times* is more fundamentally a keen description of the psyche forged out of socioeconomic conditions. It exposes personality types, their emotive and reactive make-up, and the origin and process of their symptoms. The language its characters rehearse and particularly the poses they strike result from the mind's accommodation to a new familial environment, a by-product of the machine—the great power loom. Their linguistic and paralinguistic adaptations result in a dialectic where love dominates life in the absence of its direct expression, fancy preoccupies the mind while it is ridiculed, and feeling—particularly in the male—is glorified while it is denigrated. In the fictive time-space of mid-nineteenth-century Coketown both a psychopathology of the family and its rhetorical expression is voiced. Dickens had to describe a psychic condition with a vocabulary that itself was a symptom of the disease.

He saw his fictive society against a backdrop of an earlier agricultural state, thus naming the parts of his novel sowing, reaping, and garnering, and framing its time in spring (I. 4. 11), summer (II. 8. 137), and autumn (III. 6. 201). Winter is absent; the great question mark at the end. These are growth stages, psychological as well as vegetative. How do agricultural and industrial growth differ? How do people, particularly the family unit, psychically grow, mature,

61

and die in the age of steam? After the Reformation the nature of the family radically changed, according to some becoming sternly "patriarchal," according to others richly "affective."[2] No such elemental split seems to have occurred; rather power (the patriarchal) and love (the affective) became fixed in an uneasy bondage within the family, the terms Wife, Husband, Mother, and especially Father undergoing redefinition. Robbed of the rich "network" of legal and social services held by the family in ancient and medieval times (Lacy, 9, 15–32; Given, 42), and now provided by the State, the family was thrown back upon itself, had to justify itself as an entity tied together only by the cords of the emotions. Law and state replaced religion and family as the cement that held society together. Crime was divorced from sin (Sharpe, 4, 15–17), and punishment from family action. Entertainment which had taken place in the public arena was forced from the marketplace, tavern, or pilgrimage (Bakhtin, 7–19; Heywood, 1–23; Whitmore, 192–247) into the confines of the home and family.

In the age of nascent capitalism, after 1750, there is a stress on the "inner life" of the family, which is signalled by a lowering of the marriage age and a slight increase in family size (Anderson, 232; Levine, 62; McFarlene, 27ff).[3] Gradgrind has five children—often thought pointless for only two have an active role in the novel; Louisa marries at just over nineteen (I. 3. 10–11; I. 15. 75) to a much older man—while preindustrial marriage generally took place between those of the same age (Laslett, "England" 146). Wherever technology is found, the nuclear rather than the extended family is found (Stoianovich, 177–181), with a stress on children rather than relations. The family changed from a more functional to a more affective unit. As it weakened politically and economically, it changed psychically. With the narrowing of its activity in public space came an expansion of its inner life in the private space of the home, what historians have labeled its domestication but which Dickens in *Hard Times* describes as its dislocation. The shift in the nature of the family is marked by redefinition in vocabulary. The very word economics, for instance, derived as it is from the Greek οἶκος or "house," was no longer referred to in terms of the household unit. The family became mythologized, maintaining itself as a unit by godly commandment (paterfamilias) and supporting itself by sacrificial rite (feminine love).

Woman's function is reduced to her love; man's affection is replaced by his function. Dickens' novel for good reason centers on the industrialization of weaving, the very sign of woman's traditional status and economic position (Ste. Croix 180–181). Every Homeric woman—mortal or immortal—is never found without her distaff. Here mechanical frame and loom replace her distaff.

In the fifteenth century, the water power revolution stripped her of another function, the two or three hours of grinding duties to feed her family (Reynolds, 124). Four centuries later the attrition of her functional value in terms of household economy was enormous. With attenuated functional value, women became aliens inside and outside the home. They were justified as moral agents, as repositories of love and beauty; that is, for themselves not for their function. After his educational system failed in Louisa, Gradgrind does not so much question its utility as its applicability to females: "it [the educational system] would be difficult of general application to girls" (III. 3. 183). Later, Louisa is praised for having no function. She "beautifies" life precisely because she holds "no fantastic vow, or bond, or brotherhood, or sisterhood, or pledge, or covenant" (III. 9. 226). Women became the fertile matrix for great moral battles between function and love. Wives are destroyed. Marriage kills off Mrs. Gradgrind, Mrs. Blackpool, Mrs. Jupe, and to all intents and purposes Mrs. Bounderby. Sibling and romantic love are confused. Louisa malfunctions in the expression of her emotions to her brother and to her would-be lover.

Female functionalism in terms of family economics reciprocally affected male functionalism. Dickens in *Dombey and Son* (1846) had documented an earlier stage in the transition of the family from farm to firm. Mercantilism affected awkward family relations, particularly the sexual ones between husband and wife. The first Mrs. Dombey is a procreating object; the second Mrs. Dombey a sexual curiosity. The "father" and "son" of the title are equivocal terms, undergoing redefinition because of economic imperatives; a father and a son are something between partners and relatives. Emotion publicly stripped from males found clumsy expression in the family. Sons deny motherhood. Bounderby and Bitzer in *Hard Times* effectively eliminate motherhood, matricides by intent. Fatherhood is lethal. Mr. Gradgrind tries to withdraw his affections from his daughter; Mr. Jupe nobly parts from his.

In a wild interplay of actions and reactions among the Gradgrinds and Bounderbys, the Jupes, Sparsits, Bitzers, and Blackpools, the roles of father and mother, husband and wife, brother and sister, bachelor and spinster are psychically reestablished. It is on this all too fragile, this all too unprofound psychic surface where the matter of the novel exists. It is here that we find the causes and motives for the awkward reticence, indirection, and circumlocution that mark all the relationships in the novel.[4] Characters conform to an oblique communication code. To understand the code, the pathos of the moment must be deciphered. For after all, it is of the essence that the novel is an exposé of ordinary people interacting in the daily course of daily life.

For instance, the three mysteries of the novel, where is Mr. Jupe? who robbed the bank? what happened to Blackpool?, are not exploited as means to uncover monumental truths but to map the characteristic ways that feeling finds expression. Mr. Jupe's whereabouts is every day fixed in the pathetic pattern of Sissy's carrying about the bottle of nine-oils. The robber's identity is manifested in Louisa's pathetic doubts about her brother's complicity. Blackpool's disappearance stimulates the pathetic faith of Rachael. The structure of *Hard Times* is therefore regressive—events are not cumulative but repetitive, bound to a single psychic pattern. Its paradigm may be described as: 1. daily "incompatibility" (Dickens' word), in which males and females are ill formed and wrongly joined; 2. daily misdirection, in which communication of all kinds between and among the sexes is oblique—a pattern of avoidance marked by the heart's silence or dumbness to its desires; 3. daily disaster, in which relationships break up and end rather than grow and resolve.

The regressive structure of the novel is a template of the repressive nature of its language; that is, a language that moves action ahead while harking back to loss. On the purely pathological level, action is impersonalized by a varied catalogue of gestures and tics, from Bitzer's parroting of formulas (echolalia) to Mrs. Gradgrind's mental torpidity (bradyphrenia). A veritable pathopoiesis results, each compulsive movement manifesting a feeling in the absence of its direct expression. On the rhetorical level, Dickens creates a structure of naming. Throughout the text, he humorously plays with the designation, "ology." The suffix carries all the weight of its origin in λόγος, "logos." Logos means "word" or "name" but signifies a complex of values from thought and discourse to reason and conversation; in fact, it refers to all that gives meaning to existence. On her deathbed, Mrs. Gradgrind wishes to find the word or name for all that is missing in Gradgrind's philosophy. She knows that the word is not a Gradgrindian "ology." She struggles, but before she can find the word she dies. The narrator comments: "It matters little what figures of wonderful no-meaning she [Mrs Gradgrind] began to trace upon her wrappers" (II. 9. 152–153). Dickens insists that to see into his characters it is only the "unsaid," the "unlogos" that will do. With no pen, Mrs. Gradgrind writes no words on no paper. It is the "wonderful no-meaning" that gives meaning to existence. It is the "wonderful no-meaning" that is the rhetorical counterpart to the no-actions and the no-statements of all the characters. On the language level, Foucault calls a similar occurrence society's "procedures of exclusion" (*Le Ordre*); that is, structures society uses to avoid the expression of what it does not permit, the prohibited. Here, what is not permitted or withheld expression is nevertheless stated; it might be called a rhetoric of exclusion. The rhetoric exposes what is in the mind of characters by what is excluded in acts and words. Dickens uses exclusion as a tool to satirize the inadequacy of the linguistic formula of Gradgrind's school and Bounderby's factory. Gradgrind wishes his students to form themselves on the factory model of a language that expresses a one to one relationship with "thingness." Such a mathematical formulation eliminates the space between word and phenomenon, the space where ambiguity and emotion slip in at the back door. Therefore, he wishes a definition of a horse in terms of genus and differentiation, stripping language of either cultural or personal connotation. Bitzer's scientific enumeration of the qualities of a horse is preferred to Sissy's perplexity about how to define. Louisa and Tom keep "conchological" and "mineralogical" cabinets: "the specimens were all arranged and labelled, and the bits of stone and ore looked as though they might have been broken from the parent substances by those tremendously hard instruments their own names" (I. 3. 8). The very act of naming is then an act of destruction—of breaking reality from the word meant to explain it. In Bounderby's factory the same process occurs. At his marriage breakfast, Bounderby vaunts that he is "a man, who when he sees a Post, says 'that's a Post' " (I. 16. 83). Expression is an exact equation: one word equals one thing. But what functions satisfactorily in his factory cracks in daily life. Bounderby accuses Blackpool of refusing out of fear to spy on his fellow workers. Blackpool denies the accusation not by an assertion of his reasons but by refraining to speak—"nowt to sen." The no-statement is filled in as the content of his psyche—ethical, human, religious. The unsaid has no meaning and all meaning. Therefore, Bounderby is constrained to respond in words that mock his own attitude about language: "I know what you said; more than that, I know what you mean, you see. Not always the same thing, by the Lord Harry! Quite different things" (II. 5. 112). It is appropriate that he swears by the Lord Harry, or the Devil, for it is the devil who represents splitting word from thing—the diabolic being even in etymology a "carrying away" as opposed to symbolic, a "carrying together."

In presenting the psychic activity of a new family type, Dickens replaces expression by indirection, the frontal attack by the gesture. Language of the public space (factory and worker) was too shallow to function effectively in the private space (home and family); it detached and split rather than unified and glued the world and the self. In a linguistic tour de force, Dickens supported his psychological investigation with a virtual philosophical theory of language. "Wonderful no-meaning" is hunted in "no-naming," "no-stating," and "no-acting." This notion may be refined, at least briefly, by stating a few forms into which his language falls: 1. "no-meaning" discovers meaning when of two significations for a sign the intended one is false while the unintended is true (amphiboly). Louisa thus logically interprets the woman in Blackpool's room as his "wife," but the woman is Rachael—not his wife but whom he wishes were his wife (II. 6. 12); or Tom intends that Blackpool's appearance nightly at the bank will be logically perceived as a sign of guilt should the bank be robbed (II. 6. 125–126) while the hidden truth is that innocence will be sacrificed. Signs rather than having direct meaning stand for the presuppositions of the interpreters. 2. "No-naming" discovers meaning by the substitution of an epithet for a personal name (antonomasia). Children in the school are designated by numbers; workers in the factory are called "hands." The rhetoric of no-naming is fixed in the references to nicknames. Nicknames indicate not just identity but attitude. Mrs. Gradgrind's perplexity about nicknaming gets at a psychic truth: the word can be a kind of medicine to relieve anxiety. Her problem is what to call Bounderby after he marries her daughter. Gradgrind won't permit nicknames (I. 2. 2). If nicknames like "Joe" aren't permitted, and she can't call him mister, and the name Josiah is "unsupportable" to her, what shall she name him (I. 5. 78–79)? Her dilemma originates because she cannot call son a man who is as old as she is; the integration into her family of such an old man upset family order and strained the available language.[5] She solves her problem by a no-name; he becomes a letter, "J" (II. 9. 151). Cecelia is Sissy, an expressive name that indicates family and social order, while "J" indicates detachment and predicament. 3. "No-stating" discovers meaning by the personification of the absent (prosopopeia). The personification is of psychic conditions. The Sparsit-Bounderby relationship is almost totally unexpressed in their direct conversations. Mrs. Sparsit apostrophizes Bounderby's portrait (II. 10. 156; III. 9. 224–225). What she refrains from expressing and acting out to him in person, she speaks to his portrait, thereby retrieving for us some of her hidden feelings. 4. "No-acting" discovers meaning in unexpressed acts tied to withheld words (anastrophe). This is the most used device to capture not only suspense but all the unexpressed hopes, desires, and dreams of the characters. For example, Louisa does not know how to act in Blackpool's rooms. She says that she is ignorant of "how to speak" (II. 6. 121), but she also refrains from doing: "She [Louisa] stretched out hers [her hands], as if she would have touched him [Blackpool]; then checked herself and remained still" (II. 6. 122). Psychic content is built at the expense of expression.

Dickens chronicles by a vast psychic and linguistic system family history, or more accurately, family psychohistory in *Hard Times*. His subject is the domestic family and its intricate battle to survive under industrial capitalism, how it is welded together, how it thinks and loves, how it is perverted and dies.

> II. THE PSYCHIC HISTORY: "It was now . . . The Magnetic Age: the age of violent attractions, when to hear mention of love is dangerous, and to see it, a communication of disease." Sir Austin in Meredith, *The Ordeal of Richard Feveral* (1859).

The opening of *Hard Times* documents an act of psychic surgery. A new training ground, the school, was a prerequisite for the new ethical and emotional thinking required by the new economic and social world. Emotions, which have no practical value, would be replaced by "facts," which can aid in economic life. The school is the training ground for the middle-class psyche; the factory is the training ground for the working-class psyche. Bounderby is the professor of the novel's second school. The factory required altered behavior from workers, machine teaching man its rhythm,[6] even as Blackpool complained of the machinery working "in his own head" (I. 10. 49). One of the most astounding side-effects of the operation on the emotions is the surface calm of the patients. Though the surgery is fundamentally a violent act, it is performed calmly, responded to almost silently. Silence reigns in Coketown, save for the rhythmic beating of the power looms. They are its heartbeat. When the second Mrs. Dombey does not return home one night, Dombey himself breaks down her locked door and thereafter strikes his daughter who tries to comfort him *(Dombey,* 616). Jonas Chuzzlewit screams and "hauls" about his wife, Mercy Pecksniff, so that she fears "bloodshed" *(Martin Chuzzlewit,* 764–766).[7] But the psychological violence in *Hard Times* is executed silently. Relationships with self, others, and even things are quietly taut. The attempt to fashion the mind on the economic formula of trade—quid pro quid—left the psyche distressed. Emotion evicted from public life found uneasy expression in the family; love prohibited to males found unstable shelter in females. A side-effect of the psychic operation is infertility—the death of the family. Tom and Louisa will produce no children; Blackpool and Rachael will never marry. Bounderby, Bitzer, and Harthouse personify futile bachelorhood.[8] In a world where the family is dislocated by economic and social forces, where the psyche is deformed by education, characters express themselves in twisted language and hunt their selves in twisted relationships.

Nowhere is the psychic condition of the family better seen than in Mr. Thomas Gradgrind's relationship with wife and daughter. He is not monolithic, impenetrable, and cold. His sentiments at times unseat him (I. 5. 20–21). He is unaccountably kind to Sissy, for instance. He excuses his feeling by the rationalization that success with such poor matter as she will prove his system. Reluctantly he admits that "he had become possessed by an idea that there was something in this girl which could hardly be set down in tabular form" (I. 14. 71). "Tabular form" is a stale metonymy whose origin is the *tabula* or writing table, a flat surface or board upon which wills, accounts, and letters were once written. So the *tabula* defines communication in terms of lists and public accounts; for instance, God's commandments were written into a tablet. Typically in this novel, the metaphor—Sissy being compared to what is not tabular—catalogues an absence: her worth is what "could hardly be set down." The "idea," the atabular, appears obliquely just beneath the surface of the action, at the point where verbal expression and psychic desire conflict. The absence defines the presence or the sum of Gradgrind's actions, his calculated existence as a public man, teacher, and M.P. But he is a man "possessed" by a formless "idea." The idea, the private man, peeks through. The idea is expressed even though Gradgrind has no vocabulary for it. This akinesia is typical of him when he confronts feeling; the articulate man displays a stickiness of mind. When her father left Sissy, Gradgrind had taken her in against the sound advice of Bounderby (I. 8. 37). In the negotiations for her at the circus, the "idea" appears in glances and movements. Circus folk read in Gradgrind what he does not realize is in him. Childers looks at Gradgrind with "hope." But most importantly the absent "idea" forces its presence upon him when their idiom pops out of his mouth, the idiom being atabular in form: "Why has he [Jupe] been—so very much—Goosed? asked Mr. Gradgrind, forcing the word out of himself, with great solemnity and reluctance" (I. 6. 24). The idea's atabular form is the common idiom of the other, the circus. Gradgrind forces the word out with "solemnity," as if it were a word in a religious rite, an untouchable thing both magical and lethal at the same time. The socially loaded word "goosed," meaning hissed, is really a non-word that mimics the hissing of the goose to express an attitude and feeling of disapproval. His "reluctance" to use the word is a sign of psychic stricture. Such words are metaphoric, expressing social norms and the grey area between desire and permissibility. They are a psychic shorthand. In the same circus atmosphere, Bounderby will object to the circus word "Cackler," and indeed Childers will have to translate the expressive particular term to its inexpressive general form "speaker" (I. 6. 24). Such linguistic acrobatics are commonplace in the novel. Feeling requiring suppression in public life is expressed over and over again by circumlocution, signs, and absence.

Gradgrind's manner in relation to females displays the silent truth beyond the surface of his words; his innate affection suffers from public image. Straight away we learn that Gradgrind "was an affectionate father after his manner" (I. 3. 8). Nothing could be more important than the modifying phrase—"After his manner." The sole bit of information we have about his past, his manner, is that he had sold hardware. His past is business; his manner is geared to it. The ex-hardware man has modified his character with a manner. As the idea of fatherhood became reduced in its legal, political, and economic extensions, the demand for another dimension — affection—increased.[9] For instance, the notion of a "confidence," a trust beyond the kind of business affiliation of *Dombey and Son* was expected of the relationship. Harthouse notices that had such a confidence been present between Gradgrind and his son their relationship might have been different (II. 7. 131). At one point, Louisa is in a state of tension: "a fire with nothing to burn" (I. 3. 10); something had "crept" into her head (I. 4. 14) which stunted could only grow malignantly. Again the expression takes the form of negation; a fire cannot exist unless it burns. The "unfire," which is the fire, thus may give neither light nor heat, yet both are present. This is a psychic expression of schizophrenia, literally the broken-off mind. But her symptoms are the physical manifestation of his anxiety—his broken-off mind. Whenever she hints at tensions by broken-off words or physical tics, Gradgrind himself becomes ill at ease. He attempts to preserve his equilibrium by cutting himself off from inconvenient sentiments. But the strength with which he stops the onrush of sympathy shows the concomitant strength of the now deemed pertinent family feelings, the strength of what is absent. Louisa says to her father: "I was tired. . . . I have been tired for a long time" (I. 3. 10). But she doesn't know from what; exhaustion is the state resulting from the pursuit of the unknown absent. Gradgrind cuts her off, cuts off any investigation of her exhaustion, of what is too mysterious to be categorized as data, as tabular. Nevertheless, Gradgrind reacts, silently within himself. Non-statement or non-action is the sign of his state. His instincts function without his practical consent. His state and his perplexity rankle, for he is unable to get what she said (or did not say) out of his mind. He walks along "in silence" for half-a-mile after the conversation, exactly like the meditating Abraham about to sacrifice his son Isaac. A slowness of mental activity, almost a frozen mind (bradyphrenia), marks his emotional state when it comes to family love. Finally, he "gravely broke out." Surely Dickens' ear was to the grindstone of the psychic expression of his period. "Gravely" and "broke out" conflict. The grave, what is heavy and solemn, conflicts with the eruptive and effusive "broke out." What breaks out is a nothing with regard to the situation. Bradyphrenia becomes bradyphrasia—his speech is slow and heavy and does not express his psychic state. He broke out not in tears or in anger, but in an appeal drawn from the language not of family but from the imperatives of public life, admonishing her to heed her friends who would think her vagueness silly (I. 3. 10–11). Blunting Louisa's nascent expression of emotion, he blunts his own.

Gradgrind began the process to reduce emotional stimuli by mating years before with an unwomanly woman. Mrs. Gradgrind is a non-entity, without even a first name to distinguish her as separate from her husband. She is deprived of sexual identity, being a "transparency of a small female figure, without enough light behind it" (I. 4. 12). Gradgrind's emotional bradyphrenia is the sum of her character. Like Bitzer, she involuntarily parrots the words spoken by others (echolalia), a condition frequently present in catatonic schizophrenia. For instance, she castigates Louisa by telling her to "go and be somethingological directly" (I. 4. 14)—the "ologies" belonging to her husband's vocabulary. On the image level, Mrs. Gradgrind is the final product of the early stage Louisa. Mrs. Gradgrind is a "transparency . . . without enough light," while Louisa is a "light with nothing to rest upon" (I. 3. 10). Once again Dickens defines character by absence. Neither the transparency with too little light nor the light with no resting place may be seen. Mrs. Gradgrind is the mother reduced to a comic and useless figure. Her symbolic symptom is a constantly "throbbing" head (I. 4. 13). Her head began to split as soon as she married Gradgrind and never stopped thereafter (I. 16. 78). These headaches are attributed by Louisa to life lived in the world of facts (I. 4. 14), at the tabula. The more the world, Hermia, dominated the domestic life, Hestia, the more women became displaced; the more the term motherhood is stripped of economic significance, the more it was redefined in terms of love of children and husband. "Husband," on the other hand, originally only a Germanic term for the master of a house, now solely expressed a relationship to a woman, both legal and affective. Gradgrind attempts to reduce psychic tension—born of the growing demand for affection in marriage and fatherhood—by reducing the femaleness of his wife and daughter.

In Bounderby the same psychic conflict is almost eliminated by excess, by overabundance. The mark of his character is an abnormally rapid mental activity (tachyphrenia) marked by volubility or rapidity in speech (tachyphrasia). The hint of his conflict is, as in Gradgrind, his avoidance of femininity, but he avoids not by passivity but by intimidation. He is a "bounder," cocksure, wielding vulgarity as a weapon, in his creation of new boundaries, limits, shapes. The narrator speaks of him as a God, one with "Divine Right" (I. 12. 61). On the linguistic level, he vulgarizes the terms family, state, hero by a process of deformation and then reformation. He creates myth or μυθός —the words out of which reality is made. He uses myth to such a degree that he structures both world and people by it. He builds with the fiction of his "humility" the other that he would be; the narrator thus calls him the Bully of Humility. The public, other self he creates (Hermes) dominates the private, inner self (Hestia). Bounderby is self-made; he is one who by sheer will pulled himself up by the bootstraps out of a poor and wicked family to become great. The myth of the self-made man, the new hero, is tied to the death of the family. He posits this death in a scene that has Mrs. Gradgrind for its audience and his birthday for its subject. He is so voluble that his words overwhelm her while in his tale he attacks fictive women. Rechristening himself Bounderby, he consciously destroys the Pegler family—his real father and mother. This substitution of an epithet for a name (antonomasia) discovers a withheld psychological condition. Changing his name, he escapes meaning that proceeds from the family; at the same time under the assumed name he self creates a new type. He is a self-made man born of a self-made language; he is the child of his own words. He destroys every trace of the gentle woman who is his mother, Mrs. Pegler, and of his father who is called the "best" of husbands (II. 6. 19). What Bounderby does is replace his "ideal" fam- ily—the gentle mother and good husband—with an ideal "no-family" in mythic terms. Exiling his real mother from ever seeing him (or to put it correctly, from his seeing her), he commits a kind of matricide. But Bounderby goes further. He creates and then abuses a fictive mother and grandmother. With each retelling of his fictive autobiography, he destroys his female side—a kind of gynecide. The male is heroic to the degree he is a bastard, one who makes it on his own in the same way as Gide later linked the bastardy of Oedipus to his greatness (*Oedipus* 1930).

Bounderby's pursuit of Louisa, young enough to be his daughter, is a sign of his malady. Outwardly like Mrs. Gradgrind, Louisa is unfeminine, the product of a sexually egalitarian education. Yet he proposes to her not because she is asexual but because he expects to find in her all the feminine charms with none of the difficulties. He seeks to release on her all his emotions. Nowhere is the split between man and words better represented than in his ability to talk of other things while his heart is preoccupied with Louisa: "He spoke of young Thomas, but he looked at Louisa" (I. 4. 13). He babbles out words (tachylalia); he talks of other things, of what is not on his mind. His words negate his thoughts, but his body reveals them. Typically, he will say, "Well, Louisa, that's [stemming her father's anger] worth a kiss" (I. 4. 16). His training makes him speak of the kiss as an exchange for help, while emotionally he needs the fulfillment the kiss provides.

His body bursts from its shell, his head swells from its skin, his face erupts into fiery red (I. 4. 11; II. 5. 116). His rapid mental activity is out of bounds of his body. His tachyphrenia is so endemic that no situation in which he acts is free of it. One of the more curious, but no less typical relationships in the novel is between Bounderby and Mrs. Sparsit. On the conscious level, Bounderby regards the woman as a possession. He dominates others with a flood of words that uses her nobility to quell opposition and to control behavior (e.g., I. 7. 36). Her worth is that she will be the captive nobility, the "captive Princess" (I. 7. 33), that demonstrates the captor's strength. But their relationship, like all other relationships between men and women, functions mechanically on the program of a series of unstated assumptions. One of the best ways to see this is to compare Bounderby's telling Sparsit he will marry Louisa with Gradgrind's asking Louisa to marry Bounderby. It is curious the extent to which these two scenes run parallel. First, the subject is the same: a marriage proposal between Bounderby and Louisa. Next, the manner of handling the announcement is the same: Louisa is told to marry someone she does not want to marry; Sparsit is told she is barred from marrying someone she wants and from being his housekeeper. Both Gradgrind and Bounderby expect the women to react with emotion; neither does. Sparsit, like Louisa, outwardly accepts what she inwardly repels. That Bounderby is aware that Sparsit's attachment to him is more than professional is signalled by Bounderby himself who, though never expressing any desire for her, thinks she will faint away at the news of his forthcoming marriage. He is aware of what neither verbalizes: that she cares to be his wife, a feeling that puffs no doubt a side of him he doesn't acknowledge—his sexual vanity. Finally, the two scenes are alike in their effects on the males: if Gradgrind is upset by Louisa's cold response, Bounderby is "far more disconcerted than if she [Sparsit] had thrown her box at the mirror or swooned on the hearthrug" (I. 16. 80).

Her fumbling with this workbox encodes her psychic state. The box is constantly in her hands. It is a sexual symbol, a place to receive needles and pins and to store the cloth of life. While Bounderby is telling her of his decision to marry, she of course has her box with her and works on a piece of cambric: "she picked out holes for some inscrutable ornamental purpose" (I. 16. 80). Her actions speak without words. She is a gross caricature of

Penelope, always pictured with distaff, always waiting for her man, a man always in danger of being snared by sirens. Sparsit thinks of Bounderby as a victim, particularly of Louisa's snares. That Tom noticed in his sneering way that she wished to marry Bounderby (II. 3. 104) and that she was like a mother, calling her continually "Mother Sparsit," indicates the complexity of this relationship. She functions like a mother, taking over domestic duties, but fits into the economic framework of a housekeeper. In Freudian terms, she is the desired mother from a higher class worthy of such a son (Rank, 69). She is a sign of his inner emotional dilemma and a symbol of his outer victory over class. With her genteel sewing what better figure to represent the domestic side of cloth manufacture which his power looms have assaulted and destroyed.

Emotional and class signs and symbols that hover about this relationship are fixed in a single act: Bounderby's dismissal of Sparsit. Bounderby does not face her or himself, but nevertheless encodes in his words and acts what he would hide. He sticks "an envelop with a cheque in it in her little basket" (III. 9. 224). The cheque, an economic promise, replaces the sexual promise of the man. He deposits money in her "box" and withdraws self.

Bitzer parallels Bounderby more than in the alliteration of their names. He is the perfected state of the new mythic hero—the Industrial Man. He is the echo of Bounderby. He acts without acting, for his actions are repetitive of others. He repeats definitions without personal imput (I. 2. 3); he repeats Gradgrind's philosophy without concern for human relationships (III. 8. 218–219). His language is the ideal shape of all others—a parrotlike repetition of the words spoken by others (echolalia). A Hermes, he begins as a messenger of the banking god, spying and informing on mankind for Bounderby while conniving to usurp his position. Bounderby dies of a fit in a Coketown street (III. 9. 225), a final paroxysm that appropriately ends his excess of words in an excess of movement. But Bitzer continues to climb the mythic ladder (III. 9. 225).

After his father dies, Bitzer—echoing his idol Bounderby—gets rid of his mother. Bounderby's myth is Bitzer's reality. He does not exile her into anonymity in the country, rather he has her shut up in the Work House. Like Bounderby, he provides her with an allowance, "half a pound of tea a year" (II. 1. 88). To the perfected type such an allowance is a weakness. To him the idea of the family is ludicrous. It is provident to be single, and it is perverse to have a family according to his ethic, for Bitzer says, "I have only one to feed, and that's the person I most like to feed" (II. 1. 90). Even "hearing" of "wives and family" conditions makes Bitzer "nauseous" (II. 1. 90).

The industrial ethic sought to retrain the affections, "gratitude" for instance and its consequent "virtues" (III. 8. 219). Bitzer is simply the advanced state of what Dickens saw as the new malady—Industrial Man. The sleeping Bitzer emits a kind of "choke" (II. 8. 139). The noise is just the non-word to characterize his stifled life. The choke is a sign of tension incipiently present in him, the tension between organic desire and social morè. What he despises, intrigues him—the forbidden world of fancy. In the same way as Louisa, dragging Tom after her, is intrigued by the circus, Bitzer runs after something, a circus character—Sissy. He does not simply wish to catch her but to establish a relationship with her, his void, his unexpressed torment exposed in his need to torment her. The two were already metaphorically linked in the opening classroom scene. Now Bitzer redirects the relationship by making faces at her as any child might do. But the faces are frightening, ill-adapted to creating a relationship. They are manufactured emotions. They seem "cruel" to Sissy, and she runs away from him (I. 6. 20). His "faces" are his ethic. Like all else about him they are imitations; they are unfeeling because there is nothing behind them. He "knuckles" his forehead, "blinks rapidly," "chokes," all the nonverbal signs of his condition.

Bitzer, a Hermes figure, represents movement, mobile wealth, and public space; Sissy, a Hestia figure, represents fixed hearth, domestic affection, and private space. Educated to be a Hermes, Louisa's sex prevents fulfillment of her role. Absence dominates her. Awaiting a sign from her mother that never comes, or a kiss from her brother that proves too little, Louisa is a figure who might have become something wonderful but doesn't. At the end of the novel, the narrator characterizes her future as an absence: "a thing [wife and mother that] was never to be (III. 9. 226).

Very early, Louisa is curious about family relations, about what binds husband to wife, parent to child. Although her only extended conversation with Sissy Jupe begins with school matters, themselves inherently parental, it ends with Louisa directly asking Sissy about the emotional ties that unite a family. Louisa pointblank inquires, "Did your [Sissy's] father love her [Sissy's mother]?" (I. 9. 45). More than the words, the manner with which they are spoken reveal their intent, for "Louisa asked these questions with a strong, wild, wandering interest peculiar to her; an interest gone astray like a banished creature, and hiding in solitary places" (I. 9. 45). The differentiation between what she expresses and what seethes in her creates a charged atmosphere. The normal love essential to her being is the "banished" monster.

Love is the perversion, what ''has gone astray'' to hide ''in solitary places,'' while cultivated conduct is accepted in its place—such emotional displacement is the very basis of the pathology of Coketown family life. Louisa here is like Florence Dombey, believing she is to blame for her father's hatred for her and thus trying to reshape ''her wrong feeling'' (*Dombey*, 372). What baffles Louisa is her own wrong feelings. She is baffled by the forms and structures of family ties expressed in the paradox of Sissy's father loving yet leaving her. Her recourse rather than to feel is to collect more data about the biography of the man so as to still by neutral facts her nascent feelings (I. 9. 45–46).

Louisa's own father is near physically but distant emotionally. She has only a professional (a teacher) relationship with him. With her mother, she does not even know how to be cordial, Sissy being ''more pleasant'' than Louisa ''can ever be'' (I. 9. 43). Love goes ''astray'' with her parents and with all of Louisa's relationships. Her love for her brother, her marriage, and her attraction to a lover on both the plot and the psychic levels are one unit. The intensity of her feelings for her brother spurs her to action. Accepting a man, Bounderby, who is old enough to be her father, she first gives passive comfort to the perversion of love, to fulfilling the desires of her brother. Refusing a man, Harthouse, who is young and alluring, she next gives active vent to her confusion about love, to the man who purposely links himself with her brother, his eligible surrogate.

Professor Deneau calls the brother-sister relationship ''abnormal'' (373) As important as the label is, the manner of the malady, the shape the perversion takes is more important. Tom actively uses Louisa while passively accepting her love. She passively accepts usage while actively loving him. Whenever these active and passive forces meet, language fails. Circumlocution, indirection, and finally silence prevails. For instance, one of her most revealing statements about her relationship with Tom is a non-statement. In the scene where Tom lays his plan before her for escape from home, she interprets his words as an expression of love for her. She looks into the fire and wonders about ''you [Tom] and me grown up'' (I. 8. 41). She burns like a fire, at once life-giving warmth and self-destructive force. What is the content of her wonder? The precise nature of her thoughts is inexpressible, cut off from all conscious awareness. She wonders ''unmanageable thoughts'' (I. 8. 41). Louisa's feelings for her brother are too complex for her to handle; they are deep but inchoate. Such formlessness is that mysterious fount out of which tension universally grows. Tension exists on the level of the taboo—the desire never to be directly expressed or experienced. Louisa does not know how to distinguish sensual passion from fraternal affection.

Tom fosters the "unmanageable" thoughts. He fosters her taking the roles of mother and wife, not because he understands what is "unmanageable" but because he wants ease. To "enjoy" himself, he will exploit Bounderby's willingness to do "anything" for Louisa (I. 8. 40). She is his victim, exactly like the mothers and wives in the novel are victims of their sons and husbands. When later Tom explains to Harthouse why Louisa married Bounderby, he stresses two important reasons: her having "no other love" than the old gruff magnet, and her being left at home without her brother would be "like staying in jail" (II. 3. 103). He realizes that she has no experience in love and whatever love she knows is wholly experienced for him. He induces her to marry, offering himself as consolation. Marrying this man, she and he will be "much oftener together . . . . Always together, almost" (I. 14. 72). Knowingly, he trades Louisa to secure his pleasure. Unwillingly, he puts himself in the place of her lover, indeed of her husband. Three scenes direct the siblings as if they were about to elope: 1. They will escape from paternal tyranny; 2. They will establish a new home; 3. They will always be together. These scenes preface Gradgrind's request to Louisa to marry Bounderby. Not Gradgrind's but Tom's previous arguments sway Louisa. They are Tom's "marriage proposal." After the marriage breakfast, Louisa is "a little shaken" and not her usual "reserved" self. She physically manifests her error. She cannot cling in her shaken condition to her legal husband; instead she clings to Tom (I. 16. 83). Love misused and misdirected distorts reality.

Such love cannot be experienced verbally. It is expressed by the responses of the body. She blushes and becomes animated when Tom enters the room. That Harthouse tries to raise the same blush, stimulate the same animated response indicates that he understands their sexual nature. He wishes to replace her brother as her lover.

After she left Bounderby, Louisa explained her reasons for marrying him. Each concerns Tom: she could be "useful" to him and express "all the little tenderness" of her life (II. 12. 166). Her tenderness arose, she explains, because she knew "so well how to pity him." If she does not exactly share the same kind of distress that Tom feels (compassion), she experienced the same matrix out of which he grew and so she wishes to help and comfort him (pity). If we catalogue the elements that compose the matrix, we have a classic condition for sibling incest: 1. a weak mother (Meiselman, 263); 2. a father who is distant, physically or emotionally (Meiselman, 263–265); 3. a sharing of a mutual condition (Maisch, 205); 4. a similar education (Meiselman, 269–277); 5. a brother with no other female relationship (Meiselman, 269–277). Brother-sister here, as it is so often, is equivalent to mother-son incest (Maisch, 14; Foward, 96). She comforts him and suffers for him as if he were her son and at the same time bestows her acts as if she were his wife—kisses him, offers tenderness to him, sells all she has to protect him (II. 7. 131), faints when he is in trouble (II. 8. 139).

Sibling incest has a long history in literature. Dickens in *Hard Times* shifts its traditional use from explaining political corruption (e.g., Amnon-Tammar, 2 Sam. 13–19), exploring religious morès (e.g., Hartmann von Aue, *Gregorius*, 1195), and especially probing philosophical questions (e.g., Lope de Vega, *La fianza satisfecha*, 1614?), or just titillating the senses (e.g., Seneca, *Oedipus*) to the drama of its growth and expression. Dickens had frequently followed tradition. For example, he generally pictures sister-brother relationships as idyllic, an outgrowth of the Romantic notion of *amitié fraternelle*—love deepened by a knowledge of a blood relationship (e.g., Chateaubriand, *René*). In *Martin Chuzzlewit*, Tom Pinch and his sister Ruth set up house together after he—a pure knight in armor—rescues her from an intolerable position (661). But in *Hard Times* all changes. He scorns the rebellious or philosophical use of sibling incest. More than this, he pictures the female side of sibling incest. Before him only Ford, in *'Tis Pity She's a Whore* (1633), and Defoe, in *Moll Flanders* (1722), had touched the female viewpoint. But neither considered the internal drama, for their brothers and sisters did not even grow up together. Dickens takes the theme and places it in the camp of what could happen and does to any ordinary brother and sister. Before Freud, Dickens demonstrated incest's mechanics in the capitalistic system.

That mechanism is fixed in the climactic bedroom scene. Louisa anxiously awaits Tom's return home after questioning by the police about the bank robbery (II. 8. 144–146). While she waits, "time lagged wearily," "darkness and stillness . . . thicken." The gate bell rings for a moment. Tom has come home. Then, "the circles of its [the bell's] last sound spread out fainter and wider in the air, and all was dead again" (II. 8. 144). First, time is stopped, "lagged wearily." Next, space changes quality, "thickens." Lastly, waiting has charged Louisa's emotions; police questions have frayed Tom's nerves. A moment out of time is carefully constructed to permit a suspension of what usually governs conduct. Time and space, the sole matrix of norms, fade. The figures in the scene are no longer bound by their biographies; they are simply two humans, subject to one law—mortality. Louisa, entering his bedroom, tells Tom that she has come to him stripped not only of clothes but of identity. She is "barefoot, unclothed, undistinguishable in darkness," exactly she says as will be "through all the night of my decay until I am dust" (II. 8. 145). She is not his sister, but a woman. She is not related (taboo), but mortal (like all others). In only her "loose robe," she kneels beside Tom's bed. She draws his face to hers. Like a lover, "she laid her head down on his pillow, and her hair flowed over him as if she would hide him from everyone but herself" (II. 8. 145). Again a gesture takes the place of words, the letting down of the hair an ancient sign of female abasement and sexual availability.[10]

Louisa is overwhelmed by the wealth of the emotions both sensual and maternal that she hardly understands: "in the energy of her love she took him to her bosom as if he were a child" (II. 8. 145). An unspoken love binds her to him. The subconscious secret she holds in her heart parallels the conscious guilt Tom holds in his head. She begs Tom to verbalize what she suspects—his guilt in ravaging the bank vault.

The novel is filled with such distorted and perverted relationships, each conducted in a complex language of denial that pits desire against reality. The lower-class marriage follows the formula. Understandably, Blackpool has been misinterpreted, caught as he is in that uncharted territory between the drives of the psyche and the imperatives of society. On the psychic side, he has been condemned to facile appreciation as "too good" or "all good" (Leavis, 248; F. Smith, 108), on the social side, to narrow evaluation as "diagramatic" or "neutral" (Williams, 93; S. Smith, 83). Blackpool is neither a reflection of some real working man, a figure the sociological critics have in mind when they castigate Dickens' characterization and praise Mrs. Gaskell's (Carnall; Gallager; S. Smith), nor a one-dimensional allegory, the figure of Good in some medieval morality play. Blackpool is a complex prototype, a factory worker perplexed by ambient abundance and intelligence that results in depletion and injustice. What is mirrored in his character is what does not function in his society. For him the explanation of all problems is fixed in a single term "muddle," a term that is the icon of his character and Dickens' explanation of his psychological state. Muddle and his name Blackpool are forms of the same idea, a denial of clarity—the muddying or blackening of a pool of water. The use of a word, muddle, that negates understanding defines his psychic state. When the social scene loses its laws—here of economic and family structure—language falters and perplexity follows. This is rather like the perplexity the Greeks must have felt about incest. It muddled their sense of order to such a degree that they had no single word for it, calling it by negations; for instance, "the unmarriage marriage" ($\check{\alpha}\gamma\alpha\mu o\nu \ \gamma\acute{\alpha}\mu o\nu$). What must have been Blackpool's perplexity if scholars still debate the dynamics of early industrial England, one proving that capitalism bettered working conditions (Hartwell, 135–146), another that it brought psychological upheaval (Hobsbawm, 119–134).

Blackpool's temperament may be suggested by positioning his emotions on a map of fixed forms. Blackpool lives in a city, a "kinetic structure," where activity takes place across the range of polarities from work to entertainment. But he must also face a system of norms, a "social context" whose demands cut across morès and law, the rules of marriage and courtship and the regulations of employer and union. Where these intersect his personal desire, a "human dimension" (these terms are adapted from Mandrou's historical psychiatry), the hidden self emerges.

The Blackpool captured in the kinetic structure reveals two things: Coketown mutilates human growth and reduces people to their economic function. Gradgrind annihilates "the flowers of existence" (III. 1. 169) and Sparsit exults that "the harvest of her hopes" will be Louisa's moral decay (II. 10. 156–157). In such a space, Blackpool is an oddity. However respected he may be, he is a loner in the mass of activity that defines the city: "he had been for many years a quiet silent man, associating but little with other men, and used to companionship with his own thoughts" (II. 4. 110). The city enforces isolation in its very structure. Streets are narrow; and true to the Victorian cityscape (Dyos I. 360), homes are a function of the shops to which they are attached. Jupe's home is on a narrow street, as is Blackpool's; and both working-class men live above stores (I. 5. 21; I. 10. 51). Whenever the worker's home is not tied to economics (the shop), it is tied to Death. Dickens weds death to the home in the image of the ladder—the counterpart to Sparsit's staircase that predicts moral fall. Workers move with difficulty up the staircase of success, but with ease down the ladder that carries them to death. Though Blackpool's room was "clean," its "atmosphere was tainted" (I. 10. 52), for it was a room to whose window "the black ladder had often been raised for the sliding away of all that was most precious in this world to a striving wife and a brood of hungry babies" (I. 13. 63). The dirty outer city (Hermes) is contrasted with the clean inner room (Hesita); the space that holds a precious wife and children (Eros) is punctured by the black ladder that separates them (Thanatos). The room becomes the meeting place of life's polarities: Hermes-Thanatos and Hestia-Eros. Rather than a refuge, the home becomes a part of the muddle.

In this world of kinetic activity, work infects Blackpool's leisure time: "Old Stephan was standing in the street with the old sensation upon him which the stoppage of the machine always produced—the sensation of its having worked and stopped in his own head'' (I. 10. 49). Even in his dream the loom at which he works becomes a machine that brings death (I. 13. 66).

Set against the anxiety about dying are "holiday" and "honest dance" (I. 5. 19), each a manifestation of fancy defined as entertainment that wards off work. So afraid is the bourgeoisie of entertainment that it must struggle on in "convulsions" (I. 5. 19). The workers did not belong to the churches of the city (I. 5. 18). Rather they took "opium" and "drank." Even worse they did "low singing" and "low dancing" in "low haunts" (I. 5. 18). All the "lows" are the unvoiced but implied morality of the bourgeoisie. Entertainment is a mark of separation, a mark of the suspicion of one class about another. We never see Blackpool entertained. He is the convulsed result of the fear of fancy. His only joy seems to be contact with Rachael, walking hand in hand with her and thereby feeling "brightened" (I. 10. 51). But even this activity is restricted by the morality of his world. For a married man to walk with an unmarried woman was scandalous (I. 10. 50–51).

Examined from the standpoint of the "social context," Blackpool becomes far more complex and tainted and his wife far less simple and malignant than is usually thought. In the social context, institutions designed to unify individuals and facilitate communication break down. Marriage and unionization that should bring security at home and at work mirror each other in their futility.

What reduced the Blackpool marriage to an unholy alliance, one that causes each, in fact, to distort reality—she through drink and he through despair? How did the woman become a "self-made outcast" (I. 13. 64)? What made her "drunken," "begrimed," "foul" (I. 10. 52)? The marriage took place some eighteen or nineteen years before we meet them (I. 11. 55; I. 13. 67). Little is said of her background, but nothing indicates that she was unlike any other working-class girl. Indeed, she worked with and was a friend to Rachael (I. 13. 64), which shows that at least she kept good company. Before marriage, Blackpool himself admits that as a girl she was quite "pretty" and had "good accounts of herseln" (I. 11. 55). After marriage Mrs. Gradgrind's head began to ache; after marriage, Blackpool's wife drinks. Blackpool professes that he was "not unkind to her" (I. 11. 55). But this is a negative response. When she began to go bad, he says that he tried to be "patient" with her (I. 11. 55). Again the word is significant, originating as it does in πασχω, to suffer. The word denies and reveals what he feels; he suffered her. Throughout the novel, she is not even called Mrs. Blackpool. She is permitted no identity. She is a reflection of Blackpool's dilemma, the "evil spirit of his life" (II. 6. 119).

Marriage blackens his life. What seems to have happened to him is that as a youth he chose the flesh—the "pretty" girl—and as a man he regrets his choice. Blackpool tries to escape the muddle, thinking even of suicide as a means: "I ha' gone t' th' brigg [bridge], minded to fling myseln ower, and ha' no more on't. I ha' bore that much that I were owd when I were young" (I. 11. 55). The last phrase emphasizes that he has a sense of being cheated in his youth, cheated in his marriage, that he had grown old too soon, that he anticipated marriage to cure what he suffered in youth. He had married on Easter Monday (I. 11. 55), a time of the year associated with freedom and rebirth—among the Hebrews Passover, a feast to celebrate the liberation from slavery in Egypt, among the Christians a feast to celebrate the resurrection of Christ. Could the anticipation of happiness meet the reality of marriage, especially in his changing world?

In his relationship to his work the same conditions prevail as in his marriage. The two are tied together by a "promise" to Rachael. A pregnant ambiguity hides the exact wording of the promise in the same way as the wording of the commandment in his dream remains hidden and Mrs. Gradgrind's final message has "no meaning." Each frustrates the expression of deep asocial desires. The promise is diverted from its particular impetus, found only in the Copy Proofs (after line 26 in I. 13. 68 and Textual Note 252), a promise to stem open anger against culpable bosses who passively accept industrial accidents, to its final form in the novel: an oblique pledge to refrain from passive violence (I. 13. 68–69), the violence he felt for his wife. The substratum of pledge and promise is the same: to stem his rage. As a pledge against violence, the promise is one thing, but it becomes quite another when reattached to its original source—to stem open anger against bosses. Bounderby mocks Blackpool for having made no promise to the boss who paid his wages (II. 5. 113). The snide remark condemns Bounderby but also undercuts a truth. Blackpool makes no promises to keep faith with any of the social forces around him, no promises to either boss or to union. He enforces his own isolation. The discontinuity between the man and the social context in which he moves is apparent in both his excommunication from the Union and his death in the industrial landscape.

But it is only in the third area, the "human dimension," that we discover the extent of Blackpool's perplexity and the effect of economic conditions on his psyche. His dream stands at the center of this dimension, splitting his asking for a divorce (or freedom) and his condemnation to a marriage (or imprisonment). The dream expresses elements floating in his daily life: 1. a desire for a "new marriage" (I. 12. 62) though he is already married—the dream impetus; 2. a symbolic murder and adultery—the dream thought; 3. a fusion of feelings about marriage and factory—the dream work; and 4. an obscure and haunting sensation of futility and death, personal mortality and meaningless existence—the dream "navel" (Freud 5. 525), a layer that goes so deep it is practically beyond perusal. Dickens exposes the tragic substratum of this "navel" only later in the novel: "Even Stephen Blackpool's disappearance was falling into the general way, and becoming as monotonous a wonder as any piece of machinery in Coketown" (III. 5. 194). The dailiness of life dulls all feeling, whether noble or ignoble, with the indifference of the machine. In Blackpool's so-called "ambiguous dream" (F. Smith, 108), something of both the dilemma of this everyman of Coketown and of all men is captured.

Blackpool's state before the dream is dominated by thoughts of death on the one hand and marriage on the other. Both are brought out in his conversation with Bounderby—the figure of the father confessor. Death takes two forms, his own—suicide (I. 11. 55); and his wife's—murder (I. 11. 57). Marriage also takes two forms, his divorce from his wife and his desire for union with Rachael. The codes of law—not Church ethics—which he looks to for solutions bind him in every way. He may not flee his marriage nor "hurt" his wife (I. 11. 57); he may not commit bigamy nor "live wi" Rachael (I. 11. 57). Rachael then tries to calm him, first when his soul is compared to "wild waters" and "the raging sea" (I. 12. 59) and then just before the dream when he will not let her touch him and has a "violent fit of trembling" (I. 13. 65). Again in this state his mood is dominated by death and marriage, but a new ingredient is added: a sense of injustice and hopeless existence. He hopes for a "new marriage" that both he and Rachael want, but about which—in the typical technique of the book—they never speak. The hope is intermixed with the idea of "home" and thus "pleasure and pride" (I. 12. 62). He thinks of Rachael seeing others marry while she may not and this thought "smote him with remorse and despair" (I. 12. 62). The injustice of all this is stressed by his seeing a light in the window of his small room, the window where the ladder of death had been, and thinking that ladder would carry away a good wife or child while his wife lived on. Again without words being used, without Blackpool saying anything, Rachael senses the intension of his heart: " 'for that I,' says Rachael, 'know your heart, and am right sure and certain that 'tis far too merciful to let her [Blackpool's wife] die" (I. 13. 64). After this his eyes twice fall on the bottle of medicine that improperly drunk would poison. The first time he reads its letters he turns "a deadly hue" (I. 13. 64); the second time "a tremble passed over him" (I. 13. 65).

Thoughts of murder and death are surrounded by a sense of hopelessness—"the dreadful nature of his existence, bound hand and foot, to a dead woman, and tormented by a demon in her shape" (I. 12. 62). The woman he married, the woman before him, has no being. She is like every other woman in this novel; she is an absence, a "shape" that in this case has become demonic. This hopeless state, filled with thoughts of death and marriage—impossible opposites, the one to preserve what the other destroys—gives him the feeling of blowing up, of becoming bigger, different: "Filled with these thoughts—so filled that he had an unwholesome sense of growing larger, of being placed in some new and deseased relation towards the objects among which he passed, of seeing the iris round every misty light turn red—he went home" (I. 12.63). Blackpool himself is now absent; his vision is blurred, his body lost, his sense of presence disrupted, his ability to act turned off by a "red" light. He goes home; he goes to a shelter that provides no protection.

What he feels, he now dreams. His pre-dream state and his dream crisscross. The dream also places him in a "new deseased relation" to the world, and the dream also is composed of the same double layer of materials: on one side marriage, adultery and bigamy and on the other death. The dream confirms the hopelessness of human existence. In the dream, he had long set his heart on a woman—not Rachael but the "pretty girl" who here, exactly as the wife in his daily life, is never named. Anticipation of joy and anxiety for the future mark his premarital state in the dream, again exactly as in his youth when he had also anticipated marriage. Suddenly as the marriage ceremony in the dream is being performed, his mental state is fixed in an image: "a darkness came on, succeeded by the shining of a tremendous light." Since the light burst forth from above in "fiery letters" out of a line of the commandments and the burning words are dispersed all over the church, we may consider this written light to be the psychic expression for fatherly authority, for societal law. But what precisely are the words that the fiery letters spell out? Because he dreams of a marriage ceremony and because at this very moment in his waking life he is blocked from a divorce (I. 11. 54–59), blocked from a "new marriage" (I. 12. 62), the words of the commandment must be: "Thou shalt not commit adultery." That is, his marriage is permanent. Permitted neither divorce by the codes of man nor adultery by the laws of God, his high hopes for marriage prove frivolous; his life is a dead end.[11] All turns dark in the dream, for marriage is self-murder. The dream scene now transforms from the space of hope to one of hopelessness. The someplace, the particular church that celebrates the prospect of joy, becomes a universal no-place, without extension, where "if all the people in the world could have been brought into one space, they could not have looked . . . more numerous'' (I. 13. 66). This is the place of the second death, the final judgment. Here all ''abhor'' him, the counterpart of his avoiding in life all social contact. He feels condemned, persecuted by all and everything. His marriage and his life are both dead ends. The marriage ceremony and the last rites are one, administered by a single clergyman who links both scenes. Now a superimposition occurs, like a double-negative in photography; the no-place is overlayed with the most real place of all, the work place. In the same no-place, Blackpool stands under his looms and listens to the burial service. Neither marriage nor work supports him. His work, the loom that he works at, becomes the mechanism of his death. He looks up at it as if it were a noose, and then ''what he stood on fell below him.'' The cloth looms here and throughout the novel remind us of the Fates, spinning out the cloth of life with no purpose but to destroy its makers. Marriage has become hanging; its ceremony of hope is a ceremony of death. Hearing the service read distinctly, he knows futility. Marriage and work, the twin foundations of his life—and of everyman's—lead but to the same end, to personal extinction.

With this manifestation, the final transformation in the dream takes place. Blackpool returns to familiar places but with the unfamiliar sense of condemnation, the same way he had previously felt ''filled'' and in a ''deseased relation to the world.'' The unnamed commandment in the first part of the dream is now mirrored in a ''nameless, horrible dread.'' Dickens' rhetoric of exclusion is ever at the center of his method. Blackpool is condemned to wonder without hope, to seek what cannot be known, and to cover what cannot be hid. The unnamed dread is caused by an unnamed ''shape.'' Because all ''grew into that form,'' the ''shape'' itself has no proper shape. The unnamed, the unshaped is of course the greatest negation of all those things sown into the imagery of the novel: death. Blackpool knows he is condemned to hopelessly wander in search of happiness, to never realize the beatific vision in a ''new marriage'' with Rachael, to see all die and decay around him. His ''hopeless labour'' is to prevent others from seeing the unnamed face of death. The very last words of the dream fix the image of death in an unnamed ''printed word'' that infects the home, the ''drawers and closets,'' the cityscape, the ''streets,'' and work itself, the ''chimneys of the mills assumed that shape.''

Life is futile; marriage is hopeless. Condemned to ''miserable existence,'' ''aimless wandering,'' the marriage ceremony and the burial ceremony are one. Marriage is a reminder of mortality. The waking dream becomes a nightmare.

Blackpool tries to deal with his situation in the same way as the villains, Bounderby and Bitzer. Like them, he constructs a dream world in which to live. Bounderby and Bitzer build myths around themselves; Bounderby, the myth of his rise to success, Bitzer, the myth of his inevitably reaching the level of his idol Bounderby. One stage in the myth was to get rid of the mother and to deny family. Bounderby exiles his mother; Bitzer imprisons his in a workhouse. Both sever themselves from family ties. Blackpool tries to get rid of his wife. First, he paid her off to stay away from him and is proud that with her gone "I ha' gotten decent fewtrils [trifles] about me agen" (I. 11. 56). Next, he would divorce her, or as he puts it: "be ridded o' this woman" (I. 11. 56). Lastly, in a hypnopompic state he would murder her, passively doing nothing while his wife mistakenly poisons herself (I. 13. 66–67). He plunges into myth by fantasizing that "if he were free to ask her [Rachael, to marry him], she would take him" (I. 12. 62). Forced into a purely symbolic marriage with Rachael, untouched by the carnal, he can experience neither fulfillment nor disappointment. The symbolic marriage deludes Blackpool into thinking he is free, no longer, as he puts it, "bound" to "a dead woman" (I. 12. 62). But of course he is bound and only his death will free him.

To explore lower-class family life necessitated Dickens' reversing the roles of the typical husband and wife. Only by reversing the roles could he expose not only the female's but the male's need to love and sacrifice. This may be seen by contrasting Blackpool's marriage to a parallel working-class marriage, that of Mrs. Dithridge in Collins' *Man and Wife* (1869). One mirrors the other. Blackpool supports a morally corrupt and psychologically abusive wife; Mrs. Dithridge supports and eventually kills a physically abusive and drunken husband (220–223). A husband could with impunity beat and rob his wife of her dowry, but the opposite was not permitted (Holcombe, 21–22). Blackpool plays the female role—allows his wife to take his property, allows her to dominate him sexually and financially.

Blackpool may not be a realistic description of the contemporary factory worker, but he is an effective symbol of the dilemma, psychic and social, which the working man of Coketown knèw: the "muddle." Dickens is right; "I have done what I hope is a good thing with Stephan, taking his story as a whole" (letter to Foster, July 14, 1854).

Only the circus family is uninhibited by the mores that bind and distort reality and thus the psychic condition of all the others.[12] Nevertheless, circus relationships have their own peculiarity. Contrary to the rest of the novel, circus folk live, at least metaphorically, in extended or multiple families (for definitions, Laslett, "Intro." 29–32). Circus people marry within the circus family. Jupe marries a circus dancer. E. W. B. Childers marries Josephine Sleary. The diminutive, child-like Little Kidderminster, who once played Cupid, marries a widow, once a tightrope walker, now grown fat. It is as if the child were marrying his mother. Indeed, Mr. Sleary remarks that she is "old enough to be hith mother" (III. 7. 213). Marriage here is endogamous, slightly incestuous by the nature of the tightly knit circus world.

Close to the end of the novel a clown at a circus performance tells a curious riddle, one which may serve for the novel's psychological icon; that is, the riddle like the novel is concerned with the structure of threes, the psychological stages of sowing, reaping and garnering, or youth, maturity, and old age. In attendance, Gradgrind, Louisa, and Sissy listen, tensely awaiting the final solution to another riddle—the riddle of Tom and the bank robbery. Is he safe, what will become of him and of the family? The clown's story is the verbal equivalent to their psychological tension. It is "about two legs sitting on three legs looking at one leg, when in came four legs, and laid hold of one leg, and up got two legs, caught hold of three legs, and threw' em at four legs, who ran away with one leg" (III. 7. 212). The narrator calls this "an ingenious Allegory" and solves it as "relating to a butcher, a three-legged stool, a dog, and a leg of mutton" (III. 7. 212). Allegory is deep layered, obliquely revealing what cannot be stated openly. It is a psychological map that followed correctly leads to the labyrinth of the mind. Behind the literal level of the butcher and the mutton there are others. This riddle belongs to a group called "leg riddles," the most famous of which is the one the Sphinx poses to Oedipus. Her riddle opens with four but ends up with three legs. Almost all end with one leg less than they begin, either a leg disappears or, as in the clown's story, "runs away." The clown's allegory is in fact the classic form of an old and wide-spread riddle. In many cultures, both Eastern and Western, Primitive and Modern, leg and foot are freely employed as symbols for the penis. Oedipus' name, from οἰδάω (to swell) and ποús (foot) is not only appropriate for one who solves such a riddle but is also a reminder of the erect or swollen penis. In short, the clown's "Allegory" and the Sphinx's riddle are the tame guises for the anxiety filled primal scene where the foot or leg, equaling the penis, "runs away" into the vagina. The clown's riddle is worded exactly the same as one that Géza Róheim discusses: "Two legs sat on three legs and ate one leg; / Then came four legs and took one leg from two legs; / Then two legs hit four legs with three legs; / So that four legs dropped one leg." Róheim says that "in yet another version [of the riddle], however, the object [dropped] is at last called by its right name [penis]. Two people lie in one bed. The observer first sees four legs (i.e., the father on all fours), the two outstretched legs of the mother, and finally one leg which, as in most variants, mysteriously disappears. We may suspect that the riddle of the Sphinx is concerned with the primal scene and the fact that her death coincides with its solution suggests that she is herself its object'' (7).

Whether or not it is simply a coincidence that Dickens chose a riddle with such implications to appear at the end of the novel is immaterial. The riddle encapsulizes a psychic environment. All relationships in the novel are riddled by anxiety. Like the great riddle-giver herself, the Sphinx, the women here are anomalies, mysterious riddles. They are not only sexually neutralized, like the Sphinx whose lower body belies gender, but are intellectually destroyed, enigmas but never solvers, victims of the classic prejudice: 'Ρᾷον ἐρωτᾶν ἤ ἀποκρίνεσθαι (Plato, *Republic* i. 336c). Taking up Oedipus' role as detective, males solve economic questions but are blind to themselves. The result is mutilated characters, stilted relationships, and biting tensions. Rather than comfort, the bells of the eighteen denomination churches of Coketown drive people ''sick'' and ''nervous'' (18). The people drink and take opium. They anesthetize themselves to the relentless ''monotonous'' work whose effect is expressed in a ''craving'' for relief. They must ''vent'' their emotions (I. 5. 19). For the expression of emotion in language, they substitute a psychological rhetoric of exclusion. As a result ''Fancy'' has to ''struggle'' on in ''convulsions'' (I. 5. 19). Dickens' whole vocabulary is psychological, particularly when he deals with marriage. He speaks of ''suppression'' (II. 7. 127), ''alienation'' (II. 9. 150), and ''incompatibility'' (III. 3. 184). The people's favorite reading is significantly the bawdy and raucous Defoe (I imagine *Moll Flanders,* with its innocent incest), for what they are concerned with are the world of business, and the relationships of men, women, and children—with families and with ''human nature, human passion, human hopes and fears'' (I. 11. 57).

More than with social and economic problems, Dickens in *Hard Times* is concerned with the psychic effects of the new industrialism. A new personality type is evolving whose ideal is the lobotomized Bitzer. In this novel the genotype is not yet heroic.

The novel's end is structured as a final absence: to see in the present what we the readers will be like in the future, to see life as if our actions were to be judged from the grave. But the warning seems double-edged, for only Sissy among the characters seems to escape from the general dissolution of family life. Even the allusion to the Writing on the Wall at the end is to words whose meaning is elusive, names that may be seen but have no meaning—save to those with godly vision—and a warning about the degeneration of a family. The *mene, mene, tekel, parsin* that Daniel interprets for King Belshazar predicts his family's doom. Desire rather than fulfillment, thought rather than action, a language of absence rather than presence persists to the very end of the novel and is absorbed into a still greater pattern of absence. The book's three parts—as we have said—parallel its time sequence of spring, summer, fall. But the fourth season, the fourth temperament, is absent: winter. Winter, the dead season, is the unnamed destroyer. The final word of the novel is "cold."

NOTES

1. Critics have rarely been interested in *Hard Times* as a psychological study and never as a portrait of the reciprocal relationship of social forces and family history; that is, with the development of the psyche (see for instance Manheim, 342). A typical formulation is that the novel's characterization is so concerned with describing a "system" that it lacks "life" (Calder, 76–77). Sadock stresses the need to evaluate "the breakdown of interpersonal communication under the stress of laissez-faire industrialism" (215) but does not do so. Only Benn, Lougy, Wilson, Johnson, and Barickman have touched on the psychological nature of the work. Benn shows that the conflict in using both allegorical and human characterization causes dullness; Lougy that *Hard Times* should be read as a "romance," in the sense that Frye defines the word in *An Anatomy of Criticism* (and therefore with psychological types), and adds that the work struggles between Eros and Thanatos; Wilson that contemporary censorship forced Dickens to "submerge" his "sensuality" (5); Johnson that the characters were created to appeal to the ordinary Victorian family and thus are prim; Barickman, et al., that Victorian fiction expresses the "tension" effected by partriarchal values (viii) and that the father's "flawed sexuality"(89) affected his children, particularly females.

    Other critics of *Hard Times* fall into two groups, those concerned with the novel's bipolar structure or its artistry, and those concerned with its social, economic, and political implications. Among the many in the first group, we may mention: Leavis, who finds the design and vision of the first two chapters carried out in a "comprehensive" way (227–228); Watt, who treats Dickens' "symmetrical structure" (xxiii–xxvii) and his "symbolic method" (xxx–xxxii), while acknowledging his concern with "the evil practices of Victorian industrialization" (x); Hirsch, who finds Leavis's view meaningless and thinks that the characters do not fulfill their symbolic potential nor can they be taken seriously; Sadock, who finds that Leavis's appreciation is not criticism but simply "preference" for "organizational economy," an economy resulting in loss of "richness of characterization" (209); Sonstroem, who examines the work's imagery revolving around Fancy, concluding that Fancy means "imaginative play" and "fellow feeling" (520); Winters, who finds the characterization falters when the author's life and his characters are at odds; F. E. Smith, who believes the balance of Fact and Fancy "so carefully arranged" is "false" (103); Gallagher, who argues that the novel is organized on the metaphoric principle of social paternalism. Among the many in the second group, we may mention: Ruskin, who finds the social criticism accurate; Whipple, who attacks Dickens for equating economic laws with their harsh effects on individuals, resulting in his failure to investigate the interior of such characters as Bounderby; Shaw, who saw Dickens herein as a kind of Karl Marx aware of "social sin"; Orwell, who summed up Dickens as a naive "moralist" and reduced *Hard Times* to preaching that "capitalist ought to be kind not that workers ought to be rebellious" (6); Holloway, who castigates the misconstruing of contemporary politics (159–174) and thus the failure to delve into the "deepest levels" of human experience (167–174); Carnall, who attacks Dickens for deliberate historical distortion of both workers and unions, thus creating "insulated individuals" intent on giving vent to their lust for power (45–46); Gilmour, who argues against Holloway and for the soundness of Dickens' view of utilitarian education; Welsh, who shows the way a journalistic approach helped to develop the metaphor of the city as a monster or machine; Fielding, who finds error of fact and theory in Holloway and who stresses the historical accuracy of Dickens' view of education; Sheila Smith, who argues that the symbols of Coketown are inadequate to describe correctly the lower class, particularly Blackpool.

2. Lawrence Stone thinks that the "restricted, patriarchal, nuclear family" dominated other types already by about 1750; Steven Ozment offers the opposite conclusion, that the Reformation was a time of liberation for women and for children, and that the family under Protestant impulse became humanized.

3. Over the course of history what constitutes a family—kin, degree and kind of kin, servants, inmates—has varied. Family here means no more than the economic unit composed of those who live in the same dwelling. We use the term without distinction of conjugal, extended, or multiple (Laslet, "Intro." 28–46). The functional aspect of the family seems to sit on safer grounds than its constitution. While the reproductive unit remains the same throughout history, a more complex kinship system exists in pre-industrial society (Goody, 119). Although a simplification of structure or composition of the family occurs in industrial society, the size of the family is subject to controversy. Laslett indicates that family mean size remains constant at about 4.5. Size in the long run may have decreased somewhat, but the size of Preston—a city Dickens knew—seems to have slightly increased during the nineteenth century (Anderson, 232–233). The assumption of the extended family predating the nuclear family is under attack, especially in England. Agricultural society in England seems to have functioned in the nuclear family, but that does not preclude a difference in the way it functioned.

4. Emotion seems to have coursed along a more direct route to expression in ancient literature. For example, during a violent battle, Paris flees the field for Helen's bed: ἀλλ' ἄγε δὴ φιλότητι τραπείομεν εὐνηθέντε οὐ γάρ πώ ποτέ μ' ὧδέ γ' ἔρως φρένας ἀμφεκάλυψεν [Come on! Let's enjoy ourselves by going to bed and making love: for not even up to this moment has passion (erōs) so entirely seized my senses (phrēn); *Il.* 3. 441–442]. For an incisive summary of Foucault's position on Greek sexuality, see "Le souci de la vérité," 19; and for his view of repression during the nineteenth century as the key to the sexualization of women and everything else, see *La Volonté*, 137 and passim.

5. "In pre-industrial England marriage came relatively late, and took place between people of about the same age. Therefore, the proportion of single persons was high on both sides" (Laslett, "England." 146).

6. Travers Twiss at Oxford in 1844 commented on the factory's power to reconstruct the psyche, rescuing workers of the old domestic hand-loom system from drink, sexual licence, and female exploitation (65), and the factory's power "to raise the condition of women" (71).

7. Dabney sees aggression and violence as the result of "mercenary marriage" (70–71). Sonstroem believes that the "pervasive violence" of *Hard Times* cannot be accounted for by the "action" but only by the "imagery" (523). The point is that the violence is internalized, perceptible only in the paralinguistic code. In Sophocles' *Oedipus,* the code is externalized in expression. Oedipus and Tiresias curse and shout at each other freely, the vulgar word προπηλάκιζε even being used (316–462). When Oedipus learns what he has done, he shatters the air with his lamentations, screaming: αἰαῖ, αἰαῖ, δύστονος (1308).

8. Ancient states sometimes imposed penalties against bachelors (MacDowell, 86). Here both the bachelor and spinster are norm. Dr. William Ballantyne Hodgson, Dickens' contemporary, attacked the character of Bitzer by saying that economic science did not teach celibacy or filial cruelty (see Gilmour, 221). That celibacy was a concern of the time is graphically demonstrated by the subtitle of George Drysdale's 1854 anonymously published tract *The Elements of Social Science, or . . . the only cure of the three primary social evils, poverty, prostitution, and celibacy.*

9. An ancient comparison may be appropriate to show the radical shift in perspective. Hrethel feels the loss of a son only as a loss of honor and meaning given to life by inheritance and patronymics (Beowulf, 2435–2470), very "different from the usual responses to such tragedies today and they illustrate the central position of kingship obligations in Anglo-Saxon life" (Chickering, 263).

10. See Numbers 5.18. The degree to which this episode parallels one in Melville's *Pierre* is astounding: "she [Isabel, Pierre's sister] fell upon Pierre's heart, and her long hair ran over him in ebon vines" (XXXVI, 362). A recent article on hair in Victorian literature discusses neither passage (Gitter).

11. Winters (229–230) believes the words are: "thou shalt not kill," and that the dream expresses Blackpool's guilt for an unexpressed desire to murder his wife. But he does express his desire with such clarity that Rachael realizes it. To explain the second half of the dream by recourse only to this commandment seems doubtful.

12. For a discussion of the circus see Gallagher 76–77 and Butwin, who failing to note the words "ingenious Allegory" calls the riddle discussed below an "inane joke" (130).

WORKS CITED

Anderson, Michael. "Household Structure and the Industrial Revolution; Mid-Nineteenth Century Preston in Comparative Perspective." In *Household and Family in Past Times.* Eds. Peter Laslett and Richard Wall. Cambridge: University Press, 1972, 215–235.

Bakhtin, Mikhail. *Rabelais and His World.* Trans. H. Iswolsky. Bloomington: Indiana University Press, 1984.

Barickman, Robert, Susan MacDonald, and Myra Stark. *Corrupt Relations: Dickens,*

Thackeray, Trollope, Collins, and the Victorian Sexual System. New York: Columbia University Press, 1982.

Benn, J. Miriam. "A Landscape with Figures, Characterization and Expression in *Hard Times*." *Dickens Studies Annual* 1 (1970): 168–182.

Butwin, Joseph. "The Paradox of the Clown in Dickens." *Dickens Studies Annual* 5 (1976): 115–132.

Calder, Jenni. *Women and Marriage in Victorian Fiction*. New York: Oxford University Press, 1976.

Carnall, Geoffrey. "Dickens, Mrs. Gaskell, and the Preston Strike." *Victorian Studies* 8 (1964): 31–48.

Chickering, Howell D. "Commentary," In *Beowulf*. Trans. and ed. Howell D. Chickering. New York: Anchor, 1977.

Collins, Wilkie. *Man and Wife*. 1870; New York: Dover, 1983.

Dabney, Ross H. *Love and Property in the Novels of Dickens*. London: Chatto and Windus, 1967.

Deneau, Daniel P. "The Brother-Sister Relationship in *Hard Times*." *The Dickensian* 60 (1964): 173–177.

Dickens, Charles. *The Life and Adventures of Martin Chuzzlewit*. Ed. P. N. Furbank. New York: Penguin, 1981.

———. *Dombey and Son*. London: Everyman's, 1964.

———. *Hard Times*. Eds. George Ford and Sylvère Monod. Norton Critical Edition. New York: Norton, 1966.

Dyos, H. J. and D. A. Reeder. "Slums and Suburbs," in *The Victorian City: Images and Realities*. Eds. H. J. Dyos and Michael Wolff. 2 vols. London: Routledge and Kegan Paul, 1973, Vol. I, 359–386.

Fielding, Kenneth J. *"Hard Times* and Common Things." In *Imagined Worlds*. Eds. Maynard Mack and Ian Gregor. London: Methuen, 1968, 183–201.

Forward, Susan, and Craig Buck. *Betrayal of Innocents: Incest and Its Devestation*. Middlesex,: Penguin, 1979.

Foucault, Michel. "Le souci de la vérité." Interview by François Ewald. *Magazine Littéraire* (May 1984): 18–23.

———. *La Volonté de Savoir*. Vol. I of *Histoire de la Sexualité*. Paris: Gallimard, 1976.

———. *L'Ordre du Discours*. Paris: Gallimard, 1971.

Freud, Sigmund. *The Interpretation of Dreams*. Trans. James Strachey. Vols. 4 & 5. In *The Standard Edition of the Complete Psychological Works*. Eds. James Strachey, et. al. 24 vols. London: Hogarth, 1955.

Gallagher, Catherine. *"Hard Times* and *North and South:* The Family and Society in Two Industrial Novels." *Arizona Quarterly* 36 (1980): 70–96.

Gilmour, Robin. "The Gradgrind School: Political Economy in the Classroom." *Victorian Studies* 11 (Dec. 1967): 207–224.

Gitter, Elizabeth G. "The Power of Hair in the Victorian Imagination." *PMLA* 99 (Oct. 1984): 936–954.

Given, James Buchanan. *Society and Homicide in Thirteenth-Century England*. Stanford: Stanford University Press, 1977.

Goody, Jack. "The Evolution of the Family." In *Household and Family in Past Times*. Eds. Peter Laslett and Richard Wall. Cambridge: University Press, 1972, 103–123.

Hartwell, R. M. "The Standard of Living." *Economic History Review* 16 (August 1963): 135–146.

Heywood, William. *Palio and Ponte*. 1904. New York: Hacker, 1969.

Hirsch, David M. *"Hard Times* and Dr. Leavis." In Dickens, *Hard Times*. Eds. George Ford and Sylvère Monod. Norton Critical Edition. New York: Norton, 1966, 366–372.

Hobsbawm, Eric. "The Standard of Living during the Industrial Revolution: A Discussion." *Economic History Review* 16 (August 1963): 119–134.

Holcombe, Lee. *Wives and Property: Reform of the Married Woman's Property Law in Ninteenth-Century England*. Toronto: University of Toronto, 1983.

Holloway, John. *"Hard Times:* A History and A Criticism." In *Dickens and the Twentieth Century*. Eds. John Gross and Gabriel Pearson. Toronto: University of Toronto Press, 1962, 159–174.

House, Humphrey. *The Dickens World*. London: Oxford University Press, 1942.

Johnson, Pamela Hansford. "The Sexual Life in Dickens's Novels." In *Dickens 1970*. Ed. Michael Slater. New York: Stein and Day, 1970, 173–194.

Lacey, W. K. *The Family in Classical Greece*. London: Thames and Hudson, 1972.

Laslett, Peter. "Introduction." In *Household and Family in Past Times*. Eds. Peter Laslett and Richard Wall. Cambridge: University Press, 1972, 1–89.

———. "Mean Household Size in England Since the Sixteenth Century." In *Household and Family in Past Times*. Eds. Peter Laslett and Richard Wall. Cambridge: University Press, 1972, 125–158.

Leavis, F. R. *"Hard Times:* An Analytic Note." In his *The Great Tradition*. New York: New York University Press, 1963.

Levine, David. *Family Formation in an Age of Nascent Capitalism*. New York: Academic Press, 1977.

Lougy, Robert E. "Dickens' *Hard Times,* A Romance as Radical Literature." *Dickens Studies Annual* 2 (1972): 237–254.

MacDowell, Douglas M. *The Law in Classical Athens*. Ithaca, N.Y.: Cornell University Press, 1978.

Macfarlane, Alan. *Marriage and Love in England: Modes of Reproduction* 1300–1840. Oxford: Blackwell, 1986.

Maisch, Herbert, *Incest*. Trans. Colin Bearne. New York: Stein and Day, 1972.

Mandrou, Robert. *Introduction à la France Moderne; Essai de Psychologie Historique 1500–1640*. 2nd Ed. Paris: Albin Michel, 1974.

Manheim, Leonard F. "Dickens and Psychoanalysis: A Memoir." In *Dickens Studies Annual* 11 (1983): 335–345.

Meiselman, Karin Carlson. *Incest: A Psychological Study of Causes and Effects with Treatment Recommendations*. San Francisco: Jossey Bass, 1978.

Melville, Herman. *Pierre or The Ambiguities*. Eds. Harison Hayford, et al. Evanston, Ill.: Northwestern University Press, 1971.

Orwell, George. *Dickens, Dali and Others*. New York: Harcourt, 1944.

Ozment, Steven. *When Fathers Ruled: Family Life in Reformation Europe*. Cambridge, Mass.: Harvard University Press, 1983.

Rank, Otto. *The Myth of the Birth of the Hero and Other Writings*. Ed. Philip Freund. New York: Vintage Books, 1964.

Reynolds, Terry S. "Medieval Roots of the Industrial Revolution." *Scientific American* (July 1984): 123–130.

Róheim, Geza. *The Riddle of the Sphinx or Human Origins*. Trans. R. Money-Kyrle. 1934. New York: Harper Torchbooks, 1974.

Ruskin, John. "A Note on Hard Times" (1860). In *The Dickens Critics*. Eds. G. H. Ford and Lauriat Lane. Ithaca, N.Y.: Cornell University Press, 1961, 47–48.

Sadock, Geoffrey Johnston. "Dickens and Dr.Leavis: A Critical Commentary on *Hard Times*." *Dickens Studies Annual* 2 (1972): 208–216.

Shaw, Bernard. "Introduction to *Hard Times*" (1912). In *The Dickens Critics*. Eds. G. H. Ford and Lauriat Lane. Ithaca, N.Y.: Cornell University Press, 1961, 125–135.

Smith, Frank Edmund. "Perverted Balance: Expressive Form in *Hard Times*." *Dickens Studies Annual* 6 (1977): 102–118.

Smith, Sheila M. *The Other Nation: The Poor in English Novels of the 1840s and 1850s*. Oxford: Clarendon Press, 1980.

Sonstroem, David. "Fettered Fancy in *Hard Times*." *PMLA* 84 (May 1969): 520–529.

Ste Croix, G. E. M. de. *The Class Struggle in the Ancient Greek World*. London: Duckworth, 1981.

Stone, Lawrence. *The Family, Sex and Marriage: England 1500–1800*. London: Weidenfeld and Nicolson, 1977.

Thompson, E. P. *The Making of the English Working Class*. New York: Pantheon, 1964.

Twiss, Travers. *Two Lectures on Machinary Delivered Before the University of Oxford in 1844*. Shannon, Ireland: Irish University Press, 1971.

Watt, W. W. "Introduction." In Dickens, *Hard Times*. Ed. W. W. Watt. New York: Rinehart Editions, 1958, vii–xxxiii.

Welsh, Alexander. "Satire and History: The City of Dickens," *Victorian Studies* 11 (March 1968): 379–400.

Whipple, E. P. "On the Economic Fallacies of *Hard Times*." In Dickens, *Hard Times*. Eds. George Ford and Sylvère Monod. Norton Critical Editions. New York: Norton, 1966, 323–327.

Whitmore, Mary Ernestine. *Medieval English Domestic Life and Amusement in the Works of Chaucer*. 1937. New York: Cooper Square, 1972.

Williams, Raymond. *Culture and Society*. New York: Columbia, 1958.

Wilson, Angus. "The Heroes and Heroines of Dickens." In *Dickens and the Twentieth Century*. Eds. John Gross and Gabriel Pearson. Toronto: University of Toronto Press, 1962, 3–11.

Winters, Warrington. "Dickens' *Hard Times:* The Lost Childhood." *Dickens Studies Annual* 2 (1972): 217–236.

Viewing and Blurring in Dickens: The Misrepresentation of Representation

James R. Kincaid

"When people say Dickens exaggerates," fumes an irritated George Santayana, "it seems to me that they can have no eyes and no ears"; their ears are plugged up and their vision narrowed and clouded by purely conventional "notions" of what things are (65–66). Santayana suggests pretty clearly that he *does* have eyes and ears, quite unconventional ones too; he further suggests that we had better come similarly equipped if we are to read Dickens. But read Dickens how? And what does it mean when we say we are reading Dickens—or watching him? Santayana's suggestion is, in fact, quite a tame one: he thinks that by escaping from conventional ways of seeing, hearing, and interpreting, we can live cheek by jowl with the *real* Dickens and the *real* world. Such formalist notions—defamiliarizing in order to "make the stone stony," to get back to palpable reality—now seem wistful fantasies. This real Dickens is a very elusive customer, much like those "fabulous animals" Tony Weller objects to: griffins, unicorns, and kings' arms (ch. xxxiii). We can join in the hunt, of course, and there is no question that we are beckoned to do so by the novels. There is also no question that with unconventional eyes and ears we can spot more interesting things, even if not the thing itself.

Correspondingly, the most fascinating films playing off of Dickens, it seems to me, have been those that approach the novels with the most bizarre of squints. Face the novels head-on and you find them, like the sky at Marseilles in *Little Dorrit*, staring blankly back at you. A film-maker, like a Dickens reader, has to be prepared for a good many jolts, no matter what our own conventional expectations may be. Dickens does not merely re-form our eyes and ears; he confuses them by asking them to be turned in too many directions at once, by giving a clear signal that then vanishes, by offering a confounding variety of interpretive possibilities. Films, like readers, can only pretend that they have "got it," then, since there is no "it" to get.

My subject is the slippery and uncertain nature of perspective and of representation in Dickens. Such a thesis rests solidly on one grand cliché: that nineteenth-century novelists loved to fool around with both physical and moral perspective. There is, however, another cliché lurking behind my thesis that should make us as uncoordinated and wobbly as Mr. Pickwick on the ice: namely, that Dickens is a "cinematic novelist." What can that mean? In its naive form, this "cinematic" notion suggests that there is a movie right there in the novel: all one has to do is slip a camera into the book, follow the directions in the pages, and let the movie emerge. I do not mean to attack what I am sure everyone will agree is a ludicrous notion (held by no one making films); but, instead, to examine some of the ways in which the whole question of representation is made both difficult and problematic in the novels, how what at first seems clear becomes blurred. Most of all, I want to argue that a film-maker must construct, not represent or reflect, a Dickens novel.

But first, a digression to suggest that in one novel, *The Pickwick Papers*, Dickens did often write in a manner to give some apparent support to the naive "cinematic" idea. One can locate passages that not only appear to provide clear and uncomplicated details but also to give directions as to the angle from which we are to view these details. Partly to illustrate this point and partly to indulge in the pleasure of quoting Dickens' remarkable prose, I'll give a couple of examples. The first picks up with Sam Weller's approach to Goswell Street and to Mrs. Bardell's cheery home, occupied at the time by that worthy person, her son, and her two friends, Mrs. Cluppins and Mrs. Sanders—all later to be stars in the suit against Mr. Pickwick for breach of promise:

> It was nearly nine o'clock when he reached Goswell Street. A couple of candles were burning in the little front parlour, and a couple of caps were reflected on the window-blind. Mrs. Bardell had got company.
> Mr. Weller knocked at the door, and after a pretty long interval—occupied by the party without, in whistling a tune, and by the party within in persuading a refractory flat candle to allow itself to be lighted—a pair of small boots pattered over the floor-cloth, and Master Bardell presented himself.
> "Well, young townskip," said Sam, "how's mother?"
> "She's pretty well," replied Master Bardell, "so am I."

"Well, that's a mercy," said Sam; "tell her I want to speak to her, will you, my hinfant fernomenon?"

Master Bardell, thus adjured, placed the refractory flat candle on the bottom stair, and vanished into the front parlour with his message.

The two caps, reflected on the window-blind, were the respective head-dresses of a couple of Mrs. Bardell's most particular acquaintance, who had just stepped in, to have a quiet cup of tea, and a little warm supper of a couple of sets of pettitoes and some toasted cheese. The cheese was simmering and browning away, most delightfully, in a little Dutch oven before the fire; the pettitoes were getting on deliciously in a little tin saucepan on the hob; and Mrs. Bardell and her two friends were getting on very well, also, in a little quiet conversation about and concerning all their particular friends and acquaintance; when Master Bardell came back from answering the door, and delivered the message intrusted to him by Mr. Samuel Weller. (ch. xxvi)

There are certain decisions for a film-maker left open by this passage—whether to give an invented sample of the women's "quiet conversation" about "particular friends," for instance. Still, it is hard to escape that shadow on the window-blind, the movement from outside to inside the house, the cozy domestic details, the patter of Master Bardell's small boots, the refractory flat candle, the wonderful dialogue between Sam and the young Bardell. All these details and the sequence in which they appear amount to interpretations, of course, but the interpretive function is here partly disguised, the mode of seeing and recording being generally so conventional as to give the illusion of being natural.[1] The scene thus may seem pretty clear and authoritative —uncharacteristically so, as I will argue.

But before getting on to what is characteristic, let me quote one more passage, the dream of an uncreative and lazy film director or writer willing to cater to what an audience may be presumed to take to be real or natural. This is a meeting between Sam Weller and his affectionate, beleaguered father. We pick this up near the end of an extended, precise, and "cinematographic" description of Tony Weller and his attire:

His hair, which was short, sleek, and black, was just visible beneath the capacious brim of a low-crowned brown hat. His legs were encased in knee-cord Breeches, and painted top-boots: and a copper watch-chain, terminating in one seal, and a key of the same material, dangled loosely from his capacious waistband.

We have said that Mr. Weller was engaged in preparing for his journey to London—he was taking sustenance, in fact. On the table before him, stood a pot of ale, a cold round of beef, and a very respectable-looking loaf, to each of which he distributed his favours in turn, with the most rigid impartiality. He had just cut a mighty slice from the latter, when the footsteps of somebody entering the room, caused him to raise his head; and he beheld his son.

"Mornin', Sammy!" said the father.

The son walked up to the pot of ale, and nodding significantly to his parent, took a long draught by way of reply.

"Werry good power o' suction, Sammy," said Mr. Weller the elder, looking into the pot, when his first-born had set it down half empty. "You'd ha' made an uncommon fine oyster, Sammy, if you'd been born in that station o' life."   (ch. xxiii)

There's not a lot one would want to do with this apparently prescriptive passage, I suppose (though there is something disorienting about the notion of walking up to a pot of ale as if it were a person or a building), but my point is precisely that Dickens almost never gives us this sort of aid to conventional seeing, hearing, and even smelling. Much more frequent are disruptions, instructions that are difficult or impossible to decipher, blurrings.

Often, where we expect description, we receive instead interpretation, reminding us, really, that all representation is a matter of interpretation, of words and not neutral observation. Here is Pip's description of a box-tree that grows, if that's the word for it, in Miss Havisham's garden: "one box-tree that had been clipped round long ago, like a pudding, and had a new growth at the top of it, out of shape and of a different colour, as if that part of the pudding had stuck to the saucepan and got burnt" (ch. xi). This stylistic habit of playing exuberantly and unexpectedly with objects and figures is so common in Dickens that Orwell identified it as *the* Dickensian style, "the florid little squiggle on the edge of the page" (61). The effect of such squiggles is to push representation into the realm of wild, fanciful interpretation and to defy any sort of neutral visualizing. Here are a couple of more examples. From *Little Dorrit*, a part of a long description of the guests at Pet Meagles' marriage: "There were three other Young Barnacles, from three other offices, insipid to all the senses, and terribly in want of seasoning, doing the marriage as they would have 'done' the Nile, Old Rome, the new singer, or Jerusalem" (ch. xxxiv). How does one *see* undercooked and underseasoned Young Barnacles? Similarly, in *Martin Chuzzlewit*, the narrator spends many pages talking about Todgers's, but the result of all this talk is not to pin the place down, locate it for us in some perceptual field. Rather, the emphasis is on its "mystery," as to character and even location. Postmen familiar with the neighborhood despair of finding it, and even those who live there must be content to abide in mystery: "But the grand mystery of Todgers's was the cellarage, approachable only by a little back-door and a rusty grating: which cellarage within the memory of man had had no connection with the house, but had always been the freehold property of somebody else, and was reported to be full of wealth: though in what shape—whether in silver, brass, or gold, or butts of wine, or casks of gunpowder—was a matter of profound uncertainty and supreme indifference to Todgers's, and all its inmates'' (ch. ix).

It is not just Todgers's which is shrouded in ''profound uncertainty''; we too are bound to reach a kind of terminal befuddlement, partly because we are in Dickens bombarded with a cascade of ''seem's,'' ''appear to be's,'' and similar qualifiers. That things only ''seem'' to be, places what they *are* in some problematic never-never land and robs any particular perspective of final authority. In much the same way, Dickens' habit of describing one thing in terms of another suggests the hopelessness of locating an essence. All this figurative language amounts to a kind of waving toward solidity, an admission of relativity in these matters, an indication that the best we can do amounts to an approximation. Here is Pip, trying to describe the figure of Magwitch retreating across the marshes:

> At the same time, he hugged his shuddering body in both his arms—clasping himself, as if to hold himself together—and limped towards the low church wall. As I saw him go, picking his way among the nettles, and among the brambles that bound the green mounds, he looked in my young eyes as if he were eluding the hands of the dead people, stretching up cautiously out of their graves, to get a twist upon his ankle and pull him in. (ch. 1)

The pointed reference to ''my young eyes'' draws us to note the singularity of the spectacularly grisly image, to realize that the image is a trope and an extravagant one, that the young boy is casting about wildly to find a simile that will suggest something of his fear and his compassion. One recalls that this scene represents Pip's ''first most vivid and broad impression of the identity of things,'' including the impression ''that the small bundle of shivers growing afraid of it all and beginning to cry, was Pip.'' That is, Pip learns his separateness and, by implication, the sad, frightening fact that his only material for bridging that separateness between himself and ''things'' is language, an impossibly inadequate substance. In his attempt to capture and hold the convict and his own ''small bundle of shivers'' he goes chasing after words. And he takes us on the same chase—after the wildest of geese. As Magwitch approaches the gibbet that once held a pirate, Pip tries yet another brilliant figure: ''as if he were the pirate come to life, and come down, and going back to hook himself up again.'' There is a desperation hidden in these linguistic maneuvers, signaled by the very extravagance of the figurative devices, a sense that there are no direct equivalencies between words and things. Pip, however, can read himself and his experience only through words, and words can never provide him with the reading materials he needs.

A more explicit indication of the impossibility of reading (and showing) is provided in Poll Sweedlepipe's wrestling with his own inevitable illiteracy when confronted with the indecipherability of Young Bailey:

> Mr. Bailey spoke as if he already had a leg and three-quarters in the grave, and this had happened twenty or thirty years ago. Poll Sweedlepipe, the meek, was so perfectly confounded by his precocious self-possession, and his patronising manner, as well as by his boots, cockade, and livery, that a mist swam before his eyes, and he saw—not the Bailey of acknowledged juvenility, from Todgers's Commercial Boarding House . . . but a highly-condensed embodiment of all the sporting grooms in London; an abstract of all the stable-knowledge of the time; a something at a high-pressure that must have had existence many years, and was fraught with terrible experiences. And truly, though in the cloudy atmosphere of Todgers's, Mr. Bailey's genius had ever shown out brightly in this particular respect, it now eclipsed both time and space, cheated beholders of their senses, and worked on their belief in defiance of all natural laws. . . . He became an inexplicable creature: a breeched and booted Sphinx. There was no course open to the barber but to go distracted himself, or to take Bailey for granted: and he wisely chose the latter. (ch. xxvi)

Notice that this passage, which begins with what appears to be a good-natured exposé of Poll's credulity, quietly moves to include one and all, every "beholder," including us. We are all "cheated" of our senses, made to abandon "all natural laws," forced to acknowledge that Bailey is "inexplicable." Like Poll too, we cannot inquire too closely into the mystery of this Sphinx. That way madness lies. We must "take Bailey for granted," that is, rely casually on the conventional assumption which tells us that words are truly descriptive and that our senses speak to us accurately and naturally. But the same passage that encourages such an attitude as the only one available and sane also exposes its purely conventional status, its artificiality. Language can provide neither authoritative images nor an inroad to essences—but we must pretend that it does. Dickens' play with the limitations of language is relentless. He sometimes even allows his words such priority that they take over the presumed reality being represented, most obviously when a metaphor simply becomes a character: Mrs. Merdle as "bosom," Pancks as "Steamboat."

Even those devices ordinarily used in realistic fiction to provide the illusion of solidity refuse, in Dickens, to stand still and do their job.[2] The most obvious of these devices, the proliferation of presumably solid concrete objects, is both employed and subverted. The objects are never just *there*; they swing into the viewer's eyes, crowd about him, take on a threatening life of their own. Here, for instance, is Pip waiting in Mr. Jaggers's office: "there were some odd objects about, that I should not have expected to see—such as an old rusty pistol, a sword in a scabbard, several strange-looking boxes and packages, and two dreadful casts on a shelf, of faces peculiarly swollen, and twitchy about the nose'' (ch. xx). Faced by these twitchy noses and the swelling faces, Pip goes on with his catalogue, as if he hopes to overcome his sense of the unexpected and the strange by enumerating the inanimate objects about him. But the objects refuse to remain inanimate, and Pip can no longer stabilize and control them: ''I wondered whether the two swollen faces were of Mr. Jaggers's family, and, if he were so unfortunate as to have had a pair of such ill-looking relations, why he stuck them on that dusty perch, for the blacks and flies to settle on, instead of giving them a place at home. . . . I sat wondering and waiting in Mr. Jaggers's close room, until I really could not bear the two casts on the shelf above Mr. Jaggers's chair, and got up and went out.''

Sticking with *Great Expectations*, we can observe how apparently explicit descriptions are not allowed to run on very long without an interruption which has the effect of blurring the image. Pip's attempt to disguise the returned Magwitch is given in great detail, but the detail merges quickly into non-imagistic interpretive figures: ''I can compare the effect of it [powder applied to Magwitch], when on, to nothing but the probable effect of rouge upon the dead; so awful was the manner in which everything in him, that it was most desirable to repress, started through that thin layer of pretense, and seemed to come blazing out at the crown of his head'' (ch. xl). Note that this passage sticks to details—rouge, a corpse, the crown of his head—but then insists on the necessity of a comparison (or ''probable'' comparison) and, further, makes the terms of that comparison impossible to visualize. What is it that is blazing out at the crown of his head? What is this ''everything''? And why are we given a ''probable effect'' rather than a certain one?

This same sort of uncertainty is often produced by a habit which we might term a kind of surrealistic dissociation, where people and actions are oddly carved up, parts swallowing up wholes. Here, from *The Pickwick Papers*:

> Mr. Justice Stareleigh . . . was a most particularly short man, and so fat, that he seemed all face and waistcoat. He rolled in, upon two little turned legs, and having bobbed gravely to the bar, who bobbed gravely to him, put his little legs underneath his table and his little three-cornered hat upon it; and when Mr. Justice Stareleigh had done this, all you could see of him was two queer little eyes, one broad pink face, and somewhere about half of a big and very comical-looking wig.   (ch. xxxiv)

Notice that the surrealistic exuberance becomes so great here that Mr. Justice

Stareleigh does indeed seem to be "all face and waistcoat," equipped, unlike the rest of us, with only two eyes, a hat, and a wig. His legs, which seem at one point to have rollers attached, at another point to be wooden and detachable, at another to be the real article, if a trifle short, are, in any event, syntactically equivalent to his "little three-cornered hat." It's a bit like Mr. Potato Head: you get a certain number of faces, eyes, wigs, and so forth to arrange at your convenience and as it suits your fancy; but none of them really connects organically with the others.

Even conventional set pieces, apparently filmable as they are, often are subtly disrupted by a similar kind of surrealistic dissociation, an inexplicable shift of visual fields that disallows any attempt we might make to naturalize the description, bring it into a coherent focus. Another way to put this is to say that the mode and tone shift with dizzying rapidity from, say, melancholic-sentimental to comic-grotesque. A good example occurs at the end of the second chapter of *David Copperfield*. David, along with Peggotty, is in Mr. Barkis's cart, slowly retreating from a happy home that we sense will be happy no longer:

> I am glad to recollect that when the carrier began to move, my mother ran out at the gate, and called to him to stop, that she might kiss me once more. I am glad to dwell upon the earnestness and love with which she lifted up her face to mine, and did so.
> As we left her standing in the road, Mr. Murdstone came up to where she was, and seemed to expostulate with her for being so moved. I was looking back round the awning of the cart, and wondered what business it was of his. Peggotty, who was also looking back on the other side, seeming anything but satisfied, as the face she brought back into the cart denoted.

The cinematic directions seem quite clear, even as regards the placement of the camera: shoot from David's point of view, receding from the house; stop receding movement and focus on Mrs. Copperfield; back up to scene of her kissing David; move in to close-up of Mrs. Copperfield's face; begin receding, again from David's point of view; frame with the cart's awning the image of Murdstone angrily remonstrating; slowly distance the scene; close-up of Peggotty's dissatisfied face swinging back around; move to forward motion of the cart. All this seems reasonable enough; in fact, it is far too reasonable, too visually coherent. It overlooks the marvelously grotesque effect of the modal shift in this predominantly sad scene: "the face she brought back into the cart." It is as if Peggotty had dropped her face out of the cart and barely managed to catch it and haul it back before it rolled away in the dust. The verbal shift undermines the apparent primacy of the visual here and abruptly returns us to the instability of language. Dickens' astonishing ability to upset all applecarts (or Barkis-the-carrier carts) reminds us that vision and perspective are never naturally determined, that they are matters of habit and convention only.

The whole procedure I have used thus far has also been a matter of habit and convention: displaying all-too-ripe passages from here and there to illustrate what is suggested to be everywhere. I acknowledge that there is a kind of critical hucksterism involved here, something equivalent to peddling those little boxes of strawberries with the only edible ones glorying the top and all the disfigured or green ones stuffed beneath. Selectivity is necessary, of course: who would want to hear even such a brilliant commentator as Stanley Fish go slow-motion through a Dickens novel word-by-word? Still, a brief look at a couple of longer passages might partly justify my smaller picking and choosing: first, the way the disrupting techniques I have mentioned are combined in the first chapter of *Little Dorrit*; second, the way *David Copperfield* and other later novels make the problem of perspective impossible to solve (or duplicate) and how they, even more challengingly, question the notion of the individual, the self, from our perspective, the actor.

The first chapter of *Little Dorrit* combines and controls these local blurring techniques in such a way as to throw the whole issue of representation into doubt.[3] The chapter opens calmly enough, with a conventional, easy-to-take, one-sentence paragraph: "Thirty years ago, Marseilles lay burning in the sun, one day." Few openings could be less demanding, less of a strain on our ordinary habits of reading and perceiving, though one might possibly notice the mildly heightened term "burning" and wonder if something more than heat is being hinted at. Such assurances as we are able to receive from the first sentence are, however, quickly dissolved in a strange and terrifying play with this image of a blazing sun: "Everything in Marseilles, and about Marseilles, had stared at the fervid sky, and been stared at in return, until a staring habit had become universal there." The notion of staring as a kind of "universal" blindness is suggestive of a horrifying universal illiteracy. Where does meaning reside, if not in the light? Perhaps even more unsettling is the mixing of humans and objects, granting equal blinding power to each. Worse, the passage goes on to explode this equality, allowing superior power to the objects and making the humans the losers in this staring contest: "Strangers were stared out of countenance by staring white houses, staring white walls, staring white streets." Humans take refuge in any darkness they can find from a whiteness that simply reflects a universal and impersonal meaninglessness. They finally stop looking altogether: the sea is "too intensely blue to be looked at." Marseilles, thus, becomes invisible, merely "a fact to be strongly smelt and tasted." When we switch inside the prison, a pit of darkness which "had no knowledge of the brightness outside," we are in no better shape as regards accurate perception—or perceptions of any kind. Rigaud's eyes are emblematic: "They had no depth or change; they glittered, and they opened and shut. So far, and waiving their use to himself, a clockmaker could have made a better pair." Even his hair has "no definable colour." One cannot see, then, inside or out—into or out of. The only person with knowledge is Cavalletto, but he has no better eyesight than anyone else: "How can I say? I always know what the hour is, and where I am. I was brought in here at night, and out of a boat, but I know where I am." How absolutely uncinematic (or at least unmimetic) this is. One situates oneself in the light that is darkness only through some mystical process that cannot be explained, much less easily reproduced on film.

Many of the novels, particularly the later ones, pointedly raise a confusion as to perspective: to what extent can a film accept the privileged view of the narrator, and how can one escape it? There are also problems as to structure or pattern: how is the story or film to be formed, and who is to tell it? Finally, one wonders how legitimately or interestingly one can employ actresses or actors in filming Dickens, whether the sharp outlines of a person (or a personality) might not avoid one of the most important suggestions in the text: that humans are not to be understood in reference to sharply-defined, self-contained integers but in reference to amalgamation, merging, absorption. Films using actors seem implicitly biased towards individualistic assumptions,[4] assumptions which are attacked by Dickens' novels but by no Dickens films that I know of.

To start with the simplest matter, perspective, is to start with something not very simple. How close does a camera want to get to David Copperfield's eyes and his troubled heart? David admits that he invents histories for some people, histories that "hang like a mist of fancy over well-remembered facts," and adds the startingly self-enclosed and self-limited statement: "When I tread the old ground, I do not wonder that I seem to see and pity, going on before me, an innocent romantic boy, making his imaginative world out of such strange experiences and sordid things" (ch. xi). Where do the "experiences" and "things" end and the romantic and imaginative inventions take over? Further, what are we to do with a self-pitying mode? How can a camera turn in on itself and weep for the injustice it has suffered?

Perhaps there is no real problem, as most of the films of the novel have illustrated: cast a sweetsie, moderately androgynous boy in the role of the child and surround him with the monsters he sees, monsters unqualified in the bestiality. Basil Rathbone, in this case, makes a good Murdstone. But he is David's self-pitying version of Murdstone only, one that even David hints may be incomplete, colored and distorted by the child's jealousy and by his rage at being excluded from the undivided attention of his mother. David later wants to portray Murdstone as an indiscriminate (hence impersonal and desexualized) fiend, preying on one widow after another. But David the child knows better or, rather, lets us see more: "He seemed to be very fond of my mother—I am afraid I liked him none the better for that—and she was very fond of him" (ch. iv). We hardly need Freud in attendance here to see the sexual jealousy at work, but what film has noted the child's distorted vision and portrayed the love between the two adults? What film has been willing to emphasize Murdstone's terrible and obviously sincere grief at his wife's death, a grief coldly but selfishly observed by the child: "Mr. Murdstone took no heed of me when I went into the parlour, where he was, but sat by the fireside, weeping silently" (ch. ix). There is, in other words, a great deal that David notes but doesn't register, doesn't allow to penetrate into an area that would call for interpretation. The question is how interesting films can be that follow his practice.

As David matures (a pretty loaded term in this context), he develops a habit of removing people he knows from social, class, and economic contexts in order to explain them and deal with them in isolated, psychological terms. He is a relentless individualizer. All this is understandable, of course, since he would like to present himself as the hero the first sentence of the novel coyly announces, a figure uninfluenced by his surroundings and youth, a self-sufficient, industrious fellow, made by himself. Thus, he is remarkably blind to the class-induced snobbery of Steerforth, refusing to acknowledge it even when Steerforth tells him of it, abducts Em'ly, and is drowned. In fact, the drowning represents a great psychological bonanza for David, since it allows him to maintain the notion that one—or David at least—is captain of his own fate. Similarly, when Uriah Heep presents to David a scorching indictment of the hierarchical social and educational system that instills hypocritical 'umbleness, David ignores altogether the wider implications and remarks only that Uriah's remarks provide him with a fuller insight into Uriah's personality, his "detestable cant," his "base, unrelenting, and revengeful spirit" (ch. xxxix).

David's curious personalizing and individualizing habit raises questions about how he sees his own life, what form or structure he is attempting to impose on it—and to what extent a film-maker might be guided by it. The problem is made severe by David's confused and contradictory efforts to provide a clear framework himself. What kind of causal connections can he draw between events and his own developing self? Well, the problem turns out to be that David both needs and abhors the whole notion of causality. He both is and is not the product of what he has encountered. When he arrives at Dover, for instance, and is secured against further incursions from the Murdstones,[5] he announces in the chapter title, "I make another beginning" (ch. xv), a beginning, furthermore, that he hopes will wipe out the first one. His first beginning, after all, had been tainted powerfully by the brutal intruder Murdstone, by Creakle, by his degradation in the warehouse—perhaps also by his guilty and, for the time, undisturbed love for his mother. So, he resolutely attempts simply to cancel that earlier passage in his life. "Thus I began," he says, "my new life, in a new name, and with everything new about me." "Like one in a dream," he drops with finality the curtain on his old life: "I only know that it was, and ceased to be; and that I have written, and there I leave it" (ch. xiv). The cadences ring with the blunt assurance of the funeral bell, appropriately enough, since David is trying to arrange the murder of his earlier self. He is, like his name, brand-new—or so he insists. Later he puts the point even more insistently, perhaps over-insistently: "That little fellow [his former self] seems to be no part of me; I remember him as something left behind upon the road of life—as something I have passed rather than have actually been—and almost think of him as of some one else" (ch. xviii).

This attempt to dislocate his life is still an attempt to see that life as a linear path, a road, albeit a road he can manipulate, creating dead ends or denying that it was he who was on it before. David is, in other words, undertaking a novelistic task that is self-contradictory. He both does and does not want an E. M. Forster sort of "plot." He would, on one hand, like to formulate his narrative as a causal and clear line of self-development: a series of events and reactions to those events that will explain his maturation, his notorious ability to discipline his heart and so forth. In part, David is striving to write a straight-line Horatio Alger story, describing the ability of a strong character to mold the shape of his own destiny.

We recognize, however, that this clear developmental model for understanding is countered by a contradictory one that the Victorians would have understood as "catastrophic.[6] David's many new beginnings depend on a cancellation of what came before, not a smooth progression from it. Notice how many times he speaks of himself starting anew: most extensively when he gets to Dover, but also when his mother marries, when he is sent to school, when he lands in London, when he becomes a "new boy" at Dr. Strong's, when he marries Dora, when she dies, when he ascends to Agnes. The straight-line form is thus shadowed by a radically disconnected one, the disconnections being attached to David's need both to explore and to forget parts of his life. This great novel of memory also doubles back on the very function of memory, attempting to erase its uncomfortable disclosures. It would be wrong to say that this is a self-consuming novel—it is far too complex for that—but David (or a part of him) would very much like for it to be so. "The remembrance of that life is fraught with so much pain to me, with so much mental suffering and want of hope" (ch. xiv): all that suffering wars against the coherent narrative the adult author is trying to fashion.

Joining in this war against a coherent single plot is a backcurrent that perversely refuses to run uphill in the direction David wants, but keeps circling back to home, to David's infancy, refusing to advance very far for very long. All this is rather familiar material, and I will not repeat the evidence that would link Dora or Agnes to David's mother and his nurse. The perception, however, that he is trapped trying to tell a progressive narrative with materials that refuse, finally, to budge from a stasis, an idealized infancy and young childhood, haunts the novel. I think most readers have a sense, concurrent with other possibilities, that David's story is over after a few chapters, that he can engage only in a series of sad repetitions, retracing a cyclic, non-progressive pattern.

Adding more murk is the argument advanced by some critics that David has a straight-line story to tell, all right, but that the line leads downward, not upward. According to this reading, David travels on a road that leads away from beauty, youth, playfulness (figured either in his mother or in Dora) to a dreary, account-book, pinched-in life. His report of what it is to be a novelist, one might say, sounds very much like the latest business school graduate discussing his workdays with I.B.M.: he identifies "the source of my success" as "a patient and continuous energy," "habits of punctuality, order, and diligence," the acquisition of "steady, plain, hard-working qual-ities," "thorough-going, ardent, and sincere earnestness" (ch. xlii). This surely is a portrait of the artist as an organization man. No need for imagination or skill; just get to the office early and work straight through coffee breaks! The question is how we are to understand this development in David, this subtle and pathetic acceptance of the Murdstonian ethic of firmness, energy, and self-control. One positioning of this perception runs like this: David as an infant finds himself in a situation most wondrously fulfilling but also most dangerous: a complete absorption in his beautiful and coquettish mother. He is her lover, a position not untainted with guilt, as his terrifying dream of his father breaking through the ground at the appearance of a rival makes clear. Murdstone enters, violently carries out the revenge of the father and offers to David his only way of dealing with the Oedipal dilemma:[7] deny his love for his mother and emulate the rigidity and firmness of Murdstone. David does, it is true, adopt the role of imitation-Murdstone reluctantly, attempting to deny his presence by seeking out substitutes for his mother and nurse, attempting, that is, to return to the pre-Murdstone days. Still, by the end of the novel, this argument claims, David has made the sad, ironic "adjustment," killing off his mother (Dora) and adopting the Murdstone position. Whatever one thinks of such formulations—and this is only one of many that might describe the same pattern—it does seem clear that the novel may be seen as insisting on an advance that is really a decline, a successful working out of problems that is really a capitulation to them.

To get back to our hypothetical film or film-maker: what does one do with these four patterns: linear and progressive, discontinuous and catastrophic, cyclic and static, linear and regressive? One can choose among them; one can, doubtless, represent somehow the possibility of all four.

Making a film that embodies four diverse and often contradictory narrative structures would surely be a tough assignment, leaving all but the most ingenious floored. But there is an even more difficult problem for a film-maker lurking just around the corner. The four patterns mentioned above all leave undisturbed the notion of the individual, the self. However disturbed or discoordinated, the self is at the center. We still tend to take for granted the notion of the individualized self and are likely to imagine that Dickens did also. That self, as with David, is contained and marked off, its boundaries as distinct as the sharp black lines delineating a cartoon character. That self is formed (as in a mold), develops clearly from that core, and goes through life, as it happens, with largely tenuous connections with other selves so formed. Defined in isolation, the self tends to live in isolation. David's narrative and his life depend on such notions, which is why, I suggest, he feels so uncomfortable with the self-less Micawbers.

It is not just that the Micawbers seem impecunious, wildly able to teeter-totter gaily in defiance of the commercial and economic reality about them. They seem to be a different order of beings (or being). They live in an amorphous, largely undifferentiated state, with a variety of children, willing to share happily the nourishment which runs without stint from Mrs. Micawber's ever-ready founts. The Micawbers embody, I am suggesting, a notion of being that is without clear boundaries, that is out-flowing, accepting, absorbing.[8] As such, they exist in a more radical non-pattern that subverts all four of the models we have proposed. The Micawbers neither advance nor decline; they refuse to acknowledge the pressures of time, of linear or discontinuous narratives, of cyclic movement or of stasis. David is, to them, both an equal, a child, and, later, "Friend of my youth! Companion of my earlier days!" Their language always wipes away boundaries; their characteristic gesture is an embrace or—one is tempted to say but shouldn't—an erasure. David is not happy to meet Mr. Micawber in Canterbury, uneasily tries to explain him in terms that have nothing to do with Micawber's state of being, is churlish and grumpy during his grand and illogical unmasking of Uriah Heep, and finally ships the Micawbers off to Australia, where, in the last words we hear from him, he is writing a narrative of his own. Justly so, since David's cannot contain him and his antagonistic notion of what "being" amounts to.

This same assault on individualistic postulates is brought to the surface clearly in such images as the union of Amy Dorrit with Arthur in *Little Dorrit* and of Magwitch/Miss Havisham/Joe with Pip in *Great Expectations*. Arthur Clennam is told by Ferdinand Barnacle: "You have no idea how many people want to be left alone. You have no idea how the Genius of the country . . . tends to being left alone" (ch. xxviii). He is right. The end result of rampant individualism is shown in the novel to be a nation of individuals busy pushing others off, isolating themselves in frightened little cabins, wanting nothing but to be left alone. The definition of a human being as an individual, then, is inhuman. There is no genuine possibility of connection, of love, of sanity. Human society becomes a Gilbert and Sullivan pool table, with the balls careering wildly, never to find a pocket or a home. The only solution is a rejection of the idea of individual essence, an acceptance of such figures as the "nothing" called Amy Dorrit coalescing with the "nobody" called Arthur Clennam, of the proud and wealthy Pip absorbing himself into the convict Magwitch, both his father and his child.

To return again to our filming, how do you represent "characters" who do not conform to post-Enlightenment notions of individualism? Put a figure on the screen, even with gauze in front of the camera, and one risks eliciting conventional mimetic assumptions about what constitutes a "character." My contention is that Dickens pushes on us possibilities that should make all of us, not just screenwriters and directors, scratch our heads and squirm a little.

I do not, of course, mean to suggest that Dickens is unfilmable. Obviously, films, and brilliant ones, can be made and have been made. But what is it that is being filmed? Dickens, we might say, puts up astonishingly sophisticated resistances to interpretation, offering us his own blank stare just when we most need help and playing with the very process of interpretation. A film, then, is necessarily an interpretation of an interpretation (or a non-interpretation), not a reflection. But, then, so is interpretive commentary. Both, finally, are constructions, not reconstructions. There is a story that W. C. Fields, on being asked why he added juggling to Mr. Micawber's repertoire when there was nothing about juggling in the text, said, "Dickens forgot it." That's the right idea. Dickens, with his various obfuscating squiggles going all over hell and gone, would have loved juggling. He was, after all, the most consummate juggler of them all.

NOTES

1. In fact, even this passage is not all that naturalistic, what with the personified and stubborn candle, the pattering and possibly unoccupied boots, and the walking head-dresses—not to mention the implied comparison between the pettitoes and Mrs. Bardell, Mrs. Cluppins, and Mrs. Sanders.
2. See Dorothy Van Ghent's eloquent analyses in "The Dickens World: A View from Todgers's," *Sewanee Review* 58 (1950): 419–438 and *The English Novel: Form and Function* (New York, 1953), pp. 125–138.
3. I am very much indebted to my colleague, Professor Jane K. Brown, for many of the ideas on the opening of *Little Dorrit* presented here, ideas which I am shamelessly cribbing from her. The fact that her conclusions as to the interpretive possibilities in this chapter and the novel as a whole differ from mine gives me no little discomfort. I would also like to thank Professors Lesley Brill, Cathy Comstock, and Jeffrey Robinson for many valuable suggestions used throughout.
4. I recognize the parallel here to Charles Lamb's brilliant argument—usually dismissed as perverse—on the inevitably impoverishing and limiting effect that actual productions of Shakespeare's plays must produce. The imagination can entertain many, even contradictory possibilities, enriching possibilities that are narrowed by the interpretive choices actors and directors must make. Hamlet can exist for us in dozens of forms as we read. We are, suggests Lamb, better off not seeing Olivier, or anyone else, reduce that sumptuous banquet to the mere baked beans of "a man who could not make up his mind."
5. Aunt Betsey's victory over the Murdstones is an equivocal one at best, since it gives them just what they want, a relief from any further responsibility for a child who is a mere encumbrance: "Now I must caution you," says Murdstone to Aunt Betsey, "that if you abet him once, you abet him for good and all; if you step in between him and me, now, you must step in, Miss Trotwood, for ever. I cannot trifle, or be trifled with. I am here, for the first and last time, to take him away. Is he ready to go? If he is not—and you tell me he is not; on any pretence; it is indifferent to me what—my doors are shut against him henceforth" (ch. xiv). Having no more use for David, the Murdstones are simply freed to run off to other cruel exploitations.
6. These alternate models for understanding made war on one another throughout the

nineteenth century, most obviously in the sciences and most particularly in reference to explanations of the earth's origins and changes, where the biblical, catastrophic model had to do battle with the evolutionary, developmental model culminating in Darwin. The same contest was staged in medical thought, where children's growth was understood both in catastrophic terms—the child as a different sort of thing magically transformed by puberty—and in developmental terms—an incomplete version of the adult-in-making.

7. Much more subtle and complete psychoanalytic readings of *David Copperfield* and of other Dickens novels are offered in the well-known writings of Leonard Manheim and Michael Steig.

8. Such conceptions of over-flowing being are not uncommon in nineteenth-century fiction, though they are usually presented as having a tragic end, as in *Wuthering Heights, Frankenstein, The Mill on the Floss, Moby-Dick*. The discourse of child-lovers, Lewis Carroll's being most prominent, often comments wistfully on the fact that such ideas are realized only in the imagination, often because the child is unaccountably resistant to them.

WORKS CITED

Dickens, Charles. *David Copperfield*. Ed. Trevor Blount. New York: Penguin Books, 1976.

———. *Great Expectations*. London: Oxford University Press, 1953.

———. *The Life and Adventures of Martin Chuzzlewit*. Ed. P. N. Furbank. New York: Penguin Books, 1981.

———. *Little Dorrit*. Ed. John Holloway. New York: Penguin Books, 1980.

———. *The Pickwick Papers*. Ed. Robert L. Patten. New York: Penguin Books, 1978.

Orwell, George. *Dickens, Dali and Others*. New York: Harcourt Brace Jovanovich, 1946.

Santayana, George. "Dickens." In *Soliloquies in England*. London: Oxford University Press, 1922.

Miss Wade and George Silverman: The Forms of Fictional Monologue

Carol A. Bock

Miss Wade in *Little Dorrit* and George Silverman in his "Explanation" are portrayed as neurotic individuals, isolated from other people by their idiosyncratic perceptions of reality. Both alienate those who would show them affection by behaving in a manner that they believe is self-suppressive but which can only be construed as morbidly egocentric. As studies in the psychology of self-effacement, their stories reflect Dickens' deepening understanding of the complexities and dangers in self-renunciation. As character studies undertaken in the first person, "The History of a Self-Tormentor" and "George Silverman's Explanation" are also formally interesting since they employ in prose methods similar to those used in dramatic monologues.

Deborah Thomas (*Dickens*, 124–131) has referred to both narratives as dramatic monologues because she senses in them the unresolved tension between sympathy and judgment that Langbaum identifies as the salient characteristic of that form. Careful examination of the two narratives will reveal, however, that in fact neither really achieves this balance between sympathy and judgment. Miss Wade's narrative does, of course, temper our distaste for her by providing an account of her personal history; but while the effect of the introduced story is to refine our assessment of her character, ultimately, our critical judgment of her personality predominates over our sympathetic understanding of her as a victim. In Silverman's "Explanation," on the other hand, the peculiarities of narrative style discourage us from adopting either a judgmental or a sympathetic attitude toward the speaker. Instead, we relinquish the practice of forming moral opinions about character and join the

113

narrator in his sincere if ineffectual attempt to understand the deformities of his personality. In each case, Dickens has deliberately adopted the narrative perspective most appropriate to the purpose of his tale: the judgmental ironies of Miss Wade's narrative allow it to fulfill its didactic function within the novel's larger moral design, while the ambiguous ironies of the "Explanation" establish Silverman's narrative as an ethically neutral study of a character towards whom the author remains emotionally ambivalent. Though Thomas is justified in arguing that the works are prose approximations of the dramatic monologue, further study of their generic properties is needed to refine her claim that both are dramatic monologues in Langbaum's sense of the term. Careful examination of narrative point of view will allow us to differentiate more cautiously between the distinctive forms of these two works and will further our appreciation of the richness of Dickens' art by presenting him as a conscious fictional craftsman in what has normally been thought of as a poetic mode.

Responding to Forster's objection to the introduction of Miss Wade's narrative in *Little Dorrit*, Dickens defended his use of the inserted tale on the grounds that her history could be presented as a coherent and essential part of the larger narrative: "In Miss Wade I had an idea . . . of making the introduced story so fit into surroundings impossible of separation from the main story, as to make the blood of the book circulate through both" (Dexter, 2:776). Though Forster apparently doubted Dickens' success in this attempt, most readers have little difficulty seeing "The History of a Self-Tormentor" as an illustration of the novel's thematic interest in psychic self-imprisonment, and one can easily demonstrate the tale's fundamental unity with the "main story" of *Little Dorrit*. Intended as a coherent strand in the novel's moral design, Miss Wade's narrative functions as an exemplum illustrating the psychological and ethical dangers of rampant personal will. Lionel Trilling has remarked that *Little Dorrit* is a novel guided by "an imagination under the dominion of a great . . . moral idea" and that it teaches in the manner of *Piers Plowman* and *Pilgrim's Progress* the necessity of transcending individual personal will (589). The role of Miss Wade's narrative can be understood within this larger context of ethical purpose. Viewed within this broader thematic framework for which it was designed, her narrative has a fable-like effect, for it makes a cautionary statement by depicting Miss Wade as a victim of her own unlicensed, and therefore perverted, self will.

If "The History of a Self-Tormentor" is to point this moral lesson effectively, however, Miss Wade cannot be allowed to speak through the dramatic monologue form as Langbaum understands it. According to Langbaum, the dramatic monologue is written from an ethically objective perspective, one that ignores considerations of moral values and elicits sympathy for an immoral or psychologically aberrant position; the effect of the dramatic monologue is to cause the reader to suspend temporarily his judgment of a reprehensible or unlikeable speaker in the interest of understanding his or her character (96). It is true, of course, that the insertion of Miss Wade's narrative provides us with a fuller understanding of her decidedly unpleasant personality. We are forced to refine our perception of her as it has been developed in the novel's third-person point of view because the introduced story not only clarifies the nature of her emotional deformity but also attributes that deformity, in part, to external sources. We learn, for example, that much of her asperity derives from a painful consciousness of her illegitimacy, a fact of her existence for which she is clearly not responsible. We also see that she has been deceived and abandoned by a man who understands her insecurities and is thus able to exploit them in his own interest. Given this information about her personal past, we cannot read her account without, in Trilling's words, "an understanding that amounts to sympathy" (585).

Such sympathy is not, however, the quality that Langbaum refers to in his discussion of the dynamics of the dramatic monologue form, and Miss Wade's narrative does not ultimately controvert our ethical assessment of her venomous character. Though the unfortunate facts of her personal history—her illegitimacy, her abandonment, etc.—may temporarily arouse our pity for Miss Wade, Dickens' heavily ironic presentation of her character prevents us from sympathizing with her in the way that we sympathize with, for example, Browning's Duke of Ferrara.

The opening words of "The History of a Self-Tormentor" immediately alert the reader to the manner in which the narrative must be read:

> I have the misfortune of not being a fool. From a very early age I have detected what those about me thought they hid from me. If I could have been habitually imposed upon, instead of habitually discerning the truth, I might have lived as smoothly as most fools do. (663)

Even the most naive reader is unlikely to take this self-assessment at face value, particularly since we have been predisposed to be critical of Miss Wade by the earlier portions of the novel. These introductory remarks prepare the reader to find the meaning of this tale by reversing, or at least radically modifying, Miss Wade's perception of the truth. We are prepared from the outset to see that, in fact, Miss Wade is a kind of vicious "fool" for perversely distorting the truth she witnesses; the rightness of this initial response is borne out by her manner of persistently misinterpreting the facts of the tale she tells. She sees the compassion of her schoolmates as "insolent pity" and their forgiveness of her bad temper as "vanity and condescension" (663). Her best friend's capacity for pleasing others is, in Miss Wade's eyes, a "plan" to "drive [her] wild with jealousy" (664). Repeatedly, she places the most despicable constructions on the kindest intentions of those around her and unconsciously draws attention to the inaccuracy of her vision by insisting on her own perspicacity. Over and over again, she claims that she "saw it clearly," "knew very well," "knew before hand," "understood," "divined," "penetrated" to a knowledge that "a fool" would not have perceived. In each case, of course, we see that Miss Wade's assessment of the situation is false, and her claims to percipience are an ironic indictment of her distorted vision. Consequently, the effect of her narrative is not simply to deepen our understanding of her personality, though it assuredly does that as well. More importantly, her history is a cautionary tale which dramatizes the destructive consequences of imprisoning oneself within the narrow confines of an egocentric vision imposed upon life through a perverse assertion of personal will.

"The History of a Self-Tormentor" is, as Dickens had hoped it would be, coherent with the moral pattern of *Little Dorrit* precisely because Miss Wade is not allowed to elicit a response of sympathy which would controvert our ethical judgment of her character. Though Langbaum does not precisely define the term sympathy in his discussion of the dramatic monologue, his repeated use of words like "dazzling," "appreciation," and "overwhelm" suggests that he is referring to a fascination with a speaker's character—our admiration for the virtuosity with which Browning's duke, for example, reshapes reality in accordance with his own egocentric perception of the truth. The compassion we feel for Miss Wade when reading her narrative is clearly sympathy of a very different order.

Admittedly, Miss Wade is psychologically more interesting than the author of "A Madman's Manuscript," an interpolated tale from *Pickwick* which describes the insane speaker as gnashing his teeth, rattling his chains, and rolling on the straw in his cell. Sociologically, "The History of a Self-Tormentor" is also a great advance over Dickens' early depictions of psychological aberrance because, in *Little Dorrit*, we are presented with a sophisticated analysis of the ways in which personality and social institutions impinge on one another, limiting and imprisoning the individual. Technically, however, Miss Wade's narrative is essentially similar to "A Madman's Manuscript," an early monologue which announces its narrator's obvious unreliability in its title and opening line:

A Madman's Manuscript

"Yes!—A madman's! . . ." (139)

As in Miss Wade's narrative, we immediately recognize that the speaker's interpretation of events will be grossly inaccurate and that our task will be simply to reinterpret his blatantly distorted account of himself. We are not fascinated with either the madman or Miss Wade, as we are with Browning's duke, for example, because Dickens' presentation of them is so overtly ironic that it disallows our interest in them as psychologically complex characters.

Miss Wade's personality is, to be sure, a *potentially* fascinating illustration of psychological abnormality. Given Dickens' remarkably accute insights into aberrant behavior, it is tempting—especially to a modern reader—to read "The History of a Self-Tormentor" in isolation from the rest of the novel as an ethically neutral case-study of classic masochism.[1] However, such a reading not only does violence to the aesthetic integrity of *Little Dorrit*, but also glosses over the clues Dickens has placed within the short narrative itself to guide our judgment of Miss Wade's character. Conscious that the intense energy of her personality could easily subvert her ethical function in the novel by too fully engaging the reader's interest, Dickens is careful to present her narrative from a point of view which forestalls our sympathy and inhibits our tendency to identify with a first-person speaker. In explaining his decision to introduce Miss Wade's narrative, Dickens refers to his need to place the reader "on a level with the writer" so that the "idea" of the novel can be clearly conveyed (Dexter, 2:776). Dickens achieves this desired change in perspective by shifting to first-person narration and presenting his speaker by means of heavy irony, a mode which, as Wayne Booth remarks, creates a sense of community between the writer and the reader at the expense of the object treated ironically (27–31). Consequently, from the very outset of her story, we see the truth to which Miss Wade is blind, and we understand her character as she cannot understand it herself. Our attitude towards her is thus not one of balanced sympathy and judgment, but one of superiority and condescension, a stance which is reinforced by the judgmental running title that Dickens later added as a guide to our assessment of her "Distorted Vision."

If we are to call Miss Wade's narrative a dramatic monologue then, we must do so on the basis of terms other than Langbaum's tension between sympathy and judgment. We do not sympathize or identify with the speaker of this narrative; instead, we ally ourselves with what we sense to be the judgmental position of the implied author, an attitude that is clearly signalled by the blatant ironies which betray her perverse nature. Though "The History of a Self-Tormentor" is devoid of humor, Miss Wade's tale can perhaps be best compared to the kind of dramatic monologue that Ralph Rader describes as evoking a posture of "comic condescension" on the part of the reader (139). As with Browning's "The Bishop Orders His Tomb" and "Soliloquy in a Spanish Cloister," we look upon Dickens' narrator from a position of superiority because we immediately apprehend the nature of her blindness and understand her better than she understands herself. Presenting Miss Wade's character through a dramatic monologue of comic condescension thus allows Dickens to defuse the potential power that otherwise might accrue to her intense personality and to place her within the novel's moral pattern as a prisoner of jaundiced vision and perverted self will.

While "The History of a Self-Tormentor" is presented as an exemplum illustrating the dangers of self-centered vision, "George Silverman's Explanation" is an ethically neutral study of the consequences of such an approach to life. The ironies involved in Silverman's self-revelation are consequently more subtle than those employed in Miss Wade's narrative, and the author's attitude toward the narrator is less critical. The result of Dickens' narrative technique is to create a work that is highly charged with ambiguities, and the effect on the reader is to forestall the tendency either to condemn or to vindicate the apologist's vision of truth.

Though Dudley Flamm is wrong when he claims that Miss Wade's "days of torment are over" (21)[2], his comment perceptively connects her narrative's lack of ambiguity to its purely retrospective point of view. Distorted though her vision is, she writes with authority and conviction so that her present state of mind is not a primary concern to herself or to the reader. Silverman's narrative, on the other hand, is characterized by hesitancy and self-doubt, qualities that draw attention to the confession as an ongoing project in self-analysis. Unlike Miss Wade, who writes her history to justify her character to another individual, Silverman writes his explanation purely "for the relief of [his] own mind, not foreseeing whether or no it will ever have a reader" (Thomas, *Charles Dickens*, 406).[3] Even so, he finds it so "very difficult to begin," that he requires two false starts before his narrative truly gets under way:

FIRST CHAPTER

It happened in this wise:
    —But, sitting with my pen in my hand looking at those words again, without descrying any hint in them of the words that should follow, it comes into my mind that they have an abrupt appearance. They may serve, however, if I let

them remain, to suggest how very difficult I find it to begin to explain my Explanation. An uncouth phrase: and yet I do not see my way to a better.

SECOND CHAPTER

It happened in *this* wise:

—But, looking at those words, and comparing them with my former opening, I find they are the selfsame words repeated. This is the more surprising to me, because I employ them in quite a new connection. For indeed I declare that my intention was to discard the commencement I first had in my thoughts, and to give the preference to another of an entirely different nature, dating my explanation from an anterior period of my life. I will make a third trial, without erasing this second failure, protesting that it is not my design to conceal any of my infirmities, whether they be of head or heart. (379)

Silverman's manner of speaking in these opening chapters presents the reader with a more challenging interpretive task than do the overt ironies of Miss Wade's introductory comments. We sense that the speaker suffers from a chronic lack of self-confidence, and that sense allows us to view Silverman, like Miss Wade, from a posture of condescension. On the other hand, the narrator's awareness of his own confusion, demonstrably evident in the apologetic manner of his introduction, narrows the gap between what we know about Silverman and what he knows about himself. From the outset of the "Explanation," we assume that this tale will be to some degree colored by the "infirmities" that affect Silverman's perception of the truth, but his consciousness of these infirmities prevents us from simply adopting an attitude of superiority toward him. In his willingness to try to understand himself, Silverman is a more appealing character than Miss Wade, who alienates the reader by perversely insisting on the justice of what we understand to be a perverted view of life. Moreover, much of the appeal of Silverman's narrative is registered by our sense that the author is not sitting in ironic judgment of his narrator but is, to some degree, using the speaker's voice to project an exaggerated account of his own feelings.

The autobiographical overtones of "George Silverman's Explanation" have been explicitly acknowledged by Edgar Johnson and Michael Slater, the latter surely stretching the case by identifying little Sylvia with Maria Beadnell and Adelina Fareway with Ellen Ternan (216). It is perhaps more plausible to argue that George Silverman is created out of Dickens' personal past in the same way that Pip and David derive their orphaned existence from the traumas of the author's childhood experience. As a fictional correlative for Dickens' understanding of his own emotional history, the narrative is, in Johnson's words, "haunted by Dickens' troubled consciousness of ambiguities within himself'' (2:1071). The narrator consequently exists in relation to the author as a kind of artificial self: a fictitious persona created in clear disjunction from the artist yet at the same time serving as a mask through which he can present an aesthetic exaggeration of his own concerns.

Beginning his narrative for the third time, Silverman discovers that indirection is paradoxically the most efficient and logical means for getting to his explanation: ''Not as yet directly aiming at how it came to pass, I will come upon it by degrees. The natural manner, after all, for God knows that is how it came upon me!'' (379). Attempting to justify an event that occurred well into his mature life, Silverman finds that he must return to the place of his birth, an ''unwholesome cellar'' in Preston, to account for his misconstrued adult behavior. Like Miss Wade and indeed like Dickens himself, he recognizes that his emotional nature has been irrevocably determined by his experiences in infancy and childhood. Like the whole host of protagonists created, at least in part, out of the author's emotional past, Silverman has been made to feel morbidly sensitive about himself and his low origins. Unlike Miss Wade, however, he does not review these experiences purely in an attempt to justify his psychological abnormality.[4] Instead, his narrative is heavily flavored by an attitude of self-conscious guilt. His experience with Lady Fareway has left him ''suspecting . . . that [he is] a repulsive object'' (405), and his explanation is written in an attempt to learn ''how not to have a repugnance toward [him]self'' (385). Clearly, he belongs to the tradition of autobiographically based protagonists who, with varying degrees of self-awareness, pursue the goal that Esther Summerson articulates: ''I would try . . . to repair the fault I had been born with'' (18). Unlike Esther's narrative, however, Silverman's story is infused with a mood of saddened defeatism, as the narrator implicitly acknowledges that he cannot repair his emotional deformity through his ''quiet gift of explanation'' (395). The last of Dickens' completed works, Silverman's narrative is perhaps the bleakest reflection of the author's diminishing faith in the power of the individual to transcend the damaging effects of his personal past.

Trapped within the morbid perception of himself as soiled and unworthy, George Silverman is driven by an obsessive need for self-effacement as a means to assuage the sense of guilt and self-loathing that he cannot exorcize. Deeply committed to the morality of self-sacrifice, he explicitly associates it with his own potential for love, as his decision to avoid little Sylvia illustrates:

It came to my mind now, that I might try to prevent her taking the fever, by keeping away from her. I knew I should have but scrambling board if I did; so much the less worldly and less devilish the deed would be, I thought. . . . Out of this holding her in my thoughts, to the humanizing of myself, I suppose some childish love arose within me. I felt in some sort dignified by the pride of protecting her, by the pride of making the sacrifice for her. As my heart swelled with that new feeling, it insensibly softened about Mother and Father. It seemed to have been frozen before and now to be thawed. (386)

Silverman's self-suppressive behavior here engenders in him a new capacity to love, but it is a self-pitying perversion of normal love, tainted by pride and fruitlessly directed away from a vital, affectionate girl toward his dead, unloving parents. Later in life, he acknowledges that Adelina Fareway returns the love he feels for her, but he refuses to let their relationship grow since he is convinced of his unworthiness to be her lover. Silverman's failure in love is, then, directly attributable to his neurotic need for self-renunciation, the very quality which, in *David Copperfield*, for example, guarantees salvation through love. "George Silverman's Explanation" thus represents an important shift in Dickens' thinking. It suggests that by 1868 he had begun to reevaluate the concept of renunciation, seeing it no longer as a means for overcoming one's sense of guilty participation in a sordid and corrupt world, but as a product of those guilt feelings and as a quality that radically incapacitates the individual for relationships of personal love.

Because Silverman's habitual self-effacement is presented as no less obsessive or egocentric than Miss Wade's rampant self-assertion, the "Explanation" reflects Dickens' growing despair about the possibility of transcending personal will. As such, it reassesses the feasibility of the moral lesson implied in *Little Dorrit*. Miss Wade's self-torment is presented as a cautionary example, and the judgmental ironies that inform her narrative suggest that we, as readers, are capable of perceptions and responses that she, the object of our condescension, is not. The narrative posture adopted in "The History of a Self-Tormentor" thus makes it a more hopeful story than the "Explanation" precisely because Miss Wade's delusions are so obvious that they do not deeply engage our sympathies. In George Silverman, however, we are confronted with a speaker whom we view from a posture of simultaneous identification and disjunction, as he struggles to break beyond the confines of his own limited vision to a more truthful understanding of himself and his relationship to other people.

"The narrator's position toward the other people" is, as Dickens acknowledged, the "main idea" of this story (Dexter, 3:533). Silverman never does fully comprehend that his habitual need for self-effacement is an obsession stemming from a fundamentally egocentric response to life, and that other people are to some degree justified in seeing him as hypocritical and selfish, as Lady Fareway does. Distorted though his self-assessment may be, however, George Silverman is distinguished from a narrator like Miss Wade by his perceptive insights into his own character and by his desire to "repair the fault" in his emotional nature. He recognizes, as Miss Wade does not, that his greatest fault is a neurotic sense of guilt and self-loathing, and he accurately identifies the source of his deformed nature in the brutalizing experience of his early childhood:

> There were two or three rats at the bottom of one of the smaller pits of broken staircase when I craned over and looked in. . . . And when they started and hid themselves, close together in the dark, I thought of the old life, . . . in the cellar.
> How not to be this worldly little devil? How not to have a repugnance toward myself as I had towards the rats? I hid in a corner of one of the smaller chambers, frightened at myself, and crying. . . . I tried not to think about it. (385–386)

He is able to trace the process by which his character was formed, and acknowledges, as Miss Wade does not, that his attitude towards himself may be unhealthy: "It was in these ways that I began to form a shy disposition; to be of a timidly silent character under misconstruction; to have an inexpressible, perhaps a morbid, dread of ever being sordid or worldly" (387). At such points in the narrative, the gap between what we know about Silverman and what he knows about himself is closed, and we view him not from a posture of condescension, but from a position of identification which we sense that the author has at least temporarily adopted. In short, we are invited by Dickens neither to judge nor approve of his character but to explore with the protagonist the causes and consequences of his narrow and faulty perception of life.

Dickens was conscious that in writing "George Silverman's Explanation" he was creating a work significantly different from anything he had previously produced. His enthusiasm for the story is evident in a letter he wrote to Wills during the last stages of its composition:

> I am glad you see a certain unlikeness to anything in the American story; and I hope that when you see it complete, you will think still better of it. Upon myself it has made the strongest impression of reality and originality!! And I feel as if I had read something (by somebody else) which I should never get out of my head!! The main idea of the narrator's position towards the other people, was the idea I *had* for my next novel in A.Y.R. But it is very curious

that I did not in the least see how to begin his state of mind, until I walked into Hoghton Towers one bright April day with Dolby. (Dexter, 3:533)

Dickens' letter furnishes clues which can help define the generic properties of this remarkable narrative. Silverman is created as a speaker who stands in clear disjunction from the author, his story being written "by somebody else." At the same time, the narrative is clearly one that is powerfully meaningful to Dickens—something he would "never get out of his head"; this suggests that Silverman may also function as a mask facilitating the expression of feelings the author shares with his narrator. Most significantly, the letter establishes the symbolic significance of setting, an element totally lacking in Miss Wade's story. Hoghton Towers, a ruin next to the farm where George is quarantined after his parents die of fever, functions as an objective correlative for Silverman's "state of mind." Silverman's description of the ruin is almost lyrical, and it is clear that he recognizes its juxtapositions of beauty and decay as a symbolic reflection of his own inability to grow beyond his morbidly introverted nature:

What did I know then of Hoghton Towers? When I . . . got in among the ancient rooms, many of them with their floors and ceilings falling, the beams and rafters hanging dangerously down, the plaster dropping as I trod, the oaken panels stripped away, the windows half walled up, half broken; . . . when all over the house I was awed by gaps and chinks where the sky stared sorrowfully at me, where the birds passed, and the ivy rustled, and the stains of winter-weather blotched the rotten floors; when down at the bottom of dark pits of staircase, into which the stairs had sunk, green leaves trembled, butterflies fluttered, and bees hummed in and out through the broken doorways; when encircling the whole ruin were sweet scents and sights of fresh green growth and ever-renewing life, that I had never dreamed of,—I say, when I had passed into such clouded perception of these things as my dark soul could compass, what did I know then of Hoghton Towers? . . . I knew that all these things looked sorrowfully at me. That they seemed to sigh or whisper, not without pity for me: "Alas! Poor worldly little devil!" (385)

This passage not only demonstrates Silverman's intuitive understanding of the fault in his character but also presents him as having an aesthetic sensibility, a capacity for imaginatively projecting the pathos of his inner life into an exteriorized vision of compelling beauty and symbolic value. In this respect, he is like his creator, who discovers in the narrator's situation a fictional equivalent for a privately felt dilemma. Given the peculiar narrative perspective employed in the "Explanation," and given the prominence of Hoghton Towers in Dickens' conception of the work, it may be best to compare "George Silverman's Explanation" not to a dramatic monologue of balanced sympathy and judgment but to the mask lyric: that type of poem, like Eliot's "The Love Song of J. Alfred Prufrock," in which we understand the speaker to be "an artificial person projected from the poet" and the setting to be a symbolic "correlative of a private emotion" which the poet shares with the speaker (Rader, 140 and 150).

Readers of "George Silverman's Explanation" are quick to note the similarity between Dickens' narrator and Eliot's Prufrock, the apologist who sings a diffident love song to explain his fundamental impotence. Hesitant to "presume" to explain himself, Prufrock initially evades "the overwhelming question" of his failure just as Silverman circles around his explanation, coming at it indirectly and "by degrees" as the least painful approach to his confession. But Prufrock and Silverman are united by more than their shared diffidence, for both are created from a narrative perspective peculiar to the mask lyrical mode. Both stand as projected masks which facilitate the expression of feelings they share with their creators, and both find themselves in settings that are symbolic evocations of the emotions they describe. Admittedly, Silverman's narrative is not managed with the consistency and confidence evident in Eliot's poem. The entire second installment—a satirical attack on evangelicalism—seems to be tonally incompatible with the rest of the narrative, and Hoghton Towers is not as effectively pervasive as Prufrock's fog-muffled afternoon. Nevertheless, Silverman's story is remarkable in the way that it anticipates the ambiguous ironies of the modern mask lyrical form.

This narrative perspective is not a point of view commonly found in Dickens' writing. It evolved only at the end of his career, perhaps partly in response to his darkening vision of human potential, certainly in response to his interest in human psychology. Dickens' practice in writing the autobiographical novels may have contributed to this evolution in narrative technique, though the differences between the "Explanation" and *Great Expectations* and *David Copperfield* are more striking than are the similarities. George Silverman is distinguished by the inadequacy of his self-knowledge from Pip and David, who are intended as reliable historians of their emotional pasts; in neither of the two autobiographical novels do we recognize the intense subjectivity of a self-conscious narrator engaged in the painful task of introspective analysis. Dickens' search for a more diffident voice may have resulted in the creation of Esther Summerson, a sympathetic narrator who tells her life story with much of the same self-consciousness that characterizes Silverman's tale. The creation of George Silverman seems to have been a deliberate compromise between sympathetic narrators like David, Pip, or Esther and wholly ironic characters like Miss Wade or the author of "A Madman's Manuscript." In

Silverman, Dickens found a narrator with whom he could deeply sympathize, whose life he could fashion as a correlative for his own emotional history, but who, at the same time, would stand in complete disjunction from himself. Published approximately two years before his death, "George Silverman's Explanation" is, not surprisingly, the most technically sophisticated of Dickens' first-person narratives. As a prose anticipation of the modern mask lyric, it is a remarkable advance over the blatant ironies of Miss Wade's dramatic monologue of comic condescension and demonstrates the skill with which Dickens designed each of his monologues to fulfill its intended purpose.

NOTES

I would like to thank the National Endowment for the Humanities for the opportunity to write this paper at the University of Rochester under the guidance of George H. Ford during his 1984 Summer Seminar on "The Novels of Charles Dickens and His Development as a Writer."

1. Edmund Bergler, in "*Little Dorrit* and Dickens' Intuitive Knowledge of Psychic Masochism," interprets "The History of a Self-Tormentor" as a study of a masochistic personality but attempts to establish the narrative's coherence with the rest of the novel by demonstrating the masochistic tendencies of other characters in *Little Dorrit*. Amy, he claims, illustrates "nice" masochism in contrast to Miss Wade's repellent behavior. Bergler does not relate these observations to the novel's thematic concerns.
2. For other discussions of "George Silverman's Explanation," see Harry Stone, "Dickens's Tragic Universe: 'George Silverman's Explanation'," *Studies in Philology* 55 (1958); M. K. Brady, "An Explanation of 'George Silverman's Explanation'," *The Dickensian* 36 (1940); Barry Bart, " 'George Silverman's Explanation'," *The Dickensian* 60 (1964).
3. All further quoations from "George Silverman's Explanation" will be taken from this edition, page references being cited parenthetically within the text of the essay.
4. Only once does Silverman succumb to this tempation:

> A worldly little devil was mother's usual name for me. Whether I cried for that I was in the dark, or for that it was cold, or for that I was hungry, or whether I squeezed myself into a warm corner when there was a fire, or ate voraciously when there was food, she would still say, "O you worldly little devil!" And the sting of it was, that I quite well knew myself to be a worldly little devil. Worldly as to be wanting to be housed and warmed, worldly as to be wanting to be fed, worldly as to the greed with which I inwardly compared how much I got of those good things with how much Father and Mother got, when, rarely, those good things were going.
>
> (380)

This apparently excrescent passage might reasonably be compared to Dickens' own indignant outburst against his mother in the autobiographical fragment: ''I do not write resentfully or angrily: for I know how all these things worked together to make me what I am: but I never afterwards forgot, I never shall forget, I never can forget, that my mother was warm for my being sent back [to work at Warren's blacking factory].'' A product of Dickens' mature years, Silverman's narrative is, as a whole, purged of such violent indignation.

WORKS CITED

Booth, Wayne. *A Rhetoric of Irony*. Chicago and London: University of Chicago Press, 1974.

Dexter, Walter, ed. *The Letters of Charles Dickens*. Nonesuch Edition, 3 vols. Bloomsbury: Nonesuch Press, 1938.

Dickens, Charles. *Little Dorrit*. The New Oxford Illustrated Dickens. London: Oxford University Press, 1953. All quotations of Dickens' novels are taken from this edition; page references are cited parenthetically within the text of the essay.

Flamm, Dudley. ''The Prosecuter Within: Dickens's Final Explanation,'' *The Dickensian* 66 (1970).

Johnson, Edgar. *Charles Dickens: His Tragedy and Triumph*. 2 vols. New York: Simon and Schuster, 1952.

Langbaum, Robert W. *The Poetry of Experience: The Dramatic Monologue in Modern Literary Tradition*. New York: W. W. Norton, 1957.

Rader, Ralph. ''The Dramatic Monologue and Related Lyric Forms.'' *Critical Inquiry* 2 (Autumn 1976).

Slater, Michael. *Dickens and Women*. Stanford, Calif.: Stanford University Press, 1983.

Thomas, Deborah A, ed. *Charles Dickens: Selected Short Fiction*. New York: Penguin Books, 1976.

————. *Dickens and The Short Story*. Philadelphia: University of Pennsylvania Press, 1982.

Trilling, Lionel. ''Little Dorrit.'' *Kenyon Review* 15 (1953). Originally printed as an introduction to *Little Dorrit* (London: Oxford University Press, 1953), reprinted in *The Dickens Critics*, eds. George H. Ford and Lauriate Lane, Jr. (Ithaca, N.Y.: Cornell University Press, 1961).

Charles Dickens in *The Land We Love*

Julian Mason

The years 1867–68 saw the return of Charles Dickens to America. Actually he had hoped to return for a reading tour earlier, but the American Civil War had prevented that (Johnson, 1001). In the aftermath of that war an interesting, but now seldom noticed, pro-Southern periodical, *The Land We Love,* was published in Charlotte, North Carolina from May 1866 through March 1869, when it was absorbed by the *New Eclectic* of Baltimore. *The Land We Love* devoted very interesting attention to Dickens, especially through a series of three informative essays about his reading tour.

The magazine had been established by and was edited by General Daniel H. Hill, a South Carolina native, 1838 graduate of West Point, and veteran of the Mexican War. In 1849 he had become a professor of mathematics at Washington College in Virginia, and in 1854 had moved to Davidson College, where he remained until in 1859 he became superintendent of the North Carolina Military Institute in Charlotte. During the Civil War he had been significantly involved in various campaigns as a leader of Confederate troops, after which he returned to Charlotte and, with James P. Irwin and J. G. Morrison as partners, began publishing his monthly magazine. It included historical, agricultural, literary, military, and political essays, and regularly had book reviews of both literary and other publications. It also included new poetry and fiction (though Hill really did not like fiction). The emphasis of its contents and editorial positions was on the South and its heritage, and its authors were Southerners, including Hill himself. However, it also contained favorable reviews of works by such Northern authors as Holmes and Whittier, and unfavorable treatment of Longfellow. And it paid a good bit of attention to past and contemporary English writers, including Milton, Cowper, Tennyson, George Eliot, and Dickens. Among the poems by better known Southern writers were reprintings of ones by Poe and Washington Allston and new

127

poems by Paul Hamilton Hayne and Henry Timrod. In 1867 Hill's magazine claimed twelve thousand subscribers in thirty-two states, including a significant number in the North. Hill's continuing interest in education emerged in speeches and articles and his serving as President of the University of Arkansas from 1877 to 1884. He died in Charlotte in 1889.

The magazine's first notice of Dickens occurred in a review of *Our Mutual Friend,* which probably was written by Hill himself, in its issue for August 1866. (Though there is an apology that the war had delayed this review of the novel, it was reviewed in *The Atlantic Monthly* as late as May 1867.)

> It may be thought that we have been culpably tardy in so late a notice of this production of the most prolific and popular pen of the age. Many of our readers, however, as with ourselves, have been cut off, by "force of circumstances," from access to the current literature of the day, and some of them may not even now have read a work which has fallen into our hands only within the last month.
>
> We do not propose to give an abstract of the story, nor an analysis of its characterizations.
>
> Both are forbidden by the space at our command, and by our consciousness of incompetency for so delicate a task. In the number and variety of its *droll* characters—in delineating which Dickens excels all living authors, and is excelled, if at all, only by Walter Scott among the departed—this last work will be found not inferior to the most successful of its predecessors. We may not, indeed, find a Wilkins Micawber, a Weller, father or son, nor a Pecksniff; but what is wanting in the striking individualizations of the *dramatis personae,* is fully supplied in the unprecedentedly large assemblage of actors in the scenes, any one of whom would have sufficed to rescue the book from dullness and thus from oblivion.
>
> It is sufficient to say of this work that its moral tone is unexceptionable. We pity the man or woman who goes to a novel for his religion, whether of doctrine, rites, church order, example, precepts, or devotion. We are satisfied, so far forth, if it inculcate nothing erroneous in faith, or immoral in practice.
>
> A friend at our elbow who, for personal reasons perhaps, feels a deeper interest in this feature of the book than we may be supposed to feel, wishes us to express our gratification that Mr. Dickens has at last presented the world with a clergyman who is neither a boor nor a hypocrite, neither a fool nor a scoundrel. It is true. Mr. Silvey performs no important part in the progress or denouement of the story, yet he is a gentleman and a Christian. His wife—and our friend thinks the author deserves thanks for this also—is a lady.
>
> One thing we must regret—that Mr. Dickens should, by the title of his book, have given weight of his immense popularity to extend and perpetuate so gross a solecism in language as that current phrase, "Our Mutual Friend," "the low vulgarism," as Macaulay stigmatizes it, "for our *common* friend."

Given the high praise of Dickens imbedded in this review, it is not at all surprising that *The Land We Love* should have paid some attention to Dickens' return to America and his very successful reading tour. However, it is extremely interesting to find that Hill published a total of twenty-eight pages about it, in three, sometimes remarkable, essays, which seem to have been overlooked by Dickens scholars. These essays were written by Thomas Cooper De Leon, who apparently attended one or more of the Dickens readings (probably in New York) and whose brother Edwin was a speaker at the farewell dinner for Dickens. Cooper De Leon was a native of South Carolina who had attended Georgetown University, after which he worked in Washington until he left to serve in the Confederate Army. In 1865–66 he edited the *Cosmopolite Magazine* in Baltimore, and was in New York in 1866–67 as a writer for several newspapers and magazines and as a translator of French novels. In 1866 he published an anthology of Southern poets, and in 1868 he moved to Mobile, where he was to live for the remainder of his life, as managing editor, and after 1877 as editor, of the *Mobile Register*. He also was a theater manager, organizer in 1873 of the Mobile Mardi Gras Carnival (which he managed for twenty-five years, also designing carnivals for Pensacola, Vicksburg, Baltimore, and Albany, N.Y.), and in addition was a poet, essayist, parodist, novelist, short story writer, memoirist, and playwright (including an 1873 play, *Jasper,* based on Dickens' *The Mystery of Edwin Drood,* which was produced in 1873–74). One of his plays, an 1870 New York produced burlesque, titled *Hamlet ye Dismal Prince,* is said to have been the first American play to run for one hundred nights. Among the national periodicals, his work appeared in *Harper's, Appleton's, Leslie's,* and *Lippincott's.* It is not strange that a man of such interests would have found the theatrical readings by Dickens to be fascinating.

De Leon's first Dickens essay was a little over twelve pages long, was titled ''Mr. Dickens' Readings,'' and in most ways was the most interesting of his three essays on Dickens, especially in its report on Dickens' reading per se and its comparison of his reading with those by various others then providing dramatic readings or other oral presentations in the United States. The essay opens with praise for its subject, and then establishes a context for his readings, before focusing on them per se:

* * *

The wide range of modern fiction has no name more universally known and more deservedly popular than that of Charles Dickens.

Wherever the English language is spoken—from the remote towns of Australia and the Cape to the log hut of our western prairies—his sharp, clear-toned photographs from actual life have made it a household word.

And this result is due—as it only could be due—not to the peculiar, quaint humor, to the roaring furor to the dramatic, and sometimes sensational, effects of his best known works; but to that deep vein of humanism that we find ever underlying these.

It is generally agreed that humor, condensed, original and often bizarre, is the great characteristic of Charles Dickens. In effect this is true. . . .

Humor alone; even such humor as is his alone—could never have raised an English writer to the third if not the second place in modern fiction. There can be little doubt that, save Thackeray and Bulwer, he is the first British novelist of the century, in ability as well as popularity. More widely known than either, it would still demand something more than the graphic and quaint use of his wonderful pencil;—something more appealing than admirable caricature of every day character to raise him to equality with the caustic, analytic dissections of the former, or with the polished, beautiful—if sometimes overstrained—conceptions of the latter.

And this something is the substratum of humanism, underlying and cropping through, ever and again, the softer formation of fun, humor and pathos imposed upon it.

For Charles Dickens is the Apostle of homely truth—of real and human nature.

Drawing his text from the plain book of every day life—sometimes from its very darkest pages—he preaches in strong and comprehensible language the gospel of that truth which appeals to the strong common sense of the masses; of that truth which alone comes home to them to be analyzed, dessicated—used.

In America, perhaps even more than among his own compatriots, Mr. Dickens is known and appreciated.

That much addressed personage, the General Reader, is found universally among us: while in the older civilizations his aspirations are repressed by tradition and circumstance, and his practice cramped to a routine from which he may not depart.

In America the wonderfully distributed machinery of cheap publications—comparatively little known over the water—no less than the morbid craving among us for independence and mental equality, put the writings of all great Englishmen in the hands of thousands who cannot afford to buy a book of which the copyright has been purchased—not stolen.

For the last twenty years any American who read at all would have felt it a reproach not to have been familiar with at least the general style and tone of the great master of character-fiction. A little before this he had shot from obscurity into fame; his name was in the mouths of all men, and his books—although the gigantic system of brain-theft was then in its infancy—had crossed the water by hundreds. But more than this, Mr. Dickens had been to America.

He had been received with some hospitality and a vast deal of flunkeyism. Literary tuft-hunters, illiterate rich men, in short all the goodly company of the snobs—fell down before him and kissed his feet.

A man like him naturally sees a vast deal more than was visible to ordinary eyesight. In his American trip in '42, Mr. Dickens saw a vast deal that was good, a great deal that was comic and not a little that was despicable in the varied classes of Americans he met.

The result was two books—"American Notes," bearing directly upon the manners, habits and future of our people; and "Martin Chuzzlewit," part of which is given to a similar, but lighter, sketch.

They were received with howls of dismay and rage. Those who had before been the wildest partisans of their author, were first struck dumb, then vied with each other in voluble vituperation.

No books ever written produced, half the outcry and indignation these called up. The choicest vocabularies of abuse were showered upon their author, he was denounced in unmeasured terms for falsehood, prejudice, and for the blackest ingratitude.

He was declared despicable—beneath contempt: and then—his books sold by tens of thousands. But the few people who kept their tempers, and who were candid enough to look from Mr. Dickens' impartial standpoint, saw nothing very horrible in either book. Mr. Dickens came to America as an observer, and preceded by a reputation for a wonderfully active sense of the ridiculous. It was natural that he should put into type, for sale, any thoughts on America, as he did thoughts on every other subject, and with this strong light, the Americans were deliberately to work to make him think as peculiarly of them as possible.

Following the bias they gave him, he chose some of the most ridiculous. . . . These he grouped together—broadcast in outline, and colored highly with the most ludicrous tints. He made a very funny, and not an entirely untrue, book. It was not a flattering likeness, but it was still a likeness, while yet a broad caricature.

It certainly was not magnanimous conduct in Mr. Dickens to hold up to public derision abroad, the petty absurdities that thrust themselves so persistently under his nose. . . .

But, Mr. Dickens, like all men who write for both money and fame, desired to make a telling and saleable book, and by exploiting this new field, he accomplished his purpose fully.

Gradually the howls of indignation over the "Notes" sunk into silence; then the groans ceased likewise, and finally the majority of American readers began to believe what the candid few had all along thought—that the books were not flattering, not generous or evenly just; but that they were very funny and not very malicious.

Parallel passages would only show that where an odd custom was ridiculed, a really solid quality was recorded; and there may be some doubt if under the laughter and the sneers there is not as much of praise as blame.

But the books served to send the name of "Boz" into the most remote corners of the land; and hands that first stretched out . . . with raging spite, continued their grasp with calmness, then with amusement, and finally with undeniable admiration. Hence Sam Weller, Micawber, Quilp, Betsey Trotwood, Swiveller, Bella Wilfer and Bradley Headstone have acquired an individuality of their own;—a solid, palpable personality that removes them far away from the world of fiction and puts them on the footing of the every-day intimate whose umbrella we take and for whom we lay an extra plate at table.

. . . .

Suddenly the news came that Mr. Dickens was coming to America!

Grasping the sudden boon of a new item, six hundred and five editors nibbed fresh quills and sighed with joy. Six hundred and five paragraphs appeared almost simultaneously, each one assigning a different reason for the visit. . . .

At last it was definitely settled that he was coming to gratify American admirers with a series of those unique readings that had so delighted his own countrymen. There was but one expression and that of unqualified delight from the people; and there were but few instances, even in the press, where the time-mellowed, if not forgotten, bitterness of the "Notes" and "Chuzzlewit" was well-shaken, much diluted with twaddle and administered to the public in daily doses.

They were of little effect, however. Whatever cause our people have to hate Mr. Dickens; however little reason they may have to forgive him, they surely have practiced a charity that is beyond commendation.

New York and Boston vied with each other in claiming the first roar of the lion. But finally it was settled that the dwellers at and near the Hub were to be thus far blessed. Expectation all over the country rose to tiptoe and peered into the future with vague speculation as to what he was like and how he would do it.

Then the news of the farewell dinner came. We heard how some of the mightiest of England's men of letters had assembled to bid him Godspeed! How his greatest living rival had spoken eloquent and manly words of feeling adieu; how enthusiasm had brimmed over into almost bathos.

. . . .

Then came the thrilling moment for the sale of tickets at Boston!

Ticknor and Fields were ready for the fray!

Midnight came:—cold, foggy, marrow-piercing as only midnight in Boston can come. Just on the vibration of the twelfth stroke, a man was seen to pause before the cradle of American Literature. —He looked up eagerly—longingly at the brown house as if he would pierce its centre and magnatize out the best tickets of the front bench.

He was a sharp visaged man with eye-glass and umbrella. —Moreover, he wore a long tailed dress-coat under a short overcoat, and his feet gloried in a pair of solid "Arctics."

He paused. He rubbed his hands; he sighed the sigh pleasurable. Happy man! He was on time!

Suddenly appeared to him a female—a masculine female.

Brown of skirt and stout of foot, she flourished a bulky cotton umbrella—with a flourish that seemed to say with a nasal twang, look I am here!

Then the crowd came. There were more sharp visaged men with "Arctics;" more masculine females, more, or less, brown of skirt—more, if not less, determined in port. They came by twos, by threes, by scores.

Boston assembled before Mr. Field's doors. By 2 a.m. Boston arranged itself in a queue and aided by such refreshing ditties as "Old John Brown"—and by the presence of a police force—waited until 7 a.m. in deep adoration of the great, good man she had come to worship.

. . . .

At last seven came and with it the opening of the ticket office. —Then even police could scarce repress the ardor of the worshipers; and, as the fortunate first come was first served with tickets, and bore his trophies down the blue-nosed, shivering line, cheers rent the foggy welkin at the pluck and stamina that had achieved success in the great and good cause!

All the tickets were sold before half the crowd was satisfied; and then came the news that the steamer was in sight. Straight from ticket-office to wharf, moved that solid mass of Boston humanity; and the "coming man" only escaped an ovation by landing at an unexpected point in the bay, and fleeing to the shelter of the Parker House in a cab.

Did a solid town ever make a more absurd display. Verily are we a unique people! Nor do the Chinese sound their gongs more loud!

Mr. Dickens read in Boston.

He was listened to by crowded, cultivated, and doubtless, appreciative audiences. He was, doubtless, rated at his true value—as an artist. But as a man! He would have been toadied, teaed, and Cambridged *ad nauseam*, had he not, in self-defence, refused to move from the quiet and secluded path he had chosen.

It was too bad! Here had the Modern Athens pocketed its wrath, its criticism, and its self-respect to prostrate its neck before the Juggernaut—and lo! the Juggernaut refused to trouble itself to roll on. Jenkins wrote with a pitiful moan:—"He will not have a public dinner!—He won't even dine with a friend!—And, after a quiet tea each evening he goes early to bed.''!!!

Business, society, music, The Great Organ—the very Sun of Literature itself stood still!—during this red-lettered era in the life of Boston. The Athenians breathed, ate, drank, dreamt of Dickens! . . .

When Mr. Dickens came to New York, it was natural to expect her more cosmopolitan tone and her excess of sensations would leave a more unbiassed judgment of his powers as a reader. The difficulties created by the bad arrangement of his agent, made an unpleasant impression in the beginning. The tickets for the readings were allowed to get into the hands of speculators, who held them at prices sufficiently enhanced to drive away many of the author's most real and warm admirers.

It was gross mismanagement, if nothing worse, in Mr. Dolby to allow sharpers to get the choice seats by scores, at two dollars, and hold them at twenty: but it was a very pleasant sensation to stand at the door of the hall and see these keen gentry, on sundry occasions, forced to sell out at ridiculously low prices.

New York, too, was already prepared in the way of comic lecturers and readers; for this season she had been infested with them, of all ages, countries, and sexes. And it was a great test of the strong personal hold Mr. Dickens had upon the American people, that they were willing to give up every other entertainment, and submit to be swindled for the sake of hearing him.

Among the mass meetings of lecturers, old and young, grave and gay, who paved his way, were specimens of his fellow-countrymen.

"Mr. Arthur Sketchley" was the first in the field. Many Americans knew him favorably as a contributor to the *London Fun*, from which journal his

rather humorous sketches of an English Mrs. Partington—whom he christened, "Mrs. Brown,"—had been copied into our papers.

This Cockney lady, he transported to America, and introduced to his audience. But her troubles were purely English troubles, and her dialect purely
Cockney dialect; so, although Mr. Sketchley, otherwise Rose, is a florid,
pleasant, and very English gentleman, and evidently has much fun in him,
he rather failed to impart it to his hearers.

With the rarest exceptions people who set out to specially amuse, fall below
their own and their auditors' standard. All professionally funny lecturers seem
to protest earnestly against being as funny as they can; and to drearily declare
"if fun were as plenty as blackberries, they wouldn't be funny on compulsion."

So it is with "Mr. Arthur Sketchley." His lectures aim solely to amuse.
They are occasionally odd and laughter-moving, with many a dreary hiatus.
He is neither so quaintly humorous as Dr. Bagby, nor so broadly ridiculous
as Artemus Ward:—and funny lecturing is one of the few paths in which one
does not go safest in the middle.

The Hon. Mrs. Theresa Yelverton had also consented to give readings in
New York, as she is now doing in the South. Privately requested by Bennett,
pere, to read in public from her private correspondence, she declined . . . but
agreed to read certain poems, such as "Locksley Hall" and "Sheridan's
Ride." This she did in a fashion to convince us she was not a Mrs. Siddons
nor yet a Fanny Kemble.

Mrs. Yelverton may be a much injured lady; the sympathy of our people,
North and South, may be due to her wronged womanhood: but, in the matter
of public readings, beyond a peradventure, she sins far more than she is
sinned against.

In his New York readings, Mr. Dickens had neither of these draw-backs.

He was not a funny lecturer; and the *Herald* was very far from taking his
part.

His sole mission was to introduce to their American friends such of his
brain children as had by their force of character already made a reputation
away from home. He appeared in the double character of parent and stage
manager and proposed "to show them, not as known to others, but as known
only to their maker."

The very great difficulty of this must be obvious when we reflect that, in
most instances, to do it he had to unmake impressions which were already
formed and which, even if erroneous, had become fixed.

That he generally failed to accomplish his task in no manner detracts from the very great merit of the effort.

The very great peculiarity of Mr. Dickens' characters is their everyday naturalness. Even when odd and eccentric far beyond any people we know, still they have an oddness and eccentricity that *might* very readily belong to any living man.

There is nothing we cannot account for in Sairy Gamp, in Swiveller, in Micawber, or in Sir Leicester Dedlock. Even Quilp, while improbable, is not unnatural. But this strength belongs more specially to his earlier works: And in the latter ones we see, or think we do, sometimes a combination of opposites in the same character.

The Boffins and Mr. Venus we leave with an unsatisfied feeling that they are not friends of ours. They are strained in their oddity as in their goodness, and we leave them with a sense that they may leave us. In Obenreizer, too, we mark that clashing of opposites that renders him a nonentity the moment the Christmas story is done: and Madame Dor has that *oneness* of eccentricity that goes far to mar some even of the earlier creations.

But when, in the earlier works we meet a new face, it has a nature, a solid entity about it that convinces us it is an old acquaintance with a new name and new surroundings. We are taken by the hand and led through troubles and pleasures with which we honestly sympathize; and at the end we take leave with *Au revoir!* not *Adieu!* .

Ever thereafter where memory summons up that character it rises in the palpable substance of a real friend; and we love, pity, respect or despise the earlier characters of Dickens' works with just the same sincerity we do those who have pleased, or aided, or injured us in life.

In meeting these people, too, every one forms his own estimate of them, both as to the person and as to character. If I choose to conceive my Sam Weller as two inches taller than yours, he is just that much taller in reality to me. If, as we talk together, I clasp Bella Wilfer's hand in mine and find it slim and taper and soft, why should you tell me your Bella's digits are chubby and blunt.

Every illusion spoiled is a sensibility shocked.

When, therefore, Mr. Dickens reads to one thousand people and fails to present one thousand Sam Wellers, or Bella Wilfers,—varying, it may be, infinitesimally, but still varying somewhat—Mr. Dickens must in some sort fail to please.

It is safe to say that no one ever yet saw a fully satisfying representative of Hamlet, Mercutio, or Ariel. These creations are familiar to our minds' eye from an ideal we have involuntarily made; an ideal we would find it difficult to describe in language, but which is still as perceptible to the inner sense as if photographed upon it. However great may be the artist who attempts to give us his ideal, he is sure in some small degree to shock our preconception and to leave an unsatisfied feeling that something is still wanting.

In a somewhat more material way we form our ideal of the less aetherealized characters of Mr. Dickens: and because they are more human and more consonant with our own natures than the others, the conception of them is even clearer, more palpable and stronger in detail. Each one of the people we meet in Dickens-land is one great, salient characteristic, relieved and displayed by a surrounding of lesser ones that in no way detracts from it. This faggot of attributes is the character; and the shell that contains it we form to suit ourselves.

Were Mr. Dickens the greatest of actors, the best of readers, and the most perfect of mimes, in one person, he could not but fail to jar these prejudices in his hearers, unless indeed in each one of them the hidden springs of thought worked in just the same grooves, with just the same direction, and from just the same motors.

Asked not long since by a clever lady for an analysis of one of his characters, Mr. Dickens replied:

"Madam, an author never dreams of any character of his as known to you."

In the critical sense of that term, Mr. Dickens is not a great reader.

His voice is not naturally sweet and sympathetic; and, whether from its over-use, or from advance of years, it is now husky and dry.

To those who remember the marvellously sweet, wonderfully educated, and thoroughly magnetic organ of Fanny Kemble—that voice which shocked us one second with the gross growling of Caliban, held us bound the next by the solemn dignity of Prospero and than lulled us into a delicious trance with the perfect music of Ariel's songs; that voice in which the very Romeo of our fancy pleads—our ideal Timon rails, and the very Puck himself chuckles and shakes with frolic laughter—to such, the first ten words of Charles Dickens send a cold shiver of disappointment.

The hearer begins to speculate as to what has made his great fame, as a reader; imperceptively he warms, and the hearer warms with him; he is quaint, broadly humorous, frank, generous, tender; he revels in a carnival of screaming fun—then suddenly melts into the softest pathos.

His hearer is spell-bound, led to the end, and sits a moment like a very Oliver, involuntarily "asking for more."

Then the inquiry comes—"what is it?"

He certainly has not a good voice; the Sam Weller he shows us is not the Sam Weller we know; and—oh, gracious! he isn't handsome!

Mr. Dickens in person, is not tall, lithe, and somewhat too spare for good proportion. The analytical eye at once discovers, however, a springiness and elasticity of muscle that—as much as his florid skin—shows a high physical condition. For despite the immense brain-labor, so wearing and long continued, despite his hard struggles in early life, and his domestic ones in later, years still set lightly on his head, and his frequent walk from Gads-hill to the Strand—a clear sweep of thirty miles, which he does in a morning without fatigue—would break down many a younger man.

This well-conditioned and muscular body, Mr. Dickens delights to dress in a caressing style. He heaps upon it the daintiest and most expensive clothes—not always chosen with a perfect accord with the years that he seems to refuse to acknowledge. In fact, the huge lappels, the broad braids, tight pants and very swell gloves in which he indulges, leave the great novelist somewhat open to the charge of being an "old beau." And when he inserts a small bouquet in the broad lappel, he but adds an exclamation mark to the expression.

Dressed then in the highest fashion of full dress, Mr. Dickens seats himself at the small table and turns his face slowly to his audience.

It is a very marked face, full of strong will, seamed with thought, and perhaps with repressed passion; but with a steady and controlled expression habitual to it.

But it is not a handsome face, nor yet an aristocratic one. But for the high and rather massive forehead—broadening at the temples and receding somewhat in the centre—and the quick, restless fire in the eye under the bushy brow—the features might be heavy. And the slope of the jaw,—half displayed, half hidden by the white goatee and moustache, might indicate severity and cruelty but for the mobile lips—quick to the most sensitive curves of humor or the gentlest touches of pathos.

No. Mr. Dickens is not handsome; but there is a self-dependence and power in the face that does away with the little fopperies of dressing the beard and training the somewhat scanty hair into "beau-catcher" curls over the brow.

One has hardly time to take in these details.

He hardly nods to his audience, plunges at once into his subject and sends the chill of disappointment to its very centre.

He is not what we thought: he is even ordinary. After the sonorous, rounded periods of Vandenhoff—the fairy music of Fanny Kemble—Mr. Dickens is no reader!

Even while this thought flashes through the crowd, some well-known character is introduced. Be it Pickwick, the Marchioness, or Bob Sawyer, the reader throws himself into the character and *acts* it perfectly. He does not read—in fact the whole performance is rather recitation than reading—but he talks, thinks, moves, laughs and grimaces just as Pickwick, or Bob Sawyer, or the Marchioness would do—or as he thinks they would do—under the circumstances.

Fanny Kemble changes utterly at every change of person; but she changes only by the wonderful modulations of her matchless voice. There is no gesture—no movement of figure or face.

Mr. Dickens is the perfect opposite. He regularly acts the character he personates. He seems to try and swell into Tony Weller, to shrivel into the Marchioness, or to wriggle into Jingle. He not only attempts to act as they would in their places, but to look as they would while so acting.

This last is the weak point of his effort. He is an admirable actor—an almost perfect mime. But no human face can attempt to represent in rapid succession a bloated old visage, a pinched, dried set of features, and the tender devotion of young womanhood—and fail to degenerate into ineffective grimace.

Turn away your head and listen to Mr. Dickens. The reading is very good, in spite of the voice: the characterization—though perhaps at variance with your own—is most admirable; and the rapid and complete change from the touching to the droll—from almost painful pathos to irresistible fun—is really marvellous.

You feel that the master-spirit is there: that you put your hands in his and are led behind the scenes of that great life-drama you have before only seen from the front. At his bidding the scenery rolls back, the bare machinery of thought stands displayed; the actors are actors no more, but men and women like us, who laugh and love and sin—who are happy or miserable as they make themselves so.

The curtain falls—the lights are out, and we have come to the front again; but we bring with us an insight into stage mysteries, new and thought-producing. We have seen the puppets so familiar to us, but we have seen them by a new light; have been taught the secret of the springs and pullies that put them in motion; and have seen them worked by the great master-hand that made them.

If, on closer inspection, they do not seem exactly what we supposed them;

if their motions are more stiff, or their grooves of action differ from the ones we made for them;—we at least know what they were meant to do. And we can tell how far that mission was accomplished.

One great point of Mr. Dickens' writings is that he is always the stage manager.

He makes his characters, drills them, dresses them and puts them on the stage. He lets them talk and act to a certain point—but when a great idea is to be evolved, he steps from behind the curtain, motions them to silence, and talks in his own proper person to the immense audience. And he talks with the effect noted in the commencement of this article. But if that talk is effective in the broken pauses of the characters who are acting for us, it is easy to comprehend it must be tenfold more so, when the stage manager sweeps away the puppets and becomes, in himself, actors, play, machinery and footlights.

Such are the "readings" of Mr. Dickens, if readings they can be called.

They are wonderful combinations of reading, mimicry, acting and animal magnetism—especially of the latter.

For there are some far better readers; there are many more exact mimics; there are thousands of better actors: but the electric genius of the man fuses all these into a magnetic amalgam that once touched cannot be let go until the battery stops working.

There is something indescribable; a subtle essence of sympathy that can only be felt, not described, that puts him *en rapport* with the most antagonistic spirits and makes them his, while the spell is upon them.

Of Mr. Dickens' pecuniary success it is useless to speak. In any city in America where there is money to spend for amusement, his tickets will sell faster than they can be offered for sale.

Of his artistic success there is equally little doubt, if we look at him not only as a reader, but as an exponent of character.

Still his path has not been strewn altogether with roses. He is said to be a peculiarly vain man and to possess the pleasing belief that Perfection, like Charity, begins at home.

The American press is hardly competent testimony in this regard; but granting it true, he could even then scarcely fail to be sickened and disgusted by the crawling, loathsome flattery with which the far greater proportion of our journals have slathered him. Even those pleasant spoken people who call Mr. Dickens "a vulgar snob," must grant him to be at least a very sensible specimen of snobbery. And as such the filthy flattery with which he is bespattered must turn sour to him.

Then an interference with his religious belief or with his domestic associations—be they what they may—can hardly be justifiable in a discussion of his merits. So long as there is a strong moral tendency and an inferred religious tone in all that Mr. Dickens writes, the constant charge of atheism must fall to the ground.

With his family troubles and his personal relations in the privacy of his personal life, the critic of the public man has nothing to do.

Only the most vulgar and low bred pruriency could warrant a prying through the key-hole of a door not opened to the public.

Who can complain if a new edition of the "Notes" shall out-Chuzzlewit Chuzzlewit?

What honest man can fail to believe that such exhibitions as that at Boston, are fair targets for the sharpest-feathered arrows of ridicule. (421–432)

*   *   *

De Leon's essay continues for another page, primarily challenging whether either New York or the country is improved in 1868 beyond the estimate made of them by Dickens in 1842 as worshipers of money. This longest of his three essays was published in the March 1868 issue of *The Land We Love* when Dickens was well along in his reading tour, which had begun at Boston on December 2, 1867 and was to end on April 20. From evidence in De Leon's essay and his own life, we can presume that he heard Dickens read (at least once, if not more) in New York, which site was alternated with Boston on a weekly basis from early December through early January. In view of De Leon's comments on Dickens' reading, it might be noted that during most of his tour Dickens was plagued with a very painful foot and with nasal and respiratory illness, sometimes severely so (Johnson, 1080–1094 *passim*)—and still made such an impression! This first of De Leon's essays is quite valuable because of the information it gives about how Dickens performed his dramatic magic, the impressions he made, and how he compared with others, especially Fanny Kemble, who was so widely praised and sought after for several decades, beginning in the 1840s, on both sides of the Atlantic for her readings of Shakespeare.

De Leon's second Dickens essay, published in the August issue, was the shortest of the three, only five pages long. Its subject was the famous testimonial dinner sponsored by the New York Press for Dickens at Delmonico's restaurant in New York on Saturday, April 18, just at the end of his tour. The dinner was given on behalf of the journalists of the whole country.

Dickens was so sick that he was very late arriving and left early (Johnson, 1092–1094). However, the evening was a success, which is reflected in De Leon's account of it. The essay opens with: "Mr. Dickens has 'been,' he certainly has 'gone,' and there are many who declare admiringly that he has most emphatically 'done it'." He goes on to report that Dickens' tour had been "one long and steady ovation." As De Leon put it, "The people welcomed Mr. Dickens of their own free will; the people saw him, heard him, and thrust their greenbacks upon him; and finally—when all else was done, the accredited representatives of the people—the Press—fed him" (324). He reports on the august preparations for the dinner, its demands on the hosts ($15 for an invitation), and what took place, creating drama out of waiting for the late arriving Dickens.

> The parlors were filled with, perhaps, as bright a set of men as could be collected between walls. The great guns of disquisition, the columbiads of argument, the mortars of monthly literature, the small arms of paragraphing, and the pop-crackers of reporting—all these were there—arranged *en barbette* for the grand Salvo to the Field-Marshal of the Pen. But as the evening of doubt settled down over what was to be the grand field—one by one the loud reports of the columbiads fell into silence; the mortars grew black; the small arms ceased to crackle, and even the pop-crackers lost their fizz!
>
> In plain English, Mr. Dickens was late, very late—and every one of his two hundred hosts began to look very blue, and to feel very hungry.
>
> . . . .
>
> Finally, cloudy doubts vanished, and the sun of Dickens shone upon the great two hundred; albeit the foot of Dickens was in a flannel shoe, while he leaned upon a friend and a stick. There was a subdued buzz of welcome, but it was understood the guest was too sick for formal introduction; and—Bohemia behaving itself pretty well on the whole—the dinner began.
>
> There are no better dinners in the world than can be gotten up in America; New York dinners are perhaps the best here; and it is probable Delmonico's are the best in New York.
>
> Therefore, all the details of the feast, eating, drinking, and appointment—which must be taken for granted—were all that could be desired; and more than one guest declared that a more appropriate and excellent dinner, of the kind, was never seen on either side of the Atlantic.
>
> The guest of the evening sat at a centre table, at the head of the great saloon, with the British flag draped above his head. He was flanked by Mr. Greeley, of the *Tribune*, who presided, and by Mr. Raymond, of the *Times*.
>
> Seven other tables ran across the room, so arranged that almost every one might see the lion of the occasion. Then there was fast and furious mastication—violent thrust of fork, and fierce lunge of knife: There was popping of corks, gurgling of fluid and chinking of glass:—and then, all was still. (325)

Then De Leon reports the other oral events of the evening, with, of course, most attention to the remarks of Dickens himself, who was "suffering most fearful twinges of gout, and being besides, as hoarse as the raven of his own *Barnaby Rudge*" (326). He reports with some skepticism Dickens' favorable remarks about the improvement of the U.S., also not being sure he would himself fully agree with such assessment. However, De Leon concludes finally that "We can feel that he really meant what he said; and can even honor him for a full and frank confession of an error of his youth" (327). On the other hand, he points out that Dickens' promise to write disclaimers to be added to all future printings of his earlier offensive writings about the country "would seem an admirable advertisement for new editions" of those very books; and De Leon is offended by Dickens' remarks about improvement in British attitudes toward Americans, which, in defiant contradiction, De Leon claims still are typically ones of "fierce loathing—with contempt not unmixed with fear" (327).

In a more conciliatory mood, De Leon notes that Dickens "will eat no more dinners with us for the present; but, for the sake of literature, we should hope he eat many another hearty one elsewhere" (328). De Leon concludes the essay with the following, which includes mention of his brother Edwin (who, in addition to having been editor of the influential pre-war Washington newspaper mentioned below, also was noted as a scholar and diplomat):

> One fact may interest your readers. When the order of the dinner was shown to Mr. Dickens, he made but one comment:—"I am *very* glad the Southern Press was not omitted."
> When that toast was offered, Mr. Greeley, in a few happy remarks introduced Mr. Edwin De Leon—the Editor of the *Southern Press* in the days before the flood—as "its genealogical representative;" and he briefly responded with a statement that the South had ever appreciated the Guest of the Evening; and that he hoped the press of the two sections, "so long dissevered, discordant—beligerent"—might now reunite in the great work of peace and good will towards men.
> Such was the Dickens' Dinner, or rather, such was Mr. Dickens at the dinner.
> That there was some sincerity in the utter recantation he made seems proven by the fact that, next evening—after his last reading in America—when un-toasted, undined and unwined, he said, substantially, the same things in the self-same matter.   (328)

(It might be noted that Dickens' remarks about the U.S. at the Delmonico's dinner were quite gracious and magnanimous, whatever their impetus, and that what he said on that occasion is supported in part by what he was saying in letters to those back home.)

De Leon's third Dickens essay, eleven pages in length, appeared in the September issue of *The Land We Love* and is the least valuable of the three in that it is much less informative about Dickens and his American visit, but is more a continuation of De Leon's reflections upon Dickens' Delmonico's remarks, which had begun in the preceding month's essay. This essay's title is "Mr. Dickens and His 'Debt of Honor'." De Leon begins by quickly summarizing the Delmonico's dinner, and then moves to classify that event as not so much intended to honor Dickens as it was a vulgar celebration of the American press itself.

> But the significance of the Dickens banquet lay not in the celebration of itself by the press of the United States, nor yet in the good feeling that undeniably prevailed at the festive board; but in the amends voluntarily made by the illustrious guest, as a farewell peace-offering for all the hard things he had said of America in his *American Notes* and *Martin Chuzzlewit*. Mr. Dickens, indeed, retracted nothing contained in those two wretched fictions, but he gave hearty utterance to the favorable impressions made upon him by the America of to-day, and promised that every future edition of *American Notes* and *Martin Chuzzlewit* should contain this tribute by way of appendix. The promise has been kept, and a late number of *All the Year Round* pays the "Debt of Honor" by publishing the Postscript hereafter to accompany the works in question. (415)

De Leon goes on to downplay the forgiving nature of Americans toward Dickens during his tour, pointing out that most of those offended by him in his writings after his visit in the early 1840s had long ago departed and that the passage of twenty-five years, along with Dickens' further literary and recent performing successes, easily would account for much of the good feeling on both sides during his 1867–68 tour. So, the success of the much publicized dinner in New York should have been no surprise. However:

> With regard to the *amende honorable* of Mr. Dickens, it is just a little curious that he himself should have overlooked the true nature of his offence, and that it should not have occurred to him that no correction, of the unfair picture of the American society given in *Martin Chuzzlewit* and the *American Notes*, could possibly meet the case at all. The picture *was* unfair, because it withheld all the more favorable merits, while it exaggerated all the weaknesses and vices of the American people and character. That these weaknesses and vices did exist, though in less degree than was represented, most intelligent Americans are now prepared to admit. But the fullest retraction of the slanders in these books could not excuse Mr. Dickens for having written them; still less can praise of the Americans of the present day excuse him. The unpardonable sin of Mr. Dickens was that, true or false, these books were acts of gross ingratitude to a people who had lavished upon him a hospitality, without a precedent for its cordiality and its profusion. True or false, these books should hever have been written by the man whom America, foolishly yet generously, had delighted to honor. The universal American home had been his home for the time, and

it was a poor return, indeed, for the kindness of a whole people to cover them with inextinguishable ridicule.

. . . .

Herein lay Mr. Dickens' grievous fault. He does not seem to recognize it, and therefore he cannot see that no tribute he may now pay to the American people can atone for it. But we recognize none the less the manliness and magnanimity of his remarks at the New York Dinner, embodied in the Postscript just published in *All the Year Round*. They were made of his own free will, at a time, the very eve of his departure, when he had nothing to gain by them, when fine words would sell no additional tickets for his Readings, and when America could do nothing more for him, except grant an International Copyright. We would not imply by this exception that Mr. Dickens had the matter of the Copyright in his mind in the promise he gave and has so faithfully kept. We believe his tribute to the American people of the present day to have been wholly unselfish and sincere, as it was frank and manly, and as it was also (in our judgment) of no real value whatever.   (417–418)

De Leon next quotes, from the printing of them in *All the Year Round*, the full paragraphs which Dickens now indeed had appended as "A Debt of Honor" to reprintings of the two of his previous works which had offended many Americans. The paragraphs consist mostly of his remarks at Delmonico's. In response to these, De Leon contends:

As a general proposition the weight of testimony, the impartiality of the witness being considered, depends upon the opportunity the witness has had for accurate observation of the matters concerning which he testifies. —With regard to Mr. Dickens, neither upon his first nor his second visit to America, was he an impartial witness. In 1840, he came to secure an International Copyright and failed. In 1867–'68, he came to make money, and succeeded beyond his most sanguine expectations. Both the failure and the success disqualified him as a fair, not to say as a dispassionate, critic of American society. But giving him the fullest credit for impartiality, he certainly had no means of forming an intelligent opinion of the social, moral, and intellectual condition of America, upon his recent visit. The extent of his journeyings was extremely circumscribed. —The state of his health and "the nature of his avocation here" enforced upon him, as he tells us himself, a privacy which he honors the American people for respecting. He had no glimpse of the domestic life of the country outside the little aesthetic circle of poets, publishers and philosophers of Boston. . . . He attended no public entertainments but his own. He did not go to church, for the reason, as was happily suggested by some wag of the daily newspapers, that he felt no interest in American politics. In short, he saw nothing but what could be seen out of the windows of railroad cars, inside fashionable hotels, and from the platforms of lecture halls. The testimony of such an observer, as to the social, moral and intellectual condition of a great country, is surely of no importance whatever.   (419)

De Leon does accept the contention of increased U. S. material wealth, railroads, and population since 1840 and the abolition of "the damning sin of slavery, which, upon the occasion of his former visit, gave Mr. Dickens such constant quietude" (420). However, he points out that during his recent tour Dickens did not visit the South, "the fairest and alas! the most desolate portion of the country. . . . He was well aware that the only class in the South who could enjoy his Readings, had no money to spend in such literary entertainments" (420). At some length De Leon takes issue with Dickens and claims that there has been deterioration in the country in regard to its general morality and religion, citing various highly publicized scandals in government, high society, the press, the church, and the theatre; and lest anyone think his "gloomy view of the social, moral and intellectual condition of the Northern states has been inspired by the petty feeling of sectional prejudices," he quotes a long passage from "the ablest and most independent of the weekly journals of New York City" (423) which tends to support his contentions. De Leon ends this essay: "But flatteries like those of Mr. Dickens will rather retard the day by blinding men to the true condition of affairs, and it is certain that there is small hope of a higher culture and a purer Christianity for a people who already believe themselves the wisest, best and greatest of mankind" (424).

The attention given to Dickens in *The Land We Love* is both interesting and informative, especially De Leon's accounts of Dickens reading and of the Delmonico's dinner. Also illustrated is the fact that despite the strongly overt Southern partisanship of *The Land We Love*, it clearly did not wish to participate in a cultural secession; and the skill and success of Dickens, in De Leon's words "a magnetic amalgam," helped greatly to make this decision an easy one.

WORKS CONSULTED

Atchison, Ray M. "*The Land We Love*: A Southern Post-Bellum Magazine of Agriculture, Literature, and Military History." *The North Carolina Historical Review* 37 (1960): 506–515.

Chaudron, Louis deV. "Sketch of the Author." *Four Years in Rebel Capitals*. By Thomas Cooper De Leon. 1892 ed., 5–12.

Churchill, R. C. *A Bibliography of Dickensian Criticism 1836–1975*. New York: Garland, 1975.

"De Leon, Edwin," in *Southern Writers: A Biographical Dictionary*. Ed. Louis D. Rubin, Jr. et al. Baton Rouge: Louisiana State University Press, 1979.

De Leon, T[homas] C[ooper]. "The Dickens' Dinner." *The Land We Love* 5 (1868): 323–328.

[De Leon, Thomas Cooper.] "Mr. Dickens and His 'Debt of Honor'." *The Land We Love* 5 (1868): 414–424.

———. "Mr. Dickens' Readings." *The Land We Love* 4 (1868): 421–433.

"De Leon, Thomas Cooper." *Dictionary of Alabama Biography.* 1921 ed.

———. *Dictionary of American Biography.*

———. *Southern Writers: A Biographical Dictionary.* Ed. Louis D. Rubin, Jr. et al. Baton Rouge: Louisiana State University Press, 1979.

———. *Who's Who in America, 1912–13.*

"The Dickens Banquet." *The New York Times* 19 April 1868: 8. (Includes Edwin De Leon's remarks.)

"Hill, Daniel Harvey." *Dictionary of American Biography.*

Johnson, Edgar. *Charles Dickens: His Tragedy and Triumph.* 2 vols. New York: Simon and Schuster, 1952.

Kent, Charles. *Charles Dickens as a Reader.* Philadelphia: Lippincott, 1872.

The Land We Love. 6 vols. Charlotte, N. C.: 1866–1869.

Rev. of *Our Mutual Friend*, by Charles Dickens. *The Land We Love* 1 (1866): 302.

Slater, Michael, ed. *Dickens on America and the Americans.* Austin: University of Texas Press, 1978.

Sweetser, Kate Dickinson. "Dining With Dickens at Delmonico's." *The Bookman* 49 (1919): 20–28.

Van Amerongen, J. B. *The Actor in Dickens.* 1926. New York: Blom, 1969.

Wilkins, William Glyde, ed. *Charles Dickens in America.* New York: Scribner's, 1911.

Dickens, Drama, and the Two Realities

Richard Lettis

Dickens' fascination with the stage has probably received more attention than anything else about him except his novels. Every aspect of his interest and participation in the world of drama has been mentioned—his constant attending of stage events, from a Macready production of *King Lear* to the humblest puppet show; his attempts to write plays on his own and with others; his assistance to both amateur and professional playwrights; his early thoughts about acting as a career; his acting in and directing and producing of amateur performances, ranging from those in which his children played roles for family entertainment to that offered before the Queen; his involvement with dramatizations of his own stories, and his public readings from them; his own critical commentary. With drama we are at the very heart of Dickens' interest in the arts; as James Payne said, "The subject . . . which most interested him . . . was the dramatic—nay, even the melodramatic—side of human nature" (2: 216).

In his "A Christmas Tree," a record of his earliest childhood memories as recalled in an imaginary trip down a Christmas tree composed of his first awareness of things, Dickens tells us of the impressions made upon him by the stage:

> And now, I see a wonderful row of little lights rise smoothly out of the ground, before a vast green curtain. Now, a bell rings—a magic bell, which still sounds in my ears unlike all other bells—and music plays, amidst a buzz of voices, and a fragrant smell of orange-peel and oil. Anon, the magic bell commands the music to cease, and the great green curtain rolls itself up majestically, and The Play begins! The devoted dog of Montargis avenges the death of his master, foully murdered in the Forest of Bondy; and a humourous Peasant with a red nose and a very little hat, whom I take from this hour forth

149

to my bosom as a friend (I think he was a Waiter or an Hostler at a village Inn, but many years have passed since he and I have met), remarks that the sassagassity of that dog is indeed surprising; and evermore this jocular conceit will live in my remembrance fresh and unfading, overtopping all possible jokes, unto the end of time. Or now, I learn with bitter tears how poor Jane Shore, dressed all in white, and with her brown hair hanging down, went starving through the streets; or how George Barnwell killed the worthiest uncle that ever man had, and was afterwards so sorry for it that he ought to have been let off. Comes swift to comfort me, the Pantomime—stupendous Phenomenon!—when clowns are shot from loaded mortars into the great chandelier, bright constellation that it is; when Harlequins, covered all over with scales of pure gold, twist and sparkle, like amazing fish; when Pantaloon (whom I deem it no irreverence to compare in my own mind to my grandfather) puts red-hot pokers in his pocket, and cries "Here's somebody coming!" or taxes the Clown with petty larceny, by saying, "Now, I sawed you do it!" when Everything is capable, with the greatest ease, of being changed into Anything; and "Nothing is, but thinking makes it so." Now, too, I perceive my first experience of the dreary sensation—often to return in after-life—of being unable, next day, to get back to the dull settled world; of wanting to live for ever in the bright atmosphere I have quitted; of doting on the little Fairy, with the wand like a celestial Barber's Pole, and pining for a Fairy immortality with her. Ah, she comes back, in many shapes, as my eye wanders down the branches of my Christmas Tree, and goes as often, and has never yet stayed by me!   (*Household Words*, 2: 292)

The passage tells us almost all we need to know about Dickens and drama, from the exclamation marks and the word selection—"wonderful," "vast," "magic," "great," "majestic"—to the descriptions, to the final comment. The descriptions support the sense of a magic world, one superior to the dull sublunary where inanimate things require human exertion: here, the lights rise and the bell rings apparently of their own volition, and the curtain rolls itself up. The bell is like no other bell on earth, just as the dog and humorous peasant are like no dog or man Dickens has known elsewhere, and the latter's conceit surpasses all other jokes for eternity. But though this is a special place, it is not a mere imaginary place; it is not at all "unreal." One uses the physical senses to respond to it—all five senses, if the peel comes from an orange that has been been touched and tasted. Dickens feels a personal relationship with the peasant; he remembers him as he would remember any man he had met elsewhere, and is as unsure of his occupation as he might be of that of anyone after many years had passed. Pantaloon is virtually a relative. The dog's wisdom is surprising, and the man's joke is the epitome of humor, but dog, man, and joke are still of this world, just as the avenging of the master, and the starving of Jane Shore, and the murder by George Barnwell are, though somehow more telling than vengeance, starvation, and murder can be in the real world, still just as real. The wonder and magic of that which is both real and somehow better than real, which one can enjoy whether it produces unmatchable laughter or provokes to bitter tears, is explained near the end of the passage: all has been created by human thought, which means that the harsh inflexible rules of reality have been lifted. But the magic lies both in this fact and in the fact that all appearance of human agency has been removed: again, a bell rings and music plays and the curtain lifts without benefit of human exertion. The stage is a magic world precisely because, first, unlike the dull settled world, it is made by man to his liking; and second, all evidence of human effort has been removed, and the thing seems, like the real world, to occur by itself.

The only defect of this magical world—a world of "fanciful reality," as Dickens' friend John Forster called it for him (I: i, 13)—is that, though the peasant's conceit may prevail to the end of time, the performance does not; one must at last return to the "dull settled world" created without human thought—that is, without imagination—and with all too much evidence that all is accomplished by heavy human labor. The last sad sentence expresses the lifelong attempt of Dickens to consort with this immortal fairy in various forms (which must include, one assumes, writing his novels), and his lament, like Keats's knight on the cold hill side, that she insists on leaving him.

It would be too much to say that this mythic reality was the sole cause of Dickens' fascination with the stage. He was attracted to much that had precious little reality of any sort in it—to bad plays as well as good ones, wretched performances as well as convincing ones; he loved the circus, magicians, animal acts, anything that could be called entertainment. And certainly the play was often for him, as much as for anyone, an escape from life. When like David Copperfield he found life sloppier than he had expected, he sought the stage as a man in an air-raid seeks a shelter. "Whenever he felt in need of distraction," Forster says, "whenever he was restless, or unhappy, he broke out in a violent bout of theatricals" (VI: v, 159). He went to a play, or acted in a play, or directed, or helped put on a dramatization of his own novels, or read from them, and the escape from the dull settled world made him feel better. He did more than this: not only did he escape into the theatrical, but he brought the theatrical into his own life, appearance, personality, character, and work (see, e.g., Woolcott, 14; *Dickens Theatrical Reader*, 3–4; and Kent, 13). George Dolby said that, though quiet and reserved among strangers, Dickens was often "on" with his close friends, entertaining them like a performer. It was "a phase in Mr. Dickens's nature, which was apparent only to a limited circle of friends with whom he felt himself quite

at his ease, and to entertain whom, in that genial way of which he seemed
to be sole possessor, he would take any amount of pains and trouble'' (35).
Forster said that

> He seemed to be always the more himself for being somebody else. . . .
> "Assumption has charms for me so delightful—I hardly know for how many
> wild reasons—that I feel a loss of Oh I can't say what exquisite foolery, when
> I lose a chance of being someone not in the remotest degree like
> myself."   (X: iii, 399)

The motivation for such escape was not merely, as it would have been in
most others, dislike of self, or need to disguise self from self; as Sir Arthur
Helps penetratingly commented, Dickens "never dramatized himself to himself" ("In Memorium," *Macmillan's Magazine* 22 [1870]; repr. *Interviews*,
2: 335). Perhaps it was not even dislike of the misery that Self sometimes
encountered. As with Dostoevsky's Undergrounder, it was rather the intolerable sense that the self must always be what it is, always in the world in
which it finds itself, unable to be anything else in any other reality, bound
by the inflexible laws of existence in Blake's fallen world, in which Nothing
is capable of changing itself into Anything else, and thinking can make nothing
so. As the trip down the Christmas tree so clearly shows, the theater freed
Dickens from the immutable.

So, no doubt, did the novel, poetry, music, all art. But Dickens believed
that the stage offered more than any other art form; it was, he said, "at once
the most obvious, the least troublesome, and the most real, of all escapes out
of the literal world" ("The Amusements of the People," *Household Words*
[3/30/50] 1: 13; all dates refer to the nineteenth century unless otherwise
identified). The highest form of drama, tragedy—"the noblest flight of human
genius" (Stone, 626)—was the most real: "the Art that of all others strikes
to the Soul like Reality" (*Speeches* [7/21/58], 276). At times he spoke of the
play as pretense, or of the actor as "a friend who has beguiled us of a moment
of care, who has taught us to sympathize with virtuous grief cheating us to
tears for sorrows not our own" (*Speeches* [4/6/46], 76), but far more often
it was the conviction of reality that drama conveyed of which he spoke, and
of that reality as an improvement upon the world's, or at the least as a
representative of the world at its best. In the actor's art, he said, "we always
find some reflection, humorous or pathetic, sombre or grotesque, of all the
best things that we feel and know" (*Speeches* [4/14/51], 122).

Upon occasion, apparently, Dickens found this kind of power to touch what
we feel and know in the real world; when he did, he said he preferred it even

to drama. When his father was imprisoned in the Marshalsea for debt, and Dorrit-like had held a meeting in which he got up a petition for bounty with which to drink the King's health on his birthday, young Charles sat in the corner, watching: "I would rather have seen it than the best play ever played" (Forster, I: ii, 31). But such an instance was rare; far more often it was the theater that "placed us for a time in a wider and less selfish world in lieu of that which is so much with us early and late" (*Speeches* [4/2/55], 186).

In "A Curious Dance Round a Curious Tree," Dickens wrote what Harry Stone has called "a theory of dramatic catharsis"; it clearly defines the attraction of play as escape from the unhappy consequences of harsh reality, while preserving all the excitement of life. While visiting St. Luke's Asylum, he says he might instead

> have betaken myself to that jocund world of Pantomime, where there is no affliction or calamity that leaves the least impression; where a man may tumble into the broken ice, or dive into the kitchen fire, and only be the droller for the accident; where babies may be knocked about and sat upon, or choked with gravy spoons, in the process of feeding, and yet no Coroner be wanted, nor anybody made uncomfortable; where workmen may fall from the top of a house to the bottom, or even from the bottom of a house to the top, and sustain no injury to the brain, need no hospital, leave no young children; where everyone, in short, is as superior to all the accidents of life, though encountering them at every turn, that I suspect this to be the secret (though many persons may not present it to themselves) of the general enjoyment which an audience of vulnerable spectators, liable to pain and sorrow, find in this class of entertainment (*Household Words* [1/17/52]; repr. Stone, 384).

The move from madhouse to playhouse is significant. Like the demented, the dramatist distorts reality, but he does so by thought, and creates a world that, instead of incapacitating him, proves beneficial.

For Dickens, then, a strong part of the magnetism of the play lay in its combination of verisimilitude and improvement upon reality. Neither of these achievements was of great value without the other: anything (outside of the necessary magic) that hinted at the unreality of the dog of Montargis was a fault; anything that exposed the peasant as incapable of uttering the superlative conceit was a mistake. Although Dickens could enjoy almost anything upon the stage, however bad, again and again he criticized actors, producers, and playwrights who erred in either offending reality or failing to improve upon it. Over-acting was one of the great sins, fatal in a good theater and certain to succeed in cheap private theaters where amateurs sought a quick and easy reputation; Dickens gave advice on how to do the Duke of Gloucester there:

"Orf with his ed" (very quick and loud; —then slow and sneeringly)—"So much for Bu-u-uuckingham!" Lay the emphasis on the "uck"; get yourself gradually into a corner, and work with your right hand, while you're saying it, as if you were feeling your way, and it is sure to do ("Private Theatres," *Evening Chronicle* [8/11/35]; repr. *Theatrical Reader*, 50).

Even a poor actor was tolerable if he avoided such unbelievable excess; Dickens said of the performance of one such that it was "a great comfort to have that kind of meat underdone" (Pilgrim *Letters* [2/21/44], 4: 50). But good acting eschewed over- or underacting, and strove for verisimilitude. Dickens praised a performance by the son of Charles Mathews—"His acting throughout was easy, gentlemanly, and humourous, without being in the slightest degree overstrained"—and commented on his doing an Italian dance:

It was not the cold artificial dance of an actor going through a figure, because it was his part, or the burlesque posturing of a low comedian, determined to raise a laugh at all hazards: it was the sunny, sparkling joyousness of an Italian peasant, revelling in the beauty of everything around him, and dancing for very lightness of heart and gaiety. Anything more elegant and delightful we never saw (Review in *Morning Chronicle* [1/11/36]; repr. Carlton, 23–24).

Mechanical and thoughtless acting also damaged verisimilitude. Dickens spoke of actors in one play who "never looked at one another, but delivered all their dialogue to the pit, in a manner so egregiously unnatural and preposterous that I couldn't make up my mind whether to take it as a joke or an outrage" (Pilgrim *Letters* [12/13?/44], 4: 239). Forster said that the French actor Plessy "enchanted" Dickens (VII: v, 162); perhaps he did at one time, but near the end of his life Dickens wrote, "the Lord deliver us from Plessy's mechanical ingenuousness!" (Hogarth *Letters* [5/2/70], 2: 510). (Perhaps he was referring to Plessy's writing.) *Unnatural* was one of his favorite pejoratives; its opposite, along with such words as *truthful* and *lifelike*, was a favorite compliment. He found in an Italian theater "the most extraordinary acting I ever beheld. As an exact copy of the life out of doors; set before one without much art—not heightened here, and kept out of view there, but presented broadly and plainly as the real thing itself is—it's quite wonderful" (Pilgrim *Letters* [2/25/45], 4: 273). One of the things he most admired in the acting of his friend Charles Macready was its "tremendous reality" (Pilgrim *Letters* [9/1/43], 3: 548). He liked that performance that seemed not so much aimed at the audience as realizing itself, conveying the sense that the actor did what he did—like the peasant dance of Young Mathews—because it was in him to do it, not because he wished to create an effect. Robert Keeley was a remarkable Verges who "threw Dogberry into the shade" because "he was so lost in admiration of that portentous jackass, and became so much more and more absorbed in the contemplation of him as he became more and more ridiculous, that he in a manner appropriated Dogberry to himself" (*Nonesuch Letters* [3/3/69], 3: 709). And Charles Fechter's Iago was great because in the role he avoided

> the conventional ways of frowning, sneering, diabolically grinning, and elaborately doing everything else that would induce Othello to run him through the body very early in the play. Mr. Fechter's is the Iago who could, and did, make friends; who could dissect his master's soul, without flourishing his scalpel as if it were a sign-of-the-Saracen's-Head grimness; who could be a boon companion without *ipso-facto* warning all beholders off by the portentous phenomenon; who could sing a song or clink a can naturally enough, and stab men really in the dark,—not in a transparent notification of himself as going about seeking whom to stab ("On Mr. Fechter's Acting," *Atlantic Monthly* [8/69]; repr. *Collected Papers* 1: 119).

Dickens was sensitive to anything on the stage that struck a wrong note. He commented on a play with which he was helping Charles Fechter:

> When I went over the play this day week, he was at least 20 minutes, *in a boat, in the last scene*, discussing with another gentleman (also in the boat) whether he should kill him or not; after which the gentleman dived overboard and swam for it. Also, in the most important and dangerous parts of the play, there was a young person of the name of Pickles who was constantly being mentioned by name, in conjunction with the powers of light or darkness; as, "Great Heaven! Pickles?"—"By Hell, 'tis Pickles!"—"Pickles! a thousand Devils!"— "Distraction! Pickles?"   (Forster, VIII: vii, 248)

When in another performance an actor twenty years too old to play Caesar walked on the stage in that role and said, " 'He calls me Boy'—a howl of derision arose from the audience" (Collins *Letters* [3/4/55], 22–23). The same actor held a map of London in his hand and pretended it was a Roman scroll, to the further destruction of the scene. Dickens objected to the custom of having "the Senate of ancient Rome represented by five-shillings' worth of supernumery assistance huddled together at a rickety table, with togas above the cloth and corduroys below" ("Macready as 'Benedick,' " *Examiner* [3/4/43]; repr. *Collected Papers*, 1: 144–146) Props were useful but dangerous: in *Nicholas Nickleby* Dickens laughed at dramatists who built plays around them (in the novel, they consist of a pump and two washing tubs), and he did his own readings on a stage without background of any sort to show "how much a single performer could do without the aid and stimulus of any of the

ordinary adjuncts of the stage; how many effects of a genuinely startling
character could be produced without the help of scenery, costume, limelight,
or mechanical contrivance'' (Dolby, 442). Some props did more harm than
good: because Greek costumes (and names) had become associated in the
public mind with stage farce, Dickens feared their effect on an audience in
serious drama, and advised his friend Bulwer to change the locale of his play
from Greece to Russia (*Nonesuch Letters* [10/14/67], 3: 560). He urged Macready to remove a picture from a scene:

> Do have upon the table, in the opening scene of the second act, something in
> a velvet case, or frame, that may look like a large miniature of Mabel, such
> as one of Ross's, and eschew that picture. It haunts me with a sense of danger.
> Even a titter at that critical time, with the whole of that act before you, would
> be a fatal thing. The picture is bad in itself, bad in its effect upon the beautiful
> room, bad in all its associations with the house.
>
> (Pilgrim *Letters* [12/10/42], 3: 392)

Properly used, of course, a costume or prop could add to the reality of a
scene, not only by conveying the appearance of the world, but by giving an
actor a concrete thing to which he could react. Dickens admired the manner
in which the French actor William Lemaitre, playing a guilty murderer,
covertly examined his clothes for bloodstains, started when he saw the color
of wine brought to him, and used the murder weapon to reveal his mental
state (Forster, VII: v, 159–160). On the whole, Dickens seems to have felt
that the theater of his time did much better with scenery—with ''pictorial
effect'' (Hogarth *Letters* [1/1/67], 2: 315) than with other parts of performance;
he did not say why, but it is no bad guess that he found props, like Lemaitre's
walking staff, often more capable of conveying reality, and of evoking emotion, than the actors and plots could do.

But the worst offender against the mythic reality of drama, in language,
acting, and story, was convention. Dickens despised the plays of John Mad-
ison Morton (''those dismal Morton comedies'') (Pilgrim *Letters* [8/6/47], 5:
144) because they teemed with iterated clichés. The convention of poetic
inversion, at least when poorly done, was harmful: he spoke of one play
which was ''made up of expressions so curiously inverted that it is difficult
on first reading them to understand their meaning'' (Pilgrim *Letters* [9/13/41],
2: 382). Conventional characters were among the main causes of the inferiority
of nineteenth-century drama; T. E. Pemberton said that managers often failed
to adapt Dickens' novels to the stage with any success because of this fault:

As plays, [the adaptations] are altogether different from their predecessors. The

> *dramatis personae* cannot, as that of the sentimental comedy and heavy mel-
> odrama, be summarily and arbitrarily put into the various conventional classes
> amongst which stage managers distribute the "parts." One cannot be safely
> given out at once to the "heavy father" of the company; another to the "smart
> servant"; a third to the "low comedian"; a fourth to the "juvenile tragedian";
> a fifth to the "chambermaid" or a sixth to the "sentimental young lady."
> Dickens's characters are too much like nature for that. (159)

Dickens called attention to the same fault in the work would-be playwrights
submitted to him: "The father is such a dolt, and the villain *such* a villain,
the girl so especially credulous and the means used to deceive them so very
slight and transparent, that the reader *cannot* sympathize with their distress"
(Pilgrim *Letters* [9/27/39], 1: 587–588). And he supplied his own list of
conventional roles, complete with conventional plot:

> There is a rightful heir, who loves a young lady, and is beloved by her; and
> a wrongful heir, who loves her too, and isn't beloved by her; and the wrongful
> heir gets hold of the rightful heir, and throws him into a dungeon, just to kill
> him off when convenient, for which purpose he hires a couple of assassins—a
> good one and a bad one—who, the moment they are left alone, get up a little
> murder on their own account, the good one killing the bad one, and the bad
> one wounding the good one. Then the rightful heir is discovered in prison,
> carefully holding a long chain in his hands, and seated despondingly in a large
> arm-chair; and the young lady comes in to two bars of soft music, and embraces
> the rightful heir; and then the wrongful heir comes in to two bars of quick music
> (technically called a 'hurry'), and goes on in the most shocking manner, throw-
> ing the young lady about as if she was nobody, and calling the rightful heir
> "Ar-recreant—ar-wretch!" in a very loud voice, which answers the double
> purpose of displaying his passion, and preventing the sound being deadened
> by the sawdust. The interest becomes intense; the wrongful heir draws his
> sword, and rushes on the rightful heir; a blue smoke is seen, a gong is heard,
> and a tall white figure (who has been all this time, behind the arm-chair, covered
> with a table-cloth), slowly rises to the tune of "Oft in the stilly night." This
> is no other than the ghost of the rightful heir's father, at sight of which the
> wrongful heir becomes apoplectic, and is literally "struck all of a heap," the
> stage not being large enough to admit of his falling down at length. Then the
> good assassin staggers in, and says he was hired in conjunction with the bad
> assassin, by the wrongful heir, to kill the rightful heir; and he's very sorry for
> it, and won't do so any more—a promise which he immediately redeems, by
> dying off-hand without any nonsense about it. Then the rightful heir throws
> down his chain; and then two men, a sailor, and a young woman (the tenantry
> of the rightful heir) come in, and the ghost makes dumb motions to them, which
> they, by supernatural inference understand—for no one else can; and the ghost
> (who can't do anything without blue fire) blesses the rightful heir and the young
> lady, by half suffocating them with smoke: and then a muffin-bell rings, and
> the curtain drops ("Astley's," *Evening Chronicle* [5/9/35]; repr. *Theatrical
> Reader*, 44).

Clearly, the muffin-bell and the blue smoke have only the most distant kinship with the magic bell and green curtain of the "Christmas Tree" world of drama. In "The Theatrical Young Gentleman," Dickens laughed at the theater-goer who could appreciate only conventional acting, and was "very acute in judging of natural expressions of the passions, and knows precisely the frown, wink, nod, or leer, which stands for any of them, or the means by which it may be converted into any other; as jealousy, with a good stamp of the right foot, becomes anger, or wildness, with the hands clasped before the throat, instead of tearing the wig, is passionate love" (*Theatrical Reader*, 48–49). Of a play he saw in Italy, Dickens said, "I have seen the same thing fifty times, only not at once so conventional and so exaggerated" (Forster, VII: v, 167). His great dislike of French classical drama is probably owing to the conventions of the form—conventions so venerable and therefore so unalterable that they both attracted a Thackeray character in *The Newcomes* and put him to sleep. "One tires of seeing a man," Dickens said, "through any number of acts, remembering everything by patting his forehead with the flat of his hand, jerking out sentences by shaking himself, and piling them up in pyramids over his head with his right forefinger" (Pemberton, 232).

As some of the above quotations show, the value for Dickens of verisimilitude lay in its contribution to the creation of feeling. Accompanying such key words of praise as *truthful, natural*, and *real* are the equally important *fresh, vigorous, tender, gallant, passionate*, and *affecting*. The sense of reality was essential to drama because an audience will not feel unless it believes; for Dickens the value of all art lay primarily in its enabling us to respond to the world in a way in which, in our own daily contact with it, we are unable to do. Drama, with its unique blend of verisimilitude and capacity for evoking emotional response, was (when well performed) the most nearly-perfect evocation of which art was capable. Again and again, Dickens' admiration of a dramatic performance couples reality and feeling. Writing to a friend, he described himself as being, in a dream, "as real, animated, and full of passion as Macready . . . in the last scene of *Macbeth*" (Hogarth *Letters* [2/27/51], 1: 287–288). He praised Fanny Stirling, who "has so gracefully and captivatingly, with such an exquisite mixture of art and fancy and fidelity, represented her own sex" (*Speeches* [2/14/66], 359). Once, he expressed admiration for an actor, La Font, for being so realistic that it was "Nature's triumph over art" (Hogarth *Letters* [5/9/53], 353), but what he far more frequently admired was the refinement of nature by art, in such a manner that the nature of the spectator was refined (by his emotional response) as well. Acting that was true to life, so that it could be believed and could speak to the audience about its world—not about some ideal or artificial place where feeling could not be believed, but its own world—must be united to acting that at the same time moved the spectator. Charles Fechter, in Hugo's *Ruy Blas*, combined "French suddenness and impressibility" with the Englishman's slower and more deliberate rise to fury, to produce "a powerful concentration of human passion and emotion [that belongs] to human nature." The power of the emotion he conveyed lay in its immediacy: "When he is on the stage, it seems to me as though the story were transpiring for the first and last time" ("On Mr. Fechter's Acting," *Atlantic Monthly* [8/69]; repr. *Collected Papers*, 1: 116)—as opposed to those dreary scenes in which conventional acting reminded him of sitting through a thousand like performances. Good acting, even when it expressed a proper state of mind, was not good if it omitted emotion: Dickens urged Mark Lemon to get an actress in a play of his to "shew more feeling. She lost it in the endeavor to look frank. It is quite right that she should be frank, but it is altogether out of nature not to be more touched and touching" (*Nonesuch Letters* [4/25/52], 2: 390). Here nature and feeling are, indeed, one.

Of reality and emotion, emotion is for Dickens the more important: the first is necessary because it makes possible the second. He could even tolerate and find enjoyable unrealistic acting that enabled one to feel: in the Queen's Theater he said he saw "the prettiest piece of acting I have seen for a long time. It is burlesque acting (I am sorry to add) but quite original and singularly graceful and pleasant" (*Nonesuch Letters* [12/25/68], 2: 692). Even if the acting were exaggerated it might do its job, if it avoided the deadly drag of conventionality, looked attractive, and elicited response.

Several of the quotations above have added still another quality to Dickens' ideal stage presentation: the visual. The magic coupling of verisimilitude and feeling could not achieve its goal of uniting man through emotion—"one touch of nature makes the whole world kin" (*Speeches* [3/1/51], 115)—unless it exerted a powerful aesthetic ocular effect upon the viewer. The audience at a play should see a picture that, as much as any painting, both pleased and made sense to him. This was one of the great virtues of Fechter:

> Picturesqueness is a quality above all others pervading Fechter's assumptions. Himself a skilled painter and sculptor, learned in the history of costume, and informing those accomplishments and that knowledge with a similar infusion of romance (for romance is inseparable from the man), he is always a picture,—always a picture in its right place in the group, always in true composition with the background of the scene ("On Mr. Fechter's Acting," *Atlantic Monthly* [8/69]; repr. *Collected Papers*, 1: 118).

Dickens read many plays, but his written comments are almost exclusively on performances, and often he calls attention to the performance as *seen*. He complimented Samuel Phelps, co-manager of Sadler's Wells, on "the great beauty of all the stage arrangements" (Pilgrim *Letters* [8/29/47], 5: 153–154) in a performance of *Cymbaline*, and urged Fechter to "give the public the picturesque, romantic drama" (Hogarth *Letters* [2/4/63], 2: 223). He commented on the dress of actors: Mrs. Nisbett's "attire was picturesque in the extreme, composed of bright colours and glittering ornaments after the gypsy fashion, but full of barbaric grace, and calculated to set off to advantage the fine form and features of the wearer" (Review in the *Morning Chronicle* [9/7/35], repr. Carlton, 13). He noticed stage lighting; indeed, the thing he discussed at most length about a performance of Goethe's *Faust* was "Stage management remarkable for some admirable, and really poetical effects of light" (Hogarth *Letters* [2/19/63], 2: 225).

But the picture should not only be striking; it should be readable, understandable. Dickens is not famous for use of the word *rational*, but he frequently applied it to good drama. The play was "the most rational of all amusements" (Pilgrim *Letters* [2/28/43], 3: 447), and the public owed Macready's acting company at Covent Garden "a debt of gratitude for the intellectual and rational enjoyment which they had afforded" (*Speeches* [1839], 3). Like a good Victorian, he thought art should bring learning as well as pleasure, and spoke of "the instruction and delight we have derived from the rich English drama" (*Speeches* [1839], 3). As always, he refused to limit art to the cognoscenti: drama was "a powerful and useful means toward the education of the people" (*Speeches* [4/6/57], 229). Some of his best comments are on the cognitive capacity of performances: Fechter's Hamlet was great bcause it was "the most coherent, consistent, and intelligible Hamlet I ever saw" (Hogarth *Letters* [3/16/62], 2: 207–208), and Macready's *King Lear*, already remarkable "for a masterly completeness of conception," was made still more so by his reintroduction of the Fool (omitted for centuries), whom Dickens shows linked to and illuminating Lear and his daughters, as well as balancing the sublimity and grandeur of the scenes in which he appears by his "quiet pathos" and homely nature ("The Restoration of Shakespeare's *Lear* to the Stage," *Examiner* [2/4/38]; repr. *Collected Papers*, 1: 123–124). *Intelligent* must be added to the list of Dickensian favorites for actors: Rose Cheri playing Clarissa Harlowe is praised as offering "A most charming, intelligent, modest, affecting piece of acting" (Pilgrim *Letters* [1/27/44], 4: 14). Much as Dickens loved stage devices—"tags," as he called them—that could startle and entertain, he disapproved of mere show that displaced sense; after a performance of *The Black Crook* in New York he decided that, despite the flamboyance of the thing, "The people who act in it have not the slightest idea of what it is about," and he could not understand why it had been "playing every night for sixteen months (!)" (Forster, X: i, 324).

For Dickens, then, the play at its best was realistic, picturesque, rational, and productive of feeling. So it may be for many lovers of the stage, but for Dickens this combination produced a mythic reality in which he believed as firmly as he did in that lesser, harsher, barer reality which most of us accept as the only truth. Dickens could not live without an alternative to the dull settled world, with no fairy immortality, no wands to wave, nothing to be made so by thinking, nothing to be anything else, two and two always four, as Dostoyevsky's Undergrounder lamented, and the planets, as Blake resented, as confined to their chartered rounds as the Thames to its banks. The Undergrounder was defeated by reality; Blake predicted its destruction in the Millenium; Dickens tried to loosen its inexorable grasp in his own time. The world of imagination—of fiction, art, and especially of drama—was not for him a mere pretense affording temporary escape, but a separate and equal reality. He spoke often to Forster about the overpowering reality of his own stories and people (see, e.g., Forster, II: i, 70), and most valued that praise, Forster said, which recognized them "as bits of actual life, with the meaning and purpose on their part, and the responsibility on his, of realities rather than creatures of fancy" (Pilgrim *Letters* [1/18/47], 5: 9). He often spoke of his characters as real: the deaths of Little Nell and Paul Dombey seem to have affected him as strongly as the loss of his own baby Dora (Pilgrim *Letters* [10/29/44], 4: 207). Sometimes he seemed to feel that his "fanciful reality" was the true reality: he was fascinated by a remark made by a Spanish monk who showed Titian's painting of the Last Supper to Sir David Wilkie, and said that he often thought that the figures in it were "in truth the Substance, we the Shadows." Having left off writing *Dombey and Son* for some time, he said that at last he "began to doubt whether I ever had anything to do with a book called Dombey, or ever sat over it, day after day, until I half began, like the Monk in poor Wilkie's story, to believe it the only reality in life and to mistake all the realities for short-lived shadows" (Pilgrim *Letters* [1/27/47], 5: 13). Living among the shadows, he peered into the picture of imagination and saw the real reality there: "when . . . I sit down to my book, some beneficent power shows it to me, and tempts me to be interested, and I don't invent it—really do not—but *see* it, and write it down" (Forster, IX: i, 272). Such was the power of this process, Forster said, that it never permitted Dickens to complete a story as he had planned it (IV: v, 338).

II

As real as Dickens' fictional world was to him, and as great as he was at conveying it to others, he seems never to have felt satisfied that he had made it sufficiently real or clear. Elsewhere, in a study of Dickens' work with his illustrators, I have attempted to demonstrate the extent to which he tried to use visual art to assist his fiction in creating mythic reality for his readers ("Dickens and Art," *Dickens Studies Annual* 14 [1985], 93–146). Dickens' interest in book illustration began with the plates in his childhood books, which as an adult he sometimes remembered more vividly than the texts. The Gad's Hill library contained many illustrated books; it has been argued that Dickens' interest in painting and illustration was an important influence upon his fiction. His first book was originally conceived by its publishers as a series of plates that he was to connect by supplying a narrative; though Dickens quickly reversed the process, so that he was in charge and the artist illustrated his text, the idea of Pickwick grew out of a picture by Robert Seymour (the illustrator), and a pattern was established: Dickens used a series of artists (eighteen in all, including many of the most famous painters of his time) to illustrate most of his subsequent works. He dominated his illustrators, selecting them, usually giving them not only the subjects for illustration but exact instructions on how the picture should appear (once, though the illustrations were in black and white, he even mentioned color), and requiring second or third drawings when the first did not please, even in such slight details as a hat or a pipe. He did everything he could to help his artists catch the sense and spirit of the works they were to portray: he sent them copy, explained at length what he was after in a chapter or number, and even read entire numbers to them. Once, when he was on the continent and an illustrator didn't please him, he arranged a meeting at Bale to be sure that the artist got it right.

The impression left by a review of Dickens' work with his illustrators is that, had he been able to draw, he would never have left the pictures in his books to others—not even to such artists as John Leech and George Cruikshank. For him the illustration was not a pleasant addendum, a lagniappe to attract buyers; it became a vital part of his work designed to convey his imaginative reality even beyond the ability of his pen. He could not see it, write it down, and draw it, as well, but he did the next best thing: he got the finest talent he knew to draw it for him, guiding and cajoling and sometimes browbeating them until their imaginations could produce something as close to his own as was humanly possible. Often his directions for a picture included far more than any artist could have depicted: Hablot Browne once complained he would need almost a mile of perspective to include everything for which Dickens had asked (Pilgrim *Letters*, 3: 543n). The directions indicate an impatience with the limitations of the picture as aid to his fiction: Dickens often called upon his artist to describe action, as though somehow the picture could be made to move. Sound, too, was desired: Dickens supplied dialogue for the characters, and even mentioned such things as a knock at the door. Obviously he did not believe his artists could include such things, but the tone of his letters indicates that he wished they could: he yearned for an art form that could make his stories come alive for his readers—as alive as anyone in the unimagined world of reality. Art could render life beyond the limitations of prose, but not even art could provide voice and action. Only the stage could do that.

Dickens shared the predilection of his age for narrative art: he was drawn to and made acute observations upon any picture (by Hogarth, for example, or by his friend Daniel Maclise) that told a story and aroused emotion. In painting, in literature, in drama, he objected to anything that might detract from the effect of the story. Much as he was fascinated by theatrical gimmickry, for example, he drew a distinction between *dramatic* and *theatrical*, to the detriment of the latter: "in the former case a story is strikingly told, without apparent consciousness of a spectator, and . . . in the latter case the groups are obtrusively dressed up, and doing (or not doing) certain things with an eye to the spectator, and not for the sake of the story" ("Insularities," *Household Words* [1/19/56], 626). "For the sake of the story"; certainly everywhere in his work with his illustrators, Dickens' first concern is that. That fault in an illustration which called forth his strongest reaction was one in which the artist failed to follow the narrative. The worst such instance occurred when John Leech put the wrong character in a scene near the end of Part II of *The Battle of Life*. Dickens wrote Forster:

> When I first saw it, it was with a horror and agony not to be expressed. Of course I need not tell *you*, my dear fellow, Warden had no business in the elopement scene. *He* was never there! In the first hot sweat of this surprise and novelty, I was going to implore the printing of that sheet to be stopped, and the figure taken out of the block. But when I thought of the pain this might give to our kind-hearted Leech; and that what is such a monstrous enormity to me, as having never entered my brain, may not so present itself to others, I became more composed; though the fact is wonderful to me.
>
> (Pilgrim *Letters* [12/12/46], 4: 679)

Any novelist would be pained by a faulty illustration, but Dickens is more than pained: he is devastated. A picture drawn contrary to his story is a "monstrous enormity," almost a kind of threat to the imagined reality that the story is as it exists within his brain. It is "wonderful" to Dickens that anything contrary to that imagined reality can exist; he has to convince himself that others will not find it monstrous too. It is almost like science fiction, in which some departure from cosmic law may threaten existence itself.

Dickens did at times criticize his illustrations as works of art, good or poor in themselves, but his greatest concern was that they faithfully visualize his fiction. Browne's representation of Mrs. Pipchin and Paul for *Dombey and Son* was "frightfully and wildly wide of the mark"; Dickens felt he had been "utterly misrepresented" (Pilgrim *Letters* [11–12/46], 4: 671). Fred Stone was obliged to make Boffin (for *Our Mutual Friend*) more likeable and droll, as Dickens had intended him; and Browne was directed to show the Sergeant in *Pickwick Papers* as younger, slyer, and more knowing (Hogarth *Letters* [2/23/64], 2: 247; Pilgrim *Letters* [1/37], 1: 222). For *Nicholas Nickleby*, Dickens told Browne that in a picture "I don't think Smike is frightened enough or Squeers earnest enough—for my purposes" (Pilgrim *Letters* [2/39], 1: 513). He found cuts by Doyle and Leech for *The Chimes* "so unlike my idea" that he, "with the winning manner which you know of, got them with the highest good humor to do both afresh" (Pilgrim *Letters* [12/2/44], 4: 234). "You know," he wrote to John Forster in 1846, "how I build up temples in my mind that are not made with hands (or expressed with pen and ink, I am afraid), and how liable I am to be disappointed in these things" (Pilgrim *Letters* [12/12/46], 4: 679). His highest praise was reserved, not for the artist who drew the best illustration, but for those who did what John Leech managed for *Master Humphrey's Clock*: "this is the very first time any designs for what I have written have touched and moved me, and caused me to feel that they expressed the idea I had in my mind" (Pilgrim *Letters* [1/30/41], 2: 199). When Cattermole sent him watercolors of two of his illustrations for *The Old Curiosity Shop*—one of Little Nell's grave, and one of the interior of the shop—Dickens expressed similar satisfaction: "It is impossible for me to tell you how greatly I am charmed with those beautiful pictures, in which the whole feeling and thought and expression of the little story is rendered to the gratification of my inmost heart" (Pilgrim *Letters* [12/20/42], 3: 397). And when W. P. Frith, after doing a picture of Dolly Varden for *Barnaby Rudge*, later painted Dolly again, and also Kate Nickleby, Dickens is reported to have said, "All I can say is, they are exactly what I meant" (Pilgrim *Letters*, III: 373n4).

III

Though illustration sometimes helped Dickens to convey what he meant, it was for him a flawed vehicle. Its inadequacies were three: it could not move, it could not speak, and it had to be done by somebody else. He continued to use illustration as long as he published books, but at the same time he discovered another visual art that offered him, in his pursuit of a means of fully realizing his fiction, the great assets of motion, sound, and best of all, self-production. He discovered the stage.

We have already seen that Dickens loved the theater from infancy; before he was through he was to write for it, act upon it, direct, devise a portable stage—do almost anything that could be done in connection with it. He was a poor playwright, an ingenious deviser, a very good to excellent actor, and (in amateur productions, as in all these activities) a supreme director. But his greatest triumph in connection with the stage came in the last years of his life, when he trod the boards to read from his own works. He had always been aware of the kinship between the novel and the play, and was always interested in what could be done for a novel by dramatic representation. Speaking at the Royal General Theatrical Fund, he said it was appropriate for him to chair the meeting because

> Every good actor plays direct to every good author, and every good writer of fiction, though he may not adopt the dramatic form, writes in effect for the stage. He may write novels always, and plays never, but the truth and wisdom that are in him must permeate the art of which truth and passion are the life, and must be more or less reflected in that great mirror which he holds up to nature. (*Speeches* [3/29/58], 262)

Forster said that Dickens' "higher calling" included the lower one of acting; he also quoted Ruskin as saying that in his novels Dickens "chooses to speak in a circle of stage fire" (V: i, 374; VII: i, 120).

In 1844 Dickens informed Robert Keeley, actor and, with his wife, manager of the Lyceum, that he objected "to the *principle* of adapting novels for the stage," but in all probability he had in mind only the unauthorized adapting of his own novels—without recompense, without power to approve, even without the opportunity, usually, to help them be something better than horrible. In conferring his blessing on Frederick Yates's production of *Nicholas Nickleby* at the Adelphi, he wrote that his

> general objection to the adaptation of any unfinished work of mine simply is, that being badly done and worse acted it tends to vulgarize the characters, to

destroy or weaken in the minds of those who see them the impressions I have endeavored to create, and consequently to lessen the after-interest in their progress. No such objection can exist for a moment when the thing is so admirably done in every respect as you have done it.

(Pilgrim *Letters* [11/29?/38], 1: 463)

Long before this Dickens had adapted a piece of his own short fiction for the stage, and he was active in helping others to do the same; he had no objection to making a novel into a play, as long as the poor novelist had something to say about it. As editor, he seems to have been alert to the advantages of either genre as he considered work submitted to him. As early as 1838, he wrote to Theodore Martin, of a piece submitted for *Bentley's Miscellany*, that it was "not, I think, quite the thing for us, but why don't you turn it into a two-act comedy? It would make an excellent little piece for the stage and looks so like one even now, that when I read it I could scarcely help thinking you had originally written it in that form" (Pilgrim *Letters* [12/28/38], 1: 479). When Wilkie Collins tried to dramatize his novel *Armandale*, he apparently consulted Dickens, who sent him detailed advice (Collins *Letters* [7/9/66], 132). In 1859 he even wrote to Regnier in France to inquire whether *A Tale of Two Cities* might be dramatized for the French stage (it was not) (Hogarth *Letters* [10/19/59], 2: 121).

Dickens was most often involved in the matter of translating novel into play by his assistance to some of the unrelenting horde of theater managers who found great profit in subjecting his works to the process. Sometimes plays of his serialized works would be on the stage before he had finished the novel, with the flattest and tritest working out of his plot to an improbable ending. Forster says that the plays made from Dickens' books were "the subject of complaint with him incessantly" (IV: iii, 305). Upon occasion, for little other reason than to see his work represented by something less than the abominable (just as he could hardly bear to see his scenes and characters misrepresented in illustrations), he would, when given the chance, oversee and improve the production. "I really am bothered to death by this confounded *dramatization* of the Xmas Book," he wrote in 1846 about *The Battle of Life*. "Unless I had come to London I do not think there would have been much hope of the version being more than just tolerated—even that, doubtful" (Pilgrim *Letters* [12/19/46], 4: 680). He could not allow the creatures of his imagination to be just tolerated, and so somehow he found time to help. He felt his hard work on the *The Battle of Life* production paid off:

The scenery and dresses are very good indeed. . . . The great change from the

ball-room to the snowy night is most effective, and both the departure and the
return will tell, I think, strongly on an audience. I have made them very quick
and excited in the passionate scenes, and so have infused some appearance of
life into those parts of the play. But I can't make a Marion, and Miss May is
awfully bad. She is a mere nothing all through.

(Pilgrim *Letters* [12/21/46], 4: 682)

Drama, as means of conveying creatures of the imagination, obviously had
its own defects, when Dickens was not the performer. But he kept trying;
when he wrote to Robert Keeley that he could not supply a prologue to the
rendering of *Martin Chuzzlewit*, he added, "I will gladly come down at any
time you may appoint . . . and go through it with you all" (Pilgrim *Letters*
[6/22/44], 4: 150).

One or two of Dickens' letters convey a sense of pleasure taken in such
work, but Forster says that on the whole these "efforts to assist special
representations were mere attempts to render more tolerable what he had no
power to prevent" (IV: iii, 305). Unable to halt a production of *A Tale of
Two Cities*, he "devoted myself for a fortnight to the trying to infuse into the
conventionalities of the Theatre, something not usual there in the way of Life
and Truth" (Forster, X: ix, 324). When Benjamin Webster, whom he admired,
brought out a version of *The Haunted Man*, Dickens begged him not to
perform it, saying he was "quite persuaded and convinced that if you bring
the piece out tomorrow night, it will not succeed" because of its "slovenly
and imperfect state" (Pilgrim *Letters* [12/18/48], 5: 459) The play was a
success, but only because, as Dickens wrote Angela Burdett Coutts, "I discovered yesterday that barbarous murder was being done upon me at the
Adelphi, and was fain to go down there and pass the day in bettering their
interpretation of my haunted friend" (Pilgrim *Letters* [12/19/48], 5: 460).

T. E. Pemberton gives us an idea of the kind of thing that must have driven
wild the author who could not bear to have the reality of his imagination
mangled: in one performance of *The Chimes*, he said, "the actress who was
to play the blind girl, Bertha, was suddenly taken ill, and unable to appear;
but the stage-manager was equal to the occasion, and sent on another young
lady *to read her part!!!*" (172). Little wonder that Dickens described himself
as being "direfully slaughtered" by such productions, called the cast of one
performance "black despair and moody madness," and, at a performance of
Nicholas Nickleby at the Surrey, "in the middle of the first scene . . . laid
himself down upon the floor in a corner of the box and never rose from it
until the drop-scene fell" (Pilgrim *Letters* [11/27/46], 4: 663). Watching the
rehearsal of another version of the same novel, he objected to "sundry choice

sentiments and rubbish regarding the little robins in the fields which have been put in the little boy's mouth by Mr. Stirling the adapter'' (Forster, II: iv, 100). Dickens quotes some of the sentiments: ''I've heard that good people that live away from this place feed the pretty harmless robins when the cold days and dark nights are on—perhaps they would feed me too, for I am very harmless—very. I'll run to them at once, and ask them.'' Mrs. Keeley, who played Smike, is supposed to have said, ''I shall never forget Dickens' face when he heard me repeating these lines. Turning to the prompter he said, 'Damn the robins; cut them out' '' (Pilgrim *Letters* [1/23?/38], 1: 459, and see note).

But if Dickens would gladly have cut out all the adaptations of his novels that disgraced the stage in his time, clearly it was because of their poor quality, not their dramatic representation of his fiction. He himself was largely responsible for the dramatization of one of the novels of his master, Scott; it was his desire, he said, ''to put Scott, for once, upon the stage in his own gallant manner.'' The performance was ''*an enormous success*,'' in good part because ''there is scarcely a movement throughout, or a look, that is not indicated by Scott. So you get a life romance with beautiful illustrations, and I do not expect ever again to see a book take up its bed and walk in like manner'' (Hogarth *Letters* [1/6/66], 2: 286). Dickens did not make allusions to his Lord lightly; there was for him a true sense of the miraculous in the realization of the novel upon the stage. (The quotation suggests, too, something of a sense of the need of the novel to complete itself by the miraculous transformation.) Frustrated by the failure of others to come close to doing for him what he helped do for Scott, he at last decided to do it for himself: he would adapt and produce and act in his own stories.

It has been assumed that Dickens gave the series of readings in the last years of his life because 1) he wanted to make money; 2) he loved contact with an audience, and delighted in their applause; and 3) his marital life was in such disarray that he sought escape in any kind of activity, and may even in the exhausting schedule he set for himself, while in increasingly poor health, have sought death. One more reason must be added: Dickens believed passionately in his mythic reality, searched all his life for means by which to render it ever more completely and intelligibly to his audience, and found in his readings a vehicle for realizing it, even beyond the combined powers of his prose and his artists' illustrations.

Few men or women are perfectly happy in their work; nearly all know moments of ennui, frustration, erosion, and despair. Dickens loved his desk and pen as much as any writer, but on a surprising number of occasions he declared his dissatisfaction with his occupation. Writing was imprisoning anguish: "Men have been chained to hideous prison walls and other strange anchors 'ere now, but few have known such suffering and bitterness at one time or another, as those who have been bound to Pens" (Pilgrim *Letters* [6/2/43], 3: 500). Facing the task was particularly trying: beginning his favorite novel, *David Copperfield*, he wrote that "deepest despondency, as usual, in commencing, besets me" (Pilgrim *Letters* [2/49], 5: 494). He described his condition while beginning a work: "sitting, frowning horribly at a quire of paper, and falling into a state of inaccessibility and irascibility which utterly confounds and scares the House" (Pilgrim *Letters* [10/5/48], 5: 419). To end a novel, on the other hand, made him sad: finishing *Bleak House*, he said he felt "sorrowful, which is rather the tendency of my mind at the close of another long book" (Hogarth *Letters* [8/27/53], 1: 364).

He spoke constantly of the restlessness he felt when he tried to write: "I go wandering about at night into the strangest places, according to my usual propensity at such a time—seeking rest, and finding none" (Pilgrim *Letters* [3/2/46], 5: 419). As he was first thinking of *Bleak House*, he said that, "I sit down between whiles to think of a new story, and, as it begins to grow, such a torment of a desire to be anywhere but where I am; and to be going I don't know where, I don't know why; takes hold of me, that it is like being *driven away*" (Forster, VI: vi, 96). To another friend at the same time he wrote of beginning to write as a kind of illness: "Violent restlessness, and vague ideas of going I don't know where, I don't know why, are the present symptoms of the disorder" ([8/17/52], Johnson, *Heart of Dickens*, 184). He seemed impelled like the Ancient Mariner to describe this anguished state, especially endured as he began a novel:

> At such a time I am as infirm of purpose as Macbeth, as errant as Mad Tom, and as ragged as Timon. I sit down to work, do nothing get up [sic] and walk a dozen miles, come back and sit down again next day, again do nothing and get up, go down a railroad, find a place where I resolve to stay for a month, come home next morning, go strolling about for hours and hours, reject all engagements to have time to myself, get tired of myself yet can't come out of myself to be pleasant to anybody else, and go on turning upon the same wheel round and round and over and over again until it may begin to roll me toward my end.   (*Nonesuch Letters* [5/4/55], 2: 658)

He often spoke, too, of the difficulties he had in writing. Driven by his restlessness to walk eighteen miles under a hot sun, he felt ill and "could as soon eat the cliff as write about anything" (Pilgrim Letters [8/29?/43], 3: 547). Trying to write in Paris, he told Forster that he "Couldn't begin, in the strange place; took a violent dislike to my study, and came down into the drawing-room; couldn't find a corner that would answer my purpose; fell into black contemplation of the waning month; sat six hours at a stretch, and wrote as many lines'' (Pilgrim *Letters* [12/6/46], 4: 622). Sometimes he blamed his state on his location: staying in a friend's house near Kensington, he said, ''This odious little house seems to have stifled and darkened my invention'' (Forster, IX: v, 292). When he began *Bleak House*, he said that ''It is dreadfully difficult to work at the new book on these dull days'' of January ([1/13/52], Johnson, *Heart of Dickens*, 193).

It was not always easy to see what he wished to write down. Having difficulty with the sixth number of *Dombey and Son*, he hoped, ''Perhaps I shall get a rush of inspiration'' (Pilgrim *Letters* [2/7/47], 5: 675). Sometimes the muse would not come: ''I have been, and am, trying to work this morning; but I can't make anything of it, and am going out to think'' (Pilgrim *Letters* [7/28/49], 5: 583). (Thinking, we remember, was the force behind the fairy wand.) Working on *Bleak House*, he lamented his inability to ''grind sparks out of this dull blade'' (Forster, VII: ii, 123). And while trying to see something for *Hard Times*, he experienced ''a great pressure of Wooden-Head-edness on gifted author'' ([4/20/54], Lehmann, 128). When he succeeded in seeing and writing down, the effect was debilitating: ''There are some things in the next 'Copperfield' that I think better than any that have gone before. After I have been believing such things with all my heart and soul, two results always ensue: first, I can't write plainly to the eye; secondly, I can't write sensibly to the mind'' (Hogarth *Letters* [9/24/50], 1: 263). So much so that his P. S. declared him ''not equal to the flourish'' under his signature. ''What a dream it is,'' he wrote to Macready, ''this work and strife, and how little we do in the dream after all. Only last night in my sleep, I was bent upon getting over a perspective of barriers, with my hands and feet bound. Pretty much what we are all about, waking, I think?'' (Hogarth *Letters* [3/15/58], 2: 53). Pretty much what he experienced when trying to see and write down, certainly.

More and more, in the last years, Dickens expressed dissatisfaction with his work. ''I have grown hard to satisfy, and write very slowly, and I have so much bad fiction, that *will* be thought of when I don't want to think of it, that I am forced to take more care than I ever took.'' Possibly, at the end, he even came to dislike his task. While he was working on *The Mystery of Edwin Drood*, George Dolby asked him ''how he liked returning to the writing of a serial story, and he replied at once that he 'missed the pressure' of former days; which I took to mean that as his circumstances were comfortable now, the work was irksome'' (435). Was the pressure that of making money? Some years earlier, Dickens associated the pains of writing with a greater need: getting ready to start *Bleak House*, he told Mary Boyle, "This is one of what I call my wandering days before I fall to work. I seem to be always looking at such times for something I have not found in life" (Hogarth *Letters* [7/22/52], 1: 326). His son Henry wrote that his father "was haunted at times . . . by a dread of failure, or of a sudden waning of his imaginative powers" (repr. Collins, *Interviews*, 1: 159).

Is all this, after all, no more than most writers feel as they undergo the agony of creating? Perhaps, but not many writers have been so driven to express so often and so darkly the pangs of giving birth. Probably not all writers find the sense of suffering, of inadequacy, increasing through their careers, certainly not when the last work they complete is as great as *Our Mutual Friend*. But an examination of the dates of the above quotations indicates an increasing dissatisfaction: before the 1840s, Dickens had hardly a word of complaint; afterwards, he speaks ever more frequently of his restlessness, his pain, his ill moods, the difficulty of writing, the need for inspiration, the greater difficulty in pleasing himself, and the yearning for something. One thing is certain: during these years, despite his statement to Forster that he "had never thought of the stage but as a means of getting" money (I: iv, 50), he told many people that he not only thought often of a career in the theater, but sometimes said that he would have preferred it to that which he chose. "I have often thought," he wrote Forster in 1844, "that I should certainly have been as successful on the boards as I have been between them" (Pilgrim *Letters* [12/30–31?/44], 244). He told Grace Greenwood that "he believed he had more talent for the drama than for literature, as he certainly had more delight in acting than in any other work whatever" (repr. Collins, *Interviews*, 2: 236) In 1842 he wrote "that nature intended me for the lessee of a National Theatre—and that pen ink and paper have spoiled a Manager" (Pilgrim *Letters* [5/21/44], 3: 244). "I have always had a misgiving, in my inmost heart, that I was born to be the manager of a Theatre. And now, I am quite sure of it" (Pilgrim *Letters* [9/27/45], 390).

When he finished a long and exhausting job of producing, directing, and acting in an amateur performance, instead of sighing with relief, he was unhappy:

> I have no energy whatever—I am very miserable. I loathe domestic hearths. I yearn to be a Vagabond.
>   Why can't I marry Mary! Why have I seven children—not engaged at sixpence a night apiece, and dismissible for ever, if they tumble down, but taken on for

an indefinite time at a vast expence, and never—no, never, never—wearing
lighted candles round their heads!
   I am deeply miserable.
   A real house like this, is insupportable after that canvass [sic] farm wherein
I was so happy. What is a humdrum dinner at half past five, with nobody (but
John) to see me eat it, compared with *that* soup, and the hundreds of pairs of
eyes that watched its disappearance!   (Pilgrim *Letters* [11/47], 701)

The call to another amateur production, he said, "stirs my blood like a
trumpet" (Nonesuch *Letters* [9/30/50], 224).

Months before he died, he expressed his desire once more; Charles Kent
tells the famous story:

   Going round by way of Lambeth one afternoon, in the early summer of 1870,
   we had skirted the Thames along the Surrey bank, had crossed the river higher
   up, and on our way back, were returning at our leisure through Westminster,
   when, just as we were approaching the shadow of the old Abbey at Poet's
   Corner, under the roof-beams of which he was so soon to be laid in his grave,
   with a rain of tears and flowers, he abruptly asked, "What do you think would
   be the realization of one of my most cherished day-dreams?" adding instantly,
   without waiting for my answer, "To settle down for the remainder of my life
   within easy distance of a great theatre, in the direction of which I should hold
   supreme authority."   (263–264)

IV

   Everyone dreams of finding a thing to do that is less wearisome and more
rewarding, but when such dreams are the idle wishes of the moment, the
dreamer usually does not know much about the other something (which is
why it seems better). Dickens knew all there was to know about drama. On
more than one occasion he spoke of the exhausting labor it required, and of
the frustration and disappointment it could create. Yet he was drawn always
to the stage, and as years passed he seemed more and more attracted, for all
the irritation he expressed to Forster, to the idea of having his own work
represented upon it. Gradually, he worked his way toward the idea—overriding
the objections of such friends as Forster and Angela Burdett Coutts—of
eliminating the objections to such representation (the poor adaptation and
poor performances) by taking on the task himself.
   He had always enjoyed reading from his works. As we have seen, he read
to his illustrators; he also read to Forster to get his critical reaction; and he
read to groups of friends for mutual pleasure, the most famous occasion
probably being that sketched by Maclise in 1844, when he read from *The*

Chimes. To convey meaning in this way to his reader, to perceive that he comprehended—that was what Dickens wanted. "It was as if," said Edmund Wilson, "he had actually to embody, to act out in his own person, the life of his imagination" (59). If Dickens was, as some have argued, challengeable as actor in the plays of others but supreme in his own readings, this is surely the reason. (For some, it should be noted, Dickens' acting was also characterized by the ability to reach his audience, to make them feel. A review of his performance as Richard Wardour in *The Frozen Deep* said that

> Mr. Dickens has all the technical knowledge and resources of a professional Actor; but these, the dry bones of acting, are kindled by that soul of vitality which can only be put into them by the man of Genius, and the interpreter of the affections. . . . Altogether, the audience return home from Tavistock House rather indisposed for some time to come to be content with the time-honoured conventionalities of the public stage [*The Leader* (1/10/57); repr. Collins, *Interviews*, 2: 239–240].)

Several perceptive members of Dickens' reading audience employed analogies to art to describe the effects he achieved. We have seen how Dickens attempted to use illustrations to realize his characters beyond the limits of fiction; now some of those who heard his readings seemed to feel that he was picturing his imagined world in another but similar way. The *Cheltenham Examiner* spoke of a scene in *Nicholas Nickleby* that "was 'painted' " by his reading "with a vividness and pathos which told with thrilling effect" ([1/8/62]; repr. Collins, *Public Readings*, 251). The *Scotsman* said of his readings that "His works could have no more perfect illustrator" ([12/8/68]; repr. Collins, *Readings*, xlvii). Kent went beyond illustration: Dickens' description of scenes "were not simply word-painting," he said, "but realization" (repr. Collins, *Interviews*, 2: 246). And later commentators, attempting to convey the effect of his readings, also have referred to art. Philip Collins concluded from his extensive study of commentary on the readings that "To hear [Dickens] read, instead of reading the book oneself, was like meeting someone instead of getting a letter from him—or like seeing a stereoscopic instead of a two-dimensional photograph, or a great painting instead of an engraving of it" (*Readings*, lv).

Like illustration in the books, the reading platform became for Dickens a medium for conveying what his daughter Kate called the "excessive realism of his mental vision," which made whatever he read about so real for him that he sometimes disliked illustrations of books he had previously read because "the picture in his mind was often so vivid as to preclude the possibility of its being conceived in any other way'' (Perugini, 129). That which he "really did not" imagine but "saw," and then tried to realize by writing down and by using drawings, he now attempted to realize by acting. By most accounts, he realized superbly. Kent said that "he realized everything in his own mind so intensely, that listening to him we realized what he spoke of by sympathy" (repr. Collins, *Interviews*, 1: 124 . Turgenev said that "there were several first-class actors in his face alone who made you laugh and cry" (Collins, *Readings*, lviii), and Charles Kent said that he brought conviction and reality even

> to the very least among the minor characters. . . . A great fat man with a monstrous chin, for example, was introduced just momentarily in the briefest street-dialogue, towards the close of [*A Christmas Carol*], who had only to open his lips once or twice for an instant, yet whose individuality was in that instant or two so thoroughly realized, that he lives ever since then in the hearer's remembrance. When, in reply to some one's inquiry, as to what was the cause of Scrooge's (presumed) death?—this great fat man with the monstrous chin answered, with a yawn, in two words, "God knows!"—he was before us there, as real as life, as selfish, and as substantial.   (95)

Dickens had done for the fat man what the actor described on his Christmas tree had done for the peasant: made him real to the viewer.

George Dolby said that Dickens took "scarcely less pleasure and delight in his public readings than in the pursuit of his legitimate calling" (447); I wonder if he did not take at least as much—I almost dare say more. Once, to Edmund Yates, he himself said that he did. He would like, he told Yates, to have been a great actor. But you are a great novelist, Yates protested. "That's all very well," Dickens replied, "but I would rather have been a great actor, and had the public at my feet" (Collins, *Interviews*, 2: 205). The final image is uncharacteristic: Dickens always hated the lionizing process, and surely did not mean at his feet to worship, but to hear. The readings gave him, in any case, what the novels could not. Writing to Forster, who had always opposed the public readings, he said, "I must do *something*, or I shall wear my heart away. I can see no better thing to do that is half so hopeful in itself, or half so well suited to my restless state" (*Life*, Ley Edition, 646; repr. Collins, *Readings*, xx). To Wilkie Collins he wrote that he wanted to "escape from myself. For, when I *do* start up and stare myself seedily in the face, as happens to be my case at present, my blankness is inconceivable—indescribable—my misery amazing" (Collins *Letters* [8/29/57], 81). Forster and all his followers have attributed this "restless state" solely to the marital troubles of the time, and no doubt the readings were a relief from that unhappiness: Philip Collins points out that Dickens' first private reading from his work in 1847 and his return to the idea of public readings in 1857–58 both coincided with troubles in his private life (*Readings*, xxi). But great as those troubles were, they may not have been the sole cause of his unhappiness. Forster himself says that in the mid-1850s Dickens' "books had lost for the time the importance they formerly had over every other consideration in his life" (*Life*, Ley edition, 646; repr. Collins, *Readings*, xxi). No doubt there were several reasons for this; I suspect that one was the frustration he felt with the limitations of his art, the desire to find some impossible medium that could establish immediate contact with his audience, and could convey more powerfully than his novels his own imaginative reality. If so, how well we may now understand the irresistible attraction readings had for him—so irresistible, many believe, that he died rather than give them up. Here was his desire, realized; here were his characters, "before us there, as real as life . . . and as substantial." Dickens had finally found the way, even beyond the art of illustration, to show his readers what he meant. The *New York Tribune* saw his readings as "only the natural outgrowth of what he has been doing all the days of his life. To have heard these readings is to have witnessed the spontaneous expression of a great nature in the maturity of its genius" ([12/10 & 11/67]; repr. Collins, *Readings*, liii). In *David Copperfield*, Agnes tells David how his "old friends . . . read my book as if they heard me speaking its contents." When he wrote his books, as we learn from several anecdotes, Dickens often wrote out loud; G. H. Lewes said that "Dickens once declared to me that every word said by his characters was distinctly *heard* by him" (*Interviews*, 1: 25).

Dickens would seem to have been an even better actor in his own roles than in those written by others: as Angus Wilson says, "accounts differ" (94) about his performances in amateur productions, but though there were adverse criticisms of his readings, as well, opinion varied far less. Admiration began with "the cunningly contrived and admirably lighted platform, which was the outcome of his keen eye for theatrical effect" (Pemberton, 135), and ended with the entire performance—"a whole tragic comic heroic *theatre* visible, performing under one *hat*" (Froude, 2: 270), as Carlyle put it. Charles Kent said he indeed had the power of the Ancient Mariner to mesmerize his audience (97). Edgar Johnson goes into more detail:

> In the public readings of Dickens's last dozen years he attained to the very peak of his career as a dramatist and actor. The dramas and the comedies he himself enacted, alone on his own stage, were indeed dealt with according to his own pleasure and his own judgment, for he molded them out of his own

writings, and the players, "a skilled and noble company," every member of which was his own protean self, were absolutely under his command. In essence, he had achieved his "cherished day-dream" of holding supreme authority over a great theater.   *(Theatrical Reader, 357)*

Several reviewers join Kent in refuting—at least for the readings—Forster's contention that Dickens' ability was limited to the comic: the *Scotsman* said that in his readings "he was as clever a comedian" as Charles Mathews, but with "a power of pathos to which even that most versatile of players has not the slightest pretension. Hence his reading is not only as good as a play, but far better than most plays, for it is all in the best style of acting" (*Scotsman* [11/28/61]; repr. Collins, *Readings*, xvii). Professor Adolphus Ward also thought him as good in "pathetic" roles as in humorous, but argued that "he isolated his parts too sharply" (repr. Collins, *Readings*, lxi) which I take to mean that he tried too hard to make his characters distinct from each other—no doubt because he took pride in his ability to do so, but also because he wanted so much to make clear to all what he meant by each. Several reviewers commented on this ability: Dickens "to an extraordinary extent assumes the personality of each," and "All the characters seem to live" (Priestly; repr. Collins, *Readings*, 4). His face, said Leigh Hunt, had "the life and soul of fifty human beings" (Patterson; repr. Collins, *Interviews*, 1: 20).

Professional actors apparently approved as much of Dickens' theater in a hat as did laymen. Early in 1870, among twelve scheduled readings, he gave three in the morning so that actors could attend. Dolby said that "He succeeded, to perfection, in the presence even of so thoroughly critical an audience" (442). The great Charles Macready—who was, as Philip Collins notes, a severe judge of actors—said that Dickens "reads as well as an experienced actor would," and was heard "undisguisedly sobbing and crying" (Collins, *Readings*, lvii) at the private reading of *The Chimes*. After hearing readings from *David Copperfield*, Macready was rendered speechless, Dickens says, and finally managed:

> No—er—Dickens! I swear to Heaven that, as a piece of passion and playfulness—er-indescribably mixed up together, it does-er-no, really, Dickens!—amaze me as profoundly as it moves me. But as a piece of art—and you know—er—that I—no, Dickens! By—! have seen the best art in a great time—it is incomparable to me. How is it got at—er—how is it done—er-how one man can—well? It lays me on my—er—back, and it is of no use talking about it!(*Nonesuch Letters*, 3: 276–277)

He wrote that it was "altogether a truly artistic performance" (Nevil Macready; repr. Collins, *Interviews* 1: 31). And when he heard the Sikes-Nancy scene, he could say no more than "in my—er—best times—er—you remember them, my dear boy—er—gone, gone!—no, it comes to this—er—TWO MACBETHS!" (*Nonesuch Letters*, 3: 704).

As in all things, one of the keys to Dickens' success as reader was hard work. Dolby said that "seldom . . . do we find a man gifted with such extraordinary powers, and, at the same time, possessed of such a love of method, such will, such energy, and such a capacity for taking pains." In preparation for his reading at St. James's Hall in 1866, Dolby said, Dickens rehearsed "considerably over two-hundred times" (8) in less than three months. Of the first fifty readings he got up for public performance he wrote to Forster that he had "*learnt them all*, so as to have no mechanical drawback in looking after the words. I have tested all the serious passion in them by everything I know; made the humorous points much more humorous; corrected my utterance of certain words; cultivated a self-possession not to be disturbed; and made myself master of the situation" (Forster, VIII: vii, 258). When did he not? Only once did he find himself "out" of a part, and this he caught well in advance of the performance. "Imagine my being so entirely out of 'Dombey'," he wrote Wills from Paris, "that I have been obliged to go down this morning and rehearse it in the room" (Lehmann [1/29/63], 324).

But another factor in his success was the ability to make his stories real to his audiences; it was a delight to him that he could do so, and he reveled in their responses to him both as creator and performer. It was, after all, the ability many of his readers admired in his novels. "What a power he has," Macready exclaimed, "of penetrating his reader with his idea" (Pollock; repr. Collins, *Interviews*, 1: 31). The same was said of his speeches: they "seemed to come from the very heart of the speaker and to go straight to the heart of the listener" (McCarthy; repr. Collins, *Interviews*, 2: 295). To Maclise, who had expressed his appreciation of Dickens' acting of Richard Wardour in *The Frozen Deep*, he said, "the interest of such a character to me is that it enables me, as it were *to write a book in company* instead of in my own solitary room, and to feel its effect coming freshly back upon me from the reader" (Dupee, *Letters* [11/3/51], 191).

To convey meaning in this way to his reader, to perceive that he comprehended—that was what Dickens wanted.

Critical response to the readings lends support to the idea that they improved his audience's understanding of his work. It was said that his performance of *The Chimes* "added much to his admirers' awareness of the qualities to be found in this story" (Collins, *Readings*, 77). (Philip Collins, from whom

I take this quotation, expresses surprise that, in view of the comparatively limited success of *The Chimes* as a reading, Dickens spent so much time revising it; perhaps the reason lies in his conviction that the reading revealed qualities not previously found.) Kent said that when he read he disappeared, and his characters stood before them; the minor characters, whom "no one had ever realized" before hearing him read, came "with the surprise of a revelation" (repr. Collins, *Interviews*, 2: 245). Whittier thought that hearing him act his character was "as if their original creator had breathed life into them" (Pollard; repr. Collins, *Interviews*, 2: 300). Kate Field attested to Dickens' ability to bring his characters to life; after seeing his reading from *Dombey and Son* she said of Toots,

> You may have loved him since childhood, . . . but until you have made acquaintance through the medium of Dickens, you have no idea how he looks or how he talks. When Toots puts his thumb in his mouth, looks sheepish, and roars forth "How are you?" I feel as the man in the play must feel when, for the first time, he recognizes his long-lost brother.
>
> (70; repr. Collins, *Readings*, 128)

One critic said that in Dickens' reading of "Sikes and Nancy" Fagin "seems actually before us" (*Glasgow Daily Herald* [2/23/69]; repr. Collins, *Readings*, 469); another wrote of Dickens' performance of Nancy that "Here the acting of Mr. Dickens is much beyond his writing" (*Bath Chronicle* [2/4/69]; repr. Collins, *Readings*, 469). Still another asserted that the readings lent greater reality to certain scenes which were deficient in that quality in the novels; in "Bardell and Pickwick," Dickens had "succeeded in giving the scene an air of probability which in the original version it does not wear" (*Chester Chronicle* [1/26/67]; repr. Collins, *Readings*, 197). Collins notes that in this reading Dickens' "conception of the characters differed significantly from the usual interpretations" (*Readings*, 197); it is as if Dickens were saying, "No, *this* is how what I have written should be understood." Kent thought his reading of the storm scene from *David Copperfield* brought to the listener the violence of the episode better than the novel could do; it "was the realization to his hearers . . . of a convulsion of nature" (repr. Collins, *Readings*, 217). Good scenes became great ones: "What has struck you heretofore as a diamond no better than its fellows is magically transformed into a Kohinoor. And when I say 'magically transformed,' I mean it in all soberness" (Field, 92). Lesser things were improved: a reviewer said that hearing Dickens reading "Barbox Brothers" made it "very much more agreeable and interesting than a private perusal" (*Yorkshire Post* [2/1/67]; repr. Collins, *Readings*, 422).

Though Turgenev admired Dickens' reading, he contrasted it to that of Gogol, who "did not seem to care whether there were any listeners or what they were thinking of" (Collins, *Readings*, lviii). Several viewers objected to Dickens' tendency to the theatrical. But if he strove for effect, perhaps the term *theatrical* in its pejorative sense is not appropriate: the difference between Dickens and Gogol is not that one loved his work and lost himself in its reading to the exclusion of his audience while the other sought merely to impress, but that Gogol was content with making his reading perfect unto itself while Dickens believed that no performance—written or spoken—could approach perfection unless it reached its audience, unless it produced a re-action that was both emotional and cognitive. Members of his reading audience testify again and again how penetratingly he had done this. "I was dreaming dreams," the novelist Dick Donovan (J. E. Preston Murdock) said. "Charles Dickens had carved his name on my heart. . . . He seemed to . . . stir within me feelings and desires of which up to then I had only had a vague con-sciousness" (Kent, 95). Robert Lytton (the poet Owen Meredith) wrote Dick-ens: "You play with the heart . . . as tho' it were a creature of your own construction" (Collins, *Readings*, 218).

None of this is to say, of course, that Dickens was not also drawn to the reading stage by the attraction one supposes many authors must feel: simple applause. In many places, some of which we have already seen, Dickens wrote of the tremendous appeal audience response had for him. When Douglas Jerrold facetiously supposed that Dickens had given up *Martin Chuzzlewit* in order to write a comedy, he replied,

> I have my comedy to fly to. My only comfort! I walk up and down the street at the back of the Theatre every night, and peep in at the Green Room Win-dow—thinking of the time when "Dick—ins" will be called for, by excited hundreds, and won't come, 'till Mr. Webster . . . shall enter from his dressing room, and quelling the tempest with a smile, beseech that Wizard if he be in the house (here he looks up at my box) to accept the congratulations of the audience. . . . Then I shall come forward and bow—once—twice—thrice—Roars of approbation—Brayvo—Brarvo—Hooray—Hoorar—Hooroar—one cheer more. (Pilgrim *Letters* [8/13/43], 3: 510)

It is facetious, certainly, but it does not mask nor does it intend to mask the real pleasure Dickens would take were such a thing to occur. It hardly occurred as he imagined it, ever, for him as dramatist, but it did for him as actor, and did as much as could ever have been dreamed for him as reader of his own works. But the pleasure lay not merely in the applause; it came also from the comprehension.

Even on the reading platform, however, Dickens had some difficulties in showing what he meant. Even in this joining of the powers of fiction and stage, he did not create the perfect medium with which to reach his audience. He experienced two major difficulties. First, as some criticisms we have already seen have indicated, in his desire to realize his imagination he pressed too hard. Some readers have felt the same way about his novels, and have attributed the pressing to a similar motive. If in his works "the desire for effect [was] too obstructive," said G. H. Lewes, it was owing to his effort to use his "power effectively" to reach and improve "the lot of the miserable Many" ("Dickens in Relation to Criticism," *Fortnightly Review* [1872] 16; repr. Collins, *Interviews*, 2: 241). In his readings, said Francesco Berger, "he allowed himself certain mannerisms of voice and gesture which in the theatre, he would not have resorted to." A reviewer argued that in the pathetic passages of the readings Dickens was "too effective—too stagey, in fact" (*Scotsman* [11/28/61]; repr. Collins, *Readings*, lix). Kent, who loved everything Dickens did, wished that his voice as Bob Crachitt, crying for Tiny Tim, had been "a shade less dramatic" (repr. Collins, *Interviews*, 2: 255). In his reading of "The Poor Traveler," said *The Saturday Review*, he used "a series of little turns or tricks adopted by which an idea is continually brought round and round, and forced upon the attention. . . . Mr. Dickens . . . threw out the whole strength of his power of reading to make them tell. . . . He has . . . thrown away the genuine success he might have achieved, by having recourse to the paltry artifices of stage effect" ([6/19/58]; repr. Collins, *Readings*, 154). This straining for effect has been interpreted as a simple attempt to impress, to draw applause. There was, R. H. Hutton said, "something a little ignoble in this extravagant relish of a man of genius for the evidence of the popularity of his writings. Dickens must have known that theatrical effects are by no means the best gauge of the highest literary fame" (*Spectator* [2/7/74] 175; repr. Collins, *Readings*, lxii). So important a contemporary scholar as Philip Collins agrees with Hutton: "It is a judgment . . . which must carry some weight" (*Readings*, lxii). Perhaps, but the load is lessened, surely, by what we have seen. Before an audience that could understand him, Dickens eschewed mere theatrical effects in his readings, and sought apperception at least as much as he sought approbation. Mr. Collins himself attests to this: "many accounts," he says, ". . . show that he gave his audiences that enriched sense of the power and subtlety of a text which a critical commentary attempts to convey by analysis and argument" (*Readings*, lxiii). Disliking exegesis as he did, Dickens provided it for his novels only by acting them. In his criticism of Dickens for striving for effect,

R. H. Hutton also unintentionally explained why he did: Dickens, he said, "had too much eye to the effect to be produced by all he did. . . . He makes you feel that it is not the intrinsic insight that delights him half so much as the power it gives him of moving the world. The visible word of command must go forth from himself in connection with all his creations" (Collins, *Readings*, lviii). In popular plays, Dickens certainly did appreciate stage effects, but he never confused them with good art, and if at times he used them in his readings, it was not owing to poor judgment or to the desire for a cheaply-bought reaction, that made him do so. Hutton's last sentence provides the key: for Dickens the play was not in itself the thing, but only the thing by which he might catch the imagination of his audience. To put it more accurately, it was not a Mousetrap; it was a portal to his mythic reality, and he used what he had to use to draw his listeners through it.

Dickens' second problem in his readings was that in his effort to go beyond his own novels he encountered the same kind of difficulty which he had so well defined years earlier, when his friend Macready had, after establishing himself as a tragic actor, taken on the comic role of Benedick. Among several problems, Dickens suggested that

> First impressions, too, even with persons of a cultivated understanding, have an immense effect in settling their notions of a character; and it is no heresy to say that many people unconsciously form their opinion of such a creation as *Benedick*, not so much from the exercise of their own judgment in reading the play, as from what they have seen bodily presented to them on the stage. Thus, when they call to mind that in such a place Mr. A. or Mr. B. used to stick his arms akimbo and shake his head knowingly; or that in such another place he gave the pit to understand, by certain confidential nods and winks, that in good time they should see what they should see; or in such another place, swaggered; or in such another place, with one hand clasping each of his sides, heaved his shoulders with laughter; they recall his image, not as the Mr. A. or B. aforesaid, but as Shakespeare's *Benedick*—the real *Benedick* of the book, not the conventional *Benedick* of the boards—and missing any familiar action, miss, as it were, something of right belonging to the part ("Macready as Benedick," *Examiner* [3/4/43]; repr. *Collected Papers*, 1: 144).

Reviewers and students of Dickens' readings have noted a similar problem. When he undertook such favorites as Mrs. Gamp or Sam Weller, Collins says, "audiences were easily disappointed by the outcome . . . if it clashed with their own cherished notions of how the character must be played" (*Readings*, 184). The imaginations of the readers of Dickens' novels created the same difficulty for him as earlier actors had made for Macready: they created pictures with which he was forced to compete. Doubtless this was the difficulty one Bostonian had with Dickens' presentation of Sam. In the first reading of 1867 in that city, George Dolby observed a man leaving the theater early, and thinking that he might be ill, asked what was wrong. The man responded,

> "Say, who's that man on the platform reading?"
> "Mr. Charles Dickens," I replied.
> "But that ain't the *real* Charles Dickens, the man as wrote all them books I've been reading all these years."
> "The same."
> After a moment's pause, as if for thought, he replied, "Wall, all I've got to say about it then is, that he knows no more about Sam Weller 'n a cow does of pleatin' a shirt, at all events that ain't *my* idea of Sam Weller, anyhow."   (176)

The painter W. P. Frith agreed with the Bostonian:

> It seems a bold thing for me to say, but I felt very strongly that the author had totally misconceived the true character of one of his own creations. In reading the humorous repartees and quaint sayings of Sam Weller, Dickens lowered his voice to the tones of one who was rather ashamed of what he was saying, and afraid of being reproved for the freedom of his utterances. I failed in being able to reconcile myself to such a rendering of a character that of all other seemed to me to call for an exactly opposite treatment.   (1: 49–50)

(Frith conveyed this feeling to Dickens who, he said, subsequently changed his rendering of Sam.) John Hollingshead said that if Dickens' acting of Mrs. Gamp "fails to produce an impression upon the audience commensurate with its artistic merits, it is because the character . . . is so broadly and deeply impressed upon the printed page, that nearly every reader is able to build up for himself a clear idea of this great friend" (*Critic* [9/4/58]; repr. Collins, *Readings*, 184). Many viewers agreed: their ideas of Sam and Sairy had grown so in their own imaginations that not even Dickens could modify the imagined reality. As Adolphus Ward put it, Sam had "become to all of us a mythical personage incapable of realization in this imperfect world" (*Manchester Guardian* [2/4/67]; repr. Collins, *Readings*, 197).

In short, Dickens found himself, in his effort to go beyond his own novels, running into a catch-22: his very success as a writer in stirring the imaginations of his readers now blocked his further attempts to convey, through the greater immediacy of the stage, his own imagination. Not even Charles Dickens, seeking to bring to bear the combined forces of fiction, painting, and drama, could make imagination real. But the praises poured on his performances indicate that he came perhaps as close as human power can to freeing himself and others from the tyranny of the dull settled world. Intelligent critics like Kate Field commended his effort to combine fiction and theater. "Dickens," she said, "was as much born to read *Mr. Bob Sawyer's Party* as he was to create it" (Field, 92; repr. Collins, *Readings*, 365). For her, at least, Dickens managed to escape his own reality: in acting Justice Stareleigh, she said, "Dickens steps out of his own skin" (Field, 103; repr. Collins, *Readings*, 197).

Certainly Dickens was ever-alert to the reactions of his audiences, always sensitive to what they liked. After a reading from *Nicholas Nickleby* he said, "I am inclined to suspect that the impression of protection and hope derived from Nickleby's going away protecting Smike is exactly the impression—this is discovered by chance—that an Audience most likes to be left with" (Collins *Letters* [10/31/61], 106). But if he always tried to reach his listeners, he also seems to have expected them to hear intelligently, perceptively. It is significant that in the readings success appears often to have been defined by the ability of Dickens' audience to get what he meant. One viewer was struck by this. "He depended, as I remember," said David Christie Murray, "in a most extraordinary degree upon the temper of his audience. I have heard him read downright flatly and badly to an unresponsive house, and I have seen him vivified and quickened to the most extraordinary display of genius by an audience of the opposite kind" (50). This does not sound like the performance of a man who read merely to acquire evidence of his popularity. Dickens' own comments upon his readings repeatedly concentrate upon whether or not his audiences got what he meant, on whether they found reality in his readings, as well as entertainment. "Among my English audiences," he said,

> I have had more clergymen than I ever saw in my life before. It is very curious to see how many people in black come to Little Dombey. And when it is over they almost uniformly go away as if the child were really Dead—with a hush upon them. They certainly laugh more at the Boots's story of the Little Elopement than at anything else; and I notice that they sit with their heads on one side, and an expression of playful pity on their faces—as if they saw the tiny boy and girl, which is tender and pleasant, I think? (Johnson, *Heart of Dickens* [8/23/58], 362–363).

"As if the child were really dead"; "as if they saw"; is it not as if what Dickens had, as he said to Forster, not imagined but really seen and written down—a reality that he felt compelled, indeed like the Ancient Mariner, to convey to others—had finally had its complete transmission to the mental vision of others?

Always the emphasis is upon getting a reaction from his audience, especially an unusual reaction—not merely enjoyment, certainly not just applause to swell his ego, but a special, understanding response. Edward Dowden said that Dickens' eye "kept roving throughout his audience from face to face, as if seeking for some expression of the effect he was creating" (quoted in *Dickensian* [1901] 5: 66; repr. Collins, *Readings*, lviii). Dowden's intent is to disparage, but perhaps it was not merely for response to effect that Dickens was looking; some of his viewers said that he strove not for effect but for truth: "Where an ordinary artist would look for 'points' of effect he looked for 'points' of truth" (quoted by Brannan, 82; repr. Collins, *Readings*, lx), one such reviewer remarked of his acting.

"I have made one reading from DC," Dickens wrote. " . . . It seems to have a strong interest, and an expression of a young spirit in it that addresses people of sensitive perception curiously" (Johnson, *Heart of Dickens* [11/3/61], 372). After he read it at Norwich, he wrote to Collins that "I don't think a word—not to say an idea—was lost" (Collins *Letters* [10/31/61], 106). After performing it and *A Christmas Carol* in Paris, he wrote to Wills that

> You have no idea what they made of me. I got things out of the old "Carol"—effects I mean—so entirely new and so very strong, that I quite amazed myself and wondered where I was going next. I really listened to Mr. Peggotty's narrative in "Copperfield" with admiration. When Little Emily's letter was read, a low murmur of irrepressible emotion went about like a sort of sea.
>
> (Lehmann [2/4/63], 328)

Charles Kent said that during the same Paris performances, when Dickens portrayed Steerforth sincerely shaking the hand of Peggotty, then condescendingly shaking the hand of Ham, he heard a Frenchman in the front row whisper "Ah-h!" "The sound of that one inarticulate monosyllable," said Kent, "as he observed when relating the circumstances, gave the Reader, as an artist, a far livelier sense of satisfaction than any . . . imparted by mere acclamations" (123–124). James T. Fields said that Dickens liked his Paris audience best because "it was the quickest to catch his meaning" (*Yesterdays;* repr. *Interviews*, 2: 315. In his reading at Sunderland, Dickens said, he did "a vast number of new things" because of the effect of "a rapturous audience . . . and the stage together: which I never can resist" (Lehmann [9/24/58], 246). "I can most seriously say," he wrote to Bulwer, "that all the sights of the earth turn pale in my eyes, before the sight of three thousand people with one heart among them, and no capacity in them, in spite of all their efforts, of sufficiently testifying to you how they believe you to be right" (*Nonesuch Letters*, 2: 377).

WORKS CITED

Brannan, Robert. *Under the Management of Mr. Charles Dickens: his Production of "The Frozen Deep."* Ithaca, N.Y.: Cornell University Press, 1966.

Carlton, William J. "Charles Dickens: Dramatic Critic," *Dickensian* (1/60) 56: 11–27.

Collected Papers of Charles Dickens. Arthur Waugh, Hugh Walpole, and Thomas Hatton, eds. 2 vols. Bloomsbury: Nonesuch Press, 1932.

Dickens, Henry Fielding. "A Chat about My Father," *Harper's Magazine* (1914), 129. Repr. in part in *Interviews and Recollections* (q.v.), to which volume and page in notes refer.

Dickens Theatrical Reader, The. Edgar and Eleanor Johnson, eds. Boston: Little, Brown, 1964.

Dolby, George. *Charles Dickens as I Knew Him.* 1885. Repr. London: Everett & Company, 1912.

Dupee, F. W. *The Selected Letters of Charles Dickens.* New York: Farrar, Straus, and Cudahy, 1960.

Field, Kate. *Pen Photographs of Charles Dickens's Readings.* 1871. Repr. in part in *Interviews and Recollections* (q.v.), to which volume and page in notes refer.

Fields, James T. *Yesterdays and Authors.* Boston, 1872. Repr. in part in *Interviews and Recollections* (q.v.), to which volume and page in notes refer.

Forster, John. *The Life of Charles Dickens.* Introduction by G. K. Chesterton. 2 vols. London: J. M. Dent, 1927. (Though in two volumes, the book repeats the original division into book and chapter; notes in this article cite by book, chapter, and page.)

Frith, W. P. *My Autobiography and Reminiscences.* 8th ed., 1890. Repr. in part in *Interviews and Recollections* (q.v.), to which volume and page notes refer.

Froude, J. A. *Thomas Carlyle: A History of His Life in London.* 1884. Repr. in part in *Interviews and Recollections* (q.v.), to which volume and page in notes refer.

Interviews and Recollections. Philip Collins, ed. 2 vols. London: Macmillan, 1981.

Greenwood, Grace. "Charles Dickens: Recollections of the Great Writer," *New York Daily Tribune* (7/5/70). Repr. in part in *Interviews and Recollections* (q.v.), to which volume and page in notes refer.

Johnson, Edgar. *The Heart of Charles Dickens.* Boston: Little, Brown and Company, 1952.

Kent, Charles. *Charles Dickens as a Reader.* 1872. Repr. New York: Haskell House Publishers, 1973.

Lehmann, R. C. *Charles Dickens as Editor.* New York: Sturgis and Walton, 1912.

Letters of Charles Dickens. Georgina Hogarth and Mary Dickens, eds. 2 vols. 1879.

Letters of Charles Dickens, The. Pilgrim Edition, Oxford: Clarendon Press. 5 vols. V. 1, Madeline House and Graham Storey, eds., 1965; v. 2, Madeline House and Graham Storey, eds., 1969; v. 3, Madeline House, Graham Storey, and Kathleen Tillotson, eds., 1974; v. 4, Kathleen Tillotson, ed., 1977; v. 5, Graham Storey and K. J. Fielding, eds., 1981.

Letters of Charles Dickens to Wilkie Collins. Laurence Hutton, ed. New York: Harper, 1892.

Macready, Nevil. *Annals of an Active Life.* 1924. Repr. in part in *Interviews and Recollections* (q.v.), to which volume and page in notes refer.

McCarthy, Justin. *Reminiscences.* 1899. Repr. in part in *Interviews and Recollections* (q.v.), to which volume and page in notes refer.

Murray, David Christie. *Recollections.* London: John Long, 1908.

Nonesuch Letters. The Collected Papers of Charles Dickens. Arthur Waugh, ed. 2 vols. Bloomsbury: Nonesuch Press, 1937.

Patterson, Clara Burdett. *Angela Burdett Coutts and the Victorians.* London: John Murray, 1953.

Payne, James. *Some Literary Reflections.* 1884. Repr. in part in *Interviews and Recollections* (q.v.), to which volume and page notes refer.

Pemberton, T. Edgar. *Charles Dickens and the Stage.* London: George Redway, 1888.

Perugini, Katherine. "Charles Dickens as a Lover of Art and Artists," *Magazine of Art* (1/1903) 27: 125–130; (2/1903) 164–169.

Pollard, John A. *John Greenleaf Whittier: Friend of Man.* Boston: 1949. Repr. in part in *Interviews and Recollections* (q.v.), to which volume and page in notes refer.

Pollock, Lady. *Macready as I Knew Him.* 1884. Repr. in part in *Interviews and Recollections* (q.v.), to which volume and page in notes refer.

Priestly, Lady. *The Story of a Lifetime.* 1904. Repr. in part in *Interviews and Recollections* (q.v.), to which volume and page in notes refer.

Public Readings of Charles Dickens, The. Philip Collins, ed. Oxford: Clarendon Press, 1975.

Speeches of Charles Dickens. K. J. Fielding, ed. Oxford: Clarendon Press, 1960.

Stone, Harry. *Uncollected Writings from Household Words.* 2 vols. Bloomington: Indiana University Press, 1968.

Ward, Adolphus. *Charles Dickens.* 1882. Repr. in part in *Interviews and Recollections* (q.v.), to which volume and page in notes refer.

Wilson, Angus. *The World of Charles Dickens.* New York: Viking, 1970.

Wilson, Edmund. "Dickens: the Two Scrooges," *The Wound and the Bow*. London: W. H. Allen, 1952; first pub. 1941.

Woolcott, Alexander. *Mr. Dickens Goes to the Play*. Port Washington, N. Y.: Kennikat Press, 1967; first pub. 1922.

Mark Twain and Dickens: Why the Denial?

Howard G. Baetzhold

In 1909, while discussing literary matters with his biographer Albert Bigelow Paine, Samuel Clemens remarked, "I don't know anything about anything, and never did. My brother used to try to get me to read Dickens long ago. I couldn't do it" (Paine, 1500–1501). He also once said, "When I was younger, I could remember anything, whether it happened or not; but I am getting old, and soon I shall remember only the latter." And another time: "It isn't so astonishing the number of things I can remember, as the number of things I can remember that aren't so" (1269). His memory of not being able to read Dickens (though he did except *A Tale of Two Cities*) was obviously one of the things he remembered that "wasn't so." His own writings show that he *had* read a very substantial portion of the Dickens canon and, consciously or unconsciously, had borrowed important elements for a number of his own works.[1]

Because of the denial, a word is necessary about Clemens' attitudes toward the matter of literary influences in general. Though he often denied such influences, and sometimes railed at plagiarism, he did admit the possibility of "unconscious" borrowing or "unconscious absorption." On one occasion, after telling his friend William Dean Howells how he had inadvertently stolen a story idea from Charles Dudley Warner, he even wondered whether he might not be "the worst literary thief in the world without knowing it." To another correspondent he remarked that if a man knowingly appropriated ideas or language from another he would be a thief, but that unconscious plagiarism should not be considered a crime. Still, at least once, in 1876, he confessed to Howells that he often borrowed situations or ideas from other stories to adapt into his own (Baetzhold, xiii). Perhaps much of his borrowing from

189

Dickens was "unconscious," perhaps not. But there are echoes which contribute significantly to a number of Mark Twain's works.

Dickens' works were a part of the scene from Clemens' earliest recollections. In "Villagers of 1840–3" he recalls that for literature Hannibal residents favored "Byron, Scott, Cooper, Marryatt, Boz" (*HH&T*, 34). His biographer Albert Bigelow Paine notes that Keokuk, Iowa residents remembered often seeing young Sam Clemens with a book under his arm—"a history or a volume of Dickens" (Paine, 106). He obviously read a number of the novels as soon as they appeared, and may actually have set the type for the excerpts of *Bleak House* (1852–53) which his brother Orion published in the Hannibal *Journal*. In November 1856, while *Little Dorrit* was still running in monthly installments, Thomas Jefferson Snodgrass (one of Clemens' early alter-egos) in summarizing the plot of *Julius Caesar* for the readers of the Keokuk *Daily Post* alluded to Dickens' famous symbol of governmental red tape: "Missus Brutus come out when the other fellers was gone," he says; "And like Mr. Clennam at the Circumlocution Office, she 'wanted to know.' " The author may well have had the Circumlocution Office in mind also when Snodgrass in Letter No. 3 describes the difficulties of "an indigent Irish woman," bounced from official to official, when she seeks to obtain an allotment of coal from the public supply (Baetzhold, 304). And he drew on the Circumlocution Office syndrome again in "The Mint Defalcation" (*Territorial Enterprise*, 8 January 1866 [Gardner, 92n]). But his most thorough treatment of the concept came in 1870 when the protagonist of "The Facts in the Case of the Great Beef Contract" *Galaxy*, May 1878) struggled through the mazes of "the Circumlocution Office of Washington" (Baetzhold, 305).

Clemens had obviously read *Martin Chuzzlewit* (1843–44) by the time of his piloting days on the Mississippi (1857–61). Writing to his brother Orion from St. Louis in November 1860, following the birth of a child to their sister Pamela, he compared the nurse Pamela had hired to Sairey Gamp, mentioning (in Allen Gribben's eloquent understatement) Sairey's "lenient views on alcoholic refreshment" (Gribben, 190). Thirteen years later, at a dinner of the Scottish Corporation of London, Mark Twain's speech, "The Ladies," would list the delightful malaprop—she who was addicted to tilting the bottle on the "chim'ley piece" when she was so "disposed"—along with the Queen of Sheba, Napoleon's Josephine, and Semiramis, legendary queen of Assyria, as one of the "sublime women" of history (Fatout, 80). (One also wonders if Sairey's imaginary crony, Mrs. 'arris, could have furnished the name Harris for Mark Twain's traveling companion in *A Tramp Abroad* [1880]. The possibility becomes more intriguing and amusing when we know that the actual companion was Clemens' Hartford friend, the minister Joseph Twichell.)

In another letter to Orion in February 1861 Clemens spoke of a recent visit to a New Orleans fortune-teller. Among her predictions, she assured him that no matter how many times he might fall in love in the future, he would always think of Laura Wright, his newly estranged love, immediately before falling asleep at night. Noting that the clairvoyant had unfortunately been correct so far, he summoned one of Augustus Moddle's phrases to bewail his own sad state: Such a recollection (just at bedtime) "will be devilish comfortable, won't it, when she and I (like one of Dickens' characters) are Another's" (*MTBM*, 57).

That spontaneous recollection of Moddle's habitual reference to the loss of Mercy Pecksniff—notably in the letter to Charity Pecksniff in the novel's final chapter when Augustus writes, "I love another. She is Another's"—suggests (along with the affection for Sairy Gamp) a real fondness for *Martin Chuzzlewit*. Twain would also refer later to Mark Tapley's penchant to "come out strong" in an 1862 letter to a western friend William Clagget (Gardner, 92). And he may well have had *Martin Chuzzlewit* in mind in discussing the impossibility of reproducing a dialect which one has not been "bred to." After noting that he himself had never tried to reproduce cockney dialect, he observed, "When Mr. Dickens tries to produce Yankee dialect, he [showed for once mistake]. He made his Yankee talk as no Yankee" (*N&J1*, 552–553).

Dickens' depiction of Martin Chuzzlewit's "Eden" owed much to the author's impressions of Cairo, Illinois, as recorded in *American Notes*. Just when Clemens first read the latter work cannot be determined, but in 1882, when preparing to expand his "Old Times on the Mississippi" articles into the full-length *Life on the Mississippi* (1883), he reminded himself to "See Dickens for a note on Cairo" (*N&J2*, 482). And *Life on the Mississippi* itself contains several other not uncomplimentary comments about Dickens and his reactions to the American scene.

If not before, Clemens probably first read *Dombey and Son* during the river years, also. It had obviously become a favorite by the time he got to Nevada, for a letter to "Dear Mother" in the Keokuk *Gate City* lists it among the "luxuries" that he took with him on a prospecting expedition to the Humboldt mining region late in 1861 (Rogers, *Pattern For RI*, 30). But much more revealing is his letter to his friend Bill Clagget later the same month. Referring to an expected visit by some friends, he wrote:

—and when we get Billy Dixon and the other Keokuk boys here, Oh no, we won't stuff ballot boxes and go to Congress nor nothing. By no means. "I hope I'm not an oyster though I may not wish to live in crowds." Now I don't mean to say that Nipper's remark is at all pertinent, you know, but I just happened to think of "them old Skettleses," and the quotation followed as a matter of course. And equally, of course, the whole Dombey family ccame trooping after: Cap'en Ed'ard Cuttle, mariner, as Uncle Sal's [sic] successor, polishing the chrometers [sic], and making calculations concerning the ebb and flow of the human tide in the street; and watching the stars with a growing interest, as if he felt that he had fallen heir to a certain amount of stock in them; and that old fool of a nurse at Brighton, who thought the house so "gashly"; and "that innocent," Toots; and the fated Biler; and Florence my darling, and "rough old Joey B., Sir," and "Wal'r my lad," and the Cap'en's eccentric timepiece, and his sugar tongs and the other little property which he "made over j'intly" and looming grandly in the rear comes ponderous Jack Bunsley! O d—n it, I wish I had the book.   (Quoted in Gardner, 92)

Even if he was showing off his literary knowledge for his friend by mentioning that *Dombey and Son* was not immediately at hand, his closing remark also suggests that the pleasure of his reminiscences made him want to read the book again. He obviously knew it well and thoroughly enjoyed it.

He particularly liked "Cap'en Ed'ard Cuttle," mentioning him on a number of occasions in the 1860s, in 1885, and again as late as 1903. His affection was doubtless enhanced when he saw Dan Setchell's performance as Cuttle in John Brougham's adaptation of the novel in California. Indeed, in "A Voice for Setchell" (*Californian*, 27 May 1865) he defended the actor against the attacks of a rival newspaper critic and paid tribute to the power of both the performer and the character. What with a dull dramatic season, the depressing "election bosh," and a falling stock market, he said, people were settling into gloom and despair—"when Captain Cuttle Setchell appeared in the midst of the gloom and broke the deadly charm with a wave of his enchanted hook and the spell of his talismanic words, 'Awahst! awahst! awahst!' And since that night all the powers of dreariness combined have not been able to expel the spirit of cheerfulness he evoked" (*ET&S2*, 172).

In one of his letters from Hawaii in 1866, Mark Twain had borrowed Captain Cuttle's name for a passenger aboard the *Ajax*—one of a jolly group of three for whom nineteen gallons of whiskey proved insufficient to sustain them during the ten day voyage (Frear, 262). During the Hawaiian tour, also, and several times during the next few years, Mark Twain drew upon *Our Mutual Friend* (1864–65), particularly the incongruous tendency of Silas Wegg—the villainous "man of low cunning"—to "drop into poetry" upon the slightest provocation.[2] On the first occasion, endeavoring to entertain his companion Mr. Brown, who was suffering from seasickness, Twain "dropped into poetry" with a rendition of Polonius' advice to Laertes—whereupon Brown regurgitated (Frear, 367). In 1868 the phrase helped enliven a Chicago *Republican* article in which the author professed horror at the reported efforts of certain Congressmen to write verse. Ironically granting the Congress preeminence among legislatures for solemn stupidity, he added, "But I did hope it would not 'drop into poetry.' I *did* hope it would confine its dullness to prose" (*W1868*, 11). The following January he used the phrase again, to tease his Cleveland friend, Mrs. Fairbanks. A few days earlier, noting that the fragrance of his cigar still lingered in the guest room to remind her of his recent visit, she had quoted a purposely banal verse apropos of the sentiment. Replying in kind, Clemens urged her to "go up to my room & take another whiff—it does you good . . . —it softens you—it makes you 'drop into poetry' like Silas Wegg" (*MTMF*, 65).

One could go through the canon citing additional evidence for Mark Twain's acquaintance with Dickens' works, but more important are some of the other specific uses that he made of those works.[3]

Most of the evidence suggests that Clemens was not particularly fond of the *Pickwick Papers*. In December 1863 he did find that the speech of Sgt. Buzfuz at the Bardell vs. Pickwick breach-of-promise suit, which he had theretofore considered the "tamest of Mr. Dickens' performances," had been mightily enhanced for him when the actor James Stark had presented the episode at a benefit in Carson City. He even was sure, he said, that such renditions would ensure the piece's continued existence as a classic (Baetzhold, 305). But in the summer of 1885 while making preliminary notes for a speech which presumably would discuss wit and humor, he jotted: "No humor in Pickewick papers except the kind the clown makes in the circus—I mean the humorist is a million times funnier to himself than ever he can be to any reader. Every line in the book says: 'Look at me—ain't I funny!' " A little later, to support his contention that he (Clemens) had no sense of humor, he wrote: "If there is a humorous passage in the Pickwick Papers, I have never been able to find it." Subsequently he did soften his criticism somewhat by noting that "Capt. Cuttle is good anywhere, and also all of Dickens' humorous characters except those in Pickwick Papers, & the body-snatcher in Tale of 2 Cities" (*N&J3*, 163, 168, 172).

But if Clemens did not like Pickwick and his cohorts as humorous characters, he obviously knew them well. In 1852 one of his early sketches signed "W. Epaminondas Adrastus Blab," had Blab describe a young man at a fraudulent "historical exhibition," as a "cheap-looking [i.e., discomfited] 'seeker after knowledge under difficulties.' " The interior quotation marks make certain that the author was intentionally borrowing from Tony Weller's question to his son Sam, who was laboring to compose a valentine at the Blue Boar Pub in Chapter 22: " 'But wot's that you're a-doin of—pursuit of knowledge under difficulties—eh, Sammy?" (*ET&SI*, 81, 445).

Clemens must also have been attracted by the comic overtones of the name Augustus Snodgrass, for both Snodgrass and Augustus appear several times from the very early writings on, beginning with the literary efforts of Thomas Jefferson Snodgrass, already introduced. To mention only two more, the humorist presents another namesake's counterpart of the poetic Pickwickian, more "literary" than Thomas Jefferson, in one of the "incidents" in "About Magnanimous Incident Literature" (1878). There a starving young writer named Snagsby (who, incidentally, shares his name with the kindly law stationer of *Bleak House*) begins his climb to fame through the willingness of "the renowned Snodgrass" to read his manuscript and submit it for publication.[4] And in Chapter 24 of *The American Claimant* (1892), Washington Hawkins tries to destroy Sally Sellers' interest in Howard Tracy (actually the heir to the Earldom of Rossmore) by telling her that he is really S. M. (for Spinal Meningitis) Snodgrass, the horse-thief son of a Cherokee Strip doctor. He assures Sally that he is personally acquainted with Dr. Snodgrass and also with S. M.'s brother, Zylobalsamum Snodgrass.

Though the humorist's enthusiasm for Dickens was high during the Western years—he classed him with Shakespeare, Bacon, and Byron in noting that the Jackass Hill miner's cabin which he was sharing with Jim Gillis in December 1864 contained "only first class Literature" (*N&J1*, 70)—he also began to satirize Dickens' sentimentality, especially as he saw it imitated by such writers as Bret Harte.

In his own writings Mark Twain was often guilty of blatant sentimentality himself; yet he consistently deplored it in others, most vehemently in a letter to a Hannibal friend, Will Bowen, when he called it "mental and moral masturbation" (*MTWB*, 24), and perhaps most colorfully in the lugubrious effusions of Emmaline Grangerford in *Huckleberry Finn*. An early instance appears in a sketch called "Uncle Lige" in the *Territorial Enterprise* in November 1865. This burlesque in the "condensed novel" form made popular by Bret Harte, Charles H. Webb, and others, had as its announced target a "companion novelette" by his friend and former colleague, Dan DeQuille (William Wright), entitled "Uncle Henry." Yet it is difficult not to see as the target, if only at second hand, the sort of sentimental relationship epitomized by Little Nell and her grandfather in *The Old Curiosity Shop*.

In Mark Twain's sketch, the narrator, seeing the "fair-haired, sweet-faced" eight-year-old "lill Addie" standing by her uncle's chair, bursts into tears. Regaining his composure momentarily, he is moved once more when the smiling child introduces him to her Uncle Lige—"poor blind-drunk Uncle Lige." This kindly old man—"He's the best uncle, and tells me such stories!"—Like Nell's grandfather, is obviously (and hiccupingly) grateful for the attention of "lill Addie (e-ick!)," and the tears start from his bleary eyes as she kisses his "poor, blossomy face," while he slobbers benignly over his shirt front (*ET&S1*, 379).[5]

Others among Dickens' works, however, provided materials that were not subject to satire or burlesque. Some of the instances may have resulted from similar ways of looking at their subjects as much as from direct borrowing on Mark Twain's part, but in a number of cases Dickens contributed importantly.

To digress briefly, though striking differences between the two authors can be noted, there were some remarkable similarities in their attitudes and in their lives. Both judged their experiences by strictly contemporary criteria rather than relying heavily upon any tradition. Both knew poverty and hardship; both of them, uneducated by any formal standards, were taken from school at about twelve years of age and put to work—Dickens at the infamous blacking warehouse, and Clemens in a printer's shop. Both became newspaper reporters and later, for a time, furnished accounts of the doings and misdoings of the House of Commons and the Nevada legislature and U.S. Congress, respectively. In their twenties, both were jilted by sweethearts, though Dickens' loss of Maria Beadnell probably left deeper wounds than Clemens' loss of Laura Wright. Yet Clemens' memories of Laura remained a matter of concern throughout his life, and influenced several of his works.[6]

Both educated themselves through wide and eclectic reading. Both shared a gusto, a robustness, a closeness of observation, and with humor, sentimentality, and social criticism as important stocks in trade, achieved wide popularity both with their works and on the public platform. More important, both drew heavily on personal experiences to create novels that brought the vernacular idiom and the use of the first-person narrator to new levels of artistry. As Ellen Moers has pointed out, both went on the public platform to provide support for the lavish life styles that their successful writings had permitted them to establish, but partly also at the call of an inveterate love of performing. Both at times relished the experience; both sometimes found the effort demeaning (Moers, 10).

As for personal connections, their paths crossed only once, when Clemens attended one of Dickens' readings in December 1867, but later vicarious connections occurred in 1872, when Clemens obtained the services of George Dolby, who had guided Dickens' platform career in America, as manager for his English lectures, and in 1887, when the Clemenses entertained the novelist's son Charles, his wife, and daughter in Hartford. (The younger Dickens at the time was in America giving readings from his father's work.)

One striking example of similarity of outlook and attitude is reflected in the reactions of both authors to Leonardo da Vinci's *Last Supper*—in *The Innocents Abroad* (1869) and *Pictures from Italy* (1846), respectively. If Mark Twain had not encountered Dickens' work before the *Quaker City* voyage, he became acquainted with it, directly or indirectly, through Abraham Reeves, M.D., "the Doctor" of *The Innocents Abroad*. Reeves not only had a copy with him, but borrowed heavily from it in sending his own dispatches home. And Mark Twain may well have consulted his friend's copy.

In a recent article, Robert Regan has justifiably taken me to task for arguing too strongly for Mark Twain's direct "borrowing" from Dickens (36). Yet I still would insist that the two descriptions of *The Last Supper*, and the authors' reactions to what they saw as the hypocrisy of the "enraptured" tourists, exhibit a remarkable similarity.

In his chapter on Milan, Dickens describes his visit to the "dilapidated" Convent of Santa Maria delle Grazie: "In the old refectory . . . is the work of art, perhaps better known than any other in the world: the Last Supper, by Leonardo da Vinci—with a door cut through it by the intelligent Dominican friars, to facilitate their operations at dinner time." Claiming a complete lack of knowledge of the mechanical aspects of the art of painting, and with no "other means of judging of a picture than as I see it resembling and refining upon nature, and presenting graceful combinations of forms and colours," he apologizes for his inability to recognize "the 'touch' of this or that master." Thus, of *The Last Supper*, he "would simply observe that, in its beautiful composition and arrangement, there it is, at Milan, a wonderful picture; and that in its . . . original expression of any single face or feature, there it is not."

Then follows a long description of how, besides damage from damp and decay, the work of the original artist had been "blotched and spoiled" by the clumsy work of retouchers, which has utterly blurred and distorted the expressions on the faces. He would not have mentioned these flaws at all, Dickens says, had he not observed "an English gentleman before the picture, who was at great pains to fall into what I may describe as mild convulsions, at certain minute details of expressions which are not left in it." And in concluding that it must "have been a work of extraordinary merit once," he suggests that "with so few of its original beauties remaining," travelers should be content with perceiving the great skill in design and not praise details which the present painting does not possess.[7]

Mark Twain's account in Chapter 19 of *The Innocents Abroad* contains striking parallels. Placing the painting in a church rather than a convent refectory, he, too, notes the "dilapidation": "Here, in Milan, in an ancient tumble-down ruin of a church, is the mournful wreck of the most celebrated painting in the world—'The Last Supper,' by Leonardo da Vinci." Like Dickens, he denies any expertise in the art of painting: "We are not infallible judges of pictures, but, of course, we went there to see this wonderful painting, once so beautiful, always so worshiped by masters in Art." Of the picture itself:

> "The Last Supper" is painted on the dilapidated wall of what was a little chapel attached to the main church in ancient times, I suppose. It is battered and scarred in every direction, and stained and discolored by time, and Napoleon's horses kicked the legs off most of the disciples when they (the horses, not the disciples) were stabled there more than half a century ago. . . . The colors are dimmed with age; the countenances are scaled and marred, and nearly all expression is gone from them; the hair is a dead blur upon the wall, and there is no life in the eyes. Only the attitudes are certain.

Again like Dickens, he notes the surprising reactions of the tourists, who stand "entranced" before the painting, speaking only "in the catchy ejaculations of rapture." And he expands that reaction into a humorous yet biting criticism of what he interprets as blatant hypocrisy. If the tourist reactions were honest, he says, they would be worthy of envy, or would at least reveal "an astonishing talent for seeing things that had already passed away." Perhaps the eye of a practiced artist could restore the painting's former beauties, but he himself could not, nor in his opinion could those other "uninspired visitors." And his conclusion seems almost a vernacular version of Dickens' more formal judgment. Whereas Dickens remarked "I would simply observe that in its beautiful composition and arrangement, there it is in Milan a wonderful picture, and that, in its original colouring . . . or expression of any single face or feature, there it is not," Mark Twain concludes: "I am satisfied that the Last Supper was a very miracle of art once. But it was three hundred years ago."

Present in Mark Twain's account, of course, is the humor derived from "anti-guidebook" tone—the "independent" pose of the individualistic American against the "authority" of those who would tend to dictate what one's reaction should be to the "wonders" of European art and tradition.

Still, though not humorously nor satirically, Dickens makes the same sort of point.

It is even more likely that Mark Twain had Dickens in mind—specifically *David Copperfield*—when he undertook another experiment in the "condensed novel" tradition, the "Boy's Manuscript," which in turn was the source for a number of characters and episodes and one of the major themes of *Tom Sawyer* (1876). Though concrete evidence that Mark Twain had read *David Copperfield* is slight, he certainly was familiar with it. In 1866 he compared an obsequious Hawaiian official to Uriah Heep (*LSI*, 110–111). He heard Dickens read from the novel in 1867; in 1898 when offers came from Europe to dramatize his short story, "The £1,000,000 Bank Note," he borrowed the famous line from Peggoty's suitor to tell Henry H. Rogers that "Barkis is willing" (*MTHHR*, 378). And in the unfinished fantasy, "Three Thousand Years Among the Microbes" (1905), the narrator renamed one of his microbe friends "David Copperfield" (*WWD*, 472).

In the "Boy's Manuscript," as Franklin Rogers has pointed out, the source (and target of the burlesque) was very likely the type of courtship depicted in David Copperfield's wooing of Dora Spenlow. And the story makes much of its burlesque point by reducing the action of adults to those of children (Billy Rogers and his "darling Amy") and by paralleling of Billy's actions with those of the "tall young man" in their mutual adoration of the nineteen-year-old Laura Miller (*Burlesque Patterns*, 101–103).

Many of the details of course derive from the author's Hannibal boyhood, with possible aid from Thomas Bailey Aldrich's *Story of a Bad Boy* (1869). But Dickens' assistance is also highly probable, even in minor details. Billy's Amy shares her name with Little Amy Dorrit, and Bob Sawyer, the boy who "licks" Billy, with the medical student and unsuccessful suitor of Arabella Allen in the *Pickwick Papers*. Despite Mark Twain's professed lack of appreciation for Pickwick and his cronies, at least as humorous characters, this use of Bob Sawyer's name, and his later inclusion in a notebook list of characters to appear in a proposed story, "Creatures of Fiction,"[8] suggest a considerable interest in Dickens' medical student. More than that, Bob Sawyer thus becomes perhaps the most likely source for *Tom* Sawyer's surname.

As for *Copperfield* (particularly Chapters 26, 33, and 43), the actions and characteristics of Billy and David and their respective lady-loves reveal several close parallels. Both heroes hang about the houses of the adored ones, hoping to catch even a glimpse. Both walk for long distances, undergoing severe difficulties in the hope of seeing or being seen—David in severe pain from shoes too small for him; Billy playing hookey in order to walk down Amy's street and later bribing a torchlight procession which he joins to march past Amy's house—four times. Present also are the frequently broken engagement, the rival lover, and David's flirting with the lady in pink in order to make Dora jealous. Moreover, when the beautiful Laura Miller drops a geranium leaf, which both Billy and "the tall young man" simultaneously stoop to pick up as a precious keepsake, we remember that geraniums also played an important role in the relationship of David and Dora—in the greenhouse during their first time alone, in David's birthday bouquet, and in the memories conjured up for David by the scent of a geranium leaf in later years: "a straw hat and blue ribbons, and a quantity of curls, and a little black dog, being held up, in two slender arms, against a bank of blossoms and bright leaves." (Billy's Amy also wore a blue ribbon and doted on her dog Bingo as Dora did on Jip.)

Like David, who habitually speaks of Dora as "my little wife" and "dear, dear little wife," Billy several times calls Amy "my little wife." (Mark Twain also referred to "Dora, the child-wife," in his review of the Dickens reading which he attended in December 1867.) Amy and Dora themselves were also remarkably similar, especially since Dora never outgrows her childish fancies. Amy dreams of "a little cozy cottage with vines running over the windows and a four-story brick attached where she could receive company and give parties." David envisions just such a cottage for himself and Dora, and though the four-story addition is not specified, Dora's plans for entertaining, if realized, would require at least that much extra space. Such details, therefore, though not absolutely conclusive, suggest a considerable debt to *David Copperfield*.

The "Boy's Manuscript" itself, though essentially a fragment, was important in Mark Twain's own career for several reasons. Not only was it an early attempt to make literary use of what Henry Nash Smith has called "the matter of Hannibal," but it also provided the "Tom and Becky" plot element for *Tom Sawyer*, as well as a number of other scenes and episodes. And though the similarities to *David Copperfield* become less clear when additional elements and plot-strands are added, the events of the "courtship" still serve as an important unifying element for the novel as a whole.

David Copperfield also very likely contributed to *The Gilded Age* (1873), Mark Twain's collaboration with Charles Dudley Warner, on the surface the most Dickensian of the humorist's novels. One must note, however, as DeLancey Ferguson has pointed out (168), that the multiple plot, the beautiful maiden of unknown parentage, and the upright youth who ultimately wins fame and fortune were staple devices of the Victorian novel, and thus should not be considered important in assessing influence.

It is difficult to believe, however, that Wilkins Micawber was not among the several models for Colonel Beriah Sellers. One of the earliest English reviewers (*Spectator,* March 1874) commented on the resemblance, noting that he found Sellers inferior to his Dickensian progenitor, but that there was a significant difference. Whereas Micawber simply waited for something to turn up, the Colonel "turned up the most surprising Kohinoors by merely delving into the inexhaustible mine of his own inventive fancy." Both characters were largely based on their creators' relatives—Micawber on Dickens' father; Sellers on Clemens's cousin James Lampton. Dickens' basic resentment of his father's failures is perhaps somewhat apparent in his portrait of Micawber, whereas Mark Twain seems almost to delight in Sellers's extravagant schemes. Yet both authors emphasize the good-heartedness of their visionaries. And the characters are even closer relatives in their unfailing ability to enlarge upon the commonplace and minimize the unusual. To cite only one of the numerous examples, the Colonel's verbal transformation of a few turnips into a sumptuous feast (Chapter 13) exhibits the same sort of magic that prevails when Micawber, in his lowly quarters, concocts a batch of rum punch (Chapter 28). "It was wonderful," David says, "to see his face shining at us out of a thin cloud of these delicate fumes, as he stirred, and mixed, and tasted, and looked as if he were making, instead of punch, a fortune for his family down to the latest posterity." The Colonel's family also resembles Micawber's more than that of James Lampton, who had a son and four daughters. The Micawbers boasted a set of twins and two others, a boy and a girl. The Sellers family—remember that the Colonel's dreams were often grander than Micawber's—exactly *doubles* the number of Micawber children, with two sets of twins and four others. Such similarities could be overstressed, of course, but so could a denial of influence.

As an additional Dickensian element in *The Gilded Age, Martin Chuzzlewit* very likely also played a part in inspiring one of Colonel Sellers's schemes—the dream of transforming the tiny and backward Stone's Landing into a shining metropolis, which, in turn, would provide boundless wealth for the investors whom he hoped to entice. The promotion of Martin Chuzzlewit's "Eden" bears a number of resemblances. Some writers have erred in supposing that both Dickens and Mark Twain based their "land swindles" on a similar scheme involving Marion City, Missouri.[9] Although Clemens may well have known of William Muldrow's glamorized and widely publicized portraits of the Marion City-that-was-to-be, there is no evidence that

Dickens did. He did know, however, of the lavish advertisements for the ill-fated Cairo City and Canal Company which in 1837 tempted a large number of English investors. And his knowledge of that scheme, coupled with his revulsion at the condition of Cairo, Illinois, during his visit to America in 1842 (as recorded in *American Notes*) surely formed the major inspiration for "Eden."[10] And given Mark Twain's fondness for *Martin Chuzzlewit*, Dickens' "Eden" is a much more likely model than Marion City for the Stone's Landing speculation.

Although this paper purports to deal with Mark Twain's denial of Dickens, the record would not be complete without some consideration of the one novel he did not deny—*A Tale of Two Cities*. Actually, it became one of his favorite books, so much so that by 1898 he was telling his friend Henry Fischer that he read the book "at least every two years," and had recently finished it for "the 'steenth time" (Fisher, 60). It is therefore not surprising that *A Tale of Two Cities* (1859) left important traces on his own works.

When he first read the novel is uncertain. In 1863 the opening sentence of "How to Cure a Cold" (*Golden Era*, 20 September) possibly echoes Sidney Carton's final words, when Mark Twain says, that though writing to arouse the public is a good thing, "*it is a far huger and nobler thing* to write for their instruction." In "An Open Letter to Commodore Vanderbilt" in *Packard's Monthly* for March 1869, Mark Twain's picture of the Commodore's reckless driving through the park closely resembles Dickens' description of the Marquis St. Evremonde's callous disregard for the safety of bystanders. We do know that Clemens and his family used the book as one of their guides in 1869 when visiting the scenes of the Terror in Paris.[11]

Just as *David Copperfield* may have supplied details for the "courtship" episodes of *Tom Sawyer*, via the "Boy's Story," so *A Tale of Two Cities* probably helped Mark Twain introduce another of the novel's major plot strands—the grave robbery which culminates in the trial of Muff Potter for the murder of Dr. Robinson. There is no evidence in Clemens' own memories of his boyhood, nor did Dixon Wecter's detailed study of the early years turn up any instances of grave-robbers in Hannibal. But a vivid incident in *A Tale of Two Cities* features young Jerry Cruncher stealing from home in the dark to peer fearfully through a cemetery gate as his father and two companions ply their "honest" nocturnal trade (Book 2, Chapter 14). So, too, does Tom Sawyer leave his bed and, hidden from sight with Huck Finn in the graveyard, observe Dr. Robinson, Injun Joe, and Muff Potter as they exhume Hoss Williams's body.

But there is much more of *A Tale of Two Cities* in *Huckleberry Finn* and

A Connecticut Yankee. In *Huckleberry Finn,* Dickens' novel joins with Carlyle's *French Revolution* (another favorite) and other classics of "prisoner literature" to undergird Tom Sawyer's "rescue" of Jim in the book's final episode. Tom's prescription for the ink to be used in the prisoner's journal—"Many makes it out of iron rust and tears; but . . . the best authorities uses their own blood" (Chapter 35)—recalls that Dr. Manette, in his Bastille cell, kept his journal by writing "with rusty iron point" in "scrapings of soot and charcoal from the chimney, mixed with blood" (Book 3, Chapter 10). Tom's directions to Huck for fetching a doctor, blindfolding him, and putting "a purseful of gold into his hand" (Chapter 40) also closely parallel Dr. Manette's experience just before his incarceration, when the Evremonde brothers summon him to treat the victims of their violence (Book 3, Chapter 10).

Walter Blair suggests parallels to the attitudes of the British-to-the-core Miss Pross (Book 3, Chapter 7) in the argument of Huck and Jim about the French language (Chapter 14), and to Jerry Cruncher's browbeating of his wife for hindering his career by her penchant for "flopping" (praying) in Pap Finn's "lambastin' " of Huck for putting on "airs" and for learning to read. In the latter instance, however, Joseph Gardner has found an even closer parallel in *Our Mutual Friend,* where Gaffer Hexam berates his son Charley for learning to read and write and thus consider himself superior to his parent (155–156). Both may well have contributed. As Blair also notes, there seems to be additional borrowing from *A Tale of Two Cities* in the Bricksville "lynching bee" (Chapter 22), where the progress of the unreasoning mob in Bricksville, which reacts almost as a single organism, closely follows the pattern of action of a similar mob in London (Book 2, Chapter 14).

Blair's analysis shows that the materials from Dickens are absorbed into the very heart of Mark Twain's book. Huck and Jim's discussion of the French language delineates character, emphasizes an early stage of their relationship before the development of Huck's appreciation of Jim as a person, and contributes through its humor to the depiction of life on the raft. Pap Finn's speeches help characterize him, motivate important subsequent actions, and castigate the prejudice, ignorance, and hypocrisy of mankind. The "lynching bee" not only brings the period to life but also explicitly pronounces one of Mark Twain's harshest denunciations of human cruelty, conformity, and cowardice (Blair, *Twain and Huck,* 128, 311–315; "French Revolution," 21–35).

Before leaving the discussion of the possible presence of Dickens in *Huckleberry Finn,* one should also note that two writers have seen important parallels to *Great Expectations.* J. M. Ridland cites Pip's struggles with conscience over helping Magwitch, the resemblance of his older sister to Miss Watson, and the collision of the Thames river steamer with Pip's rowboat. And Nicholas C. Mills, in two much more detailed comparisons of the books, examines the attitudes of the boys to society, the nature and influence of home and society upon them, their moral and psychological decisions.

To return to *A Tale of Two Cities,* its presence in several episodes of *A Connecticut Yankee in King Arthur's Court* (1889) is perhaps less familiar. In developing this novel's major theme of man's slavery to ideas perpetuated by monarchy, aristocracy, and the Established Church, Mark Twain drew upon almost all ages of Western history from the Roman era to his own, and especially that of the French Revolution. To forestall charges of anachronism, his preface admitted that the laws and customs portrayed did not necessarily exist in sixth-century Britain and declared that "it is only pretended that inasmuch as they existed in the English and other civilizations of far later times, it is safe to consider that it is no libel upon the sixth century to suppose them to have been in practice in that day also." And along with Carlyle, Taine, St. Simon, and others, Dickens contributed significant episodes to the novel's attack on "medieval" practices and the habits of mind which fostered them.

During their quest to rescue a group of captive princesses, the Yankee and his companion Sandy (the Demoiselle Alisande La Carteloise) stay for a time at the castle of Queen Morgan le Fay (Chapters 17 and 18). At one point when a page boy accidentally brushes against the Queen's skirt, she nonchalantly stabs him. Surprised at the Yankee's shocked reaction, she is even more surprised when he does not view her offer to pay the boy's parents for the inconvenience as a truly magnanimous gesture. Here we seem to be in the presence of the haughty Marquis St. Evremonde, whose actions, attitude, and comments are almost exact counterparts of Morgan le Fay's. In the episode already mentioned, when the Marquis' speeding coach crushes the peasant child, Evremonde tosses a coin to the grief-stricken father and rides on "with the air of a gentleman who had accidentally broken some common thing and had paid for it, and could afford to pay for it" (Book 2, Chapter 7). Two chapters later he recalls an earlier incident when (in a reaction much like the Queen's) an indiscreet peasant was "poinarded on the spot for protesting some insolent delicacy respecting his [the peasant's] daughter."

Very likely, too, the curse uttered by the page-boy's grandmother owes something to Dickens' vivid description of the howl of the French boy's father and of Madame Defarge's knitting "with the steadiness of fate" as Evremonde's carriage departs. And the Queen's command, "To the stake with her!'' all but translates into action the Marquis' remark: "You dogs. I would ride over any of you very willingly, and exterminate you from the earth. If I knew which rascal threw at the carriage, and if the brigand were sufficiently near, he should be crushed under the wheels.''

As in *Huckleberry Finn*, Dickens here, too, helped Mark Twain introduce one of the novel's major concerns. For besides presenting another example of aristocratic callousness, the episode also leads into the Yankee's discussion of the influence of "training" in the lives of human beings. The matter of "training," in turn, becomes influential in the Yankee's ultimate defeat.

A Tale of Two Cities seems also to be reflected in the case history of two of the prisoners whom the Yankee releases from Morgan le Fay's dungeons. This tragic pair had been rash enough on their wedding night to try to deny their feudal lord, Sir Breuse Sans Pite, his *droit du seigneur*. Not only had the young wife "spilt half a gill" of Sir Breuse's "almost sacred blood," but the husband committed a doubly unpardonable sin by daring to lay hands upon the nobleman and fling him bodily into the parlor amid "the humble and trembling wedding guests," leaving him there, "astonished at this strange treatment" (Chapter 18). Sir Breuse, of course, could not condone such an insult, and within the hour, since his own dungeons were cramped for space, had asked Morgan le Fay to "accommodate" his prisoners. And there "in her bastile" [sic] they had languished ever since, neither knowing whether the other was dead or alive.

That incident and its effects echo the experience so painfully described by Dr. Manette in the same journal entry (Book 3, Chapter 10) that probably inspired Tom Sawyer's instructions to Huck about procuring and paying a doctor. Manette's record describes his abduction by the Marquis St. Evremonde and his brother in order to treat a young man and his sister, victims of the younger Evremonde's lust and brutality. The ravished girl, the recent wife, and more recent widow of one of the Marquis' tenant farmers had resisted the younger Evremonde brother in vain. When her own brother sought revenge, he was fatally wounded by the latter, an action which left both Evremondes feeling "besmirched" at having been obliged to draw a sword and dispatch this "crazed young common dog," as if he were a gentlemen. Manette's efforts to help prove futile; and though the Evremondes swear him to secrecy and reward him with a "rouleau of gold," three days later their henchmen force him into a coach and drive him secretly to the Bastille to begin his long imprisonment.

Besides these parallels, several other details suggest that Dr. Manette's story was in Mark Twain's mind as he wrote. Both the appearance and actions of the husband, thirty-four though he looked sixty, resemble those of Dr. Manette when his daughter and Jarvis Lorry first see him at his cobbler's bench in the Defarges' garret (Book 1, Chapter 6). In the Bastille, Manette suffers the same treatment by his jailers, who refuse to answer questions about his young wife, or even to tell him if she is alive. And is it a coincidence that the periods of incarceration are analogous? Manette was "buried alive" for "almost eighteen years"; the Arthurian pair graced Morgan's dungeons for nine.

But whereas Dr. Manette is ultimately restored to family and to health, Mark Twain suggests that although the Yankee restores the pair to their friends, their experience will probably leave their minds "wandering in some far land of dreams and shadows."

Those friends, too, no doubt reflected the same "dumb, uncomplaining acceptance" of wrongs and hardships that the Yankee described on another occasion. Hence the borrowings from Dickens' examples of aristocratic cruelty help dramatize Mark Twain's overriding premise that the people's acceptance of the "superstitions" of monarchy and aristocracy "enslaved" not only the bodies but the spirits of the common people. The reactions of the prisoners, in turn, also helped the Yankee reach the conclusion that whereas he had hoped to engineer a peaceful revolution, such attitudes could not be rooted out without "a Reign of Terror and a guillotine."

Another of the themes that emerge from *A Connecticut Yankee* is the identity of "slavery" no matter what the era. When the Yankee and King Arthur wander incognito in order that the King may know first-hand the realities of his realm, they observe additional examples of that mental and physical bondage. And *A Tale of Two Cities* again seems to have evoked an episode which in turn produced one of the novel's most explicit comments on the universality of that "slavery" to custom and tradition. Surely Mark Twain was remembering Dickens' dramatic symbolic chapter, "Fire Rises," in which "Monseigneur" is murdered and his chateau burned (Book 2, Chapter 23) when he came to write his chapter "The Tragedy of the Manor House" (Chapter 30).

Leaving the sadness of the "Small-Pox Hut," the Yankee and King Arthur, from the top of a small hill, observe a red glow in the distant blackness. While they ponder the source of the fire, the wind rises, flashes of lightning and rumbles of thunder signal an approaching storm. Dickens' episode also features a rainy night, lowering darkness, and watchers on a hilltop. Soon the "raging . . . red-hot wind" that roars in Dickens' chapter finds its fearsome counterpart in the roar of human voices at Abblasoure, as the mob of villagers pursue and hang all those in any way suspected of involvement in the burning of the manor house and murder of its lord. Results of their pursuit are gruesomely revealed as the King and the Yankee push through the "almost solid blackness" to investigate the cause of the red glow. Bumping into a soft object, they are horrified when a lightning flash reveals a corpse dangling from a tree limb. With subsequent flashes they see many other trees similarly decorated.

That Mark Twain was thinking of the French Revolution is obvious when the Yankee, in order to placate King Arthur, agrees to help find the "villains" who had actually burned the manor and says (again for the king's benefit): "If they were merely resisters of the gabelle or some kindred absurdity I would try to protect them from capture; but when men murder a person of high degree and likewise burn his home, that is another matter." More specifically, the reference to the gabelle—the salt-tax which French peasants found so oppressive—may well have been inspired by Dickens' symbolic Monsieur Gabelle, the village postmaster and tax collector who figures largely in the "Fire Rises" chapter.

The dangling corpses also appear in Dickens' novel. His summary of the violent night notes that with daylight the crowd surrounding Gabelle's quarters had dispersed, sparing the tax-collector's life "for the while." But, he adds, "within a hundred miles, and in the light of other fires, there were other functionaries less fortunate . . . whom the rising sun found hanging across once-peaceful streets. . . . Also there were other villagers and townspeople . . . upon whom the functionaries and soldiery turned with success, and whom they strung up in their turn."

Mark Twain's treatment of the Arthurian mob and the hangings at Abblasoure seem almost to dramatize that summary comment. But in partly reversing the situation, he introduces an irony not present in the original. There is no celebration of the death of the oppressor, as in Dickens. And it is the people of Abblasoure who, though they are glad the crime has been committed, are hunting down and executing not the "functionaries" of their feudal lord, but their fellow-townspeople. Ironically, almost all become the "functionaries" of oppression because of a sense of "duty" to their former master.

Dickens' symbolic picture of the fire that soon was to engulf all of France serves primarily, then, as a means for Mark Twain once more to denounce the subjugation to tradition, fear, and a misguided sense of duty to one's "betters." And he projects that sort of "slavery" into future centuries by comparing these people to the "poor whites" in the American South, who subverted their own "freedom" by helping perpetuate the power of the large slaveholders. In terms of the novel's plot, also, this episode results in the meeting with Marco and Dowley, which, in turn, results in the King and the Yankee being sold as slaves themselves, to learn first-hand the delights of that institution.

Given the evidence, why, then, the denial to Paine in 1909? The reasons, I would suggest, were both personal and professional. They resulted from the emotions of the moment, from an actual dimunition of appreciation over the years, and from a lifetime devoted to projecting a particular sort of public image.

On the personal side, the mood of the moment was certainly important. In what proved to be the last year of Clemens' life, he and Paine were returning home from the Saint Timothy's School in Baltimore, where Clemens had delivered an address at the graduation of Frances Nunnally, a young friend whom he had met on his trip to England in 1907.[12] On such an occasion the author almost certainly would have thought about his own schooling, or lack thereof. The comment about Dickens actually followed a general denial of knowledge about books and authors. After mentioning that he felt "like a barkeeper entering the kingdom of heaven" when approaching one of Jane Austen's novels (she was a favorite of his friend Howells) and citing Mrs. Clemens' embarrassment at having to admit to a visitor that her husband did not know the writings of Thackeray and several other greats (again an exaggeration), he had commented, a bit plaintively it seems, "I don't know anything about anything, and never did." As the train rolled along, he continued his reflections on literature, life, and learning.

Struck by two poems in the *Saturday Times Review*—one by Willa Cather, the other by Kipling—he read them to Paine and said of the latter, "I could stand any amount of that." And a short while later, obviously looking back over his own lifetime, he said: "Life is too long and too short. Too long for the weariness of it; too short for the work to be done. At the very most the average mind can master only a few languages and a little history" (Paine, 1500–1502).

Although he had read surprisingly widely, as Alan Gribben's *Mark Twain's Library* amply demonstrates, there is no doubt that Clemens felt uncomfortable about what he perceived as his lack of learning. Any comparison which he might have made to his more formally educated contemporaries like Lowell, Longfellow, or Emerson, or to his good friend William Dean Howells, whose lifelong career as editor and reviewer had provided a much broader acquaintance with literary works than Clemens' own more eclectic reading had done, would have intensified that feeling.

As Joseph Gardner suggests, that discomfort was probably partly responsible for Clemens' oft-stated insistence that he preferred factual knowledge to fiction or poetry (94). Though belied by his actual range of reading, the familiar comment, "I like history, biography, travels, curious facts and strange happenings and science, and I detest novels, poetry and theology," is typical. Confident that he could absorb and understand factual material and insecure about the sort of knowledge that required a critical ability, presumably attainable only through formal education, he tended to disclaim knowledge of (or even interest in) matters literary.

As a minor matter on the personal side, Clemens' recollection that his brother Orion had pushed him to read Dickens may have contributed its bit to the denial. Though he continually offered imperious advice to his elder brother, he characteristically resented any attempt on Orion's part to do the same.

There were also signs over the years of a real lessening of appreciation of Dickens' works, separate from the professional "pose" which I shall describe shortly. In a letter to Howells in August 1887 Clemens implicitly acknowledged a change in attitude perhaps influenced by his current political and social views. Commenting on the changes that time had made in his own outlook on several matters, he wondered how those who claimed that the Bible "means the same to them at 50 that it did at all former milestones in their journey" could tell such a lie. "They would not say that of Dickens' or Scott's books. *Nothing* remains the same" (*MTHL*, 2:595–596).

By this time Matthew Arnold's unfavorable review of General Grant's *Memoirs* (1887) had helped fuel the anti-British fires that were to flare up in several unpublished attacks and ultimately in *A Connecticut Yankee in King Arthur's Court* (1889). And whereas, both in the published version of *Life on the Mississippi* (1883) and in chapters ultimately omitted, Mark Twain had defended the uncomplimentary picture of the American scene painted by Dickens and other British tourists, now he included Dickens along with Arnold and others who, in his opinion, had grossly misrepresented the United States. Since his antipathy toward British critics of America was profound during these years, the implicit condemnation of opinions voiced in *Martin Chuzzlewit* and *American Notes* suggests a real loss of affection for Dickens.

Perhaps more important, one of the elements of Clemens' adverse reactions to the *Pickwick Papers* seems to have broadened in later years to include Dickens' work in general. In 1895 during his world lecture tour, while discussing literary matters with an interviewer from the Sydney (Australia) *Morning Herald,* he at first cited Dickens among important writers who were keenly aware of the pathos, or even tragedy, behind every humorous situation—even placing him among the "bright host who have gained niches in the gallery of the immortals." But then he qualified his praise to admit—at the risk of seeming "willfully heretic"—that he had lost much of his earlier admiration: "I seem to see all the machinery of the business too clearly, the effort is too patent. The true and lasting genius of humour does not drag you thus to boxes labeled 'pathos,' 'humour,' and show you all the mechanism of the inimitable puppets that are going to perform. How I used to laugh at Simon Tapperwit [sic], and the Wellers, and a host more. But I can't do it now, somehow, and time, it seems to me, is the true test of humour" (Quoted in Budd, 11).

Since that statement of 1895 reveals a broadening of the "Look at me—ain't I funny?" note of 1885, it is possible that in the emotion of the 1909 conversation with Paine, Clemens may have expanded his earlier disenchantment into the almost complete rejection of Dickens' works.

But the Australian interview also reveals a touch of a third and perhaps the major influence of that rejection—the professional pose that Mark Twain projected throughout his life. At one point in the interview, after repeating his preference for the "heavier" sorts of literature—"history, biography, travels"—he claimed only slight acquaintance with "modern writers of fiction," though he later excepted Rudyard Kipling, whose works he knew well. "I have always had a fear," he said, "that I should get into someone else's style if I dabbled among the modern writers too much, and I don't want to do that." And then: "As I have never studied any of the great models, I can outrage them with impunity."

That last statement, especially, reflects the image that Mark Twain established early and maintained throughout his career—the "original" who owed nothing to books or literary traditions but only to his own experience; the "independent" observer; the self-confident American, often brash and disrespectful, unimpressed by reputation or status, suspicious of things foreign, and, as a traveler, refusing to acknowledge beauties or excellences that his own observations did not reveal. At times it seems almost as if he were saying, "Here I am, a boy from Missouri. Didn't have much schoolin', but I've been around, and I've seen a lot, and I've made it!"

About 1890, for instance, he told a correspondent that he or she was "exactly right" in surmising that all of his fictional creations came from life with which he was familiar. But then he went on to explain that he was familiar with more than just "boy-life out on the Mississippi," through his many experiences as soldier, prospector, miner, newspaper reporter, river pilot, printer, lecturer, investor, publisher, and author. Declaring such personal experience "the most valuable capital or culture or education usable in the building of novels," he concluded: "I surely have the equipment, a wide culture and all of it real, none of it artificial, for I don't know anything about books" (*Letters*, 2:543). It is true, as Alan Gribben has pointed out, that the reference to his varied experiences, as well as some of his other denials of literary influence, had to do with his sense of the importance of actual observation over vicarious experiences (xxvii). But such statements also contributed importantly to the "unliterary" image that he wished to project.

One major force in the shaping of Mark Twain's literary image was his concept of the audience for whom he wrote. His contracts with publisher Elisha Bliss called for the books to be sold by subscription, and as Hamlin Hill has convincingly shown, the perceived audience for such books seriously affected their form and content. Those volumes "aimed at enticing the common man, the masses, the rural, semi-literate, usually Midwestern customer who had rarely bought a book before." And, though a part of Samuel Clemens yearned for "literary" respectability and for the knowledge which his voracious appetite for reading could bring him, Mark Twain drew on his own sense of kinship with this audience in projecting the various facets of his image, knowing that such readers would not look favorably upon a writer with "literary" pretensions. As one of the newspaper reviewers of *The Innocents Abroad* put it in an excerpt contained in a salesman's prospectus for the volume: "The eyes with which he sees are our eyes as well as his. . . . And thus the book becomes a transcript of our own sentiments"; and as another commented: "He sees like an American, thinks like an American, reasons like an American, is an American, blood and bone, heart and head, and this is the secret of his great success" (Hill, 26, 30). Many of Mark Twain's sentiments do, of course, reflect his own background. But some of his professed "American" preferences—for the simple as opposed to the sophisticated, for the "real" as opposed to the fanciful—are clearly designed to appeal to his readers.

A similar sense of audience and a similar projection of the "unliterary" image may be observed in a frequently quoted letter to Andrew Lang in 1890. Actually, that letter was essentially a self-serving attempt to enlist Lang's support in counteracting the harsh British criticism of *A Connecticut Yankee in King Arthur's Court*. Some months earlier Clemens, with heavy irony, had told his English publisher Andrew Chatto that his book was written for England, not America, and would attempt to repay the many English efforts to teach Americans "something for our betterment," by "trying to pry up the English nation to a little higher level of manhood in turn." Now to Lang, after granting that "the top crust of humanity—the cultivated—" are "worth nourishing and preserving with dainties and delicacies," he argued that catering to that faction was neither dignified nor valuable since there was small satisfaction in "merely feeding the overfed." And then he completely reversed his earlier statement to Chatto: "I have never tried in even one single little instance to help cultivate the cultivated classes. I was not equipped for it, either by native gifts or training. And I never had any ambition in that direction, but always hunted for bigger game—the masses. I have seldom deliberately tried to instruct them, but have done my best to entertain them. To simply amuse them would have satisfied my dearest ambition at any time, for they could get instruction elsewhere" (*Letters,* 2:525–528).

In general, the letter argued that critics should adopt separate standards for judging works that appealed to the "cultivated classes" and those designed for "the Belly and the Members"—the masses. But despite the speciousness of the specific situation, the sense of the particular audience is clear. And Mark Twain's realization that such an audience would not consider as one of themselves a writer who pretended to literary learning certainly contributed to the image the humorist projected.[13]

In terms of Mark Twain's reactions to Dickens, many elements of the "pose" I have described may be observed in Twain's review of the reading he attended in 1867, as reported to the San Francisco *Alta California*. He was in New York that Christmas season for a reunion with his *Quaker City* shipmates, and was delighted when Charles Langdon invited him to join his parents and sister Olivia to attend the novelist's performance at Steinway Hall on December 31. Enthusiastic as he had been about Dickens' works up to this time, he must have welcomed the chance to see the famous author in person, not to mention the opportunity to meet the girl whose picture he later claimed had captured his heart when Langdon showed it to him during their Mediterranean voyage.

The very opening of his report reveals the brash Western reporter's somewhat condescending attitude toward the visiting British "lion":

> Promptly at 8 p.m., unannounced and without waiting for any stamping or clapping of hands to bring him out, a tall, "spry" (if I may say it) thin-legged old gentleman, gotten up regardless of expense . . . with a bright red flower in his buttonhole, gray beard and mustache, bald head with side hair brushed fiercely and tempestuously forward, as if its owner were sweeping down before

a wind, the very Dickens came! He did not emerge upon the stage— . . . he strode . . . in the most English way and exhibiting the most English style of appearance—straight across the broad stage, heedless of everybody.

Continuing in the same vein, he observed that Dickens in person was less attractive than his pictures, which themselves were "hardly handsome," noting that the author's "fashion of brushing his hair and goatee so resolutely forward gives him a comical Scotch-terrier look about the face which is rather heightened than otherwise by his portentous dignity and gravity."

But then for a paragraph his tone changed considerably, and one might sense in the more formal description some evidence of Mark Twain's genuine admiration for Dickens. Still, one must also consider his characteristic humorous device of painting an elaborate word-picture only to undermine the "effect" with "realistic" or "vernacular" observation:

> But that queer old head took on a sort of beauty bye and bye, and a fascinating interest, as I thought of the wonderful mechanism within it, the complex but exquisitely adjusted machinery that could create men and women, and put the breath of life into them and alter all their ways and actions, elevate them, degrade them, murder them, marry them, conduct them through good and evil, through joy and sorrow, on their long march from the cradle to the grave, and never lose its godship over them, never make a mistake.

The undermining then began with "I almost imagined I could see the wheels and pulleys work. This was Dickens—Dickens!" And the reporter followed that hyperbole with the further "down-to-earth" conclusion that "Somehow this puissant god seemed to be only a man after all. How the great do tumble from their pedestals when we see them in common flesh, and know that they eat pork and cabbage and act like other men."

The *Alta* correspondent did find the stage setting impressive in its reflection of "style" and flawless showmanship. But the reading itself proved disappointing. Taking issue with the extravagant praises bestowed by the critics of the New York *Herald* and *Tribune*, Mark Twain cited the distracting huskiness of Dickens' voice, the general monotony of the whole performance, and especially the reader's seeming inability to move his audience: "His pathos is the beautiful pathos of his language . . . it is glittering frostwork." Whereas he should have been able to make such a "bright and intelligent audience . . . laugh or cry or shout at his own good will or pleasure," he did not do so.

More specifically, he found Dickens "a little Englishy in his speech," pronouncing Steerforth "St'yawfuth"; the rendition of Peggoty's search for

Em'ly was "bad"; episodes featuring "Dora, the child-wife" and the storm at Yarmouth in which Steerforth drowned "not as good as they might have been." He did like "Mrs. Micawber's inspired suggestions as to the negotiations of her husband's bills," but concluded that the performance as a whole was far inferior to what Dickens' reputation had led the audience to expect."[14]

Joseph Gardner contends that the critical remarks in the *Alta* review illustrate one of Mark Twain's "well-known impulses, the impulse to attack overtly or covertly established renown whenever and wherever he encountered it" (96–97). Very possibly. But that characteristic is also part-and-parcel of the American and Western "pose," so often exemplified in *The Innocents Abroad* and other works—the reluctance to kowtow to "authority," in this case, especially, the critics of the New York papers, and the refusal to be impressed by status or reputation.

Mark Twain's jibes at the New York critics' "extravagant praises" probably reflect both of the above elements. Here was the Western reporter proving himself superior to the "big-city boys." The New Yorkers, by the way, had also mentioned the huskiness of Dickens' voice, but invariably noted that the distraction quickly disappeared as the reader warmed to his task. (Clemens would not have been aware that Dickens had been fighting a severe cold and that week was performing against the advice of his doctor.) And both the pose and his own feelings could have combined in the typical American condescension toward the foreigner and the "Englishy" way Dickens walked and spoke. But given his real feelings toward Olivia Langdon, it could only have been the brash Western humorist appealing to his audience which resulted in the sort of flippancy evident in the description of his companion at the reading as "the beautiful young lady with me—a highly respectable white woman."

That the persona was in command in 1867 is further suggested by a later account of the reading which Clemens dictated for his autobiography in 1907, as part of a discussion of the "Author's Reading" as a form of platform entertainment. Strong approval of the theatrical stage setting remains, but the flippancy and "superiority" are gone. Now Clemens declares that Dickens read "with great force and animation, in the lively passages, and with stirring effect," and did not merely read, but acted. Rather than being "not so good as it might have been," he now remembers the stormy scene of Steerforth's death as "so vivid, and so full of energetic action that the house was carried off its feet, so to speak" (*MTE*, 214).

Perhaps this more favorable memory was partly influenced by the fact that, as he said, the occasion had made "the fortune of [his] life" by introducing him to the future wife whom he came to idolize. Moreover, his own later experiences on the platform had taught him that lecturing and "reading" required very different skills. His first attempts had been "ghastly," he said, and hence he no doubt had come to appreciate Dickens' expertise more fully. But there remains the probability that he did not at that time feel the necessity to impress an audience with an appeal to American or Western superiority, or "be funny"—for instance, to take pot-shots at Dickens' appearance or his "Englishy" ways. And so in some respects, the recollections forty years later may represent a truer reaction to the reading itself than his earlier review.

One additional facet of Mark Twain's "professional" attitude which could have contributed to a lessening of his appreciation of Dickens is a corollary of the tendency to "put down" the famous. Gardner suggests that the emphasis on the "puissant god's" seeming "only a man after all" when seen in the flesh, constitutes a covert attack on the widespread idolatry of Dickens, and that this attitude, along with the subsequent overt satire of such idolatry, also implies a sense of professional rivalry, if not actual jealousy (97).

Shortly after Dickens' death (June 1870), Mark Twain announced "The Approaching Epidemic" in his "Memoranda" column in the *Galaxy* magazine for September 1870—a flood of tributes to the great novelist would pour forth from every quarter. Typical among these would be the many lectures and readings, including such gems as "Remembrances of Charles Dickens, A Lecture by John Jones, who saw him once in a streetcar and twice in a barbershop," or "Heart Treasures of Precious Moments with Literature's Departed Monarch" by Miss Susan Amelia Tryphenia McSpadden, who will until death wear a glove to protect "the hand made sacred by the clasp of Dickens." But if there is indeed an implicit sneer at Dickens' unworthiness of the pedestal on which his idolaters had placed him, there is also more clearly a resounding slap at the kinds of literary leeches who would seek to capitalize on even the slightest acquaintance with the master.

A delightful further jab at such idolatry is recalled by one of Mark Twain's favorite anecdotes. As reported in a letter to Frederick J. Kitton, when news spread in 1867 that Charles Dickens was to return to the United States, a large meeting was called in New York to plan a proper welcome. Reminiscences of Dickens by those present were enthusiastically cheered. Finally someone spotted Henry C. Robinson, a Hartford lawyer and good friend of Clemens who had actually seen Dickens during the latter's earlier visit in 1842. The cheers were uproarious. Nothing would do but for Robinson to relate his experience. With impressive solemnity he described the "unforgettable" moment when, "passing the City Hotel, in my ancient town of Hartford, . . . I suddenly stopped, as one that is paralyzed; for there, in the great bay window, alone—and meetly solitary in a greatness which could be no otherwise than companionless—sat one whom all the universe knew—Dickens! Eagerly I pressed my face against the pane, and in one moment was lost, absorbed, enchanted. Presently I saw his lips begin to open: was he going to speak to me?—to me? I verily held my breath. And—gentlemen—he *did* speak to me!'' Thunderous applause! And then the audience noticed Robinson walking calmly off the platform. Cries of ''Hold on, hold on! What the nation did he say?'' ''Well,'' said Robinson, ''he only said 'Go 'way, little boy, go 'way!' '' (*N&J3,* 302, n. 9).

There may have been some sense of rivalry, especially when Mark Twain's fame was increasing during the 1870s, and newspaper reviews of his lectures fairly frequently compared his performances with those of Dickens. And when the reviewers of *The Gilded Age* commented on the resemblance between Sellers and Micawber, the affront to his desire to be considered ''original'' might well have rankled. Hence a touch of professional jealousy also could have contributed its bit to the growing disenchantment.

Mark Twain's enthusiasm did cool over the years. But evidence shows that Dickens continued to occupy an important place in the reading of the whole Clemens family. Therefore the *complete* denial to Paine still remains somewhat surprising. Other elements no doubt entered in, but, as I have attempted to show, the major ones seem to have been, first, the mood of the moment—the old man's sad sense that despite lifelong efforts at self-education through wide reading, he still remained relatively ignorant of matters literary; second, his exaggeration of a diminished affection for Dickens' works into an almost complete rejection; and third, Clemens' ever-present sense during this period that he was speaking to his official biographer, who would ultimately present to the world the portrait of the self-made original from Missouri and the West, rising by his own untutored efforts to international eminence as an immensely popular and financially successful author and, in later years, as a public figure whose ''independent'' opinions were sought on almost any important issue that appeared in the news.

So successful was the creation of the ''unliterary'' image that its modification has taken many years, and is still going on. But now, at least, we can smile at Stephen Leacock's assertion in ''Two Humorists: Charles Dickens and Mark Twain'' in 1934 that there is ''no record and no internal evidence to show that either was influenced by the work of the other'' (122). He was right about Dickens, of course, since the British author died in June 1870 at the age of 58, only two months after John Camden Hotten began the piracies that introduced Mark Twain's sketches to British readers, and only one month after Hotten's publication of *The Innocents Abroad*. But he was totally wrong about Mark Twain's debt to Dickens.

Even so, Dickensians and Twainians alike will, I think, support Leacock's general observation that these two authors represent the "highest reach of the written humor of the nineteenth century" and perhaps "the world's supreme reach" now that the humor of the radio, the movies, and more recently, television have all but supplanted the humor of the written word.

NOTES

1. Alan Gribben's monumental "reconstruction" of *Mark Twain's Library* (Boston: G. K. Hall, 1980) has allowed an updating of Joseph Gardner's excellent *PMLA* article of 1968, as well as my own study in *Mark Twain and John Bull* (1970), by providing a list of the volumes of Dickens actually owned by Mark Twain. The following list indicates alphabetically those works which it is certain that Mark Twain had read. Those preceded by asterisks were editions in his own library; the others bear the dates of first publication: *American Notes for General Circulation* (1842), *Barnaby Rudge,* (1841), *The Battle of Life: A Love Story* (London: Routledge, 1889), *Bleak House* (n.p., n.d.), *A Child's History of England* (1853), *A Christmas Carol* (1843), *David Copperfield* (1849–50), *Dombey and Son* (1847–48), *Great Expectations* (London: Chapman and Hall, n.d.), *Little Dorrit,* (2 copies, Leipzig: Tauchnitz, 1856–57; New York, J. W. Lovell, 1883), *Martin Chuzzlewit* (1843–44), *Master Humphrey's Clock* (Leipzig: Tauchnitz, 1846), *Nicholas Nickleby* (1838–39), *The Old Curiousity Shop* (2 copies, London: Chapman and Hall, 1858; Boston: Ticknor and Fields, 1858), *Oliver Twist* (1837–39), *Our Mutual Friend* (2 copies, London: Chapman and Hall, n.d.; New York: Appleton, 1878), *Pickwick Papers* (1836–37), *The Poems and Verses of Charles Dickens* (New York: Harper, 1903), *A Tale of Two Cities* (New York: J. W. Lovell, 1882).

   Moreover, in the library of Theodore and Susan Crane at Quarry Farm, near Elmira, N. Y., where the Clemenses spent many summers, Mark Twain had access to the 55–volume Household Edition of *The Works of Charles Dickens* (New York: Hurd and Houghton, 1866–70). A number of the 42 extant volumes now in the Gannett Tripp Learning Center, Elmira College, contain Mark Twain's pencil markings and occasional marginalia.

   In addition, though absolute evidence is lacking, Mark Twain very probably knew *Pictures from Italy* (1846) and *Sketches by Boz* (1836) and possibly *The Uncommercial Traveller* (1861), *Edwin Drood* (1870), and at least "The Noble Savage" in *Household Words*, reissued in *Reprinted Pieces* (1858).
2. He had probably read the novel in the San Francisco *Golden Era*, where it was still appearing in January 1866, the last installment in England having been published in November 1865.

3. For evidence of Clemens' knowledge of those works listed in Note 1 but not mentioned in this article, see Baetzhold, *Mark Twain and John Bull;* Gardner, "Mark Twain and Charles Dickens"; and Gribben, *Mark Twain's Library.*

4. Collected in *Tom Sawyer Abroad, Etc.,* Author's National Edition, 328–330.

5. It is possible that Mark Twain also had the shrewish Jenny Wren's care of her alcoholic father in mind (*Our Mutual Friend*), but the burlesque has more bite when compared with *The Old Curiosity Shop.*

6. See my "Found: Mark Twain's 'Lost Sweetheart'," *American Literature* 44 (1972): 414–429.

7. Since there are so many editions of Dickens' and Mark Twain's works that page references to a specific edition would be of minimal help in identifying the sources of quotations, I refer (in the text) merely to chapter titles or numbers.

8. Unpublished Notebook, 32I (old numbering), TS, 26.

9. See, for example, Ellen Moers, *New York Review of Books* 20 (January 1966): 14.

10. See my "What Place was the Model for Martin Chuzzlewit's 'Eden': 'A Last Word on the Cairo Legend'," *Dickensian* (1959): 169–175.

11. For other mentions of the novel, see Gribben, 191–192, and Baetzhold, *passim.*

12. To note another minor parallel: Dickens, too, participated in an academic ceremony six months before his death when he distributed prizes and certificates to outstanding students at the Birmingham and Midland Institute (Johnson, 2:1143).

13. As an additional element of kinship with Dickens, one might note that the latter once sneered even more strongly at the "cultivated classes": "I have no respect for their opinion, good or bad; do not covet their approval; and do not write for their amusement. I venture to say this without reserve, for I am not aware of any writer in our language having a respect for himself, or held in any respect by posterity, who has ever descended to the taste of this fastidious class" (quoted in Wagenknecht, 180).

14. All quotations from *Alta California,* 3 February 1868, reprinted in *Twainian* 7 (1948): 4.

WORKS CITED

Baetzhold, Howard G. *Mark Twain and John Bull: The British Connection.* Bloomington: Indiana University Press, 1970.

———. "What Place was the Model For Martin Chuzzlewit's 'Eden'?: A Last Word on the 'Cairo Legend.' " *Dickensian* 55.3 (1959): 169–175.

Blair, Walter. "The French Revolution and Huckleberry Finn." *Modern Philology* 55 (1957): 21–35.

———. *Mark Twain and Huck Finn.* Berkeley: University of California Press, 1960.

Budd, Louis J. "Mark Twain Talks Mostly About Humor and Humorists." *Studies in American Humor* 1 (1974): 4–19.

ET&S1, ET&S2. Mark Twain. *Early Tales and Sketches.* Edgar M. Branch and Robert H. Hirst, eds. Berkeley: University of California Press, 1981.

Fatout, Paul, ed. *Mark Twain Speaking*. Iowa City: University of Iowa Press, 1976.

Ferguson, DeLancey. *Mark Twain: Man and Legend*. Indianapolis: Bobbs Merrill, 1943.

Fisher, Henry W. *Abroad With Mark Twain and Eugene Field*. New York: Nicholas Brown, 1922.

Frear, Walter F. *Mark Twain and Hawaii*. Chicago: Lake Side Press, 1947.

Gardner, Joseph. "Gaffer Hexam and Pap Finn." *Modern Philology* 66 (1968): 155–156.

———. "Mark Twain and Dickens." *PMLA* 84 (1969): 90–101.

Gribben, Alan. *Mark Twain's Library: A Reconstruction* 2 vols. Boston: G. K. Hall, 1980.

HH&T. Mark Twain's Hannibal Huck & Tom. Walter Blair, ed. Berkeley: University of California Press, 1969.

Hill, Hamlin. "Mark Twain: Audience and Artistry." *American Quarterly* 15 (1963): 25–40.

Johnson, Edgar. *Charles Dickens: His Tragedy and Triumph*. 2 vols. New York: Simon and Schuster, 1952.

Leacock, Stephen. "Two Humorists: Charles Dickens and Mark Twain." *Yale Review* 24 (1934): 118–129.

Letters. Mark Twain's Letters. 2 vols. Albert Bigelow Paine, ed. New York: Harper's, 1917.

LSI. Letters From the Sandwich Islands. G. Ezra Dane, ed. Stanford, Calif: Stanford University Press, 1938.

Mills, Nicholas C. "Social and Moral Vision in *Great Expectations* and *Huckleberry Finn*." *Journal of American Studies* 4 (1970): 61–72.

———. "Charles Dickens and Mark Twain." *English and American Fiction in the Nineteenth Century: An Antigenre Criticism and Comparison*. Bloomington: Indiana University Press, 1973.

Moers, Ellen. "The 'Truth' of Mark Twain." *New York Review of Books*, 20 January 1966: 10–15.

MTBM. Mark Twain, Business Man. Samuel C. Webster, ed. Boston: Little, Brown, 1946.

MTE. Mark Twain in Eruption. Bernard DeVoto, ed. New York: Harpers, 1940.

MTHHR. Mark Twain's Correspondence with Henry Huddleston Rogers. Lewis Leary, ed. Berkeley: University of California Press, 1969.

MTHL. Mark Twain-Howells Letters. Henry Nash Smith, William M. Gibson, eds. Cambridge, Mass: Belknap-Harvard University Press, 1960.

MTMF. Mark Twain's Letters to Mrs. Fairbanks. Dixon Wecter, ed. San Marino, Calif.: Huntington Library, 1949.

MTWB. Mark Twain's Letters to Will Bowen. Theodore Hornberger, ed. Austin: University of Texas Press, 1941.

N&J1, N&J2, N&J3. Mark Twain's Notebooks and Journals. Frederick Anderson, et al., eds. Berkeley: University of California Press, 1975, 1979.

Paine, Albert Bigelow. *Mark Twain: A Biography.* 3 vols. New York: Harper & Brothers, 1910.

Regan, Robert. "Mark Twain, 'The Doctor,' and a Guidebook by Dickens." *American Studies* 22 (1981): 32–55.

Ridland, J. M. "Huck, Pip, and Plot." *Nineteenth Century Fiction* 20 (1965): 286–290.

Rogers, Franklin R. *Mark Twain's Burlesque Patterns.* Dallas: Southern Methodist University Press, 1960.

———. *The Pattern for Mark Twain's "Roughing It."* Berkeley: University of California Press, 1961.

Wagenknecht, Edward. *The Man Charles Dickens.* Boston: Houghton Mifflin, 1929.

W1868. Washington in 1868. Cyril Clemens, ed. Webster Groves, Missouri, 1943.

WWD. Mark Twain's Which Was the Dream? and Other Symbolic Writings of The Later Years. John S. Tuckey, ed. Berkeley: University of California Press, 1966.

For additional details about Mark Twain's knowledge of and use of Dickens' works, see Baetzhold, Blair, Gardner, and Gribben. For further examination of the whole subject of Mark Twain and Dickens, see items listed under Dickens in the Index to Thomas Tenney's *Mark Twain: A Reference Guide* (Boston: G. K. Hall, 1977) and successive annual supplements in *American Literary Realism*.

Prisoners of Style: Dickens and Mark Twain, Fiction and Evasion

Robert Tracy

> I have never felt that reading was better than an error, a part of the fall into the flesh, a mouthful of the apple.
> —Yeats to Robert Bridges, 20 July 1901

> He said it was the best fun he ever had in his life, and the most intellectual.
> —*Huckleberry Finn*, chapter 36

Near the end of the sixteenth chapter of *Adventures of Huckleberry Finn*, Mark Twain, apparently frustrated at his own inability to make the story work as he wanted it to, suddenly introduces a steamboat which smashes the raft on which Huck and Jim are traveling:

> She was a big one, and she was coming in a hurry, too, looking like a black cloud with rows of glow-worms around it; but all of a sudden she bulged out, big and scary, with a long row of wide-open furnace doors shining like red-hot teeth, and her monstrous bows and guards hanging right over us. There was a yell at us, and a jingling of bells to stop the engines, a pow-wow of cussing, and whistling of steam—and as Jim went overboard on one side and I on the other, she come smashing straight through the raft.
> (16:80; Blair, *Mark Twain*, 150–151)[1]

It is an impressively final catastrophe, an act of violent destruction. But having written it, Mark Twain unwrites it a few pages later by unsmashing the shattered raft. Huck finds that Jim has, after all, survived, and has been

" 'patchin' up de raf'. . . . She was tore up a good deal—one en' of her
was—but dey warn't no great harm done. . . . Ef we hadn' dive' so deep en
swum so fur under water, en de night hadn' ben so dark, en we warn't so
sk'yerd, en ben sich punkin-heads . . . we'd a seed de raf' . . . she's all
fixed up agin mos' as good as new' " (18:95).

This habit of altering or shaping events by a few strokes of the pen is fairly
common in *Huckleberry Finn*. Jim's initial plan to escape simply by crossing
the river, and his sensible idea of hitching a ride on a raft to do this, is
thwarted; he waits for and intercepts a raft, intending to leave it at dawn,
when he would have been carried " 'twenty-five mile down de river,' " and
then " 'swim asho', en take to de woods on de Illinoi side,' " but when
" 'a man begin to come aft wid de lantern' " (8:39) he must leave the raft,
and hide on Jackson's Island. It is plausible, but a little contrived. So is the
sudden fog which prevents Huck and Jim from recognizing Cairo—the object
of their journey. Mark Twain did not want his characters to follow their own
plan and go up the Ohio River, since he himself did not know the Ohio, and
also because their entry into Free territory would effectively end the story
(Smith, Introduction, viii).

These moments of authorial manipulation are sometimes seen as flaws, or
as evidence of Twain's changes of plan. But I think they are also reminders
of the writer's control over what happens, and they occur because *Huckleberry
Finn* is to some extent a book about making fictions, and about fiction-makers'
ability to control events and to write scripts which must be followed—as when
Tom prepares for the imprisoned Jim "a mournful inscription," or rather a
series of inscriptions, beginning *"Here a captive heart busted,"* and promises
to "block them out" for the unlettered Jim to copy, "and then he wouldn't
have nothing to do but just follow the lines" (38:217).

Mark Twain suggests a writer's freedom to alter and control reality when
he invites his reader—in the fifteen or so pages between the smashing and
unsmashing of the raft—to contemplate Emmeline Grangerford's unfinished
drawing,

> of a young woman in a long white gown, standing on the rail of a bridge all
> ready to jump off, with her hair all down her back, and looking up to the moon,
> with the tears running down her face, and she had two arms folded across her
> breast, and two arms stretched out in front, and two more reaching up towards
> the moon—and the idea was, to see which pair would look best and then scratch
> out all the other arms; but, as I was saying, she died before she got her mind
> made up.   (17:87)

By deliberately calling attention to the artist's control over apparent reality,

Twain hints at a basic uneasiness about the enterprise of fiction. He underlines this uneasiness by introducing into his novel characters who try to assert an author-like control over their fellows. Tom Sawyer is the most conspicuous of these. In the early chapters of *Huckleberry Finn* he uses material from romantic novels he has read to create and then control his robber gang, insisting that they behave in conformity with what is " 'in the books. Do you want to go to doing different from what's in the books, and get things all muddled up?' " (2:9). In the final chapters, he again demands conformity to romantic fiction, this time as his price for assisting Huck to free Jim from imprisonment. Nor is Tom the only character in *Huckleberry Finn* who creates and imposes scripts on others; the King and the Duke are also fictionally creative, as are certain other characters.

A similar calling attention to fictionality, and a similar uneasiness, seems to pervade many of Dickens' novels, and especially *Great Expectations*. Dickens' own authorial manipulation is obvious in the existence of the two alternate endings—as mutually contradictory as the suicidal maiden's three sets of arms. He too deliberately calls attention to the possibilities of fictional manipulation by introducing into his narrative such figures as Magwitch and Miss Havisham, who control Pip and Estella, respectively, by preparing written directions which they must follow. Magwitch has sent Jaggers written instructions about Pip's education; when Estella, "in obedience" to Miss Havisham, meets Pip in London, she reminds him that " 'We have no choice, you and I, but to obey our instructions. We are not free to follow our own devices, you and I'." Pip comments that her "tone" is "as if our association were forced upon us and we were mere puppets" (33: 279, 285; Tracy, "Reading").

This mutual and self-conscious preoccupation with the act of fiction, the manipulation of characters and events, seems to me the most striking point of resemblance between Dickens and Twain, and between two of their books that often invite comparison, *Great Expectations* and *Huckleberry Finn*. In each book, a poor boy is "sivilized." He learns how to read and write, so well that he eventually writes his own autobiography. That autobiography describes a certain loss of innocence and spontaneous natural behavior as a consequence of literacy, and a certain guilty separation from, and mistreatment of, an older, simpler, unlettered male friend—Joe Gargery, Jim. That auto-biography also describes an experience of being "written"—conscripted—into a scenario by someone else. Pip finds himself acting out the story of a poor boy turned into a gentleman, a story Magwitch first imagines, and then writes in his orders to Jaggers. Huck acts out Tom Sawyer's fictions and plays an English valet in the King's and the Duke's plot to steal Peter Wilks's gold.

Though there is no direct evidence that Mark Twain read *Great Expectations* before writing *Huckleberry Finn,* his early enthusiasm for Dickens makes it extremely probable that he had done so. So does a comparison of the two books: at times, *Huckleberry Finn* seems like *Great Expectations* turned inside out, or shaken and reassembled in a kaleidoscope. In both books a fugitive is helped to escape by a boy who is himself something of an outcast, and whose conscience struggles between the conflicting claims of law and his own heart. Pip and Huck both come to love the fugitive they are assisting. In each book a river—the Thames, the Mississippi—broods over much of the action, and offers the fugitive an avenue of escape. Dickens and Twain both present conventional moral teaching negatively: Mrs. Joe and Miss Watson preach the same repressive doctrines, and the houses where they preside are shown as prisons. Society is seen as a veneer barely concealing an underlying cruelty: Jaggers's wealth is based on criminals, his housekeeper is a tamed murderess; Southern society is based on slavery and operates through murder, cruelty, and mob action. The garbled Shakespearean speeches of the King and Duke recall Wopsle/Waldengarver as Hamlet. Pap's disconcerting reappearance, looking like a man already dead, reminds us of Magwitch's initial appearance, seemingly out of the grave of Pip's father, and of his later reappearance in Pip's rooms (Gardner; Ridland).

But these resemblances of plot and episode are less important than the way both novels, as first-person narratives, present themselves as conscious acts of writing, but also suggest that literacy is a threat to truth and natural spontaneity, and raise doubts about the morality of fiction and fiction-making. The fictions created by Magwitch and Miss Havisham play havoc with the lives and natural affections of Pip and Estella; Magwitch and Miss Havisham themselves have been forced to follow a script by the arch-plotter Compeyson; and behind Compeyson lurks Charles Dickens, not quite as "behind or beyond or above his handiwork, invisible, refined out of existence, indifferent, paring his fingernails," as Stephen Dedalus tells us the artist ought to be.

Dickens often employs characters who are themselves creators of fiction within the books in which they appear: Old Martin Chuzzlewit creates a false version of himself and imposes it upon Pecksniff as part of an elaborate plot; Micawber plays Uriah Heep the same trick in *David Copperfield*; Sydney Carton pretends to be Charles Darnay; Noddy Boffin plays the miser, modeling his behavior on written lives of misers, in *Our Mutual Friend*. Like Magwitch and Miss Havisham, these characters use fictions to alter what seem to be the fixed destinies of the characters they manipulate, changing those destinies almost as easily as Mark Twain restores the smashed raft.

For Mark Twain, this kind of self-consciousness about fiction-making and the power of authors is chiefly confined to *Huckleberry Finn*, though there are interesting foreshadowings in *The Adventures of Tom Sawyer*—which originated, apparently, in an attempt to parody David Copperfield's courtship of Dora—and in *The Prince and the Pauper*. *Tom Sawyer*, at times sentimental, at times ironic, evokes boyhood and its attitudes for grown-ups. But Tom is already a reader of melodramatic fiction, and he uses his reading to manipulate his playmates' games. Then the melodramatic stories he reads, and the expectations they arouse, are unexpectedly realized. The boys play at being Cooper's Indians, but later they are threatened by the genuinely savage Injun Joe. They pretend to be pirates, and are later tracked by a murderer. They speculate about buried treasure, as it is found in "the books," but in fact a buried treasure does appear. The haunted house *is* haunted, by dangerous criminals. Tom imagines romantic situations in which he will die heroically for Becky, but then must act with real bravery to save her life. Tom's romantic fictions are unexpectedly endorsed by Mark Twain's development of the plot, even as he ridicules them. Twain's own identification with Tom, his own taste for romantic melodrama, and his apparent eagerness to flaunt his power, as author, to manipulate events, causes *Tom Sawyer* to veer from nostalgic idyll into thriller. Twain makes Tom's romantic fictions turn real and dangerous (Smith, *Mark Twain*, 81; Tracy, "Myth").

Twain began *Adventures of Huckleberry Finn* in the summer of 1876, immediately after he had completed *Tom Sawyer*, but he abandoned the novel in frustration, with the wrecking of the raft near the end of chapter 16; he wrote chapters 17–18 between mid-October 1879 and mid-June 1880, chapters 19–21 between mid-June 1880 and mid-June 1883; and the rest in the summer of 1883 (Blair, *Mark Twain*, 199). Between 1876 and 1883 he also completed *A Tramp Abroad* (published 1880), *The Prince and the Pauper* (1882), and *Life on the Mississippi* (1883; partly serialized, 1875). In *The Prince and the Pauper*, Twain returns to boyhood again, but this time in the alien setting of sixteenth-century England. Nevertheless, we can recognize elements that link the book to both *Tom Sawyer* and *Huckleberry Finn*. Some of these are mere parallels of plot or character: Tom Canty's drunkard father behaves like Pap, and Tudor mobs are as impetuous and cowardly as those Huck encounters along the river. Miles Hendon protects but also defers to the King—a ragged fugitive who has lost his identity and been given another—and their relationship is a sketch for the protective and reverential elements in the relationship of Huck and Jim. And, though Huck and Jim laugh at the tales of dispossession which the King and the Duke tell, that tale is one that Mark Twain himself has already told quite seriously—the tales of the lost Duke and the lost but rightful King of France are variants of Mark Twain's story of Edward VI as tattered vagabond, and of Tom Canty's temporary usurpation of his throne. Twain was to rewrite the Duke's story again, more or less, in *The American Claimant* (1892), in which Colonel Mulberry Sellers claims to be rightfully an English earl.

Twain's ability or willingness to treat the romantic stories of the King and the Duke seriously by presenting them as true or plausible in fictions of his own represents an endorsement of implausible melodrama similar to that employed in *Tom Sawyer* when the imaginary treasure turns out to be real. He also employs it within *The Prince and the Pauper*. Tom Canty has told himself stories about being a prince, and has drawn upon his reading to create elaborate games for his playmates. He forms them into a court, with himself as prince: "Daily the mock prince was received with elaborate ceremonies borrowed . . . from his romantic readings (2:19; Blair, *Mark Twain* 189–197). Tom finds court life as stuffy and confining as Huck finds life at the Widow's when his dream is unexpectedly realized, and he becomes Prince of Wales, then King of England—a thorough endorsement of his romantic dreams. And if Tom Canty has been reading romantic tales of court life, Prince Edward seems to have been reading some work like *Huckleberry Finn,* at least the passages that object to propriety and celebrate the pleasures of wearing rags and not having to wash—he is eager to play at being a beggar boy by dressing in Tom's rags. When both are unexpectedly locked into their fictions, Tom discovers the restraints of royal life, but Prince Edward must confront the very real danger, deprivation, cold, hunger, and squalor of the beggar's life. Twain's romantic fictions have an odd way of becoming true after they have been revealed—even mocked—as romantic fictions, an indication of his uneasiness with fiction itself, and at the same time his addiction to it. It is a kind of magic. And it is dependent on another magic, the dangerous dual art of reading and writing, with its destructive, yet necessary effect on natural behavior—a kind of secular version of the Fortunate Fall.[2]

Twain's uneasy treatment of fiction turning into truth is uneasy enough to evoke its contrary. If fictions can become true, apparent truth can also become fiction. *Huckleberry Finn* throws us off balance at the start. In an extraordinary passage, especially for a book that has so often been read as a celebration of the simple, spontaneous, natural man, Huck warns us that he is only a literary artifact. "You don't know about me," he begins, without you have read a book by the name of "The Adventures of Tom Sawyer," but that ain't no matter. That book was made by Mr. Mark Twain, and he told the truth, mainly. There was things which he stretched, but mainly he told the truth.

(1:3)

Few works of fiction begin with so clear and so insistent a statement of their own fictionality, their dependence on *another* book—which is not, it seems, completely trustworthy. We are almost ordered to put down *Huckleberry Finn* and read *Tom Sawyer,* if we have not already done so. But *Tom Sawyer,* while "mostly a true book," contains "some stretchers." A fictional character not only proclaims his own fictionality, he criticizes his own creator for making up stories. We are in an unexpectedly metaphysical realm, forced to grapple with questions of narrative reliability and the nature of a fictional character's existence. Twain jeopardizes the reader's willingness to suspend disbelief and treat Huck's adventures as true, and he does this quite deliberately.

Huck's assertion that he owes his existence to a piece of writing is followed almost immediately by his account of life at the Widow Douglas's house. He stresses the discomfort of enforced table manners and clean clothes, and his own nostalgia for his old life of rags and hogsheads—to which he briefly returns. But gradually Huck accommodates: "I liked the old ways best," he tells us, "but I was getting so I liked the new ones, too, a little bit" (4:15).

In *Tom Sawyer,* we see Huck Finn primarily through Tom's eyes, which we know are clouded by a commitment to romantic fictions. Tom envies Huck's "gaudy, outcast condition" and sees him as a "romantic outcast" (6:47–48), just as Prince Edward sees Tom Canty's life as romantic and enviable. Events refute the Prince's romantic views. In *Tom Sawyer* there is no explicit counter-view of Huck's life, but his introduction as "the juvenile pariah of the village" hints at his isolation and perhaps at his hardships. When Tom, Huck, and Joe Harper reappear after they are thought to be dead, Huck sneaks "sheepishly in the rear," and while the other boys are embraced and welcomed, "poor Huck stood abashed and uncomfortable, not knowing exactly . . . where to hide from so many unwelcoming eyes" (17:131) until Tom appeals to Aunt Polly to greet him. In *Huckleberry Finn,* Huck's reveries are often improvisations on the theme of loneliness. When he reads the Grangerfords' copy of *Pilgrim's Progress,* he notes that it is "about a man that left his family it didn't say why" (17:85); clearly Huck wonders why a man *would* leave his family. Earlier, at the Widow's, he is "in a sweat to find out all about . . . Moses and the Bulrushers" when the Widow reads the story to him (1:4), presumably because Moses is another outcast child who is taken into a respectable household. It is significant that all Huck's improvisations along the River, when he must account for himself to strangers, present him as the survivor of a large family (Solomon).[3]

Huck is both practically and imaginatively attracted by the possibility of ceasing to be a pariah and becoming part of society. Even respectability has its charms. And both social acceptance and respectability are closely associated with learning to read and write. Life at the Widow's includes going to school, and Huck learns to "spell, and read, and write just a little . . . the longer I went to school the easier it got to be" (4:14). When Pap appears, he recognizes that reading has changed Huck into a person with status, and bitterly resents the change. He promises to beat Huck if he catches him going to school, a promise that spurs Huck to continue: "I didn't want to go to school much, before, but I reckoned I'd go now to spite pap" (6:21). Pap's objections are reminiscent of Mrs. Joe's, in *Great Expectations*, as Joe explains them: " 'she ain't over partial to having scholars on the premises . . . and in partickler would not be over partial to my being a scholar, for fear as I might rise. Like a sort of rebel, don't you see?' " (7:79).

Books and reading are an even more effective enforcer of respectability in the hands of Tom Sawyer, who uses them to force Huck to conform. When Huck runs away from the Widow's, at the very beginning of the book, Tom "hunted me up and said he was going to start a band of robbers, and I might join if I would go back to the widow and be respectable. So I went back" (1:3). Tom invokes "the books" whenever a member of the gang questions one of its practices, but it is important to notice that these books, and the glamor Tom hopes they will shed on his robber gang, are Tom's chief means of compelling Huck's respectability. Tom also invokes books to thwart Huck's objections to fictions in which he cannot believe, as a further method of enforcing conformity. When Huck complains that the crowd of "Spaniards and A-rabs . . . camels and elephants" that the gang attacks are no more than "a Sunday school picnic, and only a primer-class at that," Tom insists that enchantment has concealed the exotic, and invokes the authority of *Don Quixote* (3:13). Huck is skeptical, but Tom's books have done their part in weaning Huck away from his old raffish ways. And Tom no longer envies Huck his freedom.

Though Tom Sawyer disappears from the book at this point, and does not reappear for some time, the intimate relationship he has helped to create between literacy, the reading of romantic fiction, the insistence that romantic fiction is true, and the enforcement of social propriety, is maintained during his absence by other characters who share his literary tastes and his opinions, and who use fiction as a means of coercion. Much has been made of the sense of spontaneity, of freedom, which pervades the rafting chapters, and many readers of *Huckleberry Finn* remember these chapters more vividly than the rest. Twain creates a wonderfully lyric mood as Huck and Jim together develop a perfect community on the raft, a place of equality and brotherhood—though we rarely forget that it is threatened from the river's banks.

Yet Tom Sawyer's avatars continually appear to remind us of his world of romantic fictions, and his use of fiction. When Huck and Jim explore the wreck of the *Walter Scott*—a steamboat named after one of Tom's favorite authors—they are in danger from a gang of real robbers; like the robbers in *Tom Sawyer*, they seem almost to have been evoked by Tom's book-fed imagination. Later Huck finds himself involved in the feud between the Grangerfords and the Shepherdsons—an adaptation from Scott's chivalric fiction, and especially from those feuds between Highland clans over which he threw the cloak of romance. Like the robbers of the *Walter Scott*, the Grangerfords and the Shepherdsons act out Tom's romantic fictions, and in doing so reveal their implicit cruelty and danger. When the King and the Duke appear with their tales of exalted birth and lost rights, they too represent the fictions that fill Tom's mind and which he insists on endowing with life.[4] The Duke turns Jim into a written fiction, which is partly true, by printing a handbill describing Jim as a runaway slave, and recommends tying Jim with a rope when strangers are near; " 'Handcuffs and chains would look still better,' " he remarks, " 'but . . . too much like jewelry. Ropes are the correct thing—we must preserve the unities, as we say on the boards' " (20:113); later they turn Jim into a "*Sick Arab*" (24:132). The raft journey is haunted by Tom Sawyer's literary imagination.

Huck, who has already rebelled against Tom's version of the Sunday school picnic, implicitly repudiates Tom's fictional mode in the fictions he creates himself—though he simultaneously yearns for Tom's participation and endorsement. When he creates the fiction of his own murder in Pap's cabin, he leaves clues to a brutal and unromantic story for others to read, though he wishes Tom were there to "throw in the fancy touches" (7:29). His various accounts of himself as a survivor of a decimated family are little sketches in a grimly realistic mode, in keeping with what we perceive as the reality of life along the Mississippi. Huck seems to be trying to escape from Tom's world of fiction just as Jim is trying to escape from slavery. Huck is able to confront the issue of slavery, to struggle with it, and to free himself from the social contract that accepts slavery as legitimate. But he is not as easily able to free himself from Tom's fictions. When Jim is recaptured by the institution he has fled, Huck is recaptured by Tom's literary imagination. Jim is imprisoned in his cell, but both Jim and Huck are imprisoned in Tom's books and the rules they impose.

Tom's re-entry into the novel, and his elaborately literary schemes to free Jim, have puzzled or disturbed critics ever since Ernest Hemingway made one of his characters remark that " 'All modern American literature comes from . . . *Huckleberry Finn*,'' and then add, " 'If you read it you must stop where the Nigger Jim is stolen from the boys. That is the real end. The rest is just cheating.' "[5] Tom turns Jim's imprisonment into an elaborate literary game of rope-ladders, coats of arms, disguises, diaries, messages scratched on walls and tin plates, moats, secret tunnels, and all the trappings of escape fiction—in both senses of the phrase. And he cites his literary authorities, among them Casanova, Benvenuto Cellini, Baron Trenck, Henri IV, and Dumas' *The Man in the Iron Mask* (35:200–204).

It is significant that Tom re-enters the book at the moment when Huck ceases to plot his own story, after he has successfully improvised turns of plot and so controlled events, from his staging of his own murder to his concealing of Peter Wilks's gold. Approaching the Phelps farm, he abandons himself to Providence—or to Mark Twain: "I went right along, not fixing up any particular plan, but just trusting to Providence to put the right words in my mouth when the time come; for I'd noticed that Providence always did put the right words in my mouth, if I let it alone" (32:184). Does Huck suspect, once more, that he is being written? Providence obliges with a Dickensian coincidence. Tom Sawyer is expected at this very farm, and Huck is accepted as Tom; he is able to intercept Tom, who arrives as the impersonation of his good-boy brother, Sid.

To Huck's astonishment, Tom agrees to assist in freeing Jim. His willingness to help causes him to fall "considerable" in Huck's estimation. "Tom Sawyer a *nigger stealer*! . . . I couldn't ever understand . . . how he *could* help a body set a nigger free, with his bringing up" (33:189; 42:243). And Tom characteristically redefines what they are about to do: " 'When a prisoner of style escapes, it's called an evasion. It's always called so when a king escapes, f'rinstance' " (39:224). Jim and Huck have both become prisoners of style—that style Tom Sawyer "would a throwed" (18:163) into the plot to save Peter Wilks's gold, and will now impose upon the simple question of Jim's freedom.

Tom's motivations are neither as ignoble, as exploitive, nor as silly as they seem. They are a testimony to the importance of romantic fictions as transformers of reality, and the dangerous power these fictions have—it was Mark

Twain, after all, who paid Sir Walter Scott the compliment of blaming the Civil War on him (*Life*, 46:501). The charge, which is based on the Southern taste for Scott's fiction and the Southern tendency to self-identify with his cavaliers, implies an enormous respect for the power of romantic fiction, a respect Mark Twain shares with Tom.[6]

Tom's elaborations on the theme of Jim's escape is in harmony with the robber gang material at the beginning, and the similar material at the end of *Tom Sawyer*. They share with that material the function of enforcing respectability. In *Tom Sawyer*, Tom has been rewarded for his romantic imagination by thrilling adventures and a treasure "put . . . out at six per cent." Judge Thatcher expects him to become "a great lawyer or a great soldier. . . . He said he meant to look to it that Tom should be admitted to the National military academy and afterwards trained in the best law school in the country." Huck too has been rewarded, for his assistance to Tom and for saving the Widow Douglas from Injun Joe's attempt to notch her ears and slit her nostrils; his "wealth and the fact that he was now under the widow's protection, introduced him into society—no, dragged him into it, hurled him into it (*Tom Sawyer*, 35:254–255).[7] Tom's fictions become a means of keeping Huck respectable and conforming.

Tom has discovered that events both confirm and reward his fictions. In writing *Tom Sawyer*, Mark Twain has found a way of exploiting both his sentimental picture of boyhood and lost innocence and his natural tendency to manipulate the plot in the direction of that romantic fiction he so often ridicules—to add a lurid glare to the soft light of reminiscence. And he finds a way of retreating from too explicit an admission that the cherished world of his boyhood was built on human slavery, or that Huck's aid to Jim would return Huck to pariahdom.

Tom plans to turn Jim's escape into an evasion in both senses. He will make the unpopular business of a slave attaining freedom romantic, and therefore respectable. He will even substitute the right romantic word. And in doing so, he can evade both Jim's legal freedom, already established by Miss Watson's will, and even the moral issues about Jim's right to freedom which Huck has confronted. Jim can be controlled through fiction, and made into a romantic escapade rather than a moral issue.

Jim escapes three times in *Huckleberry Finn*. The first of these is when he runs away, intended to cross to the free soil of Illinois. This is the simplest plan, but perhaps the most dangerous, because it is the predictable plan of a runaway slave. Even Pap has figured this out, and manages to get money out of Judge Thatcher " 'to hunt for' " Jim " 'all over Illinois with' "

(11:49). Though Jim's plan is thwarted, nevertheless he has decided on his own right to freedom, and has freed himself.

It is important to remember that he does this because he fears being sold down river rather than because he objects to being a slave. But once away, he begins to accept the ideas of the Abolitionists, and even to plan the "theft" of his own family—to Huck's horror. The trip along the river, and their life together, prepare for Jim's second escape, the moment when Huck recognizes, against such social and religious sanctions as he knows, that Jim must be free. Jim's freedom is accepted by a white person, and recognized as morally necessary. But Huck's decision is a private one. It has received no public legal or emotional sanction, and has no chance of doing so. It is operative only in the isolated miniature community of the raft, and endangered there.

Jim's third liberation takes place off stage, also as a result of the operations of moral conscience. As Tom eventually admits, Miss Watson " 'was ashamed she ever was going to sell him down the river, and *said* so; and she set him free in her will' " (42:241). Unlike Huck, Miss Watson has been able to make her moral decision public and effective—by writing a legal document rather than a fiction.[8]

Tom knows perfectly well that truth rather than fiction will free Jim in this legal way, as Miss Watson had intended. But his sense that romance is needed to make her decision attractive and therefore respectable directs his complicated games of evasion. He intends to re-state Jim's liberation, not in practical or moral terms—this has already been done—but in the respectable terms of romantic conventions. A right and moral act must be made romantic and chivalrous and impractical:

> what he had planned in his head, from the start, if we got Jim out all safe, was for us to run him down the river, on the raft, and have adventures plumb to the mouth of the river, and then tell him about his being free, and take him back up home on a steamboat, in style, and pay him for his lost time, and write word ahead and get out all the niggers around, and have them waltz him into town with a torchlight procession and a brass band, and then he would be a hero, and so would we.	(Chapter the Last: 243–244)

But as we know, the plan fails. Tom is wounded, and Jim refuses to leave him. " 'He had a dream,' " Huck tells the Doctor, with unconscious accuracy, " 'and it shot him.' 'Singular dream,' " the Doctor comments drily (41:231). Tom's fiction has again evoked a genuinely dangerous response, and real dangers replace fictional ones.

With Tom wounded, Jim and Huck free themselves from his fiction and refuse any longer to follow his orders. When Tom can no longer control them, he must tell the truth about Jim's freedom, and the arrival of Aunt Polly demolishes the false identities of Tom and Huck. Grey truth replaces gaudy fictions. Though Tom briefly believes that he has succeeded in freeing Jim "with style," and Jim praises his effort, declaring that " 'It 'us planned beautiful, en it 'uz *done* beautiful; en dey ain't *nobody* kin git up a plan dat's mo' mixed-up en splendid den what dat one wuz'," even Tom hints at waning faith. He exultingly reminds his friends that *they* would have been able to rescue Louis XVI and " 'whooped him over the *border*' " (40:229–230). But subconsciously he is remembering an enterprise much like his own, the botched attempt to rescue Louis XVI and the royal family and convey them to safety across the French border, known in history as the Flight to Varennes. That enterprise ended in ignominious recapture, as does Jim's escape.[9]

Jim frees himself from Tom's fiction by refusing to leave his wounded rescuer. Huck significantly allows Jim to make the decision and to express it; " 'Say it, Jim,' " marks a change from the imposition of words and postures on Jim that has prevailed, and with those words Huck recognizes Jim's right to be free from the slavery of fiction as well as from the more obvious form of slavery.[10] Jim rebels out of genuine misplaced love for Tom, and so evades the dangerous fictional adventures Tom has planned for him before telling him that he is free—adventures that would have destroyed *Huckleberry Finn* by extending the mood of the Phelps Farm episodes indefinitely. Tom's plan would have made it almost impossible to bring the novel to a close.

Huck frees himself from Tom's fiction by agreeing with Jim's refusal to leave Tom, and by ignoring Tom's instructions about the blindfold and the bag of gold which are to be part of fetching a doctor to treat Tom's wound—Tom's last effort to turn what is happening into romantic fiction. And as they thwart Tom's fictions, and attempt to control events themselves, Jim seems to look ironically over his shoulder at Mark Twain. " 'I doan' budge a step out'n dis place, 'dout a *doctor*; not if it's forty year!' " he declares, specifying more or less the period between the time when the events of *Huckleberry Finn* are supposed to be occurring, the "Forty or Fifty Years Ago" of the title page, and the time when the novel was written. In a sense, Jim does wait "forty year." The Doctor's arrival brings about Jim's recapture, and Tom's eventual abandonment of his fictions for truth, if only temporarily.

Tom's plotting has been motivated by an eagerness to tell not the true story, but the right story. Like Pip when he returns from his first visit to Miss Havisham's, and describes to Joe, Mrs. Joe, and Pumblechook his activities there, the waving of flags and swords, the feeding of veal cutlets out of a silver basket to four dogs, Tom has made an episode more interesting and satisfying to his hearers, but less true. Pip's lapse into fiction-making occurs just after he has met and fallen in love with Estella, who is herself a romantic fiction created by Miss Havisham. Estella is to function in Pip's life as a romantic obsession, as episodes in romantic fiction function for Tom Sawyer. Though Pip subsequently admits to Joe that the flags and dogs are fictions, and accepts Joe's redefinition of these fictions as lies, he remains in thrall to the fiction that is Estella, and is later trapped in Magwitch's fiction of creating a gentleman.

Tom and Pip both remain prisoners of fictions, and their inability to free themselves threatens each novel's ability to achieve closure. Dickens attempts to do so by a kind of circularity. The Pip who, at intervals, admits his mistreatment of Joe, foreshadows for the reader the sadder and wiser Pip who reveals himself eventually as the author of *Great Expectations,* and in doing so explains the ironic distance from his own childhood experiences that the narrator often adopts. But Pip remains a prisoner of those experiences, because of his own guilty compulsion to write about them. Pip has no future, only a past, which he must sustain by writing about it. His obsessive return to his own past is his story, completely enclosed in his book. His inability to marry and begin an independent adult life emphasizes this. Here he resembles David Copperfield, Martin Chuzzlewit, and other Dickens heroes. Though David and Martin are described as marrying and begetting children, they too seem unable to move out of their fictioned past. David also writes obsessively about that past, and bases his present happiness on his early sufferings; he does not really suggest a future. Martin does not narrate his own adventures, but in the last few paragraphs of *Martin Chuzzlewit,* and in the allegorical frontispiece (which appeared, as was customary, with the *last* monthly part), Tom Pinch is shown evoking all that has gone before on his organ in the medium of music rather than words; Pinch represents the book's narrative voice, equally unable to break free from the past. Everything leads us back into the written text rather than forward out of it. Pip, David Copperfield, Tom Pinch remain trapped in their books, evoking forever the events which comprise those books.

Huck Finn does seem able to evade that obsession with the fictioned past and to break free into a future outside the text. His adventures along the river are a series of discrete episodes, separated from one another by the nature of rafts and the nature of rivers. Huck rarely uses his memory, in contrast to Tom's elaborate recollections of books he has read. Once Huck has lived through an episode, no matter how horrific, he does not refer to it again—with one important exception. Unlike the Widow's house, and the house of the Grangerfords, with their juxtaposed books and respectability, the raft is free of writing and reading. But when writing and conformity to society's attitudes invade the raft, they invade it together, and bring with them that retrospection which we have seen in Dickens' novels—that immobilizing and yet potentially ennobling retrospection. Huck has lost Jim to the King and the Duke, who have sold him to Silas Phelps as a runaway. Huck sees his effort to help Jim to freedom as having landed him in a worse—because unfamiliar—slavery, and thinks of writing to Tom Sawyer or to Miss Watson to tell them where Jim is. He draws back from doing so because he knows Jim will be scorned as "ungrateful. . . . And then think of *me*! It would get all around, that Huck Finn helped a nigger to get his freedom; and if I was to ever see anybody from that town again, I'd be ready to get down and lick his boots for shame." Huck does write the letter, after an unsuccessful attempt to pray ("I was letting *on* to give up sin, but away inside of me I was holding on to the biggest one of all. . . . You can't pray a lie.") Huck acutely analyzes his own spiritual crisis (have the Shakespearean parodies brought the King's attempt to pray in *Hamlet* III, iii to Mark Twain's mind?). But when he has written the letter, he begins to remember events of the trip:

> And got to thinking over our trip down the river; and I see Jim before me, all the time, in the day, and in the nighttime, sometimes moonlight, sometimes storms, and we a floating along, talking, and singing, and laughing. But somehow I couldn't seem to strike no places to harden me against him, but only the other kind. I'd see him standing my watch on top of his'n, stead of calling me, so I could go on sleeping; and see him how glad he was when I come back out of the fog; and when I come to him again in the swamp, up there where the feud was; and such-like times . . . and how good he always was; and at last I struck the time I saved him by telling the men we had small-pox aboard, and he was so grateful, and said I was the best friend old Jim ever had in the world, and the *only* one he's got now; and then I happened to look around, and see that paper. (31:178–179)

And then, in a famous passage, he tears the letter and decides to " '*go* to hell.' "

Here, writing, Huck's new skill and part of the process which is to make him respectable, is closely associated with social conformity, from which the pariah Huck of *Tom Sawyer* was excluded. Writing and respectability combine to bring about the betrayal of Jim—and Huck abandons his own characteristic vocabulary for the "soul-butter" of society's moral clichés as he invokes Providence.[11] Reading leads to respectability and so to social, moral, and even verbal entrapment. Pip is much more corrupted by literacy and the education of a gentleman and faces the same struggle when he is called upon to recognize Magwitch's claim upon him and to treat him as a human being, because social respectability has become of paramount importance to him as a means toward the supreme fiction of Estella. Huck and Pip redeem themselves through the same process of recalling and recording the past and its crises. Huck's recollection is the novel so far in miniature, including his own earlier near-betrayals of Jim; Pip's recollection includes his betrayals of Joe. But Huck's decisive repudiation of conventional morality, as his "sound heart" wins over his "deformed conscience,"[12] frees him forever from that retrospection which can become a prison. And at the same moment, Mark Twain evades specific moral commentary of any kind, and manipulates the reader into making his or her own judgment about Huck's action.

At the end of the book, the only aspect of the past that Huck thinks about is Pap, and he refers to him partly as an excuse for not joining Tom's next fiction. Pap, he learns, will never appear again. Huck does not return to St. Petersburg and the Widow Douglas. Instead he projects his own escape from his past, from Tom's fictions, and even from any further role in fictions by "Mr. Mark Twain." In the final paragraph, Huck seizes control of his actions, to impose a decisive closure on the book and to suggest an independent life for himself outside its pages.

Huck's narration of Tom's evasion plans implicitly criticizes their elaborate improbabilities, and he quotes Aunt Sally's explicit comments about the absurdity of the grindstone, the rope-ladder, and the other props Tom has demanded. Huck himself does not directly challenge Tom's plans, but his detailed description of them, and of his own sensible objections, are part of his narrative. As author, he can suggest shortcomings in Tom's fictions. He implicitly rejects Tom's control when he fetches the Doctor without any romantic precautions, and he emphasizes the real danger to Tom and to Jim invited by Tom's fictions.

Huck's final escape comes out of the extensive implied criticism of Tom's fictional clichés and of Tom's authorial manipulation. By describing them and noting his own objections, Huck has manipulated the reader into recognizing their absurdity and danger. In doing so, Huck has raised important aesthetic issues about fictional truth and plausibility, and about a novelist's responsibilities toward the characters he has created. His parting shot is to declare his own independence from fictions and from authorial manipulation. After mildly ridiculing Tom's habit of flaunting the bullet taken from his wound—itself a reminder that fictions can turn into dangerous truth—Huck permanently resigns from the profession of author, and presumably from that of fictional character: "and so there ain't nothing more to write about, and I am rotten glad of it, because if I'd a knowed what a trouble it was to make a book I wouldn't a tackled it and ain't agoing to no more" (Chapter the Last: 245).

When Huck wrote those words, Tom Sawyer and Mark Twain were already plotting a sequel to *Huckleberry Finn,* involving getting "an outfit, and go[ing] for howling adventures amongst the Injuns, over in the Territory, for a couple of weeks or two" (244). Huck's initial effort to avoid any part in this sequel, on the grounds that he cannot afford the outfit because by now Pap must have spent all his money, is thwarted by the news that Pap has been dead for some time. It is then that he immediately moves to end *Huckleberry Finn* by announcing that he will not take part in Tom's project, and will not narrate any other adventures nor write any other book. He also refuses to participate in Aunt Sally's equally unattractive project of imitating the Widow and scripting him into respectability: "Aunt Sally she's going to adopt me and sivilize me and I can't stand it. I been there before." Huck refuses to return to the mood of the book's earliest chapters, dominated by the Widow's "sivilizing" process and Tom's fictions, which reinforce that process. He will not be swept into a recapitulation of what he has already written, nor any re-enactment of other people's scripts.

Like Don Quixote, who refuses to follow the adventures written for him by the author of the spurious Part II of *Don Quixote,* and takes the road to Barcelona because the writer described him as traveling to Saragossa (Part II, chapter 59), Huck evades adventures sent and controlled by another. Huck will evade Tom's future romantic fictions about Indians, and Aunt Sally's well-meant scenario of redeeming an outcast and making him part of conventional society. He will move into the undefined Territory ahead, a provisional sort of place where notions of legality and respectability are comparatively fluid, not yet codified in writing—an unscripted place where we cannot follow. He will "light out . . . ahead of the rest," ahead of Tom and his fictions, Aunt Sally and her rules, the whole shallow pretense at civil life and culture which the towns he has visited along the river embody.

We recognize how successfully he has evaded any further role as fictional character or narrator when we read Mark Twain's various attempts to use him in sequels to *Huckleberry Finn,* and we come to realize that his certainty that the book must end shows that his literary judgment was superior to his creator's. To read the unfinished "Huck Finn and Tom Sawyer among the Indians" and "Tom Sawyer's Conspiracy,"[13] and the published *Tom Sawyer*

Abroad (1894) and "Tom Sawyer, Detective" (1896) is to see Mark Twain vainly struggling to control Huck as narrator and as participant in Tom's fictions.

Twain makes Huck the narrator of each of these sequels, and each one describes events that occur very soon after the final episodes of *Huckleberry Finn*. "Huck Finn and Tom Sawyer" attempts to carry out Tom's plans as described in the final pages of *Huckleberry Finn*; *Tom Sawyer Abroad* opens with a reference to "the adventures we had down the river the time we set the nigger Jim free and Tom got shot in the leg' " and implies that Tom's romantic schemes had ended as gloriously as he wanted them to: "we three come back up the river in glory, as you may say . . . and the village received us with a torchlight procession and speeches, and everybody hurrah'd and shouted . . . it made us heroes" (*Abroad*, 1). This is stretching the truth a little, to say the least. "Tom Sawyer, Detective" opens "the next spring after me and Tom Sawyer set our old nigger Jim free the time he was chained up for a runaway slave down there on Tom's uncle Silas's farm in Arkansaw" (*Abroad*, 107), while "Tom Sawyer's Conspiracy" is set at about the same time: "Well, we was back home and I was at the Widow Douglas's . . . again getting sivilised some more along of her and old Miss Watson all the winter and spring, and the Widow was hiring Jim for wages so he could buy his wife and children's freedom some time or other" (Blair, *Hannibal*, 163). This last version revives Miss Watson, on whose death Jim's freedom depended. In 1902, at work on one last effort to make Huck tell another story that would be a sequel to *Huckleberry Finn*, Twain admitted to Howells that he was "making Huck Finn tell things that are imperfectly true. . . . He exaggerates. . . . Still, I have to keep him as he was, & he was an exaggerator from the beginning." A few years later he apparently destroyed the manuscript, after deciding that his characters "had done work enough in this world and were entitled to a permanent rest," and "for fear I might some day finish it" (Blair, *Hannibal*, 19–20). He eventually came to share Huck's perception that the story was ended, once and for all.

The sense of a narrative spinning its wheels, refusing to go anywhere, which pervades "Huck Finn and Tom Sawyer among the Indians" is characteristic of all four of these unsuccessful sequels. Twain wrote its nine chapters in the summer of 1884, just after reading proof for the Phelps farm chapters of *Huckleberry Finn* (Blair, *Hannibal*, 81–82). In them he returns to those chapters' preoccupation with romantic fiction, this time with the novels of Fenimore Cooper as his target. Tom, Huck, and Jim do get into Indian country after Tom has persuaded his reluctant companions by glowingly describing the Red Man's nobility, generosity, and general superiority. The Indians they meet turn out to be treacherous murderers, who pretend friendship for and then murder most members of a pioneer family with whom the boys have joined forces. They carry off Jim and two daughters of the family. " 'Tom, where did you learn about Injuns—how noble they was, and all that?' " asks Huck:

> He give me a look that showed me I had hit him hard, very hard, and so I wished I hadn't said the words. He turned away his head, and after about a minute he said "Cooper's novels," and didn't say anything more, and I didn't say anything more, and so that changed the subject. I see he didn't want to talk about it, and was feeling bad, so I let it just rest there, not ever having any disposition to fret or worry any person.   (Blair, *Hannibal,* 109)

An impossibly competent and heroic frontiersman appears to pursue the Indians, and then the futile narrative breaks off—nor is it too soon. Twain himself obviously knew that the story was a failure. He had already exhausted the theme of literary fooling with Tom's earlier fictions. The attack on Cooper is soon over, and though his noble Indians have been revealed as rascals, Twain must create a character out of "the book," very much like Leatherstocking, to pursue them. Brace Johnson, the frontiersman, is a Cooper or Tom Sawyer hero come to life. As often in Mark Twain, the story develops by endorsing, to some extent, the romantic fictions that have already been satirized. Twain evades what is crucial to his pursuit plot, the probability that one of the girls has been raped, and Huck tells an impeding lie by insisting that she is dead and that he has buried her body. Once Jim is captured, Tom and Huck seem to forget about him for long periods, though they are supposedly trying to rescue him. It is all strained and unnatural. Events quickly and violently destroy Huck's and Jim's faith in Tom's fictional Indians, but the reader has no faith in Huck, Tom, or Jim. Mark Twain cannot make his puppets perform for him, nor can he make Huck tell a sustained story. The balloon journey in *Tom Sawyer Abroad* and the Sherlock Holmes parodies in "Tom Sawyer, Detective" and "Tom Sawyer's Conspiracy" are equally adrift and equally unconvincing.

Huck's declaration of independence at the end of *Huckleberry Finn* is forever, and he cannot be forced back into any of his old roles: naive observer, Sancho Panza to Tom's Don Quixote, juvenile pariah, Jim's faithful friend. When he uneasily begins "Huck Finn and Tom Sawyer among the Indians," which depends on *Huckleberry Finn* as *Huckleberry Finn* depends on *Tom Sawyer,* he does not invoke the earlier book, but instead dismisses it: "That

other book which I made before, was named 'Adventures of Huckleberry
Finn.' Maybe you remember about it. But if you don't, it don't make no
difference, because it ain't got nothing to do with this one" (Blair, *Hannibal*,
92). The other sequels begin with vague and not quite accurate references to
Huckleberry Finn.

Unlike Pip or David Copperfield, unlike Mark Twain, Huck Finn frees
himself from the fiction in which he has been trapped, and from an obsession
with that fictional past. He breaks free of fiction and the narrating of fiction
for good with his final decisive closure of *Huckleberry Finn*, which leaves
him standing *outside* the book. The last words are "THE END, YOURS TRULY,
HUCK FINN." "The End" are conventionally the last words of a work of
fiction, but Huck slips past them. After those words, outside the fiction, there
is Huck, "TRULY" at last. He has evaded any further internal manipulation
by Tom, any further external manipulation by Mark Twain. Books are not
condemned, but abandoned, as he leaves that whole entrapment in letters,
words, print, pages, which thwart his spontaneity and freedom. He becomes
his own man, TRULY HUCK FINN.

In June 1984 I had the privilege of meeting the South African playwright
Athol Fugard. He told me that his plays often develop out of a word or two
overheard, or someone he has passed on the road, or some similar random
experience. On one occasion, he became fascinated by a photograph on display
outside a cheap photographer's studio in Port Elizabeth. It was a photograph
of a Black man wearing a broad-brimmed hat and a suit that did not fit very
well. He had a cigar in one hand and a pipe in the other, and on his face the
broadest happiest smile imaginable. "What could possibly, in South Africa,
make a Black man smile like that?" Fugard asked some of the Black actors
with whom he works. The answer: "Having his pass-book [the written document which allows him to live where he lives and work where he works]
in order." The pass-book writes such a man into society but at the same time
defines him. He cannot evade what is written about him, nor the limitations
that writing imposes. Jim is in a similar state when he is defined in words
and print in the handbill describing him as a runaway slave which the Duke
has prepared to justify Jim's presence on the raft. The printed paper seems
to preserve Jim's freedom, but it also enslaves him. True freedom is not being
written nor printed nor defined in a book.

Mark Twain almost explicitly acknowledges the resemblance between a
writer's control of his characters and a slave-owner's control of his slaves.
In his *Autobiography* he tells us that the Phelps farm is modelled on a real
farm once owned by his uncle, John A. Quarles. "In *Huck Finn* and in *Tom*

Sawyer, Detective I moved it down to Arkansas," he adds. "It was all of six hundred miles, but it was no trouble; it was not a very large farm—five hundred acres, perhaps—but I could have done it if it had been twice as large. And as for the morality of it, I cared nothing for that; I would move a state if the exigencies of literature required it." One of the Quarles slaves, "Uncle Dan'l," was Jim's prototype:

> a middle-aged slave whose head was the best one in the negro quarter, whose sympathies were wide and warm, and whose heart was honest and simple and knew no guile. He has served me well these many, many years. I have not seen him for more than half a century, and yet spiritually I have had his welcome company a good part of that time, and have staged him in books under his own name and as "Jim," and carted him all around—to Hannibal, down the Mississippi on a raft, and even across the Desert of Sahara in a balloon—and he has endured it all with the patience and friendliness and loyalty which were his birthright.   (*Autobiography,* I, 96, 100)

The tone is facetious, but clearly recognizes a writer's power of manipulating and controlling, a power indifferent to "morality."

Huckleberry Finn ends in evasion, and in literal and literary failure. Mark Twain loses control of his book and his characters. He has struggled to find or develop a literary form through which he can express the fluid possibilities of American life. The literary models available to him—the novels of Scott, Dickens, and other European or British writers—were inadequate because they ultimately affirm a complete and stable society, and act as guides to that society. Reading and writing threaten Pip morally, but direct him to a place in society which is limiting but acceptable. David Copperfield is similarly directed: he learns that an ability to narrate novels gains him Steerforth's approbation and protection, and so a recognized—but narrowly defined—place in the miniature society of Mr. Creakle's school, after he has earlier been defined in writing as one who bites; writing stories becomes David's way of finding his social place. Martin Chuzzlewit abandons the literally as well as socially fluid Eden, which does not conform to its fictional plan and resists any attempt to impose design upon it.

The society Mark Twain is exploring is one without true maps or guides, and resistant to design or definition. It is fluid and open, and cannot be comprehended in existing literary forms, though Tom and Mark Twain both attempt to impose them. A society that claims to be unaware of limits, and is unshaped because of its still incomplete movement into the unmapped spaces of the West, defies the closure that the novel, as Mark Twain knew it, demands. Apart from the passages of free floating on the river in a vessel that cannot really be navigated and can only go as the current takes it, where Twain does suggest freedom without definition, and apart from Huck's vernacular idiom, which communicates effectively and eloquently while resisting traditional grammatical and verbal categories, Twain is unable to find a literary form to present the undefined nature of American life. He senses the need for new social and moral dimensions, and hints at them through Huck; he also senses the need for new and less confining literary methods, but fails to develop them. He does not achieve for the novel the formal innovation that Walt Whitman and Emily Dickinson were achieving for poetry.

Pip and David Copperfield are enclosed in their books and in the elaborately codified society those books reflect, a society whose codes are expressed in written and printed words which must be read. The absence of those codes, as Henry James pointed out in his book about Hawthorne (1879), created severe formal problems for the American novelist, and made closure almost impossible. The book that Huck has written condemns the society he had so yearned to join. Mark Twain struggles with his paradox, the natural man who comes out of a book and must write another book. Closure cannot be imposed once the idea that there are no socially defined limits has been admitted. Huck finally selects his own society, then shuts the door.

NOTES

1. Citations to *Huckleberry Finn, Great Expectations,* and other frequently reprinted texts prefix chapter number to page reference.
2. Fiction does not, of course, depend on literacy, but even oral storytellers usually follow a traditional pattern. Both Dickens and Twain often imply a close link between literacy and fiction-making.
3. Huck successively describes himself as Sarah Williams, a girl with a sick mother, who is seeking help from an uncle; George Peters, a runaway whose parents are dead; a boy whose pap, mam, sis, and Miss Hooker are about to drown on a wrecked steamboat; a boy seeking help for pap, mam, and Mary Ann, who are dying of smallpox on a raft; George Jackson, only survivor of a large Arkansas family; a boy from Pike County, Missouri, who lost all his relatives except " 'me and Pa and my brother Ike' " and then saw Pa and Ike drown.
4. The King evolves out of rumors that Louis XVII survived the Revolution, and more directly from one particular claimant, Rev. Eleazar Williams (1789?–1858), a missionary among the Iroquois in New York state, who had somehow forgotten his childhood and the French language; the King's plan (20:111–112) to become a missionary to pirates hints at this source. The Duke claims a real but extinct title. The third and last Duke of Bridgewater, described as a man who seldom washed, died in 1803, leaving no heir to his title. He built a canal between Liverpool and Manchester. By taking advantage of certain laws, he set up a trust

to accumulate money until twenty-one years after the death of the last person to die among the many persons named in the deed creating the trust. That death occurred in 1882, and the trust was dissolved in 1903. Perhaps Twain saw a newspaper account of the 1882 death, and this suggested a title for his vagabond peer. See Falk, 108, 118–119, 129.

5. Hemingway gives the remark to a character in *Green Hills of Africa* (1935). Most critics have agreed that there is something seriously wrong with the Phelps farm chapters, which relegate Huck and Jim to comic sidekicks and indulge Tom. Two typical comments are O'Connor's, who calls these chapters "a serious anticlimax," and Smith's, who writes, "The perplexing final sequence on the Phelps plantation is best regarded as a maneuver by which Mark Twain beats his way back from incipient tragedy to the comic resolution called for by the original conception of the story" (*Mark Twain,* 114). T. S. Eliot and Lionel Trilling have rather half-heartedly defended the episode. Eliot justifies it on formal grounds, arguing that the book ends where it began, in the world of the child. Trilling suggests that the farm chapters allow Huck to relinquish center stage and fade back into the obscurity he prefers. Carrington is clearly on the right track when he sees the ending as obeying aesthetic rather than moral requirements. Among recent defenders of the farm chapters, Holland ("Authority") considers the ending to be Twain's admission that one cannot set a man free. Levy argues that Huck is "a Southern boy consistently" (36). His commitment to Jim's freedom is private, not public, and does not challenge society's assumptions. Huck's acceptance of Tom's leadership is part of his lack of self-worth, which invariably defers to Tom and to society's prejudices; Mark Twain is consistent to Huck as boy, and does not try to turn him into a social/moral crusader. Bell suggests that the evasion chapters reject "The idea of goal, the telic tendency of plot . . . in favor of the idea that play is the essence of art" (267). Since Huck's journey has been pointless (Jim is already free) and without a destination, its ending must repudiate " 'Persons attempting to find a motive in this narrative.' "

6. Twain stresses Tom's fictional proclivities and implicitly equates him with Scott as one responsible for the War in the unfinished "Tom Sawyer's Conspiracy," where Tom proposes a civil war as an adventure: "And it don't seem right and fair that Harriet Beecher Stow and all them other second-handers gets all the credit of starting that war and you never hear Tom Sawyer mentioned in the histories ransack them how you will, and yet he was the first one that thought of it" (Blair, *Hannibal,* 167). Tom's touch can be seen in the nocturnal rituals and grandiose titles of the Ku Klux Klan and such related organizations as the Knights of the White Camelia, the Invisible Empire, and the White Rose, all founded after the Civil War; many details of the evasion parody these rituals. Early in the book, Tom sends "a boy to run about town with a blazing stick . . . the sign for the Gang to get together" (3:12), thus inventing the Klan's Fiery Cross, or rather adapting it, as the founders of the Klan did, from Scott's *The Lady of the Lake,* where the "Cross of Fire" summons the clansmen to arms (Canto III, x–xix). Tom's preoccupation with Arabs reminds us that a steamboat is called the *Lally Rook* (32:185), named for Thomas Moore's popular work of romantic orientalism, *Lalla Rookh.*

7. Huck does not refer in *Huckleberry Finn* to his own earlier heroism in saving the Widow Douglas. Is he being modest, or is Mark Twain playing down the melodramatic possibilities of St. Petersburg? The boys inherit the real treasure of a real robber gang from a real murderer in *Tom Sawyer,* events at odds with the village as scene of idyllic boyhood. See Tracy, "Myth."

8. Holland points out that Miss Watson's document cancels out the objective meaning of Huck's decision, and that she writes it at about the same time Huck writes and then destroys his letter telling her where Jim is ("Raft," 75). Do the two writings cancel one another out? And is Huck's choice of "hell" (lower case) doubly ironic? In "Tom Sawyer's Conspiracy" Tom learns to set type and print in order to further his fictions. Twain introduces the printer's term *hell*, which Huck misunderstands (" 'Tell the devil to go to hell and fetch a hatful . . . of old type'. . . . It gave me the cold shivers to hear him''); Twain explains it in a footnote as "printer's term for broken and otherwise disabled type" (Blair, *Hannibal*, 189), that is, letters which can no longer be used to make words, to communicate. Huck destroys and scatters the letter he writes but does not send. The sequels suggest that Jim's freedom is precarious despite its legality. In "Huck and Tom among the Indians" we learn "there was white men around our little town that was plenty mean enough and ornery enough to steal Jim's papers from him and sell him down the river again." In "Tom Sawyer's Conspiracy" Jim, suspected of murder, is in danger of lynching, even though "he had always been a good nigger, and everybody knowed it; but you see he was a free nigger this last year and more, and that made everybody down on him, of course, and made them forget all about his good character" (Blair, *Hannibal*, 93, 217).

9. Tom presumably recalled the episode from Carlyle's *French Revolution*, Book IV. The people of Varennes gather to seize the King, like the posse assembled in *Huckleberry Finn*. Tom's leg wound, and the mission to fetch a doctor, recall John Wilkes Booth's broken leg after the assassination of Lincoln, and the involvement of the unfortunate Dr. Samuel Mudd, who set it. Jim escapes in Aunt Sally's dress; Booth was rumored to have tried to escape in the dress of a Negro woman.

10. See Holland ("Raft," 68). This is the real moment when Huck recognizes Jim's freedom; the smallpox episode and the letter episode prepare us for this. Huck's hints that there is a dangerous infection aboard the raft are true (16:77). The infection is equality and freedom. Huck discovers an inner sustaining self to replace the socially conforming self he has been trying to develop.

11. Smith (Introduction, xxiv). Smith explores the use of vernacular speech in the novel. Though Huck explicitly tells us he is writing, the book *feels* oral—we hear Huck's voice.

12. In a notebook entry of 1895, Twain speaks of *Huckleberry Finn* as "a book of mine where a sound heart & a deformed conscience come into collision & conscience suffers defeat" (Smith, Introduction, xvi). Huck's frequent use of present tense makes the book sound like a running account rather than a recollection in tranquillity, unlike the distancing of past events in the narrations of Pip and David Copperfield.

13. Blair (*Hannibal*) prints "Huck Finn and Tom Sawyer among the Indians," "Tom Sawyer's Conspiracy," and "Tom Sawyer's Gang Plan a Naval Battle," which sinks after a few pages. Twain worked on "Among the Indians" in the summer of 1884, "Conspiracy" probably in the summer of 1897, and "Naval Battle" probably in 1900 (*Hannibal* 372–377).

WORKS CITED

Bell, Millicent. "*Huckleberry Finn*: Journey Without End." *Virginia Quarterly Review* 58 (1982): 253–267.

Blair, Walter. *Mark Twain and Huck Finn*. Berkeley and Los Angeles: University of California Press, 1962.

————, ed. *Mark Twain's Hannibal, Huck & Tom*. Berkeley and Los Angeles: University of California Press, 1969.

Carrington, George C., Jr. *The Dramatic Unity of Huckleberry Finn*. Columbus: Ohio State University Press, 1976.

Dickens, Charles. *Great Expectations*. Angus Calder, ed. Harmondsworth: Penguin, 1967.

Eliot, T. S. Introduction to *Huckleberry Finn*. London: Cresset, 1950.

Falk, Bernard. *The Bridgewater Millions*. London: Hutchinson, 1942.

Gardner, Joseph H. "Mark Twain and Dickens." *PMLA* 84 (1969): 90–101.

Holland, Laurence B. "Authority, Power, and Form: Some American Texts." *Yearbook of English Studies* 8 (1978): 1–14.

————. "A 'Raft of Trouble': Word and Deed in *Huckleberry Finn*." *American Realism: New Essays*. Eric J. Sundquist, ed. Baltimore: Johns Hopkins University Press, 1982, 66–81. First published in *Glyph 5* (1979).

Levy, Alfred J. "The Dramatic Integrity of Huck Finn." *Ball State University Forum* 20 (1979): 28–37.

O'Connor, William Van. "Why *Huckleberry Finn* Is Not The Great American Novel." *College English* 17 (1955).

Ridland, J. M. "Huck, Pip, and Plot." *Nineteenth-Century Fiction* 20 (1965): 286–290.

Smith, Henry Nash. Introduction to *Huckleberry Finn*. Boston: Houghton Mifflin/Riverside, 1958.

————. *Mark Twain: the Development of a Writer*. 1962; repr. New York: Athenaeum, 1974.

Solomon, Eric. "*Huckleberry Finn* Once More." *College English* 22 (1960): 172–178.

Tracy, Robert. "Myth and Reality in *The Adventures of Tom Sawyer*." *Southern Review* 4 (1968): 530–541.

————. "Reading Dickens' Writing." *Dickens Studies Annual* 11 (1983): 37–59.

Trilling, Lionel. Introduction to *Huckleberry Finn*. New York: Rinehart, 1948.

Twain, Mark. *Adventures of Huckleberry Finn*. Henry Nash Smith, ed. Boston: Houghton Mifflin/Riverside, 1958.

————. *The Adventures of Tom Sawyer*. Berkeley and Los Angeles: University of California Press, 1982.

————. *Autobiography*. New York: Gabriel Wells, 1925. *The Works of Mark Twain*, vol. 36.

————. *Life on the Mississippi*. *Mississippi Writings*. New York: Library of America, 1982.

————. *The Prince and the Pauper*. New York: NAL/Signet, 1964.

————. *Tom Sawyer Abroad; Tom Sawyer, Detective*. Berkeley and Los Angeles: University of California Press, 1982.

Charles Dickens, *Martin Chuzzlewit*, Mark Twain, and The Spirit of American Sports

John Dizikes

"Oh where will you go?"
"I don't know," he said. "Yes, I do. I'll go to America!"
"No, no," cried Tom, in a kind of agony. Don't go there. . . . Don't go to America!" (Ch. 12)

However dreadful an experience it was for Martin Chuzzlewit to go to America and however arbitrary it was for Dickens the novelist to interrupt his narrative and send him there, we can surely agree that it was a fortunate thing for Dickens' readers, who, as a consequence, were presented with that famous gallery of American grotesques—Jefferson Brick, La Fayette Kettle, Elijah Pogram, General Choke—even if American readers didn't think so at the time. Dickens and Martin visited a culture whose games and whose spirit contrast strikingly with the attitudes towards sport in England. In Jacksonian America there existed an immense tension between the effort to remain free of social restraint, while at the same time strenuously attempting to create forms that would contain that freedom—the contrast, in short, between play and organized games. In Western societies, paradoxically, play flourishes best the more sharply and coherently defined society is; the more open and undefined it is, the more play becomes transformed, perhaps as a kind of compensation, into organized games.

As a visitor, Dickens observed the general cultural situation of the United States in the 1840s not as a case study in the degeneracy or distortion of old forms and ideas and values, but, as it were, anthropologically, as a culture evolving new forms, not necessarily better or worse, but different ones; and he tried to understand what it was in the situation of the culture that made it different. His response to America was profoundly shaped by that cultural situation, and this is one of the explanations for the schizophrenic quality of his response: the exaggerated vehemence of the burlesque; its obsessively repetitive quality; and also, by contrast, a deeper kind of fitful, but profound, exploration—or groping—toward understanding an unfamiliar situation. On top is satire, broad and energetic, but tiresome and overdrawn, satire that is consistently caricature; below it is something else, more interesting and original—and never fully followed up.

For example, Dickens meant it when he had Tom say that going to America was a kind of "agony," agony in the original meaning of the word as a type of game, a contest, an anguish of mind or sore distress which is the result of a struggle. The optimistic young Dickens imagined, as idealistic people do, that the ills of society might be avoided if we could only begin again, could dismantle the old order and return to a state of nature. The trip to America (*American Notes* plus *Chuzzlewit*) is the record of Martin's, and Dickens', agony; here was (almost) the blank page, the new beginning; here was Dickens seeing the future and being appalled at the immense human cost involved in starting over. Something as profound as this is needed to explain the disproportionate anger of the book. That something elemental had been touched in Dickens seems clear from those unforgettable scenes in Eden, that terrific picture of squalor and demoralization for which no one at all, British or American, had been prepared—and for which Charles Dickens was certainly not prepared; the sense of hopeless despair (the same quality is found in the *Notes* as well as *Chuzzlewit*) that is the most memorable, powerful part of the American section of the novel—indeed, of all of it. (There is a striking parallel between Dickens and that group of American frontier writers who were his contemporaries, those tellers of tall tales—particularly Hooper and Harris—whose stories also picture a society on the verge of disintegration from which comes the grimmest of American humor and which in turn gives us a connection with Mark Twain and the deepest visions of *Huckleberry Finn*.)

This view of culture as play, as evolutionary contest, is the basis for a second example of the agonized Dickens in America, and an explanation of an often quoted passage near the end of Chapter 16. Martin has made the acquaintance of Mr. Bevan, who informs him that in America satirists such as Swift or Juvenal could "not breathe the air." What Mr. Bevan means is that such satirists would be slandered and persecuted for telling unpopular truths (Tocqueville's tyranny of the majority, which, if unchecked, leads to intellectual conformity). This would appear to be a flicker of awareness from down below, awareness that the playing field for conventional satire has not been laid out. Dickens was in as much danger as Martin was in Eden of sinking into a swamp; or, in less hyperbolic language, American social forms were not sufficiently finished and crystallized to allow for penetrating comedy of manners, though they allowed—invited, in fact—burlesque and parody. America was too abstract. Reality outdid art. It was what, even a century later, Evelyn Waugh felt when confronted with Forest Lawn.

Some of the sporadic, fitful, Dickensian insights in *Martin Chuzzlewit* seem more revealing about the causal factors of institutional modification going on in America than the broader parodies of character types. The first of these comes from Colonel Diver, editor of the New York *Rowdy Journal,* which the colonel describes, much to Martin's surprise, as "the organ of our aristocracy in this city."

> "Oh! there is an aristocracy here, then?" said Martin. "Of what is it composed?"
> "Of intelligence, sir," replied the colonel; "of intelligence and virtue."

Perhaps Dickens here was consciously echoing Thomas Jefferson's definition, three decades earlier, of the only kind of elite that would be proper for a democracy—an aristocracy of virtue and talent. Anyway, "intelligence and virtue," Colonel Diver says, adding, "And of their necessary consequence in this republic. Dollars, sir" (Ch. 16).

Here Dickens has provided for us the central factor in the evolution of the American sporting culture: judged by European standards, the top and bottom of the class system were missing. In the United States there was no aristocracy in the traditional sense, that is, one based on name, established rank, land-holding; one that united political and social and economic power and whose position was unchallenged by those below. Nor was there a peasant class, fixed to the land as a rural labor force; a slave class at the bottom of society is not at all the same thing as a peasant class. Instead of aristocrats and peasants, there were plutocrats and farmers. This may seem obvious enough, but it has been the source of great contention and confusion in American social history. It is not that there were no classes—far from it; there were, and are. But the social basis of the American class system was different. Indeed, the reality of the American class system, and the unwillingness of Americans to acknowledge it, is one of the main thrusts of Dickens' satire in *Martin Chuzzlewit*. The coach driver says to Martin about America: "All men are alike in the United States, ain't they? It makes no odds whether a man has a thousand pound, or nothing, there." This is a nice double hit by Dickens: it does, we know, make a difference; yet the real difference is how much money, not whose money, it is. Another objection often made is the opposite one: that there was, or had been, an American aristocracy of the old sort, which existed in some regional clusters—the seacoast South, and in New York. But even the proponents of this view seem willing to agree that these clusters never formed a coherent national social elite. Anyway, the characteristic of these isolated regional enclaves has been from early on the effort to preserve their social purity by yielding political power, while struggling ferociously to maintain their economic position, not just against the proletariat, but even more against the tidal wave of plutocratic nouveaux riches—the theme of the stories of Edith Wharton and, in our own day, of Louis Auchincloss.

Dickens is, of course, one of the great chroniclers of industrial laissez-faire capitalism colliding with the remnants of the old feudal order, the chronicler of the achievements, and especially of the horrors, of the clash between capitalist utilitarian rationalism and the inherited irrationalism of the past. We take for granted what was rather remarkable: Dickens could imaginatively do justice to the position of both parties. He relished the rich diversity of the chaotic jumble of the old order without romanticizing it, because he saw how it obstructed the quest for human justice; at the same time he was horrified at the inhumane abstractness of utilitarianism while recognizing the progressive power in it. He is the creator of both *Pickwick* and *Hard Times*.

Arriving in the United States when the industrial revolution was well under way, it has usually been assumed that Dickens was the ideal observer, come at the ideal moment for a comparative evaluation. And in some ways he was. Yet it does him a disservice not to see how much more complex his position actually was and how this is related to the lopsided and curious focus of his fictional report. In the American situation there was very little of the old order resisting the new one. This is what complicates Dickens' satirical point of view, complicates by drastically oversimplifying it. In the agonized conditions of Eden, Dickens found himself baffled. He needed the presence of a coherent culture against which to play off the astonishing crudities and brutalities of the new American capitalist order, as something more inward than farce. Where was he to find this? In the slave-owning planter class, with its bogus aristocratic pretensions? No. (An urban version of this is the Norrises, who are antagonists, not allies.) Yet the alternative, the free play of social type, produced that most dreadful of all American grotesques, Mr. Scadder, whose nature is as amoral as that of the natural birds of prey to which he is compared. In Mr. Bevan Dickens tried to imagine the cultural type he needed, with the resulting vapidity and unbelievability that are so obvious. The Bevan type is itself displaced and really as foreign to America as is Martin; that is what they have in common. Dickens had to make up what didn't exist, and even his extraordinary inventive powers were no substitute for a missing social structure.

Dickens did not know or care about the situation of American sportsmen as a group. But in their plight he would have found dramatized what he was up against as observer. More than any other social group, American sportsmen were determined to re-establish the past, to reclaim their British inheritance, not in some mood of hopeless reaction, but as a means of finding some secure and solid ground in a place where everything was forever swampy, like the Edens they so often lived in.

The sports that they tried to transplant were those of the mid nineteenth century: field sports, hunting and fishing; sailing, running, and walking; above all, thoroughbred horse racing. These sports were, of course, rural, close to nature, rooted in custom, not rules; they were also a powerful way in Britain of tying together rural and urban life by means of a settled and orderly round of social/sporting seasons that brought city and country together, something we see most memorably in the works of another of the early Victorian British novelists, Anthony Trollope. The British aristocracy and middle class had evolved the institutions that defined all this: jockey clubs, yacht clubs, gambling houses, seasons, customs, rules. Insofar as rules were needed, they were altered only occasionally and were enforced informally, by the power of a small, intimately connected social elite whose word was law, whether the law was written in words or not. For example, the decisions of the Newmarket Jockey Club about horse racing were adhered to everywhere in the land, though it ostensibly adjudicated only for the one race course at Newmarket. It didn't matter where it was; society was homogeneous, unified.

Even more remarkable was the evolution of the British idea of sportsmanship, an idea closely associated with, but not identical to, the figure of the British gentleman. This idea of true sportsmanship was that of competition—often fierce, grasping, even reckless—but within rules. It was the concept of competition restrained by something larger than rules, beyond rules: fair play. Of course, it was violated in practice, and yet this concept was immensely powerful, shaping not only conduct within the games, but the games and sports themselves. The image of the British sportsman—British equipment;

dress; and, most of all, sporting style, laconic, casual, understated—spread throughout the world, where it had a continuing vogue in many countries. The idea of sportsmanship also spread, but it took hold much more superficially. In addition, the British sporting style may best be understood as an immense elaboration of, but retention of, the idea of sport as play, play taken as activity that is to some degree spontaneous, uncontrolled, improvised, freeflowing, pointless. It is an end in itself; essentially, control of the action, so far as control resides within rules, is left to the players.

And how successful were the Americans in recreating these stabilizing British sporting ideas and institutions? They failed. They built their racing courses and gave them the old names and tried to reproduce the old forms and manners and styles. But they could not do it. They went on trying and failing, and everything they did turned into something else. They could not build and nurture and maintain turf courses that in England were the result of decades of adaptation, conforming to the landscape, looping, and meandering. Americans hacked out tracks in the woods and raced their horses on these straight dirt paths; or, when more ambitious, they built ovals of dirt and raced their horses there—nothing permanent, nothing lasting very long. They emphasized speed more than endurance and shortened the length of their races. There was a country landscape, but no country culture in the British sense; in America the only successful tracks were those near cities for there were no aristocratic patrons of racing; in America horse racing was a business, and it had to attract its audience from cities for the business to succeed. And American sportsmen were entrepreneurs, from Andrew Jackson at the Hermitage, to Richard Ten Broek, New York gambler and promoter.

This was also the case in the history of American yachting. Americans took the light, fast, cheaply built, and cheaply discarded vessels built for commerce and contraband-running in the War of 1812 and gradually converted them into the speediest ships afloat—utilitarian, functional, the magnificent clipper ships of the 1840s and 1850s. These were the model of their sailing ships, the kind of ship—the *America*—with which John Cox Stevens challenged the British in 1851, winning the America's Cup. Commerce and sport were united as forms of competition. And, finally, the most important American ball game of the time, cricket—which at first seemed likely to become established as the national game, with playing fields and teams in New York, Philadelphia, Boston, and points west—did not take hold. So dependent on a sense of leisure, of poise, of patience, cricket turned out to be unexportable—to the United States anyway.

Change, not continuity, was the order of the day. So many of these traditional sports and games depended on the steady patronage of a small elite, patronage possible where there was surplus capital to expend—not as business, but as play. There was great potential (and much actual) wealth in America, but most of it was in the form of land. In America one might own vast tracts of land, land on a scale beyond the dreams of European avarice—yet, for all that, one could be poor, "land-poor," that extraordinary, perplexing phrase.

In this respect Dickens' vision of Eden was vivid and acute. Remember that Martin had come over to go into domestic architecture, virtually the last thing needed in the world to which he came, in the East as well as the West. Imagine it in sporting terms. What if Martin Chuzzlewit, in addition to trying to build a plantation house instead of that log cabin, had also wanted to establish a jockey club, build a race course, buy some blood stock, and hold a racing meet? Who, in Eden, was there to do the labor? Where would the capital have come from? Who would have come? How long would it have lasted?

Henry James wrote about Hawthorne's efforts, at this same time, to write his romances: "It takes a great deal of history to produce a little literature." And to paraphrase James further: "the flower of sporting art blossoms only where the soil is deep." In this early entrepreneurial phase, American capitalism fluctuated between hard, grinding materiality and speculative fantasy. In Mark Twain's novel *The Gilded Age,* Mr. Hawkins, on his deathbed, urges his family to hang on to their "Tennessee acres"—that pie-in-the-sky, acres-in-the-sky dream of a fabulous future:

> I am leaving you in cruel poverty. . . . But courage! A better day is coming. Never lose sight of the Tennessee land. Be wary. There is wealth stored up for you there—wealth that is boundless.

The sales pitch of Mr. Scadder. There was wealth in the Tennessee lands, but it took the TVA and the Atomic Energy Commission to develop it.

But what about the British ideal of good sportsmanship? Surely material and social conditions need not have affected that. Certainly, in the Jacksonian years this ideal is found in all the American sporting literature, in the diaries and letters of American sportsmen. Yet this also was under assault, the victim of the same absence of definition, of boundaries, of defined social structure—victim, too, of the buoyant sense in America that failure really need not be final. Sportsmanship is associated with the idea of shame; beyond rules and laws, beyond winning and losing, the real penalty for the bad sport was embarrassment or shame. But to free oneself from the past, especially a puritan past, was, for Americans, more and more to emerge as unashamed—unashamed of their vulgarity, unashamed of their bankruptcies, of their lowly origins.

It became a cardinal belief of that Prince of American bad sports, P. T. Barnum, that notoriety was an asset, not a liability. When he had become world famous for the utterly shameless delight he took in his frauds and deceptions, Barnum was asked by Madame Tussaud's if he would be willing to be enshrined in wax—or did he shrink from the notoriety? "Willing?" he replied, "Anxious! What's a show without notoriety!" And what were moral and social conventions but a show, an amoral form of entertainment. Barnum believed that those who swallowed his humbug were chumps, not victims, deserving scorn not pity. "It pays to be shifty in a new country," Simon Suggs used to say. It pays to be wary, to be smart. Another of Dickens' insights. Colonel Diver says to Martin: "We are a smart people here, and can appreciate smartness."

> "Is smartness American for forgery?" asked Martin.
> "Well!" said the colonel, "I expect it's American for a good many things that you call by other names. But you can't help yourselves in Europe. We can."   (Ch. 16)

Even Dickens couldn't have imagined a character quite on Barnum's scale of audacity, of shameless gall. Barnum is one of the chief figures in the development of the sporting equivalent of the con man—the gamesman—who plays against the rules as much as against his opponent. Those who play by the rules perish by them. Rules are vestiges of the past, and the past is a form of tyranny. And if the rules, in addition, are the imported artifacts of another culture, then right and patriotism are united in shaking free of them. Short cuts and waving the flag—how delightful! Thus, good sportsmanship, in its British version, was more and more seen as something to break away from—yet another of those ages-old straitjackets of inhibition and convention. Europeans perhaps had no choice, but Americans could start over.

In the booming, industrializing, reconstructed America of the 1880s and 1890s, the uncertain, unformed sporting culture that Martin Chuzzlewit had struggled to understand was replaced by one that was defined and well established. America moved decisively from play to games, and throughout the power of American nationalism was pervasive. Cricket gave way to baseball; basketball, the one important game invented by Americans, was in its rudimentary stages; American football, a curious mixture of rugby and soccer, was evolving steadily into something very different from each. The impact of the industrial system was everywhere apparent.

Mark Twain could take this sporting culture for granted as offering him one of his most important metaphors in *A Connecticut Yankee in King Arthur's Court* (1889). There it is striking how much the hero-narrator Hank Morgan stands Dickens on his head; he introduces into backward, medieval, Catholic (for Twain these words are synonyms) England some of the very things that Dickens had found most offensive in *Martin Chuzzlewit,* especially the institutions of public relations and the popular press. But Twain's situation is, as satirist, also very complex. The con-man gamesman was a type Twain was profoundly familiar with all his life, had studied all his life, understood inside and out. He was inextricably intertwined with Twain's view of himself; that arch games-playing manipulator, Tom Sawyer, is Twain himself. A satirist who embodies the contradictions that are the subject of his satire strikes one as a volatile state of affairs, with explosive potential. So it was. Twain's most pessimistic view of life and of human nature was one in which the gamesman was fated always finally to be triumphant.

Twain would thus not have been at all surprised by the ever increasing gamesmanship in American sports. Games have become more and more separated from nature, emphasizing man-made surfaces, stressing technique and equipment. The pattern and rhythm of American games are ones of broken sequences, not free-flowing movement. There is a considerable emphasis on position, on control of the field, and on preplanned sequences of plays. Players can be substituted as a series of interchangeable parts; and even time is divided up, manipulated, made a part of the calculations and action. And all this leads inexorably away from the field of play and from the players to control from the sidelines—from off the field. In no other sporting culture is the coach, the manager, the all-seeing mastermind, so central a figure as in America. And, of course, as play becomes game, game becomes entertainment, not an end in itself, but a part, another product, in a complex industrial commercial system.

And this has led, in turn, to the abandonment of the older notion of fair play as something decisive beyond the rules themselves. The contest is narrowed solely to what is, or is not, within the rules; and with its narrowness there comes at the same time a growing ambiguity about the rules themselves, a greater sense of the rules as entirely part of the game .itself, rules to be revised, tinkered with, modified—rules not inherited, but calculated and managed—a way to attract an audience, to ensure advantage for one group or style. The contest has become triangular, against the opponent and against the rules, without contravening them into illegality. A contemporary baseball player, having studied the rule book in spring training, said to his fellow players: "Boys, you've heard the new rules read. Now the question is: what can we do to beat them?"

Masonic Symbolism
in *The Moonstone*
and *The Mystery of Edwin Drood*

William M. Burgan

"I am not a Freemason," Dickens informed a friendly inquirer in 1850 (*Letters*, 2:244).[1] Although followed by an expression of polite interest in certain reading matter that his correspondent had offered to send, the disclaimer of membership could hardly be firmer. Yet Masonic symbolism pervades both *The Mystery of Edwin Drood* (1870) and its famous precursor in the genre of detective fiction, Wilkie Collins's *The Moonstone* (1868). Whether or not Collins and Dickens were Freemasons in the strict sense, both seem to have written for two audiences at once—a group of insiders alerted to the Masonic context, and a group of outsiders completely unaware of its relevance.[2]

The uncomprehending outsiders probably included many who *were* Freemasons in the strict sense, since the hidden signals are often too bawdy to have been acceptable to ordinary, middle-class Victorians. On the other hand, Dickens and Collins were surely not playing this game with the sole aim of amusing each other. Their code may well have furnished an anecdotal and technical point of departure for Henry James's mischievous parable, "The Figure in the Carpet." But unlike James's Hugh Vereker, Dickens and Collins had no need to invent their pattern, or to wait a lifetime for some reader to find it turned inside out in a temple at Bombay (James, 15:251).[3] The signals are too strong, and too heavily indebted to an objective, pre-existent iconology, to suggest extremes of patient isolation.

The evidence for this conjecture lies in the way the novels echo not only Masonic ritual, but also a number of non-fictional writings that trace Freemasonry to its origins in pagan mysteries, in Gnosticism and Rosicrucianism, and in hermetic codes and plots associated with the Stuarts. In the first and second parts of this essay, I shall concentrate on the demonstrable relationship of the texts to Masonic or quasi-Masonic sources. Then, having tried to show why at least some hypothesis of hidden signalling seems unavoidable, I shall discuss the impact of this practice on our perception of the total works of art in which it appears.

What emerges from the Masonic context is an emblematic counterpoint of incessant and protean irony—of contrasts, polarities, foreshadowings, *double entendres*, dialectical syntheses and mirror-image reversals. W. L. Wilmshurst observes of "Jachin and Boaz," the two pillars at the entrance of the temple:

> In one of their aspects they stand for what is known in Eastern philosophy as the "pairs of opposites." Everything in nature is dual and can only be known in contrast with its opposite, whilst the two in combination produce a metaphysical third which is their synthesis and perfect balance. Thus we have good and evil; light and darkness (and one of the pillars was always white and the other black); active and passive; positive and negative; yes and no; outside and inside; man and woman. (164)

The imagery of this philosophy in Hindu art, as also in the art of the pagan mysteries from which Masons derive many of their emblems, is of course explicitly sexual.

I

One curious parallel between *The Moonstone* and *Drood* concerns the sexual symbolism—conscious or unconscious—associated with Rachel Verinder and Rosa Bud. In itself, Rosa's full name seems too whimsical to raise even a suspicion of conscious *double entendre*. But in conjunction with her often-reiterated nickname, *Pussy,* even *Rosa,* and *Rosebud* become suspect. And the utterly gratuitous mention of *John Thomas* in Chapter 11, soon followed by a long, blush-filled dialogue on the importance of not calling one's sweetheart *Pussy* in casual conversation, raises doubts held at bay only by Victorian acclaim for the purity of Dickens' humor (*Drood*, 89, 92, 94–95).

The analogous case in *The Moonstone* concerns the theft of Rachel's diamond. Twice enacted by her lover and future husband, this bizarre charade has attracted much speculation about the author's unconscious concerns. Sue Lonoff gives the Freudian approach sympathetic attention in *Wilkie Collins and His Victorian Readers.* "Recalling the Victorian maxim that a young girl's virginity is her most precious possession," she writes, "and the statement in the Prologue that the diamond's luster waxes and wanes on a lunar cycle, I am inclined to agree with Charles Rycroft that the theft is a symbolic defloration." Although finding that this interpretation accords well with the violence of Rachel's initial rage, followed by the warmth of her forgiveness when she realizes that her lover-thief meant no harm, Lonoff questions the extent of conscious design: "For all his boldness, Collins could hardly have meant to imply what post-Freudian critics discern, nor would his readers have fathomed the sexual implications of the theft, let alone a nightgown stained as its owner passed through his sweetheart's doorway." But then, resisting the tendency to credit Collins's unconscious with the whole symbolic resonance of the action, Lonoff suggests that he may have deliberately altered his original design in response to a detail of his reading:

> Collins was sexually one of the more sophisticated men of his era, and he would have realized that the moon and precious gems have been female symbols since antiquity. On one of the pages that he read in [C. W.] King's [*Natural History of Precious Stones*] there is a description of a diamond that the Indians had tried to fashion in the shape of a Yoni, the symbol of the female genitalia; it was broken in two in the year of the Sepoy mutiny. We shall never know whether this description affected his plans. But we do know that he originally intended to call his novel *The Serpent's Eye* and to make the Indian priests worshipers of snakes, and that in the planning stages he altered the title to one more emblematic of his purposes. The theft is perpetrated, traced, and solved by men: but at the heart of the story is a "young girl" who inherits and perpetuates the domestic values dear to the hearts of the Victorians—after she has lost her Moonstone.
>
> (210–211)

The statue said by C. W. King to have borne the diamond *yoni* depicted Parvati, Siva's consort seen in her benign aspect. This detail strengthens the sense of a possible correspondence between Rachel's jewel and Rosa's nicknames, since the same Hindu goddess plays a central role in a second problem posed by *Drood*, the question of whether John Jasper worships the consort of Siva in her alternative, ferocious aspect as Kali, goddess of Destruction and patroness of Thugs (Duffield, 581–585; Edmund Wilson, 70–77).

The inference that Collins, at least, had Hindu symbolism consciously in mind gains support from his contemporaries' opinion that he had modeled a charming eccentric in *The Moonstone* on a well-known writer named Hargrave Jennings. When this earnest publicist of Masonic and Rosicrucian "secrets" died in 1890, obituaries in both the *Times* (14 March: 9) and the *Athenaeum* (15 March: 342) remarked that he was considered the original of Collins's

Ezra Jennings. Wilmshurst's twentieth-century guide to *The Meaning of Masonry* explains the function of the name "Ezra" in the Royal Arch Ceremony by treating it as a Hebrew derivative of "Osiris," and a sign of advanced progress "from West to East," or in other words towards the regeneration symbolized by dawn (163–164). Appropriately, Ezra Jennings dies facing the dawn, with the word "Peace" on his lips (516).

There is indeed a great deal about Osiris in Hargrave Jennings's exposition of such subjects as *The Indian Religions; or, Results of the Mysterious Buddhism*, "by an Indian Missionary" (1858), *The Rosicrucians: Their Rites and Mysteries* (1870), *The Obelisk* (1878), and *Phallism: A Description of the Worship of Lingam-Yoni in Various Parts of the World and in Different Ages* (1889). We shall shortly have a chance to examine Ezra Jennings's services in bringing about the marriage of Rachel and her lover. But first it will be useful to take a closer look at the history and special properties of the diamond left her by her uncle.

The Moonstone at first adorns the forehead of the God of the Moon in the temple of Siva Somanatha, Siva the Lord of Soma (34).[4] *Soma* denotes both a sacramental, Hindu drug (probably hallucinogenic) and its heavenly counterpart, the *amrita* or elixir of immortality.[5] It also means *the moon*, since the crescent moon is the cup from which the thirsty gods drink. The emptying of this cup, as the moon wanes, and its regular refilling by the sun (of which Siva is also lord), defines the monthly cycles that measure the giant cycles of time. Hence the crescent in Siva's forehead, just beneath the solar fire of his third eye: he is preeminently a god of time, and of the destruction wrought by time (Kramrisch, 108; Moor [1810], 36; Coleman, 64); and he is a god of justice (Moor [1810], 36). His temple at Somnauth (*Moon's Lord*) was unsurpassed by any in India until Sultan Mahmoud of Ghizni sacked it in 1024 (Zimmer, 1:266).

As the first narrator of *The Moonstone* explains, it is to keep the God of the Moon out of the hands of the Sultan and his followers that three Brahmins remove it from the temple just before the attack. They take it to Benares, where Vishnu the Preserver appears to them in a dream, commanding that the Moonstone be watched night and day, and prophesying ruin for anyone who steals it. The idol now has a temple of its own. But it falls victim to a second Mohammedan raid at the beginning of the eighteenth century, when the followers of Aurungzebe destroy the shrines at Benares. The idol is "broken in pieces," and in due course the stone from its forehead becomes an ornament in the handle of Sultan Tippoo's dagger. Bearing out Vishnu's prophecy, Tippoo is killed in 1799, during the British assault on his fortress at Seringapatam. But the Moonstone is stolen yet again, this time by John Herncastle, a British officer who murders one of its guards to get it, and who later wills it to his niece, Rachel Verinder, thus precipitating the events of the detective story (34–37, 70). The last chapter of the novel shows us the diamond restored to the forehead of the Moon God. He is seated on "his typical antelope," above a crowd of worshippers. From this vantage point, his diamond "looks forth" over the city of Somnauth bathed in moonlight, and the novel closes with the words: "So the years pass, and repeat each other; so the same events revolve in the cycles of time. What will be the next adventures of the Moonstone? Who can tell!" (526).

Since the diamond in that final scene "looks forth" from the god's forehead, and since Siva's third eye sometimes functions as a solar flamethrower (Moor [1810], 52), it is tempting (and, I think, faithful to Collins's intention) to identify the stone with Siva's embodiment of destruction as well as time. At the literal level, however, there is a hitch. In Indian painting and sculpture, Siva holds his typical antelope with one hand, as we might hold a tame bird or squirrel; he does not—and for reasons of scale *could* not—ride it. The discrepancy between Collins's imagery and traditional portrayals of Siva is clarified in a classic, early-nineteenth-century study, Edward Moor's *Hindu Pantheon*. Chandra, a relatively unimportant deity, is God of the Moon, and rides an antelope; but he is closely associated with Siva, who in fact is sometimes known as *Siva Chandrasekra,* Siva "moon-crowned." The mightier god "is also frequently seen with Chandra's emblem, the antelope," and "is, indeed, in one of his forms, expressly called the Moon" ([1810], 289). In short, Collins does something very odd. Choosing for his locale the home of Siva as Lord of the Moon, he refrains from ever speaking Siva's name, and places within the temple a statue of a far less powerful moon god—adorned with a jewel strongly suggestive of Siva's most distinctive attribute. Writing in 1832, Charles Coleman calls attentions to the "resplendent gem" sometimes placed "in the centre of [Siva's] forehead" to represent his third eye (97).

Now, Moor comments that Chandra is linked with Vishnu, though still more closely with Siva ([1810], 289). But the placement of the stone in the forehead of an idol at one of Siva's best-known temples seems deft rather than fortuitous. For the total absence of Siva's name from the text accompanies a close, emblematic fit between his peculiar nature and the events of the story. Just as he is a god not only of destruction but of generation (hence the dualism of his consort, Kali/Parvati), so Collins closes the main action of the novel by having pious Brahmins smother the last of the Moonstone's many thieves, and by having Rachel's husband announce that she is pregnant. With concrete enactments of Destruction, Generation, and Justice neatly in place, it remains only to return the stone to moonlit Somnauth, with a final, poetic flourish on the cyclical nature of Time. But why hide so much light under a bushel?

The first answer that comes to mind—and a true one as far as it goes—is that Siva is not mentioned because he is unmentionable. At the center of all his temples stands his chief emblem, the *linga* or phallus. Inevitably, he and his consort dominate the exposition of sexual symbolism in Moor's *Hindu Pantheon* ([1810], 382–398); and although Moor identifies the third eye with solar fire (36, 52), he also suggests that "it is the symbol . . . of the sacred *Yoni*," and that certain positions of the pupil indicate differing phases of the moon (100, 408; plates 2, 5, 13, etc.). In *Oriental Fragments,* he repeats the lunar, female interpretation with emphasis (467–468, 478–481; plates 4, 5).

Moor's reputation as a knowledgeable guide is not the only reason for suspecting that Collins read him. The chapter on "Linga and Yoni" in *The Hindu Pantheon* closes with a story about two Brahmins, whose patriotic willingness to serve as ambassadors to England exacts a temporary loss of caste ([1810], 397–398), a fate strikingly similar to that of the Brahmins in *The Moonstone* (525–526). And *Oriental Fragments* offers minute descriptions of Sultan Tippoo's treasures, together with vivid anecdotes of British plunder after the fall of Seringapatam (a good friend of Moor's, charged with evaluating the jewelry for legal distribution among officers of the conquering army, witnessed much selling and receiving of stolen goods, as did Moor himself) ([1834], 22–26, plate 111, 35–48, 74–76).

In *The Gnostics and Their Remains,* C. W. King follows Moor in terming the eye painted by Saivites on their foreheads "the most expressive symbol of passive nature" ([1864], plate 13, 229–230), and discovers a more obvious version of that symbol in "the Nizam's" diamond. This is the gem identified by Sue Lonoff as a possible model for the Moonstone, and King describes it in language he will repeat almost word for word the following year, when discoursing on diamonds at large in his *Natural History of Precious Stones.* Parvati, the Hindu version of Isis, he writes,

> still bears in her hand . . . the *yoni,* or *bagha,* as her distinctive symbol. Similarly her consort, Siva, wields the phallus. Thus, the Nizam's Diamond—the largest known for certain to exist, weighing 340 carats—exhibits the evident attempt of the unskilful native lapidary to reduce it into such a form, and to mark the longitudinal orifice.   ([1864], 154)

Thomas Inman reads the third eye as an image of sexual union—pupil is to eye as *linga* to *yoni*—in his *Ancient Faiths Embodied in Ancient Names* (2:649). The first volume of this anti-clerical fantasia on the phallic basis of all religious rites appeared some time in 1868 (the serialization of *The Moonstone* began in January of that year) and was followed in 1869 both by a second volume, and by *Ancient Pagan and Modern Christian Symbolism Exposed and Explained,* a concisely annotated gathering of plates from the larger work. Inman's illustrator, who bases the cover design for Volume Two on an engraving of Siva in *The Hindu Pantheon,* is so bent on enhancing the female reference of the third eye that he replaces the pupil with a single line down the center of the oval, as though punning on the most blatant *yoni* in Moor (*Ancient Faiths,* 2:xxxiv; *Ancient Symbolism,* plate 16; cf. Moor [1810], plates 13, and 42: fig. 4) (See Figs. 1, 2, and 3 pp. 264–266.)

Inman, a doctor rather than a linguist or historian by profession, says that *Ancient Faiths* began in an effort to explain why "*John* and *Jack* are synonymous." *John,* behind which he detects *yoni* as well as *Jehova,* turns out to mean "the Androgynous Sun." Another god associated with the sun is *Bacchus,* whose name perhaps derives from Hebrew *Pachaz* ("to be jolly"); *Bacchus* is also known as *Jacchus,* from Hebrew *achaz* ("the one who conjoins"), or perhaps *yakash* ("to ensnare") (1:v, 26–33). Hence *Jack.* Inman thinks that the secret of reading names lies in religious "paronomasia," and his lists of erotic, visual puns sound like notes for *The Interpretation of Dreams.* The "Mother of gods and men," he tells us, may be indicated by "a door, a ring, a myrtle leaf, a lozenge, a fish of oval form, a fruit cleft like the apricot, a cavern, a fissure, a spring of water, a ship, an ark, a dish or plate of certain form, a cup, a half moon, an eye, a systrum, a speculum, a barley-corn, a wheat-ear, a fig, a pomegranate" (2:456).

Inman comments appreciatively on the likeness between a particular Hindu symbol—grouped with a number of forehead eyes—and a comparably female Assyrian door (2:649). He may have been one reader who did fathom "the sexual implications of . . . a nightgown stained as its owner passed through his sweetheart's doorway." After stressing the importance of the triangle "in the mysteries of India, and amongst the Freemasons generally," he explains that "with its apex uppermost, it typifies the phallic triad," while "with its base upwards, it typifies what is known to anatomists as the Mons Veneris, the Delta, or the door through which all come into the world" (1:145–146). The two figures together—familiar as the Shield of David or Seal of Solomon—prove to have a place in the imagery of the Royal Masonic Arch, and of the "celebrated gates of Somnauth" (1:146–147).

The meaning of Somnauth for Victorians is ultimately traceable to the

Fig. 1. Siva. "Taken from Moor's *Hindu Pantheon*" for the cover of Thomas Inman, *Ancient Faiths Embodied in Ancient Names* (1869), Vol. 2. The present reproduction, which shows the drawing as it appears in Plate 16 of Inman's *Ancient Pagan and Modern Christian Symbolism Exposed and Explained* (1869), was made from a copy in the George Peabody Library of the Johns Hopkins University.

SIVA

Fig. 2. Siva. Edward Moor, *The Hindu Pantheon* (1810), plate 13 (detail).

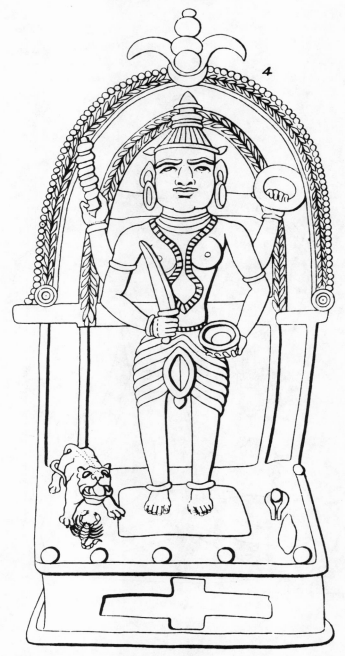

Fig. 3. Devi (Parvati/Kali). Edward Moor, *The Hindu Pantheon* (1810).

smashing of its temple *linga* by Mahmoud. This Islamic insult to Siva's votaries received an extra measure of attention from nineteenth-century scholars, because James Mill happened to have gotten the facts wrong in his *History of India*. His successors took pains to set the record straight.[6] But the Somnauth gates were "celebrated" because of a much greater blunder than Mill's. During the Afghan Campaign of 1842, Lord Ellenborough, the Governor General of India, decided to restore to Somnauth the temple gates that Mahmoud had carried off to Ghizni. The gesture was meant to rally loyal Hindus to the crown, while impressing Mahmoud's rebellious descendants with the power of British rule. Unfortunately, it soon became clear that the gates torn from the sultan's tomb by Ellenborough's general in the field were mere copies of the originals, and that the temple at Somnauth would have to be built from scratch to receive them, having been razed and replaced over four hundred years earlier. Resolutions condemning the Governor General for lack of judgment were moved in both houses of Parliament. The ensuing debate brought the vanished temple to life in the imaginations of many Victorians (Archbold, 513–518; Imlah, 113–115).

Ellenborough's parliamentary critics accused him of making the government in India ridiculous, of fostering enmity between Moslems and Hindus, and above all of sponsoring idolatry. The missionary societies presented angry petitions. Macaulay stressed that the god in question was "Siva the destroyer" not "Vishnu the Preserver," and that worship of Siva gave rise to "the very worst forms of prostitution" (*Times*, 10 March 1843: 3–4). In the House of Lords, the Marquis of Clanricarde took a more lighthearted approach:

> If the Government intended to act upon the proclamation—if the gates of Somnauth were to be applied as the Governor-General had proposed, of course the temple must be rebuilt—a body of Brahmins must be established therein—a corps of priestesses must be forthwith engaged, and an idol must, with all due diligence, be manufactured. (Laughter.) Their lordships, of course, knew what would be the character of the idol. What he, as an economist, should like to be informed of was, whether the Government intended to advertise for designs and estimates (renewed laughter), for, in that case, he thought he might promise to the house that there would speedily be laid on the table one of the most curious documents that had ever been presented to Parliament by a Government. ("Hear," and laughter.) (*Times*, 10 March 1843: 2)

Punch responded with a satire titled "The Gates of Somnauth," in which Ellenborough puts his trophies up for auction in London. "Time, the Great Leveller" has destroyed their first home. An allegorical drawing shows Time at work, silhouetted against a toppling dome; fragments of pillars fly through the air, but one tall column in the background remains intact (Fig. 4; see pp. 270–271). The auctioneer's advertisement evokes "The Temple of Siva" and its "Two Thousand Hindoo Maidens. . . . *With gazelle eyes, and cheeks 'crimson as cleft pomegranates'* " (the phrase in single quotation marks is from Byron's *Don Juan,* III, xxxiii, 3). *Punch* thinks that such historic associations should appeal to a buyer like "the late lamented Marquis of Hertford" (soon to be resurrected as Lord Steyne in *Vanity Fair*).[7] The illustrator shows a "lodge-keeper," in profile closely resembling Time, opening his newly-acquired Park Gates to a woman wearing a large, plumed hat (76; Fig. 5).

Wilkie Collins's neatly labeled packet of notes on the Indian background of *The Moonstone*—now in the Morris L. Parrish Collection at Princeton University—is as silent as his fictional text on the subject of Siva. One hesitates to suggest that he "withheld evidence" from posterity, while apparently going out of his way to be helpful. But that conclusion is hard to avoid, and in the long run the contents of the packet actually support it. For they make explicit the link between Somnauth and the imperial scandal we have just examined. In recommending Somnauth as a possible setting for the forthcoming novel, a foreign office expert whom Collins credits with having supplied useful details for the ending of the story comments parenthetically, "you know the Lord Ellenborough story about the gates from Ghazni." The same informant deals at length with the question of foreign spectators' access to ritual "abominations" in Hindu temples. An Englishman might look on at any "ordinary religious ceremony . . . with tolerable safety, if he were civil and fair-spoken." But although "obscene orgies" still occur, the participants are unlikely to perform in front of anyone they recognize as an outsider, and a foreigner would have little hope of passing for a native ("Burton's pilgrimage to Mecca would be a joke to it"). Nevertheless, if Collins wants "hints on some very atrocious Hindoo orgies," he will find them in "a collection of Wheeler's letters or articles in the Englishman about 1862 or 1863, on the trial at Bombay known as the case of the Maharajs" (Wyllie, sheets 1–4; published with the permission of Princeton University Library).[8]

Rather than try to devise an orgy fit for *All the Year Round,* Collins quietly begins the diamond's career with an allusion sure to offend no one, while reminding a few insiders of "the linga of historical celebrity." That phrase is from an article on "Somnauth" in the 1857 edition of Edward Thornton's Indian *Gazetteer.* No doubt the place-name and the reference to Sultan Mahmoud meant little to most members of the crowd who lined up weekly to buy fresh installments of *The Moonstone,* a quarter of a century after the uproar about Lord Ellenborough. Even in 1843 there must have been many readers of "The Gates of Somnauth" who failed to recognize a *linga* in the standing column, or *yonis* in the cleft pomegranates. But Mark Lemon, the editor of *Punch,* and Douglas Jerrold, his leading humorist, were Freemasons (Price, 69), and as such they encountered precisely this symbolism every time they entered a temple.

In an essay on Rosicrucianism and Masonry published in 1824, Thomas De Quincey mentions that Jachin and Boaz "have an occult meaning to the Free-masons," which he declines "publicly to explain." His accompanying footnote refers to "the account of these pillars in the 1st Book of Kings, vii. 14–22, where it is said—'And there stood upon the pillars as it were *Roses*'." De Quincey adds: "This may be taken as a free translation of the first passage in verse 20. Compare 2d Book of Chron., iii. 17" (*Works,* 13:424–425). The King James Bible specifies "pomegranates" in both places.

The reason for De Quincey's circumlocution surfaces in F.-T. B.-Clavel's *Histoire Pittoresque de la Franc-Maçonnerie et Des Sociétés Secrètes, Anciennes et Modernes* (1843). Glossing his allegorical frontispiece (Fig. 5; see p. 272), Clavel explains that the columns "B" and "J" "figurent les deux *phallus,* générateurs, l'un de la lumière, de la vie et du bien, l'autre, des ténèbres, de la mort et du mal, qui entretiennent l'équilibre du monde." At the top of each pillar is a pomegranate, emblem of "l'organe féminin, qui recoit et féconde le germe bon ou mauvais qu'y depose l'un des deux principes." The joining of male column and female capital—in white and black pillar alike—expresses the union of Nature active and passive, "à l'exemple du *lingam* des Indiens" (75).

The architectural features called "roses" by De Quincey and "pommes de granade" by Clavel are known in Masonic ritual—and, I believe, normally displayed in Masonic decor—as "pommels or globes" (Mackey, 1:299; 2:575). When John Herncastle's cousin catches him in the act of murder and theft, the bloody dagger in his hand flashes fire from the stone set "like a pommel" in the end of the handle (37). The fire here is pure destruction. But in due course the diamond will shed a gentler, lifegiving light as well.

The figure in the Masonic carpet is not a particular image but a cosmic, sexual metaphor, endlessly varied in its riddling incarnations. Analyzing the most famous of Masonic emblems, the compass joined with a carpenter's square, Jean-Pierre Bayard first touches on the oriental contrast of heavenly circle, earthly square, and then invokes the androgynous figure in a seventeenth-century, hermetic engraving, where the male, right side holds a com-

These unique and interesting Gates were placed by the original proprietors at the Temple of Siva. However, one of those accidents for which

Time, the Great Leveller,

is so justly celebrated, about eight hundred years ago removed them from their pristine situation. But, to use the lava words and glow-worm thoughts of the Governor-General—

"THE INSULT OF EIGHT HUNDRED YEARS IS AVENGED!"

Fig. 4. Time, the Great Leveller. Drawing for "The Gates of Somnauth," *Punch* 4 (1843). 76.

Fig. 5. Lodge-keeper. Drawing for "The Gates of Somnauth."

Fig. 6. Frontispiece. F.-T. B.-Clavel, *Histoire Pittoresque de la Franc-Maçonnerie* (Paris, 1843).

pass, while the female, left side holds a square (343). Clavel's pomegranates on pillars reflect the same dualism; and they resemble Collins's pommel on a dagger, just as De Quincey's roses on pillars resemble Hargrave Jennings's rose on a cross. According to Edward Moor, the union of male and female underlies the Royal Arch jewel of the Triple Tau, "the monogram of Thoth, or Taaut, the symbolical and mystical name of *hidden wisdom,* and of the Supreme Being among the ancient Egyptians" ([1834], 284, 293). It will be recalled that Royal Arch imagery also includes the Seal of Solomon. In a second, Masonic version of that figure, the "male" triangle is white, the "female" black, with values corresponding to those of Clavel's black and white pillars (Mackey, 2:800).

In its contrasting roles and its various disguises, the *linga-yoni* combination presides over Collins's emblematic program. Rosanna Spearman lives and dies in the shadow of the destructive principle (indeed her name, disfigurement, and hopeless passion recall the name and fate of Rosa Dartle in *David Copperfield*). On the other hand, Rosanna's rival in love gains the unclouded light of good fortune by assisting at the simulated theft of her own jewel.

Rachel's triumph furnishes the climax of a charade already under way by the end of the first weekly installment. As Penelope Betteredge tells her father what she has just overheard between the Brahmin "jugglers" and their clairvoyant boy, she pauses over their reference to some unnamed "It": "Has the English gentleman got It about him?" She quotes the phrase a second time, then asks her father, "What does 'It' mean?" Treating her question as a joke, Betteredge proposes with a wink that they wait and ask Franklin Blake. But he ends the chapter by warning his readers, "you won't find the ghost of a joke in our conversation on the subject of the jugglers," since Franklin Blake "took the thing seriously," and believed that " 'It' meant the Moonstone" (52).

According to Eric Partridge, both "it" and "thing" served in the nineteenth century as euphemisms for "pudend," and in literature this usage of "it" goes back at least to Elizabethan drama. James T. Henke cites an instance from Marlowe's *Jew of Malta,* in which Barabas tells Lodowicke: "Win it and wear it" (138). Here, the antecedent of "it" is a metaphorical "diamond," which Lodowicke now understands to be the Jew's daughter, having previously thought that the stone was a literal gem for sale. In the earlier exchange—which is relevant not so much because of "it" as because of a female diamond that rivals the moon—"foiled" means "placed against a dull background," and also "deflowered":

Lodowicke. What sparklle does it give without a foile?
Barabas. The Diamond that I talk of, ne'er was foiled:
    But when he touches it, it will be foild: [*Aside*.]
    Lord *Lodowicke*, it sparkles bright and faire. . . .
Lodowicke. How shows it by night?
Barabas.   Outshines *Cinthia's* rayes:
    You'll like it better farre a nights than
    dayes. [*Aside*.] (Marlowe [1981], 287)[9]

The first time the Verinders' butler, Betteredge, describes the Moonstone in his narrative, he recalls how Rachel and her guests first "set it in the sun, and then shut the light out of the room," admiring how "it shone awfully out of the depths of its own brightness, with a moony gleam, in the dark." Collins's extracts from C. W. King authorize this display of mineral magic ("Notes," Item 6), which rouses Betteredge to exclaim that "I burst out with as large an 'O' as the Bouncers themselves" (97). Partridge attests the female character of the letter "O" in *Shakespeare's Bawdy*, while Hargrave Jennings assigns the same meaning to "the Egg, O," carried in Greek mysteries ([1870], 216).

True to the conception of cyclical time, the denouement of *The Moonstone* features an artificial re-enactment of the theft, which turns out to have resulted from Franklin Blake's morally innocent sleepwalking under a heavy dose of opium, a form of *soma* dear to Collins himself. Ezra Jennings bills the re-enactment in advance as an "experiment." Rachel's aunt, Mrs. Merridew, (another punning reference to *soma*)[10] thinks it would be "an outrage on propriety" for her to allow her niece "to be present (without a 'chaperone') in a house full of men among whom a medical experiment is being carried on" (457). She also believes that experiments always end in "explosions" and that she must take special precautions in Rachel's behalf (468–470). Rachel promises her aunt not to stir from her own part of the house when the experiment takes place at nine o'clock (469). At eight o'clock, Ezra Jennings observes Rachel tenderly hovering over Franklin, who will soon wake up from his trance, on a sofa in the sitting-room adjoining her bedroom. She is so rapt that she is "not even able to look away from him long enough to thread her needle." Pleased at having made this reconciliation possible, Jennings departs, closing the outer door. Mrs. Merridew would have discovered the couple together, but for Rachel's hearing the sound of the old lady's dress in the hall, and rushing to intercept her with a warning of "the explosion!" Mrs. Merridew allows herself to be led into the garden, and afterwards felicitates Franklin on "the truly considerate manner in which the explosion had conducted itself,'' explosions having become ''infinitely milder'' than they were when she was a child (482–484).

In retrospect, we notice a rich grouping of allusions to Siva at the birthday dinner before the first, opium-induced theft. Franklin Blake manifests his overdosed condition by a flood of almost manic wit, including advice to a cattle-raiser that ''the proper way to breed bulls [is] to look deep in your own mind, evolve out of it the idea of a perfect bull, and produce him'' (104). A member of Siva's retinue more important than the antelope is Nandi, the wonderful bull, an embodiment of justice and fertility, regularly placed at the entrance to the shrine, facing the linga within (Kramrisch, 26; Moor [1810], 47, 58, 343). The table conversation veers embarrassingly to the subject of the dead in their graves—Siva has charge of cemeteries. The Indian drum heard during dinner affords another, more urgent reminder of this invisible guest: the sound of the drum beats out the rhythm of his cosmic dance. The pretended Indian jugglers are simulating the behavior of Saivite mendicants, who make their way by begging in imitation of their lord, recommending themselves through feats of juggling, fortune-telling, and the like, supposedly made possible by yogic aspiration to his divine powers (Kramrisch, 36, 43, 45–46; H. H. Wilson, [1832], 186, 192). As Rachel's hectic party nears its end, and the theft of the diamond approaches, Betteredge takes comfort in the thought that ''Old Father Time'' will sooner or later bring the carriages round (111).

In light of this density and consistency of cryptic reference, it seems reasonable to give a bawdy rather than a Freudian reading to certain alternations in Franklin Blake's demeanor—''The prospect of doing something—and what is more, of doing that something on a horse—brought Mr. Franklin up like lightning from the flat of his back'' (78). Franklin asks to have the best horse in the stable saddled at once. Not long afterwards, we are told that ''he had left us at a gallop; he came back to us at a walk. When he went away, he was made of iron. When he returned, he was stuffed with cotton, as limp as limp could be'' (119). A few pages later we find ''the resolute side of him uppermost once more. The man of cotton had disappeared; and the man of iron sat before me again'' (127).

By no means all of the sexual symbolism in *The Moonstone* is distinctively Indian. As expounded by Hargrave Jennings, the phallic fire-worship at the core of occult tradition expresses itself in innumerable forms, on every continent and in every age.[11] For example, he gives rather unexpected grounds for identifying the Moonstone with the kind of rose garden dear to Sergeant Cuff:

In the "tables" alternating with tying-knots, of the Order of the Garter,—which "Most Noble Order" was originally dedicated, be it remembered, to the Blessed Lady, or to the Virgin Mary,—the microcosmical, miniature "King Arthur's Round Table" becomes the individual female *discus*, or organ, waxing and waning, negative or in flower, positive or natural, alternately red and white, as the Rose of the World, *Rosamond, Rosa mundi*. ([1870], 168)

Jennings finds in the motto of the Order a meaning that he puts unforgettably, if a little obscurely: " 'YONI' soit qui mal y pense" (169). A later edition of *The Rosicrucians* contains a diagram of "The Round Table of King Arthur. From the Original, preserved in the Court-House of the Castle at Winchester." The seats at the table are correlated with thirteen "lunations," two seats apiece, except for a "Royal Seat. / Sun. / Phallos," which counts for two, and appears to be directly united with the large rose at the center of the table. The inner petals of the rose are white, the outer ones red (Fig. 6; see p. 277) (1907, plate 4).[12]

One thinks at once of the white roses, blush roses, and dog roses that engage Sergeant Cuff whenever he turns from solving crimes to raising flowers. Collins marks this imagery the moment it enters the novel. "This is the shape for a rosery," says Cuff on seeing the Verinders' garden: "nothing like a circle set in a square" (134). As a symbol for the meeting of heaven and earth, the shape Cuff admires is reproduced and analyzed in E. C. Ravenshaw's paper on two Hindu *jantras* or "pocket altars," which he presented to the Royal Asiatic Society in 1849. This was only six years after the Ellenborough fiasco, and Ravenshaw devotes the rest of his talk to exploring the historical connection between Hindu and Royal Arch uses of the Double Equilateral Triangle or Seal of Solomon, "the chief ornament of the celebrated so-called gates of Somnath, taken from the tomb of Mahmud at Ghazni" (76, 79 [Figs. 8 and 9]. More generally, the circle in a square is implicit in the juncture of compass and square as interpreted by Bayard, and explicit in much hermetic and Rosicrucian literature (Jung, 106; Ferguson, 159). While it is hard to know how seriously Collins intends the transcendent reference of such figures, there is no mistaking his intent to show vigorous, unashamed sexuality allied with goodness and justice, or to base fictional form on the idea of a pattern underlying the apparent chaos of human fates.

Collins's interest in hidden pattern takes many forms, including a recognizably Masonic habit of orienting dramatic action to the solstices. The two main festivals of Freemasonry are those of St. John the Baptist on June 24 (Midsummer Day), and St. John the Evangelist on December 27. Clavel refers

THE ROUND TABLE OF KING ARTHUR.

From the Original, preserved in the Court-House of the Castle at Winchester.

"SANGREALE"— or "HOLY GRAIL."

LUNATIONS.

13 Lunations.

2 = "Sun—Moon."   ("Light—Dark.")   Royal Seat.

26 Knights.   SUN.

"PHALLOS."

12 (Twin)-Knights.
(1 Place, each
    Knight : for
    "1 Mystic Luna-
    tion ")
1 each, 24
1 Knight, 2 Pl

Total, 26

These are t
Mystic Guards
the Holy – t
"SANGREALE
        or
HOLY GRAAL
        or
GRAEL

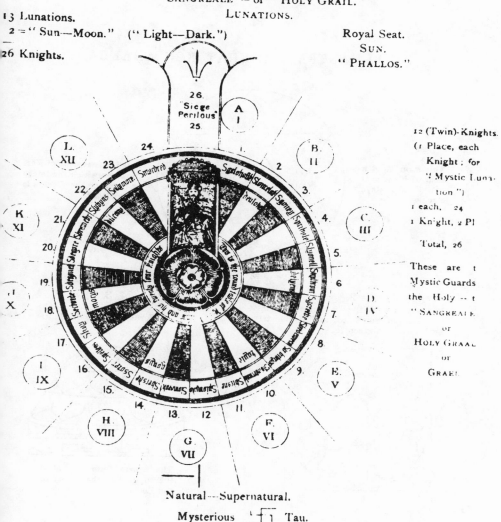

Natural — Supernatural.

Mysterious ⌐⌐ Tau.

Fig. 7. The Round Table of King Arthur. Hargrave Jennings, *The Rosicrucians* (1907), plate 4 (detail).

PLATE I.
1.
SRI JANTRA, OR, KHAT KON CHAKRA.

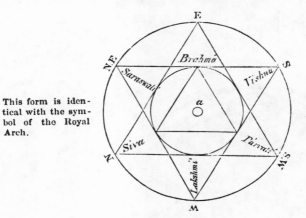

This form is iden-
tical with the sym-
bol of the Royal
Arch.

a, is the centre or " Kar-
nika " on which the image
or name of the Devata is
to be placed.

2.

Bird's eye view of the Sri Jantra, showing
the leaves of the Lotus, and double triangle forming the centre.

3.

Elevation of the Sri Jantra.

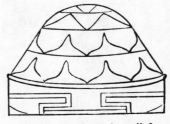

The square base is called
" Bhúpur," or the " City of
the Earth."

Fig. 8. Double Equilateral Triangle and Circle-in-Square. E. C. Ravenshaw, "Note
on the Sri Jantra . . . ," *Journal of the Royal Asiatic Society of Great Britain and
Ireland* 13 (1852) plate 1 (detail).

Plate II.

1.

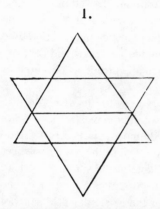

David's Shield and Seal of Solomon.
From Biblical Encyclopædia, vol. i ,
p 42.

2.

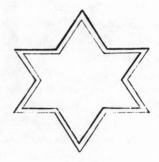

Double triangle carved on the Som-
náth Gates, or Doors of the Tomb
of Mahmúd of Ghazni.

3.

Buddhist double triangle.

4.

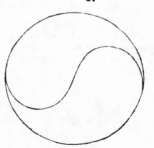

The Tae kieh.

Fig. 9. Seal of Solomon, and Double Triangle of Somnauth Gates. Ravenshaw, plate 2 (detail).

to "St. Jean d'été" and "St. Jean d'hiver." He also links Jachin and Boaz with these seasonal opposites, and so with the central myth of Freemasonry: the murder, burial, and exhumation of Hiram Abif, architect of Solomon's temple. Clavel sees this tale, and its ritual enactment in the initiation of a Master Mason, as an allegory of "la mort fictive du soleil" at the winter solstice. His frontispiece shows the murder of Hiram flanked by the deaths of Balder and Osiris, two other versions of the archetype on which he thinks all the great myths are based (75). And Charles William Heckethorn explains that despite the honor paid to John the Baptist as a herald of "light," the sign of the zodiac entered by the sun at the summer solstice may mark a time of troubles, since "Egypt at this period is enveloped in clouds and dust, by which means the sun, which figuratively may be called truth, is obscured or disguised" (2:38).

Anyone who doubts that Collins constructed plots with this symbolism in mind has only to check the dates in two of his earlier novels, *The Woman in White* and *Armadale*. In the former, the villainous Sir Percival Glyde marries Laura Fairlie on December 22, the precise date of the winter solstice. The following summer, on June 21, the precise date of the summer solstice, the equally villainous Count Fosco, who lives in St. Johns Wood, and who lists among his titles "Perpetual Arch-Master of the Rosicrucian Masons of Mesopotamia," takes advantage of Marian Halcombe's illness to read her diary, and to make his own, exultantly evil entry in it (217, 358–360).

In *Armadale*, the owner and devoted repairman of an elaborate clock prepares a guest for its wonders by advising him—

> At the first stroke of twelve, Mr. Midwinter . . . keep your eye on the figure
> of Time: he will move his scythe, and point it downwards. You will next see
> a little printed card appear behind the glass, which will tell you the day of the
> month and the day of the week.   (195)

Readers who take the hint will discover, by lining up various dates and days of the week, that on Midsummer Day the murderous Lydia Gwilt is first seen in the flesh by the two Allan Armadales. She will later hoodwink and betray both of them. One of them has already seen her in a dream, which the Midsummer scene precisely reenacts; the other, who alone takes the dream seriously, is generally known by the name of the gypsy who rears him, "Ozias Midwinter."

In *The Moonstone*, Rachel Verinder's birthday occurs on June 21. On that day in 1846, her uncle meets with the rebuff that causes him to will her the diamond. He dies "about a year and a half" later—or in other words at or near the winter solstice—having arranged for the jewel to pass to Rachel on her next birthday. So the catastrophe occurs at the summer solstice of 1848, when Franklin Blake innocently takes the diamond from its cabinet, due to the heavy dose of opium slipped him by Dr. Candy. The artificial birthday party, staged by Ezra Jennings, takes place a year and four days later. The additional four days allow for the experiment to begin on a Monday (*Somvar,* which is Chandra's day as well as Luna's [Moor (1810), 286]), and also for the correlation of the happy outcome with retribution for the true thief, Godfrey Ablewhite.

Twice yearly—at Christmas (Midwinter Day), and at Midsummer Day (507)—Godfrey Ablewhite must pay three hundred pounds to the beneficiary of a trust fund in his care; having squandered the principal, he steals the Moonstone on June 22, and pawns it on Midsummer Eve to meet his obligation. He arranges to redeem his pledge at the end of one year. Collins explains the three-day interval between the payment on Midsummer Eve, 1849, and the actual transfer of the stone into Godfrey's hands, as a futile scheme to elude his Brahmin pursuers (512). He is killed less than twenty-four hours after the reconciliation of Rachel and Franklin.

II

Dickens uses the same seasonal polarity as Collins. Edwin Drood intends setting out at Midsummer "to wake up Egypt a little" (54–55). He never makes the journey, but instead disappears shortly after midnight of Christmas Eve. No trace of him afterwards "revisit[s] the light of the sun" (136), a phrase emphasized by repetition. Two nights later, on December 26 (the Feast of Stephen, patron saint of stonecutters), Canon Crisparkle walks to Cloisterham Weir, where he is troubled by his memory of a passage from his reading, "about airy tongues that syllable men's names." This memory arises so "unbidden" that he tries to "put it from him with his hand, as though it were tangible" (142). In Milton's *Comus,* the character troubled by remembered fantasies "Of calling shapes, and beck'ning shadows dire, / And airy tongues, that syllable men's names / On Shores and desert Wildernesses" (207–209) is that "misled and lonely Traveller" (200), the Lady. A moment before, she has heard the revelry of Comus and his band. Now she finds only silent darkness in the place where she had imagined them to be.

Unable to locate the source of his uneasiness, Crisparkle returns the next morning, the Feast of St. John the Evangelist. He now spots Drood's gold watch, caught in the timbers of the weir, and swims through the icy waters to recover both it and the stick-pin lodged nearby in the mud at the bottom. Without speculating on the turns of plot by which Dickens would finally have integrated this baptism into the solution of the crime, we may gloss its likely, pivotal importance by means of another quotation from *Comus*. The Indian word "Thug" means "deceiver," and the first, official, nineteenth-century British report on Thuggee likens the typical Strangler to Circe's child, Comus, who says of himself,

> I under fair pretence of friendly ends,
> And well plac't words of glozing courtesy,
> Baited with reasons not unplausible,
> Wind me into the easy-hearted man,
> And hug him into snares.
>   (160–164; cf. Sherwood, 332)

In the text of *Comus*, the Lady's lines about "airy tongues" follow almost at once. They show that she intuits the nature of the deceit she must fight, though her immediate situation puzzles her. Her words thus form an apt, Providential warning for Mr. Crisparkle. I am not suggesting that he had been reading reports about Thuggee—but Dickens certainly had! The dating of Crisparkle's adventure to coincide with the feasts of Stephen and John will prove equally deliberate, as we explore the whole network of Masonic allusions in *Drood*.

The name "Jennings" appears once in that novel, when Miss Twinkleton, the schoolmistress of the Nuns' House, interrupts her own lecture on the evils of Rumour to chastize one of her students: "Miss Jennings will please stand upright" (65). Dickens' reputation as a humorist who scorned indecency has gone almost unchallenged for so many years that a finding of bawdy intention in this line will seem over-eager, especially since *upright* in its normal, complimentary sense is an expression dear to Masons. But *Drood* appeared in the same year with *The Rosicrucians*, and the phallic "upright" appears with great frequency in that work.[11] Jennings has a habit of reinforcing its mystic significance with quotation marks: "the succeeding array of phallic figures will be found interesting, as tracing out to its progenitor or prototype that symbol which we call the 'upright' " ([1870], 223); "the Architectural Genealogy of the 'Tower' or 'Steeple' displays other phases of the alterations of the 'upright' " (228). Sometimes the quotation marks change partners:

There seems little or no reason to doubt that the much-disputed origin of the pointed Gothic arch, or lancet-shaped arch, and the Saracenic or Moorish horseshoe arch, is the union and blending of the two generative figures, namely, the "discus" or round, and the upright and vertical, or "phallic," shape, as indicated in the diagrams on pp. 238, 239. These forms, in their infinite variety, are the parents of all architecture. (235)

To compare *Drood* with *The Rosicrucians* is to be struck by an apparent overlapping of interest in a variety of subjects. Magnetism and mesmerism fascinate Jennings no less than Dickens. "A spark of that mysterious fire that lurks in everything" (107) is a phrase from *Drood,* but in *The Rosicrucians* this notion of ubiquitous, latent fire is as important as the upright. Like Dickens, Jennings quotes from Milton's *Comus,* a poem cited by Heckethorn as an example of Rosicrucian influence in literature. We are told more than once that John Jasper leans against a sundial, "setting, as it were, his black mark upon the very face of day" (170), as he terrifies Rosa with his declaration of love. Jennings points out that there are few churchyards in England "without a *phallus* or obelisk," on top of which "is usually now fixed a dial." He touches more than once on the image of stars as letters in a mysterious alphabet, spelling out the shape of things to come, an image Dickens uses in connection with Mr. Grewgious (160). Jennings discusses a number of classical deities whose names appear in *Drood*—Apollo, Diana, Minerva, and Venus (58, 166)—and expatiates at length on the Wandering Jew (Dickens describes Miss Twinkleton as "a sort of Wandering Jewess" [17]), on the gypsies (Dickens likens Helena Landless to a gipsy [44, 54]), on the Tartars (Rosa Bud falls in love with Mr. Tartar), and on Egypt, Isis, and the Great Pyramid of Cheops, all of which come up in connection with Drood's proposal to serve the Empire as an engineer (21). If Dickens has a heroine named *Rosa Bud,* the author of *The Rosicrucians* can match him with *Rosa mundi,* and with *Bhudd.*[14] In a moment we shall consider Jennings's interest in both *Jack* and *jasper.* Since his true quarry in *The Rosicrucians* is the union of male and female darkly coded in every alphabet, language, legend, religious belief, philosophical concept, architectural style, heraldic device, nursery rhyme, or fashion in hats, caps, and helmets since the beginning of history (with cosmic analogues predating the Creation), we may finish Dickens' side of the list with *Pussy,* and with some throwaway lines about the mysterious P J T, whose initials adorn a lintel in Staple Inn. The narrator speculates that this inscription may signify, "Perhaps John Thomas," later adding that this "tinderous and touch-woody" individual must have been "Pretty Jolly Too" (89, 93, 99).

In a passage of dialogue running six pages (8–13), Dickens manages to include Rosa Bud's nickname, *Pussy,* nineteen times, though it refers to an absent person, and to match this with thirty-five repetitions of John Jasper's nickname, *Jack,* which can double in slang as a bawdy abbreviation of *Jack-in-the-Box* (Hargrave Jennings derives the phallic meaning of *Jack* from *Iacc* and *Bacchus,* presumably echoing Thomas Inman, whose learning he admires—[1870], 55, 333). Drood's toast, "Pussy, Jack, and many of 'em! Happy Returns, I mean" (9), recalls Partridge's sample of poetic bawdy, "Aeneas, here's a health to thee, / To Pusse and to good company!" (*Dictionary*). On a single one of the six pages, the repetitions of *Pussy* and *Jack* are interspersed with eight repetitions of *Crack* (9), ostensibly a sound effect for a nutcracker—*nutcracker* being a Victorian slang equivalent of both *pussy* and *crack* (Burton, 92, n. 46). As noted earlier, the name *John Thomas* is soon followed in the text by Mr. Grewgious's speech admonishing Edwin Drood not to refer to Rosebud as *Pussy* (92, 94–95).[15] The whole dialogue could be excerpted and reprinted under the heading, "Homage to Laurence Sterne."

The best external warrant for these inferences of *double entendre* lies in yet another grouping of parallels with the names of the cast in *Drood*. The villain of that novel is John or Jack Jasper. Describing a Gnostic gem bearing the image of a "Cynocephalus, crowned, with *baton* erect, adoring the first appearance of the new moon," Jennings states that it is made of yellow jasper, and refers interested readers to a line drawing in C. W. King's *Gnostics and Their Remains* (40). In writing about the Gnostics, King deals at length with mystery religions and secret societies. He undertakes to show the causal basis for the many correspondences between Freemasonry and the mysteries of antiquity—a basis that makes nonsense of claims alleging a secret, unbroken tradition of Masonry, starting in the days of Noah. But King shows considerable respect for Rosicrucian as well as more ancient sources of modern Masonry. He asserts that the whole tradition springs from India, and he treats its symbols with less excitement and greater frankness than Jennings.

It must be said in fairness to Jennings and King that neither would enjoy being classed with the other. Jennings considers King a dry-as-dust antiquarian, full of useful information but without a glimmer of insight into the wonders in his care ([1884], 149–150). King sees in Jennings a "masonic" vulgarian whose research is a farce ([1887], 393). Theirs is the mutual scorn that pits scholarship at its most lucid against occultism at its most portentous. As probable readers of both, however, Collins and Dickens are harder to place, especially in view of their role as pioneers of detective fiction. Detective stories normally demand little learning, and ignore the unseen. Yet these early practitioners build whole novels as extended puns on two meanings of "mystery": "secret rite" and "puzzle." The mysteries of Parvati and Siva, Isis and Osiris, lie embedded in the mysteries of the stolen jewel and the vanished engineer. And whatever may have been the social matrix of this game—which does have a decidedly "Masonic" look about it—the aloof, anti-Masonic King seems to have been as important to Dickens as to Collins.

To begin with, King mentions jasper some sixty times, because the supposed magical properties of the stone appealed to the makers of amulets. In addition to *jasper*, and to every one of the classical and Egyptian gods already cited in connection with *The Rosicrucians*, King's anticipations of names in *Drood* include *Helena*, *tiler*, and *tope*.[16] An edition of *The Gnostics* that came out seventeen years after *Drood* enables us to add *Hiram* and *Constantia* to the list of matching pairs ([1887], v, 402, 406), a possibility that cautions us against assuming that Dickens took the other names from King, and at the same time rules out casual explanations for the cluster as a whole. Since King cannot very well have arranged his historical facts to fit the names of a detective story, the historical Constantia, granddaughter of the historical Helena, must have something to do with Dickens' *Constantia*; and Dickens' *Constantia* must, in turn, have something to do with his *Helena*, a name he gives his dark-skinned heroine from Ceylon. Moreover, this last connection must belong to a semaphore untrammeled by narrative logic. For Constantia in *Drood* is not a person but a wine from the Cape of Good Hope, forced by Mrs. Crisparkle down the throat of her son, whenever that kindly and submissive clergyman seems to her in need of a pick-me-up (79).

The grandmother of the historical Constantia was the Empress Helena, mother of Constantine. She and her granddaughter figure in *The Gnostics and Their Remains* as elements of an argument concerning the derivation of the round form of the Temple Church in London. The design of this "Templar" monument recalls the form of the Church of the Holy Sepulchre—built in Jerusalem to commemorate Helena's finding of the True Cross—and also the form of Constantia's tomb. King's point is that the circular shape characterizes a number of early Christian buildings quite lacking in Gnostic associations, and need not be assumed to have an occult meaning in London ([1887], 402). The example happens to illustrate his preference for common sense over mystic "keys." But the more likely source of Helena's role in *Drood* is the legend that she found the True Cross, and commemorated the event by building the Church of the Holy Sepulchre on the site of a pagan temple. Helena's legend—eked out by a stage prop representing "a cathedral"—figures in the ceremony of initiation into the Masonic degree, "Knight of the Holy Sepulchre" (Richardson, 126). The setting of *Drood* also centers on a cathedral, and especially on the accompanying crypts and tombs, and one of the novel's major themes is the difference between true Christianity and various forms of pseudo-Christian, pseudo-civilized idolatry, from Jasper's double life to the Dean's bland hypocrisy. According to Arthur Waite's authoritative *Encylcopedia of Freemasonry,* the ritual for the "Knight of the Holy Sepulchre" recalls that for the degree of "Rose Croix" strongly enough to suggest plagiarism (1:444).

The blend of Freemasonry and Rosicrucianism in the Rose Croix degree seems in any case essential to Dickens' symbolic program. Following the initials "PJT" over the door leading to Hiram Grewgious's rooms is "1747," the date of the founding of the "Rose Croix" under the sponsorship of the Stuart pretender, Prince Charles Edward, recently arrived in France after the collapse of his fortunes in the Rebellion of 1745 (Mackey, 2:637–638). Clavel observes that "le premier centre d'administration des hauts grades fut établi à Arras en 1747, par Charles-Edouard Stuart lui-même" (167). (His escape owed much to Flora Macdonald, step-daughter of Hugh Macdonald of Armadale, Skye: such names and associations are plainly more in the nature of secret handshakes than political gestures.) *Tiler,* the word echoed in "Perhaps Joe Tyler"—a second attempt at guessing the name behind the initials (89)—signifies the Masonic functionary charged with guarding the secrecy of a lodge meeting, and is used with that meaning in King ([1864], 190). In addition to the congruence between *roses* as a "free translation" for *pomegranates,* and *Pussy* as a nickname for *Rosa,* Thomas De Quincey's essay on Rosicrucians and Freemasons anticipates the *Drood* names of *Neville*—a Masonic partner of Oliver Cromwell's, according to a legend that De Quincey finds absurd (13:435)—and *Dachery,* a scholarly editor (13:445; Dickens adds a "t" before the "ch"). De Quincey also anticipates Jennings and King in discussing "the holiest masonic name of Hiram," the biblical architect revered by Masons as "a type of Christ" (445).

In real life, the letters over the door assigned by Dickens to Hiram Grewgious designated the president of Staple Inn in 1747, "Principal John Thompson" (Chancellor, 258, 260). Dickens takes pains to replicate the pattern of this black and white inscription, as follows:

$$P$$
$$J \qquad T$$
$$1747$$

A purported transcript of secret Masonic ceremonies states that during the initiation of a Mark Master Mason, the Master presents the candidate with a keystone bearing in circular form the letters:

$$
\begin{array}{ccc}
 & H & \\
T & & W \\
S & & S \\
T & & K \\
 & S & \\
\end{array}
$$

These initials stand for "Hiram Tyrjan, Widow's Son, Sent To King Solomon," and they mark "the stone which was set at naught by [the] builders, which is become the head of the corner." The Masonic candidate who receives the keystone must beware of being rejected with better reason, "as unfit for that house not made with hands, eternal in the heavens" (Richardson, 48–49). The manual's instructions for the degree of Intimate Secretary include the further admonition, "Brother, the color of your ribbon is intended to remind you of the blood of Hiram Abif, the last drop of which he chose to spill, rather than betray his trust" (137). The first time Dickens shows Hiram Grewgious at home, he tells us, "The largest fidelity to a trust was the life-blood of the man" (89).

A full list of counterparts to names in *Drood,* culled from three works dealing with the tradition of mystery religions and secret societies, will thus include *Jennings, Apollo, Diana, Juno, Minerva, Venus, the Wandering Jew, Tartar, Isis, Cheops, Rosa, Bhudd, Jack, jasper, Helena, Constantia, Hiram, tiler, tope, Neville,* and *Dachery.* Moreover, Edwin Drood's first name is traditionally honored as that of the earliest titled patron of Freemasonry in England, and Dickens' preparatory notes show *Edwyn,* the old-fashioned spelling used in a classic, seventeenth-century source on this topic, coming in a close second behind *Edwin,* five trials to six (Cardwell, Appendix A; Mackey, 1:231; 2: 570).

Other details strongly suggestive of Masonry are Miss Twinkleton's globes, terrestrial and celestial (17), Drood's present of gloves to Rosa (13), the two-foot rule and hammer of Cloisterham's literal stonemason, Durdles (29), and the scarf that suddenly forms part of Jasper's attire on the eve of his nephew's disappearance (128, 130). Celestial and terrestrial globes are "symbols of the universal extension of the Order"; it was the custom to give newly-initiated Masons white gloves to present to their sweethearts; the 24-inch gauge and the Mason's gavel form part of the initiation of an "Entered Apprentice"; and a black scarf is featured in the first stage of initiation into the degree of

Rose Croix (Mackey, 1:290, 298, 299; Heckethorn, 2:41). The last of these items is of particular interest, because Jasper's "great black scarf" has stirred more critical interest in the Hindu background of *Drood* than any other detail in the story.

The question of whether Jasper is a Thug has divided *Drood*-lovers since 1930, when Howard Duffield published an essay entitled, "John Jasper: Strangler." Dickens' illustrator, Luke Fildes, had written that Jasper was to have used his scarf to strangle his nephew, and this disclosure, recalling the Thug practice of using sashes for the performance of their art, seemed to Duffield to impose vivid, logical coherence on a number of otherwise un-related details, and so to establish that Dickens had Thuggee in mind. For example, Dickens pointedly associates the word "destruction" with Jasper, and shows him taking as much interest in burial sites as if he were a Thug planning to dispose of a corpse. Like the choirmaster, Thugs assiduously identify themselves with "the most respectable classes." Thugs drug their victims before strangling them; Jasper shows his mastery of such tricks when he incites a violent quarrel between his nephew and Neville Landless, after serving them "mulled" wine, and again when he gains access to the locked cathedral at midnight by tempting the drunken verger with a specially prepared bottle. Thugs prey on travellers: Drood is about to set out on a journey, and seems to have disappeared just after midnight, a time favored by Thugs for murder. The cry of a rook in sight of a river was considered a favorable omen by Stranglers; Jasper hears such a cry a week before the crime (Duffield, 584–587).

Duffield points out that stranglers had turned up in such novels as Eugene Sue's *Wandering Jew* and Meadows Taylor's *Confessions of a Thug,* as well as in Dickens' own periodicals (587). Numerous further facts attesting the topicality of Thuggee in journalism as well as fiction have come to light since 1930 (Jacobson, 526–537). But Duffield's parallels were enough to convince Edmund Wilson, who added yet another of his own. According to John Forster, an essential clue in the solution of the mystery was to have been a gold ring that would resist dissolution in the quicklime used by the murderer to get rid of the body. Unknown to Jasper, Drood is carrying such a ring in his breast pocket on the night of their last encounter. Wilson found in a major, Victorian account of Thug superstitions the warning that evil would befall the expedition that selected for its first prey a man with gold on his person (Wilson, 72; Thornton [1837], 90; cf. Sleeman, 133–134).

Richard Baker, Philip Collins, and Wendy Jacobson are among the scholars who have faulted the Duffield/Wilson thesis for its disregard of plausibility

Fig. 10. Flora and Kali-Hecate-Medusa. *The Mystery of Edwin Drood,* monthly number cover (detail).

Fig. 11. Kali-Hecate-Medusa. Note the rearing serpents over the forehead.

and consistency, values that mattered as much to Dickens as surprise (Baker, 74–77; Collins, 291–310; Jacobson 536–537). Jasper is violently jealous, and his behavior accords perfectly with what Dickens told Forster—that the killer was to realize the needlessness of the crime soon after committing it. When he learns that Drood and Rosa had broken their engagement, and agreed to be merely good friends to one another henceforth, the choirmaster clutches his hair, shrieks, and falls to the floor in a swoon, apparently unconsoled by thoughts of Kali. Why would Dickens carefully develop the psychology of this talented, sophisticated cynic, driven to ruin by desire for a woman, only to disclose at the end that the source of his violence is attachment to a naive Hindu cult? On the other hand, if no such revelation lay in readiness for the climax, what is the meaning of the network of correspondences unearthed by Duffield and Wilson?

The simplest answer is that Dickens, like the author of *The Moonstone*, has fashioned two sets of clues—one set literal, the other emblematic. Collins arranges for Siva ("Old Father Time") to attend Rachel's birthday party, together with his bull, his graveyard, his mendicants, and his drum. Parvati's diamond is there too, disguised as Siva's *yoni*-like third eye. But Betteredge and Franklin Blake are not Hindus, nor has the Moonstone ever adorned a statue of Parvati or Siva.

The source cited by Edmund Wilson concerning a strangled victim with gold on his person also mentions the Thugs' dread of beginning an expedition in December (Thornton, 79). Jasper's behavior during that month would be oddly reckless in a literal worshiper of Kali. But there is no evidence that he knows anything at all about Thug lore. What he (probably) knows is that a Christmas Eve party will serve admirably for framing Neville as Edwin's murderer, and that gold will resist dissolution in quicklime. Hence the December reconnaissance with Durdles, and the disposal of Drood's watch and pin. On the other hand, Jasper is decidedly a Thug in the eyes of Dickens, who shapes the action to fit a hidden, analogical pattern. As might be expected, *The Gnostics and Their Remains* features a lengthy discussion of Siva's consort, Kali, pointing out her kinship with Hecate and Medusa, and touching on the ferocity of her votaries, the Thugs (a composite image of this female horror appears on the cover of the *Drood* monthly numbers, opposite Flora's [Figs. 10 and 11]).

A comparison of Hindu iconography in *Drood* and in Bulwer Lytton's Rosicrucian *Strange Story* shows that the choirmaster is even more a "Siva-figure" than he is a Thug. Jasper's prototype in the earlier novel is Margrave, a singer, pianist, and dancer of charismatic powers, and also a mesmerist assassin: "the light of his wondrous eye seemed to rest upon us in one lengthened, steady ray through the limpid moonshine" (126–127). The narrator likens Margrave to "an incarnation of the blind powers of Nature, beautiful and joyous, wanton and terrible and destroying! Such as ancient myths have personified in the idols of Oriental creeds" (195). The Thug who serves this villain's veiled mistress has no evident function beyond removing all doubt as to the identity of the idol chiefly concerned (221).[18]

Jasper is an avatar of the same god, more realistic than Margrave without being any less symbolic. Hence his musical genius (Siva is "Lord and Teacher of Music" [Kramrisch, 106]); his complexion "pale as gentlemanly ashes" (77) (Siva, "King of Dread," is "often painted as if rubbed over with ashes" [Moor (1810), 38]); his "almost womanish" ways (118) (Siva "called *Ardha Nari*" is "*half woman*" [Moor (1810), 98; plates 7 and 24]); his lust coupled with a mania for destruction; his interest in tombs; his specters summoned at midnight; and his brooding on those vistas of time that sustain the ecstacy of murder in an opium dream, afterwards making—by their absence—a stale anti-climax of the actual experience of killing. Hence, too, Jasper's affinity with fire, and with the moon. Before setting out on his "night with Durdles," the choirmaster sits at the piano "with no light but that of the fire . . . until it has been for some time dark, and the moon is about to rise" (103). Within the cathedral, Dickens then evokes the white and black, good and evil, of Masonic pillars and temple floor:

> They enter, locking themselves in, descend the rugged steps, and are down in the Crypt. The lantern is not wanted, for the moonlight strikes in at the groined windows, bare of glass, the broken frames for which cast patterns on the ground. The heavy pillars which support the roof engender masses of black shade, but between them there are lanes of light. (106)

The mystery in such writing renders facile contrasts between "emblem" and "symbol" as irrelevant to *Drood* as to *The Magic Flute*.

III

Part of King's usefulness for the student of Collins and Dickens lies in the attention he pays to the semantics as well as the imagery of his talismans. He discourses at length on the element of secrecy present in symbols that not only stand for concepts but serve as means of concealment and secret recognition. The Gnostics have their analogues of the "masonic grip" ([1864],

121). *Richardson's Monitor of Free-Masonry* also affords some insight into possible forms of double talk. Masons wishing to warn a brother away from a poor bargain, and lacking the chance to slip him a word in private, are advised to tell him publicly it will be to his advantage to buy, using formulaic language already agreed on to mean the exact opposite of what it says (93).

Something similar happens often in *The Moonstone*. Betteredge tells us we won't find the ghost of a joke in his conversation with Penelope, because "It" means the Moonstone. But we do find the ghost of a joke: we find that the Moonstone means "It." As the moment of Franklin Blake's glad awakening draws near, Rachel Verinder does not look down to thread her needle: but her needle will be threaded by Franklin Blake. Partridge traces the bawdy use of this expression to the nineteenth century, and Edward Moor illustrates the kinship between British and Indian folklore by showing that just as the Hindus regard cleft rocks and trees as *yonis,* bringing luck to all who pass through them, so a recent book on Irish legends records the same superstition at Innisfallen, where squeezing through the hole in a certain tree is called "threading the needle" ([1834], 514).

Collins never says that the idol serves Siva Somanatha, or that the diamond in its forehead marks this relationship; he tells us instead that the stone is under the protection of Siva's opposite, Vishnu. Unlike the diamond *yoni* described by King, the Moonstone never belongs to the Nizam. It belongs instead to the Nizam's rival, Sultan Tippoo (the bitter conflict between these two Indian princes, including the Nizam's alliance with the British at the time of Tippoo's fall, is fully reported in a source Collins acknowledges having consulted for background on the storming of Seringapatam) (Hook, 1:223n).[19]

John Reed has shown the reversal in the Moonstone's relation to the Koh-I-Noor: the Brahmins recover the spoils of an imperialist thief—Rachel's uncle—and restore it to India at the very time when Queen Victoria receives a fabulous diamond commemorating the first two hundred and fifty years of the East India Company. To get the Moonstone, the Indians have smothered that pluperfect Victorian hypocrite, Godfrey Ablewhite, "in the near vicinity of Lime and Leadenhall streets where the House of the East India Company stood in 1849" (Reed, 287–288). It seems fitting that they should have returned the stone to the site of "the Lord Ellenborough story."

Dickens enjoys reversals as much as Collins. Deputy, the urchin who catches sight of Jasper scouting the Cathedral and its precincts at night, pays for his indiscretion by being picked up, shaken, and nearly choked. In fact, he "forces his assailant to hang him, as it were" (110). But the nonsensical refrain of Deputy's song, "Widdy widdy wake-cock warning," suggests that one day the noose will be on the other neck. *Widdy* is slang for both *widow* (Masons are "Sons of the Widow") and *gallows*. "Wen I ketches him out arter ten," though literally referring to Durdles, puns on *Jack Ketch*—slang for *hangman*—picking up a theme sounded at the beginning of the chapter in jokes about breaking "our worthy and respected choir-master's neck" (101, 110–111; cf. 32, 36).

Thugs often used a yellow garment to function as Kali's murderous "handkerchief" (Sherwood, 343; Sleeman, 128), and they always entrusted their most sacred emblem, the pick-axe, to the "cleanest, most sober and careful man" among them (Sleeman, 109). Dickens entrusts it to the town drunk, Durdles, who is never clean, wears a yellow kerchief, and lives in company with "mechanical figures emblematical of Time and Death" (29, 102).[20] But that does not mean that Durdles himself is evil. Quite the contrary. One source of critical speculation that Jasper may have his good or "tragic" side is the fact that Dickens takes pains to show him looking devotedly at his nephew. Another is that St. John the Evangelist twice mentions jasper as a substance used in building the Heavenly City (Vogel, 63; Beer, 163, 179, 181). For that matter, the Gnostics thought jasper would "drive away evil spirits, fevers and dropsies, check lust, prevent conception, render the wearer victorious and beloved, and stanch the flow of blood" (King [1864], 130). But Chesterton recognizes with his usual acuteness the double-take required of us by that line about the devoted look: the horror is that this "devotion" is lethal, not loving (221). And though we have no reason to think John Jasper begets children or suffers from dropsy, his name embodies in every other respect a reversal as crisp as the use of *David* to name a hero whose villainous rival is *Uriah*.

The basic metaphor of contrast in *Drood* is the mirror-image reversal of Thuggee and Masonry. Each group consists of a body of initiates into secret mysteries, who make known their membership through signs that only their fellows can recognize, and who communicate with one another in coded slang. Dickens suspends these good and evil versions of fraternity like masks flanking the stage of a drama that does not literally involve either one. The story at the core of Masonic legend and ritual tells that the master builder, Hiram Abif, was murdered by some of his workmen while the temple of Solomon was still being built. The temple, fated in due course to be destroyed entirely, was thus flawed from the outset by a tragedy of betrayal. But God's house—as the ceremony of the Mark Master Mason reminds us—is not made by hands, and the building of the true temple goes on, with human beings for stones. This metaphor of working among ruins to recover and complete what was lost in the murder of Christ underlies the image of Cloisterham, with its fragments of old wall and its fixation on the past, and above all its tendency to honor the wonderful monuments as tributes to itself.

Jane Vogel rightly stresses the Christian, allegorical thrust of some ostensibly jocular references to St. Stephen in this text (63).[21] To her emphasis on martyrdom, I would add the theme of the spiritual church versus its material shell. Before he is put to death, charged with having claimed that Jesus would destroy the temple in Jerusalem, Stephen confronts his accusers with a brief history of the Jewish people, the point of which is that they have always mistaken prophets for troublemakers requiring to be ignored, exiled, or killed. When Moses led them out of slavery, they became nostalgic for Egypt and its idols. And when they replaced the movable tabernacle of their wanderings with a splendid, permanent building, they made an idol of that, forgetting that "the most High dwelleth not in temples made with hands" (Acts, vii, 2–53). In *A New Encyclopedia of Freemasonry*, Arthur Waite observes of the ritual of Helena's degree, "The Holy Sepulchre":

> It is testified in behalf of the Candidate that he has served the Church and its members, yet he says on his own part that for want of an abiding-place he and his fellow-servants in Christ can only build their Temples and Tabernacles in the heart. . . . The Church is therefore within, and so is the ordained priest. (1:445)

Keeping a round table in his rooms, living under the doorway commemorating John Thomas and the tiler and the union of the Rosy Cross with Freemasonry, Hiram Grewgious stands in the same figurative relationship to these insignia as John Jasper to his scarf, his mulled wine, his choir, his friend the mayor, and his Gate House (the name recalls that of Gatehouse Prison in London). Generation, *re*-generation, and brotherhood here struggle against their opposites. The two antagonists are metaphorically the Mason and the Thug, and it makes no more sense to ask whether Grewgious attends lodge meetings than to ask whether Jasper communicates with other Stranglers in slang. As Jacobson points out, one of the features of Jasper's situation that casts doubt on his (conscious) devotion to Thuggee is the fact that he has no accomplices. He is utterly alone. His success in drawing harmonious sounds out of his choir is purely mechanical—"I/It," never "I/Thou." Mr. Grewgious, too, at first appears solitary, flinty, "angular." But it soon becomes apparent that his somewhat dogged way of doing his duty builds community, kindness, the conspiracy of the good. Before long, he is working in real harmony with that other Cloisterham singer, the Widow's Son, Mr. Crisparkle, and with Rosa, Helena, Neville, and Tartar. Not the least striking mark of his conspiratorial flare is his service to the plot, which for Dickens means service to Providence (Nelson, 11–14). It is Grewgious who brings Drood to the state of mind in which he leaves the gold ring in his pocket, rather than continue the pretence that he and Rosa are a promising couple for marriage.

If Jasper is not literally a Thug, there is one less reason to think he is schizophrenic; if he is, however, a Thug emblematically, there is also one less reason to think he is innocent; and if *widdy* and *ketch* foretell his doom, he is going to hang. But it is hard to say how much these inferences may owe to my own, prior attachment to the view of the unwritten ending first sketched by Forster, and afterwards tentatively fleshed out by Philip Collins. Moreover, just as the study of Masonic echoes may yield highly debatable insights into the ending, so fixation on the ending may distract attention from the difference inescapably made by those echoes in our perception of the text. What they affect most deeply is not our guessing about the plot but our awareness of the kind of book we are reading. By the same token they radically alter our sense of Dickens' relation to his audience.

We tend to think of the Victorian period in literature as one in which the intellectual sport and learned allusiveness of earlier centuries were severely hampered by the aim to reach a large audience. But such a formula does not fit Dickens, who among great writers reached the largest audience of all. Nor does it fit Collins, who among popular writers comes closest to deserving the adjective, "great." I don't think either man's pleasure in creating a sub-text for insiders disproves his sincerity as a friend of the many who had never read C. W. King. Still, the insiders' game does reveal the need felt by the two most popular of gifted writers for a freedom to invent, to joke, to be difficult and "shocking," that the mass of their readers would have neither understood nor forgiven.

NOTES

1. I wish to thank Carla DeFord for calling my attention to this letter. The present essay grew out of a talk given as part of a panel on "Popular Culture" at the Victorian Studies Alumni Conference, Indiana University, Bloomington, on February 24, 1984. I am indebted to Steven Elwell and Beth Kalikoff, my two respondents on that occasion; to Michael Dietz, who introduced me to the invaluable *Richardson's Monitor of Free–Masonry*; to L. Thomas Williams, who offered many insights into Masonic analogues (such as the Rose-Croix version

of Jasper's scarf) and into Bulwer Lytton's Rosicrucian methods; and to Linda David, David Frasier, Jerry Herron, and David Warrington, who offered useful suggestions and criticisms.

2. In a discussion of *Barnaby Rudge*, Marsha Schuchard states that Dickens *was* a Mason (352).

3. James's hapless narrator imagines a temple of Vishnu; an alternative possibility is the most famous of Siva's temples, the cave of Elephanta in Bombay harbor.

4. Collins does not name the temple. But in "the holy city of Somnauth" there was only one "famous temple." The article on the city in *The New Encyclopaedia Britannica: Micropaedia* (Chicago: Encyclopedia Britannica, 1983) speaks of "the temple of Siva (Shiva) as Somanatha—i.e., 'lord of the *soma*,' a sacred intoxicating drink, and, by extension, 'lord of the moon'."

5. For a Victorian exposition of *soma* as ritual drink, in a book Collins is known to have consulted, see Wheeler, 1:12–15; the rains accompanying both occasions when opium plays an important part in *The Moonstone* may reflect Wheeler's statement that offerings of *soma* were especially dear to Indra, the rain god; in a "vigorous hymn," the gods are said to long for *soma* "as bridegrooms long for their brides."

6. See Simpson's footnote, Moor (1864), 300–301; Horace Hayman Wilson (1832), 170, 194–195; (1840), 21; (1848), II:251n; Elphinstone, 1:554–555n; Nolan, 1:596n; and Martin, 1:67.

7. The information that Hertford served as the original of Thackeray's Lord Steyne is included at the end of the article on his father, Francis Seymour, in *The Dictionary of National Biography*. Also named by *Punch* as a possible buyer for Siva's gates is a nobleman whose private life seems to have been under attack at this time: see the note in the *Times*, 16 September 1843, "Lord Frankfort and His Family."

8. Wyllie is responding to questions put in Collins's behalf by Eden, a mutual friend. Strictly speaking, therefore, "you" refers to Eden not Collins. But even if Collins did not know the Lord Ellenborough story initially, and was thus guilty of a rather startling gap in his expertise as a journalist who had researched the Sepoy Mutiny, Wyllie's letter would presumably have aroused his curiosity. It is noteworthy that he chose Somnauth as a setting in preference to another, also in Kattiawar, more strongly recommended by Wyllie, namely, Dwarka, the birthplace of Krishna.

9. For "foil'd," see the entry for that word in Henke, and in Pendry's glossary (Marlowe 1976); see also Irving Ribner's notes to II, iii, 55–56 (Marlowe 1963).

10. Zimmer characterizes the earthly counterpart of the heavenly *amrita* as a "dewlike elixir," derived from the stalks of a plant in which "king moon" dwells; this juice forms "the basic ingredient in the sacrificial drink offered to Indra and the other gods in the diurnal rituals of the Vedic period" (I, 164). The tiresome evangelical, Miss Clack, describes her own efforts to calm an erring mortal as "Manna in the wilderness . . . dew on the parched earth!" (306), while Ezra Jennings, recalling the effects of opium on Franklin Blake, states that "the sublime intoxication of opium gleamed in his eyes; the dew of a stealthy perspiration began to gleam on his face" (475). Manna = (merry) dew = opium = soma, gift of the moon. Hargrave Jennings raises the possibility that the first syllable of "Rosicrucian" puns on "*ros*," "dew," a thesis granted tentative support by Frances Yates in *The Rosicrucian Enlightenment* (47, 69, 221). For a Masonic reference to "vivifying dew," see Wilmshurst, 119.

11. Though preferring a different approach, George Eliot's Reverend Casaubon takes no greater pride than Hargrave Jennings in having found "the key to all the

mythologies" ([1870], 327). The phrase itself, almost identical with the title of Casaubon's opus, appeared in *The Rosicrucians* in the year when George Eliot began—"about the opening of November" (Haight, 431–32)—to write the story of Dorothea Brooke. In Jennings, the key is specifically the fall from androgyny into sexuality, "the appearance of 'woman' upon the scene [as] an 'obtrusion,' in the sense of a thing unintended" (327). Jennings is never more cryptic or reverent than when referring to primordial or celestial androgyny; one wonders whether Collins has this in mind in stressing the feminine side of Ezra Jennings—"some men are born with female constitutions—and I am one of them!" (422). Eliot's *Middlemarch* notebooks show a serious interest in Hinduism; among many other facets of that religion, she notes that Siva "brings the lingam as sign of Life and Death (= orgiastic worship in Greece)" and cites "Creuzer's opinion, strongly contested by others," that Dionysus is a Greek adaptation of Siva ([Pratt and Neufeldt], 223).

12. See also Jennings's commentary, in which he equates the dark of the moon with red, the light with white: "The whole refers to King Arthur and his Knights of the Round Table, set round as sentinels ('in lodge') of the *Sangreal, or Holy Graal*—the 'Sacrifice Mysterious,' or 'Eucharist.' " The table itself is "the same object as that enclosed by the mythic garter, 'garder,' or 'girther' " (323-324).

13. For other instances of "upright," see Jennings, 1870: 10, 17, 58, 63, 82, 91, 92, 97, 106, 109, 110, 148, 161, 215, 222, 229, 230, 232–234, 282, 304, 331. See Steig for a cogent critique of the *a priori* assumption that Dickens abstained from bawdy humor.

14. For the following topics, see the pages indicated in Jennings (1870)—magnetism: 100, 158, 284; mysterious fire: 70–79, 203, 204, 208, 335; *Comus:* 117; sun-dial: 148; "alphabet": 71, 74, 123, 148, 210; Apollo, Minerva, Diana: 100; Olympus: 113; Venus: 7, 66, 147, 193; Wandering Jew: 16–17; gypsies: 63, 110, 119; Tartars: 115, 280, 319–320; Great Pyramid of Cheops: 98, 105; Rosa Mundi: 169; Bhudd: 117.

15. See Partridge (1984) for *pussy, John Thomas, jack,* and *crack,* and also for *poker,* which Dickens uses as a proper name in the "Sapsea Fragment," reprinted in Cardwell as Appendix C (232–235).

16. For commentary on the special properties of jasper, see King (1864), 74, 112, 130; for other instances in text, see 48, 56, 70, 76, 77, 100,101, 105, 113, 118, 134, 139, 140, 142, 186; for instances in "Description of Plates," see 201–208, 210, 212–218, 222–225, 233–237; for other names or terms corresponding to characters' names in *Drood,* see 17 (topes); 146 (Helena), 190 (tiler); and for names of various deities, see 2, 23, 39, 41–42, 54, 59, 60, 67, 85, 105, 139, 149, 157, 162, 165, 199, 223, 233.

17. Cohen terms the sinister figure on the cover "a threatening Amazon" (216). But see *Goostics* (1864) 76, 169–71, 199, 207, 223, and plates III, fig. 5 × fig. 5; Neumann, plate 70; Eliot (1981), plate 3; and compare the knife of fig. 3 and the serpents of fig. 11 in the present essay with the attributes of Hecate and Medusa on the jasper gem shown in Zazoff, plate 225, fig. 1706.

18. Lindsay stresses the importance of *A Strange Story* as a forerunner of *Drood* (406). Cf. the analysis of Rosicrucian allusions in Lytton's *Coming Race,* in Williams, 112–167.

19. Hook discusses the Nizam at a number of earlier points (e.g., 170–173, 176–177)—necessarily so, for that prince plays a key role in the political as well as military history of the war. On Collins's reversals, see Leavy, 96.

20. Hill stresses the relevance of Holbein's *Dance of Death* to the imagery associated

with Jasper and Durdles, and adduces Death's pickaxe in Holbein's *Alphabet of Death* (141–147).
21. Vogel also seems to me correct in finding *rood* embedded in Edwin's last name (64). Given Masonic habits of mind, Dickens may be punning on *rood* and *Druid*, carrying through the one idea of the meeting of pagan and Christian religions.

WORKS CITED

Archbold, W. A. J. "Afghanistan, Russia and Persia." *British India*. H. H. Dodwell, ed. Vol. 5 of *The Cambridge History of India*. 5 vols. Cambridge: Cambridge University Press, 1929. 483–521.

Baker, Richard. *The Drood Murder Case*. Berkeley: University of California Press, 1951.

Bayard, Jean-Pierre. *Le Symbolisme Maçonnique*. Paris: Editions du Prisme, 1974.

Beer, John. "*Edwin Drood* and the Mystery of Apartness." *Dickens Studies Annual* 13 (1984): 143–191.

Burton, Richard, trans. *The Perfumed Garden of the Shaykh Nefzawi*. 1886. Alan Hull Walton, ed. London: Neville Spearman, 1963.

Chancellor, E. Beresford. *The London of Charles Dickens*. London: Grant Richards, 1924.

Chesterton, G. K. *Appreciations and Criticisms of the Works of Charles Dickens*. London: J. M. Dent, 1911.

Clavel, F. T. Bègue. *Histoire Pittoresque de la Franc-Maçonnerie et des Sociétés Secrètes Anciennes et Modernes*. Paris, 1843.

Cohen, Jane R. *Charles Dickens and His Original Illustrators*. Columbus: Ohio State University Press, 1980.

Coleman, Charles. *The Mythology of the Hindus*. London, 1832.

Collins, Philip. *Dickens and Crime*. Bloomington: Indiana University Press, 1968.

Collins, Wilkie. *Armadale*. 1864–66. New York: Dover Publishers, 1977.

———. *The Moonstone*. 1868; rev. 1871. J.I.M. Stewart, ed. Harmondsworth: Penguin Books, 1966.

———. "*The Moonstone* (The Novel) / Notes Extracted from books and letter from Mr. Wyllie (Since Deceased) who kindly gave me the information on which I founded the 'Epilogue' at the end of the Story," ms. Morris L. Parrish Collection, Princeton University, Princeton, N. J.

———. *The Woman in White*. 1859–60. Julian Symons, ed. Harmondsworth: Penguin, 1974.

De Quincey, Thomas. "Historico-Critical Inquiry into the Origin of the Rosicrucians and the Free-Masons." *Works*. David Masson, ed. 14 vols. London: 1896–97. 13:384–448.

Dickens, Charles. *Letters of Charles Dickens*. Walter Dexter, ed. 3 vols. Bloomsbury: Nonesuch Press, 1938.

―――. *The Mystery of Edwin Drood*. 1870. Margaret Cardwell, ed. Oxford: Clarendon Press, 1972.

Duffield, Howard. "John Jasper: Strangler," *The Bookman* 70 (1930): 581–588.

Eliot, George. *A Writer's Notebook 1854–1879, and Uncollected Writings*. Joseph Wiesenfarth, ed. Charlottesville: University of Virginia, 1981.

―――. *George Eliot's Middlemarch Notebooks*. John Clark Pratt and Victor Neufeldt, eds. Berkeley: University of California Press, 1979.

Elphinstone, Mountstuart. *The History of British India*. 2 vols. London, 1841.

Ferguson, John. *Encyclopedia of Mysticism and Mystery Religions*. New York: Crossroad, 1982.

"The Gates of Somnauth." *Punch* 4 (1843): 76.

Haight, Gordon S. *George Eliot: A Biography*. Oxford: Clarendon Press, 1968.

Heckethorn, Charles William. *The Secret Societies of All Ages and Countries*. 2 vols. 1897. Hyde Park, New York: University Books, 1965.

Henke, James T. *Courtesans and Cuckolds: A Glossary of Renaissance Dramatic Bawdy (Exclusive of Shakespeare)*. New York: Garland Publishing, 1979.

Hill, Nancy K. *A Reformer's Art: Dickens's Picturesque and Grotesque Imagery*. Athens: Ohio University Press, 1981.

[Hook, Theodore.] *The Life of General The Right Honourable Sir David Baird, Bart*. 2 vols. London, 1832.

"House of Commons, Thursday, March 9: The Somnauth Proclamation." *Times* 10 March 1843: 3–6.

"House of Lords, Thursday, March 9: Lord Ellenborough's Proclamation." *Times* 10 March 1843: 2–3.

Imlah, Albert H. *Lord Ellenborough*. Cambridge, Mass.: Harvard University Press, 1939.

Inman, Thomas. *Ancient Faiths Embodied in Ancient Names*. 2 vols. London and Liverpool, 1868–69.

―――. *Ancient Pagan and Modern Christian Symbolism Exposed and Explained*. London and Liverpool, 1869.

Jacobson, Wendy S. "John Jasper and Thuggee." *Modern Language Review* 72 (1977): 526–537.

James, Henry. *The Novels and Tales of Henry James*. 26 vols. New York: Charles Scribner's Sons, 1922.

Jennings, Hargrave. *The Indian Religions; or, Results of the Mysterious Buddhism.* London, 1858.

———. *The Obelisk: Notices of the Origin, Purpose, and History of Obelisks.* London, 1877.

———. *Phallicism Celestial and Terrestrial, Heathen and Christian: Its Connexion with the Rosicrucians and the Gnostics and Its Foundation in Buddhism, with an Essay on Mystic Anatomy.* London, 1884.

———. *Phallism* [sic]: *A Description of the Worship of Lingam-Yoni in Various Parts of the World and in Different Ages, with an Account of Ancient and Modern Crosses . . . and Other Mysteries of Sex Worship.* London, 1889.

———. *The Rosicrucians: Their Rites and Mysteries.* London, 1870.

———. *The Rosicrucians: Their Rites and Mysteries.* 4th ed. London: George Routledge, 1907.

Jung, C. G. *Word and Image.* Aniela Jaffe, ed. Bollingen Series 97: 2. Princeton, N. J.: Princeton University Press, 1979.

King, C. W. *The Gnostics and Their Remains, Ancient and Medieval.* London, 1864.

———. *The Gnostics and Their Remains, Ancient and Medieval.* Second Edition. London, 1887; rpt. San Diego, Calif.: Wizard's Bookshelf, 1982.

Kramrisch, Stella. *Manifestations of Shiva.* Philadelphia: Philadelphia Museum of Art, 1981.

Leavy, Barbara Fass. "Wilkie Collins's Cinderella: The History of Psychology and *The Woman in White.*" *Dickens Studies Annual* 10 (1982): 91–141.

Lindsay, Jack. *Charles Dickens.* New York: Philosophical Library, 1950.

Lonoff, Sue. *Wilkie Collins and His Victorian Readers: A Study in the Rhetoric of Authorship.* New York: AMS Press, 1982.

"Lord Frankfort and His Family." *Times* 16 September 1843: 5.

Lytton, Edward Bulwer. *A Strange Story.* 1861. Boston, 1892.

Mackey, Albert G. *An Encyclopaedia of Freemasonry.* Rev. William J. Hughan and Edward L. Hawkins. Chicago: Masonic History Company, 1927.

Marlowe, Christopher. *Complete Plays.* Irving Ribner, ed. New York: Odyssey Press, 1963.

———. *Complete Plays and Poems.* E. D. Pendry, ed. London: J. M. Dent, 1976.

———. *Complete Works.* Fredson Bowers, ed. 2nd ed. Cambridge: Cambridge University Press, 1981.

Martin, R. Montgomery. *The Indian Empire.* London, [1858–61].

"Mr. Jennings." *Athenaeum* 15 March 1890: 342.

Moor, Edward. *The Hindu Pantheon.* London, 1810; rpt. Los Angeles: Philosophical Research Society, 1976.

————. *The Hindu Pantheon*. Rev. W. O. Simpson. Madras, 1864.

————. *Oriental Fragments*. London, 1834.

Munck, Johannes, trans. and ed. *The Acts of the Apostles,* rev. William F. Albright and C. S. Mann. Garden City, N. Y.: 1967.

Nelson, Harland S. "Dickens' Plots: 'The Ways of Providence' or the Influence of Collins?" *Victorian Newsletter* 19 (1961): 11–14.

Neumann, Eric. *The Great Mother*. Trans. Ralph Manheim. New York: Bollingen Foundation, 1955.

Nolan, Edward Henry. *The Illustrated History of the British Empire in India and the East, from the Earliest Times to the Suppression of the Sepoy Mutiny in 1859.* 2 vols. London, [1858–60].

"Obituary" (Hargrave Jennings). *Times* 14 March 1890: 9.

Partridge, Eric. *A Dictionary of Slang and Unconventional English*. Paul Beale, ed. New York: Macmillan Company, 1984.

————. *Shakespeare's Bawdy*. 1948. New York: E. P. Dutton, 1960.

Price, R. G. G. *A History of Punch*. London: William Collins, 1957.

Ravenshaw, E. C. "Note on the Sri Jantra and Khat Kon Chakra, (Six-Angled Wheel), or Double Equilateral Triangle." *Journal of the Royal Asiatic Society of Great Britain and Ireland* 13 (1852): 71–80.

Reed, John R. "English Imperialism and the Unacknowledged Crime of the *Moonstone*." *Clio* 2 (1973): 281–290.

Richardson, Jabez (Benjamin Day). *Richardson's Monitor of Free-Masonry*. 1860. New York, [1872].

Scholem, Gershom G. *Major Trends in Jewish Mysticism*. 2nd ed. New York: Schocken Books, 1946.

Schuchard, Marsha. "Freemasonry, Secret Societies, and the Continuity of the Occult Traditions in English Literature." Diss. University of Texas at Austin, 1975.

Sherwood, Richard C. "Of the Murderers Called Phansigars." In Sleeman, Appendix 5: 327–362.

Sleeman, W. H. *Ramaseeana, or A Vocabulary of the Peculiar Language Used by the Thugs*. Calcutta, 1836.

"Somnauth." *The New Encyclopaedia Britannica: Micropaedia*. 15th ed. 1983.

Steig, Michael. "The Intentional Phallus: Determining Verbal Meaning in Literature." *Journal of Aesthetics and Art Criticism* 36 (1977): 51–61.

Thornton, Edward. *A Gazetteer of the Territories Under the Government of the East-India Company, and the Native States of the Continent of India*. London, 1857.

————. *Illustrations of the History and Practices of the Thugs*. London, 1837.

Vogel, Jane. *Allegory in Dickens*. University: University of Alabama Press, 1977.

Waite, Arthur Edward. *A New Encyclopaedia of Freemasonry*. 1921. New York: Weathervane Books, 1970.

Wheeler, James Talboys. *The History of India from the Earliest Ages*. 9 vols. London, 1867.

Williams, L. Thomas. "Journeys to the Center of the Earth: Descent and Initiation in Selected Science Fiction." Diss. Indiana University, 1983.

Wilmshurst, W. L. *The Meaning of Masonry*. 1927. New York: Bell, 1980.

Wilson, Edmund. *The Wound and the Bow*. 1941. New York: Farrar Straus Giroux, 1978.

Wilson, Horace Hayman, ed. James Mill, *The History of British India*. 9 vols. London, 1848.

————. "Sketch of the Religious Sects of the Hindus." Asiatic Society of Calcutta. *Asiatic Researches* 16 (1831): 1–136; 17 (1832): 169–314.

————. "Two Lectures on the Religious Practices and Opinions of the Hindus; Delivered Before the University of Oxford, On the 27th and 28th of February, 1840." Oxford, 1840.

Wyllie, [John William Shaw]. Letter to Eden. n.d. Collins, "*Moonstone . . .* Notes."

Yates, Frances. *The Rosicrucian Enlightenment*. Boulder, Colorado: Shambhala, 1978.

Zazoff, Peter, ed. *Antike Gemmen in Deutschen Sammlungen: Hannover, Kestner-Museum; Hamburg, Museum für Kunst und Gewerbe*. Wiesbaden: Franz Steiner Verlag GMBH, 1975.

Zimmer, Heinrich. *The Art of Indian Asia: Its Mythology and Transformations*. Joseph Campbell, ed. 2 vols. New York: Pantheon Books, 1955.

Recent Dickens Studies: 1985
Brought Together Very Curiously

Jerome Meckier

"Only connect!" The shibboleth of Margaret Schlegel—"That was the whole of her sermon"—became a Dickensian watchword in 1985. Critics unwilling to repeat it had no more chance of finding themselves in print than an Ephraimite of fooling the Gileadites. For twelve months, with only two notable exceptions, Bloomsbury's decision that connectivity is the primary study of man proved more of a siren's song than utterances from Bakhtin or Derrida. It was as if, turning into 48 Doughty Street, one found oneself, instead, at 46 Gordon Square with Vanessa and Clive Bell, or with Adrian and Virginia Woolf at 29 Fitzroy Square.

During the past year, Dickensians examined Dickens and his novels in conjunction with, among other persons, places, and things: allegory, Horatio Alger, Hans Christian Anderson, Eric Berne, the Bible, Chesterton, coincidence, Collins, Conrad, cricket, dream theory, drink, an eighteenth-century nobleman named Charles de Marquetal de Saint Denis de Saint Evremond, *Jane Eyre,* feminism, John Forster, the Literary Fund, Gogol, Hawthorne, the Hermit of Hertfordshire, Hobbes, homosexuality, R. H. Horne, industrialization, Irving, Kafka, language, Alice Lemon, F. R. Leavis, the Rev. David Macrae, Harriet Martineau, masochism, onomastics, popular entertainment, providence, protest novels, Reade, Charles Rowcraft, Shakespeare, Shaw, Ellen Ternan, a Turner painting, Tolstoy, veneer, the visual arts, and windows.

More than forty years ago, Humphry House set out to show the "connexion between what Dickens wrote and the times in which he wrote it." The goal was to ground the fictive world of Dickens' novels more firmly in the concerns of Victorian society, thus demonstrating the pertinence each had for an understanding of the other. By 1962, in *Dickens and Crime*, Philip Collins wanted to "relate" Dickens' "writings about crime to the events, ideas, and literary conventions of his age." As Dickens' personality and *oeuvre* took precedence to the age that produced them both, Collins suggested that one could automatically illuminate the period the more light one shed on its greatest novelist. Since then, the Dickens connection has come steadily into its own: the tendency to scrutinize Dickens and something, whether it be Carlyle, charity, or suspended quotations, is no longer a plaintive methodology used to argue for the Inimitable's importance; it springs from a resolve to capitalize on his growing centrality as the Loadstone Rock of Victorian studies. Determining how events and personalities impinged upon Dickens or the significance he continues to have for them, Dickensians throughout 1985 testify to his escalating usefulness as both indicator and referent.

I

Angus Easson enjoys the distinction of having written the year's only essay on Dickens' earliest publications. In "Who is Boz? Dickens and his Sketches" (*The Dickensian*), he decides that Boz never developed into a consistently realized persona, like Elia or Mr. Spectator. Instead, Easson argues for a receptive consciousness: a tripartite combination of perceiving eye, responsive mind, and creative imagination. Yet it seems unfair to measure the shortlived, periodic Boz against Addison and Steele, who, with helpers, wrote a daily paper. Lamb's essays, signed "Elia," spanned more than a decade (1820–33). Neither Steele nor Lamb created a consistently realized persona for his first appearance in print. To illustrate the coalescence of receptivity, responsiveness, and imagination, Pickwick, not Boz, is your man. Despite several interminably long paragraphs, this essay nicely supplements DeVries's fine book.

In another matter involving identity, Juliet McMaster contends that Jack Bamber, whom Mr. Pickwick meets at the Magpie and Stump, does not relate a story about himself. The argument of "Who *is* Jack Bamber? More about the Old Man and the Queer Client" (*The Dickensian*) is that the teller is not Heyling, the vindictive central figure of the inset tale in Chapter 21, but the rascally lawyer who abets his client's schemes for revenge. Whoever Bamber is, one should emphasize, Dickens' point would seem to be the evolving Mr. Pickwick's wisdom in not adopting him as a role model.

James E. Marlow's delightfully anachronistic point about Mr. Pickwick is that the immortal gentleman's theory of language fails to take into account Derrida and the semioticians of the 1980s. In "Pickwick's Writing: Propriety and Language" (*English Literary History*), the resilient hero is belabored as the patsy of positivism. He presupposes that language is a system of signs referring to the actual world instead of to itself. Had he realized that the *signified* has no priority over the *signifier,* he might not have misread Bill Stumps's signature. A victim of the "semiotics of virtue," Pickwick is easily duped by Job Trotter's grief: he interprets signs the way they are meant to be read, as if all semiosis were not difference, that is, as if displays of feeling actually furnished foolproof guides to the nature of someone's heart. For a skilful deconstructionist like Buzfuz, who can wring hidden fire from reference to a warming pan, the untutored Pickwick is no match. He is not convicted for breach of promise but for his assumption that the mimetic operations of justice can restore a past event to complete presence for review by a jury.

Imprisoned, Pickwick finally learns to "decenter his focus." He awakens from "the dream of a full and immediate presence closing history, the transparence and indivision of a parousia, and the suppression of contradiction and difference," quite an enlightenment. His "immersion into the ways of language" is then complete, and he is reborn a post-modern linguist, although not as good a one as Sam Weller, the novel's "model of a flexible point of view" who is ahead of his times instinctively.

Read with a straight face as the story of a man who "like most of us, has not vigorously examined the composite ideology he espouses," Marlow's twenty-four-page essay would be just another elaboration of a critical truism: Pickwick cannot view the world in the Pickwickian or dispassionate sense with which he starts off. But the same piece becomes the year's cleverest if one detects an excellent parody of current critical ideology. That Marlow's proposal is ultimately modest, that it says little at length in a jargon-filled manner, is part of the joke. Instead of a Victorian novel falling victim to the deconstructionist approach of an imposing critic perched outside it, the hero within the novel is reprimanded by Dickens for entertaining reactionary, anti-deconstructionist sentiments about the spoken and written word. The reviewer for *Blackwood's Magazine,* stranded in the wilderness of *Little Dorrit,* was a fool to yearn for "the old natural, easy, unconscious Pickwickian style," which had problems of its own. On the other hand, contrary to the nihilism behind an art and language pointing only to themselves, deconstructionism is allegedly salvific for Mr. Pickwick.

Language for Jingle, says Marlow, is for fiction and escape (absence), not the medium of truth and permanence (presence) Pickwick tries to make it.

Escape also impresses Jim Davis as the reason Henry Irving never tired of playing Jingle even after he became a famous Shakespearean actor. In "'Jingle' Without 'The Bells'" (*The Dickensian*), Davis calls Irving's appearance in Albery's 1871 adaptation of *Pickwick Papers* "one of the most successful Dickens cameos of the century." Albery's version, which concentrated on early episodes from Dickens' novel, excluding those in the Fleet, enabled Irving to step out of character and display his virtuosity. This was especially true when he played the conscience-less Jingle and Mathias, the man of stern conscience in *The Bells*, as parts of the same evening's program. Witty reviewers could not decide if they preferred *Jingle* without *The Bells* or vice versa.

If Marlow's remarks on *Pickwick Papers* trifle with Derrida, the year's essays on *Nicholas Nickleby* and *Oliver Twist* are merely trifles. Gary H. Day intends to establish "The Relevance of the Nickleby Stories" (*The Dickensian*). He finds that "The Five Sisters of York" and "The Baron of Grogzwig" are informed by the same themes pervading the rest of the novel. This is hardly a new connection. Gary Schnarnhorst believes that Horatio Alger vulgarized in his juvenile fiction features of Dickens' early novels. In "Dickens and Horatio Alger, Jr." (*Dickens Quarterly*), he attributes the American mythology of success for the industrious to Alger's oversimplifications of *Oliver Twist* and *Nicholas Nickleby*.

Barely more substantial is Brian Rosenberg's view of "Physical Opposition in *Barnaby Rudge*" (*Victorian Newsletter*), the "most oppositional" of Dicken's novels. Characters overtly dissimilar yet thematically connected convey Dickens' sense of a world in which contrast and separation are dominant principles. Paradoxically, opposition serves as the strongest form of bonding, as in the contrapuntal pairing of Gabriel Varden and Barnaby Rudge the elder. According to Rosenberg, Dickens considered social and personal conflict inevitable and unresolvable. Thus, one might add, he subsequently posed a threat to the more optimistic outlooks on human relationships adopted by Mrs. Gaskell and George Eliot.

Sylvère Monod's *Martin Chuzzlewit,* in the Unwin Critical Library, is an entire book devoted to a single novel. The critic aims his remarks at serious students and knowledgeable non-academic readers, neither of whom will be disappointed. But Dickensians already familiar with the novel's publication history, the controversy regarding its American episodes, and the niche it occupies in the Dickens canon may find Monod both insightful and simplistic.

Regrettably, *Martin Chuzzlewit,* a pivotal performance for Dickens, is not a novel Monod sufficiently admires.

Martin Chuzzlewit is Janus-faced, the last of Dickens' early novels and the first of his later, better-constructed, increasingly satirical productions. Disillusionment with civilization's fresh start in America forced Dickens to reevaluate his conception of human nature. If basic flaws, crudely similar to those found in England, had quickly emerged, making the new society a step backward, then republics of the imagination had to be discarded as utopian fantasy. A general down-grading of expectations, the so-called darkening vision of Dickens' later fiction, soon followed. Back from America, Dickens could no longer entertain Rousseauean daydreams of a bygone edenic state. Nor could he embrace historical process as a steady, linear climb to perfection since centuries-old England was as acquisitive as brand-new America. The mother country had simply acquired a veneer of politeness to cover its hypocrisies. Dickens discovered that he preferred the restraints of custom and tradition to the wide-open state of affairs in America but neither place seemed likely to improve voluntarily or heed the reforms he suggested.

Monod's opening chapter on "Dickens' Pre-*Chuzzlewit* Days" and another on Chapters I–XIV, the pre-American episodes, create a' false impression. It sounds as if the author recognizes that Dickens' seventh novel in six years constitutes a dividing-line (pre-*Chuzzlewit*/post-*Chuzzlewit*), with the journey Martin and Mark take to America as the point of crossover. Yet the remainder of this study tries to excuse, not justify, Dickens' disappointment with America. Instead of a gateway to the later fiction, Monod sees a "desire to revert" to the leisurely style of *Pickwick Papers;* he demotes *Martin Chuzzlewit* to a novel that "does not show much progress since the days of *Oliver Twist.*" One cannot downplay the American episodes as "extemporization" because they only occupy one-seventh of the novel's chapters. Nor should Dickens' disenchantment with America be blamed on "the intense weariness" constant travelling produced in a novelist who had been "working inordinately hard for years."

Cataloguing the novel's deficiencies in a concluding chapter mistitled "The Evolution of Dickens's Style and Method within *Martin Chuzzlewit,*" Monod lists organizational problems, "creakings" of the narrative machinery, excessive use of coincidence, and "unevenness" in the writing. These flaws are not imaginary. They are also ubiquitous in Dickens' preceding novels. But the discrepancy Monod complains of between Dickens' growing seriousness and the attempt, admittedly his "last," to "present a comic solution" ought to indicate a novelist with a changing perspective. *Martin Chuzzlewit* is the product of Dickens' growing awareness that deficiencies in society and human nature are more deep-seated, time-honored, and interrelated than the creator of Pickwick had suspected.

Although a Frenchman writing about an English novel in which American scenes prove pivotal, Monod is at his customary best when analyzing Dickens' use of language. He questions Dickens' pride in his ability to render on paper critical verbal differences between English and American speech. Equally suspect is the novelist's use of such differences as infallible clues to a nation's character. Chapters on "Pecksniffery," Tom Pinch ("The Salt of Pinch"), "Crime and Punishment" in *Martin Chuzzlewit,* and the novel's minor characters are all highly readable but pale before discussion of "Mrs. Gamp and Mrs. Harris" because Monod treats "Gampese" as a separate language. He works out the rules and patterns for a style of utterance that registers the nurse as an "oral/aural" achievement.

Monod claims that Sarah Gamp, not the American scenes, gave *Martin Chuzzlewit* a boost similar to the push the circulation of *Pickwick Papers* received from Sam Weller. Since she appears in only eight of fifty-four chapters, however, this proves how crucial even one-seventh of a novel can be. As Monod recognizes, sales of *Martin Chuzzlewit* were "alarmingly low" only by comparison with previous triumphs. Moreover, if Dickens had secured copyright protection in 1842, transatlantic proceeds might have made *Martin Chuzzlewit* the biggest moneymaker he had ever had.

Dvora Zelicvici defends the "architectonic design" of Dickens' eighth novel in "Tema con Variazioni in *Dombey and Son*" (*Modern Language Studies*). She argues for a three-part structure featuring variations on Pride: this capital sin colors Dombey's relations with his son (Chapters 1–20), his dealings with Edith and Florence (21–50), and finally destroys his business (51–60). Dombey impresses Zelicvici as Dickens' "first sustained and insightful study" of self-incarceration in "a psychological and spiritual prison." Unfortunately, the contention that the novel's weaknesses are not structural falls short of exonerating Dickens, at least as Zelicvici formulates it. She points to a stylistic deterioration that saps the novel's strength as pathos and melodrama replace satiric irony. This leaves matters as badly off as before, only in a different regard. One could counter that the replacement is essential if Dickens is to work out Dombey's salvation; thus it reveals flaws in conception or results from them. One cannot answer Dickens' critics by promoting one aspect of his art at the sacrifice of another.

For Linda Zwinger, the flaw in *Dombey and Son* is neither stylistic nor structural but ideological. She argues in "The Fear of the Father: Dombey and Daughter" (*Nineteenth-Century Fiction*) that critics should pay greater attention to the women in the novel who are literally in fear of Dombey. Instead, since Moynahan's seminal essay, the focus has been on the iron-hard Dombey and his fear of a softening feminine mystique.

Unlike William Dorrit, Boffin, and the avuncular Captain Cuttle, Dombey can dispense with the ministrations of a daughter, even in his wifeless, motherless household. As a result, the powers Dickens routinely conceded to figures like Nell, Florence, Agnes, and Amy Dorrit lose their humanizing impact. Where the father is powerful, that is, not unthreatening, the ideology that consecrated home and hearth as a virtual church begins to break down. Dickens comes close, Zwinger maintains, to "revealing the hollowness" of domesticity as a semi-religious ideal in a resolutely patriarchal society.

Lest that happen, the novelist contrives to have Florence and Edith admit the errors of their ways. An Edith not quite guilty of adultery apologizes to a Florence completely innocent of any disloyalty who in turn begs her father's forgiveness for leaving his house. Florence is readmitted as the mother of Dombey's grandson, a replacement for Paul, not as an emblem of budding womanhood, masculinity's enemy. Both of the women in Dombey's life, says Zwinger, confess to "violating the domestic space with unseemly rebellions against its culturally sanctioned power structure." Woman's domestic influence was not stronger than capitalistic power, Zwinger charges in her conclusion; Dickens knew it yet stopped short of saying so.

This indictment of the lip-service Dickens allegedly paid to the efficacy of an unselfish love like Florence's falters on several counts: it omits Gradgrind and Hexam from the examination of powerful father-figures and minimizes Dickens' generally unfavorable treatment of the *pater familas* and his surrogates. They are often incompetent (Trent), cruel (Ralph Nickleby), overbearing (Pumblechook), and sometimes hypocritical as well (Pecksniff, Casby the sham Patriarch). Dickens' dislike of Dombeyism, the new urban business mentality, seems unmistakable to all but Zwinger. She must shrug off Dombey's breakdown as an unnecessary capitulation. Otherwise, she cannot insist that the patriarch, unlike Florence and Edith, never appears as confessant.

Insufficient connection, the split between Dickens' presentation of Copperfield's turbulent history and the unexamined basis for the hero's literary achievement, furnishes the slim pretext for "*David Copperfield:* The Decomposing Self'' (*Centennial Review*). Surely, one replies, the arguments for this kind of breakdown have worn thin. The novel ought to be allowed to testify for itself as David's attainment of personal and artistic selfhood; it shows what he can do. To the extent that *David Copperfield* is autobiographical, it offers the same basis for the protagonist's compositional urge that Dickens had himself: severe early disappointments, capacity for hard work, a generous, observant nature, and a need for self-justification. What really decomposes in Simon Edwards's essay is the critic's grasp of his material and all sense of direction.

The most rambling of potpourris, this piece ranges from *In Memoriam* and England in 1850 to comparisons between writing novels and proliferation of the railways. Edwards also covers Poe, gender confusion, and Heep's masturbatory propensities. The "historical parameters of the resolution of the social/sexual/productive crisis in relation to Tennyson" supposedly "govern" concluding remarks on *David Copperfield*. But by then one might as well be in Krook's shop trying to decipher a mysterious document in a dim light. Edwards attempts to break down a connection the novel depends on but forfeits the reader's confidence by concocting too many outlandish groupings of his own.

After the glut in Edwards's essay, Edwin M. Eigner's humility at first proves refreshing. He writes "The Lunatic at the Window: Magic Casements of *David Copperfield*'' (*Dickens Quarterly*) to note "a distinct window motif" pervading Dickens' novel. Unfortunately, having cited numerous examples, he exasperates the reader to the verge of self-defenestration by confessing he has no idea what the book's many windows mean. Instead of a thesis hunting symbols to support itself, one is left with potential symbols in search of a thesis. Read as a parody of symbol-hunting, this essay improves only slightly, for it makes a convincing case for the abundance of casements. Perhaps they form an appropriate subliminal accompaniment to the novelist-narrator's review of his past. *David Copperfield* is a novel about seeing. It begins and proceeds through retrospection but ends with the hero's vision of the future as provided by the fenestral Agnes.

Alan Shelston writes the year's best essay on the novel Dickens liked best. The thesis of "Past and Present in *David Copperfield*'' (*Critical Quarterly*) is that Dickens refused to oversimplify the relationship between childhood sensibility, recaptured through memory, and adult responsibility, which continually poses new challenges. Unlike Wordsworth in *The Prelude* or George Eliot in *The Mill on the Floss,* Dickens asserts the difficulty of relating past to present. He had experienced this personally when unable to continue the autobiographical fragment he abandoned to write *Copperfield*. Despite the strongly confessional flavor of this novel, Dickens never made a clean breast of his past, argues Shelston, either in his *Bildungsroman* or anywhere else; he left that job to Forster.

Copperfield the narrator unravels his past gropingly, with misgivings, as if he lacks Wordsworth's confidence in the recollective faculty. At novel's end, David has a firmer sense of the distance he has traveled, the separation of *then* from *now*, than of days bound to each other. Uncertain initially of his own fitness for a hero's role, he writes about the arduousness required to establish moral standards for the conduct of a noble life. The message of David's life, Shelston concludes, is not that child is father of the man but that one can and must rise above circumstances. David does so, whereas Steerforth, trapped within privileges, does not.

Shelston presents an un-Wordsworthian Dickens, whose world-view, one could add, was closer to the darker uncertainties in Coleridge's best-known poems. But the article goes too far by denying David any sense of revitalization through recall. Stocktaking has brought a surer hold on selfhood and purpose. Granted, the present must still be met on its own terms. Nor does Copperfield's need for earnestness, the only reliable Victorian equivalent for faith, abate an iota. Nevertheless, it is easier for him to imagine a more tranquil future and a happy death after reviewing past travails and laying them to rest. Bolstered by Agnes, the novelist is no longer the tentative narrator of the opening paragraphs, unsure of his rememberings. He has been replaced by the successful writer-husband, unafraid of the final forgetfulness "when realities" will be "melting" from him "like the shadows" he can "now dismiss." Dickens could not face his past squarely but Copperfield seems to think that he has.

Four essays on the Esther Summerson controversy leave the problem in worse state than before. John Frazee's explanation of the relationship between "The Character of Esther and the Narrative Structure of *Bleak House*" (*Studies in the Novel*) amounts to a concession: difficulties with Esther, as both character and narrator, were the price Dickens willingly paid in order to establish a connection between Lady Dedlock's guilt and Jo's fate. Esther's mother's death becomes the emotional equivalent of the punishment meted out to society for ignoring the crossing-sweeper.

Next, in "Double Vision and the Double Standard in *Bleak House*: A Feminist Perspective" (*Literature and History*), Virginia Blain focuses on the "submerged dialectic between male and female viewpoints." Dual perspectives result from gender division. Maintenance of separate spheres for men and women ensure that society's corruption has its roots in hidden sexual hostilities which the double narrative critiques yet furthers. Blain is at her best when contrasting the third-person narrator's view, that of a male insider, with the outsider's view of a woman born out of wedlock. Still, Blain forgets that illegitimacy is not a social stigma reserved for females; nor does incipient misanthropy add to the benefits of being on the inside. The lot of Esther's unnamed co-narrator is allegedly superior because he is closer to the center of power: he more readily comprehends Chancery and the country's legal system in general. Yet the embittered man seems hardly happier for it.

Like Frazee, Blain reserves a crucial role for Lady Dedlock. Her death amounts to "a purification rite for a whole diseased society." From this observation on, the real argument is between Blain's idea of Victorian society's perspective on women and her own. Esther's taint is bestowed on her not by her mother but by the hostility toward women "endemic in a patriarchal society." Lady Dedlock emerges as "the paradigm for all the failed home-makers in the novel." Her "illicit female sexuality" threatens a social fabric put together by men. All of this seems rather hysterical. Lady Dedlock was never expected to be a Victorian Betty Crocker. She was denied her one true love, not the chance to become a prototype for Lady Chatterley. Similarly deprived of what would have been a rather conventional form of happiness, Hawdon is apparently another victim of the patriarchs but one Blain ignores.

Bleak House, Blain concludes, "deconstructs itself" by fostering the violence it sought to contain: Esther's rewards come at the expense of her mother's death, which she must witness and relate. Her narrative purges her of Lady Dedlock's stain but, simply by telling it, she accomplishes "her own clitoridectomy." If so, the ultimate loss, one fears, is not Lady Dedlock's or Hawdon's but Woodcourt's.

Merritt Moseley begins "The Ontology of Esther's Narrative in *Bleak House*" (*South Atlantic Bulletin*) with the pertinent observation that Esther is a self-conscious narrator who thinks of herself writing a story. She also realizes that she shares this task with another, for she refers to "my portion of these pages." The third-person narrator makes no similar acknowledgment of divided responsibility or of Miss Summerson. From this Moseley illogically deduces the "ontological status" of Esther's narrative: it is subsidiary. He likens it to interpolated narratives elsewhere in Dickens, such as the tales in *Pickwick Papers,* Magwitch's long account of his life to Pip, and "Miss Wade's Narrative."

Such a classification fails to improve Esther's character, which Mosely finds "distasteful." It also aborts one of Dickens' most modern technical experiments as effectively as clitoridectomy would ruin Esther's chances of fulfilling herself. The other interpolations Moseley mentions, including each of the tales in Dickens' first novel, exist as self-contained inserts or units, not as a running narrative deftly interwoven with another's. Common sense suggests the third-person narrator as the interweaver, narrator plus editor, which would entail awareness of Esther. She is subordinate only in that the project was not of her conceiving. Moseley asks one to believe that half of *Bleak House* is embedded in the other, not "a coordinate contribution" but a secondary element as large as the primary. An interpolation so king-sized seems ontologically as impossible as it would be pointless artistically.

Dickens' manipulation of the narrative, not Esther's, upsets Brahma Chandhuri in "The Interpolated Chapter in *Bleak House*" (*The Dickensian*). Examination of the original manuscript and corrected proofs has convinced Chandhuri that Chapter Two, on the Dedlocks, was merely the result of exigencies of serial publication. Dickens rearranged his material, moving some of it forward, to fill out the first month's installment, not as a thematic stroke of brilliant interpolation linking the worlds of Chancery and Chesney Wold. Why, one asks, are urgent remedies and masterful juxtapositioning mutually exclusive? Surely the first became the second even as it was being accomplished. The insertion remains ingenius no matter how mundane its cause. It illustrates the uncanny affinity Dickens felt for a popular format that he elevated to high art as effectively as Shakespeare reworked the Elizabethan revenge tragedy.

Finally, Jane A. McCusker explicates the very next chapter of Dickens' finest novel in order to rehabilitate its much-maligned heroine. Relying on Eric Berne's popular classic of modern sociology, she identifies "The Games Esther Plays—Chapter Three of *Bleak House*" (*The Dickensian*). As a result of a terrible childhood, Esther contracts an acute inferiority complex that causes her to invent games, such as habitual self-disparagement. The games are designed to disarm criticism and win sympathy and love. McCusker employs Berne adroitly to prove that Dickens cannot be artless since Esther's ways of projecting herself are not. Although this argument is straightforward, it allows insufficient latitude for altruism. Esther's commentaries on the society she encounters and her own good deeds to offset it are not invariably self-centered. One wonders why an Esther so qualified to write a book like *Games People Play* contributed to a condition-of-England novel instead.

In "Dickens's Mrs. Sparsit and the Politics of Service" (*Dickens Quarterly*), Diane Dewhurst Belcher shows a truly professional game-player at work, an expert on one-upmanship. She hails Bounderby's housekeeper as "one of the cleverest women Dickens created, and, not surprisingly, one of the most repulsive." Without elaborating convincingly on the chauvinism in this remark, Belcher studies Mrs. Sparsit's manipulations of her employer. A subtler bully than Bounderby, she destroys his marriage in an effort to re-establish her mastery over his household. Ironically, she uses Mrs. Pegler to deflate the image of Bounderby she was hired to keep inflated. The campaign Mrs. Sparsit wages against Louisa, Belcher ought to have continued, carries hints of sexual politics. One wonders if the former Powler is any better suited for romantic intimacies than the self-made man whose inflatable ego substitutes for other signs of virility. The campaign fits into a pattern of self-defeating systems and strategies Dickens satirizes throughout *Hard Times*. At novel's end, Mrs. Sparsit is advised by Bounderby, whom she calls "a Noddle"—neither a sexual nor intellectual compliment—to transfer her interfering ways to Lady Scadgers's. This is a novel in which cleverness, self-serving compared to Fancy, is not held in high moral regard: witness the failure of Harthouse's success as an orator to stand him in good stead against the normally inarticulate Sissy Jupe.

John A. Stoler's essay, "Dickens's Use of Names in *Hard Times*" (*Literary Onomastics Studies*), is Dickens and onomastics at its most rudimentary. More cleverness is required here than the realization that Dickens manifested his linguistic skills by choosing names indicative of the essence of his characters. Even the names Esther's admirers bestow upon her at Bleak House evince more imagination than Stoler's explications. He reduces "Bitzer" to bits and pieces of knowledge but decides "Sleary" has no onomastic significance for the book's themes. "Sissy" is clearly from Cecila, which means "sister," the role its bearer adopts toward the young Gradgrinds. But no attempt is made to decode "Jupe."

If Fact is the central target in *Hard Times*, D. W. Jefferson objects, there should be more of it instead of Dickens' meager portrait of Gradgrind the statistician. Jefferson rankles at the suggestion of kinship between such a caricature and powerful, thoughtful men of fact like Bentham and John Stuart Mill. In "Mr. Gradgrind's Facts" (*Essays in Criticism*), the argument is that Dickens unfairly impoverished both Gradgrind and Coketown so neither would reflect the busy public and intellectual life a true proponent or recipient of Utilitarian endeavor enjoyed in the 1840s and 50s. Coketown lacks a mechanics' institute, for example, and an athenaeum, just as Gradgrind does not seem cognizant of the latest scientific advances. He is particularly ignorant of the decade's improvements in hygiene, which could be Victorian England's greatest contribution to civilization.

Admittedly, Jefferson's protestations are more than cavils; they add up, but not to the point where he substantiates his claim that the novel's central contentions do not bear scrutiny. Dickens attacked an overly pragmatic, anti-aesthetic frame of mind rather than the specific range of that mind's contents. He calls attention to minuses, a satirist's tactic that does not oblige him to enumerate the pluses of the philosophy he questions. Much of the dystopian satire in *Hard Times* focuses on the support Dickens believed the Utilitarian outlook gave *laissez-faire* industrialism, to the smoke and other evils from which he thought some of his rivals were purblind. Not Gradgrind's IQ but his diminishment of the affective life—that is Dickens' point. It would hold true even if Dickens showed Gradgrind reading Dalton and Joule instead of criticizing circuses.

"The Dickens of *Little Dorrit*" (*American Poetry Review*) nicely offsets Jefferson's essay. Robert Coles reminds us how much Dickens knew or foresaw of the world's workings and intuited of the mind's. For the author, who teaches a course titled "Dickens and the Law" at Harvard Law School, the novelist who wrote *Little Dorrit* was a prescient psychologist and far-seeing social critic. He not only explored Clennam's mother-fixation, for example, but showed it aging him prematurely. He recognized in the Circumlocution Office and the equally symbolic Marshalsea early warning signs of the modern bureaucratic nightmare and the alienation in store for man's imprisoned and imprisoning self. Coles's tribute to an intelligent, prophetic, and, above all, realistic Dickens is an appreciation of the sort that used to be called Chestertonian, but for Edmund Wilson's Dickens. It should be mandatory reading for incoming graduate students. Like Coles's budding lawyers, they will be astonished to discover a Dickens one can mention in the same sentence with Weber, Kafka, and Freud.

Forster never mentions Charles Rowcroft, nor do Edgar Johnson and the Pilgrim Letters. E. J. Zinkhan considers this a graver omission than leaving Chadwick out of Mr. Gradgrind's consciousness. The interrogative in "Charles Rowcroft's *Chronicles of 'The Fleet Prison'*: A Source for Amy Dorrit?" (*The Dickensian*) apparently deserves an affirmative answer. Nancy Ward, the "Beauty of the Fleet," preceded the "Child of the Marshalsea" by ten years. The heroine of "The Turnkey's Daughter," one of four tales published as the *Chronicles* (1845–46), does not have a collegian for a father. But, like Amy, she must grow up "in the midst of all sorts of vice and immorality." She remains, Rowcroft writes, "uncontaminated and unharmed by the noxious examples around her."

At this point, the parallel breaks down. Instead of solacing Clennam, Nancy falls in love with a well-born prisoner and deceives her parent to assist her lover's attempt at escape. Rowcroft, who once spent fourteen months in the Fleet, may have been writing from experience, either first or second hand. In that case, Zinkhan ought to realize, the chronicler seems to be saying that uncontamination, which Dickens had already made the hallmark of Oliver and Nell, goes only so far.

Andrew Sanders goes back to the seventeenth century to find a model for Charles Darnay. His name and title derive from the French soldier and poet Charles de Marquetel de Saint Denis de Saint Evremond (1613–1703). In "Monsieur heretofore the Marquis: Dickens's St. Evremond" (*The Dickensian*), Sanders also unearths four other important influences upon *A Tale of Two Cities*. Darnay's Anglicized version of his mother's family name, D'Aulnais, seems to have been taken from a contemporary of St. Evremonde, the Countess d'Aunoy. Dickens learned about the mores of the *ancien regime,* Sanders argues, by reading Louis Sebastien Mercier's *Tableau de Paris*. He also borrowed from the journals of an English traveler, Arthur Young. Having seen France's wretched millions, Young was willing to condone "the murder of a seigneur or a chateau in flames."

· The French connection collapses dramatically when Sanders proposes a source for the fatal accident caused by Monseiur the Marquis' carriage. In *A Tour in England, By a German Prince* (1832), the author tells of running down a child years ago in Jena. Although von Pueckler-Muskau is able to blame his youthful impatience and the child involved lived, other details are strikingly similar to Dickens' account.

Philip Drew's thesis in "Dickens and the Real World: A Reading of 'The Uncommercial Traveller'" is that the thirty-seven papers Dickens wrote for *All the Year Round* between 1859 and 1867 exhibit an invaluable quality, rare elsewhere in his prose: total objectivity. Part of Geoffrey Harlow's collection of *Essays and Studies 1985* (John Murray), Drew's survey of the better papers is meant to illustrate Dickens' unbiased resoluteness as a "serious social commentator." In such pieces as "Wapping Workhouse," Dickens allegedly sees "what is to be seen" and describes it impartially. Disguised as a salesman for "the great House of Human Interest Brothers," the journalist salutes every right step he can find being taken to alleviate the plight of the multiplying urban poor. He notices several persons in authority performing their tasks conscientiously. Even an objective Dickens, says Drew, has no sympathy for criminals. Nor does he entertain the illusion that the government is able or willing to remedy society's ills. One admires everything about this essay except its constant implication that harsh criticism is a subjective response and that a novel as topical as *Bleak House* is less connected to reality than these loosely connected papers.

Great Expectations nosed out *Our Mutual Friend* as the novel most often discussed in the periodicals during 1985. Scott Foll expresses skepticism about Dickens' so-called spontaneity in conceiving Pip's narrative. He offers "*Great Expectations* and the 'Uncommercial Sketch Book'" (*The Dickensian*) as proof that the autonomy of Dickens' novel, its unconnectedness, is a myth. Different pieces in *The Uncommercial Traveller* (1860 series), Foll demonstrates, exhibit themes and images Dickens reused in his subsequent novels, *Great Expectations* in particular.

For William A. Wilson, the more important link is with Shakespeare. In "The Magic Circle of Genius: Dickens's Translations of Shakespearean Drama in *Great Expectations*" (*Nineteenth-Century Fiction*), the Shakespearean in Dickens is the novelist who deliberately blurs distinctions between comedy and tragedy, as did the Bard. Dickens reshapes the Elizabethan revenge tragedy (*Hamlet*) into a Victorian comedy of forgiveness. He also transforms the happy conclusion of Victorian melodrama and New Comedy into the bittersweetness of *A Midsummer Night's Dream*, neither purely comic nor tragic. Although Pip eventually has the power to get even with all who deceived him, he chooses to forgive instead. But, Wilson continues, an Estella who cannot forgive herself cannot translate her life and Pip's fully into comedy. One problem is that Wilson requires twenty pages to travel this far. Along the way, another difficulty emerges as some strained parallels occur: Magwitch as Hamlet's father's ghost, for instance, or Estella as a perverse Cordelia to Miss Havisham's Lear. If Pip impersonates the gentleman as unworthily as Waldengarver, born Wopsle, does Hamlet, then the play-within-the-novel is there to catch the conscience of an upstart; Pip need not play Hamlet himself.

As heavily Freudian as Wilson's essay was Shakespearean, Shuli Barzilai's "Dickens's *Great Expectations:* The Motive for Moral Masochism" (*American Imago*) purports to solve what the author claims is the novel's riddle: who causes Pip's excessive, seemingly unmotivated guilt? Blame falls on

Estella Provis. In punishing others, Barzilai decides, Estella seeks to punish herself. Since she is Pip (or both Pip and not Pip), and Pip, of course, is Dickens, Dickens punishes himself by punishing Estella. Ergo, guilt is sadism translated into masochism. Dickens allegedly has Estella mistreat Pip so the novelist can torture himself anew for rejections that formed a pattern in his mind when his mother sent him to Warren's, his sister became a music student, and Maria Beadnell said no.

Michael Haig explains "The Allegory of *Great Expectations*" (*Sydney Studies in English*) in terms of the numerous connections between the novel's characters: Estella is the daughter of Magwitch whose arch-enemy was false to Miss Havisham, Estella's mother-by-adoption, etc. The plot in which these interrelationships develop becomes an allegory for a reality in which events operate "organically as links in an unbroken chain." Haig is right to insist Pip's life starts not at birth but with Magwitch's sudden appearance, the first link in the novelist's chain. But the concept of organic chainlinks is one that both Dickens and George Eliot would consider more repugnant than he found her idea of "a wonderful slow-growing system of things" or she his emphasis on appointed times for uncovering the multitude of society's sins.

Although Dickens denied reading the Brontës, Helen von Schmidt makes a good case for thinking that he had. In "The Dark Abyss, the Broad Expanse: Versions of the Self in *Jane Eyre* and *Great Expectations*" (*Dickens Quarterly*), she contends that both novels can be read as a first-person narrator's attempt to show a self in the process of creating itself. The novels offer opposite models for determining the self's relation to the world. Von Schmidt decides that Pip and Dickens are more realistic than Jane and Charlotte. The former pair insist convincingly that the self must be created in relation to others, not out of opposition to them. Jane regards her sense of self as an endangered quantity she must keep others from taking away. Dickens' handling of Orlick as a double for Pip is also preferable to Charlotte's Bertha for Jane. Bertha is a part of herself that Jane cannot admit, whereas Pip, says von Schmidt, accepts and subdues the secret sharer he recognizes in Orlick. It seems, she might have added, that Dickens had Brontë's novel in mind on several occasions, not just in *Great Expectations* but earlier in *David Copperfield* and when creating Esther Summerson, three studies of problematic self-formation.

Carol Hanbery MacKay's "A Novel's Journey into Film: The Case of *Great Expectations*" (*Literature Film Quarterly*) defends David Lean's classic 1947 adaptation. After studying original screenplay, post-production script, and the edited film, MacKay finds only two outright lapses from fidelity to

Dickens' text: elimination of Orlick and use of a decidedly happy ending. Most of the other minor deletions and additions were simply a means to greater continuity.

MacKay applauds use of a narrator for point of view. He gives Dickensian descriptions and opens Pip's mind to the viewer. But MacKay regrets the absence of the Newgate dust that contributes to Pip's sense of guilt, and the excision of Trabb's boy. To compensate for omitting Orlick, the film distributes Pip's darker side among several of the other characters, spreading it throughout the London scene. A happy ending, MacKay adds, is defensible both as a solution to Dickens' own ambivalence and because it is in keeping with the "wish-fulfillment fantasies . . . propagated by the body of nineteenth-century fiction."

Of five essays on Dickens' last completed novel, the first three of which appeared in *The Dickensian,* Owen Knowles's is the best. In "Veneering and the Age of Veneer: A Source and Background for *Our Mutual Friend,*" Knowles describes the Victorian penchant for covering surfaces with a thin layer of seemingly superior material. Then he traces the theme of gaudily varnished surfaces masquerading as solid reality to five articles Dickens must surely have read in *Frazer's Magazine.* Their anonymous but trenchant author anticipated the satire in *Our Mutual Friend* against "Perfectly New People" when he christened the nineteenth century "The Age of Veneer."

Frank Gibbon suggests Dickens borrowed more than dust-mounds from an 1850 contribution to *Household Words.* "R. H. Horne and *Our Mutual Friend*" go together, says Gibbon, because Horne's tale of "'Dust,' Or Ugliness Redeemed" focuses on the resurrection and regeneration of a nearly drowned and impoverished man. In "'The Sensational Williams': A Mutual Friend in 1864," Michael Cotsell resurrects an article from *All the Year Round* that argued it was mere cant to dismiss as sensational anything out of the ordinary. The article reviewed *Macbeth* from an anti-sensationalist critic's point of view. Cotsell believes that Mr. Podsnap's opinions on the arts, in a passage published one month after the parodic review, are, in part, a satire against critics who find Dickens too melodramatic.

The first two chapters of *Our Mutual Friend* introduce distinct social worlds that, according to Hillis Miller, "exist side by side" but never "organize." Dickens does Gaffer's dark and primitive riverside in one style and the bright, new, insular world of Podsnaps and Veneerings in another. To demonstrate "The Coherence of *Our Mutual Friend*" (*Journal of Narrative Technique*),

Bruce Beiderwill uncovers a "shared lexis" that connects the opening chapters and continues to operate throughout the novel. A network of recurrent words and phrases creates a pervasive sense of decay as both worlds forfeit the human dimension.

Actually, Dickens regularly begins his novels by creating social circles that appear mutually exclusive but turn out to reinforce one another's contribution to the same deleterious social processes, whether communal irresponsibility or acquisitiveness. In an 1838 novel, Nicholas or Kate enter one petty tyrant's fiefdom after another. By the time Dickens writes *Bleak House* and *Our Mutual Friend*, his skill at suggesting new ramifications of pervasive problems with each additional setting has improved astronomically, as has his sense of pervasiveness. At all times, the satire is doubly effective: seemingly self-contained worlds that are seen to promote variant forms of the same social ills are both denials of fraternity and perverse instances of it.

Angus P. Collins makes a series of persuasive connections between *Our Mutual Friend* and Dickens' mounting awareness of his own mortality. He relates the novel's concern with a world of remorseless physical disintegration to the series of bereavements Dickens suffered in the 1860s. In "Dickens and *Our Mutual Friend:* Fancy as Self-Preservation" (*Etudes Anglais*), Collins theorizes that the therapeutic potential of the imagination in times of personal crisis became increasingly important to the fifty-two-year-old novelist following a circulation drop of 5,000 between the first and second numbers of his fourteenth novel. As Dickens worried about depletion of his own creative gift, characters for whom fancy is a "means of accommodation and imaginative compensation" swelled in importance. Nevertheless, concludes Collins, the Dickens who penned Jenny Wren's rooftop songs about the sweetness of oblivion simultaneously devoted himself to the work at hand, hopeful it would outlast and preserve him. This essay is particularly good at augmenting the meaning of specific passages. Many lines in *Our Mutual Friend* resonate if read in light of Dickens' unsettling fear of death and his longing for immortality through his creations.

If one critic talks about Fancy in *Our Mutual Friend*, another is surely allowed to connect the subject of Dickens' thirteenth novel with *The Mystery of Edwin Drood*. Joseph H. O'Mealy attempts to humanize an apparent murderer in "'Some stray sort of ambition': John Jasper's Great Expectations" (*Dickens Quarterly*). A recognizable type in Dickens' later fiction, O'Mealy's Jasper is the disappointed man who feels he has not received from life all he deserves. The choirmaster is Pip without an inheritance but determined to rise, no matter at what expense to others. As a reworking of Pip, however, Drood is a better choice. Ned has excellent prospects and, in Rosa, a promissory arrangement clearer than Pip's with Estella. The lustful murderer inside the outwardly respectable Jasper has affinities with Orlick, if seen as an emanation from Pip, or with a Carton no longer so self-effacing.

"*Edwin Drood*: A Boneyard Awaiting Resurrection" (*Dickens Quarterly*) seems more to the point. Marilyn Thomas examines the effect upon Cloisterham of a dying social institution, its Cathedral church. One agrees with Thomas that Jasper's dualism is the result of outdated institutions and conventions that compel him to suppress his own needs and drives. But the envy he feels for his nephew and his desires for Rosa seem to issue from a dark side of human nature unacknowledged by the Victorian ethos. No living religion or viable social institution has ever been able to eradicate the antisocial inner self that periodically threatens to take over Jasper's public personality. Thomas is correct again to hold society accountable for Drood's disappearance. Unlike recent continuers of Dickens' unfinished novel, however, she seems unduly expectant that deliverance and rebirth are in store for Cloisterham. Had Dickens completed his task, Jasper might have made subsequent presentations of duality as the modern disease in Conrad and Robert Louis Stevenson seem derivative yet confirmatory.

Conan Doyle resurrected Sherlock Holmes and Dickens may have intended something similar for Drood. So Robert F. Fleissner is not surprised by the number of writers who have borrowed the hawknosed detective to solve the disappearance at Cloisterham. In "Sherlock Holmes Confronts Edwin Drood" (*Baker Street Journal*), Fleissner reviews these effluvial efforts at length. What amazes is Doyle's own reluctance to put Holmes on the case. The doctor-novelist relied instead on seances for a solution. Although he discounted an American report of a visitation from Boz, he believed he had experienced one himself. In the course of it, the spirit divulged that "Edwin is alive and Chris [sic] is hiding him." Alerted by this fumbling of the minor canon's name, Fleissner is properly skeptical.

II

1985 was not a bountiful year for works of a biographical or bibliographical nature. Nevertheless, two books published during the period promise to remain useful research tools for the rest of the century and beyond: David Paroissien's

Selected Letters of Charles Dickens (Twayne) and J. Don Vann's *Victorian Novels in Serial* (Modern Language Association).

The latter, meriting its $50 pricetag, consolidates into 181 pages a wealth of statistical information about the nineteenth century's most novel form of publication. Tables record the divisions into serial installments for the major fictions of sixteen novelists, a total of 192 novels anatomized. The compiler gives the date each installment appeared and the sentence with which it concluded wherever an installment ending does not coincide with the termination of a chapter in the hardcover version.

For Dickens, novel and serial novel were synonymous. He established the popularity of the format, and Wilkie Collins became his only serious rival for mastery of it. Yet neither comes close to being champion numerically. Their combined total of 32 serial novels falls short of Trollope's 34 and Ainsworth's 33. Thackeray wrote two more than Dickens and exactly as many as Collins. The editor admits that the form caters to masters of suspense and delay. Yet novelists who were not enamored of such things employed the form as regularly as some who were. Thus Hardy's dozen matches Reade's, while Meredith and Marryat wrote ten apiece. One concludes that novels in serial, thanks to Dickens, proved profitable to many, perhaps even mandatory, but were aesthetically advantageous to only a few. A nineteen-shilling novel was obviously a better buy than a triple-decker at 31s 6d. But for most novelists, artistic drawbacks of serial publication in magazines—set lengths, enforced pauses, bigger problems with propriety—more than outweighed economic gains. Serial publication altered the shape of the publishing business. Except in the cases of Dickens and Collins, however, it is less certain if it had a beneficial influence on the design of the novel. That so many novelists were compelled to find the format congenial is another indication of Dickens' centrality.

In a perfunctory "Introduction," J. Don Vann lists the pros and cons of serial publication. He explains why only 25 of the 192 novels covered were issued in parts, while the majority appeared in magazines. But the compiler declines to speculate about the failure of practice to bring Trollope and Ainsworth closer to Dickens' level of perfection. Nor is enough said regarding feminine reluctance to make use of the installment novel. Alone of the major Victorians, the Brontës eschewed it entirely. The three women novelists included—George Eliot, Mrs. Gaskell, and Mrs. Humphry Ward—managed only fourteen serials collectively, one less than Dickens.

Paroissien thinks of connection as collection. His *Letters* brings together 377 pages of Dickens' most significant missives. Editors of the Pilgrim Edition will not have printed all 13,452 of the Dickens letters known to be extant until the twenty-first century. So this expedient volume, affordable as well as portable, is more than a boon to beginners not yet acquainted with Dickens' skills as a letter-writer. It also performs a service to scholars who want the key epistles always close to hand. Paroissien's argument that the Pilgrim Edition "will not, in any fundamental way, alter the authentic aspects of Dickens present in the Nonesuch Letters" seems indisputable as a defense of his book's readability.

Dickens could dash off letters as frequently and almost as quickly as moderns pick up the phone. Twelve mail deliveries daily in central London spurred on the prolific letterwriter. But the dynamo who emerges from Paroissien's selections is the same genius of creativity who could keep several novels going at once. To make such profusion into more of a story, Paroissien gathers Dickens' best letters under three headings: those on personal matters (chiefly to family and friends); those on social and political topics in which Dickens speaks as the public voice of conscience; and those containing aesthetic statements, the writer reflecting on his art. Each section begins with a short, informative essay by the editor, of which the third is the best.

In the first, Paroissien stresses the many clues in Dickens' letters to his growing displeasure with Catherine. The novelist's attempts to unwind become increasingly desperate. Having separated from his wife, Dickens, the letters show, was much less a Londoner after 1859, unless needed on business. Contrary to Johnson's biography, epistles of the 1860s reveal a Dickens preoccupied with taking care of himself. Introducing the second batch of letters, Paroissien defends Dickens against charges of inconsistency. A call both for more government action and greater individual involvement, he points out, is not a sign that Dickens' social criticism lacked a theoretical basis.

Paroissien uses prefatory remarks to the third section to challenge the contention that Dickens seldom exhibits interest in his craft or a strong sense of the artist's professional obligations. He did both as a letterwriter. Paroissien proposes the letters as compensation for the shortness of the prefaces to Dickens' novels. The letters express the novelist's confidence in literature's educational role and his unflagging view of himself as a realist. Paroissien's assessment of Dickens' belief in change, whether on the personal or social level, seems overly optimistic. Otherwise, this edition is nearly letter-perfect.

Less practical, Joel J. Brattin envisions a super-edition of Dickens' manuscripts. In "A Map of the Labyrinth: Editing Dickens's Manuscripts" (*Dickens Quarterly*), he hopes this mega-work will record all deletions and interlinear additions, no matter how legible, while preserving Dickens' spelling and punctuation. Granted, not enough has been done to identify the salient features of Dickens' manuscripts. But Brattin's project, expanded to include changes Dickens made to galleys and proofsheets, would make the often-called-for concordance to the novels a minor undertaking by comparison.

Forthcoming though Dickens was as letter-writer, his double urge toward reticence and disclosure hampered him as autobiographer. So claims Jean Ferguson in "Dickens and Autobiography: A Wild Beast and His Keeper" (*English Literary History*). The critic lists several cogent reasons why Dickens could not complete the fragment of self-exposure he began between 1846 and 1848. Dickens feared he could not adequately recapture his childhood anguish. A believer in the past's capacity to influence the present, he found his own past had a disturbing impact on his present sense of security.

At such a juncture, Forster's biography of Goldsmith came as a relief. In Ferguson's opinion, Dickens settled on Forster as a "surrogate" autobiographer. Dickens would not have to do the job himself yet could be sure it got done: a way of both playing the keeper and letting the tell-all beast elude its gag. Not only did Dickens supply Forster with information, he became a virtual collaborator. For nearly a quarter of a century, Ferguson continues, he tutored his friend on the subject of Dickens, grooming him for the task ahead. Dickens' many letters to Forster allegedly should be read in this light. A final point is less persuasive: Dickens' growing belief in irremovable barriers between individuals made him ultimately doubt that even Forster could convey the complexity of being the Inimitable. On one hand, loss of confidence in intersubjectivity would help to account for a decline in intimacy between Dickens and Forster. On the other, it turns the substitute autobiographer into another keeper of secrets.

Wendell Stacy Johnson's concept of a double urge refers to the conflict in writers between the paternal and filial. His title for the first volume of Studies in Romantic and Modern Literature reflects this concern: *Sons and Fathers: The Generation Link in Literature, 1780–1980* (Peter Lang). Johnson refers to the writer's sense of filial need for a link with his predecessors and for self-identification (or fathering of the self) through a break with the general order. Although this sounds like a biographical rendition of individual talent versus the tradition, moderns Johnson covers do not include Eliot. Besides Wordsworth, Coleridge, Byron, Ruskin, Mill, and Arnold, the author concentrates on Yeats, Joyce, and Faulkner. A chapter devoted to "The Orphan: Carlyle and Dickens" rambles from Carlyle's heroic orphans—Teufelsdröckh and Frederick the Great as rejected sons who become self-generating heroes—to Bounderby (Dickens' counterfeit orphan), Oliver and David (victimized orphans), and Pip, whom Johnson calls a visionary orphan.

Carlyle dismays Johnson as a "self-contradictory author." He is both a time-involved creature who denies time's existence and a son of teachers and fathers who is also a self-generating or "reclothed" orphan. Dickens receives better grades for parodying the self-made man and because the victimized or orphaned sons in his fiction must develop gentleness, generosity, and a "generative love." These qualities enable them to become fathers of men and doers of good deeds. For one thing, not all of Dickens' orphans, like Carlyle's, are male. For another, Oliver's prospects for parenthood seem beside the point, while Pip's, although relevant, remain problematic.

"To sum up," writes Johnson:

> if Dickens does not produce Carlylean utterances, neither does he clothe himself in the disguise of the self-sufficient, the orphan and the genius. His characters, including those who *are* orphans, appear as children generated really and spiritually by others.

John Dickens to the contrary, Charles Dickens often saw himself as a virtual orphan. Thanks in large part to the said John Dickens, he also thought sometimes of life itself as a bad parent. Nor was he averse to Carlylean utterances. Rarely after thirty-two pages does one encounter a set of conclusions every point of which cries out for qualification.

III

P. J. Robertson thinks great critics are rarer than great poets. Hence his determination to add F. R. Leavis to the likes of Johnson, Coleridge, and Arnold. In "Criticism and Creativity: Dickens and F. R. Leavis" (*Queen's Quarterly*), the Cambridge don's essay on *Little Dorrit* is said to be typical of the greatest criticism: it achieves "a moving power akin to poetic words." In Robertson's opinion, Leavis rectified the "pardonable error" of omitting Dickens from the great tradition in 1948 by devoting his 1964 Oxford lecture to Dickens' twelfth novel and "greatest book." That Leavis's belated tribute was preempted several times during that sixteen-year period of silent reconsideration, by Trilling among others, goes unnoticed. The new line-up, consisting of Shakespeare, Blake, Dickens, and Lawrence, is what matters to Robertson. This revised genealogy of English genius confirms Leavis's thesis that novelists are the Bard's successors.

With *Little Dorrit*, Leavis maintained, the novel reaches its fullest development as a "dramatic poem." In 1855, having been eighteen years a novelist,
Dickens finally stamped himself an heir to Blake as well as Shakespeare,
although it would take nearly a century until, thanks to Leavis, this arrival
was recognized. Today, Leavis seems a dogmatic critic, obsessed with rank-
ings and idiosyncratic lineages. But Robertson's partisan essay, a mixture of
paean and plea, seeks to reinstate him as the representative for "inherently
responsible" criticism. Through production of such criticism, the critic par-
ticipates in the transmission of human creativity. These are noble-sounding
aims, even if incomprehensible to adherents of reflexiveness.

One cannot argue with Robertson's Leavisite conclusion that the creative
strength of the English language has recently been going into literary criticism.
But the addition of Derrida and Bakhtin to Johnson, Coleridge, and Arnold
seems a chilling prospect. Leavis insisted on the novel's relevance to the
"heartless technological civilization" Robertson says "has evolved from
Dickens' England." Indeed, three-fourths of Leavis's revamped great tradition is expressly skeptical about the industrial-scientific-technological trium-
virate, with Shakespeare, who had a weakness for the pastoral, implicitly so.
From one point of view, Leavis remains a narrow, overly opinionated critic.
His criticism was creative in that it promoted aspects of authors vital to his
own views. From another, his criticism can be said to draw its power and
continuing relevance from convictions rooted in the truths put forth by the
great literature it dealt with. Aligning Dickens and Lawrence with Blake and
Shakespeare was not just how Leavis wrote about his world. It was also his
method of demonstrating what he considered the perennial function of criticism.

Rare birds or not, the great Dickens critics were much in evidence during
1985. Volume eleven of the *Chesterton Review* was given over entirely to
Dickens' importance for Chesterton and vice versa. Peter Rae Hunt's "Introduction" stresses the "profound effect" of this life-long connection on
Chesterton's career. In Chesterton's own "Charles Dickens: An Early Essay"
(1903), which begins the November issue, the critic equates realism and
romance as authorial devices. The actual world does not resemble a Dickens
novel any more than it is like one by Flaubert. Chesterton also underscores
the significance of Dickens' "optimism," which he finds neither false nor
feeble, and defends caricature as "subtle truth."

Hunt's "The Background of G. K. Chesterton's *Charles Dickens* (1906)" defines this important work as an attempt to rescue Dickens, not just revive him. As Dickens' reputation improved in Edwardian England, several members of the literary community, especially Gissing, praised Dickens for reasons Chesterton considered un-Dickensian. To counteract the spread of pessimism, the so-called *fin-de-siecle* gloom, Chesterton, says Hunt, spoke up for "exuberance" as the "true Dickens spirit," whether expended in attacks upon industrialism or celebrating the humor of the poor. Revival of interest in Dickens smoothed the way for Chesterton's book, yet he strove to redirect the phenomenon that helped to make his own project feasible.

The common denominator in "Chesterton's Dickens Criticism," Leo J. Hetzler contends, is a conviction that Dickens had a contribution to make to the Edwardian age and every subsequent generation. An effective reformer of injustices who was able to portray "the full essence" of the common man's nature, Chesterton's Dickens stood for England's centuries-old anti-Puritan tradition. Unlike decadents and some moderns, on whom Chesterton used Dickens as a scourge, the great Victorian novelist was not afraid to connect the soul with bodily sensations as diverse as the fear of death and the enjoyment of sunlight.

In "Chesterton on Dickens: A Closer Look," Lawrence J. Clipper settles scores with modern criticism: it has either slighted Chesterton or misunderstood him. Edmund Wilson endorsed Chesterton's prophecy that Dickens would be recognized as "incomparably the greatest writer of the time" but split Dickensians into Wilsonites and Chestertonians. In "The Two Scrooges," Wilson gave the twentieth century a "dark" or serious Dickens who could have status in academe. George Ford allegedly followed suit in *Dickens and His Readers:* like Wilson, he ignored Chesterton's awareness both of Dickens' often "mirthless" social vision and the moral and mental wounds suffered at Warren's. The unkindest cut, in Clipper's view, came from the New Criticism. It fostered the impression that Chesterton was hampered by a lack of technical jargon.

Merja Makinen examines the twenty-two-year connection between "G. K. Chesterton and the Dickens Fellowship." That span included the presidency in 1921–22, during which 48 Doughty Street was acquired. It also featured the role of presiding judge at "The Edwin Drood Trial" (1914) and countless engagements as a speaker at Fellowship functions. Oddly, no record of when Chesterton joined has been found, but he made his final appearance at a dinner marking the Fellowship's twenty-fifth anniversary.

Writing about "G. K. Chesterton on Dickens and the French," Sylvère Monod decides that Chesterton's Dickens loved France generously but not uncritically. Chesterton presents a Dickens who comprehended France and its revolution more shrewdly than his contemporaries, Carlyle included. But Monod is dubious about Chesterton's elevation of Dickens on this point; it Chestertonises Dickens, as Monod feels did many of Chesterton's other judgments.

Nearly fourteen when Dickens died, Shaw nevertheless had no personal recollections of him. But he knew of the original ending of *Great Expectations* before most readers and campaigned in 1936 for its restoration. Kate Perugini called him "Shernard Bore,"yet in 1896 he dissuaded her from tossing into the fire 137 letters Dickens wrote Catherine between 1835 and 1867. He was foreman of the jury at the Drood trial Chesterton conducted. Well before Leavis, he praised *Hard Times* and *Little Dorrit* as the stupendous accomplishments of a conscience-stricken novelist whose eyes had been opened to England's deplorable state. In *Shaw on Dickens* (Frederick Ungar), edited by Dan H. Laurence and Martin Quinn, one finds a "hero-worship" for Dickens as strong as Chesterton's and just as biased.

Shaw on Dickens contains letters to, among others, Chesterton, Kate Perugini, and Gladys Storey. It reprints the 1913 "Introduction" to *Hard Times* and Shaw's "Foreword" to *Great Expectations*. The centerpiece is a hitherto unpublished, 6000-word fragment of an 1889 essay "From Dickens to Ibsen," all twenty-two pages of which focus on Dickens. Unfortunately, it is difficult to tell where this essay was headed, which may explain Shaw's failure to complete it. Several of Shaw's unsigned or pseudonymously signed reviews of Dickens material might well have been omitted. In its place, Laurence and Quinn should have elaborated on Shaw's frequent boasts that he had pillaged Dickens for scenes and characters to stock his own plays. More so than the Dickens-Ibsen fragment, these borrowings connect Shaw's high regard for the novelist with his other love, the stage; they reveal how Dickensian a playwright Shaw was.

As a critic, Shaw had enormous blind spots. One of them encompassed everything Dickens wrote prior to 1854. Nell he dismissed as "a sort of literary onion to make you cry." Agnes is downgraded to "the most seventh rate heroine ever produced by a first rate artist." Shaw discounted all aspects of Dickens that were not Shavian, that is, useful propaganda for a socialist and Fabian. Only with *Hard Times* did Dickens, having had an unspecified epiphany, begin to see through the middle class. He condemned "the whole industrial order of the modern world'' and became a great writer by attacking the rotten base of a capitalist system based on exploitation.

Far-sighted and modern in some respects, Shaw's pseudo-Marxist Dickens is also heavily didactic and unsmiling. The burdensome legacy of Shaw's reconstructed Dickens is not just a novelist whose ignorance extends only to the world of labor; one is left with a Dickens who failed to formulate the productive, revolutionary philosophy Shaw expected from him. Lamentably, Shaw decides that Dickens had no philosophy at all. Minimizers of the novelist's intellectual prowess, such as A. O. J. Cockshut, have underrated him for decades as a result. Shaw called *Little Dorrit* ''the most complete picture of English society in the XIX century in existence'' but implied that it might as well have been taken by a camera: ''no equally gifted man was ever less of an artist and philosopher'' than Dickens. Such a pronouncement is much narrower than Aldous Huxley's disdain for congenital storytellers whose characters are not expressions of different attitudes toward life. It is in even worse taste than Shaw's use of ''Dickensites'' for Dickensians.

Edwin M. Eigner and George J. Worth disagree with the view that no widely held nineteenth-century theory of fiction existed. In their ''Introduction'' to *Victorian Criticism of the Novel* (Cambridge University Press), they argue for the coalescence of a ''majority rationale.'' Many highly intelligent, ''non-theoretical'' reviewers and essayists allegedly contributed to an aesthetic of realism that can be found by reading ''between the lines'' of what they wrote. Were this so, Victorian critics would be less partisan than Chesterton and Shaw. They would also be more single-minded collectively than either of these critics was alone. But attempts by Eigner and Worth to isolate and define the major realisms—romance-realism, didactic, objective, etc.—undermine their insistence that a key to all realisms exists. The truest common denominator not a will-of-the-wisp seems to be the hostility exponents of each brand usually felt for its opponents.

Victorian Criticism of the Novel is nonetheless an extremely handy text. It anthologizes essays by such well-known Victorian pundits as Masson, Lewes, Bulwer, and Fitzjames Stephen. Lesser lights also get opportunities to shine (George Moir, William Caldwell Roscoe, Archibald Alison, and Vernon Lee, the only woman critic in the volume besides George Eliot). As one can easily see, the selections are weighted in favor of the Lewes-George Eliot axis and against the Dickens-Collins camp. Most Victorian criticism of the novel, one could argue, was done by Victorian novelists themselves, not "between the lines" of essays and reviews but through competitions between their novels. Unbeknownst to the critics Eigner and Worth anthologize, many Victorian novels were conceived and published to correct the realism in works already exant. Such novels were thus simultaneously stories and tracts on realism.

Inclusion of Henry James, Robert Louis Stevenson, and Joseph Conrad disturbs the edition's focus. The realism disputes of the 1850s and '60s had to do with the novelists' conflicting assessments not just of society and human nature but of the capacity of each to alter for the better. Selections from the 1880s and '90s are part of another story in which aesthetic differences predominate *per se*. These differences were not so issue-oriented; they were not as often chiefly vehicles for philosophical disagreements about the merits of ethical and sociological developments, such as secularization, progress through reform, evolution, and industrialization.

Initially, bi-partisan seems appropriate as the adjective for Steven Connors' four-fold approach to *Charles Dickens* (Basil Blackwell). An ambitious would-be connector, Connors wants to uncover "a certain conceptual continuity" between different theoretical approaches. So he offers a structuralist interpretation of *Pickwick Papers* and *Dombey and Son,* a deconstructionist reading of *Bleak House,* and a Marxist critique of *Our Mutual Friend* and *Great Expectations,* a critique that contains psychological additives. He succeeds mainly in strengthening one's conviction that the new kind of theoretical critic, like the Marxist and Freudian before him, is a creature of predilections: he selects the kind of reading he intends to do arbitrarily, then chooses a text to inflict it upon.

Connors is cleverer than most of his ilk. He is indebted to Ferdinand de Saussure more than to Derrida. But this book does the new theoreticians no service by revealing them for what perhaps they are: players whose "conceptual continuity" is their decision to think of literary criticism as a game best played dispassionately, that is, without the convictions Leavis considered the hallmark of the responsible arbiter. Like Marxists and Freudians, the new theoretician is a Procrustes. Unlike the Leavisite, his predilections have no moral hold over him, for they come neither from within nor from within the text.

Literature was once used by irreverent moderns to sabotage outmoded values. It is possible to see the newest criticism as the next step, an attempt to subvert the idea that the writing of literature is a process whereby meaning or value is consciously generated. What Connors adds is a sort of intellectual cold-bloodedness. *Pickwick Papers* ceases to be amusing in his reading of it because the critic would rather look for binary oppositions, such as alternations between passivity and activity, Mr. Pickwick as passive victim and as free agent. *Bleak House* ceases to be scathing while the critic "disobediently" wonders if the domicile referred to in the title is metonymic or metaphoric, a replacement of the whole with its parts or a part signifying all. Binary tension is between contraction in the former and expansion in the latter. Such tensions, one complains, are too abstract for anyone to feel passionately about.

Actually, *Pickwick Papers* does not endlessly catalogue shifts from stasis to motion (and vice versa). It is about Pickwick's transition from a state of constant activity, in which he incorrectly believes himself free and in control, to one of forced confinement. In the Fleet, he is compelled to revise his world-view and act upon it. Moreover, the nature of his actions—liberation of Mrs. Bardell, a kindness to Jingle in return for unkindnesses—breaks the pattern of repetition in the novel with a series of reversals: getting out instead of getting even, reliance on sincerity rather than humbug, and the victimized Pickwick aiding the victimizers instead of being gulled again.

Readers unalert enough to finish *Bleak House* without a reliable sense of the relationship of part to whole should be made to read Connors' chapter twice, although, perhaps appropriately, it will not help them. Is the bleak domicile of the title Jarndyce's residence or England, or is it, one might add to the binarist's consternation, a third and fourth thing: the house given to Esther and Woodcourt and the human condition? Surely, it is each and all. Connors wonders whether chaos in Dickens' novel is represented as fog or does fog stand for the general chaos—another toss up between expansion and contraction. Surely, the relationship of fog to chaos, chaos to fog, is richly reciprocal, metaphoric and metonymic simultaneously. If deconstructionists are reluctant to break their eggs at the convenient end, no one else need be. For Connors and Derrida, unwilling to have things more than one way, the real fogginess seems to be generated by their critical strategy: they decide that Dickens' use of fog "carries a metonymic thrust which the novel does not succeed in deflecting into metaphor."

Chesterton's Dickens is a Catholic comedian, Shaw's a Fabian socialist, Leavis's a Blakean poet. Dickens was simultaneously a bit of all three and much more besides. One must be wary of metonymic critics who misjudge a part for the whole. But theoreticians who disassemble the whole on grounds that its parts do not mesh are even less trustworthy. They do not seem even to have seized upon part of the truth. Connors thinks traditional criticism operates by assumptions or imposition too, the idea of novels as windows on the Victorian world, for example, or of plot and characters having correlation with real life. If the structuralist is no better or worse than previous partisans, one wonders what the new theorizing accomplishes. One might also emphasize that traditional criticism and Victorian novelists operate from shared assumptions one cannot disregard by coining the notion of disobedience. One could also compare the value and uses of different assumptions, something deconstructionists would say is pointless or impossible, although, in choosing theirs, they have already done so.

Connors is refreshingly candid. He declares that texts have no meaning for the new theoreticians. "Systems of meaning," he writes, "are . . . not necessarily inside a text; instead, they provide a field of meaning and intention within which a particular text may derive meaning." If meaning is outside texts, what, besides raw material for the theoretician, is inside them? Connors makes the derivation of meaning a mystical process or like conducting a seance. The socialist in Shaw enlarged upon Marxist tendencies in *Hard Times* and *Little Dorrit,* but they were tendencies that caused both novels to pulsate with significance for him. Similarly, Kafka fastens onto *Bleak House* and *Little Dorrit* to write *The Trial.* Qualities both admirers of Dickens magnify appear to be present in the texts, vulnerable to exaggeration and extrapolation but not summoned from some external field. Imposition there must always be but not willful disobedience, no forcing of the text entirely against its will. That could be construed not as parody and subversion of the New Criticism but as a kind of dispassionate rape, and thus much nastier than trying to Chestertonise Dickens into the jolliest of good fellows.

One is left with the prejudices of Leavis, Chesterton, and Shaw, Victorian reviewers who did their best work "between the lines," and new theoretical approaches that do not pretend to unlock meanings within the text. Some of the most apposite commentaries on Victorian novels and their claims to be realistic, therefore, have to be found elsewhere. A good place to start is with the rivalries between the novels of the novelists themselves, *Felix Holt* as a rethinking of *Bleak House,* for example, or *North and South* as a revision of *Hard Times.* George Eliot and Mrs. Gaskell did not read Dickens disobediently in order to make him contradict himself. They wanted to contradict him, to discredit his fictions by setting up a counterpoint between his renditions of reality and their own. Reworking Dickens into their own image was not like dispassionate rape but a spirited reforming of his allegedly errant views.

Although self-serving, it was not like Chestertonising Dickens either because it did not commence from admiration.

To enhance the twentieth-century American's appreciation of vital texts, Julia Prewitt Brown offers *A Reader's Guide to the Nineteenth-Century English Novel* (Macmillan). Unlike Frederick R. Karl's similarly titled work, this guide contains no explications ready-made for the reader's adoption. Brown's idea of providing a "field of meaning" is to organize under appropriate headings "basic facts" one should keep in mind when reading Victorian fiction. She supplies information about such things as the Victorian class system, the pound's value then in dollars today, the structure of Church and Parliament in Dickens' lifetime, and the nature of a nineteenth-century middle-class education.

For Brown, Victorian fiction is "distinguished by its dense and detailed accuracy," its strivings to establish a "relation to real life." *A Reader's Guide* is the perfect restorative after Connor's four-pronged approach. It opposes a sense of context to the new theoretician's free-floating "systems of meaning." Brown seeks to countermand current ahistorical trends: she reaffirms "the importance of historical information to aesthetic readings of the novel."

"Compactness" is not only the right word for Brown's book, which has the slimness of a Victorian serial's monthly number. It is also the dominant impression she wants to give of Victorian England. Smaller and less diffuse than America, its former colony, this world-ruler's institutions and aristocracy wielded immense power. Those with authority, Brown points out, were few enough to know each other personally; noblemen, churchmen, and politicians maintained a comfortable, fluid relationship few monopolies can match. During Victoria's reign, there were only 24 dukes, 19 marquises, 111 earls, 19 viscounts, and 192 barons—a nobility the size of modern America's typical high-school graduating class.

Boundaries to the nineteenth century, as set by Brown's guide, extend from 1815 to the Second Reform Bill, the heyday of liberal, evangelical, industrial society. It saw rapid transformations from agriculture to industry, country to city, parish to central government. The flaw in the "compactness" approach to Victorian England is that one overlooks the prevalence of transition and the preoccupation, intellectually and practically, with the relationship of change to progress. Brown argues that the network of power-brokers, which included the legal system, universities, and professions, withstood the onslaught of social and economic changes for at least two generations. Consequently, her view of Victorian England is one of unity transcending diversity when it could as easily be seen the other way round. Had Brown included chapters on Science, Secularization, and Industrialization, a stronger sense of change or diversity straining against a vestigal unity would have been the result. Dickens' lifespan coincides with Brown's concept of a Victorian heyday. His novels present a time of collision between irresistible forces, not all of them alterations for the better, and immovable objects resistant to change.

Even veteran rereaders of Victorian novels can profit from Brown's painless refresher. She answers such questions as which ranks higher, a marquis or a viscount, a rector or curate. She knows which guest the social climber would find a more desirable catch for a party, the wife of a baronet or the daughter of a duke. Brown writes excellently on the rise in status and number of the professions and on topics as varied as marriage, reform, courts and prisons, censorship, and Evangelicalism.

But conversion figures she gives for the British pound, fascinating though they are, can be misleading. Perhaps the Archbishop of Canterbury's salary of £27,000 *per annum* is equivalent to five million dollars in 1985. Brown is also probably right to point out that Becky Sharp's willingness to be a "good woman" on £5,000 a year (about one million dollars) is no indication of potential virtue thwarted by circumstances. But the realization that a four-volume novel by Scott at half a guinea a volume means $500 the set in modern money or that a shilling number of a Dickens novel would cost $10 today chiefly shows how expensive inflation has made modern life. It is not an infallible sign that Victorians were willing to pay exorbitantly for great literature.

Several additional problems arise. Too many illustrations of Brown's points come from Austen, the novelist she seems to know best. Some of the imaginative parallels between Victorian and modern contain so many variables they verge on the ahistorical. A case in point is the observation that women's rights prospered in England in the 1850s by riding the wave of larger legislative reforms just as women's liberation profited in the 1960s when swept along by America's civil rights movement. Although *A Reader's Guide* is barely 137 pages long, space constraints seem to have stunted only the last two chapters. With three pages each for serial publication and Victorian realism, Brown cannot get the job done. She compares serialization to "the most demanding sonnet form." A less diminutive analogue, possibly the expansiveness of the extended musical forms used by Bach or Beethoven, would have been more fitting. Brown tries to distinguish between reality and truth when every major Victorian novelist based his claim to be telling the latter on his (or her) superior knowledge of the former.

IV

In "Vision into Language: The Style of Dickens's Characterization" (*Dickens Quarterly*), Brian Rosenberg stops just short of a deconstructionist position. Dickens' plentiful descriptions of his characters' gestures and physical appearance, he argues, do not generate hyperclarity. Instead, they are intended to show that an abundance of detailed observations is unable to pin down a fundamentally uncertain external reality. Often, Rosenberg continues, the details Dickens uses for a given characterization at one point in a novel contradict, qualify, or undermine those employed for the same purpose earlier. The more specifics Dickens volunteers, the more he emphasizes the tentativeness of physical appearance, the risk in all interpretation, and the ambiguity and elusiveness of the physical world. Rosenberg's viewpoint differs from a deconstructionist's in that Dickens is left in control of a process working against itself.

Granted, the Dickensian authorial voice is sometimes equivocal, often highly speculative, and self-consciously subjective. But these are narrative strategies similar in intent to Esther's, only far more supple and sophisticated: they are designed to involve, appease, and ingratiate. The hypothesis that the Victorian era's foremost novelist utilized his unprecedented descriptive powers to stress the limited value of appearances makes Dickens Sisyphean. It also implies that the Victorian novel's pursuit of a "dense and detailed accuracy" was largely quixotic, if not hypocritical.

Contrary to Rosenberg, Baruch Hochman explores analogies between the way one apprehends characters in a literary context and in real life. In neither case does their elusive inner complexity inevitably undercut one's initial understanding of external appearances. Hochman states that he wrote *Character in Literature* (Cornell University Press) to oppose recent critical schools that disown the human element in literature by pretending characters have nothing to do with people. This spin-off from Hochman's *The Test of Character: From the Victorian Novel to the Modern* stands up for Mr. Micawber.

His "static schemation," Hochman insists, is "no simpler in its psychologic and is potentially no less dynamic than the schematism of dynamic characters." A florid, rotund Micawber only seems simpler, but his personality is "just more evident and more simultaneous in its presentation." Hochman impugns "simplicity of structure"—E. M. Forster's timeworn distinction between *flat* and *round*. Micawber is complex and fully realized but he becomes intelligible through an "instantaneity of perception" few novelists can excite in their readers.

Dickens fashioned Micawber as a case of arrested development, Hochman continues, so the "Absence of process" in his ongoing experience and behavior is appropriate. By contrast, David grows into a constructive social role. Micawber changes uncharacteristically when he helps to overthrow Heep and restore Mr. Wickfield. Only then does he seem "incoherent" and "opaque." Hochman concludes with a positive reformulation of the phenomenology of several Dickens novels. One must rely on "flanking figures" such as Micawber, Steerforth, and Heep to understand processes going on in less stylized, less vividly rendered characters at the novel's center, such as David. The figures flanking the protagonist externalize or objectify lessons the hero must learn.

Barbara Hardy's concerns are also related to Rosenberg's yet seem even subtler than Hochman's. She wants to know how the great Victorian novelists represented feelings, how they delineated the great primitive emotions. Throughout *Forms of Feeling in Victorian Fiction* (Ohio University Press), she points to the novelists' willingness not just to analyze feelings but to manipulate those of their readers. In both instances, they moved beyond the limits of realistic representation. Consequently, stellar fictionists of "the so-called period of realism"—Dickens, Thackeray, Charlotte Brontë, George Eliot, Hardy, and James—were never simply mimetic. Hardy's two-part essay on Dickens is both sensitive and insightful. It atones for a flimsy introductory discussion of the kinds of emotional deepening Victorian novelists resorted to.

In a section on "The Passions: Surfaces and Depths," Hardy aims to improve Dickens' standing as a novelist of feelings. Even when most obsessed with surfaces—superficial rants, ravings, groans, and sighs—he also plumbs depths. Dickens' reliance on "conventional theatricalities," Hardy cautions, should not obscure his skill at "interiorizing the emotions and passions." Simple language and gesture serve Dickens well enough for expressible feelings but he devises more complex forms of representation for inner currents.

What emotions was Dickens particularly good at? Garis gave him credit for the passion of anger. Hardy broadens the spectrum to include guilt, fear, and also guilty fear since Dickens was adroit at mixing passions. From Sikes's murder of Nancy to his involvement in the fire, for example, Dickens keeps readers in touch with the common human feelings of loneliness, alienation, repression, energy, and fear, so that his villain never becomes simply a brute. Dickens earns Hardy's praise for showing Ralph Nickleby's reawakened sexual and moral jealousy, once felt for a brother, now transferred to that brother's son. Dombey's famous train journey is not only a metaphor for the passions he feels; Dickens allegedly also shows how Dombey's stricken imagination makes it so.

Throughout Dickens' early novels, Hardy argues, he was content gradually to connect internal passion with external expressions of it. Later, he became more interested in strong feelings for which no suitable outlets existed. His handling of jealousy, pride, revulsion, fear, gluttony, and sloth—all improved. As the cheerfulness of the early novels waned, Dickens' treatment of love matured. The later Dickens, Hardy concludes, "created characters who forced him to meditate more finely and more analytically on the emotional life." True enough, except that the process had to be reciprocal: deeper meditation leading to more complex characters.

In "A Question of Sentimentality," Hardy admits that a "morbid pathos" marred Dickens' investigations of the affective life. But she balances this concession with a study of his death scenes to trace a "movement away from sentimentality." Hardy considers Nell's demise worse than Smike's, which it is not. With the deaths of Paul Dombey and Jo, however, Dickens supposedly developed an *ars moriendi:* he learned how to flirt with sentimentality without lapsing into it. In Jo's last moments, Hardy decides, "Dickens at last finds a perfect voice for death." Given the foliation of death scenes still to come after 1852, this judgment seems premature. It also burdens Dickens with an artistic smugness or self-satisfaction too great even for an inimitable novelist. Finally, it is the incensed third-person co-narrator who presides over Jo's last breaths, not the Dickens who waxed sentimental over Nell and the little scholar.

V

Lois E. Chaney wrote "The Fives Court" (*The Dickensian*) to identify an allusion in Chapter One of *Nicholas Nickleby*. Dickens is referring to a building in Little St. Martin Street. Designed for raquets, it became better known for benefit boxing exhibitions. Dickens' association with "The Gads Hill 'Higham' Cricket Club," Dick Hoefnagel points out (*The Dickensian*), was more substantial. He stated an eagerness to chair meetings and supervise business affairs. The letter containing these proposals, however, could not have been written to his son, Henry, from Baltimore on 11 February 1866, the date Hoefnagel supplies. Dickens' relationship in 1864 with the committee preparing to mark the three-hundredth anniversary of Shakespeare's birth was both briefer and less cordial. As Richard Foulkes notes in "Dickens and the Shakespeare Tercentenary" (*The Dickensian*), the novelist declined to contribute to a statue of the playwright. The Bard's "best monument," Dickens informed the Working Men's Shakespeare Committee, "is his works."

With two notable exceptions reviewed at the end of this segment, recent contributions to the Dickens-and-other-people department are nearly as ephemeral as his dealings with cricket clubs and commemorative committees. In "Alice Lemon's Childhood Recollections of Charles Dickens" (*Dickens Quarterly*), Leona M. Fisher relates that Dickens was seldom "unapproachable." He delighted in playing children's games with his and Mark Lemon's children. Both men were philoprogenitive. Fisher's authority for Alice's fond recollections of Dickens is a memoir in the possession of her grandchildren.

Dennis Walder, an authority on Dickens and religion, directs attention to the novelist's previously unnoticed correspondence with a minister of the Scottish United Presbyterian Church. Letters between "Dickens and the Reverend David Macrae" (*The Dickensian*) reveal the former's search for a way of expressing the Christian fundamentals without becoming embroiled in sectarian battling. Anne Lohrli adds a brief footnote to her work on Dickens' periodicals: in "Wife to Mr Wills" (*The Dickensian*), she argues that Janet Chambers Wills, Dickens' coeval, deserves greater recognition as a "much-appreciated" member of the novelist's circle.

A two-part essay, "Miss Havisham and Mr. Mopes the Hermit: Dickens and the Mentally Ill" (*Dickens Quarterly*), is a model exercise in detecting reverberations from the novelist's life in his art. Susan Shatto describes Dickens' encounter with James Lucas and identifies the Hermit of Hertfordshire as the inspiration for "Tom Tiddler's Ground." Aspects of Lucas's mode of life at Elmwood House may also underlie Dickens' portrayal of the disappointed bride of Satis House. Shatto hypothesizes that Dickens had an "algolagnic" curiosity about human affliction. He took pleasure from the sight of suffering in others, provided they were not children (projections of himself). Dickens' "spiteful portrait" of Lucas in "Tom Tiddler's Ground," Shatto suggests, avenges Miss Havisham's mistreatment of Pip. But it also casts "unflattering light" on Dickens' claim to be an advocate of benevolent treatment for the insane.

Katherine M. Longley bases her title to "The Real Ellen Ternan" (*The Dickensian*) on Helen Florence Wickham's recollections of her "Aunt Nelly." Wickham's mother, Rosalind, met Ellen shortly after Dickens' death and lived with her until 1876, when the marriage to the Rev. George Wharton Robinson took place. According to Wickham, Ellen may have been injured in the Staplehurst accident. Also, she was clearly a friend of the Dickens family, for her notebook contained Henry's family address as well as Mamie's and Georgina's. As Mrs. Wharton Robinson, Ellen gave readings from Dickens for charity, either using Dickens' own dramatizations or shaping her own from his novels.

Were this all, the real Ellen would resemble Wagenknecht's, not Ada Nisbet's. But around the turn of the century, Ellen's attitude toward Dickens underwent "a total change." She did her last reading in February of 1897, two months before Canon Bentham's note to Thomas Wright. Did Ellen suddenly tell Robinson all? Was there a falling-out with the Dickens family? Or was the truth in danger of coming out because the Vicar of Margate was the first of those made privy to the real story to spoil the semblance of propriety that had been cast over it by common consent? Regrettably, Wickham does not know why Ellen suddenly behaved as if she wanted to forget all about Dickens. Despite some splendid photographs for illustrations, therefore, Longley's essay fails to render a definitive picture of the Ternan affair.

Connections between Dickens and other writers continue to fascinate the modern Dickensian. In 1985, the circumference of this interaction widened to encircle English, American, and European authors from both the nineteenth and twentieth centuries. Still, Irene E. Woods is only moderately persuasive when linking "Charles Dickens, Hans Christian Anderson, and 'The Shadow'" (*Dickens Quarterly*). The Danish storyteller's tale is too slight to have had much bearing upon Dickens' experiments with doubles. Scarcely more momentous is Robert F. Fleissner's query: "Is Gregor Samsa a Bed Bug? Kafka and Dickens Revisited" (*Studies in Short Fiction*). Although Kafka's commercial traveller remains "entomologically unfathomable," Fleissner traces his genealogy to Tony Jobling ("Weevle") and Grandfather Smallweed ("a grub"), just two of Dickens' many uses of "bug-like terms" for unsatisfactory human beings. As a forerunner of modern satirical novelists, one might add, Dickens frequently indulged in zoological imagery to modify enthusiasm for the idea that evolution is a sociological phenomenon as well as a scientific fact. It was no guarantee of steady social progress. Kafka wisely left details of Gregor's classification to the reader's imagination, which is not a Dickensian strategy.

More than any other Tolstoy novel, Brian Rosenberg argues, *Resurrection* recalls *Little Dorrit* and the impassioned, complex fictions of Dickens' maturity. In *"Resurrection* and *Little Dorrit:* Tolstoy and Dickens Reconsidered" (*Studies in the Novel*), the critic convincingly reverses current trends that have Tolstoy and Dostoevsky outstripping their Victorian master. Dickens was not a mentor Tolstoy assimilated and surpassed but a profound and lasting influence. Rosenberg examines resemblances between Clennam and Nekhlyudov, analyzes Tolstoy's use of an intrusive ironic voice, and interprets both works as novels about imprisonment by inhumane, unproductive institutions. The lone shortcoming is that Rosenberg seems uncertain whether Tolstoy's hostility to institutions in general takes Dickens' satire a step further by design or is simply a wrong impression the Russian got from tirades against the Circumlocution Office and the Marshalsea.

D. M. Urnov's position regarding "Dickens and Gogol" (*Series on Literature and Language*) is easy to summarize but difficult to evaluate. Writing in Russian, the critic attempts a comparative assessment of language-style. Emphasis falls on each author's innovative qualities, in particular the prominence given to descriptions of mundane habits and objects. Urnov decides that Dickens and Gogol are alike insofar as each opened a nation's prose language to the common and palpable. Such a conclusion seems to make both novelists resemble the Wordsworth of the "Preface" to *Lyrical Ballads* more than one another. It lacks the precision and utility of comparisons, like Rosenberg's, of Dickens and Tolstoy where similarities of theme, technique, and social vision can be used to point out not only affinities but influence.

Elizabeth Sanders Arbuckle's title indicates that she has two points to make in "Dickens and Harriet Martineau: some New Letters and a Note on *Bleak House*" (*The Dickensian*). The "newly seen" letters to Fanny Wedgewood (1850–60) show Martineau damning a "meddling" Dickens who is to be "distrusted on social subjects" generally, not just when writing about factories. More interesting but unrelated to the letters are echoes Arbuckle finds in Dickens of Martineau's *Life in the Sick-Room*. Dickens never took his statistics from the author of *Illustrations of Political Economy* but he trusted her account of her own invalidism when composing Esther Summerson's recovery from smallpox in Chapter Thirty-five of *Bleak House*.

Abundant connections seem to be just waiting to be made between Dickens and Martineau. Like Dickens, she had an unhappy childhood and a family that remained an encumbrance after success came. Declining family fortunes (in her twenties, however), an early fascination with literature, passion for reform, interest in mesmerism, travels in America and books about the experience, indefatigability as a walker—these are just some of the links the popular writer and contributor to *Household Words* had with her quondam editor. But the few instances for comparison and contrast that Gillian Thomas emphasizes in *Harriet Martineau* (Twayne Publishers) are either perfunctory or debatable. *Life in the Sick-Room,* for instance, is extolled for urging readers "to set aside subjectivity and isolation in favor of . . . participation in the social world." This, Thomas claims, is one of the "most persistent themes of nineteenth-century writing." She then cites *A Christmas Carol* and *Middlemarch* as proof, as if the latter pair relate to the former as effects from a cause.

Thomas recounts briefly the clash between Dickens and Martineau in 1855 over the incidence of factory accidents. Siding with the manufacturers, Martineau became part of the extended difference of opinion Dickens was also having with Mrs. Gaskell, whose response to Bounderby was Mr. Thornton. Thomas neglects to link one battle with the other, thereby obscuring how thoroughly Dickens felt himself beset by female political economists, both of whom he had invited to contribute to his journal. Martineau, of course, had severed connections in 1853, citing ideological differences.

More impressed by America than Dickens would be, Martineau took an interest in copyright that, according to Thomas, "ranges well beyond its effects on her own earnings as a writer." Admittedly indirect, the remark is nevertheless defamatory to Dickens. He spoke up at the Boston dinner for all unprotected authors, both English and American. Thomas's analyses of *Society in America* and *Retrospect of Western Travel* appear to use the Dickens of *American Notes* and *Martin Chuzzlewit* implicitly as a whipping boy. Martineau is "systematic rather than impressionistic," not averse to "extensive use of personal anecdotes," and circumspect with her anti-slavery views since her purpose in visiting America was "to learn and not to teach." Furthermore, she was favorably struck by America's vastness, the configuration of the landscape, and the good manners of most Americans.

In *The Peasant and the Prince,* continues Thomas, Martineau failed to solve the same problem Dickens succumbs to in *A Tale of Two Cities:* mob violence swings the reader's sympathy away from the downtrodden and back toward their oppressors. Yet Dickens, whose book has little to fear from Martineau's, clearly wants to show that perpetrators of violence are always losers by it. Rightly or wrongly, Dickens thought Martineau "vain," "wrong-headed," and "a Humbug." Doubtless he would have liked to beat her with the same stick he longed to use on Mrs. Gaskell but would have been taking a big risk in either case.

Once the *Cornhill Magazine* was started, Dickens experienced difficulty obtaining novels for *All the Year Round*. The newer publication paid more for serial rights and guaranteed subsequent publication in volume form. Such problems notwithstanding, John Sutherland discovers that Dickens comes off well as recruiter, businessman, and editor. From "Dickens, Reade and *Hard Cash*" (*The Dickensian*), one learns that Reade contracted for an eight-month serial. If *Hard Cash* ran beyond that, it did so at no extra cost to Dickens. Since the novel lasted forty weeks, the far-sighted Dickens received 115 pages for free, although he was not overjoyed at the bargain. Sutherland finds Dickens resourceful in attracting Reade and hard-headed when negotiating with him. But he proved sympathetic to a fellow novelist's composition problems and refrained from editing his manuscript.

Dickens' dealings with the Royal Literary Fund are a different story. Nigel Cross retells it in the opening chapter of *The Common Writer: Life in Nine-teenth-Century Grub Street* (Cambridge University Press). Dickens' struggle to reorganize the Fund lasted for almost a decade before ending in fiasco. It was a signal failure for the novelist both as a reformer and man of letters. Acutely sensitive to the widespread suffering of authors, Dickens gave his first public speech at the Fund's anniversary dinner in 1837. By 1849, how-ever, he had concluded that managers of the Fund reduced applicants to begging-letter writers. In addition, although grants only averaged £30, it cost £500 to administer £1500.

Attempts to improve management of the Fund were thwarted by a committee unresponsive to Dickens in 1855 and by a general vote against a Dickens resolution condemning mismanagement in 1856 and again in 1857. Two years later, Dickens resorted to bribery, promising administrators of the Fund "a magnificent Library" for the use of authors and the sum of £10,000 "to maintain and enlarge it." The library, Forster's not Dickens', was left to the Victoria and Albert Museum after the ploy failed.

Cross is generous with facts but frugal about motivation. He thinks that Dickens made little headway because few novelists or poets were adminis-trators of the Fund. Had Dickens been "more subtle," he adds, conservatives in the group, displeased with sharp criticism of their organization in *Household Words,* might have been more amenable to change. But the threat of collapsing into poverty, authorial or otherwise, was too keen an issue for an upstart like

Dickens to address evenly. Unlike most other middle- or upper-middle-class writers supporting the Fund, he had experienced impecuniousness personally and was never to get over fears of its recurrence. That explains his zeal to reform the Fund at a time when his colleagues wanted no more than a kind of literary club that dispensed some charity to justify its existence. Dickens' 1859 bribe seems aimed at the clubman's mentality. His disillusionment with the Fund coincides with the appearance of *David Copperfield,* the novel in which he came closest to revealing his youthful brush with indigence.

When other authors commented on the Fund, their self-concern was less commendable than Dickens'. Thackeray objected to the spectacle of eminent writers cavorting at fund-raisers: they were lowering the dignity of the profession. Granted, the press, pointing to constant internal squabbling, re-christened the Fund "the Rupture Society." But behind such remarks as Thackeray's one hears the whine that fund-raising itself is unseemly: it brings impoverished artists to public attention, thereby underlining the precariousness of the profession and damaging its standing as a gentleman's calling, something no lawyer or doctor would let happen to his vocation. Dickens' vision of a professional society of authors and artists, funded by themselves for their mutual benefit, was a working-class concept submitted to a middle-class club. Applying to such a fund for monies was like saying one was out of work (i.e., out of favor); it would be little different than seeking assistance from one's union or accepting charity from the parish.

Disgusted, Dickens broke away to found the Guild of Literature and Art. It was conceived in 1850 but did not award a grant until 1868, one year before its dissolution. In 1869, half of the Guild's assets went, ironically, to the Fund it had been created to replace. The Guild hoped to provide annuity assurance and sickness benefits for its members. It endowed a college for pensioners. Suitable residents were never found, perhaps because, as Cross realizes, the idea of entering a literary almshouse was more demeaning than sending begging letters to the Fund. Dickens satirized collegians of the Marshalsea in *Little Dorrit* but was obtuse to the euphemism himself when trying to disguise a charitable institution as a seat of learning. Cross believes the amateur theatricals staged for the Guild's benefit hurried Dickens toward public readings. But his conclusion that "Few of Dickens's projects can have been more impractical" than his involvements with Fund and Guild is the critical understatement of 1985.

A triangular interconnection as complicated as Dickens-Fund-Guild concerns S. J. Wiseman in "Lewes, Forster and Dickens: A Resumé" (*George Eliot–G. H. Lewes Newsletter*). He finds the self-centered biographer responsible for obscuring the friendship between Lewes and Dickens in the latter's later years. Lewes's notice of *The Life of Charles Dickens* in the *Fortnightly Review*, Wiseman feels, was not an attack upon the novelist but against Forster as a biographer. As Collins did privately, Lewes objected publically to what Wiseman calls "Forster's deliberate respectabilisation" of Dickens. Forster, instead of defending himself, replied to Lewes on behalf of Dickens, whom he accused the reviewer of denigrating. When Wiseman summarizes Lewes's criticisms of Dickens, however, he underestimates the force with which reservations erode the initial bursts of praise.

In "Dickens and Collins: The Rape of the Sentimental Heroine" (*Ariel*), Valerie Purton awards the palm to Collins's "rhetoric of exposition" over Dickens' "rhetoric of intensification." Wendy Lesser's point in "From Dickens to Conrad: A Sentimental Journey" (*English Literary History*) is that Conrad's irony is "an outgrowth of Dickens's complex form of sentimentality." First, Dickens is denied his due, then given too much credit.

Purton prefers *No Name*, an "underrated novel," to *Dombey and Son*. Instead of Florence's passiveness, Collins presents Magdalen Vanstone's "emotional transvestitism." Miss Vanstone not only withdraws from a female role but activates her masculine abilities. She challenges the emotional structure on which Victorian society is founded. Dickens merely enlarges his heroine's plight to attract sympathy for her. But Collins, more intellectual in his use of the sentimental register, employs an active female whose inevitable immolation reveals society's corruptness. One problem with this is the difference between the heroines' predicaments: Florence's enemy is her own father, whereas Magdalen can take arms against an unjust inheritance law that disenfranchises illegitimate children. She might better be compared with Esther Summerson. Also, given Purton's views, Magdalen's subsidence into a conventional female role at novel's end must be read as an ironical submission, a reading the text resists.

One feels that Purton's approach overrates *No Name*. Situated between *Great Expectations* and *Our Mutual Friend*, it studies loss of gentility and the assumption of false identities in an attempt to get one's money back. Thus it looks back to one Dickens novel and forward to another. Collins has mixed feelings about Magdalen's stratagems, none of which ultimately succeeds, and wants the reader to have doubts also. The unfairness of the law Collins targets becomes clearer when it drives his heroine to unlady-like schemes some will disapprove of but for which no one can entirely blame her. His point is that Mr. Vanstone's sins of omission and commission descend upon his daughters, one of whom must misbehave against law and propriety to seek recovery of their rights. Sins descend on the next generation, Collins tells Dickens, in that the children must not only suffer consequences but continue and extend the offence itself. Norah, Magdalen's passive sister, finally marries the money that should have been theirs all along. Too enraptured by the emotional transvestite Collins sees as more victim than heroine, Purton ignores this irony.

To Lesser, Dickens seems deeply progressive and deeply conservative, a writer who combines great faith in human nature with Swiftian insights regarding its deficiencies. His sentimentality was therefore self-critical; he allowed Victorians to remain skeptical while feeling a release. Conrad's "colder and more impersonal" sentimentality, Lesser continues, does not result solely from changes in London between Dickens' time and publication of *The Secret Agent*. It also develops the duality in Dickens' sentimentality "so completely as to become unadulterated irony." Conrad's humanism is admittedly the descendant of Dickens'; it is watered-down, ironically presented, yet curiously functional in places. Lesser's efforts to describe this phenomenon in terms of a "conversion of sentimentality to irony" and hence a sentimental journey do violence to logic and language. She has Conrad extending a duality so thoroughly that half of it disappears, allowing the other half to exist "unadulterated."

Edward Stokes embarks upon a larger but hardly less quixotic journey to weigh *Hawthorne's Influence on Dickens and George Eliot* (University of Queensland Press). Having re-read parts of *Bleak House* and *The Scarlet Letter* back-to-back, Stokes experienced a revelation: he decided the former was all Hawthorne. Once this train of thought got started, *Hard Times, Little Dorrit, A Tale of Two Cities,* and *Our Mutual Friend* quickly became additional stages of Dickens' indebtedness. Were these conclusions less absurd, Hawthorne's impact on Dickens' later fiction would eclipse that of Shakespeare and the Bible. In George Eliot's work, Hawthorne figures just as prominently for Stokes but over the entire career. This means the American novelist had a profounder effect upon the works from *Scenes of Clerical Life* to *Daniel Deronda* than G. H. Lewes, Darwin, or Renan.

Instead of hurdling obstacles, Stokes dodges them. Dickens disliked *The Scarlet Letter,* claiming it "falls off badly" after the opening scene. He thought Chillingworth "very poor." Nevertheless, says Stokes, Hawthorne's sadistic avenger must have "made a powerful impact on Dickens's imagination" because he modeled Tulkinghorn on him—"Both have three syllables" in their names. As does Hawthorne's novel, *Bleak House* contains a major character who has borne an illegitimate child. So Hester becomes Lady Dedlock but is also reincarnated as Esther, while Dickens combines in Lady Dedlock the sufferings of Hester and Dimmesdale. A second difficulty is that Dickens never mentions Hawthorne again. Stokes believes nonetheless that Esther's "likeness" to Phoebe Pyncheon in *The House of the Seven Gables* is "too strong to be coincidental." In addition, Clifford Pyncheon, not Leigh Hunt, is the model for Harold Skimpole.

Mrs. Transome, who plays Hester in *Felix Holt,* proves "how thoroughly George Eliot had assimilated the work of the American romancer." As far as Stokes is concerned, Rufus Lyon was inspired by Arthur Dimmesdale and Felix himself modeled on Hollingsworth from *The Blithedale Romance.* Watching Stokes's thesis unfold, one also sees the originality of Dickens and George Eliot disappear: what the critic calls assimilation begins to sound like plagiarism. Instead of George Eliot rewriting Dickens, both Victorians are merely stealing from the same source. They were apparently so awed by Hawthorne that, acting independently, they resolved to do most of their plundering of him from the same two novels.

To account for larceny on so grand a scale, Stokes does not hesitate to draw far-reaching conclusions about British fiction in the second half of the nineteenth century. Many will find these conclusions far-fetched. Stokes accomplishes the Americanization of the Victorian novel. English novelists from 1850 on "did not commit themselves more fully . . . to realism" because of "the example and influence of Hawthorne." Dickens in particular received from the American "general encouragement in the direction of sombre romance."

Contrary to Stokes, Victorian realists became thoroughly embroiled throughout the 1850s in arguments and competitions to determine who was the best realist and thus the most reliable social analyst. In the decade in which the term "realism" achieved currency as a literary standard and sparked innumerable controversies, Stokes posits a concerted retreat from any commitment to mimesis. World-famous by 1850, Dickens did not need moral support from Hawthorne. In Wilkie Collins he was shortly to find encouragement closer to home, but in the form of a skilled competitor. Throughout the 1860s, rivalry with Collins, not adulation for Hawthorne, pushed Dickens further in directions he had already elected to go during the 1850s.

Unlike Stokes, who turns Dickens and George Eliot into clones of Hawthorne, Susan K. Gillman and Robert L. Patten examine several fascinating parallels between Dickens and Twain. In "Dickens: Doubles: Twain: Twins" (*Nineteenth-Century Fiction*), they argue for three points of convergence: Dickens and Twain both began by employing conventional modes of doubling and pairing; as each novelist developed, he lost confidence in bounded worlds, boundaries in general, and a self distinct from others; finally, in different ways, Dickens and Twain became wary of creativity as an uncontained force inside them and so were left with metaphysical abysses to explore.

Initially, Dickens uses doubles to represent moral polarities or else invents contrasting pairs like Pickwick and Sam Weller to embody different ways of seeing the world. Occasionally, the phenomenon Gillman and Patten call doubling sounds more like counterpoint. This is especially the case for Dickens' second phase. Dissimilarities of feature and station separate Edith Granger from Alice Marwood, for example, but they are linked as variations on a theme by underlying similarities in their moral and psychological situations. In the 1850s and '60s, Dickens' "interiorizing" of doubles leads him to imagine a second, darker self who rises unbidden from within. This brings Dickens full circle to the use of doubles for moral polarities.

Twain began by investigating the implications of "identicality," particularly in twins, but grew increasingly skeptical about separating criminal and inhuman behavior from that which is civilized and humane. After studying wilful impostures that depended on a switch of identities, Twain moved on to impostures forced upon individuals by society. Eventually, by creating a character like Pudd'nhead Wilson, Twain studied the artist himself as an impostor. Just as Wilson appears free but ultimately remains bound by arbitrary cultural categories, the artist has an illusion of omniscience and control but is actually at the mercy of stories that grow of their own accord out of a creative unconscious he only pretends to direct.

Of the two, Gillman and Patten consider Dickens to have been more fortunate. As Boz and then the Inimitable, he took on additional identities without losing confidence in self-knowledge as drastically as the Clemens who became Mark Twain eventually did. Comparing the three decades of Dickens' career with the half century of Twain's results in a complex, fast-paced essay that demands rereading. But Dickens' premature demise, after a shorter run, suggests limitations to the threefold parallelism Gillman and Patten propose. Had Dickens lived to finish *Drood* and then gone on writing into the 1870s, a fourth point, this time of divergence, might have been required. Dickens was still in full control of his art on the day he died; the Twain Gillman and Patten present became less focused, less certain by 1890, of how or what to write. An unfinished novel remains the deepest study of human duality any Victorian novelist atempted. In June of 1870, Dickens' exploration of the metaphysical abyss may just have been entering its most critical phase.

In *Doubles: Studies in Literary History* (Oxford University Press), Karl Miller promises to tell the story of duality from the Romantic period to the present. Oddly, when the moment arrives to evaluate Dickens' contributions to the dynamic metaphor of the second self, Miller writes about Little Nell and Jenny Wren instead. The duality in question turns out to be heaven and earth. Victorian sentimentality, Miller contends, binds the individual to the community by promising him a chance to steal away to a higher realm.

A second, equally diffuse essay jauntily incorporates Dickens into a discussion of the many "Keatses" in nineteenth-century literature. The first "dual Keats" was the poet himself, an orphan who resembled a fainting girl with ringlets and lustrous eyes but had a strong torso and the powerful hands of an older man. Another is the Dickens who saw himself as a magnanimous waif, a great heart in a little body. *Little Dorrit* allegedly contains two Keatses: Amy herself and John Chivery, the latter a parody of the type. Miller then shifts to *Bleak House,* whose parody of Keats is Skimpole and "whose Little Dorrit is Esther Summerson." Casting chronology aside hardly seems to matter in a catchall book as aimless as this one.

VI

Michael K. Goldberg's "Gigantic Philistines: Carlyle, Dickens, and the Visual Arts" is one of three essays edited by Jerry D. James and Rita B. Bottoms as *Lectures on Carlyle and His Era* (University of California Press). It begins with a drumroll of charges. Like Carlyle, Dickens was "essentially" a philistine. He was wanting in systematic thought, lacking in taste and culture, burdened with a coarse mind, and "largely uncritical" of his own art. His tastes in the visual arts remained "unformed, uninformed" and "conservatively timid" throughout his life.

What Goldberg cannot explain away, despite herculean attempts, is the ambiguity of his title. Were Dickens and Carlyle larger philistines than others of the breed or monumental figures regardless of their ignorance of the era's best painters? If the latter, then the modernist position crumbles. To produce great art, one need not always appreciate it; that is, one can dispense with such prerequisites as T. S. Eliot's Harvard education, Joyce's cosmopolitanism, Mrs. Woolf's interest in the post-impressionists, and Huxley's ency-clopedic intellect.

Dickens, Goldberg points out, admired mediocrities like Stanfield and Landseer but was ignorant of Delacroix, Goya, and Degas. He thought Mi-chelangelo a "humbug" and took the detailed literalism of the Pre-Raphael-ites as a personal affront. Having reduced Dickens on art to a plane lower than Bentham on poetry, Goldberg offers three propositions, the first two of which are palliatives. He decides that Dickens and Carlyle thought of the artist primarily as an entertainer (Dickens) or a social prophet (Carlyle). Wide cultural interests, he adds, are not necessary concomitants of creative genius. But he also concludes that the philistinism of Dickens and Carlyle keeps them "remote from the sensibility of modernism."

One must register a host of objections to the sort of essay G. H. Lewes might have written. Dickens knew the popular culture of his day better than his rivals did. He may have done more to improve the popular or general public's taste than Degas did for modern art. The sobriquette "Mr. Popular Sentiment" was meant to ridicule but has its positive side. Dickens was also an expert on illustrations, surely a visual art. Goldberg admits that many of Dickens' scenes seem influenced by Victorian narrative painting and could easily become pictures, for example, the scene in which David beholds the fallen Martha Endell. People who read Proust exclusively, listen only to "filthy Mozart" (Lucky Jim's phrase), but downgrade Dickens as a plebeian taste are not fundamentally superior. They, too, may be culturally deficient. Highbrows—Dickens would have called them humbugs—have as many blind-spots as so-called philistines.

Goldberg understates the crucial distinction between an aesthetic sensibility and an artistic one. Ruskin, Pater, Morris, and even Wilde represent a stage of secularization beyond that of Dickens and Carlyle's era. The idea that the profane must be made sacred through transubstantiation into art or that life itself should become a work of art would not have suited either man. Neither was about to take so aesthetic a view of a world both often saw as an ugly, mismanaged place, a vale of tears. Modernists are hardly uniform in their aestheticism, some using it archly to suggest an unaesthetic turn of events. Mrs. Woolf's *To the Lighthouse* may be in sonata form, but Huxley's *Point Counter Point* stresses the cacophony of "the human fugue," life as art's antithesis. Conrad has Marlow exercise his impressionistic renderings on scenes of ravishment, futility, and death, one civilization preying on another as greedily as Gaffer Hexam rifles the pockets of the drowned.

One need not desist from modernizing Dickens and Carlyle because their tastes in one of the sister arts has been repudiated by time. Critics who talk about Dickens and Kafka or Dickens and Conrad mean that some of them is in him chiefly because much of him can be found in them. The darkening colors Dickens wrote into his later fiction influenced the visual artistry with which scores of writers, not just Conrad and Kafka, perceived their respective corners of the modern world.

Dickens knew at least one good painting intimately. In "Dickens and The Fighting 'Temeraine'" (*The Dickensian*), Martin Postle connects Turner's canvas with *Little Dorrit*. "The Fighting Temeraine" shows a single steam-tug towing the old man o' war. This, says Postle, gave Dickens the idea for Pancks singlehandedly directing Casby's movements. That Dickens owned Stanfield's copy of Turner's painting should not be misconstrued as more support for mediocrity at the expense of genius. Dickens was well-acquainted with Turner's work for, as Postle emphasizes, he dedicated *Little Dorrit* to him.

The case for a knowledgeable Dickens in touch with his culture also improves thanks to Catherine A. Bernard's essay on "Dickens and Victorian Dream Theory," which appeared in *Victorian Science and Victorian Values: Literary Perspectives* (Rutgers), edited by James Paradis and Thomas Postlewait. In Bernard's opinion, Dickens' fiction reveals considerable awareness of the theories of Dugald Stewart, John Abercrombie, L. A. Maury, John Elliotson, Robert MacNish, and several others. More importantly, Dickens had "an apparently intuitive insight into the autobiographical meaning of dreams."

Theorists on the continent were recognizing the dynamic relationship of dreams to the unconscious, thus preparing the way for Freud. The English, by contrast, still thought dreams reflected the dreamer's moral character, were warnings from God, or the result of liver disorders. Bernard thinks Dickens speculated about dreams more freely than many British scientists because his own experience was a better teacher. He knew about a dream's retrospective nature owing to nightmares which put him back at Warren's. After Mary Hogarth's death, Dickens learned that dreams recur. Also, he realized that dreams could not be controlled. On the role of memory in dreams and the formative nature of early experiences, says Bernard, Dickens anticipated Freud.

Surprisingly, the least satisfying portion of Bernard's essay deals with dreams and dreamers in Dickens' novels. She notes the increasingly psychological nature of both but her survey is neither complete nor in-depth. Florence Dombey, Blackpool, and, of course, Esther Summerson have their dreams analyzed, but not, for example, Scrooge. At first he attributes his nighttime visitations to indigestion, although they might more accurately be called chidings from God. Whichever the case, they seem Victorian rather than Freudian. Bernard concludes that Dickens understood more about dreams personally than he allowed his characters to demonstrate. Admittedly plausible, such an escape clause cannot fully remove the discrepancy.

Paul Schlicke has written the year's finest critical study of Dickens. In *Dickens and Popular Entertainment* (Allen & Unwin), he celebrates a popular entertainer whose championing of the people's amusements was the act of a perceptive critic of his culture, one with strong political and philosophical convictions. Dickens' defense of entertainment against attacks from the bigots of gloom was also a matter of self-defense: always a popular artist, he shared the aims of most forms of popular entertainment and felt endangered whenever they were.

English popular culture, Schlicke argues, reached its nadir during the 1830s, just as Dickens began writing about it. The factory system eroded the old rural pastimes. Railways transported citizens of an urban industrialized state to matches and resorts, thus confirming a shift from participatory activities to large-scale spectator entertainments. Industrialists thought a worker's leisure costly and unnecessary. Sabatarians decried it as an occasion for vulgar licence. Dickens saw all of these developments as signs of a great cultural upheaval: a warmer, fraternal world was being replaced by a fanciless, factual system of living in which regimented souls served the state and had their amusements doled out to them in prescribed amounts.

Dickens' "commitment" to the "values of entertainment" was as "pessimistic" as it was nostalgic. Dickens realized that music-halls, professional sporting events, and a highly commercialized mass-entertainment industry, much of which he sometimes enjoyed, were bound to win over the support of the general public whose natural inclination to want to be entertained he held sacred. Nevertheless, Schlicke shows how Dickens' early fiction began in imitation of the popular entertainments of an earlier day. He notes the dated quality of public entertainers in *Nicholas Nickleby, The Old Curiosity Shop,* and *Hard Times.* He links the importance of the child in Dickens' thinking about entertainment to the novelist's life-long predilection for the amusements he first knew as a boy. By doing all this, Schlicke proves that Dickens' "convictions about popular entertainment" were always "a function of his social conscience." Spontaneity, selflessness, and fellow-feeling, freedom, fancy, and release—entertainment was a locus for all of these "moral concerns." Had Schlicke taken the next step, he would have stressed the implicit importance popular entertainment seems to have retained for Dickens as a surrogate form of popular religion. No real replacement for Christianity, it was still both stimulus and opiate as it generated solidarity and brought peace.

Dickens' public readings, a congregating at which audiences were encouraged to vent their feelings, can be seen as both entertainment and psuedo-religious exercise. (One assumes that when Dickens refers to "release" through such performances the sublimation of sexual energies is entirely his own.) Schlicke views Dickens' dramatizations of his fiction solely as the fatal culmination of his dedication to the public's amusement, indeed as a martyrdom to that cause. Less justifiably, his concluding chapters ignore the later novels. Dickens supposedly "transferred" his concern for the fate of entertainment in the modern world to his periodicals. He satisfied a personal need to entertain by reading in public. But the darker novels are packed with amusements that fail or that seem to be expedient versions, often outright perversions, of the genuine article. A short list includes the bringing of Pip to Satis House to play, Wopsle playing Hamlet, a party at Podsnap's or Veneering's or Merdle's, Jasper's opium den, Boffin's masquerade as a miser, someone's (possibly Bazzard's) impersonation of Datchery, and, worst of all, the daily matinee in revolutionary Paris at which Madame Defarge asks The Vengeance to reserve "my usual seat."

In one of the happiest conjunctions of the year, Edward Hewett and William F. Axton team up to connect Dickens and drink. The paperback version of *Convivial Dickens: The Drinks of Dickens and His Times* (Ohio University Press) is a gratifying concoction. A combination of excellent social history and sound literary criticism, this guide to the nineteenth-century world of spirits enumerates the major Victorian potions, explains how they were made, and tells what each stood for in the language of social convention, that is, who drank what and on which occasions. Over fifty illustrations, an appendix on Dickens' cellar in 1870, and the half-dozen recipes at the conclusion of each chapter make this an intoxicating book. Hewett and Axton allude with pride to their "personal research." One's admiration for their professional thoroughness, however, is tinged with envy.

The refrain of *Convivial Dickens* is that Dickens was not gourmand, epicure, or legendary imbiber. He liked the "theatre of conviviality" for which the "prize Turkey" Scrooge sends the Cratchits or the condiments for making punch were "stage properties." In short, Dickens looked upon the preparation and consumption of food and drink as a kind of popular entertainment, one that Schlicke ought to have included in his discussions. According to Hewett and Axton, Dickens spent much of his creative energy trying to preserve the sociability he saw vanishing from the England of his adulthood. Food and drink were symbolic substances for Dickens, part of an utopian nostalgia for the world of his youth; they were also weapons in his campaign against what the co-authors call the "frost of utilitarianism and the iron fetters of urban misery." Like his devotion to popular amusements, his susceptibility to drink formed an integral part of his social philosophy.

As did Schlicke when studying the public readings, Hewett and Axton underestimate the semi-religious aspects of Dickens' fondness for gatherings at table or around the punch bowl. The number of befuddlements wonderfully described in Dickens' earlier fiction suggest his closer contact with the props of conviviality than the authors acknowledge. Such experience is not acquired vicariously. Still, *Convivial Dickens* and *Dickens and Popular Entertainment* mix well together: they reveal a strong connection within Dickens of Georgian holdover and anti-Victorian. His personal bibulosity and the extensive contribution his novels make to potabilia are reliable ways to show him becoming more anti-Victorian in spirit as the century progressed.

This point would be clearer had Hewett and Axton risked compromising their title by admitting more vocally that conviviality, like the fraternity generated by popular amusements, is a dissolving ideal in Dickens. They note, however, that the "energetically liquid" mood of *Pickwick Papers,* with its twenty-three inns, taverns, and hotels, did not last long. Most of the famous eating and drinking scenes in Dickens, they also concede, are pre-Dombey. To illustrate Dickens' changing attitude toward drink in his fiction, the co-authors recall that Dombey consumes iced-champagne, Murdstone is a wine-merchant, and split wine gives a foretaste of bloodshed in *A Tale of Two Cities.* Full of perverse entertainments, the later novels also teem with parodic conviviality.

On the other hand, it was not the Victorian age or the Dickensian but, despite a declining sociability, an age of Liquid. The most fascinating ingredient in this multifaceted book is the attention paid to such seldom-discussed facts of Victorian life as the absence of safe drinking water and the mid-century Englishman's expenditure of more on drink than on rent. Hewett and Axton also furnish a reader's guide to hundreds of once-famous eating and drinking establishments, from fast-service "slap-bangs" and "cigar divans" or dives to the elite gambling clubs. "Lamb's Wool," "Negus," "Bishop," and "Lovage" or "Love-itch" are just a few of the famous Victorian beverages Hewett and Axton bring back to life. They discuss the medicinal quality of alcohol in an age before aspirin and tranquilizers, the decline of punch as the national drink, subterfuges women had to adopt (fainting, for example) to consume alcohol, the advent of distilled spirits (gin and rum), and beer's rise to popularity as the Crown tried to curtail drunkenness.

When alcoholism became a national disgrace, a threat to the continued existence of the urban proletariat, it sparked the Temperance Movement. But Dickens opposed the closing of "wine vaults" and "gin palaces." To his credit, he saw a deeper social disease than "Blue Ruin," namely, poverty and discontent that drove stupor-seekers toward drink. The success of *Convivial Dickens* flows from its awareness that the question of food and drink for Dickens was often fraught with larger political and sociological issues.

On the brighter side, the book is a cordial reminder that the Victorians excelled not just as voracious readers and writers but as voluminous eaters and drinkers. Although Pip's parodic Messiah comes to him on the marshes on Christmas Eve, the darker Dickens of the later novels responded convivially to drink and social occasions to the end of his life. Not even a pair of visits to America or an influx of cocktails that followed him home from this side of the Atlantic could change that. *Convivial Dickens* is as good and as efficacious as any of the American Eye-openers and Antifogmatics that impressed the Inimitable.

A different sort of gaiety preoccupies Eve Kosofsky Sedgwick in the two chapters she assigns Dickens in *Between Men: English Literature and Male Homosocial Desire* (Columbia University Press). Sedgwick's definition of culture—an elaborate transaction between men concerning the possession of women—is scarcely Dickens', George Eliot's, or even Virginia Woolf's. Her conception of "male homosocial desire" or the "male homosocial eros," both of which are surprisingly characterized by intense homophobia, proves equally eye-opening: women, she claims, are the prime target of the love-hate relationships between men and the biggest sufferers from them. To substantiate this point of view, Sedgwick examines "Homophobia, Misogyny and Capital: The Example of *Our Mutual Friend*" and then takes us "Up the Postern Stair: *Edwin Drood* and the Homophobia of Empire."

Sedgwick's inordinate love of big words disables her arguments more than a Freudian-feminist bias does. She cannot simply wonder why Mr. Pickwick and Sam do not have a thing for each other. Instead, she asserts that the "constitutive elements" of the picaresque in *Pickwick Papers*

> include the hypercharged and hyperarticulated paternalism of the bond between male servant and male employer; the apparent affective sunniness and unproblematicality of its (far more open, less psychological) gynephobia; and most importantly, the structuring, "explanatory," and coercive authority, for gender as well as class relations, of an image of the family that is in fact appropriate to none of the affectional or cohabitant groupings in the novel.

Dealing with *Our Mutual Friend*, Sedgwick concedes it is "*the* English novel everyone knows is about anality." Her comments on unearned income and diffused excrement rival Earle Davis's attempt to transform Dickens' pen into "an excretory organ." But Jenny Wren's real name, Fanny Cleaver, is Sedgwick's most important clue, not to Dickensian anality exactly, but to "the homosocial/homophobic/homosexual thematics" of Dickens' last completed novel. If Jenny's real cognomen is both weapon and verb, while her first name suggests their target, then *Our Mutual Friend*, Sedgwick insists, obviously focuses on homosexual rape. Only Eugene and Mortimer, "who live together like Bert and Ernie on Sesame Street," are above suspicion. Before throwing this case out of court, however, one should ponder Sedgwick's comments about Headstone's attack on Riderhood and her analysis of the violent assault on John Harmon.

The sexual triangles Sedgwick posits in *Our Mutual Friend*—Bradley Headstone, Charley, and Lizzie, or Bradley, Eugene, and Lizzie—cannot be dismissed as figments of a post-Freudian imagination. One triangle shows Charlie willing to sell his sister to his sponsor in order to get ahead. The other illustrates the impact of class on sexual encounters or, better, encourages Sedgwick to reduce sexual encounters to an aspect of the class struggle, an un-Freudian tack. Sedgwick theorizes that homophobia or erotic rivalry between men is a manifestation of "homosocial" (i.e., homosexual) love. Like the backhanded explication of Jenny's name, the thesis Sedgwick applies to her triangle goes too far because prejudgments take over. It is unlikely that the main erotic bond in the first grouping is Bradley's yen for Charlie or Charlie's for Bradley. Yet this does not sway Sedgwick from her presuppositions. In the second triangle, therefore, neither Bradley nor Eugene wants Lizzie; rather, they express their hostility toward each other, the bad feeling between one class and another, by wooing the same woman. Men, it turns out, have not only invented rivalry between classes but have ruined female sexuality in the process by making women pawns in the struggle. They have done all of this because they love to hate each other or hate to love each other or both.

Headstone's futile attempts at "Sphincter domination" bring the essay back to matters of anality. Muscle control is Bradley's "only mode of grappling for the power that is continually flowing away from him." Although he fails to attain "leverage" with women, his murderous gripping of Riderhood is an apotheosis for his desire to "control" the anus: Bradley "caught him round the body. He seemed to be girdled with an iron ring." Inflicting death by metaphoric constipation, Headstone convinces Sedgwick that the body is "a capitalist emblem" in *Our Mutual Friend* as Marx and Freud become tangled again. Impediments to digestion are a sign of "economic individualism." But if the flow of the Thames represents time passing and dust is money, holding it in seems both futile and profitless. The most illuminating part of this chapter is a digression on differences Sedgwick perceives to have existed between Victorian upper-class and working-class homosexual relationships.

The erotic triangle involving Jasper, Drood, and Rosa strikes Sedgwick as a "recasting" of the tensions between Bradley and Eugene over Lizzie. Jasper does not love Rosa any more than Eugene was enamored of Charlie's sister. The choirmaster uses Rosa as a pawn in a struggle of male wills that is irrelevant and inimical to her. Sedgwick recognizes that Jasper loves Drood yet wants to kill him. But this duality of daylight self and darkness of heart does not look forward to Jekyll and Hyde or to the savagery inside a cultural emissary like Kurtz. Sedgwick gets around the absence of class conflict by having Jasper's plight signify the "division of the male homosocial eros," the breakdown of Victorian homosexuality into lust versus hate. If it is that archetypal, one objects, it would seem to pre-date the situation in *Our Mutual Friend,* not recast it.

Sedgwick is also uncomfortable with Crisparkle's "overfraught" concern for Neville and Tartar. Why, she wonders, does Dickens punish the homosexual panic of Jasper, a "dark" man, but protect the "blond" minor canon? Her suggestion is that Victorians thought of the undermining of their empire by subject people in terms of male rape. A long digression on the blond T. E. Lawrence being gang-raped by dark Arabs allegedly sheds light on events at Cloisterham.

Going "Up the Postern Stair," an allusion to entering by the back way, unintentionally summarizes Sedgwick's capacity to turn Dickens wrongside out. For the willful Freudian, the behaviorist of literary criticism, certain objects and situations come already "overfraught" with symbolic meaning.

If a Marxist twist and a feminine bias are added, results become truly re-markable. When the repressed, anti-social second self inside Jasper warns his nephew that the respectable choirmaster harbors a skeleton in his closet, he is to be imagined saying: "Don't come back to the Cathedral, Ned honey, or I'll have your ass."

VII

Joseph Kestner's *Protest and Reform:The British Social Narrative, 1827–1867* (University of Wisconsin Press) has more in common with Catherine Gal-lagher's *The Industrial Reformation of English Fiction 1832–1867* (University of Chicago Press) than an identical cut-off date. Both books not only revolve around a reshaping of one's conception of the Victorian novel but demote Dickens in the process. The first grants female novelists precedence over Dickens as inventors and developers of the protest novel. The second resolves that *Hard Times* and *North and South* fail for identical reasons.

If Kestner has his way, the syllabus of the future will be reorganized to incorporate nearly a dozen neglected authoresses. There will be less of Dick-ens, Thackeray, and George Eliot, more of Hannah More, Elizabeth Stone, Charlotte Tonna, Camilla Toulmin, Geraldine Jewsbury, Fanny Mayne, Julia Kavanagh, Elizabeth Meteyard, and Dinah Mulock Craik. Kestner argues that the nineteenth-century British social novel was devised and popularized by a succession of female writers. They used their narratives to protest abuses and seek reforms in what has heretofore been misunderstood as a male-dom-inated world of artists, reformers, and Parliamentary committees.

Throughout *Protest and Reform,* Kestner overstates his case. The novelists he discusses deserve to be exhumed. Formerly relegated to the status of footnotes, they merit a few paragraphs each in any responsible survey of activist fiction. But *William Langshawe, the Cotton Lord* and *Jane Rutherford; or the Miners' Strike* cannot rival *North and South* or *Shirley,* much less *Felix Holt* and *Bleak House.* Kestner's dubious yardsticks are *Sybil, Alton Locke,* and *Hard Times,* measured against which his "canon of female authors" seems better than it was. To say that Kingsley merely "summarizes the practices" of the female novelists who preceded him is debatable *per se* and ludicrous if rephrased to demean Dickens' masterworks.

The novelists Kestner seems unduly impressed by, writers of novels "with a purpose," may have smoothed the way for Mrs. Gaskell and George Eliot. Undoubtedly, they helped to elevate the novel as a serious art form by demanding that it confront social realities. To their everlasting credit, they recognized early the "transitional status caused by an industrializing economic system." Since women were often regarded as second-class citizens, these novelists quickly identified with workers as fellow-victims of economic discrimination. But the use of statistical evidence from the government in conjunction with personal feelings made for a curious mixture, in their stories, of didacticism and subjectivity.

Ultimately, such novels, unlike Dickens' or Trollope's, were casualties of their own immediacy, victims not of male-oriented critical neglect but of excessive topicality. Kestner argues that these protest novels declined too rapidly once their purposes ceased to be timely, but he never quite convinces. *Oliver Twist* appeared earlier than some of the texts Kestner resurrects. It was not about the Poor Law any more than *Middlemarch* subsequently deals with the Reform Bill. To a greater extent than either Dickens or George Eliot, Kestner's purposeful authoresses can be reduced to their most pressing concerns. They focused on specific issues that were resolved by time, if not by legislative intervention.

Kestner's approach is too mechanical. He divides his survey by decades—1830s, '40s, and '50s—rather than by issues or individual novelists. This confirms one's impression of authors who were not really novelists of ideas but tied more closely to problems of the given moment than to perennial crises in the human condition. One can talk of a "canon" of female protestors whose efforts, collectively, compare favorably with Dickens'. But no single representative from it matured from book to book as markedly as he did. Dickens figures prominently in all three of Kestner's decades. Within each chapter, Kestner summarizes the issues of the decade and the legislation that addressed them. This is followed by a survey of the pertinent novels in praise of their themes and, occasionally, their artistry. By 1860, most of the problems Kestner's authoresses took up had been settled or no longer seemed paramount. Dickens, by contrast, was just getting his third wind, while George Eliot and Wilkie Collins had yet to produce their masterpieces.

The Victorian critic W. R. Greg declared that novels by women must be "inherently defective" because of their authors' lack of intelligence and experience. This judgment is unfair, even when retooled by modern feminists to explain why Esther Summerson, ignorant of England's power system, writes poorly compared with her male co-narrator. Yet Dickens, one suspects, felt much the same as Greg. Kestner deplores the "unprofitable research" Dickens did for *Hard Times,* a novel allegedly "not in the most developed form" of the "tradition" invented by Jewsbury and Gaskell. Dickens, one counters, was writing against that tradition. He considered his novel superior to *Marian Withers* and *Mary Barton*. He believed that neither Mrs. Gaskell nor Harriet Martineau understood the negative impact industrialization was likely to have on personal relationships. Both underestimated the villainy of capitalists and the inhumanity of capitalism itself. Insufficiently aware of the evil in men and their systems, novelists like Mrs. Gaskell and, later, George Eliot were bound to misjudge the seriousness of any emergency. Dickens thought that women novelists inevitably offer shallow solutions, facile reforms based on an overly optimistic prognosis.

Kestner sets out to "reverse" the commonplace that social narrative was a male province. He succeeds only in modifying it. Stone, More, Jewsbury, Craik and company can best be likened to the parade of minor playwrights who enrich one's understanding of the great Elizabethans. Kestner insists the female novelists in his pantheon entered the field before many of their better-known successors. But Dickens soon took control, not because women protest writers were incompetent, as he believed, but due to his vastly superior artistic gifts.

Gallagher probes the "new shape" the Victorian controversy over industrialism gave to English cultural and intellectual life. She contends that novels "underwent basic changes" in their configuration whenever they took part in the discourse. Industrial novelists discovered self-contradictory tensions within the structures they employed yet made "excessively naive mimetic claims." For example, although they preached reform, depiction of both men and masters as predestined victims of circumstances made rational choices or trust in providence equally unrealistic solutions to recommend. One of the major "antitheses encountered as formal paradoxes" in industrial novels, Gallagher argues, is "between society and its literary representations." Novelists dear to Kestner—More, Tonna, Martineau—populate Gallagher's early chapters. In Chapter Seven, "'Relationship Remembered against Relationship Forgot': Family and Society in *Hard Times* and *North and South*," she applies her theories somewhat unfairly to Mrs. Gaskell and greatly to Dickens' disadvantage.

Hard Times and *North and South* suffer at Gallagher's hands because she mistakenly allots them "the same metaphoric and metonymic tropes." Both novels supposedly advocate the introduction of the cooperative behavior of private life into the public realm. Dickens and Mrs. Gaskell, says Gallagher, attempt to "make social relations personal" in the belief that the industrial system—interactions between employers and the working class—can be modeled on the associations sacred to family life. *Hard Times* and *North and*

South eventually contradict themselves because the public and private spheres they try to integrate have to be left separate. The novelists call for integration of public and private life and then disassociate the two.

On the contrary, Mrs. Gaskell integrates not only Thornton and Higgins (master and man) as friends but North and South or the differing value systems of Thornton and Margaret as husband and wife. Their progeny, one assumes, will inherit the best of both worlds. Gallagher's objections seem unrealistic: she insists that the significance of the symbolic marriage "will be lost on the observers," that is, on Thornton's mother and Margaret's Aunt Shaw. She forgets that Mrs. Gaskell's readers would be properly observant.

Divorce, not marriage, is Dickens' dominant metaphor throughout *Hard Times*. He separates Blackpool from Bounderby and from the union, Louisa from both Bounderby and Harthouse. He would separate Stephen from his drunken wife if he could. *Hard Times* suggests that the private realm's best chance is to stay clear of the public. Dickens' novel should be read as a parody of the confidence women social novelists put in improved interpersonal relationships as paradigms for industrial relations. In Dickens' opinion, friendship and marriage were likely to be the industrial system's chief victims, not its models or ideals. As Blackpool's fate indicates, Dickens foresaw a grim new world of mutually antagonistic power blocs. Individuals unable to ally themselves with either would be shunned by both. Dickens and Mrs. Gaskell were not naive at mimesis. She wrote her utopian forecast to correct his dystopian predictions. He used those predictions to broaden the issue-of-the-moment protest novels Kestner's novelists thought sufficient.

VIII

Two of the year's most highly touted studies are different from one another in every way, except for two crucial similarities. In *Dickens and the Social Order* (University of Pennsylvania Press), Myron Magnet concentrates on Dickens from *Nickleby* to *Chuzzlewit*. He finds the early Boz to be a closet Hobbesian, a conservative novelist-philosopher who masqueraded as a liberal reformer but actually supported the civilizing constraints of customs and the law. Janet L. Larson, in *Dickens and the Broken Scripture* (University of Georgia Press), takes a deconstructionist view of the later Dickens' use of the Bible. From *Bleak House* on, Dickens' faith, like his era's, steadily eroded. He no longer regarded the Old and New Testament or the Book of Common Prayer as stable sources of reassurance. His use of biblical allusions,

Larson maintains, became increasingly complicated, even contradictory, creating the kinds of dissonance between text and sub-texts that new theorists relish. Well-organized, both studies are based on painstaking research, especially Larson's, which seems to identify every reference to the Bible Dickens ever made. Both are also alike in that, despite being impressive feats of scholarship, they reach conclusions that leave one incredulous.

Can a thesis about Dickens the beginner that leaves out *Pickwick Papers, Oliver Twist, The Old Curiosity Shop,* and *A Christmas Carol* avoid being lopsided? Magnet thinks so. His book pivots around *Nicholas Nickleby, Barnaby Rudge,* and *Martin Chuzzlewit,* a non-sequential trio he treats as a "discrete stage" in Dickens' career. Between 1838 and 1844, the surprisingly truculent novelist allegedly formulated a conservative political outlook not unlike the hardening views associated with later years. It can be summed up in the catch-phrase: civilization is humanization. This phrase applies whether Dickens is reworking a historical incident, like the Gordon riots, or pointing to Cairo, Illinois, as the swindle behind all daydreams of the lost innocence of a simpler day. In both cases, Dickens realized that man's inborn aggressive instincts (*id*) need to be held in check by an internalized sense of the collective good (*superego*), a faculty only the civilized person possesses.

Magnet boasts that his "emendation" of the prevailing orthodoxy about Dickens' unbridled liberalism confers a double blessing. It exalts a Dickens "who *thinks*." It also shows that he would still be "a major English novelist" had he written no novels after his thirty-third birthday. On the other hand, one replies, a Dickens whose career climaxed with *Martin Chuzzlewit* would not be considered the second greatest writer in the language. Also, the Dickens Magnet draws toward his own ways of thinking was a more complex thinker than this study presents. Magnet concentrates on selected novels and selected parts of those novels that suggest how vocal the eventual supporter of Governor Eyre was from the outset. A Hobbesian Dickens concerned with curbing man's brutishness may be preferable to Goldberg's philistine or to slanders of Dickens as a coarse-minded non-thinker. But one should not make full-fledged and retroactive the conclusions Dickens only reached in the mid-1840s, and then not as singlemindedly as Magnet has him much earlier.

Dickens and The Social Order breaks down in its final chapters because Magnet is revealed to have been reading too many aspects of the post-America Dickens back into two of the pre-*Chuzzlewit* novels. All the evidence points to a dismayed democrat, a failed republican who had to revise his politics and lower his expectations in light of the crass, lawless, and unlettered America he found. But Magnet already has such a Dickens on his hands in

Nicholas Nickleby and *Barnaby Rudge*. So he must eliminate the shock America delivered to that part of Dickens that thought social ills the result of neglect and decline, not manifestations of man's ever-flawed nature. When Magnet talks of "disconcerted surprise," he means Dickens' intellectual gratification at encountering a "massive confirmation" of the political philosophy he had worked out long before departing England for America. The parody of a genuine fresh start that an angry Dickens said he had not come out to see was thus exactly the corroboration he had come to see after all. Contrary to Magnet, the Romantic, liberal, utopian elements in Dickens were traumatized in 1842. There are no traumas of "confirmation."

Outspoken in some places, Magnet pulls punches in others. His essay on *Nicholas Nickleby* had Dickens placing "aggression" at man's "very core." This is to mistake an effect for a cause. Tyranny and oppression in Dickens' novels stem not from euphemisms like *aggressiveness* but from the evil inherent in human nature. It is not "original human nature" that disillusions Dickens but his unshakeable sense of the tenacious consequences of a basic flaw, original sin, for which "original nature" is an evasive term designed to keep any religious flavor out of Dickens' political philosophy. Evasiveness originates from Magnet's determination to contravene Dickens' liberalism without compromising the idea of civilization as the consummate corrective. The critic wants to make early Dickens more conservative without making man so problematic that all social orders he establishes are bound to be imperfect also, both a restraint on his fallen nature and an indication, perhaps an exacerbation, of it.

Granted, admirers of a liberal, reform-minded Dickens often fail to accommodate his profound skepticism about societies and human nature. But Magnet cannot explain the impression the later Dickens conveys that the whole framework of British society is wrong. By stopping with *Chuzzlewit*, Magnet saves himself and his thesis a great deal of stress. The supporter of civilizing manners and customs, especially in the face of barbarous and unformed Americans, is certainly real. Present too is the Dickens who often found conventions, propriety, and the hide-bound conservatism of English institutions stifling enough to make life resemble a jail term. In *Bleak House, Little Dorrit, A Tale of Two Cities,* and *Our Mutual Friend,* the body politic seems as subject as the human frame to corruption from within. One of the major threats to civilization, Dickens realized early and late, is civilization itself. No political system or social order, actual or imagined, earned his unstinted praise.

Ultimately, neither the concept of a revolutionary reformer nor a champion of social order will serve to encircle the totality of Dickens. Magnet's final chapter places *Chuzzlewit* in the context provided by theories about human nature advanced by Blumenbach and Lord Monboddo. But this is done mainly so Magnet can sermonize for a conservative world-view one suspects yet again reflects his own. Wariness of human nature unleashed always kept the lid on the incendiary within Dickens. Simultaneously, his historical sense, an awareness of society's recurrent tendency to profane its heritage, whether through change for the worse or by simply decaying, made strict conservatism untenable. That civilization brings humanization better summarizes George Eliot's evolutionist philosophy; it suits her gradualism better than it fits his notion of rises and falls.

After the American visit, Dickens had to balance the perils of too little society against the stultifying effects of too much. The first leaves man's natural ferocity unrestrained; the second refers to the point at which inequalities and outmoded procedures for remedying them virtually become institutionalized. The innocence, goodness, and dedication to fair play of Pickwick, Oliver, and Nell were used to test the worth of British society. But these qualities failed a sterner exam when Dickens in America became the fourth of his innocents abroad, a social critic naive enough to hope for new beginnings even if the part of him that created Fagin, Sikes, and Quilp knew better.

The darker Dickens of the later satirical novels fears that man is trapped between his savage origins and an unpleasant present from which, despite its veneer of civility, only the worst can be predicted. This outlook offended liberals and conservatives alike. After 1842, Dickens' drive as a reformer went hand-in-hand with the increasingly dystopian prognosis that fueled it, but that drive and prognosis were anathema to both moderates and progressives.

Perusing Larson's book is like attempting to run under water: 364 pages of minute print, 95 notes to Chapter One alone. Still, this slow-reading book is a much more sophisticated effort than Vogel's *Allegory in Dickens* and more disconcerting than Walder's *Dickens and Religion*. Its reliance on Bakhtin's idea of a "dialogical play of viewpoints" is subtler, thus harder to resist, than Garrett's in *The Victorian Multiplot Novel*. Larson attempts to apply a methodology one thinks of as ahistorical to an historical phenomenon of the latter part of the nineteenth century: the ebbing of orthodox religious belief.

Relentlessly if tendentiously, Larson mines Dickens' texts for "counterpointed'' allusions and ''contradictory'' patterns of allusion to Scripture. She exposes Dickens' use of antithetical references throughout his later works, particularly in *Bleak House* and *Little Dorrit*. Battles between the different biblical books invoked within the same text convince Larson that ''a broken Scripture lies behind'' the mature work. Instead of the popular novelist with clear messages to deliver, Larson's Dickens began writing ''multiperspectival'' or multivocal works full of divergent meanings. Miscellanies of biblical allusion, Dickens' novels are marked, but apparently not marred, by irresolution, discord, and outright ruptures that only crystallize into dissonance. No longer a sender of consistent signals, the Bible itself, Larson concludes, became ''a fractured Code'' for the nineteenth century.

For once it is fortunate that the new theorists teach one to read disobediently. This dictum allows one to savor Larson's erudition without swallowing her application of Bakhtin's precepts. Larson's knowledge of Dickens' knowledge of the Bible, the single work he alluded to most, is inexhaustible, indeed, staggering. Dickens' ''subtextual'' allusions or underpatterns, his use of parallel texts such as *The Pilgrim's Progress* for Oliver's adventures and Esther Summerson's, his fondness both for enhancing allusions and jocular or parodic ones, the abundance of Jobean ironies in *Bleak House,* Dickens' hedging throughout *The Life of Our Lord* with regard to Christ's incarnation and resurrection—the invaluable insights one can glean from this study are legion. This is a large plus, even if one remains dubious about procedures and unhappy with the Dickens Larson sees as his era's foremost destabilizer of biblical meaning.

Larson's Dickens is the ''parabler.'' In his early novels, he resorts to the Bible to clarify the moral outlines of his stories. Straightforward allusions, reminders of shared assumptions on the part of writer and reader, strengthen Dickens' relationship with the Victorian audience. Starting with *Bleak House,* however, a turning-point other deconstructionists working on Dickens may not accept, Dickens ''writes in figures of which even he does not 'know' the meaning although he generates them; he remains on the outside of the very riddles'' he tells. Thus in *Bleak House*, the third-person narrator's favorite subtexts are Genesis and the Book of Job, while Esther's story is full of analogies to the Book of Esther and allusions to the New Testament. As incursions of the Jobean into Esther's narrative multiply, Dickens allegedly cannot keep his religious and skeptical voices separate. One has to be incredulous of an approach to Dickens' development which equates mastery, the so-called maturity of Dickens, with an increasing loss of direction, understanding, and control. Larson's maturing Dickens is the parabler never fully aware or in charge of the discordant puzzles he passes on to peers and posterity alike.

Aldous Huxley complained in the 1920s that the "activities of" the modern "age are uncertain and multifarious. No single literary, artistic, or philosophic tendency predominates. There is a babel of notions and conflicting theories." He proceeded to fashion his polyphonic, contrapuntal fictions so as to capture the chaos of an age without absolutes. The Victorian Dickens prefigures Huxley's interest in the multifarious but is not the portrayer, in *Bleak House* or elsewhere, of characters whose conflicting theories or attitudes toward life cancel each other out. Larson's Dickens is either less talented than Huxley or less fortunate. Esther's voice and the co-narrator's are not his creations, Larson thinks, but his own voices. The resultant double vision, two perspectives on London at mid century, is not really "multispectival" or responsive to life's different moods and aspects, but self-defeatingly contradictory.

Even if Esther's views and the third-person narrator's were as pointed a standoff as Mustapha Mond's and the Savage's, which they are not, Dickens, like Huxley, would be multivocal. He would be playing one point of view against another, which is different from getting one's voices confused or from confusing one's voices deliberately. Getting confused, whether unwittingly or unintentionally, can be two-faced, deceptive as well as self-deceiving. As a shaper of counterpoints, however, Dickens is always experimental and proto-modern, not post-modern and self-reflexive. Contradictions Huxley records are those he finds in the nature of things and in the minds and hearts of his age. Those Larson imposes on Dickens exist chiefly in Bakhtin's mind, where the idea is that "dialogical play" is generally self-revealing, indeed, self-incriminating.

Despite allegiance to Bakhtin's axiom that learning is dialogic not pedagogic, the Russian critic's Western disciples nurse a secret dislike for polyphony. They think it diminishes a work instead of adding to it, broadening through conflict and variation even as it often negates or cancels through contradiction. Many of the rules Philip Quarles formulates for the "musicalization" of fiction in *Point Counter Point* have a comprehensive or inclusive tendency, a desire to reconnoiter the multiplicities of reality with a multiplicity of eyes from a variety of angles and aspects. Bakhtin's disciples and the master himself would do well to brush up by reading Quarles' Notebook. The idea of "Majesty alternating with a joke," Quarles realizes, is not unusual in Beethoven or life itself. Yet critics like Larson bridle whenever irony and naivete, skepticism and religion, a jocular biblical allusion and a serious one, metaphor and metonomy, or references to Job and the New

Testament appear within hailing distance of one another. Quarles wants to respond to life's "fantasticality," its "modulations . . . from mood to mood." Bakhtin's followers think such an author is automatically gainsaying himself: he brings things together allegedly without being fully cognizant of the conflicts that ensue or able to capitalize on them for artistic effect.

Eventually, Larson sounds more dialogical and self-contradictory when applying Bakhtin's theories than Dickens supposedly became by alluding to the Bible. The parabler who "does not 'know' the meaning" of his parables co-exists at another point with a Dickens who "unleashes the subversive capacities of unstable Biblical allusion." This suggests intentions being realized. In one place, Dickens' use of rival subtexts, his incessant "destabilization of religious language and religious views, leads to "a reconstructed Bible" for the nineteenth century. But in another, the Bible seems at fault for supplying Dickens with "contradictory interpretations of experience." At one time, Dickens, more so than George Eliot, revises Christianity for a secular age; at another, he seems confused by the baffling source he tries to rely on.

Does *Bleak House* deconstruct or does Scripture itself, or is it the latter's turn first and then the former's? Larson appears uncertain. Do the Bible's hollow formulas fail Dickens or does he let new facts collide with old truths, either to show their inutility or condemn the perverseness of his age? Larson cannot always decide. In one case, Victorian culture has "outgrown" the biblical scheme, a statement that connotes progress. At another, the idea of a "broken" or "fractured" code suggests the untimely collapse of guidelines the era still wants and needs.

Dickens, Larson maintains, "invites rival allusions from quite different parts of the sacred book to co-exist uneasily in the same fictional world." Here, with Dickens apparently in control of his riddle, the Bible's multiplicity of mood and vision is excusable, but fictional worlds, Larson implies, should be more uniform than sacred books. Why, one wonders, cannot Esther and her co-narrator occupy different places in the same society? Why is it more false to the contrapuntal diversity of fates and fortunes perennial in real life if Job and the biblical Esther inhabit the same book (or world) than if Esther Summerson and the unnamed co-narrator do?

"While Jones is murdering a wife," Quarles notes, "Smith is wheeling the perambulator in the park." The astonishing-ness of life stems from being able to see "dissimilars solving the same problem" or "similar people confronted with dissimilar problems." The contrapuntist in both Shakespeare and Dickens knew this, but Quarles thinks the proliferation of comparisons and contrasts necessitated by a code-less world defies precedent. As Esther matures, she comes into greater contact with the bleaker realities that have shaped her fellow-narrator's views. Insinuation of his kinds of allusion into her narrative signals that maturation. But persistent reliance on happier texts than Job continues to distinguish Esther's philosophy from her co-author's virtual misanthropy. Dickens is not interested in keeping these views totally separate, resolving their differences, cancelling either or both, or endorsing one over the other. Instead of being frustrated, the reader is left with variations that not only undercut but also clarify and complement each other.

Jo's deathbed scene, which Barbara Hardy praised, strikes Larson as futile utterance, a prayer sequence "defamiliarized, truncated, unable to affirm any belief." Is this so by design or another among the "unintended effects" the critic attributes to the dialogical parabler? In one paragraph, Dickens is said to invite Victorian readers to criticize their ideology, to become surreptitious revisers of biblical tradition. In another, however, the modern critic has "to reconstruct" "unstated meanings" in Dickens' texts without being invited to by the author. With Dickens in charge, author and reader become surreptitious co-conspirators. If Dickens is not in full command of the contrapuntal allusion process, the same thing apparently happens: the twentieth-century reader dubs himself "a dialogist with the text," an active participant in the production of meanings Dickens failed to articulate fully. How can effects be unintentional yet solicit readers to do the novelist's work with or for him? Can readers of *Bleak House* have secretly revised that novel or their Bibles, as Dickens allegedly encouraged them to do, if Larson must enter the text in 1985 with Bakhtin's kit for destabilizing it?

Larson's parabler is by turns a man of unsettled beliefs and an unsettler of beliefs who is himself at times stealthy at what he does and at others the chief victim of his own stealth. The contradiction is no small matter. The first Dickens remains quintessentially Victorian but going on modern; the second, more than a *bona fide* modern, already displays post-modern inclinations stronger than Beckett's. A Dickens who is pro-Bible and anti-Bible, a Jobean exponent of the Beatitudes, makes a Beckett whose novels are also anti-novels and whose characters talk in hopes of silencing themselves seem anachronistic.

Dickens and the Broken Scripture, regardless of the monumental research effort behind it, is riddled by the contradictory stances it takes toward Dickens' involvement with his readers and his texts. The book makes a variety of statements about whether Dickens is primarily the Bible's destabilizer or himself a casualty of its destabilization. Larson's book succumbs to the "self-reflexive destabilization'' she purports to find in the novelist's use of Scripture.

Unlike Magnet, Neil Forsyth and Thomas Vargish discern in Dickens a principle of order that is providential, not simply the result of man's laws and usages. Nor is this principle boken or fractured. Forsyth sees it becoming more binding in the later Dickens. There, he argues, the delightful coincidences of the early novels are replaced by more solemn patterns and designs. In "Wonderful Chains: Dickens and Coincidence" (*Modern Philology*), the critic borrows his title from *Drood* but concentrates on *Oliver Twist, Bleak House, Little Dorrit,* and *Great Expectations.* He tries to group the last three of these as another discreet chapter in Dickens' development.

The problem Dickens faced, Forsyth maintains, was how to retain pleasure in surprise despite the darkening worlds of the later novels. Coincidences happen by chance, yet in a tragic world events must move inexorably toward a sense of foreordained completion. Dickens' solution, according to Forsyth, was to transform chance into Fate. In *Great Expectations,* where Dickens' expedient succeeds, connections made by coincidence reinforce moral connections Pip and the reader make together. The novel's plot pleases Forsyth because it becomes the discovery of remarkable connections; they are not external aids propelling it forward.

Carving out discrete periods in Dickens' career proves as perilous for Forsyth as it was for Magnet. One is asked to believe that Dickens anguished about tensions between coincidence and providence in 1852 and again in 1855 before finally resolving them in 1860. More realistically, the problem never assumed the acute form Forsyth imagines. Dickens always has a sense of the dialectic of fate and coincidence: when the incident happens, it must seem coincidental, but the novelist who can shine a backward light on events will also illuminate a fateful chain patiently forging itself. Dickens simply got better at tailoring his flair for coincidence to fit the exigencies of a plot conceived well in advance of the actual writing of the novel. Indeed, he was more insistently drawn towards plots that would express a world-view still predicated on rewards and punishments. Thus in *A Tale of Two Cities,* which Forsyth ignores, disclosure of Manette's letter during Darnay's second Paris trial is both startling and the long-delayed day of reckoning for the Evremondes.

The Providential Aesthetic in English Fiction (University Press of Virginia) is billed as a deliberate exercise in the cultivation of a historic imagination.

Thomas Vargish undertakes to explore a mode of perception Victorian novelists perfected for seeing the world. He calls it "the providential habit of
mind." This useful, compact study of Victorian values and sensibilities com-
mences with Charlotte Brontë's framing of the providential frame of mind,
treats Dickens' novels as completion of the frame, the highpoint for this
aesthetic, and concludes with George Eliot's redirection of it to an entirely
human world devoid of extraterrestrial influence.

Vargish intelligently discusses the importance of coincidence, the question
of whether God was seen to be transcendent or immanent, the era's decreasing
satisfaction with poetic justice, and contributions to the aesthetic from Defoe
to Hardy. He is not aware of the impact Gallagher saw industrialization having
on the providential frame of mind. Dickens is voted most courageous in his
use of providence: he allowed challenges to the providential order to occur
in his fictions but made it the business of his novels to repel them. In the
section given over to Dickens, the book's longest, there are segments on
providence's natural enemies (gamblers, hypocrites, and solipsists) and on
Dickens' progressively more adroit use of virtuous heroines as representatives
of divine mercy and truth. Novels receiving individual attention include *Oliver
Twist, Dombey and Son, Little Dorrit, Great Expectations*, and *Our Mutual
Friend*.

Trollope and Thackeray do not concern Vargish because the sort of mind
he studies did not interest them. But omission of Wilkie Collins is inexcusable.
Dickens and Collins argued repeatedly over the best ways to depict the workings of providence in a changing, increasingly secularized world. The Inimitable instructed his rival/disciple that all good novels were little imitations
of providence, hence explanations of God's ways. Making plainer providence's subtleties is historical recovery for Vargish but was a graver matter
to Dickens and Collins; they refused to let rapid transformations taking place
throughout society obscure a directional force they insisted was neither dead
nor expendable. Dickens preferred to build toward one or two stupendous
revelations, Collins to pile one atop another to achieve crescendos. Yet both
sensational realists wavered: providence is variously God's hand or an unwritten natural law, a built-in, impersonal moral principle that periodically
sets things to rights. As the latter, it was better able to contradict George
Eliot's idea of gradual improvement through individual and societal evolution.

Vargish sees the providential frame of mind as a smooth case of rise and
fall, a continuity from Brontë, through Dickens, to George Eliot. Actually,
it was more of a subject for continual conflict, not just between Dickens and
Collins, who differed about how much providential supervision to employ

and how soon, but between both of them and George Eliot. Her frame of mind is better described as anti-providential. What Vargish miscalls the re-direction of providence for secular purposes really constituted an attempt to replace it with a more sanguine conception of history. To George Eliot's way of thinking, which she considered more scientific than Dickens', the nature of things improves steadily, if microscopically, in a straight, upward line. Floods, fire, revolutions and the like loom large to those caught up in them, and dominate history books. But such temporary interruptions, unable to alter the contours of a much larger overall process, can easily be discounted. Dickens and Collins, George Eliot thought, were anti-progressives, myopic catastrophists who mistook a few trees for the entire forest.

Finally, the kind of thinking Vargish calls "providential" is not a quaint historical phenomenon to many of the world's major religions. It also goes on in Greene's *The End of the Affair,* Waugh's *Brideshead Revisited,* and prompts T. S. Eliot's discovery of an end in his beginnings. Vargish needlessly widens the gap between Victorian culture and the modern world. In the former, many believed in a purposive universe but that belief was subject to controversy and not all lived as if they shared it. In the latter, most claim they put no trust in providence, yet many live as if material progress and improvement of the lot of the species, if not the species itself, were still foregone conclusions and purpose enough.

Is the life process progressive and evolutionary or is it problematic, more of a battleground, with declines and falls and periodic shake-ups that appear providential and resemble judgments? The verdict in the case at issue between Dickens and his supporters, on one side, and George Eliot and hers, on the other, is not yet in. Post-war moderns complained that pointlessness seemed to be the only point that needed to be made about life after World War One. Even this, however, was a chapter in the discussion of the nature of things initiated by the Victorians, especially realistic novelists from 1850 on. Those moderns who persisted in the opinion that no point to it all could be found have been succeeded by post-moderns, so-called, who are more certain that literature, too, not just the West's Christian tradition, is a fractured code. It can only be used by creative writers to speak against itself, or else an existing work can be deconstructed by the new theorists who regard it from the start as a self-refuting artifact. Exercises in historical recovery, such as Vargish's, need not take place in a vacuum. They force one to reconsider which is truly the side-tracking irrelevancy, disagreements between Victorian novelists about how life works and how good it is, or the self-reflexive theories of Bakhtin and Derrida. These can be held dispassionately (i.e., without conviction) and used to prove that Victorian convictions, like Dickens', were either confused or self-subverting.

IX

Among the many questions from previous years still vexing Dickensians in 1985, four stand out prominently: how modern is Dickens? how much did he know, how well did he think, and how do his novels relate to the Victorian novelist's obsession with appearing realistic? Bernard thinks Dickens understood dreams better than most of his contemporaries, but Goldberg finds his grasp of the visual arts inadequate. To one group, Dickens is a master psychologist, a clear-eyed critic of modern, bureaucratic society, and a forerunner of Tolstoy, Conrad, and Kafka. For others, his alleged lack of interest in the theory behind his artistry and a preoccupation with providence, coincidence, and the chains of Fate keep him basically Victorian. Paroissien endorses Dickens' claim to be a realist. Eigner and Worth believe in a Victorian consensus on what realism is. Gallagher thinks Victorian mimesis naive. Hardy argues that novelists of the period, when dealing with the emotions, were often more than mere depicters.

Perhaps the most curious nexus is formed by Shaw, Chesterton, Leavis, Axton, and Schlicke. Although their reasoning differed widely, the first three did not approve of directions modern society was taking. Chesterton found in Dickens a corrective for the modern loss of cheerfulness. Shaw and, later, Leavis saw Dickens a staunch critic of impersonal, industrialized, technological society. Axton and Schlicke add greater acknowledgment of the connections between Dickens' nostalgia for pre-1830 England and the opprobrium his later work heaped upon the England of Victoria. They recognize the extent to which Dickens' fondness for the vanishing, friendlier world of his boyhood influenced his social criticism and darkened his apprehensions for the future. Dickens may have blacked out recollections of Warren's but not of popular entertainments and festive bowls. America, instead of offering alternatives, was even less English than England was becoming. Much of Dickens' dystopian dread, which seems even more modern when refracted by Tolstoy and Kafka, was tinged with regret for qualities of life society had left behind to get where it was. In his own time, therefore, Dickens viewed developments with the skepticism and disapproval Shaw, Chesterton, and Leavis use him to express toward their own age.

Vargish and Forsyth serve as reminders that Dickens, although fascinated by the way things come together or can be made to, was no proto-Bloomsberry. Left unmodified, Margaret Schlegel's desire to integrate traditional cultural values with the modern business world of angry telegrams would have seemed to him starry-eyed. He would equate Margaret's marriage to Mr. Wilcox with Mrs. Gaskell's use of another Margaret, Miss Hale, to ally the cultivated south with Mr. Thornton's industrial north. The Bloomsbury approach is a pseudo-religious way of loving thy neighbor and earning the blessings due a peacemaker. It is not alien to Dickens' work, as Esther Summerson's narrative shows. But Dickens felt is should be supplemented, not contradicted, by a sense of the mysteriousness, the involuntary, and the providential that also gives life its coloring. So the third-person narrator exclaims:

> What connexion can there have been between many people in the innumerable histories of this world, who, from opposite sides of great gulfs, have, nevertheless, been very curiously brought together!

Through this narrator, who emphasizes life's multifariousness, its "innumerable" stories, and its capacity for juxtapositionings, the contrapuntist in Dickens speaks. His curiosity parallels the "fantasticality" Quarles wants moderns to appreciate.

Dickens posits an endlessly fateful universe which Esther comes to recognize somewhat in her own life. Her overdue good fortune as Woodcourt's wife, Dickens insists, must be balanced by the equally appropriate presence of Hortense in Tulkinghorn's chamber and the congregation of Esther, Bucket, and an expired Lady Dedlock at the entrance to Hawdon's graveyard. Convergences nearly as marvelous, Dickens argued, occur all the time if the mind trains itself to look for them with an eye both poetic and satirical. Thus Gallagher's study of industrialization in Victorian fiction, published in Chicago, and Kestner's survey of protest novels by Victorian women, issued from Wisconsin, attest to their common misuse of Dickens to put down mimesis and masculine novelists respectively: unwittingly, both critics select von Herkomer's 1891 painting, *On Strike,* for a front-jacket illustration.

Dorothy Van Ghent was annoyed by so much bringing together in story after story. "Is it possible," Dickens wonders, "that there was some analogy between the case of the Coketown population and the case of the little Gradgrinds?" Indeed so, complained Van Ghent, whose remarks about "the violent connection of the unconnected" have been too readily accepted as a shorthand description of a Dickens novel. Karen Chase puts it less pejoratively in *Eros and Psyche.* She concludes that characters in the mature Dickens "need not establish connection; . . . they have no hope of escaping it." Neither, it seems, had Dickens in 1985. Fortunately, ponderous yokings were as infrequent as missed connections. On occasion, however, one is reminded of another of Margaret Schlegel's admonitions, this time spoken out loud to her husband: ''You shall see the connection if it kills you, Henry.''

ACKNOWLEDGMENTS

This essay has relied upon Alan M. Cohn's bibliography-checklist in the *Dickens Quarterly* and on Cohn himself, who kindly supplied several offprints of hard-to-get items. I am also indebted to the staff of Widener Library and to Inter-Library Loan at the University of Kentucky, Lexington.

Professor Roger Anderson of the Department of Slavic Languages and Literature at the University of Kentucky kindly translated D. M. Urnov's essay ''Dickens and Gogol.''

George Eliot Studies: 1980–84

George Levine

The resurrection of George Eliot from the grave dug for her by Bloomsbury and early modernism was no miracle. George Eliot was born again by being the kind of writer contemporary critics were comfortable reading. Through the middle decades of our century, the task was to demonstrate that she was not the creator of "the large, loose baggy monsters" Henry James deplored, but a novelist who could, as craftsman (and I use the masculine self-consciously), hold her own with James himself. When F. R. Leavis showed how much James owed to her, and when Barbara Hardy brilliantly established her formalist credentials, George Eliot became an entirely respectable subject and one of the few women to enter the canon.

Her morality and preaching had always been suspect; her sentimentality was condemned by Leavis even as he invited her into his great tradition; and the radical unevenness of much of her work, its lapse from tough-minded realism into mythic or romantic dream, as in *Daniel Deronda,* always required extensive apologies. Moreover, her philosophic and cerebral inclinations ran counter to the New Critical insistence on dramatic particularity. So scholars were happy to quote her letter to Frederick Harrison, refusing to write a positivist novel or to let her work lapse "from the picture to the diagram." Never trust the teller, trust the tale, was the implicit motto of George Eliot critics.

Following the 1980 celebration of her centenary in conferences at Leicester, Puget Sound, and Rutgers University, a new old George Eliot began to emerge. The four years of scholarship surveyed here indicate that the curve of George Eliot's critical fate is looping backwards. Although major studies were slow to follow the intensified interest inspired by the centenary, the floodgates seem at last to have burst, and what I discuss in this survey is often only prologue to the large studies that have emerged in the last two years.

Several important shifts in emphasis are evident in the materials surveyed here. First, while the Jamesian/Lubbockian mode that resurrected her made direct attention to George Eliot's "thought" something of a critical scandal, critics are now unembarrassedly turning to her ideas again. Second, critics seem less blinded by George Eliot's commitment to realism and by her realistic techniques. Increasingly, they are looking at her works not from the perspective of mimesis and realism, but from that of romance and myth. The gradual emergence of that old embarrassment, *Daniel Deronda,* as (with the possible exception of *Middlemarch*) the most talked about of her novels is symptomatic of this change, and is consonant with the anti-realist bias of modern criticism, and its preoccupation with questions of narrative. Third, studies of *Daniel Deronda* show that instead of thinking of George Eliot as one of the boys, the ploy of her admirers during the heyday of the New Criticism, critics are now searching for specifically feminist orientations.

(Yet one more preliminary point I cannot resist: the new developments have not been accompanied by an equivalent depth of understanding of how to spell the names of two female protagonists. A trivial matter, you might say; but after reading four years worth of criticism, I found that this old pet peeve was making me yet more peevish. Is it possible that a marvelous new reading of George Eliot could be accomplished by someone who hadn't after many readings [we hope] noticed that Gwendolen is not, after all, Gwendolyn, and that Rosamond is not Rosamund? The frequency of these misspellings invites skepticism about the degree of attention scholars have been giving to the texts. Can we pass a law that misspelling of either Rosamond or Gwendolen disqualifies critics from comment on George Eliot immediately? I suppose not, but it is tempting to ask for such legislation from MLA.)

Among the full length studies of George Eliot published between 1980 and 1984, three seem to me genuinely important, and all three unabashedly, but not exclusively, preoccupy themselves with her ideas: William Myers's *The Teaching of George Eliot* (1984); Suzanne Graver's *George Eliot and Community: A Study in Social Theory and Fictional Form* (1981); and Sally Shuttleworth's *George Eliot and Nineteenth-Century Science: The Make-Believe of a Beginning* (1984).

Myers's title would have been impossible for a serious critic only a few years ago. It echoes with Alexander Main's idolatrous, *Wise, Witty and Tender*

Sayings of George Eliot, but it accurately describes one of the most valuable of recent studies. Myers treats George Eliot's work in the context of the great writers not of Victorian England, but of modern Western culture, and he allows her the didacticism we have wanted to dismiss or deny. To begin with, he wants to make clear what she *intended.* Disregard of intention in modern criticism, he argues, is both intrinsically falsifying and particularly inapplicable to George Eliot, since she self-consciously incorporates her own critique. His first section provides as rich and intelligent an explication of George Eliot's beliefs—humanist, positivist, scientific, determinist, esthetic—as we have; in the second, he subjects these beliefs to radical critiques, using Marx, Freud, Lacan, and Nietzsche as formulators of positions that not only counter her ideas, but challenge her didactic strategy of privileged, contemplative materialism. In a superb final section, "Affirmations," he shows how George Eliot anticipated, even responded to the criticisms leveled in the second part.

As an introduction to George Eliot's ideas, the book is exceptional. But more, richly engaged and fully informed it elevates George Eliot studies to a higher position by moving her beyond the exclusively English Victorian context in which her works have tended to be studied, by taking her ideas seriously enough to argue with them, and by reading her in the context of contemporary critical procedures and assumptions.

Suzanne Graver's book does not attempt so broad a view of George Eliot's thought, but it too is very much about ideas. The subject is her social theory, as it is embodied in fictions that aspire toward an ideal, yet possible community. Graver locates George Eliot in the context of pre- and unMarxist thought, and applies a theoretical framework that developed out of the kind of theory to which George Eliot herself was committed—Tönnies's conception of Gemeinschaft and Gesellschaft.

Graver argues that George Eliot was attempting to create a community of readers to prepare the evolution of a new Gemeinschaft, mixing modernity with tradition, unifying thought and action. But this mixture creates unresolvable tension between theory and fact, multiplicity and particularity, the abstract and the concrete, a tension which, Graver argues, is an aspect of the creative openness of the art. That art can be seen both as a formulation of an intellectual program and, in its insistence on the particular, as subversive of theory.

A major question for modern students of George Eliot is how far her works are designed as empirical, "realist" studies of society, how far attempts to transform that society—and how far the two objectives are reconcilable.

George Eliot's intricate philosophical reconciliations are strained, but in Art, she believed, the ideal and the persuasive and the evaluative could enter. Still, the realistic method is heir to the individualist ethos of Gesellchaft, which, precisely, the novels are designed to criticize. Again, Graver finds in George Eliot a fundamental contradiction between organicist and individualist ideals, and these contradictions appear not only in social organization, but in George Eliot's esthetic theory and practice. (It should also be noted that Graver has published a separate essay, closely related to the materials of her book and in a sense offering a brief summary of its argument, "Modeling Natural History: George Eliot's Framing the Present" [1983]).

The enrichment of the art with ideas is manifest, too, in Sally Shuttleworth's extended study of "organicism" in the novels, *George Eliot and Nineteenth-Century Science: The Make-Believe of a Beginning* (1983). Shuttleworth tries to show how "scientific ideas and theories of method affected not only the social vision but also the narrative structure and fictional methodology." She defines a contradiction in "organicism" that has important consequences for the novels: in the early narratives, particularly *Adam Bede*, George Eliot worked in the empiricist mode of natural history, which implies an ahistorical stability, and gradualism and continuity. But, Shuttleworth shows, natural history applied to biological phenomena "requires a conception of continuing and significant change and thus of a reality that eludes ahistorical classification." For George Eliot, then, the study of Comte and Claude Bernard "entailed a reimagination of the role of the scientist from that of passive observer and collector of facts . . . to that of active and imaginative constructor of hypotheses," and thus shifted her view that the novelist was responsible primarily to record empirically. Even in *Adam Bede* the ahistorical ideal is in tension with a more dynamic and constructive science and narrative method. In a highly original reading of *The Mill on the Floss*, Shuttleworth elaborates this argument: "Neither the plot nor the commentary . . . wholeheartedly reinforces organicist conceptions of gradual uniform development." Organicism, while normally associated with political conservatism, also implies (subversively even to itself) that no object is permanently what it is: since everything changes, "there can be no fixed point of value, no grounds for assessing individual moral responsibility," nor can there be any firm closure. Shuttleworth, that is to say, opens up a politically subversive aspect of George Eliot that has too often been ignored. (An earlier essay by Shuttleworth, "The Language of Science and Psychology in GE's *Daniel Deronda*," in James Paradis and Thomas Postlewaite, *Victorian Science and*

Victorian Values: Literary Perspectives [1981], is a version of the last chapter of her book, and nicely explores George Eliot's duality about change.)

None of the other full-length studies approaches these three books in richness and significance, although many other critics have been attempting to locate intellectual sources for George Eliot's ideas. Sara M. Putzell-Korab's *The Evolving Consciousness: An Hegelian Reading of George Eliot* (1983) argues for the importance of Hegel as influence. While perhaps overstressing the significance of Hegel, she interestingly argues against traditional dualistic readings—the split between sympathy and egoism—in favor of a more dialectical one: each becomes a condition of the other. The question: how does one evolve into the other form of consciousness. The answer is in Hegel. Hegel, she says, helps us understand the apparent defeat of progressive change in George Eliot's novels (a subject that has much engaged our first three authors, and that constantly worries feminist critics). Further, "although all of her protagonists can be said to learn sympathy, comparison with Hegel's phenomenology of individual development makes it possible to describe differences among their structurally similar histories." Putzell-Korab argues not that there is direct influence, but that George Eliot's way of conceiving character was Hegelian. Along the way, she provides, among other things, a nice reading of Dorothea's dark night of the spirit in terms of a Hegelian paradigm.

Another study connecting George Eliot to German philosophers is Anthony McCobb's *George Eliot's Knowledge of German Life and Letters* (1982). But this is essentially a catalogue. The Introduction, letting nothing escape, traces all of George Eliot's relations to Germany and to German thought. (It also, oddly and briefly, summarizes her reading in English, American, Italian, and French writing!)

K. M. Newton, in *George Eliot: Romantic Humanist* (1981), also moves away from formalist analysis to emphasize the "philosophical" in "philosophical novelist." Newton argues that the emphasis on George Eliot's connection with nineteenth-century rationalism and positivism is misguided, and that "the firmer connection is with a Romantic tradition." George Eliot, he insists, developed "the anti-metaphysical implications of Romantic thinking to an extreme." Newton engages the continuing problem, which has broad implications for an understanding of her narrative techniques, of George Eliot's belief in the possibility of objective description. He argues that, following Feuerbach, she sees reality as a projection of human subjectivity. George Eliot is unusual among "advanced Romantic thinkers" in supporting "organicist" rather than "egoistic" romanticism (i.e., the views of Nietzsche), emphasizing community rather than the individual. Thus her "two main aims as a philosophical novelist" were to mediate egotist philosophies derivable from her own ideas, and to support the moral and social thought of the organicist Romantics without denying the ideas. Newton considers how George Eliot gets around Nietzsche's critique that if you take God out of Christianity, the whole system collapses. She replaces God and intellect with feeling, made super-personal by community, formerly the church. In the long run, however, the rationalist-romantic distinction is not very helpful. What matters most, I suppose, is that unlike Myers, Shuttleworth, and Graver, Newton's speculations on George Eliot's ideas don't lead to fresh readings of the novels, and his rhetoric implies an argument more startling and original than the book ultimately gives.

Philip Fisher's *Making up Society* (1981) is entirely different. Full of sharp insights, originally conceived, with a coherent vision and judgment of George Eliot's canon, it ought to be much better than it is. It attempts to trace George Eliot's treatment of society and of her conception of self, conceived always in relation to society. He traces a movement within the novels, culminating in *Middlemarch,* from a sense of society there, to be discovered, reanimated, to a sense of society as a kind of creation. Although Fisher's method is free floating and imaginative, his conclusions are often strikingly close to Graver's or Shuttleworth's. Good as much of the book is, it is marred by being written in a critical vacuum, and lacks almost any reference to a community of scholarship. The ungenerous *Daniel Deronda* section is hurt particularly because it doesn't recognize its own conventionality or the fascinating recent work that has been revising our understanding of George Eliot.

Karen Mann's *The Language that Makes George Eliot's Fiction* (1983) is one of the more ambitious of the full-length studies. Its concern, as its title makes clear, is with George Eliot's language, not her ideas, nor social context; and its methods and assumptions are closer to those of most lines of contemporary critical theory. Mann assumes, fairly enough, that George Eliot saw in language the best means to register her sense of the world, and to grasp it. Mann tries to get at the dual nature of George Eliot's language—its reference to the world and to itself (its art)—by showing how some of her most basic metaphors connect with the narrative strategies of all her fiction. The figure of the "shell," for example, metaphorically implies the relationship between "energy" and "order." While these explorations produce some subtle analyses of George Eliot's language, the attempt to demonstrate how the language generated narrative is a bit strained, despite Mann's generous enthusiasm for George Eliot's style, for its textures, its humor, and its pathos.

Mann published at least two essays during this period that turn up as chapters of the book, and they should be noted for reference: "George Eliot's Language of Nature" (1981) and "Self, Shell and World: George Eliot's Language of Space" (1982).

One of the most old-fashioned of the full-length studies is not old-fashioned in a new way. Mary Ellen Doyle's *The Sympathetic Response: George Eliot's Fictional Rhetoric* (1981) offers a neat but outdated study of the novels on the kind of Aristotelian principles that were expounded by the Chicago school in the 1950s. Doyle takes no account of the extensive and varied criticism of George Eliot through the past two decades, and her readings simply remind us of what we were saying about the novels in the 1950s. The book is not unintelligent, but it is thoroughly unoriginal.

Rosemary Ashton's *George Eliot* (1983) is an entry in the Oxford Series "Past Masters." It does not pretend to be more than an introduction, but lays out most of the received ideas about George Eliot and the novels without reference to any recent criticism and without attempting to address the complication of those positions forced by recent studies. For specialists in George Eliot the book will seem dutiful but disturbingly oversimplifying. Ashton does try to emphasize the importance of Spinoza in George Eliot's thought (further evidence of that renewed preoccupation with intellectual sources), but this is really no place to do it. Her argument runs counter to dominant views of George Eliot's intellectual development, yet she cannot stop to argue. The book imagines an audience entirely innocent of George Eliot, and offers two to three page quotations to convey her qualities. The question is whether this kind of simplification will be of service even to such an audience.

Two other volumes entirely devoted to George Eliot should be noted. The proceedings of the Puget Sound conference comprise a collection of mixed interest, edited by Gordon Haight and Rosemary van Arsdel: *George Eliot: A Centenary Tribute* (1982). The volume includes thirteen short essays, very uneven in quality. Joseph Wiesenfarth's consideration of how George Eliot used a Renaissance book of gems to develop her mythic material is illuminating, not only of *Romola* but of *Middlemarch* and *Daniel Deronda* as well.

A book by Barbara Hardy on George Eliot would ordinarily require extensive treatment. Her collection, *Particularities,* however, is of major interest primarily because it reprints several of Hardy's splendid earlier essays, notably the chapter on *Middlemarch* from *The Appropriate Form.* All of these essays, which resist the recent developments in critical theory or the great excavation of George Eliot's intellectual background, reveal Hardy's uncannily sharp eye for detail, and sensitive registrations of the nuances of the text. We can see in the earlier essays how Hardy opened the way for the kind of esthetic and formal treatment of George Eliot's art that we now expect from serious criticism. The later essays explore certain patterns of George Eliot's art, the registration of "feelings," for instance, with considerable sensitivity.

   The kind of preoccupation with the analysis of ideas and their sources that we have found in the most interesting of the full-length studies is evident too in many of the essays. In particular, critics have returned to the question of George Eliot's relation to positivism, a vexed question for many reasons, and one that will recur when we consider the essays dealing with George Eliot's narrative techiques. T. R. Wright, in "George Eliot and Positivism" (1981), convincingly argues against Gordon Haight that positivism is an important element in the novels and that George Eliot admired Comte from her first reading of him in 1851, to a degree well beyond the limits that Haight and most modern criticism has been willing to allow. Through excellent use of notebooks, letters, and journals, Wright shows that we must take Comte's influence and Comte himself very seriously if we are to read the novels with full understanding.
   In "From Bumps to Morals: the Phrenological Background to George Eliot's Moral Framework" (1982), Wright argues that phrenology can be seen as a systematic intellectual structure to the novels, and claims that Comte's cerebral theory, which emphasized moral rather than anatomical matters, is a key to understanding George Eliot's moral framework, and was deeply influential on English thinkers, particularly Lewes.
   In "Comtean Fetishism in *Silas Marner* (1981)," James McLaverty reads that novel in the light of Comtean theory. Fetishism for Comte is the first stage of man's progress. Supplementing David Carroll's classic reading of the novel, McLaverty offers "an account of how Comte's system provides the vital link between the myths of the community and its domestic life and slow progress towards civilization." Like Wright, he argues that George Eliot was pervasively influenced by Comte. McLaverty concedes that it does not require a reading of Comte to portray an indolent father and his sons benefitting from the prolonged Napoleonic wars, "but such reading was necessary in order to provide systematic links between the primitive stage of their farming, the bleakness of the home, the son's unhappy marriages, and the miser's adoption of a child." This is a good sensible use of Comte, without too much special pleading. The reading doesn't change *Silas Marner* but it does put it in a slightly new light. A brief note by Valerie Dodd, "A George Eliot

Notebook'' (1981), provides further evidence that George Eliot's interest in Comte "continued throughout her life.'' The notebook is probably from 1877 and Dodd simply describes the entries.

Comte, of course, is not the only intellectual influence critics have been discussing. E. A. McCobb, in "The Morality of Musical Genius: Schopenhaurian Views in *Daniel Deronda*'' (1983), links George Eliot to Schopenhauer, showing how the portrait of Klesmer reflects Schopenhaurian notions of musical genius. McCobb is most interesting, however, in remarks arguing both George Eliot's ambivalence about music as an ethical force, and her tendency to segregate musical achievement sexually, allowing (like Schopenhauer) woman to have talent but not genius. McCobb does not unfortunately follow up the point that George Eliot's preference for non-verbal public art or for salon or drawing room art contradicts the value she attaches to it, and he fails to take account of the fact that Daniel's mother, Alchirisi, has the force of genius in her.

J. Still finds yet another intellectual influence in "Rousseau and *Daniel Deronda.*'' Using some recent notions of intertextuality, Still argues that there is "a strong link'' between *Daniel Deronda* and Rousseau. Unfortunately, neither the notion of intertextuality and some sophistication in modern critical techniques, nor considerable knowledge of Rousseau helps to make the argument significant. George Eliot's enthusiasms about Rousseau are not unknown.

Without reference to particular intellectual influences, Carroll Viera, in "'The Lifted Veil' and George Eliot's Early Aesthetic'' (1984), provides a valuable brief study. Perhaps the most original part of the essay is the comparison of "The Lifted Veil'' to George Eliot's earliest published writing, "Poetry and Prose from the Notebook of an Eccentric.'' Viera points out some striking parallels between the fictional figures McCarthy, Adolphe, and Idone, and the protagonist Latimer. She focusses on the romantic notion of the relation between intensity of feeling and intensity of perception. "In Latimer,'' Viera argues, "George Eliot provides her fullest exploration of the hypothesis that visionary powers may lead, not to sincerity and sympathy, but to disenchantment and creative impotence.''

One of the most subtle and important considerations of the impact of ideas on George Eliot's work is in Gillian Beer's *Darwin's Plots: Evolutionary Narrative in Darwin, George Eliot, and Nineteenth-Century Fiction* (1983). Beer includes three exemplary chapters on George Eliot. It would take far too long to summarize the arguments of this book, but against those critics who emphasize the mythic at the expense of the "scientific'' George Eliot,

Beer shows that science and the mythic worked together: "Far from eschewing mystification, the extension of possibility through scientific instruments and scientific hypothesis-making actually gave . . . a fresh authority to the speculative and even to the fictive." The scientific parallels are not discrete passages, but part of a full engagement with major contemporary enquiries, and "Darwin's insights and the difficulties raised by those insights move into the substance of the novels' project."

Beer addresses an issue that recurs frequently in George Eliot criticism: the tensions between individual need and the inexorable "disclosures of law," which are all that remain against Darwin's world of endless change; and Beer's arguments are indispensable for any future treatments of the subject. She analyzes George Eliot's use of the determinist structures of science, and her strategies of escape from them, and finds, even at the end of *Middlemarch,* a repudiation of "the evenness of spun fabric (the famous web image) as a sufficient image of the potentialities of human life."

The essays on *Daniel Deronda* further explore both the debt to Darwin and George Eliot's resistances to him, especially on the subjects of descent and development. Finally, Beer explores a question of major importance to feminist study: "Can fiction restore to the female the power of selection which, Darwin held, men had taken over? And can the woman writing shape new future stories?" There is no summarizing so complex and rich a study. The George Eliot chapters are not in fact fully coherent developments of the book's larger argument, but they are extraordinary examples of the kind of consequences study of her novels in the light of contemporary scientific thought might have.

Many other studies deal with many other kinds of intellectual sources upon which the polymathic Marian Evans could draw. A brief essay by Brian Rosenberg, "George Eliot and the Victorian Historic Imagination" (1982), examines a notebook entry and locates a number of English sources for her views on history. The essay is an intelligent one but badly underestimates, I believe, the importance of continental thought to George Eliot's conception of the historic imagination. A chapter in Tess Cosslett's *The Scientific Movement and Victorian Literature* (1982) moves more ambitiously to show how George Eliot drew on scientific models of knowledge as ethical models, and to connect her ideas with those of the scientific naturalists. Another extensive treatment of the relation of George Eliot's thought to science, and particularly to Lewes and to W. K. Clifford, appears in my own *The Realistic Imagination: The English Novel From "Frankenstein" to Lady Chatterley* (1983). I refrain from comment on the value of Levine's analysis.

Sara Putzell-Korab discusses the Jewish medieval sources of some of the material George Eliot used for *Daniel Deronda,* in her "The Role of the Prophet: the Rationality of Daniel Deronda's Idealist Mission" (1982). She takes issue with William Baker, who argues that George Eliot's use of these materials denies Mordecai's rationality, and insists not only that George Eliot uses them to affirm a "rational ideal," but regards Daniel as a Hegelian, world-historical figure, and Mordecai's view of what it is to be rational as Hegelian as well.

One odd contribution to the question of George Eliot's intellectual sources is David Williams's *Mr. George Eliot: A Biography of George Henry Lewes* (1983). It is hard to know why Williams was so angry with George Eliot, but he is harshly unsympathetic in his attempt to aggrandize Lewes at her expense. His insistently snide version of the George Eliot-Lewes relationship makes her "nothing herself." Yet the biography of Lewes does not even show much sympathy for or interest in Lewes's work, particularly in science. Lewes is pictured as a long-suffering self-sacrificing figure who not only encouraged George Eliot to write, but structured the writing of the novels. Williams attempts to render the (rather unpleasant) feel of life with parsimonious, unself-confident, conventionally moral, self-obsessed Marian Evans. The unrelenting deflation of George Eliot and the making petty of their relationship continues to the last, as, in a flurry of aspirants, we hear that at her death she was "hauled in the hearse through the winter slush up the hill to Highgate, there to rejoin George Lewes."

A popular alternative reading to Williams is in Phyllis Rose, *Parallel Lives* (1983), which offers a novelistic rereading of the relationship between George Eliot and Lewes. Rose sensitively interprets their behavior, though relying on no new material. She argues that George Eliot was not the passive creation of Lewes, but that she took the initiative. Refreshingly, she insists not on George Eliot's need for love, but on her desire. (I believe Rose misreads the "happiness" of George Eliot's childhood, but after Williams's sourness her essay is certainly refreshing.) Hers is a generous and humane reading of the life—even the marriage to Cross is seen as perfectly understandable and good.

These two biographical works provide a transition to another dominant category of work on George Eliot in recent years—the feminist, where, on the whole, George Eliot has not fared well. One of the reiterated arguments is that she never allows her heroines the possibilities that she herself achieved. This charge has been powerful and difficult to refute. In "George Eliot:

Feminist Critic'' (1984), Carol A. Martin tries once more to do so, but essentially repeats a familiar and inadequate argument, that writing realistically is itself a feminist move. George Eliot, she says, was ''committed to the theory that fiction should show the destructive effects of social repression by delineating the weaknesses and not merely the strengths of individuals in an oppressed group.'' Ellen Ringler, in ''*Middlemarch:* A Feminist Perspective'' (1983), will not quite accept this standard line of defense. Although Dorothea always turns out superior to the men, the women dominant over them (and all men are flawed by moral stupidity), Ringler agrees that the feminists' uneasiness about *Middlemarch* is justified. It is not because George Eliot fails to show Dorothea as achieving what George Eliot achieved (a bad comparison, she says), but that George Eliot ''shrinks from the implications of her own novel, which demands more than sad resignation.'' We would prefer, Ringler says, ''a healthy anger'' against the ''disheartening spectacle of women's spiritual grandeur ill-matched with meanness of opportunity'' which George Eliot has so convincingly traced.

Another extensive meditation on *Middlemarch* from a feminist perspective appears in Kathleen Blake, *Love and the Woman Question in Victorian Literature: The Art of Self-Postponement* (1983). Blake considers all the main objections to reading the novels as ''feminist,'' but through careful analysis, and by taking the line that George Eliot's responsibility was to reepresent things as they are, she argues that the negative readings are incorrect: women's actions and options are embedded in the social context in largely determining ways. George Eliot's women are trapped in various ways and do not show her kind of powers because that, for the most part, is the way it was. In an interesting conclusion to her George Eliot chapter, Blake reviews the criticisms of contemporary feminists, but gives George Eliot the last word.

U. C. Knoepflmacher, in ''Unveiling Men: Power and Masculinity in George Eliot's Fiction'' (1981), answers the question in a very different way, offering very much a male critic's feminism: George Eliot's attempts ''to liberate a stifled or veiled female self are primarily enacted through her handling of male characters—her own projections on and impersonations of, a masculinity she wants to tame, subdue, or feminize.'' Male masks disguise a female desire for power. In an impressive if not entirely convincing twist, Knoepflmacher argues that George Eliot equates ''the hunger for power with a sadistic masculinity that she finds all the more threatening when it spreads from the male to the female,'' and thus is harder on aggressive females than on men.

Another treatment of George Eliot's apparent ambivalence about the woman question appears in Suzanne Graver, "Mill, *Middlemarch,* and Marriage" (1984). Graver juxtaposes Mill's *On the Subjection of Women* with *Middlemarch,* showing the similarity of their positions on marriage. Considering the criticisms that emerge from the connection both writers make between the prevailing definition of woman's nature and the conditions of the marriage contracts, Graver reveals a dilemma that clouds the critiques in each case.

Lydgate can be taken as illustration of the kinds of marital disabilities that are seen by Mill in the *Subjection* to attest to the need for changing existing customs and practices. Dorothea exemplifies the notion of woman as exalted help-meet. But the novel constantly puts to question the antagonist notions of renunciation and freedom, one fostered by rhetoric, the other by plot. George Eliot tries to do justice to both, and her analysis suggests that the prevailing definition of woman's nature was a construction of culture. Marriage was dictating not reflecting woman's nature.

Another kind of argument, a very personal reading, yet one that shows awareness of the complexities of George Eliot's positions, can be found in Rachel M. Brownstein, *Becoming a Heroine* (1982). As part of a deftly autobiographical critical study of the novelistic tradition of the heroine, Brownstein devotes a long chapter to *Daniel Deronda.* (The book is strewn with miscellaneous allusions to the major novels, as well.) Brownstein attempts an analysis of how novels shape women's imagination of themselves and how the tradition of the heroine gives women the option of ambitions to move beyond the restrictions of their lives. The greatest fictions, she argues, always contain warnings about the fictionality of the heroines' striving, the dangers of the deceits of romance, and she finds this to be the case in *Daniel Deronda.* Gwendolen's power is in the intensity of her subjectivity. *Daniel Deronda* is about what doesn't happen (about the deflation of power and identity). Brownstein's analysis, geared to her book's overall objective, is not at all haunted or deformed by that. If she does not give us a very new *Daniel Deronda,* she does show one way that George Eliot may be read fruitfully within a feminist program.

Lee Edwards also concerns herself with the "hero" in her *Psyche as Hero: Female Heroism and Fictional Form* (1984). In the course of an ambitious study aimed, I believe, at revising Gilbert and Gubar, Edwards treats *Middlemarch* as part of a long chapter on "protoheros" in nineteenth-century English novels. She sets the word "hero" against "heroine," which she cedes to Gilbert and Gubar and to the traditional angel/whore dichotomy, and argues that there is a tradition of heroism that transcends gender. The woman "hero," unlike the heroines of indirection or submission, mounts a direct attack on patriarchy and male heroism. In this scheme, of course, *Middle-march* will be found lacking because Dorothea is limited not simply by the structure of society, but by George Eliot's lack of sympathy for her aspirations. Edwards's position is debatable, but she gives us one of the clearest expositions of the case against George Eliot. Like all heroinism, George Eliot's affirms the status quo. What is missing from Edwards's analysis is a nuanced sense of the text such as we can find in some of the essays I note below, and particularly that of Mary Jacobus.

Jacobus deals rigorously with major feminist issues in "The Question of Language: Men of Maxims and *The Mill on the Floss*" (1981): how is it possible, from within a discourse that is phallocentric and an expression of the dominant culture in which woman is an inexpressible other, for a woman to express that other? *The Mill on the Floss* is a text that will allow "putting the question of our social organization of gender," and as feminist critic Jacobus will try to be "at once transgressive and liberating, since what [feminist criticism] brings to light is the hidden or unspoken ideological premise of criticism itself."

The essay analyzes George Eliot's implicit critique of the language of the dominant culture, of the "Men of maxims," and her quest for the kind of language which might undo it. Maggie's "lapses," Jacobus says, are the gaps that reveal what is specific to women's writing. They are turned against the system that brings them into being, raising the question of women's access to power and knowledge. The move from subtle analysis of the text to the theoretical question, via Irigaray, makes this a major essay in feminist criticism: how can women disengage themselves *alive* from their concepts? "The necessary utopianism of feminist criticism may be the attempt to declare what is by saying something else—that 'something else' which presses both Irigaray and Eliot to conclude their very different works with an imaginative reaching beyond analytic and realistic modes to the metaphors of unbounded female desire in which each finds herself a woman writing."

An essay almost equally impressive is Margaret Homans's "Eliot, Wordsworth, and the Scenes of the Sisters' Instruction" (1981). Homans juxtaposes Wordsworth's "Tintern Abbey" and "Nutting" to *The Mill on the Floss* to consider the implications of George Eliot's use of and divergence from Wordsworth's model of the teaching and protecting male addressing the sister: "What is the female listener . . . to do with these words that are intended to help her circumvent the painful experiences that have forged the poet's consciousness?"

Much of Homans's argument is built, incorrectly, I believe, on the view that critics have taken George Eliot as a docile follower of Wordsworth. Nevertheless, the essay valuably speculates on the importance of gender difference as "the basis of Eliot's ambivalent response to Wordsworth's instructions." The study of Maggie and of the "Brother and Sister" sonnets suggests that George Eliot's "effort to be a docile student on the model of Wordsworth's implied sister" is her "subversion" of him, "for the literal is destructive." Homans offers valuable and original demonstrations of the way George Eliot diverges from the Wordsworthian model and important suggestions about the uses of realist narrative for the recuperation of imagination for the woman writer against the Wordsworthian implication that women must be protected from it.

Susan M. Greenstein, in "The Question of Vocation: From *Romola* to *Middlemarch*" (1981), considers George Eliot's concern with vocation in the light of her place in the feminist tradition she was rather reluctant to claim. Greenstein sees *Romola* as the first and most explicit "diagramming of the vocational crisis." In the character of Romola, George Eliot explores questions to be developed differently in the later novels. *Romola,* she says, examines the question of vocation in the confines of family, while *Middlemarch* examines it in terms of the larger society. Romola's longing for a child begins George Eliot's preoccupation with adoption. The question of maternity and vocation isn't resolved. "Surely George Eliot's situation with respect to Agnes Lewes" resembles "Romola's relation to the childish and innocent Tessa," but by *Middlemarch* George Eliot had discovered how to reconcile maternity and vocation.

In "The Affections Clad with Knowledge: Woman's Duty and the Public Life" (1983), John Goode makes a complex case for George Eliot as a very strong feminist writer, but he does so without lapsing back into the simple terms of the argument as Martin formulates them. Goode examines how, in *Daniel Deronda* and *The Mill on the Floss,* George Eliot explores women's relation to fiction writing as a way of considering the question of how a woman can reconcile her public and private roles. Writing novels is the compromise "between the vocations of intellectual leadership and womanhood." Goode claims that George Eliot recognizes "the question of women as a crucial feature of the whole of political life, and that she has to find a mode of expressing this, has to push sexual politics beyond the domain of personal and domestic relations into the realm of the public life." As fiction writer, George Eliot can "participate in . . . social captainship." Goode claims that George Eliot's confrontation with sexual politics "as a question of the relative kinds of membership of social groups" rather than as a question of freedom vs. oppression gets her "beyond even the most advanced discussions of her day." Goode's argument is an important one and deserves the attention of all critics concerned with George Eliot's feminist commitments, which should include all critics interested in George Eliot's art.

Diane Sadoff's *Monsters of Affection: Dickens, Eliot and Brontë on Fatherhood* (1982) is not exclusively a feminist study. It is rather a brilliant application of psychoanalytic—Freudian and Lacanian—theory in relation to nineteenth-century fiction; but its preoccupation with the question of fatherhood predictably entails important discriminations between male and female relations to the authority of paternity. There is no space here to elaborate on the theory, but in its application to George Eliot it is valuable. Reading the novels as they work out the relations between father and daughter suggests, to start with, how pervasive (and pervasively obscured) that concern is. Through metaphors of fatherhood (subjectivity itself) she connects fatherhood with other crucial issues, like class, self-consciousness, and sexual difference. Sadoff sees George Eliot as working out of one of the dominant images of "fatherhood" of the century—the vision of the father who abandons his children but who remains loveable. The ideal authority that George Eliot seeks and tries to impose is a version of her image of the seductive father, requiring passivity before the law; yet at the same time George Eliot subverts by irony the egotism of many of her father figures (like Casaubon, but even Savonarola).

I want to turn here to the third of the dominant preoccupations in recent George Eliot criticism—the related questions of the degree to which myth rather than mimesis controls the narratives, and the implications for the study of narrative of George Eliot's work.

One of the most striking examples of this concern is Felicia Bonaparte's long essay, "*Middlemarch*: The Genesis of Myth in the English Novel: The Relationship Between Literary Form And The Modern Predicament" (1981). Bonaparte claims that *Middlemarch* is the first symbolic novel in English and that its realistic narrative is indicted by its symbolic structure. The essay regards mimetic and mythic readings as antagonist; and Bonaparte makes enormous claims for the ambitions of *Middlemarch,* in which George Eliot was trying to write "a history of the world." Whatever one's view of the overall argument, one must be impressed with Bonaparte's compilation of evidence demonstrating the novel's symbolic significance.

Commitment to the predominance of myth in narrative is often accompanied by a tendency to make very large claims for literature and to deny the literal at every turn. Bonaparte's analysis relentlessly turns all things to myth, especially names (Rosamond, rose of the world, Dorothea, gift of the Gods, Tertius, referring to Lydgate's third book of the *Fall of Princes,* in which are listed men who are seduced by women to the worship of Mammon). Rejecting both science and rigid medieval allegory, George Eliot finds a synthesis in Ladislaw, "the mythological figure of Dionysus," who "restores to an age of doubt the symbolic legacy of religion." That few people will have understood the mythic allusion "is . . . precisely its 'use.'" Bonaparte concludes with an opposition that occupies many critics: at the very moment that "empiricism makes the realistic novel possible, and in fact the idiom of the age, it engenders the crisis of faith which makes the symbolic novel necessary. And because it restores the spiritual legacy in its mythological narrative, the symbolic novel is a romance."

Harry Shaw, in "Scott and George Eliot: The Lure of the Symbolic," in *Scott and His Influence,* J. H. Alexander and David Hewitt, eds. (1982), takes the empiricist side of the opposition. He says that George Eliot wants to be able to "reduce history to the personal and the inward," but she also recognizes the "truth" of generalizations. The impulse to the particularistic and unheroic is countered by the impulse to symbolic unity in heroic figures, and Shaw argues that George Eliot is much the better novelist when she chooses the former. On Shaw's account, Bonaparte is right in her study of *Romola* about George Eliot's intention, wrong about her success: "the large cultural generalities on which the novel is based never mesh with the particularities of milieu which Eliot's realist side demands."

The other side of the argument recurs in Coral Ann Howell's "Dreams and Visions in George Eliot's Fiction" (1981). For Howells, dreams and visions are continuous with George Eliot's major speculative interests. Although *Daniel Deronda* is the obvious locus, the tensions with realism had been there from the first, and Howells traces the development of the treatment of dreams from "The Lifted Veil" through *Daniel Deronda,* revealing how even in her most realistic phases George Eliot values visions, as the possible creators they become. Peter Dale takes another, but a related tack, in his "Symbolic Representation and the Means of Revolution in *Daniel Deronda*" (1981). Accepting the argument that George Eliot is as much symbolist as realist, Dale investigates her view of the philosophical status of symbols by considering *Daniel Deronda,* the "most symbolically self-conscious novel." (One wonders how it could be more self-conscious than Bonaparte's *Middlemarch.*) Dale discriminates two kinds of symbolism, positivist, which takes the reality of the natural world, apart from mediating human consciousness (and in which the symbol is a reflection of something more fundamental and worthier of possession), and phenomenological, which assumes that the world represented can never be known. Dale claims that George Eliot espouses positivist symbolism until *Middlemarch,* which becomes a process of intellectual release from the positivist model. In *Daniel Deronda,* for almost all characters, "the mind cannot perceive or comprehend existence except through the images of its own yearning." The philosophical battle is also political, for the possibility of reform is made to depend upon the way one interprets or uses the symbol. George Eliot comes to discover that metaphor is the explicit evasion of reality in favor of a fictional structure, and *Daniel Deronda* thus reflects a rejection of positivism, and an alliance with Nietzsche and modernist thought on the power of language. Dale's essay, linking contemporary preoccupations with ideas (as in Myers's book) with myth and politics, is one of the most impressive discussions of George Eliot considered in this survey.

Another Dale essay is almost equally useful. "George Eliot's 'Brother Jacob': Fables and the Physiology of Common Life," raises important questions, which complement Bonaparte's arguments, about George Eliot's use of symbolism. "Brother Jacob," Dale argues, attempts to move "beyond the 'insane' world that destroys Maggie." Using the "fable," George Eliot turns from her normal distrust of the diagram, to allow the outline to convey moral truth. She adopts the fabular form because she believes "that what it expresses bears a close relationship . . . to what the most advanced thought of her own period was beginning to perceive about human nature"—i.e., that "contra Descartes, the human and the animal are close." The fable insists on human irrationality but appeals to man's radical susceptibility to the force of symbols.

A very different sort of study of the uses of myth in George Eliot appears in Barry Qualls, *The Secular Pilgrim of Victorian Fiction* (1981). Qualls shows how Victorian writers attempted to construct a new mythology. But he only offers a mythology derived from the tradition of Bunyan, via the emblems of Quarles, and the exhortations of Carlyle. Qualls is very good in his attention to minute details of the text, and in his remarkable knowledge of those texts, and the Bible, and Bunyan. He reads George Eliot within the large mythic patterns he has laid out, as he examines the "themes, situations, and narrative devices that constitute George Eliot's meditations on nineteenth-century English life."

Several brief studies note George Eliot's borrowing from earlier writers materials that suggest the symbolic and mythic implications of her work. I note here a few: G. A. Witting Davis, "Ruskin's *Modern Painters* and George

Eliot's Conception of Realism'' (1981)—a rather feeble effort; David Molstad, "The Dantean Purgatorial Metaphor in *Daniel Deronda,* (1983); Adrian Poole, "Hidden Affinities in *Daniel Deronda''* (1983). Poole provides an unusually sensitive reading of the novel by describing an elaborate web of interconnectedness through allusions, which, he shows, "present the most extreme vision of the possibility of cultural mortification.'' We inherit "shreds and patches,'' which suggest "energies embodied by human acts to avenge and to heal.''

Attacks on the literal in interpretation of narrative take other directions, although *Daniel Deronda* is often the point of departure. Catherine Belsey, "Re-reading *Daniel Deronda,''* in *Re-reading the Great Tradition,* edited by Peter Widdowson (1982), challenges empiricist criticism through the example of F. R. Leavis. "The conventional justification of classic realism as a serious moral undertaking,'' says Belsey, is that "it records the process of learning by experience, but also embodies the process in its own mode of address.'' Leavis ignores the "prior subjectivity'' required to interpret experience, and Belsey tries to show what, because of his failure to come to terms with that subjectivity, Leavis leaves out of his reading of *Daniel Deronda.* Daniel Cottom, in "The Romance of George Eliot's Realism'' (1982), also discusses the romance-realism dichotomy. Cottom accepts the view of George Eliot as a realist rejecting "romance'': her work "consists of a commentary upon an art antithetical to its own.'' The essay is elaborate in language and argument, but its conclusions are relatively conventional.

The anti-realist thrust of contemporary criticism is brilliantly exemplified in D. A. Miller, *Narrative and its Discontents: Problems of Closure in the Traditional Novel* (1981), which includes a long section on *Middlemarch.* Miller's argument confronts the tension in George Eliot's narratives between the empirical and the kinds of religious ambitions Bonaparte considers. The novels, Miller claims, seek to transcend the impermanence, mixed conditions, and moral difficulties of the narratable world, but since for Eliot the narratable is the true, they cannot achieve the transcendence, which becomes a dream. Miller reads with extraordinary attention to detail, and demonstrates movingly that within the terms of realism, George Eliot will not falsify, and thus she will not commit herself to the possibilities she seeks to assert or discover. With a modernist eye, Miller registers incompleteness, contradiction, evasion, and he does not submit to the sage-like voice that seems to be affirming values not quite available. His startlingly convincing reading of the famous scene between the Bulstrodes, for example, shows that it precisely does *not* create the mutual understanding that for a moment seems to transform Mrs. Bulstrode gloriously.

Miller's exceptional work, leaving the narratives in a "permanent state of suspensiveness," is paralleled in another book that uses *Middlemarch* to address problems of narrative, Marianna Torgovnick's *Closure in the Novel* (1981). Less obviously working within anti-realist assumptions, Torgovnick is pluralistic in method. Beginning with a taxonomy of endings, she does not rely on special terminology. She examines the epilogue to *Middlemarch* in the context of George Eliot's status as a philosophical novelist, of her attempts to shift the epic strain to the domestic, and of her desire to "illustrate beliefs which work for the good of those who read." The analysis is sensible, but unlike Miller, Torgovnick is susceptible to the blandishments of the Sage.

Another, even less trendy but very rich treatment of the problems of narrative can be found in Karen Chase, *Eros and Psyche* (1984). Chase considers how narrative is generated out of conceptions of personality in nineteenth-century novels. The source of George Eliot's narratives is "desire," and they are sanctioned out of the attempt of characters (and narrator) to find conscious formulations of their aims and motives. On the one hand, George Eliot attempts, through representational realism, to make us see characters' behavior from their points of view; on the other, she attempts "to provide a super-personal, objective scientific analysis which requires the representation of forces that exceed the individual will" (compare Graver's view that the tension between realism and more abstract form results from conflicting biases toward individualism and toward community). Chase's analysis of the texture of George Eliot's work subtly focusses on the contrasting metaphors of "currents" and "containing spaces," particularly in *Middlemarch*.

Before discussing studies of particular novels, I pause to consider some few essays that don't quite fit my large categories. First, David Carroll, in "The Sybil of Mercia" (1983), investigates George Eliot's reputation as "Sybil," its sources and its appropriateness. The unconventional nature of her social and intellectual circumstances made George Eliot a little frightening to her contemporaries and set her apart whether she would or no. Nevertheless, Carroll argues, although she was divided, she had an instinct to be a sage. She undercut that instinct by her distrust of formulae and her testing of authority in her fictions and essays. Yet she also compromised her own self-doubt by sanctioning Main's *Wise, Witty and Tender Sayings*. A less interesting study of another sort is Peter Collister, "Portraits of 'Audacious Youth':

George Eliot and Mrs. Humphry Ward'' (1983). Collister notes parallel developments in the two writers and discusses elements in Mrs. Ward's work that reflect her knowledge of George Eliot's novels.

Jean-Paul Forster, in two essays, considers George Eliot's use of "reticence" as an aspect of language: "George Eliot: the Language and Drama of Reticence" (1983), and "Beyond Reticence: the Power Politics Relationship in George Eliot" (1983). Reticence, according to Forster, characterizes every aspect of George Eliot's art, and confirms her concern with the power of language to represent. He analyzes in the first essay different kinds of reticence, and shows it to be the root of all evil in the novels. Yet reticence is also seen as a condition for the exploration of interiority. The second essay concentrates on the function of "dialogue" in the novels. Forster claims that dialogues constitute the true events of the narratives. The contrast between reticence and dialogue, private and public consciousness, does not finally get us very far in an understanding of George Eliot.

In *The Sense of an Audience: Dickens, Thackeray, and George Eliot at Mid-Century* (1981) Fred Carlisle devotes chapters to *Scenes of Clerical Life* and to *Adam Bede*. He studies these novels in the context of contemporary Victorian fiction reading and attempts to define the persona who speaks self-consciously to "his" audience. The readings of the particular works are sound and interesting.

Three novels have been monopolizing George Eliot studies: *Daniel Deronda, Middlemarch,* and *The Mill on the Floss. Adam Bede* has tended to slip from critical attention and returns primarily as an occasion to reject earlier traditions of interpretation. In "Infanticide and Respectability: Hetty Sorrel as Abandoned Child in *Adam Bede*" (1983), Simon Harris considers the relation of Hetty to the structure of the novel. This is a refreshing treatment of its often overlooked hostility to community. Harris shows that Hetty is not really alien to Hayslope but an inevitable product of its own overconcern with respectability. The novel, he argues, is no mere nostalgic dream of community, but the story of three confused orphans who must grow beyond the limits of their class.

David Malcolm, in "*Adam Bede* and the Unions: 'a proletarian novel'" (1983), rejects the conventional treatment of the novel as pastoral. While he strains a bit to show that it is really concerned, by indirection, with the industrial transformation in England, Malcolm is certainly correct that the novel's treatment of Methodism, of Adam as artisan, of the commercial intrusions on feudal economy, would have resonated in the 1850s when the problems of unionization, of the artisan's position, and of dissent's connection with industrialism were prominent.

Since U. C. Knoepflmacher's discussion of "The Lifted Veil" in *George Eliot's Early Novels,* and since Sandra Gilbert and Susan Gubar devoted so much attention to that story in *The Madwoman in the Attic,* it has been discussed almost as often as *Adam Bede.* Terry Eagleton, in "Power and Knowledge in 'The Lifted Veil' " (1983), uses it as an example of the way disinterested knowledge actually serves established class relations. This complex reading, originally delivered at the Rutgers Centenary Conference, elaborates a contradiction Eagleton finds in "bourgeois knowledge," its commitment to master its subject and its mystification of that subject—unpredictability, he says, is "the very dynamic of bourgeois history." One can see how he applies this view to Latimer's story: the bourgeoisie does not want omniscience, "for this could only signal the death of that very freedom and irreducible randomness which is integral to its exploitation." The essay is difficult and complicated, but makes possible an interesting new reading of the story and of George Eliot's relation to her art.

B. M. Gray's "Pseudoscience and George Eliot's 'The Lifted Veil'" (1982) is less rewarding. Gray fails to note how much attention has recently been paid to the tale as she insists (as everyone would agree) that it needs to be accounted for. Usefully, she calls attention to four hitherto unpublished letters to George Eliot from George Combe in 1852, which help bring to light George Eliot's interest in mesmerism and clairvoyance. Gray claims that "The Lifted Veil" traces experiences that correspond closely to contemporary testimonies about mesmerism and galvanism. In an essay earlier referred to, Peter Dale made excellent use of that bad story, "Brother Jacob." J. S. Szirotny is less successful in "Two Confectioners the Reverse of Sweet: The Role of Metaphor in Determining George Eliot's Use of Experience" (1984). The title is more ambitious than the achievement, which is essentially an old-fashioned image study, tracing images and metaphors of sweetness through the story.

The Mill on the Floss has managed through all the fluctuations of George Eliot's reputation to sustain its interest for many different kinds of readers. We have seen already how it engages feminist critics. An essay by Barbara Frey Waxman provides another example: "Heart, Mind, Body, and Soul: George Eliot's Female *Bildungsroman*" (1982–83). Waxman offers a rather naive and straightforward comparison of Maggie with Dorothea Brooke. George Eliot, she says, teaches "that women's sexuality must be awakened and that women's hearts and souls need to become educated even more than their minds.'' Renata R. Mantner Wasserman, in ''Narrative Logic and the Form of Tradition in *The Mill on the Floss*'' (1982) treats another recurring subject—the famous, or infamous ending. Exhausted as the subject should be, Wasserman provides an interesting new analysis. She suggests that the death of the heroine ''destabilizes the Victorian convention that the 'dark,' passionate woman must die.'' Maggie dies not from ''moral and natural necessity'' but from a kind of accident, unrelated to guilt, responsibility, moral culpability. Wasserman says that Maggie's ''impasse'' grows from George Eliot's rejection of the option of ''transcendence'' (here her conclusions parallel D. A. Miller's) and of her inability to sanction the other option—violation of the rules. The traditional novelistic movement from individual will to social maturity is thus denied Maggie as George Eliot affirms the value of a static, historical past which the book otherwise disconfirms. Rosemary Mundhenk offers a less satisfying treatment of the ending in her ''Patterns of Irresolution in Eliot's *The Mill on the Floss*'' (1983). She contests the view that Maggie's decision to reject Stephen ''constitutes the final resolution of her struggles.'' Rather the last scene repeats the pattern of vacillation consistent throughout Maggie's life. Ernest Bevan, in ''Maggie Tulliver and the Bonds of Time'' (1984), examines *The Mill on the Floss* through George Eliot's treatments of family, tradition, locale. But much of what is said here recapitulates (sensibly) George Eliot's widely known views.

In Avrom Fleishman's ambitious *Figures of Autobiography: The Language of Self-Writing* (1983), a long chapter is, understandably, devoted to *The Mill on the Floss*. Fleishman claims that the novel is not only ''a characteristic Victorian autobiographical novel but marks a crucial turning point in the use of traditional forms and figures in fictional self-conception.'' Unlike Bonaparte, Fleishman places George Eliot squarely in the empiricist tradition, showing that she rejects ''the biblical figures of traditional autobiography, with their burden of typological promise and divine underwriting of a life.'' *The Mill on the Floss* ''is at once an autobiographical novel and a critique of the entire canon of autobiographical writing.'' The essay is a valuable one for its reading of the novel in the context of traditions of autobiography.

Carol A. Martin, in ''Pastoral and Romance in George Eliot's *The Mill on the Floss*'' (1984), discusses the two genres to explore the tension in the novel between illusion and reality. Jane McDonnell, '''Perfect Goodness' or 'The Wider Life': *The Mill on the Floss* as Bildungsroman'' (1982) treats the ending in yet another way. The shift in the last part of the novel is a generic shift from *Bildungsroman* to saint's legend in part because women like Maggie had no vocational possibility into which to grow. John Levay, ''Maggie as

Muse: the Philip-Maggie Relationship in MF'' (1983), strains to show George Eliot seeking a man as muse in *The Mill on the Floss*. There is a strained identification of Philip with Pope, then with Sidney. Maggie as muse doesn't add up.

John Kucich has become one of the most interesting critics of Victorian narrative. His "George Eliot and Objects: Meaning as Matter in *The Mill on the Floss*" (1983) explores the problem of humanist subjectivity in George Eliot's work. The essay can be read fruitfully in the context of the earlier noted discussions of positivism versus transcendence, realism versus myth. In George Eliot, Kucich argues, the "conjunction of man and matter always reveals the impoverished, reductive character of human efforts to appropriate the world." In *The Mill on the Floss* there are no "natural objects"—all are infused with the taint of commerce. Kucich wants to show that George Eliot's use of humanity as the standard of value for objects is contradicted by her unease at the fact that all objects are made to subserve human interests. Thus, "her humanism . . . is severely tested by her reaction against the scientific and industrial pragmatism of her age, which helped to make all human designs on the world appear to be rapacious." Redemption can come only when objects are transformed into a "complex structure of intentions so plural that it acquires massiveness of texture," although against that massiveness characters like Maggie acquiesce into passivity.

Silas Marner continues to attract attention. Donald Hawes, in "Chance in *Silas Marner*" (1982), argues that while George Eliot moralizes against chance, chance plays an important role in all the favorable events. Godfrey is condemned for relying on chance, but Silas is not. Trust in Providence is also a trust in chance (Dolly). The inconsistency, Hawes claims, is the result of a shift in method that makes it a legendary tale. Susan Cohen, too, in an uneven essay, "A History and a Metamorphosis: Continuity and Discontinuity in *Silas Marner*" (1983), contends that the favorable chance denounced by the narrator is precisely what saves Silas. Her essay, while not very strong on George Eliot scholarship, suggests a keen critical intelligence as it explores the contradictions and evasions of the novel. The novel, Cohen argues, self-consciously sustains both metamorphosis and history, disruption and continuity. The happy conclusion suggests a thin cover over formlessness and disruption. One other *Silas Marner* essay deals with the novel's rhetoric in a way reminiscent of John Holloway, but does not take the point very far. I merely note the essay here: Mary Jane Rachelson, "The Weaver of Raveloe: Metaphor as Narrative Persuasion in *Silas Marner*" (1983).

Romola has long been a focus for discussion both of the development of

George Eliot's career and of her symbolic and mythic tendencies. Hugh Witemeyer, in "George Eliot's *Romola* and Bulwer Lytton's *Rienzi*" (1983), suggests an indebtedness denied by Bonaparte. He is particularly interested in Bulwer's theory that historical romance should be externally empirical and factual, but that it should explain the fact with the internal history of the characters, i.e., in real romance. George Anderson provides the only other extensive treatment of the novel and his very useful essay, "George Eliot and the Publication of *Romola*," is really a piece of publishing history. It chronicles Blackwood's relation to the novel, and tries to explain George Eliot's willingness to switch to Smith, Elder despite Blackwood's friendship. George Eliot does not emerge admirably. John Blackwood blamed Lewes for the defection, but unlike other members of his house, he never allowed himself to be angry with either Lewes or George Eliot, whom he seemed genuinely to like. He emerges as both the most honorable, and perhaps the shrewdest of the figures in this slightly shabby literary episode.

Felix Holt has always been a problematic text in the George Eliot canon, yet it normally evokes essays that locate important aspects of her art. Of those in this survey, Susan Cohen's "Avoiding the High Prophetic Strain: De-Quincey's Mail Coach and *Felix Holt*" (1983), is the least ambitious, concentrating on DeQuincey's essay as a possible source for the novel. The argument is tenuous, but Cohen becomes more interesting when she draws connections between the opening mail-coach sequence of the novel and its narrative method. Robin Sheets's "*Felix Holt*: Language, the Bible, and the Problematic of Meaning" (1982) tackles a major problem, the nature of the novel's language. She rightly argues, in an argument that anticipates Catherine Gallagher's brilliant 1985 volume, *The Industrial Reformation in English Fiction* (outside the official limits of this survey), that in the novel words lose their clear significance and interpretation becomes arbitrary. This has large consequences for the idea of "community" and for the possibility of politics, and Sheets's analysis of the details of the political language is excellent. Unlike Gallagher, Sheets also argues that the book shows that "language can and should be recovered." This important essay shows the connection among politics, language, and fiction writing itself. George Eliot is concerned with these issues: if a community cannot determine the purpose of a text, what is her fate as a novelist? If the meanings of words are unstable, how can she fulfill her responsibilities as a story teller? The novelist is like the electioneer Johnson: she makes money from lies.

One of the most original of the essays to be considered here is Bruce Robbins's "The Butler Did it: On Agency in the Novel," (1984). Taking off from George Eliot's painful little essay of 1865, "Servants' Logic," Robbins shows how class divisions challenged the validity of her faith in the gradual teleological movement of history toward reason. George Eliot considers the possibility that servants' logic is indeed logical, but an alternative logic to our own. The contest between the logics, especially on the issue of causality, is "surprisingly pertinent" to the controversies between Marxism and post-structuralism. Urging masters to tell their servants what to do without worrying about reasons, "she in effect abandons rationality for action." We have again the contrast between free will and determinism. Rationality depends upon power and is now a source of open concern.

Robbins's question is how agency and meaning can be reconciled, for agency makes history unintelligible. Drawing on examples from Oedipus to Thackeray to show how agents of plot are the most conventional and incoherent of literary forms, he applies the views to George Eliot. Realism, Robbins claims, chastises those who pretend to be the subject, who can control (Felix in relation to the mob, for example). It makes society intelligible but at the cost of denial of agency. Servants in George Eliot intrude at the juncture of scientific rationalism and rural organicisms. George Eliot evades the problem by allowing character to withdraw from history and plot into private commitment.

George Eliot's poetry inevitably attracts some attention because of what it can tell us about the novels. The lone consideration of the shorter poetry is Bonnie J. Lisle's "Art and Egoism in George Eliot's Poetry" (1984), which considers why for George Eliot marriage is "the only happy ending available to her heroines." In analysis of "Armgart" and "Jubal," Lisle shows that art and death are closely associated: "Self-annihilation is a debt the artist owes humanity," and, paradoxically, it is "the only way to attain . . . immortality." George Eliot's ambivalence about art and about her own happiness is manifest in her inability to depict a single character uniting Mirah and Alchirisi, "the happy wife and the great artist." But it won't do to resolve the issue, as Lisle does, by suggesting that this is a matter of personal temperament. It is reasonable to ask, as she steadfastly does not, why this disjunction is so powerful in George Eliot, and whether it occurs also in the great male writers (Tennyson?).

The Spanish Gypsy attracts more attention than its poetry may be worth because of its peculiar place in the development of George Eliot's ideas and art. Sylvia Kesey Marks's "A Brief Glance at GE's *Spanish Gypsy*" (1983) simply traces parallels between the poem and the novels. Marks makes one interesting point—that all the novels up to *Felix Holt* "portray a character who opts for the past of his experience," but *The Spanish Gypsy* and then *Daniel Deronda* portray characters opting for a hereditary past. Victor A. Neufeldt, in "The Madonna and the Gypsy" (1983), claims that *The Spanish Gypsy, not Romola,* is the turning point in George Eliot's career because in it she learns that the claims of public duty must not be satisfied at the expense of personal fulfilment. Neufeldt uses the approach of Ruby Redinger, arguing that *Felix Holt* gives us the fusion of public and private good that allows George Eliot to finish *The Spanish Gypsy,* and that in killing Zara, she purged her sense of guilt toward her father.

In the course of this survey I have already discussed many essays treating either *Middlemarch* or *Daniel Deronda,* now the twin champions in the George Eliot sweepstakes. Let me here consider the remainder, which treat a wide variety of different aspects of those novels. Harriet Farwell Adams, in "Dorothea and 'Miss Brooke' " in *Middlemarch*" (1984), reexamines the composition of the novel analyzed by Jerome Beaty in *"Middlemarch": From Notebook to Novel* (1960). The turning point in the integration of the two stories, she claims, is the famous shift to focus on Casaubon. Adams tries to show that the two stories have a similar deep source and that *Middlemarch* actually influenced "Miss Brooke." While interesting, these speculations must be read in conjunction with Beaty's definitive analysis. James R. Bennett's "Scenic Structure of Judgment in *Middlemarch*" (1984), develops an old theme, that in George Eliot knowledge can reduce moral stupidity by teaching the difference between self and world and learning of other subjective centers. Bennett tries to show how this view is dramatized in *Middlemarch* in the passages in which characters are introduced. Franklin Court, in "The Image of St. Theresa in *Middlemarch* and Positive Ethics" (1983), provides another example of how concern with ideas, particularly positivist ideas, influences George Eliot criticism these days. Unfortunately, Court belabors the obvious and then assumes a George Eliot slavishly positivist. Kenny Marotta, in *"Middlemarch:* the 'Home Epic' " (1982), takes up another of our leitmotifs, but somewhat more successfully. His concern is with the genre, "Home epic," and his analysis leads to the inevitable discussion of failures and reductions of ambition that are normally associated with the realist project. But Marotta insists that *Middlemarch* requires to be judged by "an epic standard."

The most extended discussion of *Middlemarch* is a full-length study by Kerry McSweeney, *Middlemarch* (1984). Part of the Unwin Critical Library, it is meant for students and, perhaps, as a handbook for teachers. It attempts to cover every aspect of the novel—sources, biography, textual history, critical history—and to provide extensive critical analysis. McSweeney's Jamesian critical biases are evident, but he does intelligently rehearse the major issues. While he attempts to sustain balance, his manner is heavily evaluative in the old Leavisian way, with predictably Leavisian judgments. The readings are not as authoritative as the voice seems to claim for itself. On George Eliot's side in one of the great debates about her work, McSweeney claims that there is "no discrepancy between the limited knowledge of the characters and the omniscient knowledge of the narrator." He argues, finally, in an unpredictably open way that we should put aside our preoccupation with unity. On the whole McSweeney is useful in compiling materials and presenting common sense analyses, but his arguments must be warily engaged because of their dogmatic and authoritarian tendencies.

And now, at last, we wind down chronologically with *Daniel Deronda,* an apparently inexhaustible text for recent critics. And I can begin the end with another pet peeve I have been waiting impatiently to air. In K. M. Newton, "*Daniel Deronda* and Circumcision" (1981), the fuss about Daniel's penis continues. Never has so slight and precarious a member received so much attention. Since he is concerned with Daniel's penis, Newton appropriately argues that its absence from the text is less striking than its presence would have been. What Victorian novel alludes directly to the condition of a character's sexual member? Alas, however, Newton wants also to demonstrate that circumcision is as implicit in the text as men's penises are in all novels, and that the circumcision can be used "to overcome some of the traditional objections that have been made to the Deronda plot." He shows that circumcision would not have been unambiguous evidence of Jewishness, for it was often used as a cure of masturbation. The objectionable ease with which Daniel accepts Mordecai's suggestion that he is a Jew can be accounted for if his penis had already made the suggestion. The plot is therefore reconcilable with realism!

All of the penis essays, which happily have been dwindling of late, make from my point of view an embarassing episode in critical ingenuity and distortion. Newton makes Daniel's penis an active force, and once you start thinking of it that way, a lot of George Eliot metaphors grow oddly. Newton is right to show that the absence of circumcision from the text is not significant. He goes the way of all critics when he then shows how present it really is and proceeds to make a big thing of it.

Although *Daniel Deronda* is perhaps the key George Eliot text for discussion of feminism and narrative technique, it also evokes the most source studies and, as we have already seen, symbolic interpretation. Emily Auer-

bach, in "The Domesticated Maestro: George Eliot's Klesmer" (1983), conscientiously but ploddingly notes the uses of Klesmer in *Daniel Deronda*
within the context of conventions for associating Jewishness and Music in
the nineteenth century. It badly underestimates, however, the importance of
music to George Eliot, and the seriousness with which she takes the high
romantic Germanic solemnity of Klesmer's kind of art and art theory (even
while she is capable of seeing its absurdity, and its un-English qualities).

Another essay concerned with problems of realism is Herbert Levine's
"The Marriage of Allegory and Realism in *Daniel Deronda*" (1982). Much
of Levine's discussion, as he confesses, has been conducted before. But his
application of Angus Fletcher's theory of allegory to *Daniel Deronda* is useful.
In effect, his analysis shows the value for George Eliot of using mixed modes,
allegorical writing showing her audience "glimpses of experience it did not
expect to see in the realistic mirror." James Caron takes up the old argument
about the two *Daniel Derondas* in "The Rhetoric of Magic in *Daniel Deronda*" (1983), joining the organic unity camp. Here again, the problem of
"myth" turns up, and Caron argues that the novel is unified by a "rhetoric
of magic" assimilating mythic and romantic associations. In the long run,
Caron's argument is a familiar one. Deirdre David's study in *Fictions of
Resolution in Three Victorian Novels: "North and South," "Our Mutual
Friend," and "Daniel Deronda"* (1981), is more serious. In it, she considers
the mediations between the social actuality novels represent and the desires
of their predominantly middle-class readers that things not be that way. An
ostensibly strange novel for such a subject, *Daniel Deronda* is of interest to
David because of its "irreconciliation between social and psychological realism and moral correction, and Eliot's essentially middle-class albeit learned
and intellectually serious criticism." Unlike Caron, David accepts the tradition
of the two narratives and uses it for her own purposes. The real originality
of her study, however, is in her comparison with other novels treating the
same kinds of discontinuities. (I should note, however, that David devotes
one long footnote to Daniel's penis in the course of a discussion of how
George Eliot displaces her attitude toward the working classes onto the Jews.
She speculates that maybe he never was circumcised.)

The affirmation of self-denial remains a big problem for feminist critics
of George Eliot. Missy Dehn Kubitschek, in "Eliot as Activist: Marriage and
Politics in *Daniel Deronda*" (1984), addresses the question with some originality, but with much weakness of detail and an insufficiently sharp sense
of George Eliot's career or of "politics." Kubitschek insists that in *Daniel
Deronda* politics replaces filial and romantic duties as the focus of value,"

and that mere self-denial is inadequate. "The central failure in *Daniel Deronda* is not . . . Deronda's character, but . . . Eliot's inability to construct an alternative to the unacceptable marriages which mirror the political context. Not Deronda, but Deronda's marriage remains chiefly insubstantial." Another feminist discussion of the novel is by Nancy Pell, "The Fathers' Daughters in *Daniel Deronda*" (1982). Treating a similar problem, Pell argues that *Daniel Deronda* is an exploration of the difficulties of the daughter in achieving cultural and social legitimacy within an unresponsive, if not actually menacing, patriarchal society. In *Daniel Deronda,* uneasiness about the authority of the father and active resistance to patriarchal control expand to crisis proportions as George Eliot attempts for the first time to integrate the critical perspectives of historical time and cultural distance with an intimate story of English country society. George Eliot's "appeal to great distances and alien cultures reflects the psychological truth that projection is one of the first steps toward self-recognition and possible change." Gwendolen, as a divided character, reaffirms in atonement the conventions of patriarchal power. But Pell claims that atonement is not for her murderous will toward Grandcourt, but for her betrayal of "the undoubting movement of her whole being," that is, "the promise she gave to Lydia Glasher." This is an extremely interesting and well-written reading.

Finally, we have Grahame Smith's treatment of *Daniel Deronda* in *The Novel and Society: Defoe to George Eliot* (1984). Smith argues that the novel as a form comes into being with the idea of society, and thus *Deronda,* in its change in treatment of society, marks a major turn in the development of the novel. Unfortunately, Smith's reading has a kind of enthusiastic innocence that fails to reflect the enormous amount of discussion of *Daniel Deronda* that, as this now faltering survey makes clear, has been emerging with what seems like geometrical proliferation. It is late in the game to learn that the novel is "poetic" in a new manner, that it's symbolic, that its "sense of reality is more mysterious, less rationalistic than we have seen in the earlier novels." It is not news either that the novel's analysis and definition of England "embodies, in my view, something like a total rejection."

It is perhaps appropriate that this survey thus concludes with a study that obviously pays no attention to such surveys. Having exhausted myself at the job, I know how easy it would be never to read about George Eliot again, but only to have my say. With all the brilliant work I have had the pleasure to read this past year, there were large tracts of aridity, and larger ones that reflect no knowledge of former brilliance. Often, in reading essays that did not take into account earlier work, I felt a secret sympathy—one wants, after all, that solitary confrontation with a great author that the world of scholarship denies. But of course, we know that there can be no unmediated relationship, and perhaps the major service of scholarship is that it won't allow such naivete. My encounters with all this writing about writing have not been unmediated either. Moreover, I fear that this survey itself cannot be complete. So I beg forgiveness of those whose work I have somehow missed, and of those I have misinterpreted. "Interpretations," George Eliot wrote, are, after all, "illimitable." You will be pleased to know that this survey isn't.

Index

Contents of Previous Volumes

Volume 8 (1980)

Volume 13 (1984)

Volume 14 (1985)

Volume 15 (1986)